France and the Americas

the Americas

Culture, Politics, and History

A Multidisciplinary Encyclopedia

VOLUME I

EDITED BY

Bill Marshall

Professor of Modern French Studies, University of Glasgow

assisted by Cristina Johnston

Transatlantic Relations Series

Will Kaufman, Series Editor

A B C ✦ C L I O

Santa Barbara, California   Denver, Colorado   Oxford, England

Library of Congress Cataloging-in-Publication Data
France and the Americas : culture, politics, and history / edited by
Bill Marshall assisted by Cristina Johnston.
     p. cm.— (Transatlantic relations)
  Includes bibliographical references and index.
  ISBN 1-85109-411-3 (hardback : acid-free paper) — ISBN 1-85109-416-4
(ebook) 1. America—Relations—France—Encyclopedias. 2.
France—Relations—America—Encyclopedias. 3.
America—History—Encyclopedias. 4. France—History—Encyclopedias. 5.
North America—History—Encyclopedias. 6. Latin
America—History—Encyclopedias. 7. South
America—History—Encyclopedias. 8. America—Politics and
government—Encyclopedias. 9. Framce—Politics and
government—Encyclopedias. I. Marshall, Bill, 1957– II. Johnston,
Cristina. III. Series.
E18.75.F73 2005
303.48'21812044—dc22
                                200500096

08 07 06 05 10 9 8 7 6 5 4 3 2 1

This book is also available on the World Wide Web as an e-Book. Visit abc-clio.com
for details.

ABC-CLIO, Inc.
130 Cremona Drive, P.O. Box 1911
Santa Barbara, California 93116–1911

This book is printed on acid-free paper ∞.
Manufactured in the United States of America

for Maria

CONTENTS

ADVISORY BOARD

Professor Michael Burns, Mount Holyoke College
Professor Charles Forsdick, University of Liverpool
Dr. Yves Laberge, Laval University
Professor Jocelyn L'tourneau, Laval University

SERIES EDITOR'S PREFACE

The transatlantic relationship has been one of the most dynamic of modern times. Since the great age of exploration in the fifteenth and sixteenth centuries, the encounters between the Old World and the New have determined the course of history, culture, and politics for billions of people. The destinies of Europe, Africa, North and South America, and all the islands in between have been intertwined to the extent that none of these areas can be said to exist in isolation. Out of these interconnections comes the concept of the "Atlantic world," which Alan Karras describes in his introductory essay to *Britain and the Americas* in this series: "By looking at the Atlantic world as a single unit, rather than relying upon more traditional national (such as Britain) or regional (such as North or South America) units of analyses, scholars have more nearly been able to recreate the experiences of those who lived in the past." This perspective attempts to redefine and respond to expanding (one might say *globalizing*) pressures and new ways of perceiving interconnections—not only those rooted in history ("the past") but also those that are ongoing. Just one result of this conceptual redefinition has been the emergence of transatlantic studies as an area of inquiry in its own right, growing from the soil of separate area studies, whether European, North American, African, Caribbean, or Latin American. Students and scholars working in transatlantic studies have embarked on a new course of scholarship that places the transatlantic dynamic at its heart.

In this spirit, the Transatlantic Relations Series is devoted to transcending, or at least challenging, the boundaries of nation/region as well as discipline: we are concerned in this series not only with history but also with culture and politics, race and economics, gender and migration; not only with the distant past but also with this morning. The aim, in a phrase, is to explore the myriad connections and interconnections of the Atlantic world. However, although the Atlantic world concept challenges the isolation of smaller, national perspectives, nations do continue to exist, with boundaries both physical and conceptual. Thus this series acknowledges the intractability of the national and the regional while consistently focusing on the transcending movements—the connections and interconnections—that go beyond the national and the regional. Our mode of operation has been to build an approach to the Atlantic world through attention to the separate vectors between the nations and regions on both sides of the Atlantic. We do this by offering the six titles within the series so far commissioned, devoted respectively to Africa, Britain, France, Germany, Iberia, and Ireland in their engagements with the Americas. In each case, the transatlantic exchanges are those of all kinds: cultural, political, and historical, from the moment of the first contact to the present day. With this organizing principle in mind, the object is to offer an accessible, precisely focused means of entry into the various portals of the Atlantic world.

Finally, a word about this series' origins: in 1995, Professor Terry Rodenberg of Central Missouri State University invited scholars and teachers from eighteen universities on both sides of the Atlantic to establish an educational and scholarly institution devoted to encouraging a transatlantic perspective. The result was the founding of the Maastricht Center for Transatlantic Studies (MCTS), located in the Dutch city whose name, through its eponymous treaty, resonates with transnational associations. Since its foundation, MCTS has continued to bring together students and scholars from a host of worldwide locations to explore the intricate web of Atlantic connections across all disciplines. It has been a dynamic encounter between cultures and people striving to transcend the limitations of separate area and disciplinary studies. I am pleased to acknowledge the extent to which the Transatlantic Relations Series grows out of the discussions and approaches articulated at MCTS. Therefore, although the separate titles in the series carry their own dedications, the series as a whole is dedicated with great respect to Terry Rodenberg and the students and scholars at Maastricht.

Will Kaufman
University of Central Lancashire
Maastricht Center for Transatlantic Studies

EDITOR'S PREFACE

Although the relationship between Britain and especially North America has been widely absorbed into narratives and even hagiographies involving joint endeavor, common language, and rather unequal (but not wholly so) cultural exchange, the French relationship with the Americas has a more elusive and even counterfactual ring to it. What if the British had not prevailed at Quebec in 1759? What if Napoléon had not sold Louisiana? Then the history of the New World and indeed the whole planet would have been very different. In this perspective, the fact there is no French "United States" to counterbalance or even overtake the French mother country serves only to point out that what remains is, literally, remnants. Those islands and pockets, confetti indeed of French language or even "Frenchness," would thus all share the status of Saint-Pierre et Miquelon, the Gulf of Saint Lawrence fishing outpost where French rule continued when France lost its North American empire. And although this work, like all encyclopedias, aims to be an enduring monument of scholarship and research whose use-value will last for decades, it cannot ignore its own timeliness: namely, the events of 2002–2003 when the dispute over intervention in Iraq temporarily at least overwhelmed all descriptions of the French-American relationship, reigniting in some circles a mutual phobia that has existed below or above the surface at various points within modernity. This (geo)political disagreement, coupled with the determination of French cultural elites to conduct a robust defense against globalized Anglo-American mass culture, contributed to the tendency to see "France" and "America" as antithetical entities.

And yet, the length, fullness, and very existence of this encyclopedia testify to how distorted this viewpoint is, on both sides of the Atlantic. The nonsovereignty of Quebec leads many, not least in university French departments in the United States, often even in its northeastern region, but also of course in France, to forget that there is a French-speaking nation in North America. And although the territories in the Americas in which French rule holds sway are limited in number, the fact remains that French transatlantic exchanges have and continue to be endless, to the point that the two sides can be seen as completely intertwined. Any game of spotting omissions in this enormous work is complicit with this reality. The entries fall into different types or genres that express the depth and diversity of the French Atlantic. It was, for example, the French who opened up the North American continent to European settlement, and it was the American and French Revolutions that founded the politics of the modern era. There is the history of commodities and material practices and their consequences for everyday life. And there is the vast domain of cultural and intellectual exchanges, in both high and popular terms, which testify to a process of transformation as influences and movements—jazz is one example, cinema and cultural theory are others—cross from one side to another and then return, defamiliarized and strange, sometimes misunderstood and misrepresented, to be engaged with anew. These are the emphases of Ana Lucia Araujo's and Jacques Portes's introductory pieces on France and Latin America and France and the United States, to which we can add an extra twist, namely those itineraries that pass through or even bypass the hexagon (metropolitan France), such as those of Haitians or Latin Americans in Montreal or Jewish and other immigrants to France, who then left for a third and perhaps fourth country across the ocean.

But although transatlantic studies challenges and indeed shatters national boundaries, it of course establishes new ones in turn. Parameters, new ones, are laid down. The Atlantic must be crossed, so an itinerary such as Dakar to Paris is not covered here. There is the gray area of francophone Belgium and Switzerland, covered here in part. The eastward, Asian, and Pacific trajectory of French influence has to be written out. These necessary exclusions require that we guard against the potential ethnocentrism of our approach, in which we talk about the West. The volumes therefore make clear (especially in Michael Dash's introductory essay on France and the Caribbean) that the French Atlantic is also an African Atlantic, reinscribing the African diaspora firmly within this supremely "western" space, and reminding all readers of French Atlantic culture of that history of racialized terror. And although Frédéric Bastien's essay on France and Canada justifiably emphasizes the centrality of Quebec, it and a host of other entries speak eloquently of the distinctiveness of the French relations with the native peoples of North America.

It is clear, then, that these volumes offer not only diversions and facts that are comforting in a manner akin to that supremely British pastime of trainspotting. They are also a contribution to an ongoing debate about nationhood and university disciplines that transatlantic studies seeks to enrich and that the French-American dimension illustrates in a particularly intense manner. It is these conceptual ambitions that I seek to develop in my opening essay on the French Atlantic.

Thank you to Will Kaufman for inspiring the project and to Simon Mason at ABC-CLIO for his efficiency and forbearance. I would also like to express my gratitude to the British Academy for financial support and especially to my research assistant Cristina Johnston, who has been exemplary in her patience, commitment, and stamina.

Bill Marshall, Glasgow, June 2004

TOPIC FINDER

ART AND CULTURE

Adam, Paul
Adams, Henry Brooks
Alexis, Jacques-Stephen
Allen, Woody
Annaud, Jean-Jacques
Aquin, Hubert
Arcand, Denys
Architecture
Art Deco
Art Nouveau
Artaud, Antonin
Atget, Eugène
Auster, Paul
Avant-Gardes
Aznavour, Charles
Baker, Josephine
Baldwin, James
Bardot, Brigitte
Barnes, Djuna
Barney, Nat(h)alie
Bartholdi, Frédéric-Auguste
Bataille, Georges
Baudelaire, Charles-Pierre
Bazin, André
Beach, Sylvia
Beau Dommage
Beauchemin, Yves

Beauvoir, Simone de
Bécaud, Gilbert
Beguine
Beineix, Jean-Jacques
Benoît, Jean
Bernabé, Jean
Bernanos, Georges
Besson, Luc
Bianciotti, Hector
Binoche, Juliette
Blais, Marie-Claire
Bluteau, Lothaire
Boileau-Narcejac
Bombardier, Denise
Borduas, Paul-Emile
Borges, Jorge Luis
Bouchard, Michel Marc
Boukman, Daniel
Boulle, Pierre
Bourgeois, Louise
Bourget, Paul
Boyer, Charles
Brault, Michel
Brel, Jacques
Bresdin, Rodolphe
Breton, André
Brossard, Nicole
Bryce Echenique, Alfredo

Bugnet, Georges
Bujold, Geneviève
Burroughs, William S.
Butor, Michel
Cahiers du cinéma
Camus, Albert
Capucine
Carle, Gilles
Carlson, Carolyn
Carmen
Caron, Leslie
Carpentier, Alejo
Cartier-Bresson, Henri
Cassatt, Mary
Cather, Willa
Céline, Louis-Ferdinand
Cendrars, Blaise
Césaire, Aimé
Chabrol, Claude
Challe, Robert
Chamoiseau, Patrick
Charlebois, Robert
Charnay, Claude-Joseph-
  Désiré
Charrière, Henri
Chateaubriand, François-
  Auguste René de,
  Vicomte

MILITARY

American Civil War
American Revolution
Barrin de La Galissonière,
    Roland-Michel,
    Marquis
Bonaparte, Jérôme
Bonaparte, Joséphine
Bonaparte, Napoléon
Bonaparte, Elizabeth
    Patterson
French and Indian War
Frontenac, Louis de
    Buade, Comte de
Indian Wars
Iraq War
Jones, John Paul
Lafayette, Marquis de
Lahontan, Louis-Armand,
    Baron de
Leclerc, Charles-Victor
Lévis, François
Montcalm, Marquis de
NATO
Quebec, Battle of
Rochambeau, Jean-
    Baptiste-Donatien de
    Vimeur, Comte de
Treaty of Paris (1763)
Treaty of Utrecht (1713)
Vietnam War
World War I
World War II

PLACES

Acadia
Alberta
Argentina
Baton Rouge
Bordeaux
Brazil
Brittany
Cherbourg

Chicago
Chile
Detroit
Devil's Island
Disneyland Paris
Duluth
Florida
Grenada
Guadeloupe
Guiana
Haiti
Illinois Country
Indiana
Iowa
Kentucky
La Rochelle
Lake Champlain
Le Havre
Louisbourg
Louisiana
Maine
Manitoba
Martinique
Mexico
Michigan
Minnesota
Mississippi
Mississippi River
Missouri
Mobile
Montreal
Nantes
New Brunswick
New France
New Orleans
Newfoundland
Niagara Falls
Nova Scotia
Ohio
Ontario
Ottawa
Panama Canal
Quebec

Quebec City
Rochefort
Saint Lawrence River
Saint Louis
Saint Lucia
Saint Martin
Saint-Malo
Saint-Pierre et Miquelon
Santo Domingo
Saskatchewan
Sudbury
Tadoussac
Texas
Trinidad
Venezuela
Vermont
Wisconsin

POLITICAL AND SOCIAL CONCEPTS

9/11: Political
    Perspectives
Anti-Americanism
Atlanticism
Feminisms
French Revolution
Gay Movement
Liberalism
Modernization
Noble Savage
Primitivism
Quiet Revolution
Republicanism

POLITICAL FIGURES

Adams, John
Bolívar, Simón
Bouchard, Lucien
Bourassa, Robert
Boyer, Jean-Pierre
Chirac, Jacques
Christophe, Henri
Dessalines, Jean-Jacques

Eisenhower, Dwight D.
François I, King of France
Franklin, Benjamin
Fréchette, Louis
Gaulle, General
    Charles de
Giscard d'Estaing, Valéry
Jefferson, Thomas
Kerry, John
Lang, Jack
Lévesque, René
Louis-Philippe, King
Mendès France, Pierre
Miranda, Francisco de
Mitterrand, François
Pompidou, Georges
Riel, Louis
Roosevelt, Franklin D.
Talleyrand-Périgord,
    Charles
Tristan, Flora
Trudeau, Pierre Elliott
Washington, George
Wilson, Woodrow

RELIGION
Catholic Church
Huguenots
Jesuits
Joan of Arc
Labat, Jean-Baptiste
Lalemant, Jérôme
Laval, François de
    Montmorency
Leclercq, Chrétien

Perrot, Nicolas
Provost, Joseph
Raynal, Abbé
Richelieu, Cardinal
    Armand Jean du
    Plessis de
Sainte-Hélène, Marie-
    André
Tertre, Jean-Baptiste du
Ursulines
Vodun

SCIENCE AND TECHNOLOGY
Audubon, John James
Computer Technology
Cyberculture
Dubos, René
Nuclear Technology
Project FAMOUS
Reeves, Hubert
Space Technology
Steamboats

SLAVERY
Antislavery Movements
Bigelow, John
Compagnie du Sénégal
Schoelcher, Victor
Slavery
Toussaint L'Ouverture,
    François

SPORT
Sport

THEORY
Aron, Raymond
Barthes, Roland
Baudrillard, Jean
Bourdieu, Pierre
Cabet, Etienne
Caillois, Roger
Certeau, Michel de
Cohen, Gustave
Debray, Régis
Deleuze, Gilles
Derrida, Jacques
Doubrovsky, Serge
Duvergier de Hauranne,
    Ernest
Fanon, Frantz
Foucault, Michel
Guattari, Félix
Guérin, Daniel
Lacan, Jacques
Leiris, Michel
Lévi-Strauss, Claude
Lyotard, Jean-
    François
Maritain, Jacques
Mattelart, Armand
Montaigne, Michel de
Revel, Jean-François
Rivet, Paul
Sarduy, Severo
Siegfried, André
Tel Quel
Theory
Tocqueville, Alexis de
Utopias

CHRONOLOGY OF FRANCE AND THE AMERICAS

1493   On his second voyage, Christopher Columbus sights both the main islands (Martinique and Guadeloupe) of the French Antilles but establishes no colonies because the Carib Indians still inhabit the islands.

1502   Christopher Columbus lands at Carbet on the Caribbean side of Martinique on June 15.

1524   Giovanni da Verrazzano, sailing for France, sights land around the Carolinas, discovers the Hudson River, and reaches Nova Scotia ("Arcadia") before returning to France.

1534   Jacques Cartier explores from the Strait of Belle Isle south to Gaspé Bay.

1535   Cartier, on his second voyage, sails up the Saint Lawrence River to Stadacona, a Huron Indian village at present-day Quebec City, and then to Hochelaga at present-day Montreal.

1541   On Cartier's final voyage, to what is now Quebec, he finds fool's gold and quartz that he thinks are gold and diamonds.

1562   Jean Ribaut brings 150 Huguenots to Port Royal, North Carolina.

1564   French Huguenots settle in Florida, awakening the Spanish to defend their territory.

French and Spanish begin an intermittent fight that ends only in 1580 when Gilberto Gil loses a naval battle and the French withdraw from Florida.

1595   Sir Walter Raleigh publishes *The Discovery of the Large, Rich, and Beautiful Empire of Guiana,* generating the legend of El Dorado and attracting explorers from Spain and England and then France.

Early Seventeenth Century   American, European, Arab, and other African slavers begin providing slaves to the Americas after the indigenous populations proved unadaptable. French collection stations on Africa's west coast included Goree, Senegal; El Mina, Ghana; and Ouidah, Benin. Nearly two centuries of experience as slave centers help to establish them as commercial communities.

1604   First French settlement on the North Atlantic coast at Neutral Island in Maine. Later the settlement moves to Acadia.

First French expedition to Guiana.

1605   Samuel de Champlain sails south to Cape Cod while garrisoning Quebec and developing the fur trade.

1608   Founding of Quebec City and of the colony of New France.

1626   Rouen Commercial Company sends twenty-six French settlers to establish the village of Sinnamary, who then join with additional settlers on an island later named Cayenne.

1635   French Pierre Belain d'Esnambuc arrives in Martinique. Because of the wealth their sugar plantations generate, the West Indian islands are desired by both Britain and France. Martinique and Guadeloupe remain French, but the other French islands, Dominica, St. Lucia, and Tobago, are lost by France in the Napoleonic wars.

1636   King Louis XIII permits the introduction of slaves to the French West Indies.

1642   Foundation of Montreal.

1663–1763   Guiana switches from French to English to Dutch to French control and mostly stagnates. In 1664 the French take Guiana from the Dutch; in 1667 they lose it to the English; in 1676 they take it back.

1671   French explorers reach Sault Saint Marie, Michigan, and claim the interior of North America for Louis XIV.

1673   Jesuit priest Jacques Marquette and trader Louis Joliet explore from Lake Michigan south down the Mississippi River to the Arkansas River. Hearing that the Spanish control the lower Mississippi, they turn back.

1674   Martinique officially annexed by the king of France.

1678   Rene Robert Cavalier, Sieur de la Salle, and Father Louis Hennepin pass Niagara Falls on an exploration from Canada to the American interior.

LaSalle establishes Fort Crevecoeur on the Illinois River; French Huguenots settle in Charles Town, Carolina.

1685   LaSalle reaches Matagorda Bay on the Gulf of Mexico, builds Fort Saint Louis, and begins the land trek back to Canada. His men murder him in 1687.

Establishment of Jean-Baptiste Colbert's "Black Code" that, in sixty articles, officially governs the lives of slaves until 1848.

1689   War with Britain begins. Each war has an American and a European name: first, King William's War, or the War of the League of Augsburg, 1689–1697; second, Queen Anne's War, or the War of the Spanish Succession, 1701–1714; and third, King George's War, or the War of Austrian Succession, 1740–1748. The culmination was the Seven Years' War, or the French and Indian War, 1756–1763, which ended much of France's first empire.

1697   The Treaty of Ryswick cedes the western third of the island of Hispaniola to France, which names its new colony Saint-Domingue (Santo Domingo).

1699   Foundation of the royal colony of Louisiana.

1701   Cadillac founds Detroit.

1702   The French build a fort at Mobile (present-day Alabama).

1712   Control of Louisiana is ceded to financier Antoine Crozat.

1714   At the end of Queen Anne's War, the British gain Nova Scotia and its important fishing grounds.

1717   Louisiana comes under the control of the Compagnie d'Occident.

1718   First French land grant at Baton Rouge. Foundation of New Orleans.

1719   The first African slaves arrive in Louisiana.

1720   Foundation of the fortress of Louisbourg on the northern tip of Cape Breton Island (present-day Nova Scotia).

1731   Louisiana reverts to royal colony status.

1755   Deportation by the British of the French population of Acadia.

1756–1763   French and Indian War. Initial French success at Fort Necessity (near Pittsburgh, Pennsylvania) turns to defeat as the British take Louisbourg in 1758; Quebec in 1759; Montreal in 1760; and Martinique, Grenada, and the other French Caribbean islands in 1762.

1762–1848   Martinique is occupied several times by the British. France and Britain fight over the island until 1815, when it is restored to France.

1763   The Treaty of Paris gives Canada, Cape Breton, and Louisiana west of the Mississippi to Britain and the rest to Spain. France retains Saint-Pierre et Miquelon. Also France gives Britain much of the Caribbean, but Britain returns the islands. France is finished as a major player in the New World.

1763–1765   Louis XV wants to reestablish an empire in the aftermath of his defeats by Britain. His best opportunity is in Guiana, the largest landmass left of the empire. He also needs to control the area; to preclude slave rebellions, he sends 14,000 white French settlers to Kourou on the coast. Ten thousand of them die within two years, and the survivors move to the Iles du Salut (Salvation Islands), which have a less malarial climate.

1774   The Quebec Act grants the French Canadians certain linguistic and religious privileges.

1776   American Declaration of Independence.

1783   End of American Revolutionary War.

1789   The French Revolution begins, destroying the monarch and the monarchy and instituting the First Republic.

1791   Louis XVI attempts to flee with his family to Austria. France and Austria go to war for a time in 1792.

A slave rebellion erupts in Haiti, Santo Domingo, led by Daniel Boukman.

1792–1815   Napoleonic wars grip Europe and the empires.

1793   Louis XVI and his queen are tried and executed.

Slavery is abolished in Santo Domingo.

1795   The first French political prisoners arrive in Guiana.

1798   An army of slaves, led by Toussaint L'Ouverture, defeats a British invasion force in Haiti.

1799   Napoléon returns to France, leaving his armies behind, and becomes First Consul.

1800   In the Treaty of San Ildefonso, Napoléon compels Spain to return much of Louisiana to France.

First Decade of the Nineteenth Century   The transatlantic slave trade is outlawed. France is among the nations whose navies patrol off west Africa. France also establishes bases and trading posts on the coast.

1802   Napoléon is named Life Consul.

Consul Victor Hueues reestablishes slavery in the colonies.

Napoléon sends French troops to Santo Domingo to restore slavery. The French capture Toussaint L'Ouverture. Slave revolt in Guadeloupe.

1803   An army of former slaves, led by Dessalines, defeats French forces in Haiti. L'Ouverture dies in captivity.

The Louisiana Purchase: Napoléon sells French lands west of the Appalachians to the United States.

1804   Dessalines proclaims Haiti's independence. Fired by the example of the French Revolution, the black slaves revolted, massacred the French landowners, and proclaimed the world's first black republic.

Napoléon crowns himself emperor of the French.

1807–1815 The British and the Portuguese occupy French Guiana.

1812   Conflict between Canada and the United States.

Louisiana becomes the eighteenth U.S. state.

1815   The Battle of Waterloo marks final defeat of Napoléon and confirms the restoration of the monarchy in France made the previous year.

Dominica, Saint Lucia, and Tobago are lost by France in the Napoleonic wars, which also made Britain master of the seas.

Restored French control of Guiana comes with calls for the abolition of slavery.

1817   Slave trade becomes illegal in France.

1830   The July Revolution replaces Charles X with the Duc d'Orleans, Louis-Philippe.

1837–1838 The Patriots' Rebellion in Upper and Lower Canada is severely repressed in the latter (Quebec).

1838   France recognizes Haitian independence in exchange for a large financial indemnity.

1848   Agitation for electoral reform in 1847 and 1848 culminates in the abdication of Louis-Philippe in favor of his grandson. The French prefer another republic. They elect Napoléon Bonaparte's nephew, Louis, as president of the Second Republic.

A wave of revolutionary fervor in Europe leads to France freeing 262,564 slaves, most in the plantation colonies of the West Indies and Réunion. Former slaves in Guiana leave plantations to become subsistence farmers. Former slaves also have the right to vote. Because slave revolts begin in Martinique and Guadeloupe before the decree is known there, the governors of these colonies free the slaves on their own authority. Loss of slaves leads the plantation owners to bring in contract workers from India, but labor problems persist in the sugar industry throughout the nineteenth century.

1848–1851 France experiments with Chinese plantation labor in Guiana. The effort fails, and the Chinese become shopkeepers in Cayenne; the plantations revert to jungle.

1849   Upper and Lower Canada are joined into one united province.

1851   A coup d'état by Louis-Napoléon establishes Second Empire.

1861   Napoléon III suggests Maximilian to Mexico as its emperor.

1863   A Mexican delegation offers Maximilian and Charlotte the crown in October. Maximilian accepts only if a national plebiscite indicates it to be the wish of the people.

1865   The American Civil War ends. The United States pressures France to observe the Monroe Doctrine and leave Mexico.

1866   Napoléon III withdraws French troops from Mexico. Maximilian is unwilling to abandon his supporters. Charlotte sails to Europe to seek help but finds none. Mexican republican forces slowly take control.

1867   After a seventy-two-day siege at Queretaro, republican forces take Maximilian and execute him and two of his generals.

Canadian confederation.

1870s   Establishment of the Third Republic in France.

1870   The Franco-Prussian War produces another French defeat, and France is cautious about coming into conflict with other colonial powers for the next decade. The decline of the French navy enables the British navy to maintain its dominance of the seas throughout the 1880s.

1871   Paris Commune.

1876   Ferdinand de Lesseps is chosen by the Geographical Society of Paris to head La Société Civile Internationale du Canal Interocéanique du Darien. French navy lieutenant Wyse examines the Isthmus of Panama for a suitable route for the canal.

Early 1880s   Interest revives in expansion as the French mission, the way for France to reenter the world. Movement leaders include Leon Gambetta and Jules Ferry. Advocates assume that France, to maintain its image and influence, requires either continental or overseas power. The *Jeune Ecole* of the 1880s prefigures Alfred Thayer Mahan's argument that naval power equals world power. This nationalism drives the subsequent French push for empire from the 1880s until after empire's end in the 1960s.

1883   Transport of convicts to Guiana resumes.

1884   More than 19,000 men work on the Panama Canal, the maximum number the French employ at any one time.

1885   Execution of the Manitoban rebel Métis leader Louis Riel.

1886   Dedication of Statue of Liberty in New York harbor.

1888   Work begins on the lock canal in Panama. Gustave Eiffel is to construct the canal locks.

1894   The "new" Panama Canal Company, the Compagnie Nouvelle de Canal de Panama, is organized. Liquidation of the isthmian canal company is complete. The "Panama Affair" involves prosecution of company officials. Ferdinand de Lesseps and his son, Charles, receive but never serve five-year sentences for fraud and maladministration. Ferdinand dies at age eighty-nine on December 7.

The ministry for the colonies is established.

Devil's Island, Guiana, originally a leper colony, becomes the home of political prisoners.

1896   Wilfrid Laurier becomes the first French-Canadian prime minister of Canada.

1902   Mt. Pelée erupts, destroying Saint-Pierre, Martinique, and killing 30,000 people in three minutes. Fort-de-France becomes the capital.

1904   France sells its interest in the Panama Canal to the United States for approximately $40 million. The United States begins a ten-year construction project that costs approximately $387 million.

1905   Separation of church and state in France.

1914–1918   The first U.S. troops arrive in France in 1917 as part of World War I effort.

1915–1930   Haiti is occupied by U.S. Marines.

1919   The Treaty of Versailles ends World War I. Visit of U.S. president Woodrow Wilson to Paris.

1938   After the French national assembly decides to phase out the penal colony, the final transport of prisoners to Guiana occurs.

1939   World War II begins.

1940   Fall of France to the Axis powers. Marshal Pétain signs the armistice, establishing an unoccupied zone with capital at Vichy. General Charles de Gaulle in London calls for resistance to continue.

1944   On D day, June 6, American, British, and Canadian forces invade France at Normandy, supported by the French Resistance. Paris is liberated.

1945   World War II ends.

1946   The Fourth Republic begins in France.

Martinique acquires the status of a French department. Four deputies and two senators represent it.

1947   The United States announces the Marshall Plan to aid European recovery from World War II.

1949   Creation of the North Atlantic Treaty Organization (NATO).

DDT spraying begins in Guiana. Along with public health measures begun in the 1940s, it helps to decrease mortality rates for malaria, yellow fever, leprosy, and infant mortality.

1957–1971   François Duvalier becomes president of Haiti.

1958   Colonial war in Algeria and an army revolt bring down the Fourth Republic in France. General de Gaulle returns to power and establishes the Fifth Republic.

1960   Beginning of the "Quiet Revolution" in Quebec.

1961   Opening of the Maison du Québec in Paris.

1962   France establishes a space agency with a mandate to find a new rocket site to replace the one in Hammaguir, Algeria. The site is French Guiana.

The Quebec energy minister René Lévesque nationalizes Hydro-Quebec.

1964   Kourou space center opens.

1967   President de Gaulle visits Quebec and cries "Vive le Québec libre" from the balcony of Montreal city hall.

1968   Pierre Elliott Trudeau becomes prime minister of Canada for the first time.

1969   De Gaulle resigns and is succeeded by Georges Pompidou.

1974   Election in France of President Valéry Giscard d'Estaing.

Martinique and Guadeloupe become regions of France.

1976   The separatist Parti Québécois gains power in Quebec under premier René Lévesque.

Late 1970s and into the1980s   Large numbers of Haitians immigrate to French Guiana and to Quebec.

1980   The referendum on sovereignty in Quebec ends in a 59.2 percent "no" vote.

1981   Election in France of a Socialist president, François Mitterrand.

1992   Opening of Disneyland Paris.

1995   Jacques Chirac is elected president of France.

The sovereignty referendum in Quebec ends with another "no" vote, but with a narrower margin of 50.6 percent.

2003   The French government opposes the U.S. intervention in Iraq.

INTRODUCTORY ESSAYS

THE FRENCH ATLANTIC

Bill Marshall

How might the French Atlantic work as a concept, and what received opinions does it challenge? Two books may serve as points of departure. The first and less well known is a diatribe by Guy Hocquenghem from 1979 entitled *La Beauté du métis: Réflexions d'un francophobe* (Paris: Ramsay). Hocquenghem, who has an entry in these volumes, is best known as one of the founders of the modern gay movement in France, and as the author of the first work of what we would now call gay or even queer theory, *Le Désir homosexuel* of 1972. By the late 1970s, however, Hocquenghem's preoccupations had widened to a wider critique of modernity, and in particular of that form of political and cultural modernity ushered in by 1789, namely the modern state and nationalism. *La Beauté du métis* is an extended critique of what he terms "le système france" (sic). He has a taste for provocation, as will become clear.

For Hocquenghem, France is "a country without encounters or hybridity [*métissage*]"(9). In France, the most closed country in the world, you grow up a captive. Nowhere is this more true than in the horrors wrought within the French family. French misogyny and homophobia are in part explained by this fear of contagion. The centralizing, totalizing, and bureaucratized links in France between power, art, and society, with the eye of surveillance that is Paris policing the center-periphery relation, mean that its core concept goes unquestioned, so that "france" (sic) is to the French what God is to Muslims, indescribable and unrepresentable because it is the foundation of all representations and permits no critical heterogeneity. In contrast, other nations find it easier to handle culture and difference. Whereas Britain and Spain (and also Portugal) were overtaken in size and power by their former colonies, france (sic) remained resolutely at the center of the French-speaking world, so that for the French, the British or Hispanic "cultural oceans" are incomprehensible because decentered, and French history is no more than the recrimination felt toward these less deserving nations that have stolen first place. The French nation is thus immobilized in its cultural unification, which erases from its regions

3

both their past and future (that of possible *métissage*), has an extremely uneasy relationship with the "popular," and where culture has become a compulsory public service, with any countercultural forms aspiring to state power one day. Indeed, whereas in other nations the state is the impatiently tolerated form of political domination, in France it is perceived as the apogee of civilization, the goal of every cultural expression. In contrast to the seductions, voyages, and initiations of other literatures, French novels are in vitro, part of a literature of doctors and administrators devoid of generous sensations, built around authors rather than characters, the aim being the completion of a national cultural task. Needless to say, the policing—by the Académie Française, but this extends outward—and fetishization of the language itself play a major role in this process. Unlike in other languages, "sub"-languages and variations are not encouraged and fail to create any new vectors of meaning and identity.

The simplification in Hocquenghem's polemic is almost cartoonlike. Written in 1979, *La Beauté du métis* anticipates in its preoccupations some of the key political and intellectual events of the following decade, with the emergence of the *Front national* or works by other intellectuals such as Julia Kristeva and Tzvetan Todorov on similar issues of difference and modernity. Certainly, as with many radical critics of nationhood, Hocquenghem is sometimes complicit with what he sees as the nation's suppression of its own hybridity and heterogeneity. (In other words, those who criticize nations for writing out their immigrant and minority dimension create a self-fulfilling prophecy.) The context of 1979, on the threshold of the hegemony of economic liberalism in the West in the 1980s and the accelerated globalization of the 1990s, prevents his formulating or balancing his points in the light of the downside of those developments, namely, the risk of international market forces suppressing diversity.

However, before returning to these points I would like to move, more briefly, to a second book that can serve as a starting point. Paul Gilroy's *The Black Atlantic: Modernity and Double Consciousness* (London: Verso, 1993) has been very influential in the field of postcolonial studies. It basically attempts to do two things. One is to reinscribe the black African experience of slavery and diaspora into accounts of Western modernity; the other is to challenge black nationalism and Afrocentrism from the point of view of cultural hybridity. The intercultural and transnational formation of the black Atlantic demonstrates that it is engagement with others, with difference, that constitutes what we term cultural or national identities. For this argument Gilroy deploys the ship as his central organizing symbol, seen as "a living, micro-cultural, micro-political system in motion," a new chronotope in Mikhail Bakhtin's sense of a certain historical mapping of time and space. The middle passage is thus one of a circulation of ideas, of key cultural and political artifacts, be they jazz or W. E. B. Du Bois's take on European nationalism and romanticism. The image of the ship and of the Atlantic passage begin to propose that mobility of identity aspired to by Hocquenghem and described by Michel de Certeau in *The Practice of Everyday Life* in 1980:

> A space exists when one takes into consideration vectors of direction, velocities, and time variables. Thus space is composed of intersections of mobile elements. It is in a sense articulated by the ensemble of movements deployed within it. (University of California Press 1984, 117)

Confronting these texts by Hocquenghem and Gilroy forces the question, What might happen, what might be enabled, by thinking of Frenchness as diasporic and mobile?

This suggestion goes against the grain somewhat, but in fact there are ample reasons for doing so. If we concentrate for the moment on North America, it was of course the French who opened up the continent for European settlement and development, largely because of their control of the entry to the two main river systems. But a less well-known history than the rise and fall of New France must also be attended to. Again the received wisdom is that France, with its large peasant population, has not been a country of emigration and has not produced large settler societies (with the exception of Algeria). However, the 1990 U.S. census showed that there were 13 million Americans of French descent, making them the fifth-largest ethnic group after the British, Germans, Irish, Africans, and Italians. In Massachusetts they are the second-largest such group. Patterns of French migration to or within North America have historically taken three forms:

- Huguenots after the Revocation of the Edict of Nantes in 1685, who tended to settle in the English-speaking colonies;
- those fleeing the political upheavals of the nineteenth century and the loss of Alsace-Lorraine (for example, 20,000 French immigrants arrived in the United States in 1851, and there were French-language newspapers in New York, Philadelphia, and Charleston; there was even an entirely French company of Union troops, the Lafayette guards, during the Civil War; and in total it is estimated that 353,000 French people emigrated to America between 1820 and 1900, 751,000 between 1820 and 1978);
- massive emigration, nearly 1 million people, from Quebec in the late nineteenth century to the factories and mills of New England.

The reality of this French diaspora underlines all the more the impact on the landscape and culture of the continent.

Some examples: Paul Revere was the son of a Huguenot goldsmith whose real name was Rivoire. One theory of the origin of the term "Dixie" to describe the South comes from the early nineteenth-century practice in New Orleans of issuing bilingual banknotes, with $10 bills being referred to by anglophones as "dixies." Place-names are probably too well known to invoke here, but they include the Ozarks ("Aux Arcs") in Arkansas. John James Audubon, the ornithologist, artist, and naturalist who gives his name to the Audubon Society, was born in Haiti in 1785, the illegitimate son of a French merchant, planter, and slave trader and a local Creole woman. He emigrated to the United States at the age of eighteen. Jack Kerouac, born in Lovell, Massachusetts, in 1922, had Québécois parents and did not speak English until he went to school at the age of five. Whole websites in Quebec are devoted to the genealogy of Madonna, whose mother, Louise Fortin, famously dead of breast cancer when the future singer was five, also came from French-Canadian stock and whose ancestry can be traced back ten generations to Julien Fortin, who in 1619 married a Marie Lavye at Notre-Dame-de-Vair in what is now the Sarthe.

Delving a bit deeper, other itineraries hint at what a transnational category like the French Atlantic can mean, and what a purely *hexagonal* or France-centered approach can obfuscate. Louis Hémon (1880–1913) was born in Brest and rebelled against his academic and Catholic family, turning up as a farm laborer in 1911 in rural Quebec. His novel *Maria Chapdelaine* provided for French readers one of the founding myths of French Canada, and for French Canadians it has become a site of some ideological struggle. Summing up shifting states of Franco-Quebec relations, there are three film versions, French, British, and Franco-Québécois, with the latest version seeking, for example, to emphasize mythical, magical, and poetic continuities between Brittany and the native peoples. Sergio Kokis, who was born in Rio de Janeiro in 1944 and studied psychology at Strasbourg in the 1960s, emigrated to Montreal in 1970, and has published approximately a novel a year since *Le Pavillon des miroirs* in 1994. These authors fall outside any mappings of literature confined to the nation-state or centered on Paris. Kokis is but one example of a completely underresearched dimension, namely, that of overlapping Atlantics, such as the interaction of French and Hispanic or Lusitanian cultures in the New World without which, for example, the city of New Orleans or the cultivation of coffee would not have taken the forms recognized today.

It would be unwise to propose an overarching theoretical summary of what as diverse a reality as the French Atlantic is and can be. However, it is possible to suggest what some of its specificities and characteristics may be. The first is that of the relations with native peoples in New France before the British Conquest of 1759 (and thus before the particularly catastrophic examples of French republican colonialism a century later). There is much evidence to show that on the whole the French encounter with the native peoples of North America was characterized by the greater degree, in some periods at least, of suppleness and cooperation as opposed to the expansion and extermination that tended to mark the Anglo-Saxon encounter. This was by and large due to the sparser nature of settlement, but also to the reliance on the native peoples for the undertaking of the principal economic task of the colony, namely, the fur trade. Wars with the Iroquois, for example, were usually part of a wider chess game of alliances in the North American continent between competing European powers. The Jesuits, although some met a famous martyrdom in the seventeenth century, were often successful, through their notoriously syncretizing techniques, in their conversions of native communities.

A second point is about cultural transformation. As Paul Gilroy writes about the black experience, some figures may begin as, say, French (or Breton, or Norman . . .)

> and are then changed into something else which evades those specific labels and with them all fixed notions of nationality and national identity. Whether their experience of exile is enforced or chosen, temporary or permanent, these intellectuals and activists, writers, speakers, poets and artists repeatedly articulate a desire to escape the restrictive bonds of ethnicity, national identification, and sometimes even "race" itself. (19)

In the case of Quebec, by 1759 cultural identity had profoundly changed. One of the mythical—and supremely gendered—figures within the construction of Quebec cultural identity is that of the Coureurs de bois, nomadically escaping the restrictions of the ancien régime, trading and trapping furs, commingling with the native peoples. Indeed, these processes went as far as the creation of a new "race" of people, the Métis of Manitoba, Catholic and French speaking. Revisionist Quebec historian Laurier L. Lapierre argues cogently that by 1759 the *canadiens* already formed a distinct culture, a reality intensified by the departure from the colony of the French elite personnel (with the exception of the clergy). The overlap with the British Atlantic is crucial for an understanding of the later development of Quebec, as in its parliamentary institutions or the architecture and urban space of Montreal.

The third characteristic of the French Atlantic is that of the complete unsettling of the center/periphery relationship that for Hocquenghem bedevils French culture. It also unsettles the similar binary established between "French" and "francophone." The non-decolonization of the center that these terms imply in fact perpetuates the power relationships and produces the absurd notion that France is not a francophone country. The emphasis on passages and journeys, and historically the ship, means that the only conceivable "centers," in the sense of loci of departures and arrivals, are the ports, with Brest, Nantes, and La Rochelle displacing Paris.

Fourthly, the French Atlantic is also of course a black Atlantic. The role of the slave trade and its place in a wider transatlantic commodity system, the plantation cultures of the French Caribbean and their historical legacy in Haiti, Guadeloupe, and Martinique, are well known. But just as "the Black Atlantic" propelled the African diaspora into the heart of accounts of Western modernity, so too does "the French Atlantic" render unavoidable and inevitable an engagement with that racialized terror when discussing any aspect of French modernity. The interactions of the African and French Atlantics accompany many entries in these volumes, from the author of *The Three Musketeers* to World War I, in itself a crucial historical and cultural rediscovery of France by the United States in which the experience of black GIs in a nonsegregated if colonial Republic impelled a further series of cultural transformations and exchanges.

This point about race and imperialism points to two important political dimensions to the French Atlantic. The first is that of the complementary but also competing political and cultural modernities of the American and French Revolutions. Political and intellectual developments in eighteenth-century France had a massive impact on the next century's revolutions in Haiti and Latin America. That relationship also goes to the heart of a second political point, that of the crisis of French universalism that the French Atlantic represents, be it when Toussaint L'Ouverture takes the republican discourse a little too literally in the years before 1803, or when the contemporary republic struggles to come to terms with questions of difference raised by the large Moslem population, the AIDS epidemic, or feminist agendas. It is thus important to emphasize that the French Atlantic is never a one-way street. It forces an engagement with debates around postwar modernization in Europe, the profound impact of the Marshall Plan, changed business practices, and the rise of consumer capitalism. At the same time, however, it sidesteps the cultural imperialism argument—vocal in France, for example, when Disneyland Paris opened in 1992—which posits a confrontation between two "whole," nonporous cultures. In turn, the French Atlantic also upsets the binaries and identities built around Americanness itself, in particular forcing the rediscovery and reassessment of the multilingual history and reality of the United States.

There is a concept that is at the heart of this crucial, renewed Frenchness as diaspora. In the chapter "Postulats de la linguistique" of *A Thousand Plateaus* (1980), Gilles Deleuze and Félix Guattari suggest ways in which French may indeed be "francophonized." Within their ontology of particles, flows, and codings, "minor" languages and cultures are to be understood in terms not of numbers but of the relationship between becoming and the process of territorialization and deterritorialization. Minor cultures refuse and question fixity and positions of mastery. Quebec French is minor in relationship to the vast North American anglophone majority, but also in relation to standard French. Individual utterances always imply collective assemblages. "Minor" and "major" attitudes can be adopted toward any language or culture. Quebec French can fall back on Oedipal and masculinized reterritorializations. But metropolitan French and its variants may also be made to undermine "major" culture's pretensions to the natural, normal, and universal. For Deleuze and Guattari, a "language" in the singular does not exist except as a certain unstable play of variants and constants.

The French Atlantic could conceivably, then, contribute to a process whereby "French" would be destabilized, in which seeds of becoming, in Deleuze and Guattari's terms, could trigger uncontrollable movements and deterritorializations of the mean or majority.

In 1979 Guy Hocquenghem wrote that he longed for "a france in pieces" (32), given over to multiple identities. Significantly, however, the concept of "France" here remains and has not been subsumed in another culture. The French Atlantic does not deconstruct France out of existence; on the contrary it proposes that Frenchness is more important than ever: not in the comfortable or threatened assertions of cultural nationalism, but as a diverse and creative force inhabiting spaces between cultures, shaping interactions, turning up unexpectedly, challenging assumptions.

I would like to end by quoting from a text that is truly "French Atlantic" but that bypasses France itself. It is part of the preface that Edouard Glissant wrote to the 1999 Paris Gallimard edition of *L'Homme rapaillé,* the classic collection of poems by the Quebec nationalist writer Gaston Miron. Recounting in very free direct discourse a journey made to Quebec and to Miron, Glissant recounts the winter rural scene ("here space both joins up with you and takes you out of yourself, here the tornadoes are born and build up that will hit the spaces of the Americas") before zooming back to Montreal, where Miron suggests that his poor, maligned French language, Quebec French to boot, is "a splendid streetwalker that mocks standardized unlingualism" (13–14). Glissant is astonished that here the French language, so long for him associated with domination and arrogance, is turned by the poet into a pathetic, suffering thing, and he likens it to a Caribbean Creole emerging and seeking the light of day. With Miron, Glissant expresses his determination to whip up their threatened languages and declaim throughout the world with both anguish and "stubborn hope" that they too—along with all tongues that are Creole or uprooted [*dessouchées*]—will be part of, will share and participate in, French and Frenchness.

FRANCE AND CANADA

Frédéric Bastien

Relations between France and Canada have varied greatly over the 400-year period since first colonization. They have in general been marked by an asymmetrical relationship, characterized by nostalgia on the part of the French Canadians and relative indifference on the part of the French. Franco-Canadian relations are thus articulated in relation to Quebec above all else. France has developed a direct and privileged relation with its former colony because of this central factor, and the survival in collective memory of General de Gaulle's "vive le Québec libre" of 1967. (See GAULLE, GENERAL CHARLES DE; QUEBEC.)

In the beginning, however, France took a later interest in the New World than England, Portugal, and Spain. It was only in 1534 that Jacques Cartier sailed up the Saint Lawrence River, forty-two years after Columbus's "discovery." Cartier made three voyages, getting as far as present-day Montreal, but they failed to arouse in France a project for exploiting these new territories. And not until 1608 did the French show any more interest, when Samuel de Champlain established a trading post for furs. The fur trade, and not colonization per se, was the key motivation. Although some settlers arrived, it was on a very small scale. Nevertheless Louis XIV tried to expand the colony and make it prosper, sending women and trying to develop timber and agricultural resources. (See CARTIER, JACQUES; CHAMPLAIN, SAMUEL DE; FUR TRADE; MONTREAL; SAINT LAWRENCE RIVER; TIMBER.)

These early efforts failed and France fell back on its traditional indifference toward the colony, an attitude cruelly exposed by the wars with Britain, which in North America confronted New France from its base of thirteen colonies. Although France committed few resources to it, the war in America was unpopular, and conducted with little enthusiasm by French elites. Voltaire wrote that he was like the general public, who loved peace more than they loved Canada and thought France could be perfectly happy without Quebec.

In 1763, after the end of the French and Indian War, Louis XV signed the Treaty of Paris, which ceded French North America and its 60,000 inhabitants to Great Britain. France was left with some Caribbean islands and in the North Atlantic the outcrops of Saint-Pierre et Miquelon. The colonial elites went back to France, leaving the rest of the population, mainly peasants and clergy, to their own devices, provoking among the (French) Canadians a sense of abandonment, finding themselves completely cut off from the "mother country." In its turn France quickly forgot about them. Nearly sixty years after the Conquest, Tocqueville was astonished to discover that the (French) Canadians had not forgotten the language of their ancestors, and that French remained the language of the Saint Lawrence valley. He was deeply touched by the warm welcome he received as a "Frenchman from old France," but his account of his journey aroused no interest in France itself. (See FRENCH AND INDIAN WAR; LANGUAGE; SAINT-PIERRE ET MIQUELON; TOCQUEVILLE, ALEXIS DE; TREATY OF PARIS [1763]).

A similar nonreaction occurred in 1839. The French writer Alfred de Vigny was in London, visiting the House of Lords, at the very moment when the Durham report was being debated. Lord Durham, governor-general of Canada, advocated the forced assimilation of the French Canadians after the armed rebellions of 1837–1838. Vigny tried to whip up public opinion in France, but to general indifference. In fact, it was only in 1855 that the first official contacts between France and Quebec took place, when the Emperor Napoléon III sent the warship *La Capricieuse* to Quebec City, to a warm reception from the population.

The first institutional contacts began a few years later. In 1881 Quebec premier Adolphe Chapleau made a six-month visit to France and on his return created the post of agent general in Paris, appointing Senator Hector Fabre, who occupied the position for nearly thirty years and also became the representative of Canada. The renewed interest at the official level was confirmed by the visits of Quebec premier Honoré Mercier and the first francophone prime minister of Canada, Wilfrid Laurier, who were welcomed with some emotion in France in, respectively, 1891 and 1897, although little followed from them in the short and medium term. It was not until 1927 that France and Canada officially established diplomatic relations. In spite of this and Canada's participation as an ally of France in two world wars, the links remained distant both diplomatically and in the attitudes of the two populations.

This does not mean that no one in France took an interest in Canada. Many in nationalist and catholic milieus, especially after the Franco-Prussian War of 1870, began to look upon (French) Canada in a positive light compared to France, for families remained large and religious observance strong. Charles de Gaulle was born into this kind of milieu in 1890, and from adolescence took an interest in the French Canadians. This took on a historical and political dimension when on August 1, 1940, he appealed to them from London to help save France. The problem, however, was that the French Canadians were at first sympathetic to Marshal Pétain's regime, while anglophone Canada immediately adopted the British position and supported de Gaulle. Nevertheless, the Québécois were hostile to the policy of collaboration and leaned toward Gaullism the more the Vichy regime's collusion with Nazism became apparent. During his visit to Canada in 1944, de

Gaulle was acclaimed equally in English and French Canada. (See CATHOLIC CHURCH; WORLD WAR II.)

In the aftermath of the war, France and Canada kept up cordial diplomatic relations, but they were in fact largely devoid of substance. Despite the fact that certain great French artists such as Charles Trenet and Charles Aznavour enjoyed some of their first successes in Quebec, and even if French Canadians were often imbued with French culture, and thinkers such as Emmanuel Mounier had many followers there, the links between the two communities remained minimal. (See MUSIC [POP].)

Things did not change until a further visit from Charles de Gaulle in 1960, which had important long-term consequences. Besides visiting Ottawa, Toronto, and Montreal, de Gaulle also visited Quebec City, where he met the province's leading politicians. De Gaulle retained from this visit the conviction that there was indeed a "Quebec problem," and that it had two facets. Firstly, the relation between French and English Canada was not that of equals. The francophones endured the situation of being a colonized people within Canada. Secondly, the French president also observed a malaise between the French and the French Canadians, and in particular that the latter still felt a strong resentment about being abandoned by the former colonial power.

Feeling some guilt about this, de Gaulle wanted France to come to the aid of French Canada, whose identity was threatened. Moreover, in this period of decolonization he was seeking new ways for France to maintain its world influence in political, military, and cultural domains. Since France had not been able to hold on to its empire, it could nonetheless renew close relations with those "cousins" who were also seeking links. It was obvious that a stronger French presence in Quebec could only help to maintain France's status in the world.

The link is clear between the end of the French colonial empire and the relaunch of official Franco-Quebec relations. This explains the interest taken by de Gaulle, and the timing of his policy decisions on the matter, toward the end of the Algerian war. In the early 1960s, de Gaulle asked his culture minister André Malraux to take charge of relations with Quebec. Malraux was probably chosen because the general was not sure where to begin, and thought culture was the most likely candidate. On the Quebec side, the new government of Jean Lesage, elected in 1960, was very keen to renew relations with France, and in particular to set up Quebec's own diplomatic representation in Paris. André Malraux was favorable to this idea as he wanted to set up a "Maison du Québec" in Paris that would serve as a kind of shopwindow for Quebec in France.

The project came to fruition in 1961 and the French authorities spared no effort or expense. The Maison du Québec was opened on October 4, 1961, by Malraux and Lesage, and its wide coverage in the media was unprecedented for a Quebec news story in France. In 1965, the Maison du Québec became the "Délégation générale du Québec en France" and gained near-embassy status, dealing directly with the French government without passing through the federal Canadian government. Three years later, de Gaulle instructed the French consulate in Quebec City to take responsibility for relations with the Quebec government and to bypass the embassy in Ottawa. These two institutions, the Délégation and the consulate, thus came to embody the direct and privileged relations that existed between the province and the French Republic.

De Gaulle made many other concrete and also symbolic gestures in favor of Quebec. Premier Jean Lesage was received in Paris in 1961 with the honors and ceremony due to a head of state. De Gaulle's toast contained the familiar bombast: "You are Quebec, you are the French Canadians." De Gaulle's strategy was to undo the cold war politics of two opposing blocs, and thus to carve out for France a great role in international relations. Helping the French Canadians in their self-emancipation was one of his ways of making France's presence felt in the world. He also noted to his minister Alain Peyrefitte that the French population of Canada was in danger of losing its identity, and that France had to come to its aid.

For its part, Quebec wished to build a modern state and to assert its French-speaking identity within Canada, as well as its internal competencies in matters of education and culture that were put forth onto the international scene, such as the creation of foreign delegations including the Maison du Québec in Paris. In all these respects, cooperation with France was welcomed.

The interests of the two governments thus converged. The next cooperative gesture took the form of an exhibition of French technology in Montreal in 1963, where the minister of culture was again present. Malraux's eight-day visit garnered much publicity in Quebec, and prefigured that of de Gaulle four years later. Malraux emphasized the importance of French-Quebec relations wherever he went: "Canadians? I don't know who they are, I haven't met any. I only know French Canadians. France feels remorse only toward them."

However, de Gaulle wanted to go further than a special relationship with Quebec, as he made clear in a note written in 1963, in which he expressed the wish to avoid "drowning" relations with the province in something concerning "the two Canadas." "What is more," he argued, "French Canada will become a state in its own right, and we have to act with that prospect in mind."

De Gaulle was thus without question in favor of Quebec's independence before his famous 1967 visit. His views on English Canada in this scenario were that it should avoid being absorbed by the United States and in general try to keep its distance. His vision was at least coherent, seeking to resist the polarization of the world into two blocs, emphasizing a fear of the omnipotence of the United States and a reinforcement of the American bloc if such an absorption of Canada occurred following the independence of Quebec. So beyond the political emancipation of the Québécois, de Gaulle hoped for a close alliance between the two Canadas in order to limit American influence. This was the message he conveyed to the Canadian prime minister Lester Pearson on his visit to France in 1964, while holding back from hinting at the possibility of a sovereign Quebec.

The famous "Vive le Québec libre," de Gaulle's final utterance from the balcony of Montreal city hall on July 24, 1967, was thus a faithful reflection of his outlook. However, the form it took was rather improvised. The president had hesitated about going to Quebec at the time of Expo 67, but went ahead on the insistence of Montreal mayor Jean Drapeau and of Robert Bordaz, director of the French pavilion. De Gaulle nonetheless insisted on starting his visit in Quebec City rather than Ottawa, the federal capital. Indeed his arrival by sea meant that this was where he had to set foot first, at l'Anse-au-Foulon. His speeches on that day emphasized the need for the Québécois to decide their own destiny.

None of this, however, prefigured what was to come in Montreal, first of all because it had not been planned for de Gaulle to speak from the balcony. He had arrived at the city hall and was greeting the excited crowd. His request to address them was enabled by the fact that a technician from the French public service television channel SRC had placed a microphone on the balcony despite the explicit instructions of mayor Drapeau. This allowed the president to launch into his improvised but deeply felt and rather coherent speech. The event marked a turning point in relations between France and both Canada and Quebec.

For even if Quebec's leaders at the time were not seeking independence, they were very much in favor of further cooperation between the French and the Québécois. This cooperation began under de Gaulle but was greatly amplified in the years that followed. The first exchanges were in the domain of public administration. From the 1960s onward, places were reserved for Quebec among the cohort of foreign students at the Ecole nationale d'administration. In 1968, Quebec founded its own school of this kind, the Ecole nationale d'administration publique, partly on the French model. Similarly, the Québécois were attempting at the time to set up their own system of national insurance. In 1964, premier Jean Lesage's meeting with François Bloch Lainé, the chairman of the Caisse de dépôt, which administered French savings, convinced him to imitate France in this domain. A few months later his government set up the Caisse de dépôt et placement du Québec.

At the same time, the two governments increased the number of grants available to enable their nationals to study in the other country, and also organized many short courses for professional training. Here the creation of the Office franco-québécois pour la jeunesse (OFQJ) and the associations France-Québec and Québec-France were crucial. The first was inspired by a Franco-German office for youth set up in 1962, which aimed to bring together the younger generation of French and Germans. Through short courses and other exchanges, the OFQJ brought some 100,000 young people across the Atlantic over a period of thirty-five years. The second was the focal point for everyone in France interested in Quebec and wishing to organize joint activities. The equivalent association was set up in Quebec in 1971.

Besides these three entities, cooperation in research was also one of the main axes of the France-Quebec relationship. In 1983 a magazine was set up, *Médecine science,* which was a direct result of this, followed in 1988 by the *Revue des sciences de l'eau.* Further links were created between the Centre de recherche industrielle in Quebec and the Agence nationale de valorisation de la recherche, as well as between Quebec CEGEP (pre-university high schools) and the French IUT (Instituts universitaires techniques). University research in biotechnology was also jointly conducted by the Pasteur and Armand Frappier Institutes, McGill, Sherbrooke, Laval, and Compiègne universities, and the Institut national pour la recherche agronomique. These joint research operations went hand in hand with massive increases in student exchanges, reaching thousands per year by 2004.

The two governments also cooperated in the cultural domain, over and beyond the many artists and writers who have enjoyed transatlantic success. The Québécois had long held French culture in great affection. As well as Aznavour and Trenet, radio had broadcast French songs and in turn Quebec artists and singers dreamed of and aimed for success in France. This came to Félix Leclerc in the 1950s and Robert Charlebois in the early 1970s. Among the first Quebec writers to be recognized in France were Anne Hébert and Marie-Claire Blais. (See LITERARY RELATIONS.)

At the time of the first intergovernmental cultural cooperation, the Québécois were in fact much more influenced by American culture than at any time since World War II. Cultural exchanges were thus meant to reinforce the francophone character of Quebec. In the late 1970s, a new TV channel, TVFQ99, was set up to broadcast to Quebec a selection of programs from France. In 1987, this was extended to the whole of *la francophonie* and marked the beginning of TV5. (See FRANCOPHONIE, LA; TELEVISION.)

While all this was going on, relations between France and Canada were more hard going. In cultural, scientific, or other domains, relations between Ottawa and Paris remained distant and rarely gave rise to anything concrete. This was even the case for economic relations, which never surpassed those set up between France and Quebec, despite several attempts by the Canadian government.

This failure has to do with the limits of Canadian bilingualism. More than ever, linguistic dualism is about a francophone Quebec faced with nine anglophone provinces. The federal Canadian government has failed to extend the use of French to the rest of the country. As far as cooperation with France is concerned, this constitutes a major obstacle for Ottawa, which can never be more francophone than Quebec and cannot, according to the Canadian constitution, encroach upon the jurisdiction of the Quebec government in matters of education and culture. In this way Quebec is still France's privileged partner, and this dominates Franco-Canadian relations, in which direct links between France and Quebec, begun by de Gaulle, proliferate despite the opposition of the central Canadian government.

The first issue at stake is Quebec's position in the international institutions set up by French-speaking nations. In 1968, at de Gaulle's insistence, Quebec was invited by Gabon to take part in a conference of education ministers from francophone countries in Libreville. The Canadian government was thus completely excluded on the grounds that education was a provincial responsibility. When a similar conference was held the following year, Canada and Quebec agreed on a formula allowing both levels of government to take part. The question was far from being settled, however. In 1970 francophone countries organized a meeting at Niamey in Niger that aimed to set up an Agency for Cultural and Technical Co-operation (ACCT). Canada was invited, and so the question was what place Quebec would have in the new institution, since it was demanding participation distinct from that of Canada. Ottawa was set against this idea and campaigned intensively on the diplomatic front to get the other francophone countries on its side. President Georges Pompidou of France considered that France was setting up the institutions of *la francophonie* for Quebec, and thus it was absurd to associate with Ottawa and by doing so exclude Quebec. Paris did its utmost to allow Quebec to participate in its own right, and so

Quebec gained the status of "participating government," which allowed it to join the ACCT directly.

This was just the first occasion on which France supported Quebec to the hilt against the claims of the Ottawa government. *La francophonie* continued to develop and soon a summit was organized, at which Ottawa refused any autonomous participation by Quebec. France in turn refused to join any summit without Quebec. The position under presidents Valèry Giscard d'Estaing and François Mitterrand was thus the same as under de Gaulle and Pompidou: no *francophonie* without Quebec. Ottawa thus had to temper its position, and at the first francophone summit in Paris in 1986 Quebec had its own statute of participating government.

France and Canada also collided around the question of Quebec sovereignty. Although presidents after de Gaulle did not call for independence, they nonetheless established warm relations with the Parti Québécois (PQ), assuring them of France's support if a referendum delivered a "yes" vote. In November 1976, the PQ won power in Quebec for the first time, promising a referendum on independence. President Giscard d'Estaing of France was a centrist politician relying on Gaullist votes for a majority in parliament. Although in 1967 Giscard had described de Gaulle's trip to Quebec as "a solitary exercise of power," he now unexpectedly changed his tune and swung behind the PQ. The reason was that Jacques Chirac, then leader of the Gaullist RPR Party, had been accusing Giscard of abandoning de Gaulle's legacy at a time when the PQ's election victory seemed to have proven him right. Giscard needed to show he was not straying too far from the Gaullist line on the matter. This was all the easier to do as Giscard's personal relations with Canadian prime minister Pierre Trudeau were very bad. Both men tried to present themselves as modern, flamboyant, and media savvy, and their resemblance to each other in fact increased their rivalry. (See CHIRAC, JACQUES; GISCARD D'ESTAING, VALÉRY; LÉVESQUE, RENÉ; MITTERRAND, FRANÇOIS; POMPIDOU, GEORGES; TRUDEAU, PIERRE ELLIOTT.)

Despite the opposition of the federal Canadian government, in 1977 Giscard invited premier René Lévesque to Paris and gave a public assurance of France's "understanding and support on the road you decide to take." This clearly meant that if the "yes" vote won in the 1980 referendum on sovereignty, France would back Quebec.

The scenario was repeated in 1995, even though Jacques Chirac, now president, had distanced himself from the Parti Québécois because it had applied to join the Socialist International in order to cozy up to François Mitterrand's Parti Socialiste. However, Chirac had now to deal with another PQ election victory and sovereignty referendum. In January 1995, Quebec premier Jacques Parizeau met presidential candidate Chirac in Paris. Chirac's standing in the polls had slipped and some of his allies in the RPR Party had withdrawn their backing. Among those who continued to support him on the right wing of Gaullism were precisely those who were in favor of Quebec independence. Chirac thus swung behind the PQ, declaring that France must stand shoulder to shoulder with Quebec. The Canadian prime minister Jean Chrétien was furious, declaring that Chirac had as much chance of becoming president as Quebec had of becoming sovereign. While this poisoned relations between the two men at the time, they were later reconciled. After becoming president, Chirac laid it on further a few days before the October 1995 referendum, repeating publicly that France would support Quebec if the "yes" vote won, and was even ready to take this unilateral position merely hours after the result.

In summary, then, although successive French presidents have never gone as far as de Gaulle, they have all followed in his footsteps, because factors such as existing cooperation between the two countries and the importance of the Quebec question in French internal politics have been so strong. France will not abandon its special relationship with Quebec, and Quebec is happy with that. It seems inevitable therefore that relations between France and Canada will be dominated by the France-Quebec relationship, which for Paris is more advantageous and more substantial. Whenever France has to choose between Canada and Quebec, Quebec will always win out.

FRANCE AND THE CARIBBEAN

Michael Dash

The term "Francophone Caribbean" refers principally to those parts of the Caribbean—Haiti, Guadeloupe, Martinique, and Guiana—left in the aftermath of France's overseas empire in the Americas. The history of this empire goes back to the mid-seventeenth century, when Spanish domination of the Caribbean began to be contested by the other major European powers. By the beginning of the reign of Louis XIV in 1674, France had acquired Martinique (1631), Guadeloupe (1635), and between 1646 and 1650 a dozen or so other islands, which included Dominica, Saint Lucia, Marie Galante, Grenada, and Tobago. The mainland territory of Guiana was added in 1643, and the western third of Hispaniola, called Saint Domingue, in 1697. (See GRENADA; GUADELOUPE; GUIANA; HAITI; MARTINIQUE; SANTO DOMINGO.)

These early colonies, or "vieilles colonies" as they came to be known, were the fruits of France's first experience of overseas expansion. The relationship between metropole and colony was based on trade, whereby the conquered territories provided commodities not available in Europe. Sugar became the dominant crop in the exploitation of the Caribbean colonies. With the right climate and terrain, the Caribbean colonies were perfect for sugar production. What they lacked was a massive, cheap labor force, which was drawn from slaves imported from Africa. On the brutal reality of the buying, transporting, and exploiting of human cargo, an economy was founded in which the monoculture of sugar dominated all economic activity in the colony, creating a dependence on France for manufactured goods and establishing in the colonies a hierarchical society based on race and color. (See SLAVERY; SUGAR.)

Plantation slavery in the Caribbean islands brought great wealth to the French planters, who became a local white Creole elite called "bekes." The plantation system produced a rigidly stratified society based on color: a small white plantocracy at the top, followed by poor whites ("petits blancs") who, lacking in economic power, relied on race to distinguish themselves from mixed blood "métis," freed slaves, and finally the slaves who composed the majority of the population. In the colonies there also existed a number of escaped slaves, or "marrons," who were numerous in those colonies where the terrain, for instance the mountains of Saint-Domingue or the jungles of Guiana, permitted the establishment of separate communities. Guiana in particular, with its dense tropical rain forest and deserved reputation as the white man's grave because of malaria and yellow fever, allowed slaves to escape into the unexplored interior, where they attempted to reconstitute their African past.

The French Revolution in 1789 had inevitable repercussions for France's overseas colonies. Not only was the relationship of the colonies to the metropolitan government a contentious one, the future of slavery was of chief concern. Dramatic repercussions were evident in Saint-Domingue, which was in turmoil by 1791. The British, taking advantage of the unstable situation, captured a number of French possessions in the Caribbean. Even though the French retook Martinique and Guadeloupe and narrowly averted losing Saint-Domingue, the economies of the Caribbean colonies continued to be adversely affected by insurrection, British attacks, and the disruption of the slave trade. The rise of Napoléon and the restoration of slavery in the Caribbean would lead to the shrinking of French possessions in the New World to Martinique, Guadeloupe, and the only outpost of French rule in South America, Guiana.

The last full-blown effort to assemble a colonial empire in the Caribbean was attempted by Napoléon, who envisaged a kind of French-dominated Caribbean Sea extending from Louisiana in the North to Guiana in the South with Saint-Domingue as the center of this imperial network. However, this vision was jeopardized by Napoléon's military expansionism in Europe and his attempt to restore slavery in the Caribbean, already abolished earlier by the revolution. His incapacity to put down the revolt in Saint-Domingue obliged him to sell Louisiana in 1803, and by 1804 the French had been driven out of Saint-Domingue, and Martinique and Guadeloupe had been occupied by the British. By the end of the Napoleonic wars and the time of the Restoration in 1814, France was left a much reduced imperial power. The revolution in Saint-Domingue affected more than just France's imperial designs on the Americas; instead of channeling slave discontent into fleeing into the mountains, forests, or, in the case of Saint-Domingue, into the sparsely populated Spanish side of the island, it also created the new alternative of ideologically driven armed revolt. (See BONAPARTE, NAPOLÉON; LOUISIANA PURCHASE.)

The ideal of universal human rights of the French Revolution was a particular threat to slave societies, and its effect on the Caribbean illustrates the complexity of the metropolitan-colonial relationship. In Saint-Domingue each class, whether the white colonists, the wealthy nonwhite class of freedmen, or the large black slave population, was affected in different ways by the radical changes taking place in France. While seeking greater autonomy for the colony, the white Creoles wanted the system of white supremacy and the institution of slavery to be maintained. The wealthy nonwhites saw the opportunity to demand racial equality in Saint-Domingue by asserting that the Rights of Man applied to them too. The uprising of the slaves in 1791 was as much motivated by the changes taking place in the metropole as by the divided nature of white rule in Saint-

Domingue itself. Consequently, the French Revolution undermined the institution of white supremacy, severely transforming slave society in all the Caribbean colonies, creating new leadership in Saint-Domingue, and permitting the ex-slaves to develop military skills that would eventually be used to permanently secure their freedom from France. The revolutionary gains of the first decade were consolidated under Toussaint L'Ouverture, who became governor for life of the French colony. As much as anything else, the clash between Toussaint and Napoléon would lead to the latter's fatal decision to restore slavery in Haiti and the massive resistance that led to Haitian independence in 1804. (See ANTISLAVERY MOVEMENTS; FRENCH REVOLUTION; REPUBLICANISM; TOUSSAINT L'OUVERTURE, FRANÇOIS.)

The escalating radicalism of the Haitian Revolution called into question the legitimacy of the colonial endeavor and led to the newly independent state's immediate isolation. In France's other Caribbean colonies the ascendancy of the radical Jacobin Party in France meant that there was pressure to assimilate these colonies into France and extend full citizenship to their inhabitants. The universalizing dynamic of Jacobinism came to an abrupt halt with the reassertion of the old colonial patriarchy by Napoléon, who was successful in reestablishing slavery in these colonies by 1802. The nineteenth century saw declining fortunes for the French Caribbean colonies. The disruption of the sugar trade during the Napoleonic wars led to the development of beet sugar in France. By 1848 slavery was abolished in the French colonies as abolitionists led by Victor Schoelcher prevailed over the planters who had fought for its retention. Emancipation came with citizenship and the right to vote but not capital or land. This meant that the hierarchy of plantation society was little changed as French planters retained economic control, the métis developed into a new professional class, and the majority of the population remained in a situation that differed little from slavery. The demographic and cultural complexity of the colonies was intensified with the importation of Indian labor in the latter half of the nineteenth century. Guiana, because of its sinister reputation, was proposed as a place for deportation, and a prison colony, or "bagne," was developed there at this time.

Given the piecemeal and even haphazard acquisition of the French colonies in the Caribbean, it is difficult to speak of a coherent colonial policy. Dictated by rivalry with European powers, colonial expansion was based on the assumption that colonies were meant exclusively for economic profit and political prestige. They could also solve problems in the metropole like finding a home for the landless and the jobless or, as in the case of Guiana, providing a solution for ridding France of undesirables by deportation. The moral mandate that justified colonization in the Caribbean as elsewhere was a presumed white and Western superiority over inferior and backward colonized peoples. In this regard the French differed little from the British in a race-based policy of colonial exploitation. The nineteenth century, however, meant a change in colonial policy for France, which made it very different from that of the British. The emphasis placed on centralization of power in Paris and administrative standardization led the French to conceive of a policy destined to remove all differences between colonies and the metropole. It was an ambitious plan aimed at heading off any attempt at autonomy in the colonies by transforming overseas territories and their inhabitants into carbon copies of France and its people.

Under the policy of assimilation, French colonialism projected itself as more humanitarian and modernizing than racist and exploitative. The act of emancipation in 1848 was projected as the ultimate gesture of generosity of the French Republic to its colonial subjects. Its colonial policies would not therefore be marked by the exploitative practices of the monarchy. Benign and paternalist, this policy meant a shift from a biological to a cultural racism. The assumption was that the colonized were not inherently inferior but had fallen behind in the evolution of modern society. They could become modern and progressive once they had shed their own supposedly inferior culture and embraced French values. Built on the previous short-lived experience of Jacobin universalism, abolition launched the idea of France's "mission civilisatrice" that was aimed, in theory at least, at incorporating the former slaves into the French Republican family. A policy that set out not to dominate and exploit but to liberate and enlighten was seen as particularly necessary. It responded both to the need to break with the old France of royalists and reactionaries as well as to the apparent willingness of the majority of French Caribbean people to subscribe to this myth, embodied in the figure of the French abolitionist Victor Schoelcher.

Also, having lost Haiti and having abandoned its imperial designs on the Caribbean, France would reinforce its colonial links by ostracizing Haiti as a land of black barbarity and by fostering an assimilationist policy in its Caribbean colonies, which would attempt to erase the past of plantation slavery and racial exploitation. By the end of the nineteenth century there was even early talk by colonial politicians of departmentalization of Martinique and Guadeloupe. The outbreak of war in 1914 further cemented the bond with France, as conscription laws were extended to the Caribbean colonies allowing them to give the ultimate sacrifice for "la mère-patrie." Through the institution of secular education from the 1920s on, the glories of French civilization were offered as a safe exit from the rigors of the cane fields. The celebration of the tercentenary of French settlement in the Caribbean was as a result the occasion for a display of unbridled francophilia. The successful implementation of assimilation meant both the neutralizing of Haiti and the institution of a policy that meant the denial of both cultural difference and historical experience. While it promised equality and integration, assimilation certainly did not permit recognition or reciprocity. It consequently left hybrid plantation-derived Caribbean societies with an inability to assert themselves as different. At the same time, it condemned them to legitimizing French cultural superiority. This identity crisis was further complicated by the increasing economic and political dependence of the Caribbean colonies on France and in the twentieth century the choice of departmentalization, which arguably signified the most complete form of colonization possible.

The reduction of France's empire in the Americas did not signal the end of its influence on Atlantic culture in the Caribbean nor the end of the region's impact on the metropole. Indeed, the specter of the Haitian Revolution and its potential threat to the imperial enterprise haunted the French even as they extended their empire in other parts of the world in the nineteenth century. Far from being a gulf that separated former colonies from the metropole, France's Caribbean relations survive in terms of what the former colonizing power chooses to remember and forget of its past involvement with the region. These relations also survive in terms of what France's former colonies choose not to forget about a past that preceded the revolutionary idealism of 1789. The awkward embrace of France by its former Caribbean colonies is apparent in the popular choice of departmentalization in 1946, which has become a source of bitter recrimination in contemporary writing. Even Haiti, which violently threw out the French, projects its French past as a buffer against U.S. imperialist domination. During the American occupation in the 1920s, the radicals of the nationalist movement of the time defined Haiti's cultural peculiarity in terms of its Afro-Latin heritage, even if to this day the indemnity paid to French planters to secure France's recognition of its former colony never ceases to rankle.

The new phase of French Caribbean colonialism in the nineteenth century, haunted as it was by the image of Haiti, would constitute a special imaginary space, which resulted in the absorption, feminization, and eventual effacement of the "old colonies." For instance, one would be hard put to find any systematic representation of France's Caribbean colonies in French writing. Such a lack contrasts with France's fixation with the Orient and exists despite the length of the French relationship with these colonies and their economic importance to the metropole. This pattern of avoidance and omission of the concrete realities of France's Caribbean past is reflected as such in the mimetic image of the "petite patrie" used to describe Martinique and Guadeloupe in the early twentieth century, as it is in the image of Satanism that succeeded the loss of Saint-Domingue. Documentary realism was reserved for describing the social and economic situation of the metropole and an exoticist aesthetic would dominate the representation of the Caribbean in French literature.

The silencing of the reality of the French Caribbean is apparent in the romantic period, where neither the leaders nor the specific events of the Haitian Revolution, nor the unsuccessful resistance movement led by Louis Delgres, served as sources of inspiration for the romantics. This literary disengagement from the region is apparent in the novel *Bug-Jargal* (1820) by Victor Hugo (1802–1885), which deals with the Haitian Revolution. This vivid chronicle is purportedly historical fiction detailing the dramatic events at the turn of the century in Saint-Domingue, but it does not specify a single figure in the Haitian Revolution, choosing instead to feature local color and stereotyped racial figures. Reducing one of the major events of the nineteenth century to idealizing a noble generic black protagonist and vilifying perfidious mulattoes leads to a dehistoricization of the Caribbean. The grand spectacle of nature effaces human reality in Hugo's novel. Alphonse de Lamartine's (1790–1869) first play, *Toussaint Louverture,* is no less abstract and moralizing in its depiction of an unreal landscape of tigers and snow rampant with romantic sentimentalism. The romance of the tropics and the longing for a simpler, more pastoral world are strongly echoed later by Lafcadio Hearn (1850–1904). His *Two Years in the French West Indies* (1890), written during his visit to Martinique in the 1880s, is largely a panegyric to "beautiful fruit-colored populations" who precariously inhabit this exotic space. Even someone like Hearn, who seemed genuinely interested in Martinican life, is not immune to the condescending exotic image of the Caribbean colony that became firmly established in the French literary imagination by the end of the nineteenth century. (See HUGO, VICTOR.)

As far as Martinique and Guadeloupe are concerned, French universalism in the Caribbean was reduced to the welcoming passive face of the Creole woman, which became the stock in trade for an exotic literature that marked a process of absorption and assimilation of the old colonies. The complicity of the writers from the colonies in this process has often been remarked on. For instance, the figure of the French Caribbean *doudou,* the alluring, compliant female face of the colonies, moved from a metropolitan myth to one that was adopted by local writers. This theme conveyed an image of total dependency on the metropole and a longing for absolute domination. Constituting the Antilles as a zone of pleasure and self-denial, black and colored French Caribbean writers such as Oruno Lara (1879–1924), Daniel Thaly (1879–1949), and Gilbert de Chambertrand (1890–1984) produced a poetry that evoked an infantilized, submissive tropical world. It is this love for the metropole, not fully requited up to this point, that would find its consummation in the granting of departmental status to the Caribbean colonies in 1946.

The ideal of revolutionary universalism had a different trajectory in Haiti, where from the outset the extreme application of the ideal of the rights of man had led to the defeat of Napoléon's troops and Haitian independence. French universalism meant for France's colonies the right to be French, and the emphasis was put on the generosity of the French in offering universal values to their grateful subjects. In Haiti, however, revolutionary universalism was linked to human rights and equality, and was immune from cultural and historical differences. Consequently, the idea of the French as the guardians of universalism was as absurd as the idea of a Haitian-derived universalism. Consequently, universalist thought was appropriated in Haiti in the nineteenth century by essayists who were both refuting the charges—made by Haiti's detractors—of Haitian exceptionalism and racial difference and attempting to redefine within Haiti concepts of race and nation. The most notable of these essayists was Anténor Firmin, who in his monumental *De L'Egalité des races humaines* argued for the ideal of a unitary oneness of all humankind in contrast to the conception of biological difference promoted by Joseph Arthur de Gobineau (1816–1882). If this early work argued that an "invisible chain" linked all humankind in "a common circle," Firmin's last published essays, *The Letters from St. Thomas,* sought to defetishize racial and national determinism at home. Written in exile, these letters explore the idea of universalist thought as a way of understanding global interconnectedness and cosmopolitan modernity that was well ahead of its time.

In the early twentieth century France's interests in the Caribbean were slowly being eroded by the emerging influence of the United States. In Haiti one of the more fiercely argued debates at the turn of the century was whether Haiti should espouse Latin or Anglo-Saxon values. Old European influences, it was argued, should yield to new American ideas of technological progress and shift away from outmoded ideas of classical culture. With the completion of the Panama Canal, naval control of the northern Caribbean was secured in accordance with the Monroe Doctrine, and Haiti occupied it in 1915. Increasingly, French universalism was attacked by leftist intellectuals from Martinique and Guadeloupe in France for its intolerance of the cultural difference of others and for promoting its own specificity as universal values. There were also intellectual tensions within

France between Republican universalism on one hand and nationalist particularism on the other. The extremes of the latter view were articulated by Maurice Barrès (1862–1923) and Charles Maurras (1868–1952), and its implications were not lost on intellectuals from the French colonies. Nor was the anticolonial impulse of the surrealists in the 1930s, when they attacked not only the economic exploitation of the colonial system but the literary exploitation of the exotic image of greater France.

French universalism was unmasked as legitimizing oppression by the influential but short-lived French Caribbean student movement *Légitime Défense* (1932), which had been inspired by the surrealist movement. The very title of their journal indicated their attachment to André Breton, whose movement offered the students a way of making the case for decolonization based on the importance of the idea of difference. In so doing they were the first to break so vocally with the trend in the old colonies to seek greater integration with the metropole. If the surrealists fed anticolonial thought in a radical vanguard in the French Caribbean colonies, Haitian nationalism in the 1920s reacted to the U.S. occupation of the country by asserting Haitian racial and cultural difference with the help of the ideas of Barrès and Maurras. In 1928 the Haitian intellectual Jean Price-Mars published his *Ainsi Parla l'Oncle,* which accused the Haitian elite of "bovarysme collectif" by betraying their nation because of too great an attachment to European cosmopolitan values. The only way to correct this unfortunate dependence on Europe was for the Haitian elite to pay more attention to the authentic values of Haiti, which were identified in the culture, language, and religion of the peasantry.

French universalism was now exposed as empty rhetoric, and those who adhered to it in Haiti and the French colonies were seen as traitors to their people. This anticolonial trust also found support among French thinkers such as Jean-Paul Sartre, who, in his 1948 essay "Orphée noir," pointed to the need for a reaction against European universal values through the "anti-racist racism" of négritude. The evolution of the concept of national specificity in the Caribbean would take different paths in the French Caribbean colonies as opposed to Haiti. The fate of the idea of nationalist particularism in the colonies of Martinique and Guadeloupe would rest with Aimé Césaire, whose *Cahier d'un retour au pays natal* signaled both his return to Martinique, where he dominated political life for decades to come, and his particular view of universal values. Two of the founding figures of négritude, Césaire and Léopold Senghor (1906–2001), seemed particularly preoccupied with the idea of universal values. The whole problematic of négritude was predicated on French racial theories. The end of Césaire's epic poem pleads, for instance, that the native land's "noire vibration" be linked to "le nombril même du monde." In this regard these two poets were very different from the earlier *Légitime Défense* group and from the other often overlooked founding figure, Léon Damas of French Guiana. (See CÉSAIRE, AIMÉ; SARTRE, JEAN-PAUL.)

The defeat of France in 1940 and the control of the French Caribbean by a pro-Vichy military regime created a disillusion with Vichy France that led to what Frantz Fanon reported as "an extraordinary sight" of French West Indians refusing "to take their hats off while the *Marseillaise* was being played." This turning away from the "mère patrie" meant the emergence of an interest among intellectuals in racial and regional identity. Such a shift can be seen in the pages of the magazine *Tropiques* and ultimately in the political success of Aimé Césaire in Martinique. The latter's emergence should be seen in the context of the hardship of the war years, which also meant a nostalgic attachment to pre-Vichy France and to the charismatic figure of General de Gaulle to whom the assimilationist longings of the pre-war years were attached after the end of the Vichy regime. By the end of the war in 1945 the cult of Schoelcherism was transferred to de Gaulle, and the clamor for integration into the transcontinental family of greater France intensified. Aimé Césaire saw departmentalization in 1946, ironically, as a way of decolonizing the French Caribbean colonies. It was felt that if Schoelcher had brought liberty, it would be de Gaulle's mission to continue the spirit of 1848 and bestow equality and fraternity on France's adopted children. By the 1950s the French departments began their transition from an agricultural-based economy to a consumer-oriented society with mounting unemployment.

If the postwar period led to the denial of difference for the French departments of Martinique, Guadeloupe, and Guiana, in Haiti the impact of anti-American-inspired nationalist thought and of anticolonial surrealist ideas meant that the question of cultural identity would be negotiated differently there. Haiti held interest for the surrealists not only because of a fascination with the mysteries of the voodoo religion, but also because the Haitian Revolution was seen as a major challenge to European imperial expansion. Displacement due to World War II brought Pierre Mabille (1904–1952) in 1940 to Haiti, where in 1941 he helped found the *Bureau d'Ethnologie* with Haitian intellectuals Jean Price-Mars and Jacques Roumain and the Swiss anthropologist Alfred Métraux (1902–1963). In 1945, Mabille, who had been appointed French cultural attaché, invited André Breton to give a series of lectures that coincided with an exhibition of the work of the Cuban surrealist Wilfredo Lam and Haitian intuitive artists. Even though it was never his intention, Breton's speeches, with their insistence on the surrealist promotion of absolute freedom, revived the drive force of the revolutionary universalism of 1804 and fanned a popular revolt against the then president of Haiti. Both Mabille and Breton were declared *personae non gratae* and expelled from Haiti. A few months later the Haitian president himself was driven into exile. (See SURREALISM; WORLD WAR II.)

The political impact on Haiti of these interventions by surrealists who had taken refuge from the war outside of Europe is interesting in itself. Their legacy might, however, be seen as even longer lasting when viewed from the perspective of their approach to Haitian culture. What one finds in the surrealist accounts of Haitian culture in the 1940s is an acute sensitivity to its staggering complexity and a refusal either to exoticize it or to appropriate it. Haitian culture emerges in the writing of Pierre Mabille in the 1940s as unfathomable, ever changing, both familiar and strange. This attitude to Haitian culture, which located it in the West while attempting to recognize its difference, acted as a shaping force at the time on Haitian intellectuals such as Jacques-Stephen Alexis and René Depestre. It is no coincidence that they were among the foremost of their generation to criticize the négritude movement with its sweeping, monolithic ideas of race as well as to promote a Marxist critique of the atemporal, exotic image of Haitian culture as stranded outside of history. Their interest in what they called the "marvelous realism" of Haitian culture shows their debt to the surrealists as well as their idea of a cultural dynamic in Haitian identity politics that inevitably made them targets of the totalizing racial ideology of the Duvalier dictatorship in the 1960s, which found its inspiration in European fascism and the racial mystification of négritude.

The reaction against the racial constructs of négritude, which began to be seen by such radical thinkers as the Martinican Frantz Fanon as increasingly allied with the French state and neocolonial politics, was also fed in the French departments by the legacy of ideas left by the surrealists during their passage through the Caribbean. In the context of decolonization and postcolonial thought, Edouard Glissant in the late 1950s posed a series of questions as to the nature of cultural interaction and the right of cultures to resist global assimilation through recognition of their opacity. French-based intellectuals such as Milan Kundera (b. 1929) have made the literary links between French Caribbean writers such as René Depestre and the Martinican novelist Patrick Chamoiseau. Despite these sophisticated attempts by Glissant and the later *créolité* movement, which remained enormously indebted to him intellectually, to rethink the polarizing binaries of colonialism, Martinique in particular continued under Césaire's guidance to remain staunchly loyal to France. The enthusiastic local reaction to visits by André Malraux in 1958 and by de Gaulle himself in 1960 and 1964 clearly illustrates the continuation of the relationship. In the case of the latter, the rapturous reception he received drove him to exclaim "Mon Dieu, comme vous êtes français!" (See CHAMOISEAU, PATRICK; DEPESTRE, RENÉ; GLISSANT, EDOUARD.)

No French president has had as strong a loyalty in the Caribbean departments as de Gaulle. An earlier enthusiasm for being French has been arguably replaced by a fear of being abandoned by the French. With the erosion of the departments' productive base, their dependence on the French welfare state has become a matter of glum pragmatism. Discontent with departmentalization is now as evident among the white Creole elite as it is among the colored bourgeoisie and the lower classes. Traditional business interests resent the penetration of metropolitan capital with the spread of Monoprix and Prisunics. Local administrators and teachers are unhappy with the recruitment of French teachers and administrators for posts in the Caribbean, whereas many qualified West Indians are obliged to seek jobs in France. The decline of the economy and resulting unemployment has created a restless and resentful lower class. The current creole revivalism in the Caribbean Overseas Departments is an effort to preserve a threatened cultural heritage. Much current French Caribbean writing is preoccupied with memory and autobiography and the articulation of a local particularity. However, without a sustaining productive base in the departments, revitalized creole forms and local practices are always open to exoticization and commodification by the tourist trade.

The debate over the place of the French Caribbean departments in an increasingly globalized world and in a Europeanized France is acute at the present time. Such concerns have driven the Martinican novelist Patrick Chamoiseau to entitle a recent essay, in which not only is Martinique considered occupied territory but local particularity is directly attacked by the invasive presence of French television and supermarket chains, *Ecrire en pays dominé* (1997). Fear of cultural annihilation and the visible *bétonisation* of the island departments have renewed interest in independentist politicians as is signaled by the political success of Alfred Marie-Jeanne's (b. 1936) nationalist movement in Martinique. Through the cultural politics of *la francophonie,* France has attempted to use the Caribbean departments as a base for anchoring the French presence in the region. The financing of various cultural missions in the Caribbean region and the reinforcing of links with French colonies that had been lost two centuries ago (such as Haiti, Dominica, and Saint Lucia) have created a significant enough cultural presence for French to become one of the official languages of the Organization of American States. Furthermore, these territories are key points in France's international technological, military, and commercial expansion. The airports and harbors of the Caribbean departments have been significantly modernized and France's exploration of outer space, a key element in its promotion of itself as a world power, is based at Kourou in French Guiana. (See *CRÉOLITÉ; FRANCOPHONIE, LA;* LANGUAGE.)

Nevertheless, French presence is restricted not only because of American hegemony in the region but also by the fact that its departments are embedded in a region that is heterogeneous and dominated by Hispanophone and anglophone states. Furthermore, the Caribbean region is made up of a number of regional organizations of which France is not a member, which leads to the further institutional isolation of the overseas departments from networks such as the Caribbean common market, or CARICOM; the Caribbean Development Bank; and the Organization of Eastern Caribbean States, or OECS, to which Martinique and Guadeloupe geographically belong. The anomalous nature of France's Caribbean departments in an increasingly globalized, postcolonial world harks back to that centralizing, universalist thrust in French history that minimized the importance of ethnic diversity and historical difference. France imagines it can ignore the specific nature of the Caribbean since its culture is universal. The future will determine whether what have been called the confetti of empire will continue to accept the status quo or whether what exists at present at the level of cultural nationalism can be turned into a politics of self-assertion.

FRANCE AND LATIN AMERICA

Ana Lucia Araujo

Cultural relations between France and Latin America go back to the colonial era and can be divided into three distinct periods. Until the beginning of the eighteenth century, economic exchanges predominated, and these must be understood in the context of the rivalry between England, France, the Netherlands, Portugal, and Spain over the trade in raw materials. At the end of the eighteenth and in the early nineteenth century, the nature of France's relations with the Americas was one of French cultural expansion. For nearly 500 years of cultural and economic interaction, the different countries of Latin America were often a place of refuge or asylum for French people during political crises at home. For example, in 1815 after the fall of Napoléon, many of his supporters settled in Brazil, and in the 1850s those faithful to the republican cause took refuge in Rio de Janeiro. In the twentieth century, many Latin Americans resided in Paris to partake of its cultural and artistic effervescence, but also to escape the dictatorships that afflicted their continent. Although many Latin American exiles went back to their country of origin between the late 1970s and early 1980s, a good many remained in France, forming one of its most important cultural minorities.

From as early as 1504, France maintained a constant presence on the Brazilian coast. Paulmier de Gonneville's expedition of that year covered the Santa Catarina region and probably also that of Porto Seguro as far as Bahia. Between 1516 and 1526, Christophe Jacques's two expeditions marked the beginning of the French presence in Brazil itself. In 1555, the Catholic navigator Nicolas Durand de Villegagnon wished to found a French colony there that would be a refuge for French Protestants. The colony was established in Guanabara Bay at Rio de Janeiro and named France Antarctique. The settlers included not only Protestants but also Catholics like André Thevet who published, after his return to France in 1557, *Les Singularitez de la France Antarctique, autrement nommée Amérique et de plusieurs terres et isles découvertes de notre temps.* Several chapters of his *Cosmographie universelle,* published in 1575, are also devoted to Brazil. However, the colony of France

Antarctique was often shaken by crises arising from religious differences. This and the threat of a war of religion in France prompted Admiral de Coligny (1519–1572) to recruit other settlers in Protestant Geneva. These new settlers, who arrived in Rio in 1556, included Jean de Léry, who published in 1578 the first edition of his *Histoire d'un voyage fait en la terre du Brésil autrement nommée Amérique,* one of the first detailed descriptions of the indigenous Tupinamba people. The Portuguese, led by Mem de Sá, took advantage of the crises in the colony, entering Guanabara Bay on January 26, 1560, and defeating the French forces, Villegagnon having already returned to France. Despite this setback, France continued trading Brazil wood with the natives, who were resisting Portuguese authority. In 1597 the French, commanded by Captain Jean Guérand and with the help of the Tupinamba, tried to set up a new colony in the Maranhão region, which they named France Equinoxiale. In 1612, the colony in turn founded a town, Saint-Louis du Maragnan (the present-day São Luis) on Maranhão Island in northern Brazil. But in 1615 the Portuguese once more defeated the French. The last attempt to establish a French colony in the Maranhão, in 1631 with the help of the Dutch West India Company, was also a failure. (See BRAZIL; CATHOLIC CHURCH.)

French colonization of the Caribbean also goes back to the sixteenth century, a period when privateers and buccaneers were a constant presence. From Tortuga, French privateers occupied Grande-Terre, later Saint-Domingue. It was only in 1697 that Spain recognized French sovereignty over the western part of the island. It was not just the French economy that was affected by the system of sugar plantations and slave labor set up there and in Guadeloupe and Martinique. Foodstuffs from Latin America, including the potato, maize, chocolate, tobacco, and fruits such as the pineapple, also changed French eating habits. And although sugar cane, bananas, and coffee are not indigenous to the Americas, it was in Latin America that their cultivation really took off. Coffee production was widespread in the Caribbean and was introduced to Brazil only in the eighteenth century. In the nineteenth century, Brazil became one of the biggest world producers of coffee along with Cuba, Guatemala, Costa Rica, Colombia, and Mexico, and these different varieties were widely consumed in France. At the beginning of that century the consumption of *eau-de-vie* in France was largely replaced by rum, in a transatlantic system of exchange centering on Bordeaux. In an opposite movement, Chilean wine production and its international prestige are largely due to the cultivation of grape varieties from the Bordeaux region. (See BORDEAUX; COFFEE; CUISINE; GUADELOUPE; MARTINIQUE; SANTO DOMINGO; SUGAR; TOBACCO.)

Latin American flora also played a role in European pharmaceutical practices. Examples of such plants include *quinquina* or *quina-quina* root, used by the inhabitants of Peru to treat malaria. It was introduced to France at the end of the seventeenth century, its powder diluted in wine or administered in the form of pills. In 1820, the discovery of quinine sulfate by Pelletier and Canventou marked *quinquina*'s entry into modern medicine. Ipeca, of Brazilian origin, belongs to the same botanical family as *quinquina*. Also introduced to France at the end of the seventeenth century, it was produced on an industrial scale in the early nineteenth. The botanical richness of Latin America played a crucial role in the development of phytochemistry and the use of plants in the manufacture of medicine and cosmetics. Among the trees and fruits used in French cosmetic manufacture are the guava, for its leaves, fruit, and roots have astringent properties, and the papaya, rich in vitamin A.

After the declarations of independence in the Spanish and Portuguese colonies, Latin America opened up more and more to Europe. For this early nineteenth-century period, the French in Latin America can be divided into two groups: those immigrants who settled there to improve their lot, and the travelers, artists, and scientists who stayed for a fixed period and then returned to France. French immigration to Latin America, which was particularly visible in cities such as Buenos Aires, Rio de Janeiro, Santiago de Chile, and Mexico City, encouraged new food and dress habits, and new literary and artistic influences. As early as the first half of the nineteenth century, elites in Latin America had adopted the habit of speaking and writing in French, and also slavishly imitating Parisian fashion.

The influence of French culture was intensified in Brazil after 1808, when the Portuguese court fled to Rio de Janeiro in the wake of Napoléon's armies. To develop the city's cultural and artistic life (in 1815 it became the capital of the United Kingdom of Portugal, Brazil, and the Algarve), King D. João I commanded a French artistic mission that arrived in Brazil in 1816 and founded the Fine Arts Academy as well as an art gallery. French influence in Latin American art and architecture was thus reinforced. Many French craftsmen came to work in photography, lithography, and sculpture, and as goldsmiths. French influence in Rio became very tangible. Many nineteenth-century travelers' accounts describe Ouvidor Street, which became the symbol of the profound Frenchness of Brazil's customs and fashion. As Armelle Enders points out, the street was where Rio's aristocracy could not only dress and eat *à la française,* but also read and think in French.

In the nineteenth century, the presence of French artists in Latin America contributed to the development of the first artistic institutions and also encouraged Latin American artists in their turn to go to Europe and to frequent art schools and academies there. In 1818 in Cuba, the School of Art was founded by former pupils of Jacques-Louis David (1748–1825), including the former Bonapartist Jean-Baptiste Vermay (1784–1832). In 1832, the school became the Academy of Fine Arts of Havana, sending its first interns to Paris in 1840.

At the end of the eighteenth century, Mexican sculptors—such as Emmanuel Tolsa (1757–1816), in charge of the decoration of Mexico City's cathedral—studied in Spain under French artists. Alexandre-Jean Noël (1752–1834) was one of the few French artists to spend time in Mexico in the eighteenth century. He went there on a scientific expedition in 1768, from which he brought back to France several drawings of Mexican flora and fauna. In 1863, Napoléon III launched his Mexican adventure, the aim of which was to impose Archduke Maximilian of Austria as emperor of Mexico. This of course inspired Manet's famous painting *The Execution of Maximilian.* Mexican architecture was also influenced by France. The French architect, water colorist, and etcher Henry-Jean-Emile Bénard (1844–1929) headed the construction of the Legislature in Mexico City, which was decorated by the French sculptors André-Joseph Allar (1845–1926) and Laurent-Honoré Marqueste (1848–1920). (See PAINTING; SCULPTURE.)

Fewer in number than in Brazil, some French artists nevertheless visited Argentina in the nineteenth century, including Raymond Quinsac de Monvoisin (1794–1870), who painted portraits and social scenes there before going to Chile in 1842. After visiting Buenos Aires, Adolphe d'Hastrel de Révedoy (1805–1875) published his *Album de vues et costumes* (1823), and Jean-Léon Pallière (1823–1887) his *Album de mœurs argentines* (1858). It is, however, French sculpture that took pride of place in Argentina. The architect Prosper Catelin (1764–1842) created the facade of Buenos Aires cathedral in 1823. The building of several public monuments was entrusted to French architects and sculptors such as Auguste Rodin (1840–1917), for the memorial to Sarmiento in 1900, and Antoine Bourdelle (1861–1929), for the equestrian statue of General Alvear in 1913. The monuments to the tribune Del Valle are due to Emile-Edmond Peyot (1850–1932), the statue of president Pellegrini to Jules Coutan (1848–1939), and *Doubt,* in the Plaza San Martín in Buenos Aires, to Henri-Louis Cordier (1853–1925).

Raymond Monvoisin lived in Chile from 1842 to 1854, founding the Academy of Fine Arts of Santiago. François Brunet de Baines (1799–1855) founded the city's first school of architecture. Auguste François taught sculpture in Chile for twenty years. French sculpture is visible in several monuments in Santiago, including *Don José de San Martín «el Emancipador»* by Louis-Joseph Daumas (1801–1887) and the statue of General Carrera by Augustin-Alexandre Dumont (1801–1884).

Few French painters went to Peru. In 1867, the French sculptor Guillaume (a pupil of Lebas and Cugnot) won the competition to build in Lima the monument to the Peruvian naval victory over the Spanish in 1866. However, several Peruvian artists, such as Ignacio Merino, Carlos Baca-Flor, and Alberto Valenzuela Llanos, went to France as part of their artistic training.

Many of the French artists who went to Latin America at the beginning of the nineteenth century were motivated by the search for different forms of the exotic, a process that had begun in the previous century with romantic and orientalist images. This quest for the exotic produced, on the one hand, the publication of illustrated travel writings and, on the other, the creation of paintings of tropical subjects dominated by primitivist ideas. Before going to Tahiti, Paul Gauguin (1848–1903) visited Martinique, which inspired paintings such as *Eve exotique* (1890), depicting a tropical America, referring to the idea of an earthly paradise where men and women live free, naked, and in harmony with nature. Louis Réau attests that Henri Rousseau (1844–1910) was a soldier during the Mexican expedition in 1863, from where he brought back material for the tropical subjects of his paintings. Although the truth about this journey remains uncertain, it is likely that Rousseau drew much of his inspiration from representations of the tropical forests and lush vegetation of Latin America.

The many French travelers, artists, scientists, and naturalists who visited Latin America during the nineteenth century included Ferdinand Denis (1798–1890), François-Auguste Biard (1799–1882), Jean-Baptiste Debret (1768–1848), Arthur de Gobineau (1816–1882), Edouard Manet (1832–1883), Joachim Lebreton (1760–1819), Charles Ribeyrolles (1812–1860), Auguste de Saint-Hilaire (1779–1853), and Elisée Reclus (1830–1905). Back in Europe, several of them published travel accounts, in book form or in popular illustrated magazines such as *Le Tour du monde* or the *Revue des deux mondes,* that brought out the history, landscape, fauna, flora, and people of different Latin American countries.

This interest on the part of travelers in the exotic lands of Latin America fit into the literary romanticism of the time, one of whose features was the quest for the origins of humanity, which were supposedly to be found in the virgin forests of South America, the ruins of Aztec and Mayan temples, or even in the palaces of the Near East. Once in Latin America, French travelers had two kinds of exotic fantasy. Some wished to find a lost civilization among the pre-Colombian ruins. Others identified the American exotic with a type of primitivism, and so sought out Amerindians untouched by white European contact. But by the nineteenth century a large proportion of the Amerindian population had been decimated, and most communities living near the towns had long had contact with white people. French travelers and artists such as Biard and Manet were astonished and even sometimes disappointed to encounter in Brazil so many slaves of African origin. In order to meet Amerindians, travelers had to journey to the interior, a tall order in an era of limited transportation. Several engravings illustrating this travel literature, such as those to be found in Jean-Baptiste Debret's *Voyage pittoresque et historique au Brésil* (1834–1839), tend to present an idealized image of the Brazilian Amerindian that bore little relation to reality. François-Auguste Biard, who lived for a few months with the Amazon Indians, produced extremely detailed ethnographic portraits of different tribes. But several travelers, including Biard, insisted with certainty on the moral, physical, and mental superiority of the Europeans over the indigenous population, as well as over the mestizos and those of African descent. Their vision thus became a kind of taxonomy, with the white European at the top of the pyramid and these latter groups at the bottom.

Latin American music made its debut in France at the beginning of the twentieth century. The tango, whose origin lay in a mix of African and Spanish rhythms, came to France via Argentinean bands and dance troupes. Initially, tango was the music of the gauchos and of Italian immigrants from the poorer districts of Buenos Aires. Its nostalgic music and sensual and dramatic dance steps soon propelled it into the salons of the well-off classes and then across the Atlantic. Its enthusiastic reception in France was evinced by the success there after 1927 of the songwriter Carlos Gardel (1890–1935). Gardel was in fact born in Toulouse and emigrated to Argentina at the age of two. His tragic death in a plane crash contributed to his mythical status. He was famous not only for his interpretations of classic tango such as "A Media Luz" and "El Día que me quieras," but also for starring in several films shot in France. Tango lives on in France thanks to the later generation of songwriters such as Astor Piazzolla (1921–1992), who linked it to jazz. (See ARGENTINA.)

Brazilian rhythms were the inspiration for Félix Mayol (1872–1941), who wrote the song "La Mattchiche," which became the anthem of the *Belle Epoque.* Brazilian music's influence in France began to be felt from 1919. Darius Milhaud (1892–1974) discovered its rhythms after living in Brazil as secretary to the playwright Paul Claudel (1868–1955), who served as a diplomat in Rio in 1916. Other composers, such as Olivier Messiaen (1908–1992) and Michel Philippot (1925–1996), were also influenced by Brazilian

music. The samba was introduced to France by Paul Misraki (1908–1998) and his col-
league Ray Ventura (1908–1978). Misraki, of Jewish origin, went into exile in South
America and then Hollywood during the Nazi occupation of France. His hits inspired by
Latin American rhythms include "On ne badine pas avec l'amour" (1942) and "Si Eva se
hubiese vestido" (1943).

The bossa nova, close to samba and jazz, arrived in France via the films *Orfeu Negro*
(1959) and *Bandeirantes* (1960), both directed by Marcel Camus (1912–1982). *Orfeu
Negro,* which won the Palme d'or at Cannes and the Oscar for Best Foreign Film, is a rein-
terpretation of the Orpheus myth by the Brazilian poet Vinicius de Moraes. The soundtrack, by Antonio Carlos Jobim and Luis Bonfa, was a huge hit in Europe and the United
States, opening doors for other artists such as João Gilberto. In 1966 Claude Lelouch's
film *Un Homme et une femme,* which won the Palme d'or and two Oscars, also featured
the bossa nova. The success of one of the songs on the soundtrack, "Samba de Benção,"
brought the Brazilian composer Baden Powell (1937–2000) his first gold disc in Paris. In
the years that followed, the bossa nova continued to influence French musicians such as
Pierre Barouh, Georges Moustaki, Claude Nougaro, and Michel Fugain.

This interest in Brazilian music coincided with the early years of the military dictatorship, when several Latin American musicians chose exile in France. In the 1980s, the
vogue for "world music" helped Latin American music to become better known in France
and indeed Europe. French singers such as Julien Clerc, Michel Jonasz, Jill Caplan,
Kaoma, and Bernard Lavilliers were inspired not by the samba or bossa nova but by the
music of Bahia represented by João Gilberto, Caetano Veloso, Gilberto Gil, Gal Costa,
and Maria Bethânia. In 1989 the French group Kaoma sang a track that had been a hit in
Bolivia and thus launched the lambada, whose origin can be traced to northern Brazil in
the 1930s, from where much later it traveled to other Brazilian states such as São Paulo
and Bahia. Thanks to a sexy dance, and music incorporating elements of calypso, salsa,
beguine, and merengue, Kaoma made the lambada fashionable throughout Europe.

Caribbean rhythms, often blending Latin and Hispanic styles, have also been influential in twentieth-century France, first via the American singer Josephine Baker and her
Revue nègre from 1925. At the end of that decade, Paris discovered the West Indian beguine, a rhythm from Martinique blended with Cuban conga and New Orleans jazz, in
the Cabane bambou at the Bal nègre in the rue Blomet. The star of the beguine was the
Martinican Stellio (Alexandre Fructueux, 1885–1939). Other musicians and singers such
as Don Marino Barreto and Rita Montaner disseminated the bolero, the rumba, and the
cha cha. Later, Henri Salvador, Ray Ventura, and Edith Piaf (1915–1963) were instrumental in creating a wide public for Caribbean music, Piaf recording the song "Que nadie
sepa mi sufrir" under the title "La Foule." At the end of the 1970s, salsa invaded Paris
thanks to Eddie Palmieri, Azuquita, Willy Colon, Oscar d'Leon, and Celia Cruz. In the
1980s, merengue, calypso, bolero, and cumbia reappeared thanks to Malavoi, Kali, and
Ralp Tamar. In the 1990s, zouk, a new form based on Caribbean tradition, was promoted
by groups such as Zouk Machine and Kassav'. (See BAKER, JOSEPHINE; BEGUINE.)

In the early twentieth century, many representatives of artistic modernism from Latin
America resided in Paris. Between 1920 and 1922 the Brazilian Tarsila do Amaral

(1886–1988) studied with E. Renard, André Lhote, and Fernand Léger at the Académie Julian. Antia Malfatti (1889–1964) went there in 1923 on a Brazilian government grant, and Di Cavalcanti studied at the Académie Ranson between 1923 and 1925. In Paris in 1926 the Uruguayan artist Joaquín Torres García (1874–1949), a pioneer of the movement known as constructive universalism, founded the Cercle et Carré group with Michel Seuphor. The Mexican muralists Diego Rivera (1886–1957), David Alfaro Siqueiros (1896–1974), and José Clemente Orozco (1883–1949) lived in Paris in the first two decades of the century. The influence of Gauguin, Seurat, Cézanne, and Picasso is visible in Rivera's frescoes for the Ministry of Public Education in Mexico City, in which he depicted scenes from ordinary Mexican life and from Aztec culture. Until the mid-1990s, however, it was the Argentines who formed the main Latin American community in France. Paris became the city in which figures such as theater directors and producers Jorge Lavelli and Alfredo Arias; filmmakers Hugo Santiago, Edgardo Cozarinsky, and Nelly Kaplan; and painters and sculptors Roberto Matta, Jesús Soto, and Antonio Seguí settled and worked.

The architect Le Corbusier (1887–1965), who visited Rio de Janeiro in 1929, was an important influence on modern Brazilian architecture, notably on the work of Oscar Niemeyer, one of the creators of the new national capital Brasilia. The building of the Ministry of Education and Health, based on a draft by Le Corbusier, was achieved by Niemeyer and Lúcio Costa. The Brazilians, however, reinterpreted his concepts, introducing new elements such as the curved line. (See ARCHITECTURE.)

Public spaces and architecture in France have in turn been marked by Latin American artists. Julio Silva created the pink marble sculpture in the *cour carrée* of the Forum des Halles in Paris, and Pablo Reinoso the bronze sculpture of a giant dragonfly in Poitiers. The Maison de la Culture in Le Havre was designed by Niemeyer, the Opera Bastille in Paris by the Uruguayan Carlos Ott, and the Finance Ministry at Bercy by the Chilean Borja Huidobro in collaboration with Paul Chemetov.

Latin American literature bases itself on an emancipation from Spanish and Portuguese traditions. During the nineteenth century, writers there looked to British and North American poetry, and to French romantic and then naturalist writing. The rise of modernism in the first decades of the twentieth century emphasized the need for developing the national specificity of Latin American art and literature while at the same time its profile in France was enhanced. These literary relations thus developed through a network of individual contacts. Many writers, such as Octavio Paz (1914–1998), Julio Cortázar (1914–1984), and the poet Oswald de Andrade (1890–1954), traveled from Latin America to France, while in the opposite direction came figures such as Blaise Cendrars (1867–1961), André Breton (1896–1966), and Antonin Artaud (1896–1948). However, this fascination for Latin America in the twentieth century was not far removed from the exoticism that went before. French writers sought in Latin American literature what they could not find in their own, namely, the specificity of the Amerindian, the quest for autonomy from Europe, and the questioning of the social, economic, and especially cultural order, with its insistence on cosmopolitanism and *métissage*. (See LITERARY RELATIONS.)

All this was particularly true of the surrealist movement. Blaise Cendrars, whose "simultaneism" is in some ways a forerunner and who influenced the surrealists, met in Paris two representatives of Brazilian modernism, Oswald de Andrade (the author of *Manifeste Anthropophage,* the "Cannibals' Manifesto" of 1928) and Tarsila do Amaral. He also went to Brazil, where he was struck by its hybrid mix of European, Amerindian, and African cultures. Antonin Artaud, who was involved in the early surrealist movement, traveled to Vera Cruz in Mexico in 1936. His visit became an opportunity to criticize France, and to discover the dreams and cruel rituals of Amerindian culture over and beyond the standard European romanticization. In 1938, André Breton was invited to lecture in Mexico, where he met Trotsky, Rivera, and Frida Kahlo.

The work of the Argentinean writer Jorge Luis Borges (1899–1986) had an enormous influence in France, articulated in writings by Bioy Casares, Ernesto Sábato, and Julio Cortázar. From the mid-1960s Latin American writers achieved a wide readership among a French public seeking diversity more than exoticism. These names included Carlos Fuentes, Juan Carlos Onetti, Alejo Carpentier, Augusto Roa Bastos, José Danoso, Miguel Angel Asturias, Mario Vargas Llosa, Julio Cortázar, Juan Rulfo, and Jorge Amado.

In the domains of philosophy, theory, and politics, the late nineteenth-century positivism of Auguste Comte (1798–1857) found fertile ground in Brazil. French positivism inspired many Brazilian political movements and events, such as the overthrow of the monarchy and proclamation of the Republic in 1889, as well as the "order and progress" slogan in the national flag.

In the late 1920s, French historians, anthropologists, and sociologists saw in the study of Latin American societies an opportunity to develop notions of civilization that were less ethnocentric and more suited to diversity. Brazil was at the heart of the work of sociologist Roger Bastide (1898–1974) and the geographer Pierre Monbeig, and of the structuralist anthropology of Claude Lévi-Strauss. The young Lévi-Strauss studied law and then in 1931 obtained his *agrégation* in philosophy. His ethnological career dates from 1934, when he was invited to teach sociology at the University of São Paulo. He stayed in Brazil until 1939, studying Amerindian populations including the Nambikwara, Caduveo, and Bororo tribes. This period is the source for one of his major works, *Tristes tropiques,* published in Paris in 1955, in which he explains the symbolic organization and ways of life of several Amerindian tribes in Mato Grosso state.

In the second half of the twentieth century, it was the turn of French politics to be influenced by Latin America. The ideals of the 1959 Cuban Revolution inspired a whole generation of the French Left who admired Fidel Castro and Che Guevara. The election of the Marxist Salvador Allende as president of Chile in 1970 had the same effect. As dictatorial regimes emerged in Argentina, Brazil, Uruguay, Paraguay, Ecuador, Bolivia, and Peru in the 1960s and 1970s, and after Augusto Pinochet's coup d'état against Allende in Chile in 1973, France not only supported dissidents but welcomed to its shores hundreds of political exiles. Many—such as the sociologist Fernando Henrique Cardoso, president of Brazil from 1994 to 2002—came to occupy high office in Latin American politics when they returned home. The Latin American presence in France is also tangible in the higher education sector, with the existence of research institutes and centers such as the

Institut des hautes études d'Amérique latine (IHEAL), and of scholarly publications. New technologies such as cable and satellite television (for example, the francophone TV5 is widely broadcast in Latin America), as well as the Internet, mean that Franco–Latin American relations are set to become closer than ever.

FRANCE AND THE UNITED STATES

Jacques Portes

The relations between France and the United States have always been complicated, combining fascination and misgivings. Since 2002 and the war in Iraq, a new strain has occurred: French diplomats and citizens have looked at the United States as an arrogant bully, and the Bush administration has expressed its will to punish such an irritating ally in a symbolic way: "French fries" disappeared for a while from a few Washington restaurants, contracts for the reconstruction of Iraq were denied to French firms, and personal meetings between George W. Bush (b. 1946) and Jacques Chirac were avoided. Such tensions had occurred many times before: in 1835, Andrew Jackson (1767–1845) spoke of war with France to obtain his due after the sinking of American ships during the French Revolution, and his move was resented in Paris as bad taste; Woodrow Wilson came to Paris in 1919 with his own peace plan and could not be understood by Georges Clemenceau (1841–1929), who was looking only for revenge; Charles de Gaulle had difficult relations with Franklin D. Roosevelt and Lyndon B. Johnson (1908–1973); the invasion of France by American movies was met with uproar in 1946 as in 1993. (See CHIRAC, JACQUES; GAULLE, GENERAL CHARLES DE; IRAQ WAR.)

In fact these two countries have been more often at odds than in harmony, but they have never been at war. On the contrary, they have been allies frequently from 1778 to World War II. Since then and until 2001, the United States had attracted more French tourists than any other country, and the French way of life had been largely Americanized, but this does not mean that both countries have understood each other well. (See FOREIGN POLICY, 1776–1945; FOREIGN POLICY, 1945–PRESENT.)

At the same time France gave the United States one of its icons, the Statue of Liberty, and sold Louisiana cheaply to it, which doubled its territory at the time: generous moves from a close friend.

France and America have been in competition for their democratic principles, but few French immigrants went to the United States, and those who did were scattered in a few big towns such as New York or San Francisco, and they never constituted an ethnic group that could become a link between both countries.

Scholars have argued that France and America became sister republics, but as they fought each other for universal ideas, they were necessary rivals. In fact misgivings began with the Franco-American alliance during the War of Independence: American commentators have minimized the impact of the French force and stressed the role of American patriots helped by a few exceptional individuals like the Marquis de Lafayette; on the contrary, French historians have explained that without the decisive victory of Yorktown, independence would have been long in coming. In 1800, the young American Republic was eager to abrogate the perpetual alliance signed in 1778, and to be free of any French threat. (See REPUBLICANISM.)

For the same reason, when Thomas Jefferson—a real francophile—learned of the French repossession of Louisiana, he decided to buy it to avoid a French presence in New Orleans. But before the Louisiana Purchase, the revolution came in both countries, and historians have demonstrated that revolutionary ideas traveled well between Europe and America, as a transatlantic trend to upheaval. (See AMERICAN REVOLUTION; FRENCH REVOLUTION.)

The American Revolution was first: as such it was a model for some Frenchmen before 1789. For example, Jacques-Pierre Brissot (1754–1793) went to the United States in 1788 and was impressed by the constitution of Pennsylvania and the bill of rights of Virginia, and he praised them when he returned. Many French revolutionary clubs followed suit by translating and studying the American documents. Nevertheless, the 1789 French "Déclaration des Droits de l'Homme et du Citoyen" is autonomous and not inspired by American texts, and the 1791 constitution, which kept the king, is largely inspired by England and not by the United States.

The French Revolution with all its consequences claimed to be unique and could not admit to owing something to a country as provincial as the United States: Brissot was condemned and executed in 1792, as a Girondin partisan of federalism who had brought back this dreadful idea from the American Constitution. The United States could not be a model for the French *Montagnards,* only a place of exile for a few of them who escaped the guillotine by fleeing to America, like Edmond Genêt or later Maurice de Talleyrand: they did not want to stay even when the French political situation became more hospitable to them, although some preferred to do so, like Genêt, who got married in America.

In the young republic, the French Revolution was acclaimed in its first months: Thomas Jefferson had been very close to the young and liberal French aristocrats who were at the forefront of the upheaval, but such enthusiasm was short lived, and horror came when France, under the radical Jacobin rule (1793–1794) led by Maximilien Robespierre, was governed by authentic "terrorists," and religion came under attack. In 1798, under President Adams, the Alien and Sedition Acts were implemented against French subversion at a time of quasi war between the two countries: it was no longer welcome for an American to present himself as a "sans-culotte."

The ascent of Napoléon Bonaparte did not bring better sentiments. For a man who had dreamed of being a new Alexander the Great (356–323 B.C.E.), America was an unknown and uninspiring wilderness. The sale of all the territory of Louisiana—much more than Americans would have dreamed of—was logical: Napoléon has never had any plan toward America (Louisiana was seen briefly as a granary for Santo Domingo, and nothing more). And as Napoléon was denounced as a tyrant regularly by the British press, Americans had similar views and considered him a menace to democracy.

The American and French Revolutions quickly diverged, and even the hope of establishing strong commercial links did not materialize as the United States kept its usual trading partnership with Great Britain.

The traditional friendship between France and the United States was the only link to last, and this memory was revived by necessity when the American military intervened to help defeat German invaders on French soil in 1917 and 1944, but without much depth.

To many French people—especially those who could read about or travel to America—Americans were seen as rude and devoid of any sophistication. The few French people who migrated to America were attracted only by the immensity of the continent and its resources and, as Chateaubriand wrote, they could express some regret: "France owned lately in North America a vast empire from Labrador to Florida, and from the Atlantic Ocean to the more far away lakes of Upper Canada."

For similar reasons, Indians were praised, but as a mythical people: François de Chateaubriand visited North America briefly, and his novel *Atala* (1801) had a deep impact on French opinion. During the first half of the nineteenth century, Native Americans were looked upon as "bons sauvages" and related through some mysterious ways to the Roman republic: pictures of Indian chiefs were assimilated to those of Caesar (c. 102–44 B.C.E.) or Cicero (106–43 B.C.E.). In 1845, when George Catlin (1796–1872) presented his "Indian Gallery" in Paris with authentic Indians in full regalia, he was met with sympathy but no surprise, as these clichés were already present.

Later in the century, with better knowledge, this strange perception evolved, but the French kept a keen interest in Indian people, who represented for them an image of the ancient natural order, recently destroyed by brutal American materialism. Buffalo Bill's Wild West Show, which came for the first time to Paris in 1889, was a very popular event, especially due to the presence of "real" Indians, even if some editorialists contended that they were never given an opportunity to win. But when French visitors came to the United States, they were discouraged by the terrible situation of the native peoples and stopped making comparisons between these unfortunates and the heroes of antiquity.

Nevertheless, the California gold rush provoked enthusiasm in France, and thousands of people sailed to this promised land. They formed a colony in San Francisco, with its own hospital and school system, and the first mayor of Los Angeles was a Frenchman. After the Civil War and the first intercontinental railroad, they were overwhelmed by the American invasion, but the French quarter of San Francisco was still visible when World War I occurred: quite a few of these Frenchmen were still citizens of their old country and went back to fight for their native land. (See AMERICAN CIVIL WAR; WORLD WAR I.)

During most of the century, France and the United States were neither hostile nor especially close. When the tensions of the revolutionary era subsided, no political reason jeopardized the traditional friendship, but no opportunity came to try its strength. As the French regime had a chaotic evolution, some observers looked at America as an example of stability and wondered how such a "young" country could succeed with the same constitution. At each revolution, the American model was considered, but its adaptation failed dramatically when in 1848 Napoléon III destroyed the Second Republic, which was closest to the American system.

The Civil War transformed the United States deeply. France, like Britain, was hesitant toward such an evolution. Napoléon III leaned toward the more aristocratic and rural confederation, but French radicals praised the abolition of slavery. Finally, Lincoln imposed his broader vision: the Union had to be respected. Proof of this new strength was given in 1865, when Washington signaled its opposition to French influence in Mexico: Napoléon III (1808–1873) could not impose Maximilian as emperor of Mexico. American pressure was strong enough and the end of the empire condemned this absurd adventure, but the United States affirmed it would not accept any French presence in the Western Hemisphere, in spite of the traditional friendship between the two countries.

In 1869, French Republicans praised the American political regime briefly, but only as a tool against the Second Empire. Once in power they opted for a British-oriented parliamentary system, which gave way to the Third Republic. The gift of Miss Liberty was the only result of that short period of love: conceived in the 1860s, it was completed only in 1886, when the "sister republics" had chosen two different paths.

At the beginning of the twentieth century, France and the United States were two important nations and they respected each other. French public opinion appreciated the shift from a provincial country to a modern one, with the first skyscrapers and a triumphant capitalism, but it did not have to fear such a success as America did not intervene in European affairs. The war against Spain was an astounding shock, but President Theodore Roosevelt (1858–1919), a sincere francophile, made it clear he had no intention to go further toward Martinique and Guadeloupe. French politicians, journalists, and authors were confident that their country could play its world role without any American interference; they were also convinced of the superiority of their culture: Americans' prowess was impressive, but the French had the power of the mind.

Such reasoning was comforted by American reverence toward Europe: the best artists, the top orchestras, the most favored painters were acclaimed in the United States, and the rich tycoons could buy medieval castles in France or in Britain.

French people were proud of this transatlantic pecking order and were unable to understand the real transformation of popular culture going on in the United States at that time. When the Wild West Show came to Paris, in 1889 and 1905, the spectators were enthusiastic, but reviews in the press did not know what to think: was the show a circus like Barnum, or imperialistic propaganda? They did miss the specificity of a show, which had attracted more spectators in America and in Europe than any other event before (30 million in thirty years).

Cinema was invented at nearly the same time in both countries: December 1895 in Paris and April 1896 in New York City. At the beginning, movie industries followed more or less the same pattern, but rapidly the size of the American market attracted French firms such as Lumière or Pathé: the difference grew when nickelodeons opened in the United States, as there was no equivalent in Europe. In 1914, there existed 10,000 theaters in the United States, 400 in New York, but only 189 in Paris and a few hundred elsewhere. (See CINEMA, 1895–1945.)

At the dawn of the twentieth century, the United States and France did not play in the same league, but this stability in their relationship could not survive World War I.

Throughout the twentieth century, France's power and influence declined more or less rapidly, and the United States became by steps dominant: it was not easy to manage.

World War I changed everything in the relation between the two countries. First, the whole system of international finance had been turned upside down: the United States had been in debt to Britain and France; it now became largely a creditor, and in 1915 Morgan Bank rescued these two countries from bankruptcy. From 1920, the dollar began its ascent to the role of world currency. France could not compete but could not accept such domination either. The dispute about the reimbursement of loans in the 1920s was very sharp: Americans, sticking to the rules of the book, required a complete payment, but some French people refused this on the grounds of war losses. Common understanding was at its lowest point.

Second, the Sammies (as American troops in France were then called) were welcomed, and General Pershing (1860–1948) ritually evoked Lafayette, but French chiefs of staff were not convinced by the value of these American soldiers who had never fought in a large war. They liked the trucks and tanks they came with, but they were equipped with French guns and cannons.

In 1919 when he arrived in Belgium and France on his way to the Versailles Conference, President Wilson was acclaimed by enthusiastic crowds as the symbol of American freedom and victory: that is why in nearly every town there is a Wilson Street or Avenue. But the atmosphere of the conference was not so buoyant: Wilson came with a plan and fixed the order of the debates, because he was alone in not seeking revenge or punishment on Germany. Such a position could not be accepted by Georges Clemenceau, prime minister of France at the time, whose goal was to make Germans pay for what they had destroyed while being protected from their aggressive tendencies. Finally a compromise was reached, which was far from Wilson's intentions, but he succeeded in imposing the principle of the League of Nations; in 1920, when the Senate of the United States refused to ratify the treaty, French officials had the verification of the "noble candor" of a president they never understood.

Financial and diplomatic problems between France and the United States in the 1920s were discussed in the press and at the Quai d'Orsay and State Department. In 1928, such discussions led to the Briand-Kellog Treaty (Aristide Briand [1862–1932] and Frank Kellog [1852–1943]), a Franco-American initiative to ban war forever and everywhere, which was followed by dozens of nations. A century and a half after their first alliance, the two countries gave an example to the world; of course, this treaty could not work as no nation could accept such constraint, but it was a testimony of the peace-loving nature of the people.

During the war, thousands of African American soldiers discovered France. Like all American soldiers, they had no right to mix with French people; being in a segregated army they were not free to move alone. Nevertheless quite a few of them grew aware of the freedom they found in French towns and found it difficult to go back to their country. Some of them returned to France after the war to experience life in a free country: most of them were musicians, painters, and writers who gathered on the "Black Bank" of Paris. Josephine Baker's wild dances were acclaimed as deliciously scandalous. A few white writers such as Henry Miller joined them, fleeing America's conservatism in the 1920s. (See DANCE; LITERARY RELATIONS.)

During the same period, many French people discovered American movies on the silver screen: in 1926, Hollywood movies represented three-quarters of all films exhibited in theaters. For the first time in 1928, the French government tried to set quotas against such an American invasion. The result was not perfect, but such a move was repeated later in the century. Strong competition in the movie industry began between France and the United States at that time: again French measures tried to give some protection to producers but neglected exhibitors and distributors who needed new films for their theaters. Paul Claudel, then French ambassador to the United States, was vigilant about films that were not fair to his country: they could be banned or cut.

The success of the French Communist Party was important for the renewal of anti-Americanism in France. Before World War I this opinion came from the rightists, who resented American vulgarity and its "unjust" rise to power; then the leftists denounced the United States as the icon of capitalism. The glamour of the 1920s with the prohibition of alcohol, misunderstood by everybody in France, continued to fuel anti-American opinion.

At the same time, many French people were impressed by the economic success of the United States, and by the strength of the dollar, in spite of the usual misgivings.

The Great Depression gave many arguments to leftist critique: the fall of the American economy was due to an excess of speculation, what they viewed as typical lack of balance. It was easy to say so in 1930, as France was affected by the Depression only two years later. The New Deal sounded like an interesting solution to the crisis to some French Socialists' ears, but the government of Léon Blum (1872–1950) did not last long enough to try any form of adaptation to the French context.

On the way to World War II, France and the United States could not meet, as the American Congress was eager to respect neutrality laws, even if President Roosevelt was deeply shocked by the fall of France, which could not use the American P-38 planes it had been able to buy. The American advice to Adolf Hitler (1889–1945) and Benito Mussolini (1883–1945) to restrain their thrust to conquer did not bear fruit. (See WORLD WAR II.)

The defeat of France, and the Vichy regime, put pressure on Washington: President Roosevelt kept his close adviser, Admiral Leahy (1875–1959), as ambassador in Vichy until 1942, thus infuriating General de Gaulle and Free France, then established in London. Later, American officials were eager to replace de Gaulle, whom they did not trust, with someone else. Roosevelt indeed never understood a man who had never been elected by the people and who acted like a "diva." Tensions lasted throughout the war, and the Free French efforts to improve the situation in the United States were hampered by divisions among their small group, as some exiles feared de Gaulle and his ideas. Many intellectuals and artists had settled in New York and Los Angeles, glad to be able to work in a free country: poet Saint-John Perse, movie director Jean Renoir, and film star Jean Gabin (1904–1976) spent the war in America and, in spite of mixed results for their careers, were very happy there.

After D day, the U.S. government tried to establish its own authority in liberated France, and de Gaulle had to rush to his native land to avoid such a move and be recognized as a legitimate leader before the elections: he succeeded in November 1944, but did not forget this chaotic period.

In spite of this deep antagonism, French people were liberated by American soldiers, discovering with envy their way of life as they distributed chocolate, chewing gum, and cigarettes to a population who had been deprived and starving during the previous four years. Thousands of young women married attractive and healthy GIs; sympathy toward America was intense even in the bombed cities: there was no resentment, as Vichy had hoped before its fall.

Such a hopeful situation did not last long, as Reconstruction was long and painful. Moreover the Communist Party gathered nearly a third of the vote during the first election to constitute the National Assembly: it admired Joseph Stalin (1879–1953) and the USSR's triumph in the war, denouncing American imperialism altogether. Arguments of the anti-American, anti-imperialism sort were more popular than the Communist Party, as many Frenchmen, mostly rightists, resented the decline of their country: France was indeed no longer able to impose its will, or even be independent. De Gaulle kept on trying to resist such a situation. This type of sentiment nourished a strong anti-Americanism, which appeared clearly in 1948 during the controversy about the economic agreement signed by Léon Blum and James Byrnes (1879–1972) two years before: movie producers in France claimed that it opened the gates to Hollywood mass production, and they gathered in the process Communists and also moderate actors and directors. After a few months, the parliament voted a law to protect and strengthen the French movie industry and the situation improved. Such a controversy recurred in 1981 and 1993. (See ANTI-AMERICANISM.)

During the 1940s and the 1950s, many French people were favorable to the United States: some crossed the Atlantic Ocean with productivity missions organized by the Marshall Plan, and France was the first beneficiary in Europe of the plan's funds, as one of the battlegrounds of the cold war. For example the American government financed 75 percent of the French war effort in Indochina, which it saw after 1950 as a typical anti-Communist contest. Others discovered jazz music with the same passion as they did novels by John Steinbeck (1902–1968) and William Faulkner (1897–1962).

A large political center was pro-American: the MRP (Mouvement Républicain et Populaire) and part of the Socialist Party. The CIA gave discrete subsidies to some of these groups and provoked the scission of the largest Communist union to create Force Ouvrière, which became completely independent in the 1960s. French visitors who stayed in the United States were astounded to discover shopping malls, suburbs with similar houses, and little gardens: a way of life that would take ten or fifteen years to come to France. Students were amazed by the way American universities functioned with their dormitories and social life evolving around fraternities.

At the end of the 1950s, the French discovered the music coming from America—Elvis Presley (1935–1977), Johnny Lee Hooker (1917–2001), and Ray Charles (1930–2004)—and the first rockers, as Johnny Halliday (b. 1943) Richard Anthony (b. 1938), and others chose American names, translated the hit songs, and sang them in French. A few years later, the Beatles revolution came to Europe and the United States, as the Liverpool "fabulous four" brought a pretty new sound and look. The French artists did not invent anything; they were only copiers without novelty and never made it in the United States, in spite of a few failed attempts. (See MUSIC [POP].)

There was a popular fascination for America, in spite of the strength of a political anti-Americanism.

General de Gaulle came back to power in 1958 with the intention of restoring French "grandeur": he resented any American intervention in the Algeria war and would have liked a common leadership for NATO. He could not get it and decided in 1966 to withdraw France from NATO's military command. On the other hand, he vetoed Great Britain's joining the Common Market, as he could not understand its special relationship with the United States. Always willing to promote a French international role, President de Gaulle knew perfectly his due to the United States as he knew the two countries were on the same side: in October 1962 during the Cuban missile crisis, the French president was the first to give his support to John F. Kennedy (1917–1963). (See GAULLE, GENERAL CHARLES DE; NATO.)

The Vietnam War as amplified by President Johnson was another cause of tension, as de Gaulle's proposal of a peace conference had been rejected and as American officials suspected him of being pro-Communist. In May 1968, the French student mobilization focused on the opposition to the war, as they saw it as deeply immoral and as an example of the imperial thrust of the United States. Anti-Americanism found plenty of arguments in this situation and was dominant intellectually, but had few links to the American movement against the war. (See VIETNAM WAR.)

The legacy of de Gaulle's national position and of the Vietnam War was long in disappearing. This was a time when few students took American studies in French universities, because they were unwilling to study anything American, except for a focus on blacks or Indians, presented as victims of "Amerika."

Gaullist ideas have been commonly adopted on the Right as on the Left: the United States had to be held at bay in international matters and sometimes to be resisted. Every French politician has adopted such an attitude at one time or another.

During the same period, cultural exchanges were intense, as American society gave examples of dissent and a sort of upheaval that was popular in Europe, through tours by Bob Dylan and other singers. In the United States, new directors, such as Martin Scorsese

(b. 1942) or Francis Ford Coppola (b. 1939), were inspired by the French New Wave and worked to be recognized themselves as "auteurs." A mark of this reverence can be seen in *Close Encounters of the Third Kind* (1977), in which Steven Spielberg (b. 1947) asked François Truffaut to play a role. Young teens who lived a while in the United States were enchanted, as everything seemed to be organized for them at school and on the playgrounds.

On the political level, things were more complicated: the American system was very difficult to understand for French observers. The impeachment of President Richard Nixon (1913–1994) (himself a great admirer of de Gaulle) was seen as extravagant, as his faults were only peccadilloes; his replacement by a non-elected Gerald Ford (b. 1913) was not viewed more favorably. Jimmy Carter (b. 1924) and Ronald Reagan (1911–2004) were so deeply American that they seemed alien in France, where most people were ill at ease with a newborn Christian or with a Hollywood actor. For some, such men had no credentials to become presidents. The French press was especially strident toward Reagan, who was depicted as bellicose and dangerous. On their side, officials in Washington were puzzled by the election of François Mitterrand in France, especially as he invited Communist Party members to his government: could such a man be a trusted ally? The French president had to prove his opposition to the deployment of Soviet SS-20 missiles in Europe and to give some information about a Soviet spy ring to be accepted; it was easy to do as he was not at all revolutionary.

New ideas came again from America in the mid-1980s: the rejection of Keynesianism and the adoption of monetarism in the United States were copied in France, in 1986 when the right came back to power, and made their way into the European Union as an apparent solution to a growing unemployment and a bulging deficit.

France, like the United States, changed a lot in the 1990s as both countries followed parallel paths toward globalization and witnessed the disappearance of the Communist empire. Traditional anti-Americanism had fewer and fewer adepts as American dominance could be seen briefly as benevolent: the first Gulf War in 1990 was largely supported in France, and remaining resistance came only from leftists and pacifists. Bill Clinton (b. 1946) was peaceful and did not trouble the international scene, but unlike his predecessors he was interested more in Asia than in Europe as a new continent for American commercial ambitions.

American culture was widespread in France, due to the Internet revolution and the acceleration of data and information. At the same time, the United States became the first destination for French tourists, before Italy or Egypt. Most of these people prefer American nature to the cities, except for New York City, which always fascinates. (See CYBER-CULTURE; TOURISM.)

Traditional resistance reappeared in 1993, when the last GATT negotiations threatened the French system of protection for the motion picture industry: anti-American sentiment was strong, as many people in the industry, as well as politicians, were concerned.

A first result that became more apparent was to accuse the United States of being responsible for the brutality of globalization, as first proponent of the dogma of the free market; the success of the French association ATTAC comes directly from such reasoning.

Another aspect came from the strangeness of America, which was confirmed by the arrival of George W. Bush at the White House. During the Clinton years, the failure of the health care reform, along with the leaning toward international commerce, drove the United States and France apart. American glamour still attracted many people, but they did not want to live there: they did not understand the American cult of the death penalty and were repulsed by the availability of firearms in commercial centers, which even Clinton seemed to support. Affirmative action was not understood in France and was perceived as diametrically opposed to the French goal of the integration of immigrants.

Now, unlike in the past, many European directors and actors choose to shoot one movie in Hollywood, but many of them prefer to return home after such an experience.

In spite of this prevalent opinion, French firms invested in the United States in order to profit from a large and rich market; luxury items were popular, as the success of Perrier and Vuitton showed, and so were finance and media firms such as Vivendi, even if the last ultimately failed. Some Americans investigated health benefits of drinking red wine and having lighter meals, as the French do. And for years, the French philosopher Jacques Derrida was a star in many American universities. (See FASHION; THEORY.)

A sort of balance between the two countries emerged at the end of the 1990s: less passion than before but with many fruitful exchanges.

The shock of September 11, 2001, was tremendous in America. And there was nearly unanimous French support toward the wounded United States, as the chief editor of *Le Monde* affirmed: "We are all Americans." This warm response corrected the bad impression left by the 2000 election and people forgot the first, offensive moves of President Bush before 9/11 that had antagonized the Europeans: the relaxation of air pollution quotas, subsidies to American farmers, and protective measures for the steel producers. (See 9/11: CULTURAL PERSPECTIVES; 9/11: POLITICAL PERSPECTIVES.)

But George W. Bush spoiled this opportunity, especially after the war in Afghanistan, which was more or less approved of in France. The unilateralist choice and the project of the Iraq War, based on shaky grounds, met the opposition of the French government and public opinion, as well as the opposition of many Europeans. A "reborn" anti-Americanism could develop, mixing old and new themes with passion; the distinction is rarely made between American people and the Bush administration, as tensions between the two countries become stronger than ever.

Acrimony and misgivings have been dominant in official encounters and in the press: France and the United States have been following diverging roads, accentuated by the events of 2002–2003. Happily, personal exchanges are still warm and pleasant, and such a chaotic but traditional friendship cannot die.

France and the Americas

ACADIA

The anglicized version of Acadie, the first French colony in North America until 1713, covered an area similar to Canada's three present-day Maritime Provinces—Nova Scotia (NS), New Brunswick (NB), and Prince Edward Island (PEI)—as well as the northern coast of Maine (ME).

Although Acadia no longer exists geographically, a francophone population still lives in the region and retains a strong Acadian cultural identity. Beginning in 1755 and lasting eight years, most Acadians were deported to Anglo-American colonies, France, and Great Britain after they refused to swear an oath of allegiance to the British Crown. The Acadians lived in exile until 1763, a period immortalized by Longfellow's epic poem *Evangeline* (1847). A minority of Acadians hid in remote woodland to escape deportation and returned to their former region, as did a small proportion of those deported between 1755 and 1762. During the 1760s, 1770s, and 1780s, many Acadians migrated to the Spanish colony of Louisiana, where they eventually came to be known as "Cadiens" (Cajuns). Their presence gave some areas of Louisiana a strong French character. Wherever today's Acadian populations live, they draw on popular memory and oral traditions to maintain a distinct linguistic and cultural identity.

The geographical boundaries of Acadie were never clearly mapped. In 1524, Giovanni da Verrazzano, sailing on behalf of François I, the French king, was the first European to map the coast between Florida and Cape Breton Island. He gave the name of Acadia to an ill-defined area in the vicinity of North Carolina, Virginia, or Maryland. Cartographers moved the name northward, where it eventually came to be associated with northern Maine and Canada's Nova Scotia and New Brunswick. Exploration, trade with the indigenous population, and cod fishing in the summer months continued through the 1500s. In 1598 a year-round French colony was established on Sable Island. In 1604, a fresh attempt to create a permanent settlement was made by Pierre du Gua, Sieur de Mons. The Sieur de Mons set sail from France accompanied by traders and explorers, including Samuel de Champlain. They made their base on Saint Croix Island, part of present-day Maine. They moved the following year to Port Royal (on the Annapolis Basin, NS). Severe winters, illness, and skirmishes with Anglo-American settlers

Man and woman of the Acadian country in America, in native attire, doing dance of French origin at the American National Folk Festival, Philadelphia, 1944. (Library of Congress)

and the revocation of the Sieur de Mons monopoly on the fur trade led the French to abandon the colony in 1607–1608. The French returned in 1610, but a military expedition from Virginia destroyed the post in 1613. French commercial and fur-trading interest subsequently shifted to the Saint Lawrence River.

In 1629 William Alexander, a Scottish merchant, colonized Acadia, which in his Latin charter was called Nova Scotia, or New Scotland. The Treaty of Saint-Germain-en-Laye in 1632 returned the territory to France, but the rival and overlapping French and British claims to the unbounded region were already in place.

In 1632, 300 immigrants led by Isaac Razilly arrived at LaHave, Nova Scotia, to begin a new French colony. When Razilly died suddenly in 1635, Charles Menou d'Aulnay moved the colony to Port Royal (Annapolis Royal, NS), which henceforth became the heart of Acadie. The move to Port Royal marked the start of a period of repopulation and redevelopment supported by Cardinal Richelieu. However, plans to strengthen the colony further were hampered by internal disputes, and in 1654 a successful attack from British forces in New England compounded Acadia's problems. Acadia was returned to France in 1667 by the Treaty of Breda, yet the threat from British colonies and French impotence in the face of aggression were clear. Nevertheless, the period after 1632 forged a distinctive Acadian physical and cultural landscape in isolation from both New France and New England. Significantly, one-third of Acadian immigrants came from Poitou in France, sharing a common regional dialect, which led Acadian French along its own distinct path. Unlike other European colonists who cleared wooded uplands, Acadians reclaimed fertile salt marshes from tidal zones. They developed a system of coastal and riverine dykes called *aboiteaux* that allowed freshwater to drain from marshland without allowing tidal saltwater onto it. The desalination process of the marshes took two to three years. It was a system that also kept the Acadians from land conflict with the indigenous Micmac (also spelled Mi'kmaq) and Maliseet populations. Despite these developments, the fledgling colony, numbering 400 people by 1670, continued to be endangered on three fronts. French colonial policy remained ineffective; neighboring British colonies were expanding rapidly

(Massachusetts boasted 50,000 inhabitants by 1670); and its borders were still undefined.

Proven vulnerable to attack, notably in 1690 and 1704, Acadia passed again, and definitively, into British control in 1713 by the terms of the Treaty of Utrecht. Yet the British were no more successful than the French had been in colonizing the region. Paradoxically, British colonial rule had a relatively positive impact upon the Acadians, bringing a period of peace that fostered the growth of an Acadian identity and language influenced by contact with British forces and the Micmac. In the stable political climate, Acadian communities flourished, and the birth rate rapidly increased. However, the departure of the French elite and the disappearance of any institutions of formal education led to a gradual loss of literacy among Acadians. A pawn in the colonial game, Acadian leaders could do little more than adopt a policy of neutrality, promising British leaders that they would not fight in a war with France.

Outside Acadia, the battle to control North America was intensifying, as both France and Britain protected their colonial interests though the construction of a number of forts. There were many skirmishes between the rival powers, and in 1745 the French stronghold at Louisbourg on Cape Breton Island was captured by troops from New England with British naval support. Yet Louisbourg was restored to France under the terms of the 1748 Treaty of Aix-la-Chapelle. The peace established in 1748 was short-lived, and pressure intensified in the region throughout the early 1750s. The Acadian position of neutrality no longer satisfied the British administration in Nova Scotia. In 1755 the Nova Scotia Council, led by acting governor Charles Lawrence, demanded the Acadians swear an unconditional oath of allegiance to the British Crown. The Acadians refused, and in July the council ordered their deportation. An estimated 12,000 to 13,000 people were removed. The process lasted until the end of the French and Indian War in 1763. The Acadians were primarily sent to British colonies in North America but also to Britain, France, and the Caribbean. The experience entailed a large loss of life for the dispossessed Acadians, both at sea and later, in hostile settings. Many historical accounts leave the Acadian story here, with the Acadian population in exile. However, the history of Acadia and its people continued, generating an even stronger Acadian identity after the tragedies that began in 1755.

The Treaty of Paris in 1763 ended French colonial rule in North America, but a French-speaking population remained in the continent, causing concern for the British authorities. Following the treaty, Acadians were allowed to return to the Maritime Provinces, provided they finally swore an oath of allegiance. Some Acadians did return to the former Acadia, others migrated to Quebec, many remained in the regions to which they had been deported, and large contingents settled in Louisiana. The estimated 3,000 Acadians who returned to their homeland were unable to return to their lands, which had been distributed to British colonists. They headed instead for some of the most remote areas of the Maritime Provinces, a trend encouraged by the British authorities, to avoid conflict with British settlers. Consequently, there emerged a new geography of Acadia.

The British authorities inevitably erased much of the French presence from the map, renaming and reorganizing

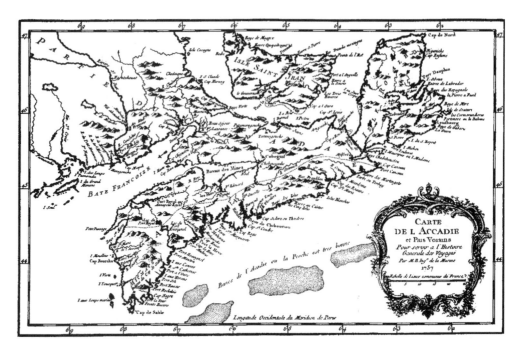

Acadia in 1757. (www.Acadian-Cajun.com)

places, territories, and institutions. They set up a colony on Saint John's Island (later Prince Edward Island) in 1769 and created New Brunswick out of Nova Scotia in 1784. A number of anti-Catholic and antifrancophone laws and policies harmed the Acadians. Catholics were prevented from owning land in Nova Scotia until 1783, from voting until 1789 in Nova Scotia (until 1810 in the other two Maritime Provinces), and from sitting in the legislature until 1830. From 1760 to 1860, the survival of Acadian communities in the Maritime Provinces was seriously threatened by the territorial and institutional dominance of the anglophone communities, which ensured that Acadians played no significant role in the political life of the Maritime Provinces before 1850. Acadian communities were scattered and isolated, making the development of Acadian insti-

tutions difficult. There were no formal Acadian schools before 1820, leaving villages dependent on an education provided by parish priests, who were not necessarily francophone. As a result, access to schools varied, and rates of literacy dropped significantly, forcing Acadian communities to rely increasingly on songs and tales to maintain their traditional identity. A significant development, however, was the opening of the Collège Saint-Joseph in Memramcook, New Brunswick, in 1854, a higher education institution teaching in French that created an educated, middle-class, Acadian elite. In 1864, Nova Scotia abandoned its tolerance of francophone schools, introducing a law that made English the only language of instruction in the province. Although a Canadian Confederation was formed in 1867, it became apparent that the new constitution did not protect the rights of francophone or Catholic minorities, when in 1871 New Brunswick also made English the only language of instruction, followed closely by Prince Edward Island in 1877. Despite these discriminatory measures from the anglophone majority and the geographical isolation that hampered the creation of a network of Acadian institutions, the Acadian population of the Maritime Provinces had reached 87,000 by 1871.

The period from 1880 to 1914, called the "Acadian Renaissance," witnessed the consolidation of Acadian institutions and the development of an Acadian national agenda as the pupils of the Collège Saint-Joseph took up positions in public life. In 1881 the first of a series of Acadian national conventions was held in Memramcook to address issues like education, religion, agriculture, emigration, and the press. A second convention was held in 1884 at Miscouche, Prince Edward Island, where an Acadian flag and anthem were chosen. Occasional conventions were held in Acadia during the next 100 years. Throughout this period, Acadians became more involved in the political life of the Maritime Provinces, taking up elected positions in provincial and national governments. Acadian schools and colleges were established, including the Université Sainte-Anne along Saint Mary's Bay, Nova Scotia, in the 1890s. The majority of Acadian parishes came to have a francophone priest, and in 1912 the appointment of an Acadian bishop was secured. While Acadian attention was focused by their political and religious leaders on promoting national institutions, the stability of the Acadian population was challenged by external economic factors, which led to emigration to the United States and to the shake-up of

traditional Acadian family models as more women entered the workplace.

The early twentieth century was a paradoxical period for Acadian communities. Despite political and social advances for Acadians, the threat of assimilation increased as larger numbers of both the anglophone and francophone populations of the Maritime Provinces moved to richer provinces and as many young men were lost in two world wars. Despite the continued threats from assimilation and economic migration, the period since 1950 has produced significant political, economic, and cultural advances for the Maritime Acadians. However, the experiences of Acadians differ according to the proportion of anglophones and francophones in each province. In the twentieth century New Brunswick became a principal home of Acadians. In 1996 Acadians represented only 3.8 percent of the Nova Scotia population and 4.9 percent of the population on Prince Edward Island, whereas in New Brunswick Acadians (some 240,000 people) made up 33 percent of the population and, as a result, have made the most significant advances there. In 1960 Louis Robichaud was voted the first Acadian premier of New Brunswick, bringing in an era of political change to the province. In 1963 the Université de Moncton, an Acadian university, was created, and education underwent reform, including the introduction of separate francophone and anglophone junior ministers for education. In 1969 New Brunswick went a step further, becoming Canada's only officially bilingual province, recognizing the status of Acadians in New Brunswick and offering them legal protection.

The political advances were paralleled by flourishing Acadian literature, theater, painting, sculpture, music, and cinema. This cultural revival began with the publication of Antonine Maillet's first novel, *Pointe-aux-coques,* in 1958, a novel concerned with identity, loss, and the threat posed by migration for the survival of Acadian culture. After 1960 there was an explosion of Acadian literature, marking a definitive transition from the traditional oral culture to a literary culture, a transition facilitated by the opening of an Acadian publishing house, Les Editions d'Acadie, at the beginning of the 1970s. These changes marked a shift away from artistic dependence on Quebec and Paris, with works published by Acadian poets, playwrights, and novelists Raymond LeBlanc, Guy Arsenault, Herménégilde Chiasson, Jacques Savoie, and Claude LeBouthillier, among others. Acadian music was also celebrated beyond its own borders during the 1970s with the popularity of traditional group 1755 and songwriters such as Edith Butler. These cultural and political developments encouraged some Acadians to consider the creation of a separate Acadian province as promoted by the Parti Acadien (1972–1982), an idea that received only limited support from the majority of Acadians.

Although Acadians in New Brunswick have both federal and provincial legislation to protect their rights, until the 1980s Acadians in Nova Scotia and Prince Edward Island have relied solely on federal protection, making it more difficult for them to achieve their political aims. For example, Nova Scotia had to wait until 1981 for the introduction of a law recognizing the status of francophone schools in the province and the introduction of a curriculum that actually included Acadian history and culture. On Prince Edward Island the same law came into effect in 1981, but with the proviso that there be enough francophone presence to warrant it. However, in January 2000 a historic ruling from the Canadian Supreme Court forced the government of Prince Edward Island to build French schools in two Acadian communities, a verdict that offers hope to many Acadian communities across the Maritime Provinces. In these two Maritime Provinces some advances have been made, but lack of access to French schools, high levels of assimilation, and loss of French as the first language have put in doubt the survival of a francophone Acadian community there.

Nevertheless, the concept of Acadia and an Acadian cultural heritage persists. In the 1990s Acadia was recognized as an important part of the Canadian cultural landscape and a valuable commodity for promoting tourism to the Maritimes as traditional industries die out. Acadian culture received international recognition with Antonine Maillet's *Pélagie-la-charrette* (*Pélagie: The Return to Acadie*), which received the Prix Goncourt in 1979, and Acadia placed itself firmly on the francophone map in 1999 by hosting the eighth Sommet de la francophonie in Moncton, New Brunswick. In 1994, the first Acadian World Congress, recognized by the United Nations Educational, Scientific, and Cultural Organization (UNESCO) as an event in its decade of cultural development, was held in Moncton to celebrate the Acadian diaspora. A second congress was held in Louisiana in 1999, and a third in 2004 in Nova Scotia, events that highlight and celebrate the role of Acadia and Acadians throughout the French Atlantic.

Kathryn Gannon

See also: Cajuns; Champlain, Samuel de;
Evangeline; François I, King of France;
French and Indian War; Louisbourg;
Maillet, Antonine; Maine; New Brunswick;
New France; Nova Scotia; Richelieu,
Cardinal Armand Jean du Plessis de;
Verrazzano, Giovanni da.

References

Brun, Régis. *Acadia Past and Present.*
Moncton, NB: Centre d'études acadiennes,
1999.

Daigle, Jean, ed. *Acadia of the Maritimes:
Thematic Studies from the Beginning to the
Present.* Moncton, NB: Chaire d'études
acadiennes, 1995.

Ross, Sally, and Alphonse Deveau. *The
Acadians of Nova Scotia Past and Present.*
Halifax: Nimbus, 1992.

Runte, Hans R. *Writing Acadia: The
Emergence of Acadian Literature,
1970–1990.* Amsterdam: Rodopi, 1997.

ADAM, PAUL (1860–1920)

Frenchman of letters, little known today but one of the key writers of the belle époque period (1890–1914).

Novelist, essayist, and a prolific journalist, Paul Adam wrote several best-sellers and was highly thought of by critics. His place in intellectual history is due to his wanderings in the politics of his time and his interest in the Americas.

As a young dandy and a member of the symbolist avant-garde, Adam was a supporter of the right-wing General Georges Boulanger along with fellow writer Maurice Barrès, and then he proclaimed that he was an anarchist. After flirting briefly with utopian Socialism and taking a restrained pro-Dreyfus stance, he then became interested in "Latinité" and ended up as a nationalist. Throughout, his major preoccupation was what he considered to be the decadence of France. The search for reme-

dies to this problem was the catalyst for his ideological itinerary.

It was in this context that in the 1900s, Adam turned more and more frequently to the American continent. His analyses and judgments, which more often than not reflected his concerns about the future of France, blew hot and cold on the subject. Nonetheless, his analyses were supported by extensive reading and also firsthand experience. He visited the United States and Cuba in 1904 and Brazil in 1912.

Adam envied what he called "les Yankees" for their taste for risk and for their society that valued action; in contrast, the Latins were said to get bogged down in endless ideological arguments. He attributed the economic power of the United States to this dynamism and to its cutting-edge technology, which he admired greatly. Adam criticized Latin countries' excessive individualism, but he was enthusiastic about the sense of solidarity that for him explained the vitality of American capitalism, seen as a system in which workers and bosses work for a common good. He was also favorably impressed by the "Yankee's" probity and the progressive attitude toward girls' education. However, the Americans were not immune to his criticism, for there are ironic passages on their bad taste and their prudishness, which he attributed to Protestantism. Adam above all calls into question democracy and universal suffrage as exemplified by the United States, for its system allows the ignorant majority to dominate and to neglect the rights of minorities.

Latin America also plays an important role in Adam's writing, mainly to do with his deep-seated germanophobia. While Germany's domination of Europe was increasing, Adam saw the only salvation for France to lie in the renewal and defense of "Latinité." He thus preached the unity of Latin countries, forming in 1916 the League of Latin Intellectual Fraternity, an organization whose aim was to develop alliances and exchanges between intellectuals and politicians of different Latin countries, including those of Latin America. Adam thus looked positively on the continent of South America, seeing it as a new incarnation of Greco-Roman culture and the continuation of its ideals. Needless to say, this interpretation ignores the native peoples. Latin America has, however, a negative side, a consequence of excessive Latin individualism that encourages endless rivalries and opens the door to dictatorship.

Isabelle Genest

> *See also:* Avant-Gardes; Brazil; Dreyfus Case; World War I.
> **References**
> Duncan, J. Ann. *Les Romans de Paul Adam: Du Symbolisme littéraire au symbolisme cabalistique.* Bern: Peter Lang, 1977.
> Parinet, Elizabeth. "Paul Adam: Littérature et politique." Mémoire de D.E.A., Institut d'Etudes Politiques, 1981.

ADAMS, HENRY BROOKS (1838–1918)

American editor, journalist, historian, novelist, and author of *Mont Saint Michel and Chartres,* an examination of the ideological unity of thirteenth-century French culture through its religious (specifically cathedral) architecture (published first privately in 1904, then in 1913), and of its companion volume, *The Education of Henry Adams: A Study of Twentieth Century Multiplicity,* an autobiographical meditation on the accel-

erating multiplicity (chaos) of his own age (winner of the Pulitzer Prize in 1919).

Born into Boston's patrician ruling class, Adams was the grandson of John Quincy Adams and great-grandson of John Adams, both U.S. presidents. In 1899 (following earlier visits to France) Adams inaugurated a yearly ritual of sojourns in Paris and travels in France that was to last (with the exception of 1912 when he was recovering from a stroke) until 1914.

Following an assistant professorship in medieval history at Harvard (1870–1877), Adams grappled with the traditional antiquarianism and party political agendas of fellow historians to formulate an independent, authoritative "science of history" grounded on scientific principles. He rejected Charles Darwin's doctrine of evolution and Charles Lyell's uniformitarian geology (a theory of geological action of uniform intensity over immense periods of time), on which natural selection was premised, as less than credible for natural and social change over historical time. Sweeping aside Darwin's followers, who had transformed Darwinian natural selection into optimistic, progressive "evolutionary" doctrines conducive to human progress and perfectibility, Adams ultimately embraced the "catastrophist" geology of his friends Clarence King and J. D. Whitney (Yale professor of geology). Catastrophism (whereby changes in the earth's history were often the result of intense outbursts of geological energy) underwrote Adams's later commitment to the energy physics of Lord Kelvin. Kelvin's heat-engine model (which Adams transformed into an analytical tool for understanding historical change) demonstrated that physical changes were driven by energy transformations from greater intensity (reconceived by Adams as "unity") to lesser intensity (reconceived by Adams as "multiplicity").

In 1895 Adams focused attention on the works of Thomas Aquinas and the architecture of the cathedrals of Normandy, including Amiens, Chartres, and the Abbey of Mont-Saint-Michel. Regarding the production of such architecture as the ultimate expressions of his historical ideal of a culture's "unity" and unified energies, he conceived of human history as a "force" that could be measured down to his own time by its motion from a fixed point in the past. In *Chartres* (to which he appended the working subtitle: "A Study of Thirteenth-Century Unity"), Adams's fixed point was supplied by the Catholic French culture of 1150–1250 (embodying the quintessential historical period of unified human energies in a unified universe) and symbolized for Adams by the powerful unifying force of the Virgin Mary.

In the *Education,* he fixed his own period as that of humankind's greatest "multiplicity." Vividly describing his repeated visits to the Hall of Dynamos at the Paris Exposition in 1900, Adams identified the centrifugal power of the dynamo as symbolic of the dissipated, chaotic energies of modern multiplicity. Using these two fixed points, he hoped to measure historical processes from medieval unity to modern multiplicity. In his *A Letter to American Teachers of History* (1910), Adams's final pessimistic pronouncement contended that man as a form of energy was susceptible to the same inevitable decay and ultimate dissipation as the Second Law of Thermodynamics predicted for the energy of the universe.

Ian N. Higginson

See also: Adams, John; Architecture.

References

Harbert, Earl, and William Decker, eds. *Henry Adams and the Need to Know.* Boston: Northeastern University Press, 2005.

Samuels, Ernest. *Henry Adams.* Cambridge, MA: Belknap Press, 1989.

ADAMS, JOHN (1735–1826)

Second U.S. president (1797–1801) and a remarkable figure in the creation of the United States.

Adams had a number of links with France and during his own administration prevented war with revolutionary France. Adams was born on October 30, 1735, in Braintree, Massachusetts, and attended Harvard before becoming a lawyer. His law career brought him into contact with Boston's political elite, with whom he discussed the plight of the colonies. He became a delegate to the First Continental Congress in 1774 and while in Philadelphia played a key role in drafting the Declaration of Independence. Adams then began a diplomatic career as commissioner to France (1778) before becoming minister to the Netherlands, where he secured recognition of American independence and negotiated a loan and treaty of amity and commerce. Adams played a key role in securing, in the Treaty of Paris of September 3, 1783, favorable terms from the British for ending the Revolutionary War. In 1785 he was appointed first U.S. minister to Britain but was unable to substantially improve Anglo-American relations. After three years in London, Adams resigned, intending to return to Massachusetts. However, in the first election under

John Adams, second president of the United States of America. (Library of Congress)

the Constitution, Adams's national standing saw him elected as the first vice president behind George Washington. The role was frustrating for a man of Adams's intellect, but that did not stop his performing it with courage and integrity, especially in casting the deciding vote in the Senate, often in support of the federal government. Although nominally a Federalist, Adams tried to remain aloof from the burgeoning party political system of the mid-1790s, which proved a fruitful tactic in the 1796 election, in which Adams prevailed over Thomas Jefferson. During the early part of Adams's administration, relations with France worsened, as the French Directory refused to accept a U.S. delegation and began a campaign to disrupt U.S. maritime trade, resulting in the sinking or capture of 300 ships. Although the Re-

publicans called for a more belligerent response, Adams recommended defensive preparations in funding a U.S. Navy. Tension with France continued as the U.S. ship *Constellation* and the French ship *L'Insurgente* battled on February 9, 1799. While demonstrating to France that the United States had assembled a significant naval force, Adams averted a declaration of war by concluding a treaty with France on September 30, 1800. Domestically, Adams signed into law the Alien and Sedition Acts (1798), which imposed harsh penalties on those who criticized government and was in turn criticized by opponents for being too authoritarian. Although Adams had helped the Federalists to a congressional election victory in 1798 by disclosing that French negotiators, named only as "X, Y, and Z," had demanded a bribe, he was unable to retain his own office when he was defeated by Jefferson in the 1800 election. In later years Adams reaffirmed an interest in the arts and sciences, having established the American Academy of Arts and Sciences in 1779, which was inspired by the French Royal Academy of Arts and Sciences. Adams would live to see his adored son, John Quincy Adams, become president in 1824 before he died on the fiftieth anniversary of the Declaration of Independence and the same day as Jefferson: July 4, 1826.

J. Simon Rofe

See also: Jefferson, Thomas; Washington, George.

References
Ellis, Joseph J. *Founding Brothers: The Revolutionary Generation.* New York: Knopf, 2000.
McCullough, David. *John Adams.* New York: Simon and Schuster, 2001.

AIDS

"A cancer that would only touch homosexuals, no, that would be too good to be true!" When, around 1981, Hervé Guibert told Michel Foucault about the American discovery of a "gay cancer," Foucault could only laugh. His reaction is emblematic of how the French gay community responded to the news, accusing American puritanism of being responsible for it. Indeed, after years of fighting for sexual freedom, the French gay community generally refused to acknowledge the possible veracity of such a "rumor." The news of acquired immune deficiency syndreme (AIDS) put an end to what Frédéric Martel, in *Le Rose et le noir,* calls a time of "insouciance."

France and the United States played central roles in the discovery of the virus. In 1981, Willy Rozenbaum connected one of his patients to cases reported in the United States by the Centers for Disease Control of a rare type of cancer—Kaposi's sarcoma—seen in homosexuals. With Jacques Leibowitch, he founded what would be called the "French work group on AIDS" in charge of finding information on a so-called gay cancer. They were in the process of discovering the virus. The team at the Pasteur Institute, headed by Luc Montagnier, was the first to isolate human immunodeficiency virus (HIV)—which they initially dubbed LAV—and published a paper on it in *Science* in May 1983. A few months later, a team led by Robert Gallo at the National Health Institute in Maryland also laid claim to the discovery, and a dispute developed, with millions of dollars at stake over blood test patents. In March 1987 French prime minister Jacques Chirac and U.S. president Ronald Reagan settled the debate, declaring both men codiscoverers. In later years Gallo and Montagnier continued to work closely together in the fight against the epidemic.

The scientific French-American relations concerning the virus, although not without rivalry, served a common goal: to understand what medicine was needed to fight what some described as a "holocaust" of the gay community. Throughout the pandemic, and to this day, American strategies have inspired the French and vice versa. In 1984 AIDES was founded by Daniel Defert, Michel Foucault's longtime partner, after the philosopher's death. Its goal was to inform the gay community of the virus and promote safer sex, but its creation was criticized by a number of militants for gay rights such as Guy Hocquenghem, who is known to have said: "Tobacco gives cancer, we all know it. Have we stopped smoking? Sex gives diseases. We should stop making love?" After the establishment of the U.S. organization AIDS Coalition to Unleash Power (ACT-UP) in 1987, its French equivalent, ACT-UP Paris, was created in 1989.

When Michel Foucault died in 1984, the cause of his death was not clearly named, although it became common knowledge. It was revealed in Guibert's novel *A L'Ami qui ne m'a pas sauvé la vie* (1990), which shows Foucault, under the name of Muzil, as a man who died from AIDS. Guibert's AIDS trilogy—*A L'Ami qui ne m'a pas sauvé la vie* (*To the Friend Who Did Not Save My Life*), *Le Protocole compassionnel* (*The Compassion Protocol*) (1991), and *L'Homme au chapeau rouge* (The Man in the Red Hat) (1992)—as well as his diary *Cytomegalovirus* (1992), are literary chef d'oeuvres that have occupied an important place in social discourse around

First ladies summit and scientific symposium on AIDS/HIV with professors Robert Gallo and Luc Montagnier. Professors Gallo and Montagnier before the conference in front of the Palace of Congresses. (Henri Tullio/Corbis)

AIDS. Although Guibert himself was neither a gay nor an AIDS activist (something for which he was reproached), his writings are at the forefront of a public discourse on the syndrome, the health care system and hospitalization, and their effects on a person's life.

A large number of writers and artists in France and the United States (as well as throughout the world) have represented the experience of HIV-positive individuals. Indeed, circulation between France and the United States took place not only by means of scientific research into AIDS but also through cultural transfers linked to the acts of mourning that it generated (the AIDS memorial quilt, for instance) and to the artistic productions connected to it. For instance, the novels and testimonials of Paul Monette, Gilles Barbedette, David Woj-

narowicz, and Alain-Emmanuel Dreuilhe; the plays of Tony Kushner and Larry Kramer; the films of Cyril Collard, Derek Jarman, and Mike Figgis; and the art of Pierre et Gilles and Keith Haring have all served to render the drama of AIDS visible on both sides of the ocean and hence encourage activism.

The tragedy of AIDS has had an important impact on another aspect of cultural circulation: American queer studies appeared on the French intellectual scene in the early 1990s, thanks primarily to the work of Didier Eribon. He organized the first gay and lesbian studies conference at the Centre Georges Pompidou in Paris in 1997, in which speakers from the United States and Canada participated. Conference papers were collected and published in one of the first volumes on the question to appear in France: *Les Etudes gays et lesbiennes* (Gay and Lesbian Studies) (1998). Eribon has also published a number of books on gay studies, among them *Réflexions sur la question gay* (Reflections on the Gay Question) (1999) and *Papiers d'identité* (Identity Papers) (2000). He is one of the most important advocates in France of what the Americans call "gay and lesbian studies."

Martine Delvaux

See also: Foucault, Michel; Gay Movement; Hocquenghem, Guy; Theory.

References

Bass, Thomas A. "Luc Montagnier on Gallo and the AIDS Virus: 'We Both Contributed.'" *The Scientist* 7, no. 24: 11.

Chambers, Ross. *AIDS Diaries and the Death of the Author.* Ann Arbor: University of Michigan Press, 1998.

Eribon, Didier. *Réflexions sur la question gay.* Paris: Fayard, 1999.

Martel, Frédéric. *Le Rose et le noir: Les homosexuels en France depuis 1968.* Paris: Seuil, 1996.

Murphy, Timothy F., and Suzanne Poirier. *Writing AIDS: Gay Literature, Language and Analysis.* New York: Columbia University Press, 1993.

ALBERTA

French explorers and fur traders arrived in present-day Alberta in the mid-eighteenth century. By the mid-nineteenth century, the French-speaking Métis people (part French-Canadian, part native) predominated in the region, but this population became a minority after the arrival of large numbers of English-speaking settlers in the 1880s. French-language community organizations nevertheless ensured the survival of francophone culture in the province through French-language education, radio and television programming, publishing, and theater. In the 2001 census, 2 percent of Alberta's population of 2,900,000 declared French as their first language, with the largest groups in the northern communities of Grande Prairie and Bonnyville.

After the British conquest of North America in 1760, Scots and Americans took over the fur trade, but French-Canadian voyageurs (canoemen) remained its labor base. Their Métis descendants worked as guides and interpreters, hunted buffalo, and developed the Red River cart to carry freight on the prairies. By the mid-nineteenth century, French was the main language of Fort Edmonton, the largest fur-trading post on the North Saskatchewan River.

In the 1840s, Catholic priests from the Oblates of Mary Immaculate arrived to found missions at Saint Albert, Lac Sainte Anne, and other centers. The most famous of these men was Father Albert Lacombe (1827–1916), who worked with the Métis, Cree, and Blackfoot for over fifty years and wrote dictionaries and grammars of native languages. Members of the Sisters of Assumption, the Sisters of Sainte-Croix, and the Filles de Jésus worked as teachers, and women from the nursing orders of the Grey Nuns, the Sisters of Charity, and Our Lady of Evron established hospitals and nursing homes.

Despite the work of *prêtres-colonisateurs* (colonizer-priests) designated by the Catholic Church in the late nineteenth and early twentieth centuries to encourage French immigration from Quebec and New England, only small numbers of settlers arrived. Some pre–World War I immigration from Belgium and France included former French army officers and members of the aristocracy who raised cattle and

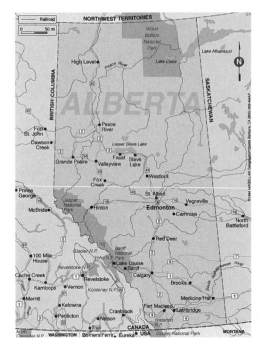

Map of Alberta. In the 2001 census, 2 percent of Alberta's population of 2,900,000 declared French as their first language, with the largest groups in the northern communities of Grande Prairie and Bonnyville. (MAPS.com/Corbis)

established in 1909 to train priests, and now trains French teachers as the Faculté Saint-Jean of the University of Alberta. The Association Canadienne-Française de l'Alberta (ACFA) was established in 1925. It publishes a French-language weekly, *Le Franco,* and in 1949 obtained a license to operate a radio station. Francophone culture continues to thrive in Alberta, with added diversity owing to more recent immigration from French-speaking areas of Africa, the Caribbean, and the Middle East.

Katherine Durnin

See also: Bugnet, Georges; Catholic Church; Fur Trade; Language; Métis; World War I.
References
Lacombe, Danyèle. *The Franco-Albertan Community.* Edmonton: ACFA Foundation, 1996.
Smith, Donald B. "A History of French-Speaking Albertans." *Peoples of Alberta: Portraits of Cultural Diversity.* Ed. Howard Palmer and Tamara Palmer. Saskatoon: Western Producer Prairie Books, 1985: 84–108.

horses on ranches south of Calgary. The best-known French immigrant from this era was Georges Bugnet, novelist, poet, and journalist. French companies present in the early twentieth century included the Revillion Fur Company, and West Canadian Collieries, which operated coal mines in southwestern Alberta.

The Northwest Territories Act of 1875 made French and English the official languages of government, the courts, and education, but in 1892 these provisions were amended in favor of English only. It was not until 1982, with the passage of Canada's Charter of Rights and Freedoms, that French-language schooling above the primary school level was again allowed, and the first French school boards were set up in 1993. The Juniorat Saint-Jean was

ALEXIS, JACQUES-STEPHEN (1922–1961)

Haitian writer and political figure, born into a family at the forefront of Haitian cultural and political life.

Alexis began his education in the Collège Stanislas in Paris and returned to complete his baccalaureate in Port-au-Prince. During his subsequent studies at the Haitian Faculty of Medicine, his political and literary passions began to emerge. He worked on the reviews *Cahiers d'Haïti* (Haiti Notebooks) and *Le Caducée* (*The Caduceus*) before joining René Depestre's militant *La Ruche* (The Hive) group in 1945. The launch of the journal coincided with the arrival in Haiti of Aimé Césaire, André Breton, and Wilfredo Lam, whose presence inspired a special edition on surrealism. Haiti's political and cultural ferment culminated in the general strike of January 1946 and did lead to the downfall of President Elie Lescot, but ultimately failed to install the democratic Socialist government envisioned by the *La Ruche* group. At the end of that year, Alexis and Depestre left to continue their studies at the Sorbonne, not realizing that for both it was the beginning of a long exile from Haiti.

Exile allowed Alexis to distill his own vision of Haiti's future, one that, like Jacques Roumain's, was never narrowly nationalist or indigenist, but sought to valorize popular tradition and also place the country in a Marxist global context. It is in *Compère Général Soleil* (1955) that this vision is most persuasively proposed; the mix of Marxism and surrealism, coupled with the memory of the massacre of Haitians in the Dominican Republic, climaxes in a stirring call for change in Haiti and the world in general. At the First Congress of Negro Writers and Artists at the Sorbonne in 1956, Alexis presented his enduring, influential theories of Haitian "réalisme merveilleux/magical realism," which essentially developed Roumain's ideas of popular culture while insisting that the particularities of Haiti could not be easily assimilated into a more general "black" or African aesthetic. These arguments fed into 1957's *Les Arbres musiciens,* which presents Haitian popular culture under threat from Americanization and the Catholic Church–led "Campagne anti-superstitieuse." *L'Espace d'un cillement* (1959) marks a movement away from rural Haiti to the urban world of Port-au-Prince and its cast of prostitutes and pimps, and

U.S. Marines literally screwing the country. His final published work, *Romancero aux étoiles* (1960), is a collection of short stories that reflects his preoccupations with resistance and Haitian self-affirmation.

A patriot and militant to the end, Alexis was killed by president François Duvalier's forces as he attempted to return to Haiti in 1961 to lead an insurrection against the dictatorship. Alexis was never universally popular with his contemporaries, yet his work remains a testament to his unquestionably committed, poetic, politically engaged sensibility.

Martin Munro

See also: Breton, André; Césaire, Aimé; Depestre, René; Haiti; Lam, Wilfredo; Roumain, Jacques; Surrealism.

References

Dash, J. Michael. *Literature and Ideology in Haiti, 1915–1961.* London/Basingstoke: Macmillan, 1981.

Depestre, René. *Bonjour at adieu à la négritude.* Paris: Robert Laffont, 1980.

Souffrant, Claude. *Une Négritude socialiste: Religion et développement chez Jacques Roumain, J. S. Alexis, et L. Hughes.* Paris: L'Harmattan, 1978.

ALLEN, WOODY (ALLEN STEWART KONIGSBERG) (1935–)

American film director and actor, born in Brooklyn.

Allen appears to many as the quintessential New York actor-director, with films such as *Annie Hall* (1977), *Manhattan* (1979), and *Hannah and Her Sisters* (1986) portraying the ironies and anguishes of middle-class life in his home city. Nonetheless, Allen's films follow stylistically in the footsteps of the French New Wave and are peppered with references to French life and culture, a reflection of the fact that for the last decade he has made a point of spending late December in Paris. The admiration is reciprocated as Allen's works fare exceptionally well in France, and there is rarely a week when his films are not playing in at least one Paris cinema.

Allen began his career in the 1950s writing jokes for newspapers and television shows and then went on to performing as a stand-up comedian before live and TV audiences. The 1960s saw his career as a cinema actor take off with Peter Sellers's *What's New, Pussycat?* (1965) for which he wrote the script. His directing debut was *Take the Money and Run* (1969), followed by a host of light, almost slapstick, comedies before his more introverted films from the mid-1970s. The 1970s and 1980s, during which Allen starred with Diane Keaton and then Mia Farrow (both partners in his personal life), is seen as his most successful period. He has now made well over thirty films. Of these, *Annie Hall* won three Oscars, *Hannah and her Sisters* won one, and *Manhattan* and *The Purple Rose of Cairo* (1985) both received the César (French Oscar) for best foreign film.

Several of Allen's productions have key scenes shot in Paris (e.g., *What's New, Pussycat?, Love and Death* [1975], *Everybody Says I Love You* [1996]) or use Paris as a leitmotif to which the characters dream of escaping. Spoofs of intellectualizing in works such as *Deconstructing Harry* (1997) lead to quips on Jean-Paul Sartre, Simone de Beauvoir, or Gustave Flaubert. In 1987 Allen appeared in Jean-Luc Godard's *King Lear,* a short modern-day satire that got limited release. More important is the influence Godard has had on Allen's productions, specifically the disjunctive documentary-style cinéma vérité that frames *Annie Hall,*

Manhattan, and *Husbands and Wives* (1992).

The punch line to *Hollywood Ending* (2002) is Allen's tongue-in-cheek tribute to French cinema: second-rate director Val Waxman makes a comeback while concealing his onset of blindness, resulting in a shambles that flops in the United States, only for Americans to be told that the French love it! Woody Allen rejects much of the Hollywood studio system and follows the influence of Ingmar Bergman, Federico Fellini, Godard, and François Truffaut, making him the most European of popular American filmmakers.

Laurence F. Grove

See also: Beauvoir, Simone de; Cinema, 1945 to the Present; Godard, Jean-Luc; Sartre, Jean-Paul; Truffaut, François.
References
Fox, Julien. *Woody: Movies from Manhattan.* London: Batsford, 1996.
Fredon, Jean-Michel. *Conversations avec Woody Allen.* Paris: Plon, 2000.

AMERICAN CIVIL WAR

In 1861, eleven Southern states, which called themselves the Confederate States of America, sought independence from the United States. However, newly elected president Abraham Lincoln did not recognize the legitimacy of the Confederate government. Instead, Lincoln's administration referred to the Confederacy as states temporarily in "rebellion." Furthermore, Lincoln's administration did everything in its power to bring the "rebels" back into the Union. But Confederate president Jefferson Davis and other Southern leaders refused to give up their cause without a fight. Outnumbered and outgunned, Davis soon realized that European aid was crucial for

Confederate survival, and he sent agents to Great Britain and France to ask for help.

The South was greatly outmatched by the North. A recent massive wave of immigration (1850–1860) had given the North a much greater population than the South. Most of the Irish, German, and Chinese immigrants settled in the North because they could get jobs in the factories. For the most part, the South did not need their services, because the South's agrarian economy relied on slave labor. It has been estimated that about 70 percent of the U.S. population was concentrated in the North at the outbreak of the war. This afforded the North a much greater supply of soldiers. Also, almost all of the nation's manufacturing capacity was in the North. It has been estimated that only about 14 percent of the nation's factories were in the South in 1860. Therefore, war materials, which could be readily churned out in the North, were difficult to come by in the South. The North held most of the mineral deposits that were necessary for making weapons. The North also boasted more than twice the South's railroad mileage. Even though the use of railroads in war was somewhat limited by where the tracks were laid, they did prove extremely helpful in the transporting of troops and supplies. The North also had most of the telegraph wire, which gave them an advantage in planning and directing military operations. Finally, the North controlled almost all the naval ships. Because of this, the North implemented the Anaconda Plan, which was a blockade of Southern ports aimed at choking the South economically, militarily, and diplomatically.

Understanding their limitations, Confederates knew that they had to end the war as quickly as possible. In order to do this, Confederate leaders determined to make very aggressive attacks on U.S. forts and the Union capital. Victories on the battlefields, it was thought, would convince the North to let the South go or at least convince Europe to intervene in the conflict in favor of the Southern cause. In general, the first year of the war went well for the Confederacy. The Battle of First Bull Run (July 1861) resulted in a Confederate victory. The Union responded with the Peninsula Campaign, but all attempts to capture the Confederate capital failed. In addition, Confederate forces were on the offensive in the East and in the West. These events on the battlefields prompted Britain and France to start pushing for mediation. They felt that the war had gone on long enough and that it was time to end it by giving the South what it wanted—independence. The Confederacy was aware that Europe needed cotton, and it used it as a bargaining chip.

Both British and French leaders favored the dissolution of the United States because they saw it as a way to slow down rapid U.S. growth, which threatened their superiority as world powers. Furthermore, by late 1861, the Union blockade of Southern ports began to take a toll on both British and French business interests, and the economic woes produced a rise in popular support for European intervention in the conflict. Even Canadian public opinion was decidedly anti-Northern. Lincoln and Secretary of State William H. Seward, however, counteracted attempts at intervention by pointing out to the British and French that they imported Northern wheat in great quantities and that it could be withheld if diplomatic relations worsened. Both Britain and France were forced to recognize that, even though they were dependent on the South's cotton, they were even more dependent on the North's wheat.

Gambling on pro-secessionist opinion abroad, Davis sent James Mason to Britain and John Slidell to France with orders to seek official recognition of the South's independence. Traveling together, the envoys attempted to run the blockade. They traveled to Havana, Cuba, and then boarded the British vessel *Trent,* only to be intercepted by the USS *San Jacinto* under Captain Charles Wilkes. The Americans forcefully boarded the British ship and took Mason and Slidell as their prisoners. The Trent Affair, as it came to be called, was the most serious diplomatic crisis of the American Civil War. Although the *Trent* was not damaged and the Union allowed the ship to go on its way, British national honor was severely bruised. And although the British really did not want war with the Americans, they adamantly held to the position that they could not allow their flag to be insulted in that way. In preparation for war, Britain quickly sent thousands of troops to Canada, got its navy ready, and demanded a release of the two prisoners and a formal apology. To make matters worse for the Americans, France declared its support of the British stand. Faced with impending war, the North backed down, and the crisis was resolved peacefully with the release of the two prisoners and a formal apology. The Confederate ministers, therefore, proceeded unencumbered to their assigned destinations.

The Battle of Antietam (September 1862), the bloodiest one-day battle of the war, was a product of a Confederate attempt to capture Washington, D.C. Unfortunately for the Confederacy, however, Union forces repulsed the attacking army, which was led by Robert E. Lee. News of the Confederate retreat resulted in greater caution in Britain. After Antietam, Britain began to adopt a wait-and-see attitude. This frustrated French Emperor Napoléon III, who longed for a permanently divided North and South, but he felt that he could not act without British support. However, future Confederate victories could make intervention a possibility once again.

Since the firing on the Union Fort Sumter by Confederate forces, which began the war, European powers had been extremely curious about the war. It was the first major industrialized war, and several countries sent official observers to report on the new methods of fighting, which were necessitated by new technologies. These foreign volunteers joined both Union and Confederate armies and took part in the war. Other European visitors took on a more detached role as mere observers. For example, France very carefully monitored the progress of the war. In the summer of 1861, Henri Mercier, French minister to the United States, arranged a visit by the emperor's cousin, Prince Napoléon. The prince toured both the North and South and reported back home on his observations. One year later, Mercier secured permission from Seward to visit Richmond, Virginia. At the capital, Mercier interviewed Confederate secretary of state Judah Benjamin, who assured the minister that the South would win the war. Mercier remained unconvinced, but he was quite impressed with Benjamin's resolve to continue the fight. In any case, of great concern to Mercier were the large amounts of cotton and tobacco that abounded in the South but would never reach France because of the federal blockade.

Besides these observers, thousands of other Frenchmen took part in the war. Many French immigrants had been attracted by the promise of a new life in the United States, and French immigration had risen steadily in the early 1800s. According to census reports, between 1850 and 1860, over 100,000 French immigrants arrived in North America. The French settled in various parts of the United States, but many headed for Louisiana. When the Civil War broke out, many Frenchmen joined in the fighting. French Zouave units, in both the Union and Confederate armies, distinguished themselves in battle. The Zouave units dressed in very distinctive uniforms, similar to the garb of French soldiers in Algiers. They wore striped or red baggy trousers, bright waistcoats, cropped jackets with braided trim, fez-style hats, and sashes tied around the waists. The most famous of these units were the Louisiana Tigers of the Confederate Army and the New York Fire Zouaves of the Union.

Several French officers also deserve mention. French-born Camille Armand Jules Marie, Prince of Polignac, served as a Confederate officer. Polignac, a veteran of the Crimean War, was a staff officer for another famous French Confederate, Pierre Gustave Toutant Beauregard. In the final year of the war, Polignac sailed to France to try to secure support for the Southern cause. Beauregard served as the staff officer of Winfield Scott during the Mexican-American War. During the Civil War, he commanded the attack on Fort Sumter, fought at First Bull Run, and assisted in the defense of Richmond in 1864. Basically, there was no theater of the war in which Beauregard did not fight. Another notable Frenchman who fought for the Union

cause was Prince Jérôme Bonaparte. Besides fighting courageously, Bonaparte left an accurate record of watercolor pictures of daily life in the Union Army.

Meanwhile, as the war was raging in North America, three European nations sought to occupy Mexico. In defiance of the Monroe Doctrine (1823), which declared that any further European colonization of the Americas would be regarded as cause for war, Spain, Britain, and France took control of Mexico under the guise of debt collection. The Union issued a formal protest against the invasion and accused the Europeans of planning to establish a monarchy. Before long, Northern diplomatic pressure, constant squabbles among the three countries, and French minister Dubois de Saligny's announcement that France supported a Mexican monarchy convinced Spain and Britain to withdraw. French emperor Napoléon III, however, ordered his troops to remain.

Determined to return France to the glory years it experienced under his uncle Napoléon I, Napoléon III had successfully intervened against Russia in the Crimean War, defeated the Austrians in Italy, conquered Algeria, acquired Nice and Savoy from Piedmont, established French Indochina, and begun the construction of the Suez Canal. Not surprisingly, to Napoléon, a French Latin American empire seemed both possible and extremely attractive. Napoléon believed that Mexican stability would attract European capital, increase European trade, supply European textile mills with cotton, and end U.S. involvement in Mexico. The first step was to remove the sitting Mexican president, Benito Juárez. On May 5, 1862, however, Juárez's army defeated a French expeditionary force near Puebla. More determined than ever,

Napoléon sent reinforcements and captured the Mexican capital on June 7, 1863. Confirming American suspicions, Napoléon then established Archduke Maximilian of Austria as emperor of Mexico.

Having acquired a foothold in Mexico, Napoléon sought to solidify the conquest by proposing joint British and French intervention in the American war. In late 1862, Napoléon asked Britain and Russia to join France in a three-power intervention aimed at securing a six-month armistice in the United States. However, neither Britain nor Russia was willing to risk angering the North with such a move. In the early part of 1863, Napoléon once again tried to bring an end to the war. After the North's defeat at Fredericksburg, Napoléon offered mediation directly to Washington. The Lincoln administration refused the offer. What is more, the U.S. Congress was so appalled by the emperor's offer that it overwhelmingly passed a resolution declaring that any future attempt at mediation by any country would be regarded as an unfriendly act.

The three-day Battle of Gettysburg (July 1863), the bloodiest battle of the war, was yet again an attempt by the Confederacy to capture the Union capital. Robert E. Lee led his men in what turned out to be the last major battle of the war. But, once again, Lee's forces were halted, and his retreat signaled the end of any hope of European intervention. British popular opinion shifted toward a pro-North stance after Union victories began to mount and Lincoln's Emancipation Proclamation was issued. The proclamation, which freed the slaves in rebelling states, served as a diplomatic weapon. It infused the war with a moral element by elevating the struggle to that of a fight against human bondage.

Aware of its implications, Lincoln wrote several letters addressed to abolitionist organizations in Britain in an attempt to appeal to the working person's sense of Christian heroism and to stir up positive reactions for his new policy. It worked. Huge rallies occurred all over Britain in support of the proclamation. Henry Adams, U.S. minister in England, wrote that, in his estimation, the proclamation had done more for the North's cause than past victories on the battlefields. Ultimately, the approval of Britain's middle class for the North restricted the British governing class from siding with the then unpopular slaveholding South.

As the Confederacy felt its chances of European intervention or recognition slipping away, it resorted to certain acts of desperation. For example, by 1864, Davis ordered Confederate agents to station themselves in Canada and try to drum up support for the Confederate cause there. Their main charge, however, was to use Canada as a base of operations from which to launch anti-Lincoln propaganda in an effort to prevent his reelection in 1864. Unable to sway the election, the Confederate agents then turned their attention to acts of sabotage in retaliation for Northern victories on the field. For example, as General William T. Sherman marched through Atlanta, Georgia, Confederate agents attempted to burn New York City by setting fire to hotels and other public places on November 25, 1864.

Napoléon believed that a permanently divided North and South would ensure his hold on Mexico, because a free South would gladly endure a French-held Mexico in gratitude for French support of Southern independence. Unfortunately for the South, however, as British interest in intervention waned, the Union threatened war against France in response to any interference. To complicate things even more for Napoléon, his advisers were increasingly reminding him that he could not afford to wage war against the Union Army at a time when Prussia was exhibiting an aggressive attitude toward France. (Their fears were apparently not unfounded: the Franco-Prussian War broke out in 1870.) Consequently, Napoléon was checked. He would not act without British support, and possibly fearing an enforcement of the Monroe Doctrine by the United States, France pulled its troops from Mexico as the American Civil War drew to a close. Without the hope of European support, the Confederacy was left to fend for itself. Consequently, the Union was preserved.

Rolando Avila

See also: Antislavery Movements; Cotton; Louisiana; Mexico; Slavery; Tobacco.

References

Blumenthal, Henry. *France and the United States: Their Diplomatic Relations, 1789–1914.* Chapel Hill: University of North Carolina Press, 1970.

Carroll, Daniel B. *Henri Mercier and the American Civil War.* Princeton: Princeton University Press, 1971.

Case, Lynn M., and Warren F. Spencer. *The United States and France: Civil War Diplomacy.* Philadelphia: University of Pennsylvania Press, 1970.

Echard, William E. *Napoleon III and the Concert of Europe.* Baton Rouge: Louisiana State University Press, 1983.

Hanna, Alfred J., and Kathryn Abby Hanna. *Napoleon III and Mexico: American Triumph over Monarchy.* Chapel Hill: University of North Carolina Press, 1971.

West, W. Reed. *Contemporary French Opinion and the American Civil War.* Baltimore: Johns Hopkins University Studies in Historical Science, 1924.

Winks, Robin W. *Canada and the United States: The Civil War Years.* Baltimore: Johns Hopkins Press, 1960.

AMERICAN REVOLUTION

The enormous financial and military effort of the French and Indian War (1754–1763) gave Great Britain absolute dominion over all North American territory east of the Mississippi. After the Royal Proclamation (October 7, 1763) that temporarily set their western border at the Allegheny Mountains, British land in North America was reorganized into nineteen provinces. East Florida and West Florida, containing 5,000 Spanish-speaking inhabitants, were added to the older provinces of Georgia, South Carolina, North Carolina, Virginia, Maryland, Delaware, Pennsylvania, New Jersey, New York, Connecticut, Rhode Island, Massachusetts, New Hampshire, Nova Scotia (including the Island of Saint John, later Prince Edward Island, and Cape Breton Island), Newfoundland (including the Labrador coast, Iles-de-la-Madeleine, and Anticosti Island), and Rupert's Land (Hudson Bay). To this area, which contained 1,628,700 English-speaking inhabitants, the province of Quebec was also added. In 1760, 63,100 francophones lived in Quebec. The British provinces were limited to the west by the Indian Territory. This extended from the Proclamation Line, which ran along the Allegheny mountain chain, to the limits of the Spanish territory. The Indian Territory, containing approximately 25,000 inhabitants, was not placed under any provincial legislation, only the sovereignty of the Crown. There remained, then, off the coast of Central America, the French islands and the British islands, the latter inhabited by 41,000 Europeans and 365,000 Africans (1760).

The Treaty of Paris (February 10, 1763) removed the French, the common enemy of the British Crown and its American colonists, from North American soil.

As a result, the need for mutual assistance was gone, and Great Britain as well as the American provinces were free to dedicate themselves to the pursuit of their own interests. Eventually, these interests conflicted. Starting in 1763 especially, the British parliament began to imagine new solutions that would reverse the negative trends of increasing administrative inefficiency and a chaotic financial situation. The public national debt of £137 million was only grazed by tax revenues of £8 million, which was just a little more than the £5 million to be paid in debt interest. The French and Indian War alone was estimated to have cost £160 million. The reorganization of the British administration had to begin from the very sector that seemed to present the most inefficiencies, the most resistance, and at the same time the most possibility for immediate economic return, that is, the entire colonial system, whose trading made up 68 percent of British public revenue. In this system the old American provinces stood out for the gap between their wealth and the modest contribution they offered to the Crown's coffers. The British parliament maintained, and not without reason, that it had paid all the costs of the French and Indian War. It had defended the interests of the American provincials, who not only paid ten times less in taxes than the inhabitants of Great Britain but also did not give military aid or even a financial contribution in return. The reorganization of the colonial system took various forms. Subordination of the provinces to the British parliament was confirmed; the entire body of laws regulating their economic and political activity, until then not applied, was put into force; and the principle that the provinces were to pay for their own administration and defense was reinforced. This policy was handled in a contradictory and inconsistent manner (between 1760 and 1775 Great Britain changed government eight times) but enjoyed nearly unanimous consent in Great Britain, at least until the outbreak of the War of American Independence (1775–1783). This war was also described by the revolutionaries as the American Revolution, and by their rivals, loyalists in America, as the War of the Rebellion. Considering its nature, historians should better call it the North American Civil War.

The new British colonial policy immediately clashed with the expectations of the provinces' elite, who were moving in exactly the opposite direction. At the very moment in which merchants and land speculators believed that they had their way clear to the west and the north and the provincial parliaments believed that they no longer needed British assistance, London blocked their expansion, taking the place of the French. The metropolitan government imposed the payment of taxes, levies, and duties that until then they had largely avoided and prevented the unlimited use of provincial currency. In addition, London did not recognize the powers of the provincial parliaments; did not withdraw its regular troops, leaving them to the orders of a unified military command; and in the end, with the Quebec Act (June 22, 1774), handed a good part of the West over to Quebec "papists." These measures, which for a century and a half had aroused nothing more than the occasional protest, instantly became intolerable. A quick glance at the events of the twelve years that passed between 1763 and the battles of Lexington and Concord (April 19, 1775), representing the beginning of the war, shows, however, how the crisis in the relations between Great Britain and the future United States accelerated. This acceleration led to a civil war that both sides believed to be avoidable up until the last moment. The 1763 Royal Proclamation was followed by the Stamp Act (March 22, 1765), which obliged the provinces to purchase a revenue stamp for documents, newspapers, almanacs, playing cards, and dice. This taxation, of little importance in itself, was interpreted by American opponents within the context of a series of new financial obligations imposed by the British parliament from the day after the French and Indian War. Rioting in the streets or symbolic demonstrations such as the so-called Boston Massacre (with three dead) (March 5, 1770) or the Boston Tea Party (December 16, 1773) led on the one hand to the unilateral convocation of the Continental Congress (June 17, 1774), in which the representatives of twelve colonies or provinces out of nineteen participated, and to the Declaration of Independence (April 4, 1776), signed by fifty-six delegates representing thirteen provinces. On the other hand, they led to the Quebec Act, which reproposed, with amendments, the broad lines of the Royal Proclamation of only a decade or so earlier.

The American Revolution had been sought by an elite that, above and beyond the law and in accordance with a new political project, had violently replaced the previous elite. Those involved at the time, from both sides, were far less certain of the inevitability of victory for the forces of the revolution than were historians following 1783. The war dragged on for a long time. In 1775 the British captured Fort Ticonderoga (May 10), but they could not defeat American resistance at Bunker Hill (June 7), a defeat that cost Thomas Gage

(1721–1787) his command. William Howe (1729–1814) replaced Gage, and the Continental Congress appointed George Washington (1732–1799) commander in chief of the Continental Army (June 15). American troops conquered Montreal (November 13) but were routed at Quebec (December 30–31), where they had met not only with the British army but also with the hostility or the indifference of the French Canadians. In 1776 Howe abandoned Boston for Nova Scotia (March 17), regrouped, and reconquered New York (August 22–25) and the entire province by the end of the year. By employing guerrilla tactics, Washington won stunning victories at Trenton and Princeton, New Jersey (December 26, 1776, and January 3, 1777). In the South, the British fleet did not succeed in conquering Charleston, South Carolina (June 28). In 1777, following the battles of Brandywine (September 11) and Germantown (October 4), Howe entered Philadelphia. However, at Saratoga, New York, General John Burgoyne (1722–1792) surrendered his 5,700-man army to Horatio Gates (c. 1728–1806) (October 17). In 1778, reassured by the turn of events in North America, France signed an agreement with the Continental Congress (February 6), and the British replaced Howe with Henry Clinton (c. 1738–1795). Clinton abandoned Philadelphia and headed toward New York, but he barely avoided defeat at Monmouth, New Jersey (June 28). In the South, the British fleet conquered Savannah, Georgia (December 29). In 1779 war operations concentrated around New York, while the Americans waged guerrilla warfare in the west against the British and the Indian nations, who mostly fought on the British side. In 1780 the British fleet took

Charleston (May 12), and Gates was defeated at Camden, South Carolina (August 16). After Gates was replaced by Nathanael Greene (1742–1786), at Yorktown, Virginia, General Charles Cornwallis, marquis Cornwallis (1738–1805), surrendered his 7,000 men to a joint French-American force led by Washington and Jean-Baptiste Vimeur, Comte de Rochambeau (1725–1807) (October 19). For all practical purposes, that was the end of the American Revolution.

All in all, by using guerrilla warfare tactics, the American revolutionaries were able to prolong the war long enough to cause French intervention and the internationalization of the war itself. This in turn caused the breakdown of the British front, that, although in favor of the war at the beginning, progressively lost its unanimity and yielded in the face of the military defeats suffered beginning in early 1781. In fact, only France's intervention on the side of the revolutionaries determined the final outcome of the war. France first supplied the Americans with logistical support and then prevented Great Britain from using its military superiority to the fullest. Therefore, with its direct intervention, France altered the balance of power in the decisive battle of Yorktown.

The American Revolution ended with the Treaty of Paris (September 3, 1783) and the independence of thirteen of the nineteen provinces or colonies that existed on North American soil when the hostilities began. Not all the provinces took part in the revolution with the same conviction, nor did the contemporaries fight with one side or the other simply according to social class, religion, or length of residence. There were merchants, planters, New Englanders, Virginians, Catholics, and Quakers among the revolutionaries as well as among the Loyalists (also called Tories), that is, those who actively sided with the British. It is a fact, however, that the revolution was predominantly led by a political bloc consisting of southern planters and land speculators from the center-south provinces. The Loyalists were numerous in all the provinces, approximately one-third of the population, and formed the majority in Georgia and South Carolina. Many, perhaps 60,000, fought alongside the British against the revolutionaries. During the war or immediately after its end, approximately 80,000 Americans (perhaps up to 100,000) left the United States. It is estimated that they represented 20 percent of those who espoused the Loyalist cause without showing it publicly and who remained in the country after the end of the war. Furthermore, as is the case during all revolutions, there were even more who tried not to side with either group.

The 12,000 (1776) residents of Newfoundland, despite the Irish origins of many of them, were not at all tempted to fight alongside the distant American revolutionaries. Neither were the 1,000–2,000 inhabitants of the Island of Saint John, a large portion of whom were of Scottish origin. The position of the 20,000 inhabitants of Nova Scotia was more complex. Many of them had arrived in the province from New England in the last fifteen years, and others were immigrants who had arrived mostly from the British Isles and from German-speaking countries. Nova Scotia was not without revolutionary sympathies, but a combination of factors gave the Loyalists the upper hand. On the one hand there were the substantial subsidies for immigration granted by the British government, especially between 1749 and 1763, which, together with the importance of Halifax as a Royal Navy military base, gave the province a certain economic prosperity. On the other side there was the multiethnic composition of the region (English, Scottish, Scotch-Irish, Germans) and the negative reaction of the population to the continuous raids by American privateers. Lastly, there was the political-religious plan proposed by a radical evangelical clergyman originally from New England, Henry Alline (1748–1784). According to Alline, whose preaching took root in the Great Awakening, Nova Scotia was nothing but the new Massachusetts, that with its revolution had abandoned the righteous path of God. The success of Alline's plan and of the resulting movement, known as the New Light, made Nova Scotians feel like a people with a unique history, a distinct identity, and a special destiny. It was their sense of superiority, therefore, that caused them not to espouse the rebel cause.

Excluded from the North American continent but favored by the terms of the Treaty of Paris-Versailles, France had immediately started to prepare for another conflict with Great Britain. The French rebuilt their navy, took advantage of trade with the West Indies, and wove a network of diplomatic relations that would heighten the isolation of the enemy country. The American Revolution did not take French officials by surprise. Indeed, several of them had expected it during the French and Indian War. Their intervention alongside the rebels in 1778 was the logical consequence of the anti-British policy operating in France at the time. What did not take place, however, was the French armed intervention on Quebec soil that many French-Canadians were nostalgically awaiting. (Only eighteen years had passed since the British conquest of Quebec.) According to the French foreign minister, Charles Gravier, Comte de Vergennes (1717–1787), a possible annexation or conquest of Canada would have given the American revolutionaries too much strength, with dangerous consequences for the future of international order. Keeping an area of friction, such as the Canadian frontier, on the contrary, would have weakened Great Britain as much as it would have the United States, all in France's interest. The Treaty of Paris was favorable to France as well as to the United States. France kept Saint Lucia and Tobago for itself and reclaimed its former possessions in India, Senegal, and Gorée (later Chad) in Africa. It also maintained fishing rights in the North Atlantic. Great Britain took back its islands in the West Indies and, like France, obtained fishing rights in the North Atlantic but ceded Minorca, East Florida, and West Florida to Spain. The latter had entered the war only on June 21, 1781.

Luca Codignola

See also: Catholic Church; Fishing; Florida; French and Indian War; Mississippi River; Newfoundland; Nova Scotia; Quebec; Rochambeau, Jean-Baptiste-Donatien de Vimeur, Comte de; Saint Lawrence River; Treaty of Paris (1763).

References

Christie, Ian R. *Wars and Revolutions: Britain, 1760–1815.* London: Edwin Arnold, 1982.

Ferling, John E. *A Leap in the Dark: The Struggle to Create the American Republic.* Oxford: Oxford University Press, 2003.

Garner Thomas, Peter David. *Revolution in America: Britain and the Colonies, 1763–1776.* Cardiff: University of Wales Press, 1992.

Lawson, Philip Graeme. *The Imperial Challenge: Quebec and Britain in the Age of the American Revolution.* Montreal/Kingston: McGill-Queen's University Press, 1989.

ANNAUD, JEAN-JACQUES (1943–)

French film director, equally well known in Europe and the United States, born in Juvisy, outside Paris.

In 1962 at the Ecole de Vaugirard in Paris, Annaud passed his BTS (a qualification as a technician in the film industry) and made his first short film, *Les Sept Péchés capitaux du cinéaste*/The Filmmaker's Seven Deadly Sins. Receiving his diploma from the prestigious French film school Institut des hautes études cinématographiques (IDHEC), he began a career in film ads at the age of twenty-three. His first feature film, *La Victoire en chantant* (also known as *Noirs et blancs en couleurs*/Black and White in Color, 1977), was a satire of colonialism that won the Oscar for best foreign film, although it was not a commercial success. His 1978 film on the milieu of football in provincial France, *Coup de tête*/Hothead, produced with Patrick Dewaere and Jean Bouise, did slightly better at the box office. Annaud won Césars for best film and best director for *Quest for Fire* (1981), the story of three members of a primitive tribe. After this success came *The Name of the Rose* (1986), an adaptation of Umberto Eco's novel starring Sean Connery, and an innovative animal film, *The Bear* (1988), which won a César for best director and France's Prix National du Cinéma. In 1991 the producer Claude Berri entrusted him with the adaptation of Marguerite Duras's novel *L'Amant* (*The Lover*), the story of a passionate affair between a teenager and a wealthy Chinese businessman, in a production starring Jane March.

Annaud shot a 3-D IMAX film, *Wings of Courage,* recounting the adventures of the pilot Henri Guillaumat who crashed in the Andes, which was first shown at the Poitiers Futuroscope in 1996. His other project that year was a film that took a clear political line against Chinese rule in Tibet. *Seven Years in Tibet,* starring David Thewlis and Brad Pitt, was the story of Austrian mountaineer Heinrich Harrer, who escaped from British troops during World War II, crossed the Himalayas, and ended up as tutor to the young Dalai Lama. Annaud's next films continued in this vein of spectacular intentional films made in English: *Enemy at the Gates* (2000), about the siege of Stalingrad, starring Ed Harris and Jude Law; and *Two Brothers* (2004), starring Guy Pearce and Jean-Jacques Dreyfus as two brothers lost, captured, and sold in the jungles of Cambodia.

Annaud is the president of the French Hollywood Circle, which brings together around 100 French film professionals working in Los Angeles. Annaud lives in that city and pursues his career choice to make films for the United States and, indeed, world market.

Jérôme Ceccon

See also: Aviation; Cinema, 1945 to the Present; Sport; World War II.

References

Bonnal, Nicolas. *Jean-Jacques Annaud: Un cinéaste sans frontières.* Paris: Maule, 2001.
Boorman, John, and Walter Donohue. *Filmmakers on Film-making.* London: Faber and Faber, 1996.

ANTI-AMERICANISM

Cultural anti-Americanism has been a feature of French discourse since at least the eighteenth century. As rhetoric, it long predates the political anti-Americanism of more recent history. Because of this well-established antipathy, modern French intellectuals inherited a cultural argument that they used to back up their political positions—attacking in particular the "simplicity," "arrogance," "Puritanism," "artificiality," and "greed" of American civilization. Seeing these terms today, it is obvious how little the anti-American critique has changed. Of course, disliking the United States is hardly uniquely French. American power has generated resentment worldwide. In addition, the historical links between the two nations and the universalist pretensions of their dual revolutions are certain to create some competitive hostility. But French anti-Americanism has characteristics that differ from mere resentment of American power or dislike of American policy. Quite apart from any political concerns, anti-American writing has repeatedly played a central role in constructions of French identity.

Tied to the French narrative of glory, decline, and decadence, critiques of America and Americanism have marked modern French history. As the United States emerged as the new colossus in the late nineteenth century, the first traces of this broad-based anti-Americanism surfaced, and intellectuals of all stripes, from reactionary to radical, began to see in America and "Americanization" the greatest threat to civilization. This sentiment was codified in the years after World War I, when it combined with political and economic concerns to make for the powerful mélange that is French anti-Americanism.

The story is rich with irony. To begin with, France and the United States are the world's oldest allies—and business and diplomatic relations have usually been excellent. In addition, the general population of France continuously demonstrates an astonishing ambivalence toward the United States. Opinion polls summarize these sentiments nicely—they tell us the United States is both the most hated and most beloved country among the French. Although political anti-Americanism has, via the Communist Party, appealed to a segment of the populace, cultural anti-Americanism has typically been an elite taste. Although it has occasionally translated into mass movements, its most dedicated proponents usually contrast American vulgarity to French *civilization,* thus legitimizing certain traditional cultural notions. It is also clear, as historian Richard Kuisel has noted, that American cultural successes seem specifically marked to undermine France's most beloved traditions—McDonald's versus the bistro, Hollywood versus cinema, belligerence versus diplomacy, the supermarket versus the village *épicier,* and so on. From this it seems a large and resilient strain of romanticism continues to inform French anti-Americanism.

This romantic anti-Americanism long predates America the superpower. For Charles Baudelaire, America stood for all of the evils of soulless capitalist society. In his writing many of the most durable themes already appeared—America's inhumanity, its childishness, and its voracious appetite for destruction of all that is "authentic." The fear, too, that the United States would "have us all Americanized" is Baudelaire's. For other commentators the threat was primarily religious—Protestant "Anglo-Saxon" America reverting to type—making a religion of work and conformity. Still others, notably Edouard Drumont and his cohort, saw the United States as symbolic of the chaotic freedom brought about by the leveling of class and order—identifying Jews as the sorcerer's apprentice of American capitalism. Although Drumont's specific link between America and Jews was later forgotten, others made use of it in different forms—from extreme right collaborationists in the 1940s to extreme left "anti-globalists" and "anti-Zionists" today. Indeed, anti-Semitism is a present, and frequently ignored, subtext of much anti-American writing.

The interwar era added nuance to the story, as France's "debt" to the United States was translated into a much more tangible debt—and loan repayment became a contentious issue. France had a number of pro-American reformers (most famously André Tardieu), but the era is better remembered by anti-American screeds such as Jean-Louis Chastanet's *L'Oncle Shylock ou l'impérialisme américain à la conquête du monde*/Uncle Shylock or American Imperialism Conquering the World and Lucien Romier's *Qui sera le maître, Europe ou Amérique?*/Who Will Be Master, Europe or America? (1928). Most famous of all was Georges Duhamel's runaway best-seller *Scènes de la vie future*/America the Menace (1930), an unrelenting and very influential attack that spares no insult. Despite the book's absurd excesses, it remains an enlightening glimpse into "America" as French dystopia.

After the crash of the stock exchange in 1929, anti-Americanism became a virtual school of French thought—one with an enormous elite following. This ideological approach defined itself against America—often equating the United States with the Soviet Union (both failures of "mass" society) and, later, Nazi Germany. Because of the protean nature of anti-Americanism, its appeal, while coinciding with the rise of the extreme right, touched a wide variety of French thinkers—everyone from Robert Brasillach to Georges Bataille. Some of the most prominent include the *jeune droite* and "nonconformist" generation—spiritu-

ally minded ex-followers of the monarchist Charles Maurras made homeless by the confusing events of the 1930s. They included Emmanuel Mounier and his journal *Esprit* followers, Georges Bernanos, Denis de Rougemont, and many others.

A book, *The American Cancer*, written by two *jeune droite* militants, Robert Aron and Arnaud Dandieu, summed up the alarm with which this generation viewed the threat from across the Atlantic. The collapse of the American economy was interpreted as a moral judgment on the corruption of American liberalism, capitalism, and civilization in general. The American cancer, Aron and Dandieu argued, was, for all its political content, ultimately a "spiritual epidemic." It has been noted that, for many of the hardy anti-Americans, Nazi Germany seemed relatively benign in comparison. A surprising number of these writers maintained their anti-American mood throughout World War II, some in the service of Vichy or collaboration, and gleefully joined in the America bashing of the *marxisant* postwar. Thus, in a very practical way, anti-Americanism showed how extremes meet.

In the postwar period, anti-Americanism has had two popular faces—Gaullist and Marxist. Although both are heir to the earlier traditions, the cultural nationalism of Charles de Gaulle and his descendants revives the chauvinistic anti-Americanism of an earlier generation. The anti-American posturing of Jean-Paul Sartre may have greater appeal, but it was finally thinner and less committed to a hostile rejection of American civilization. Aspects of the anti-American cultural critique appear in the statements of Sartre as well, but the political anti-Americanism of the cold war carried less of this baggage. Marxists had to be careful when criticizing America for its mass society, lowbrow culture, or universal, if dull, prosperity.

The very public Franco-American split preceding the U.S. invasion of Iraq in 2003 gave this old argument new life. Policy differences aside, the revival of visceral anti-Americanism in France is curious unless we take into account the deep cultural roots of this hostility. The U.S. manner of proceeding with war seemed to confirm old essentialist notions about the deeply flawed American character. Malleable and resilient as ever, the complex language of anti-Americanism now unites Gaullist politicians and Green Party activists.

Seth Armus

See also: American Revolution; Baudelaire, Charles-Pierre; Bernanos, Georges; Cuisine; Duhamel, Georges; French Revolution; Gaulle, General Charles de; Liberalism; Sartre, Jean-Paul; Theory; World War I; World War II.

References

Armus, Seth. "The Eternal Enemy: Emmanuel Mounier's *Esprit* and French anti-Americanism." *French Historical Studies* 24, no. 2 (spring 2001).

Colombani, Jean-Marie, and Walter Wells. *Dangerous De-Liaisons: What's Really behind the War between France and the U.S.* Melville House, 2004.

Kuisel, Richard. *Seducing the French: The Dilemma of Americanization.* Berkeley: University of California Press, 1993.

Lacorne, Denis, et al. *The Rise and Fall of Anti-Americanism: Changing French Perceptions of America from the Revolution to the Present Day.* New York: Palgrave Macmillan, 1990.

Mathy, Jean-Philippe. *Extrême Occident: French Intellectuals and America.* Chicago: University of Chicago Press, 1993.

Portes, Jacques. *Fascination and Misgivings: The United States in French Opinion, 1870–1914.* Cambridge: Cambridge University Press, 2000.

Strauss, David. *Menace in the West: The Rise of French Anti-Americanism in Modern Times.* Westport, CT: Greenwood Press, 1978.

ANTISLAVERY MOVEMENTS

Slavery, as discussed here, refers to a profitable trade that lasted over 400 years, involving millions of Africans transported against their will as commodities across the Atlantic.

This "respectable trade," which in many cases left those citizens involved in the trading process (both on the African and European side) vastly enriched, was not accepted by all. Indeed, opposition was expressed on both sides of the Atlantic, where people articulated in numerous ways their rejection of this dehumanization and forced migration.

The first kind of opposition came from the slaves themselves, who rejected this practice through various forms of resistance. Slave rebellions took place on land in Africa, on the slave ships, and in the New World. Some were individual actions, such as jumping overboard or starving to death, in which the captured preferred to take their own lives rather than be subjected to slavery. Suicides continued to be a common practice among the slaves in the New World. There, they also developed new strategies to fight against their condition. Such strategies involved working slowly or breaking tools and equipment, thus playing into the stereotypical view—quickly adopted by colonists—that black people were lazy and clumsy.

Some rebellions were group actions strategically organized. One of the most famous onboard rebellions was that on the *Snow Ann* on April 14, 1750, in which the captured Africans successfully managed to gain control of the ship, steering it back to Cape Lopez, where they regained their freedom, leaving onshore a handful of surviving crew members. However, such onboard rebellions were rare and usually occurred only when land was within sight.

Organized group rebellions were more common once in the New World, particularly among the maroon community. Maroons (from the Spanish word *cimarrones,* used to describe fugitive slaves) were runaway slaves organized in communities and present throughout the Caribbean and South America. The first significant maroon rebellion was led by Jean Leblanc (from Angola) and Pèdre (from Cabo Verde) and took place in 1656 in Guadeloupe. The fighting went on for fifteen days but ended in the massacre of the rebels. There were two important wars by maroons in Jamaica (1725–1740 and 1795–1796). Following the first war, a treaty was signed, and the maroons were granted some lands in Jamaica; ironically, to enjoy these newly acquired privileges, they were also expected to become slave catchers. Maroon communities existed in most places where slavery was practiced. Their most common practice was to set fire to plantations or colonial habitations, poison slave owners, and encourage other slaves to join them. However, the most successful revolt against slavery is without a doubt that led by Daniel Boukman in 1791 and then Toussaint L'Ouverture against the French in Saint Domingue.

The suppression of slavery and the destruction of French colonial society were supported by antislavery ideas in Europe, influenced by both the American Revolution (1776–1783) and the French Revolution (1789). These factors led to a vote to abolish slavery in the French Antilles on February 4, 1794. However, the decree was discarded only eight years later, on May 20, 1802, by Napoléon I. Napoléon sent his troops, led by Captain Lacrosse and seconded by the Guadeloupean Magloire Pelage, to reinstate slavery on Guadeloupe. The troops met resistance from an army led by black officers such as Joseph Ignace and Louis Deldres, who fought to the death rather than return to enslavement. Slavery was reestablished in Guadeloupe on July 17, 1802. A parallel movement took place in Haiti during that period. Toussaint's army, subsequently led by Dessalines, triumphed against the French army and forced the abolition of slavery in 1804, making Haiti the first black free nation in the Caribbean.

One of the oldest images of the antislavery movement in Europe dates back to the seventeenth century when two priests, the Frenchman Epiphane de Moirans and the Spaniard Francisco Jose de Jaca, were judged in 1681 by the Spanish Ecclesiastic Tribunal for condemning slavery and promising damnation to slave masters if they did not free their slaves. Despite the acceptance of slavery by this Spanish tribunal, religion played an important role in the fight against slavery; indeed, the antislavery movement in Europe was mostly influenced by nonconformist believers, such as the Quakers in the United States, who were the first to attack slavery and refused to possess slaves.

In Britain, Thomas Clarkson and William Wilberforce founded the first antislavery organization in Europe, the Society for the Abolition of the Slave Trade, in 1787. The group was supported by the prime minister at the time—William Pitt. It organized a number of petitions against the slave trade, and people at all levels of society happily attached their names to these petitions. Abolitionists produced literature with statistical data and drawings to inform the public of the conditions under which the slave trade was taking place. Stories were recorded from escaped or freed slaves. One of the most famous stories is the autobiography written by Equiano in 1789: *The Interesting Narrative of the Life of Olaudah Equiano or Gustavo Vassa the African.*

In France a similar movement, the Société des Amis des Noirs, founded in 1788 by the priest Baptiste-Henri Grégoire and Jacques Pierre Brissot, advocated the abolition of the slave trade. In France those associated with the fight against slavery included philosophers of the Enlightenment, who were influenced by the Quaker belief that the light of God's truth is at work in every individual, regardless of sex or ethnicity. Although these philosophers condemned the slave trade, many of them did not hold the same view of slavery. However, they were responsible for bringing the debate to the wider public in their work, an example of which can be found in Voltaire's *Candide* (chap. 19, 1759).

Until the first decade of the nineteenth century, most of these organizations advocated the abolition of the slave trade rather than the end of slavery. Although Denmark was the first European country to abolish the slave trade in 1802, the British tend to be noted as those at the forefront of the anti–slave trade movement. Indeed in 1807 Wilberforce had managed to obtain legislation against the transportation of slaves to Britain, and by 1808 it was forbidden to transport slaves from Africa to the United States. However the campaigning of the Society for the Abolition of the Slave Trade did not end there. The slave trade became illegal in France in 1817, following the Congress of Vienna, where participants were asked to sign an agreement against the slave trade. France endorsed the decision in the Paris Treaty on November 20, 1815. In 1831, the British Royal Navy was granted the right to stop and search boats suspected of breaking the law; the illegal traders were fined £100 per slave. However, the triangular trade continued in France until 1847, the date when the last slave ship left Le Havre. In England, new movements arose for the abolition of slavery by 1820, the year the Anti-Slavery Society was founded. The slave revolt in Jamaica in 1831–1832 led to the abolition of slavery by the British in 1833. In France the abolitionist movement led by Alphonse de Lamartine, Victor Hugo, Alexandre Gatine, François Auguste Perrinon, and Victor Schoelcher, to name a few, ended with the abolition of slavery in French colonies in 1848. Although in France the abolition of slavery is often associated with the name of Victor Schoelcher, it is fair to say that the industrial revolution, the development of sugar beet farming, and the various slave rebellions are some of the key factors that contributed to making the institution of slavery uneconomical.

Marie-Annick Gournet

See also: American Revolution; French Revolution; Guadeloupe; Le Havre; Santo Domingo; Schoelcher, Victor; Slavery; Toussaint L'Ouverture, François; Voltaire, François.

References

Dorigny, Marcel, and Bernard Gainot, eds. *Les Abolitions de l'esclavage.* Paris: Edition Unesco, 1995.

Klein, Herbert. *The Atlantic Slave Trade.* Cambridge: Cambridge University Press, 1999.

Walvin, James, and David Eltis, eds. *The Abolition of the Atlantic Slave Trade: Origin and Effects in Europe, Africa, and the Americas.* Madison: University of Wisconsin Press, 1981.

AQUIN, HUBERT
(1929–1977)

French Canadian novelist, filmmaker, political writer, activist, publisher, and earlier a journalist and producer for both radio and television, Hubert Aquin played an important role in the cultural upheavals of the 1960s and 1970s in Quebec and is considered to be one of the major literary figures of the period. Aquin is remembered for his innovative novels, inspired by James Joyce, Vladimir Nabokov, and the French "new novelists," among others. He was also a participant in the early debates on Quebec nationalism and became known as one of the first proponents of the separatist option.

Born in a modest middle-class setting, Aquin received a classical education from the Jesuits at the prestigious Collège Sainte-Marie in Montreal. He later attended the University of Montreal and was awarded scholarships for study in France. Aquin lived in Paris from 1951 to 1954, first as a postgraduate student and then as a journalist, and returned frequently in the 1950s and 1960s, while working for Radio-Canada and the National Film Board of Canada (NFB). In terms of his fiction, his links with Switzerland are even more significant: the plot of Aquin's first major novel, *Prochain Episode/Next Episode* (1965), is set against the backdrop of Lausanne and Lake Geneva. Aquin lived in Switzerland for a few months and unsuccessfully applied for permanent residency there in 1966. He established contacts with a number of French and Swiss writers; he notably collaborated with French critic Roland Barthes on an NFB film project.

Aquin joined the Rassemblement pour l'Indépendance Nationale (RIN), a left-wing separatist organization, in 1960. He developed his views on the issue of nationalism in a 1962 essay, "The Cultural Fatigue of French Canada," written in response to an article by Pierre Elliott Trudeau, the journalist and future Canadian prime minister. When the Front de Libération du Québec (FLQ), a group of political radicals, started a terror campaign in 1963 in favor of separation, Aquin himself evolved toward a revolutionary position. In 1964, he dramatically announced his intention to join the underground; however, it is unclear whether he had any links with a terrorist cell. Aquin was promptly arrested on minor criminal charges, which were eventually dismissed on psychiatric grounds. In his later years, Aquin shifted his interests toward literature.

Prochain Episode is largely autobiographical: Aquin's experience in the separatist movement and his subsequent arrest are transposed into a complex story of murder and international espionage. Despite its unconventional focus on narrative technique, the book became an instant success in Quebec and established Aquin's reputation as a novelist. *Prochain Episode* was eventually published in France in 1966; however, Aquin never received the same level of attention in France as he did in Quebec. Aquin went on to write three additional novels: *Trou de mémoire/Memory Gap* (1968), *L'Antiphonaire/The Antiphonary* (1969), and *Neige noire/Black Snow* (1974).

Aquin battled with depression, suicidal thoughts, and addiction to various drugs for most of his life; in fact, such themes were already present in some of his earliest literary writings. He eventually committed suicide in 1977, after months of careful preparation.

Jean-Christian Pleau

See also: Barthes, Roland; Jesuits; Quebec; Trudeau, Pierre Elliott.

References

Jameson, Fredric. "Euphorias of Substitution: Hubert Aquin and the Political Novel in Quebec." *Yale French Studies* 65 (1983): 214–223.

Sheppard, Gordon. *Ha! A Self-Murder Mystery Presented as a Docudrama.* Montreal: McGill-Queen's University Press, 2003.

ARCAND, DENYS (1941–)

Québécois film director and scriptwriter.

Born in 1941 in Deschambeault, Quebec, Arcand's first cinematic efforts were a collaborative student film, *Seul ou avec d'autres/Alone or with Others* (1962), and then three short documentaries for the National Film Board of Canada (NFB), which delved into the history of Quebec and the exploration of the North American continent: *Champlain* (1964), *Les Montréalistes/The Montrealists* (1965), and *La Route de l'ouest/The Road West* (1965). The second film plays on the contrast between the religious origin of the foundation of Montreal and its later commercial and military role, emphasized by a sequence featuring a modern-day fashion shoot in the Jeanne Mance museum. Arcand's challenge to NFB orthodoxies and the technocratizing confidence of the Quiet Revolution was expressed in the controversy around his 1970 feature-length documentary *On est au coton,* a scathing judgment of the textile industry whose screening was banned for seven years. Aspects of that film were reworked into his 1975 fictional feature, *Gina.*

Critical social commentary aided by the contrastive invocation of history characterized much of Arcand's subsequent documentary and fictional output after 1970. The 1981 documentary *Le Confort et l'indifférence/Comfort and Indifference,* on the previous year's referendum campaign for sovereignty in Quebec, uses the figure of Niccolò Machiavelli to analyze the way in which Pierre Trudeau outmaneuvered the nationalist camp and how, as the title indicates, the comforts of consumer society—and fear of their loss—had finally vanquished the dreams of a collective social and national project. These arguments are developed in fictional form in *Le Déclin de l'empire américain* (*The Decline of the American Empire,* 1986), a portrayal of a group of well-off academics spending a weekend in the country who gossip about sex and their own privileged gratifications. The title ironically and ambiguously points to the thesis of one member of the group that the prioritizing of individual rather than collective happiness leads to the decline of empires, as happened in Rome.

Although his 1970s films had known some success, *Le Déclin* was Arcand's great breakthrough on the international market, achieving far and away the biggest box-office success in France until then for any Quebec film. The follow-up, *Jésus de Montréal* (*Jesus of Montreal,* 1989), picked up the Jury Prize at Cannes and seemed to establish him as the embodiment of financially viable and indeed profitable auteur cinema. The film reworked the Christian myth via a group of contemporary actors asked to conceive and perform a new version of the passion play taking place in the park overlooking the city. Once again, Arcand combined very local preoccupations—the aftermath of the Quiet Revolution, the dramatic secularization of Quebec society since the 1960s—with issues of global relevance. In the 1990s, this judicious combination seemed to have been lost: *Love and Human Remains* (1993), based on an English Canadian play, and *Stardom* (2000), on the international fashion industry, focus too much on the global, whereas his film of that decade in French, *Joyeux Calvaire/Poverty and Other Delights* (1996), about two Montreal down-and-outs, dwells on the very local. However, Arcand made a triumphant return in 2003 with *Les Invasions barbares* (*The Barbarian Invasions*), which revisits the characters of *Le Déclin* eighteen years later, combining political insights about 9/11, globalized capitalism, and the Quebec health service with an emotional narrative of terminal illness and a father-son relationship. It won prizes at Cannes for best script and actress (Marie-Josée Croze) and the Oscar for best foreign-language film.

Bill Marshall

See also: Cinema, 1945 to the Present; Mance, Jeanne; Montreal; 9/11: Cultural Perspectives; 9/11: Political Perspectives; Quebec; Quiet Revolution; Trudeau, Pierre Elliott.

References

Coulombe, Michel. *Denys Arcand: La Vraie nature du cinéaste.* Montreal: Boréal, 1993.

Loiselle, André, and Brian McIlroy, eds. *Auteur/Provocateur: The Films of Denys Arcand.* Trowbridge: Flicks Books, 1995.

Marshall, Bill. *Quebec National Cinema.* Montreal: McGill-Queen's University Press, 2001.

Weinmann, Heinz. *Cinéma de l'imaginaire Québécois: De La Petite Aurore à Jésus de Montréal.* Montreal: l'Hexagone, 1990.

ARCHITECTURE

As far as the built environment is concerned, the exchange of ideas and forms (from city plans to decorative details) between France and the Americas is a topic of daunting magnitude. French architects, planners, and landscape designers have had significant impacts upon Latin American cities. For instance, in Rio de Janeiro, seventeenth-century military engineer Michel de l'Escolle helped create the city's regular street grid; Parisian exiles founded the first school of fine arts in the Americas, in 1816; and Le Corbusier served as consultant for the Ministry of Education, a landmark of South American modernism. In Buenos Aires, garden designers Edouard André, Charles Thays, and Jean-Claude Nicolas Forestier (who also worked in Cuba) and architect Joseph Bouvard shaped the city's open and arterial space from 1860 to 1930; René Sergent, a Parisian society architect, built elegant and palatial town houses, including the present Museum of Decorative Arts and the residence of the U.S. ambassador. The architectural connection between Franch and Latin America is rather sporadic, however, and this chronological account focuses on France's impact on Canada and on its bilateral exchanges with the United States.

French military engineers planned colonial cities (Mobile, 1711; Detroit, 1764; Saint Louis, 1780) with the kind of gridiron street pattern used for the medieval *bastides* (fortified towns). In addition to those in the province of Quebec, buildings by French settlers still exist, albeit much restored, in Louisiana and in Mississippi valley outposts (Sainte Geneviève, Missouri; Cahokia, Kaskaskia, and Fort de Chartres, Illinois). Two legacies were particularly enduring. The first affected the vernacular design of rural houses. Generally originating in Normandy, French influences migrated through Acadia and the West Indies prior to reaching the Gulf coast. Common features were tall-hipped roofs (sometimes flared) with dormers and casement windows, but construction techniques varied according to local availability of materials. Climatic variations affected form too; in particular, Louisiana plantation homes gained a Caribbean-inspired circumferential gallery. The second legacy can be seen in buildings for Catholic orders and charitable and educational institutions, ranging from the delicate Ursuline Convent (1745–1753), the oldest vestige of the French presence in New Orleans, to a series of stern and monumental hospitals and convents in gray stone in Quebec City and Montreal.

Around 1800, Franco-American intellectual kinship and military cooperation, the young republic's need for foreign expertise to build its institutions and memorialize its revolution, and a worldwide politically and economically motivated exodus of Frenchmen explain the popularity of French planning and design in the United States. Shaped during his diplomatic tenure in Paris, Thomas Jefferson's aesthetic francophilia expressed a rejection of British influence and a philosophical belief in the didactic powers of built form. His "academic village" for the University of Virginia (1817–1826) reflects Enlightenment concerns over behavior and disease control. Jefferson also helped launch the enduring love of Parisian *hôtels particuliers* (grand private houses)—their design, appointments, and related lifestyles—among American elites.

Joseph-Jacques Ramée's 1813 plan for Union College in Schenectady, New York, was the earliest model for rural and suburban university campuses, a formula presently adopted in France. Like Pierre Charles L'Enfant's 1792 plan for Washington, it fashioned the existing setting into great swaths of rolling lawns: this clear-cut dialogue between natural and man-made landscapes became a distinctive trait of American urbanism. Other major and extant contributions by French émigrés are Jean-Charles Mangin's delicate New York city hall (in association with John McComb Jr.) and, in Baltimore, Maximilien Godefroy's purist First Unitarian Church and the chapel for Saint Mary's Seminary, the first neo-Gothic structure in the United States.

A new and more durable surge of French influence lasted from the Second Empire to the belle époque. Its impact on built form operated within a fashion rationale: everything French, from furnishing to clothing, carried an aura of sophistication, mixed with the slightly risqué. France was all too happy to sustain its economy with luxury exports, to which women, whose influence on domestic design was on the rise, were particularly attracted. All around the world (and especially in New York City), stone facades, wrought iron balconies, and parquet floors helped the newly rich fulfill their ambitions in their homes and the museums and libraries they patronized.

Reasons for the transfer and adaptation to North America of the so-called Second Empire style are not yet clear. A form of "Mansard roof" marked many residential districts in North America around 1860. In the public sphere, the extension of the layout of the Palais du Louvre to house museum galleries and ministries led to the adoption of its compartmentalized and highly three-dimensional wall surfaces and prominent crested rooflines by banker William Corcoran for his private gallery in Washington; by the municipality of Boston for its city hall; and by Alfred B. Mullett, the supervising architect of the

U.S. Treasury, in a series of post–Civil War federal buildings, examples of which survive in Washington (the Old Executive Building next to the White House) and Saint Louis. In government buildings, the simplified decor and smoothened stonework betray more mechanized construction techniques and the desire to express a "good government" ethic. Montreal's central post office (demolished) and City Hall, as well as the Assemblée Nationale in Quebec City, are also grandiose public buildings influenced by the new Louvre.

By the late 1860s, the Ecole des Beaux-Arts in Paris had acquired an unrivaled reputation. Its competitive curriculum taught superior draftsmanship and authentic historical detailing, as well as how to conceptualize programs quickly and logically, devise interior decoration, and work jointly with painters and sculptors. The Ecole attracted architecture students from Europe and the Americas, and some of its French graduates crossed the Atlantic temporarily or permanently. The professional and artistic dominance of this diaspora became a source of great pride for conservative French critics. By far, the largest foreign contingent came from the United States. Designing for the powerful and wealthy, many of its members set up practice in New York City, where French ideas were filtered and dispatched all the way to Canada. Although England and Scotland held a strong grip on taste and institutions, influential Canadian architects—Montrealers Jean-Omer Marchand, William S. Maxwell, and Ernest Cormier and Toronto's John Lyle—received Parisian training.

The Beaux-Arts era coalesced the neoclassical search for order and the eclectic mind-set of the Second Empire. Town houses (in Montreal's Golden Square Mile and Washington's Embassy Row) and country estates (in Long Island and Newport) emulated *hôtels particuliers* and châteaux. Ecole alumni popularized the formula of the upscale "French flat" and played a key role in philanthropic housing reform. Stimulated by the World's Fairs in Chicago (1893) and Saint Louis (1904), the City Beautiful movement was strongly indebted to French urban design exemplars, especially Baron Haussmann's Paris; it helped produce the seminal McMillan Plan of 1902, which restored and expanded L'Enfant's vision for Washington, which had also influenced Haussmann. One among several globe-trotting Beaux-Arts-trained *urbanistes* (urban planners), Jacques Gréber put the final touch on Philadelphia's Benjamin Franklin Parkway in 1917 and helped restructure downtown Ottawa.

The Ecole taught compositional methods, in plan and elevation, applicable to buildings as stylistically diverse as the neo-romanesque libraries of Henry Hobson Richardson (who studied there during the Second Empire) and the U.S. and Canadian Supreme Courts. French-inspired styles ranged from cerebral Neo-Grec to quaint and suburban "French provincial," from ebullient Beaux-Arts baroque (in the spirit of Paris's Petit Palais) to restrained Louis XVI. Canada's château style originated in the late 1880s in the work of New York architect Bruce Price for the Canadian Pacific Railway, such as Quebec City's Château Frontenac Hotel. A tribute to the country's national origins, it blended influences from Loire valley chateaux and Scottish baronial homes and came to symbolize Canadian officialdom.

Generally larger and more specialized than in Europe, North American architectural offices achieved a modernity essentially based on technological and programmatic advances. Coupled with impeccable craftsmanship and crisp, overscaled detailing, the amalgamation of historicism and pragmatism produced masterworks such as New York's Grand Central Terminal (1907–1913). Louis Sullivan and Frank Lloyd Wright forged a new "organic" identity that influenced Scandinavian, Dutch, and German architects but had little direct impact in France. Between the two world wars, Parisian art deco was one of the sources for jazz and streamlined moderne, as evidenced in the Chrysler Building in Manhattan and the Eaton Restaurant in Montreal. Architecture, and skyscrapers in particular, came to be regarded in Europe as the most original and successful artistic contribution that the United States had made. Additionally, both Americans and Canadians produced awe-inspiring and distinctly North American World War I memorials on French soil, in Chateau-Thierry and near Arras, respectively.

After 1920, influences went in both directions, as the French began promoting the notion that U.S. cost efficiency, productivity, and superior hygiene could complement their presumably innate artistry. This idea was the leitmotif of Gréber's influential book, *L'Architecture aux Etats Unis* ("The Architecture of the United States," 1920). North American architecture inspired both attraction (for its boldness) and repulsion (for its materialism), a love-hate relationship clearly expressed in Paul Morand's *New York* (1930) and Le Corbusier's *Quand Les Cathédrales étaient blanches/When Cathedrals Were White*

(1937). Among a handful of high-rise structures built in the 1930s, the Hôpital Beaujon in Clichy (1931–1935) and the residential towers of the Quartier des Gratte-ciel in Villeurbanne (1932–1934) have clear American antecedents. Another American import was the landscaped highway, and the *Autoroute de l'Ouest* was France's superb response to the Westchester and Bronx River Parkways.

In the three decades following World War II, the United States held the same role of international artistic and architectural "fertilizer" that France had assumed around 1900. The aesthetic of the Bauhaus and Le Corbusier was given a North American twist by the likes of Walter Gropius and Ludwig Mies van der Rohe. The two typologies that had structured the fabric of most North American cities since the late nineteenth century, the tall office building and the middle-class single-family home, started shaping the French urban and suburban landscape. La Défense was begun in 1958: its skyscrapers were originally intended to have all the same height and bulk, but economics and corporate competition ended dictating a more Americanized skyline. The French saw the acquisition of an automobile as a first step toward matching North America's standard of living. Carrefour, which now operates in South America, opened its first *hypermarché* (hypermarket) in the Paris suburbs in 1963. Two years later, the mass builder Levitt launched its first neo-American subdivision near Versailles. Subsequently, the formula of the *nouveau village*—an affordable and comfortable tract house in a parklike setting—was exploited by the California-based developer Kaufman and Broad, which has become a powerhouse in the Paris region.

Since the 1970s, design for high-end corporations, mass retail, and entertainment has become as global as these sectors of the world economy. In the new town of Marne-la-Vallée, Disneyland Paris, whose theme hotels were designed by the likes of Robert Stern and Michael Graves, adjoins the clone of a U.S. megamall and a Frenchified upscale outlet center with a Ralph Lauren store. Bouygues, a major construction and media concern, selected Kevin Roche for its neobaroque headquarters near Versailles, and France's first pay channel, Canal Plus, entrusted Richard Meier, famed for his use of white enamel panels, to build its flagship studio and office structure in Paris. Christian de Portzamparc, France's sole recipient of the Pritzker Prize (the Nobel Prize of architecture) designed the LVMH Tower on New York City's Fifty-Seventh Street, a symbol of France's enduring desire to dominate the market for luxury goods.

Since the Beaux-Arts era, North American museums have been much more user-friendly and have had larger public spaces than their European counterparts. This superiority was certainly one reason French president François Mitterrand gave the commission for the Grand Louvre to Chinese American designer I. M. Pei, on the strength of his prior addition to the National Gallery of Art in Washington, D.C. These exchanges do not entail stylistic uniformization and consensus. In particular, many French architects and critics despise what they consider as the sterile and socially irresponsible gimmicks of North American postmodernism and new urbanism. History tells us, however, that transatlantic cross-fertilization between different design sensibilities has produced architecture at once beautiful and livable.

Isabelle Gournay

See also: Acadia; Argentina; Art Deco; Brazil; Carrefour; Chicago; Detroit; Disneyland Paris; Illinois Country; Jefferson, Thomas; Le Corbusier; L'Enfant, Pierre Charles; Louisiana; Mississippi; Mitterrand, François; Mobile; Montreal; Quebec; Quebec City; Saint Louis; Television; Ursulines; World War I; World War II.

References

Bacon, Mardges. *Ernest Flagg: Beaux-Arts Architect and Urban Reformer.* Cambridge, MA: MIT Press, 1986.

Cohen, Jean-Louis. *Scenes of the World to Come: European Architecture and the American Challenge, 1893–1960.* Montreal: Flammarion, 1995.

Gournay, Isabelle. "France Discovers America, 1917–1939 (French Writings on American Architecture)." Ph.D. dissertation, Yale University, 1989.

Special Jacques Gréber issue. *Urban History Review,* Toronto 29 (March 2001).

ARGENTINA

Franco-Argentine relations date back to the colonial era. Until the late eighteenth century, these relations were predominantly economic and coincided with French interests in the River Plate region. After the 1789 French Revolution, France's cultural influence in the area became increasingly important, and close relations between the two countries continued throughout the twentieth century, with immigrants moving from both sides of the Atlantic. French immigrants arrived in Argentina in the second half of the nineteenth and early twentieth centuries (most of them settled in Buenos Aires, Misiones, and Tucumán); numerous French intellectuals, artists, and literati have traveled to or resided in Buenos Aires since 1800, and countless Argentines visited or lived in Paris over a period of time, either in order to escape dictatorships or simply to relish its cultural affluence.

During the years 1776–1816, Argentina was part of the Viceroyalty of the River Plate under Spanish rule. In the late eighteenth and early nineteenth centuries, the French Revolution aroused great interest in the River Plate region. In 1810, during the French occupation of Spain (1808–1813), a rebellion against the Spanish Crown broke out in Buenos Aires, and six years later the forerunner of modern Argentina, the United Provinces of the River Plate, were formed. The provinces declared independence and in 1829 became known as the Argentine Confederation. Enlightenment ideas (from the French Revolution) and British imperial designs in Latin America overlapped with nineteenth-century romanticism and ideas about modernization to influence Argentine independence. The major task of the men of the Generation of 1837, which consisted of young intellectuals such as Domingo Faustino Sarmiento (1811–1888), Esteban Echeverría (1805–1851), Juan Bautista Alberdi (1810–1884), and Bartolomé Mitre (1821–1906), also known as the Unitarians, was to make Argentina a modern nation; in doing so, they borrowed heavily from France and especially from the romantic ideas of Victor Hugo (1802–1885).

Sarmiento became one of the most influential thinkers of nineteenth-century Latin America. His book *Facundo: Civilization and Barbarism* (1845) is a passionate denunciation of Juan Manuel de Rosas's (1793–1877) dictatorship and a fundamental text on the notion of "Argentineness." In *Facundo,* Sarmiento argues that the Argentines have searched for and found their model of civilization in Europe, especially in the "ideal" France that they have learned to love in books. In 1846, Sarmiento traveled to Paris to support the

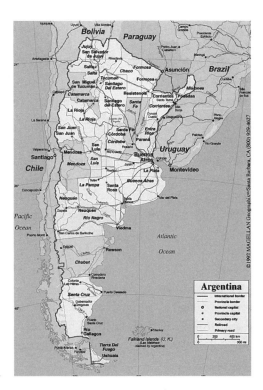

Map of Argentina. (MAPS.com/Corbis)

Franco-British blockade of the harbor of Buenos Aires, which was caused by Rosas's interference in French and British commercial interests in the region. Sarmiento sought foreign intervention, which, he believed, could lead to Rosas's demise. However, Britain and France decided to declare the blockade illegal, and Sarmiento now had to turn to the head of the French opposition, Adolfe Thiers (1797–1877), who embraced his cause in parliamentary speeches, evoking French colonial ambitions in the area. *Facundo* was thus placed in the French political arena in a way that conceptually served French colonial designs, notwithstanding that Sarmiento's opposition of civilization to barbarism never sought to project the "civilized" European colonialism against Latin American "barbarism"; instead, it was meant to target the barbarism of the Argentine Federalists led by Rosas.

By the end of the nineteenth century, France had had a huge cultural impact on Argentina, principally on its literature and architecture. Latin American "modernismo" is a movement inspired by French Parnassianism and symbolism, which emerged toward the end of the nineteenth century. Among the "modernista" poets are Rubén Darío (1867–1916), a Nicaraguan who lived in Chile and Argentina and traveled frequently to Paris, and Leopoldo Lugones (1874–1938), who was considered the national bard of Argentina. One of the most celebrated authors of the time was Paul Groussac (1848–1929), a Frenchman from Toulouse, Haute-Garonne, who moved to Buenos Aires in 1866 and stayed there until his death.

The writers of the "Centenario" (1910 was the centennial of Argentine independence) introduced the notion of the dominant work, with which they strove to give racial, cultural, and linguistic unity to the Argentines. The first book that was canonized was José Hernández's *Martín Fierro* (two volumes, written in 1872 and 1879), which Lugones and the academic scholar Ricardo Rojas (1882–1957) compared to the French epic "Chanson de Roland" of the eleventh century.

In 1926, Ricardo Güiraldes (1886–1927) published his influential novel *Don Segundo Sombra.* Güiraldes came from a family of wealthy landowners and spent part of his childhood in Europe and part in the pampa. In 1910, he went for the first time to Paris, a city that he kept visiting throughout his life (he finally died there), and whose bohemian lifestyle he very much enjoyed. Güiraldes's novel holds the tensions between his Europeanized way of life and his life in the Argentine pampa.

The French avant-garde and modernism were introduced in Argentina in the 1920s by the so-called Florida group, also referred to as the Martín Fierro group, which was identified with the literary magazines *Proa* and *Martín Fierro.* Its members included Jorge Luis Borges, Norah Lange (1906–1972), Leopoldo Marechal (1900–1970), and Oliveiro Girondo (1891–1967).

Among the most influential francophile Argentines is Victoria Ocampo, who was born in Buenos Aires, spent her childhood in Paris, and studied at the Sorbonne. In 1931, Ocampo founded the cultural magazine *Sur,* which featured the writings of influential figures in literature, history, philosophy, and the arts from Latin America, the United States, and Europe. Its contributors included Le Corbusier, Pierre Drieu de la Rochelle (1893–1945), Jacques Lacan, Jean-Paul Sartre, Albert Camus, and Roger Caillois, to mention but a few. Argentine authors included Borges, Silvina Ocampo (1903–1993), Adolfo Bioy Casares (1914–1999), and Julio Cortázar.

Caillois, who fled to Buenos Aires to avoid the Nazis during the German occupation of France (1940–1944) after he met Ocampo in Paris, launched his own journal, *Lettres françaises* (1941), in which the first translations of Borges into a foreign language appeared. Back in Paris, Caillois, as an editor at Gallimard, published Paul Verdevoye's and Nestor Ibarra's translation of Borges's *Fictions* in the series "La Croix du Sud," where he introduced the work of many important Latin American authors. In 1953, Caillois published *Labyrinthes,* a collection he formulated by combining some of Borges's fictions and essays and for which he also wrote a preface. Many translations of Borges into other languages derived from Caillois's publications. It was not until 1962 that these books were translated into English, a fact that confirmed that Borges's international status was initiated by his French translations. Borges, in turn, has had a great influence on twentieth-century French letters, inspiring, among others, philosophers such as Michel Foucault, Jean-François Lyotard, Jacques Derrida, Gilles Deleuze, Félix Guattari, Jean Baudrillard, and Lacan.

Cortázar, Argentina's most famous writer after Borges, was also closely related to France; Cortázar resided in Paris as a political exile for several years, and some of his most celebrated works are set in the French capital, including his 1963 novel *Hopscotch* (chapters one through thirty-six); in 1981, he published his book *Paris: Essence of an Image.* Among Argentina's prominent contemporary writers, Alexandra Pizarnik (1936–1972), Manuel Puig (1932–1990), and Luisa Valenzuela (b. 1938) lived in Paris.

Xul Solar (1887–1963), one of the most imaginative painters and sculptors from Argentina (also writer and inventor of imaginary languages), traveled to and stayed in Paris, Tours, and Marseilles during the first two decades of the twentieth century. In 1924, his work was exhibited in Paris as part of a show of Latin American artists, and his second major exhibition took place a year before he died in the Musée National d'Art Moderne, also in Paris (1962).

If the French capital was crucial for Solar's international recognition, the Argentine capital was a source of inspiration for the French American dadaist/surrealist artist Marcel Duchamp, who lived in the city in the period 1918–1919.

Tango has been a strong link between the Argentine and the French capitals. Born in the slums of Buenos Aires, the dance was made both respectable and fashionable in Paris in the 1920s. The most famous tango salon in Paris has been the Trottoirs de Buenos Aires (Rue des Lombards, Châtelet), whose name was inspired by a tango composed by Cortázar and Edgardo Contón and recorded by Tata Cedrón (1980). The salon, which was created in 1981 by a group of Argentine artists, writers, and musicians residing in France, soon became the place where Argentine exiles hung out. The Trottoirs de Buenos Aires held the concerts of tango legends such as the Sexteto Mayor, the Sexteto Tango, Astor Piazzolla, Osvaldo Pugliese (1905–1995), Los Dinzel, Raúl Funes (b. 1942), and Rubén Juárez (b. 1947). As in the case of Borges's work, France spread tango into other countries, turning it into a universal patrimony.

Buenos Aires, allegedly the "Paris of South America," has turned French architecture into its own patrimony. The city's boulevards; its lavish mansions and spacious parks; and the neighborhoods of El Centro, La Recoleta, and Belgrano evoke the French capital. The squares of Palermo and Belgrano replicate those in Paris; the Vatican Embassy on Avenida Alvear mirrors the Jacquemart-André Museum in the French city; and the Palacio San Martín in Calle Arenales is a construction inspired by French architecture of the eighteenth century. Similarly, the Galerías Pacífico are copies of the Bon Marché galleries in Paris, and the Centro Naval on Córdoba Avenue and the Museo Nacional de Arte Decorativo y Arte Oriental constitute spectacular examples of French architecture. The list is endless and so are the Franco-Argentine cultural exchanges from both sides of the Atlantic.

Eleni Kefala

See also: Architecture; Baudrillard, Jean; Borges, Jorge Luis; Caillois, Roger; Camus, Albert; Dance; Darío, Rubén; Deleuze, Gilles; Duchamp, Marcel; Foucault, Michel; French Revolution; Guattari, Félix; Lacan, Jacques; Le Corbusier; Literary Relations; Lyotard, Jean-François; Ocampo, Victoria; Piazzolla, Astor; Sartre, Jean-Paul; Surrealism.

References

Bethell, Leslie, ed. *Argentina since Independence.* Cambridge: Cambridge University Press, 1993.
Ferrer, Horacio. *The Golden Age of Tango.* Buenos Aires: Manrique Zago Ediciones, 1998.
Goodrich, Diana Sorensen. *Facundo and the Construction of Argentine Culture.* Austin: University of Texas Press, 1996.
Shumway, Nicolas. *The Invention of Argentina.* Oxford: University of California Press, 1991.

ARON, RAYMOND-CLAUDE-FERDINAND (1905–1983)

Sociologist, philosopher, and journalist, Raymond Aron was one of the most distinguished intellectuals of his generation. Educated at the elite Ecole normale supérieure in Paris, he spent three years in Germany (1930–1933), where he absorbed the ideas of Edmund Husserl and Max Weber, which shaped his doctoral thesis on the philosophy of history (1938). He spent the war years in London, as editor of the Gaullist review *La France libre.* In postwar Paris, he helped to found Jean-Paul Sartre's monthly review *Les Temps modernes* and

worked with Camus's newspaper, *Combat,* before joining the conservative daily, *Le Figaro,* for which he wrote regular editorials from 1947 to 1977. In parallel, he developed his career as a sociologist, gaining academic honors with a chair at the Sorbonne (1955) and later at the prestigious Collège de France. He gained international recognition with his polemical attacks on Marxism, especially in *L'Opium des intellectuels* (*The Opium of the Intellectuals,* 1955), and with his popular presentations of sociology, especially *Main Currents in Sociological Thought* (1960), which were widely translated. For much of his career, he was publicly at odds with the dominant left-wing radicalism that emerged in France after World War II under the influence of his friend and contemporary Jean-Paul Sartre. He was an adviser to Charles de Gaulle during his period of opposition under the Fourth Republic and at the height of the cold war was active in anti-Communist movements. He took sides energetically with the Western bloc, attacking Soviet totalitarianism and the failures of the planned economy while defending the social benefits of Western democratic institutions and industrial organization. Stung by de Gaulle's criticisms of Israel in the 1967 war, he began to engage publicly with issues of his Jewish identity, which he had mainly regarded as a private loyalty. He criticized the revolutionary illusions of the student insurgents in May 1968, but, distancing himself from Gaullist nationalism, he embraced a more cosmopolitan vision of liberal democracy. He associated himself with the modernizing conservatism of Valéry Giscard d'Estaing and supported a rapprochement with U.S. political and economic models. Adopting the stance of a "committed observer," he proposed a rationalist approach to political and social issues, which was informed by the French liberal tradition in the spirit of Tocqueville, but also drew on British and U.S. social and economic theory, which he was able to read in English. After a lifetime spent in the corridors of power but outside the mainstream of French intellectual consensus, Aron was belatedly reconciled with Sartre and acclaimed by the intellectual elite on the publication of his *Memoirs* (1983) shortly before his death.

Michael Kelly

See also: Camus, Albert; Gaulle, General Charles de; Giscard d'Estaing, Valéry; Sartre, Jean-Paul; Theory; Tocqueville, Alexis de; World War II.

References

Colquhoun, Robert. *Raymond Aron.* 2 vols. London: Sage, 1986.

Mahoney, Daniel J. *The Liberal Political Science of Raymond Aron.* Lanham, Md: Rowman and Littlefield, 1992.

ART DECO

Name given to a decorative and architectural style that spread into every aspect of modern life between 1919 and 1939.

Also known as "the moderne" in tribute to its French origins, art deco's geometrical designs, accompanied by playful ornamentation such as sunbursts and stylized fountains, contrasted both with the organic, naturalistic curves of art nouveau and the seriousness of the modernist style associated with Le Corbusier. The eclecticism of art deco meant that it happily raided elements from ancient Egypt, pre-Columbian America, Africa, the Far East, and the artistic avant-garde such as cubism, but in manners appropriate to the new age of speed, commerce, and consumerism and its new materials such as bakelite. This break with the past—despite the intriguing subsistence of the old alongside the new—was made all the more real by the terrible world war that had just ended.

The style's main launchpad was the Exposition internationale des arts décoratifs et industriels, held in Paris in 1925, whose aim was to restore France's competitive edge in the production of luxury goods. Cartier jewelry, liners such as the *Normandie,* but also textiles, graphic design, and typography became exemplars of art deco. Thanks to traveling exhibits, émigrés, and the interest shown by department stores, the style was disseminated throughout the world, including the United States, which did not take part in the 1925 exhibition but whose Department of Commerce report had pointed out the advantages for any nation capable of harnessing the style in "terms appropriate to modern living conditions and modern taste" (quoted in Benton 2003). The American architect and designer Eugene Schoen (1880–1957) is an example of this successful transplantation of art deco style to America.

By the 1930s and the Depression, art deco in the United States was adapting to mass production rather than the luxury end of the market and also was developing specifically American characteristics, such as its emphasis on streamlining and the proliferation of skyscrapers in New York and Chicago. Icons of American life, such as the Chrysler and Empire State Buildings, the Rockefeller Center, Miami Beach, and even the Wurlitzer jukebox, all bear the marks of art deco. In addition, Hollywood did much to disseminate the style in the art direction and set design for films such as Cecil B. de Mille's *Cleopatra* (1934), *Grand Hotel* (1932), or the Astaire-Rogers musicals.

Elsewhere in the Americas, in Canada art deco flourished, particularly in Montreal, where an architect such as Ernest Cormier (1885–1980), who had trained in Paris, created the central building of the Université de Montréal, as well as the Canadian Supreme Court edifice in Ottawa. In Latin America, art deco's combination of modernity and the (indigenous, national) past meant it could be put to use, as in the dictator Getúlio Vargas's Brazil, to mask a politics of reaction. The most famous examples of the style in Rio de Janeiro are the Central Station and the statue of Christ the Redeemer (conceived and in part sculpted by the Polish-French artist Paul Landowski).

The privations and common purpose of World War II and its aftermath saw the triumph of modernism. The challenge to it after the upheavals of the 1960s has, however, seen a rediscovery and reevaluation of the art deco style.

Bill Marshall

See also: Architecture; Art Nouveau; Erté; Loewy, Raymond; World War I; World War II.
References
Benton, Charlotte, et al., eds. *Art Deco, 1919–1939*. London: V&A Publications, 2003.
Cohen-Rose, Sandra. *Northern Deco: Art Deco Architecture in Montreal*. Montreal: Corona Publishers, 1996.

ART NOUVEAU

Art nouveau describes a movement in the visual arts extending from Europe to North America and dominant between 1890 and 1910, characterized by organic, naturalistic forms open to a wide range of interpretations, from complex fluid arabesques to simple geometric explorations and progressions.

During this extraordinarily fertile and creative period, few areas of architecture and the decorative arts remained untouched. Indeed, the language of Art nouveau proved remarkably versatile, with architects and designers exploring its potential through the design of objects as diverse as apartment blocks and lamps, book covers and posters, ironmongery and furniture.

The movement marked the end of one century and heralded the new, the label "art nouveau" coming into use at the time. At the height of the belle époque, a period noted for economic prosperity and the prominence of the middle classes, art nouveau built a bridge between the past and tradition on the one hand and growing industrialization, production, and imminent change on the other. With the rise of the new industrial classes, a new breed of patron emerged, embracing the new style and supporting its development and dissemination. The turbulence of the period and the tensions between rich and poor, conservative and radical, can be traced in the diversity of artifacts produced, from the bespoke to the mass produced.

Although seen as evoking the spirit of the age and embraced by many as a form of personal and national expression, art nouveau also provoked extraordinary criticism. It was particularly pilloried as an excess of ornament and decoration without functional substance.

Early centers of design and production flourished in Nancy, France, Brussels, and Munich, but within many countries in Europe similar movements of designers and craftsmen were evolving, often exploring national and regional identity, distinct in name and output yet recognizable as part of the wider art nouveau family: in Britain, the arts and crafts movement led by William Morris and the merchandise of the Liberty department store in London; in Austria, the secessionists of the Wiener Werkstätte; in Spain, the modernista; in Germany, the *jugendstil* movement. Basing their work around notions of regional identity, Catalan architects such as Antonio Gaudí i Cornet (1852–1926), Josef Maria Jujol (1879–1949), and Luis Domenech e Montaner (1850–1923) sought to use the narrative opportunities of art nouveau as a catalyst for artistic and political discussion and expression while reinterpreting Catalan themes and history as sources in their designs.

The 1900 Paris Exposition became the showplace for the art nouveau style and for the prosperity and creative strength of France itself, evident through the architecture of key pavilions and many of the goods and works of art displayed. The Metro stations and street furniture of Hector-Germain Guimard (1867–1942), commissioned to deal with the anticipated congestion the exhibition would create, have become the most lasting evidence of the exposition. Guimard's innovative solution involved a modular range of wrought iron and glass components that could be combined to create many alternatives. His synthesis of industrial production techniques and lightweight forms, sinuous and curvaceous, produced an effective and aesthetically challenging solution. Elsewhere, shared preoccupations and mutual interests led to creative alliances and collaborations, and the growing number of design journals and new reproduction techniques led to the wider dissemination of the style across and beyond Europe.

Art nouveau developed a parallel yet independent strand in the United States,

Poster announcing the Cincinnati Fall Festival show. Here a woman is shown wearing art nouveau jewelry. (Library of Congress)

conscious of the European work but not restricted by it, innovative and autonomous. The glassmaker Louis Comfort Tiffany (1848–1933) became known for the technical virtuosity and fluidity of his glassware including Favrile ware, whose surface sheen and iridescence amplified its curving lines. His collaboration with Greene and Greene (architects) produced some of the few notable art nouveau homes on the Pacific coast. Chicago architect Louis H. Sullivan (1856–1924) experimented with both the functional and decorative opportunities the skyscraper presented. The Carson, Pirie, Scott, and Co. store, completed in 1904, displayed a complexity of ornament seldom matched in design or realization.

The onset of World War I marked the end of art nouveau. The radical changes that ensued as a result of that war, in particular the desire to look to the future, meant that it was not until the 1960s that a resurgence in interest in art nouveau and a reappraisal of its effect and legacy led to a renewed appetite for the style.

Sally Stewart

See also: Architecture; Exposition universelle
   (1900); Painting; World War I.

References

Duncan, Alastair. *Art Nouveau.* London:
   Thames and Hudson, 1994.
Escritt, Stephen. *Art Nouveau.* London:
   Phaidon, 2000.
Greenhalgh, Paul, ed. *Art Nouveau
   1890–1914.* London: V&A Publications,
   2000.

ARTAUD, ANTONIN (1896–1948)

French actor, dramatist, essayist, poet, and scriptwriter.

Artaud was an important rallying figure for 1960s and 1970s avant-garde theater on both sides of the Atlantic, as well as for the influential group of young French intellectuals of that period who were loosely gathered around the journal *Tel Quel* (e.g., Jacques Derrida, Julie Kristeva). Born in Marseilles on September 4, 1896, he arrived in Paris in the early 1920s, where he began working in theater and initiated a correspondence with *NRF*'s editor, Jacques Rivière. The *Correspondance*—published in 1924—played a pivotal role in Artaud's intellectual development: it marked his abandonment of a poetry indebted to symbolism in favor of a writing focused on minute descriptions of what he referred to as his "sickness," his experience of his own thoughts as void. Through an obsessive reflection on his condition, Artaud would, until his death, give in with increasing vehemence to the idea of speech as alien to the uttering subject.

In the early 1930s, Artaud wrote the texts making up *Le Théâtre et son double* (*The Theater and Its Double,* 1938). In them he rejected classical theater because theater—just as much as speech—inevitably draws from a preexisting and organized cultural field and is thus unable to offer unmediated relations to things.

Like his efforts to lay the groundwork for an impossible theater of efficient signs ("the theater of cruelty"), his earlier adherence to surrealism, or his attempts with cinema in the late 1920s, Artaud's trip to Mexico in 1936 was a way for him to address his "powerlessness." He left Paris in January, reportedly to study a burgeoning social movement aiming at a return to a preconquest civilization. He returned to Paris eleven months later. In the various lectures he delivered during his sojourn and in the articles he published in local newspapers, he spoke and wrote about Europe's petrified culture, devoid of spiritual necessity: for him, culture had become a mere varnish instead of providing the way to some originary truth. He also expressed his concern about the European contamination of Mexican youth, perceptible in their predominant understanding of revolution in Marxist terms, as well as in the domain of the arts. Although he dismissed most Mexican art of the period, he wrote at length on Maria Izquierdo, seeing in her paintings an authentically Indian inspiration and a struggle with the influences of European art. In Mexico, Artaud sought the keys to a profound cultural revolution that would provide a new foundation for human beings. However, in the middle of August 1936, disappointed by what he had found in Mexico City, Artaud ventured into the Sierra Tarahumara in search of a lost tradition that would allow human beings to recover an original, organic way of communicating with the world.

In 1946, Artaud was released from the last of the mental institutions where he had been confined for the previous nine years. Until his death in Ivry-sur-Seine on March 4, 1948, he violently and incessantly returned to his incapacity to manifest, not an utterance, but something that would amount to a true creation of life.

Vittorio Trionfi

See also: Avant-Gardes; Derrida, Jacques; Mexico; *Tel Quel;* Theater; Theory.
References
Artaud, Antonin. *Selected Writings.* Ed. Susan Sontag. Berkeley: University of California Press, 1988.
Cardoza y Aragón, Luis. "Pourquoi le Mexique?" *Europe* (1984): 667-668.
Derrida, Jacques. "La Parole Soufflée." *Writing and Difference.* Trans. Alan Bass. Chicago: University of Chicago Press, 1978.

ATGET, EUGÈNE (1857–1927)

Photographer (born in Libourne in 1857 and active 1898–1927) of Paris' streets, parks, and countryside.

A former actor of indifferent success, Atget turned to a small career as an artisan-photographer, taking stock images of Paris and its environs for local historians and artists. Among the clients for his "documents pour artistes" were the Musée Carnavalet, the painter Georges Braque, and the surrealist painter and photographer Man Ray. Atget's subject matter was rather unremarkable and by no means original. His images of Paris streets followed a tradi-

tion of photographic survey that had included the work of Charles Marville (active in the 1850s) while Atget's extensive catalogue of "petits métiers"—portraits of other artisans and street sellers—continued a practice of illustrating vernacular Paris street culture that had been established by Edmé Bouchardon in the eighteenth century and Carle Vernet in the 1820s. However, Atget's major significance was in the art world (particularly centered in New York), largely due to a reappraisal of his work in the 1930s and after.

It was Man Ray who arranged for several photographs to be published in the review *La Révolution surréaliste* during 1925 and 1926, bringing the work to a new *aesthetically* interested audience, although they were uncredited, possibly at Atget's request. At this time he attracted the interest of Man Ray's assistant, Berenice Abbott, an American émigré photographer staying in Paris. When Atget died in Paris in 1927, Abbott arranged to take a substantial amount of his work (approximately 5,000 negatives) to the United States to form the Abbott/Levy Collection (with Julien Levy). The international recognition of Atget's work is largely due to the efforts of Abbott who, over the next thirty years, vigorously promoted Atget's work at the same time as her own photography echoed its rich form and plebeian subject matter. Atget's work immediately attracted interest from the photographers Walker Evans and Ansel Adams and the writers Walter Benjamin and Pierre MacOrlan, and it was through the writing of all of them that Atget came to the attention of the broader artistic community. The Museum of Modern Art in New York eventually purchased the Abbott/Levy collection in 1968 and by the late 1980s had staged four full-scale solo

Eugène Atget photograph of street musicians. (Library of Congress)

exhibitions, with accompanying monographs, under the head stewardship of John Szarkowski. These exhibitions firmly consolidated a place for Atget in the photography canon that reflected the influence his work had already had on American photographic practice, particularly the genre of documentary and reportage.

The influences of Atget's pictorial style—lustrous and velvety black-and-white images of vernacular spaces—can be seen in the work of Abbott, Evans, and Adams and also in the work of Robert Frank, Lee Friedlander, and Edward Weston. All have, at one time or another, mimicked both Atget's melancholic style and his subject matter. The influence of these photographers in turn demonstrates the huge overall impact of the style and aesthetic sensibility of Atget's work, something all the more striking in that it hides the quiet and unassuming career that the photographer himself pursued.

Sally Stewart

See also: Evans, Walker; Photography; Ray, Man; Surrealism.

References

Harris, David. *Eugène Atget: Unknown Paris.* New York: New Press, 2003.

Szarkowski, John, Maria Morris Hambourg, and Eugène Atget. *The Work of Atget.* New York/Boston: Museum of Modern Art, 1981–1985.

ATLANTICISM

A concept of Western European–North American cultural similarity and policy cooperation that existed fitfully from the early twentieth century.

U.S.-British relations were most important to this concept, but U.S.-French relations also determined its fate. Emerging most strongly after each world war, Atlanticism by the twenty-first century appeared in decline.

In the World War I era U.S. and British elites led by President Woodrow Wilson and Foreign Secretary Sir Edward Grey envisioned a dissemination of Anglo-Saxon ideals that could foster not only a liberal empire but also universal peace. France in the 1930s also sought Atlantic integration as the only insurance for French security against Germany. But various factors discredited Atlanticism at the time, including its racist implications, Wilson's collapse, transatlantic breakdowns over the League of Nations and war reparations, and the Depression.

Nazism sparked Atlanticism's revival, signaled in the Atlantic Charter of 1941. The concept enjoyed its heyday during and after World War II. Especially with the rise of the cold war, Atlanticist writers and journalists, including Walter Lippmann, Clarence Streit, Jacques Godechot, Edward Murrow, and R. R. Palmer, argued that Americans and Europeans shared a Western heritage and democratic values of protection of citizens against the state. These values were confirmed, not challenged, by the American and French Revolutions. Atlanticism provided the philosophical foundation for the Marshall Plan and the North Atlantic Treaty Organization (NATO). Britain sought to deepen its "special relationship" with the United States, while conservatives of the French Fourth Republic embraced Atlantic cooperation and U.S. aid.

The cooperative impulse alternately declined and rose until the 1980s. The Berlin crisis of 1961 helped foster a Franco-German rapprochement. Franco-American relations were strained by developments in Egypt, Algeria, and Vietnam. The formation of the European Economic Community (EEC) in 1958 (renamed in 1992 as the European Union) created a potential rival to close relations spanning the Atlantic. Under President Charles de Gaulle, France cultivated itself as leader of a European confederation not subject to Anglo-American leadership. De Gaulle blocked Britain's attempt to make the EEC a transatlantic free trade zone and also removed France from NATO's military structure in 1966. Gaullism, West German establishment of direct relations with East Germany, and the "realpolitik" of U.S. president Richard Nixon limited Atlanticist alignment in the 1970s.

In the 1980s, however, U.S. president Ronald Reagan, French president François Mitterrand, and British prime minister Margaret Thatcher cooperated over both installation of U.S. missiles in Europe and encouragement of reforms in the Soviet Union. The end of the cold war was celebrated as the vindication of Atlanticist beliefs and doctrines.

But in the post–cold war era the prospects of Atlanticism again dimmed. In 1995 U.S. president Bill Clinton reluctantly organized military intervention in the war-torn Balkans, when European nations failed to prevent ethnic conflicts in the region. In 2003 the United States under President George Bush led an invasion, joined in by British prime minister Tony Blair, of Iraq, whose dictator Saddam Hussein was under UN investigation for developing weapons of mass destruction. U.S. and British actions received heavy criticism by French president Jacques Chirac and other leaders as a show of disregard for UN authority. The Iraqi invasion challenged Atlanticist assumptions of an Atlantic community and of U.S. consultation of Europe in determining U.S. positions on global matters.

Timothy M. Roberts

See also: American Revolution; Chirac, Jacques; Foreign Policy, 1945–Present; French Revolution; Gaulle, General Charles de; Iraq War; Marshall Plan, The; Mitterrand, François; NATO; Wilson, Woodrow; World War I; World War II.

References

Fry, Michael. *Illusions of Security: North Atlantic Diplomacy, 1918–1922.* Toronto: University of Toronto Press, 1972.

Hodge, Carl. *Atlanticism for a New Century: The Rise, Triumph, and Decline of NATO.* New York: Prentice Hall, 2004.

John James Audubon. The name Audubon *remains synonymous with birds and bird conservation the world over due to the ongoing pursuits of the Audubon Society. (Library of Congress)*

AUDUBON, JOHN JAMES (1785–1851)

Ornithologist, born in Santo Domingo (now Haiti) in 1785.

John James Audubon was the illegitimate son of Jean Audubon, a French sea captain and plantation owner, and Jeanne Rabine, a chambermaid. Jeanne died in a slave uprising shortly after John's birth. He was raised by his stepmother and father in the French countryside around Nantes. It was here that he developed a love of wildlife, especially birds, and of sketching and drawing.

In 1803, aged eighteen, Audubon was sent to Pennsylvania, partly in order to avoid conscription in Napoléon's army. He lived on and managed the family-owned estate at Mill Grove, near Philadelphia, where he hunted, studied, and drew birds. It is here that he met Lucy Bakewell, whom he married in 1808. While at Mill Grove, he conducted the first known bird-banding experiment in North America, tying strings around the legs of eastern phoebes; he learned that the birds returned to the very same nesting sites each year.

Audubon spent more than a decade in business, eventually traveling down the Ohio River to western Kentucky where he set up a dry-goods store. He continued to draw birds as a hobby, amassing an impressive portfolio during this time. While in Kentucky, Lucy gave birth to two sons, Victor Gifford and John Woodhouse, as well as a daughter who died in infancy. Audubon was quite successful in business for a while, but hard times hit, and in 1819 he was briefly jailed for bankruptcy.

At age thirty-five, with no other prospects, Audubon set off on his epic quest to depict America's avifauna, with nothing but his gun, artist's materials, and a young assistant. This venture became *The Birds of America,* 435 hand-colored engravings published in double elephant folios (1828–1838), followed by a smaller, octavo-sized, version. While initiating the engraving process for *The Birds of America,* through Robert Havell Jr. of London, Audubon lived in Europe (1827–1829). In Edinburgh, London, and Paris, he was elected to learned and scientific honorary societies, and his work was acclaimed in superlatives. He developed a noble and royal patronage and a host of subscribers.

In 1840, he undertook publication of *The Viviparous Quadrupeds of North America.* By the time Audubon and his four assistants embarked on their journey up the Missouri River in 1843 to collect information on and images of western mammals, he had drawn sixty-one species. One hundred and fifty hand-colored lithographs were published in both an imperial folio size (1845–1848) and a smaller octavo edition (1846–1853).

Audubon spent his last years in senility and died in 1851 at age sixty-five, with plates for the *Quadrupeds,* but not all of the text, completed. He is buried in the Trinity Cemetery at 155th Street and Broadway in New York City.

Although Audubon had no role in the organization that bears his name, today the name Audubon remains synonymous with birds and bird conservation the world over due to the ongoing pursuits of the Audubon Society.

Martin Fowlie

See also: Bonaparte, Napoléon; Haiti; Nantes; Ohio; Santo Domingo; Slavery.

References

Audubon, John James, and Francis Hobart Herrick. *Delineations of American Scenery and Character.* New York: G. A. Baker, 1926.

Mason, Miriam Evangeline. *John Audubon, Boy Naturalist.* Indianapolis: Bobbs-Merrill, 1962.

AURY, LOUIS-MICHEL (1788–1821)

Early nineteenth-century privateer in the Americas, born in the outskirts of Paris.

Commodore Aury fought the Spanish in Florida, Texas, Colombia, Central America, and the West Indies. Despite being victimized by U.S. policies and sentiment, Aury at times worked for Americans in a capitalistic capacity. Surviving battles and the treachery of Simón Bolívar, the Lafitte brothers, and the U.S. government, Aury maintained an unwavering commitment to his republican ideals, only to die an innocent early death.

Aury served the Napoleonic navy as a sailmaker and helmsman in the West Indies. For unclear reasons, he began serving aboard a privateer vessel preying on Spanish and British shipping. Being successful, Aury purchased a vessel in New Orleans in 1810. The vessel was confiscated, and Aury was forced to leave but renewed his privateering operations. In a letter to his sister, he railed against the United States and described himself as having a few sins. In 1811 Aury's vessels entered Savannah,

Georgia, to refit. An anti-French mob burned his two ships, leaving him stranded. The French consulate in Baltimore directed him to the fight in South America against Spain, where Aury's skills raised him to the rank of commodore in the Cartagenian (Colombian) navy. The privateering contract enriched him, and he employed a trusted Frenchman, who was a member of the Association, a coalition of American businessmen in New Orleans, to dispose of his bounty and handle his finances. Disagreements with Simón Bolívar dissolved his command, but not before Aury personally led a coup and rescued 2,000 starving, besieged Cartagenians.

In 1816, exiled in Haiti, Aury contracted with the Mexican shadow government to transport an invasion force from Galveston Island in Spanish Texas to Mexico to overthrow the Spanish. En route, Aury learned that the rebel Mexican government had disbanded. The Association, which had a financial interest in Mexico, ordered the invasion continued. Despite working for his antagonists, the New Orleans Association, comprising New Orleans Americans who had constantly treated him badly, and though he chafed at having to work for them, Aury successfully raided Spanish shipping and smuggled the captured cargo to the United States. Mexican officials with the Association's invasion force arrived at Galveston and declared Aury the first Mexican governor of Texas. Aury transported them to Mexico and returning, found his camp had been confiscated by the Lafittes, who had been spying on Aury for the Spanish.

Defeated, Aury set sail for Florida. Amelia Island had recently been captured from Spain by U.S. mercenaries who needed supplies. Aury arrived and rescued the beleaguered privateers. Resuming the privateering business under the Mexican flag, he sold a half a million dollars of cargo in the United States When racism on Amelia Island, Florida, in 1817–1818 divided American whites and Aury's black sailors, Aury settled the dispute with a show of force. Aury was ousted when the United States declared Amelia Island an illegal country and invaded it. Leaving in 1818, Aury took part on Central American revolutions where he successfully assisted in removing Spain. While on a vacation on his private island, Aury was thrown from a horse and died from complications on August 30, 1821.

Gary E. McKee

See also: Bolívar, Simón; Bonaparte, Napoléon; Florida; Haiti; Mexico; New Orleans; Piracy and Privateers; Republicanism; Texas.

References

Dabney, Lancaster E. "Louis Aury: First Governor of Texas." *Southwestern Historical Quarterly* 42, no. 1 (October 1938): 112–116.

Faye, Stanley. "Commodore Aury." *Louisiana Historical Quarterly* 24, no. 3 (July 1941): 612–691.

AUSTER, PAUL (1947–)

U.S. author, born in New Jersey to an upper-middle-class Jewish family.

Auster began his writing career translating French literature. In college, his grandiose plans to become a young writer in Paris failed, and although he earned two degrees from Columbia University, he quit in 1967, remained in Paris four more years, spent some time on an oil rig, and returned to New York in 1974. Several unpublished manuscripts from that period are recalled in his memoir, *Hand to Mouth: A Chroni-*

cle of Early Failure, along with unproduced plays and a board game, Action Baseball.

Auster went on to write the films Smoke (1995) and Blue in the Face (1995), and published numerous essays, short stories, novellas, and memoirs. In The New York Trilogy (1987), which comprises City of Glass (1985), Ghosts (1986), and The Locked Room (1986), he wrote about death, homelessness, and poverty. His translations are included in A Tomb for Anatole (1983), by Stéphane Mallarmé, The Notebooks of Joseph Jourbet, Translations (1997), and The Random House Book of Twentieth-Century French Poetry (1984).

Auster's major works include In the Country of Last Things (1987), Moon Palace (1989), The Music of Chance (1990), Leviathan (1992), Mr. Vertigo (1994), The Book of Illusions (2003), and Ground Work: Selected Poems and Essays 1970–1979 (1988). The essays critique both known and relatively unknown writers such as Franz Kafka, Salman Rushdie, and André du Bouchet. They show compassion for the dispossessed and celebrate European values and artists, particularly Mallarmé and Marcel Proust, whose works Auster has translated into English. Proust most influences Auster's writing in The Invention of Solitude (1988), where he writes: "The past, to repeat the words of Proust, is hidden in some material object"—referring, in this "Book of Memory," both to the world in general and to articles from his father's memory left in his house, which become reflections of Auster's own history.

The most striking characteristics of Auster's works are the dual strains, in equal parts, of French and American culture on writing and the imaginary, with special emphasis on his love of baseball. He writes extensively about art, culture, and literature in The Art of Hunger: Essays, Prefaces, Interviews and the Red Notebook (1997).

Auster lives in Brooklyn, New York, with his wife and two children. He is published worldwide and remains a Franco-American phenomenon.

Erna Cooper

See also: Cinema, 1945 to the Present; Sport.
References
Auster, Paul. The Invention of Solitude. New York: Penguin, 1982; rpt. 1988.
———. Hand to Mouth: A Chronicle of Early Failure. London: Faber and Faber, 1997.

AUTOMOBILES

In accounts of Franco-American relations, the automobile operates both as an indicator of divergent national identities and histories and as a vehicle of evolving transatlantic relations. Although it was German engineers who first developed the internal combustion engine and adapted it for use in operative vehicles, the French automobile industry made pioneering progress in the period before World War I. There was evidence already of transatlantic exchange in this period, as engineer Louis Joseph Chevrolet moved to North America to be employed by William Crapo Dunant in 1910, but the French industry rejected working practices already associated with its North American counterpart, and an attempt in 1913 to introduce *chronométrage*, a diluted version of Taylorism, was met with industrial unrest. During this period, American motorists, such as Edith Wharton (*A Motor-Flight through France*, 1908), toured France and published accounts of their travels, but after 1918 the U.S. car industry steadily gained dominance as the automobile—and in particular affordable models such as the Ford Model T—became instrumental in processes of democratization and more general demographic change. In 1925, the United States produced 3 million vehicles, France 125,000. European francophone travelers in the interwar United States were invariably impressed by the products of American automotive engineering, but having observed working practices in car factories in Detroit, Dr. Louis Destouches published a long and highly critical report on the practical implications of Fordism (and thinly fictionalized these working practices in the North American section of *Voyage au bout de la nuit,* a novel published in 1934 under his pseudonym Louis-Ferdinand Céline).

According to Ilya Ehrenburg, in *The Life of the Automobile* (1929), André Citroën, the principal French automobile entrepreneur in the interwar period, sought to combine American styling with European austerity. Despite economic handicaps, he actively attempted to reassert the predominance of the French industry, undertaking a series of *croisières* (car rallies) that would eventually contribute to the bankrupting of his company and its nationalization. The trans-African and trans-Asian *croisières noire* and *jaune* were even complemented by a less prominent Canadian journey. Funded by the French-born business management specialist (and future intermediary between Vichy and Berlin) Charles Eugène Bedaux, and using the same Citroën-Kégresse half-track vehicles (*autochenilles*), this group attempted to cross the Rockies in 1934. With the development of a French equivalent of the Model T disrupted in 1939 by the outbreak of war, production on the main contender for this role, the Citroën 2CV, could only begin on a very modest scale and with

the sparse materials available in a carefully planned postwar economy ten years later. Although the Pons Plan privileged manufacturers who concentrated on commercial vehicles and smaller private cars, the 2CV by this time looked outmoded in relation to American cars (slowly permeating national consciousness, especially through their representation in popular culture). With critics of social changes in postwar France seeing modernization as a by-product of progressive Americanization, the American automobile came to represent a certain self-confidence and even arrogance. With the U.S. automobile industry having overtaken the technology of its French counterpart in the period following World War I, by the 1950s the gap between the two was increasingly marked: the French effort to achieve affordable motorization in a climate of initial austerity contrasted with the peak of U.S. automobile size and fantastic styling. The car came to symbolize what for many French was the hubris of postwar American culture. In an extreme outburst of anti-Americanism, for instance, the Communist poet Louis Aragon was angered by the replacement with a new Ford car of a missing sculpture from a square that honored Victor Hugo. The American car operated as a more ambivalent marker in a series of postwar French films. In works such as Jacques Tati's *Mon Oncle* (1958), Jacques Demy's *Lola* (1961), and Jacques Dhéry's *La Belle Américaine* (1961), the vehicle suggests a range of meanings, from the outlandish to the fantastic, while indicating both the material benefits and potential pitfalls of U.S. capitalism.

In U.S. cinema, the 2CV is perhaps the most common automotive marker of Frenchness. In productions such as *Ameri-*

can Graffiti (Lucas, 1973), *For Your Eyes Only* (Glen, 1981), and *Indecent Proposal* (Lyne, 1992), the car reflects meanings ranging from bohemian difference to artisanal persistence. When actual 2CVs crossed North America in the 1950s and 1960s as part of the widespread phenomenon of long-distance journeys in the unlikely vehicle, its reception was less enthusiastic. Compared to other more powerful American vehicles, the 2CV could not compete (except in extreme circumstances, such as on black ice). Although the car's technology, modern by South American standards, had served to accentuate the pre-industrial conditions of certain South American cultures (Henri Lochon, *En 2CV chez les primitifs de la Sierra mexicaine,* 1956), it had the opposite effect in the United States, where the technology was more advanced and it was greeted with incredulity. Such humiliation over appearance was compounded by the vehicle's inability, once in the United States, to reach the minimum speed limit on major roads, and this threat to French modernity of an all-engulfing American hypermodernity was given concrete form in the image of Jean-Claude Baudot and Jacques Séguéla's 2CV in *La Terre en rond* (1960) awaiting customs clearance in Rio de Janeiro, dwarfed in a crowd of large and elegant American vehicles.

Although these 2CV travelers resist, on the whole, any explicit anti-Americanism, their accounts nevertheless reveal an implicit international competitiveness, especially when their vehicles are dismissed and they are told that even a Jeep would fail to go where they dare to venture. The 2CV tends, however, to outstrip the general-purpose vehicle, by now symbolic of the American presence in postwar France.

During Cornet and Lochon's attempt in Bolivia to take the 2CV to over 5,000 meters, the accompanying American vehicle was forced to give up, whereas their French vehicle, emptied of luggage and stripped of doors and fenders, manages the climb. Similarly, as Guy Viau and his fellow travelers prepare to cross the Sahara (*Le Tour d'Afrique en 2CV de quatre jeunes Français,* 1956) they meet two sneering Chevrolet drivers. The 2CVs manage the journey with several minor breakdowns, whereas the American vehicle suffers a major breakdown, and its driver and passenger nearly die of dehydration. Faced with American mechanical hubris, French simplicity becomes a virtue.

These examples are associated with clear commercial antagonisms: U.S. consumers, little concerned with issues of fuel efficiency, were disappointed with the relative quality of most European products. The U.S. market responded to foreign imports of small cars with a series of changes in legislation: an increase in the minimum speed limit ensured that a fully laden 2CV would never be able to reach this speed; compulsory crash tests made the import of French vehicles even more difficult. Even for the engine of the epitome of French new technology, the Citroën DS, American engine oil was unsuitable and damaged seals so badly that the cars invariably broke down. In considerations of Franco-American relations, the car continues to be a vehicle of national identities and of the tensions between them: during the U.S. invasion of Iraq in 2003, for instance, there were widespread media reports of virulent anti-French sentiment in the United States being directed toward French-manufactured vehicles.

Charles Forsdick

References

Loubet, Jean-Louis. *Histoire de l'automobile
française.* Paris: Seuil, 2001.

Moustacchi, Alfred, and Jean-Jacques Payan.
L'Automobile: avenir d'un centenaire. Paris:
Flammarion, 1999.

Ross, Kristin. *Fast Cars, Clean Bodies:
Decolonization and the Reordering of French
Culture.* Cambridge, MA/London: MIT
Press, 1995.

Wollen, Peter, and Joe Kerr, eds. *Autopia.*
London: Reaktion, 2002.

AVANT-GARDES

"Avant-garde" was originally a French military term meaning "advance guard," but it is used widely within the art world to refer to a practice that is in advance of its time and portends what is, or what might be, possible. As the editors of the 1998 anthology *Modernism* describe it, the avant-garde is both a "historical moment" in the early twentieth century "when certain practitioners sought to liquidate the boundaries between art and life" and "a transformative power affecting all other practices and theories." (Kolocotroni et al., p. xviii). The avant-garde as an aesthetic and cosmopolitan trend emerged in the 1910s, stimulating writers, artists, and filmmakers on both sides of the Atlantic to explore the possibilities of art as a revolutionary experience. Encompassing various movements, manifestos and "isms," the avant-garde was at its high point in the mid-1910s and 1920s and then had a renaissance in France and the United States following World War II.

As the two primary centers for modern art in the early twentieth century, New York City and Paris were central nodes for the international avant-garde, but London, Zurich, and Berlin all played important roles in its development. It is generally accepted that the avant-garde emerged with the International Exhibition of Modern Art (the Armory Show) in Manhattan in early 1913, sponsored by the Association of American Painters and Sculptors. The mixed-media exhibits represented a sweeping away of traditional art forms and hostility toward the past, and the European émigrés Marcel Duchamp and Francis Picabia found in Manhattan an exciting cosmopolitanism not evident in Europe until later in the 1910s. The spirit of artistic adventure in the new bohemia of Greenwich Village, exemplified by the most famous of the exhibits, Duchamp's *Nude Descending a Staircase* No. 2 (1912), inspired a spirit of nonconformity and widespread disdain for orthodox aesthetics. The public response was a mixture of curiosity, bewilderment, and declamation. Despite negative reviews, artists acclaimed the Armory Show a major creative success, but not until dadaism was given its name in Switzerland in 1916 did they collectively consider the role of the avant-garde in American and European cultural life.

The cosmopolitan fertility of Zurich was the perfect place to devise art that could give reign to "free expression" and attack the foundations of decadent bourgeois culture. The experiments of Richard Huelsenbeck, the artist Hans Arp, and the poets Hugo Ball and Tzara (as well as Picabia, who joined the group in 1918) have usually been viewed as nihilistic examples of what Hans Richter has called "anti-art," in contrast to the bourgeois reverence for "Art." In their fracturing of narrative and poetic form and disdain for knowledge, morality, social progress, law, and science, dadaist anti art represented an assault on all the cherished values of Western culture. As Tzara proclaimed in 1918 in the most famous of his seven dada manifestos, "Dadaist Disgust": "Every product of disgust that is capable of becoming a negation of the family is *dada;* protest with the fists of one's whole being in destructive action."

By 1920 the branch of dadaism based in Berlin had become explicitly political in its support of Communism as "the destruction of everything that has gone bourgeois," while the Zurich dadaists moved to Paris to join the surrealists under the leadership of André Breton. Surrealism was much more engaged with the creative potential of dreams and fantasy, and in the *Manifeste du surréalisme* (First Surrealist Manifesto, 1924), Breton declared his interest in "psychic automatism" as the true function of thought, free from "any control exercised by reason" and "exempt from any aesthetic or moral concern." Surrealism shared with dada a disdain for rationalism and conventional ethics, but Tzara disliked Breton's emphasis on mysticism and "the omnipotence of the dream," the word-association games he developed from psychoanalysis, and the automatic writing experiments he shared with Philippe Soupault. The desire to "recognize value . . . wherever it exists" distanced the surrealists from the nihilistic currents of dadaist aesthetics and propelled art in "the direction of human liberation" (Breton, p. 26), leading Tzara to break with them in 1921. Surrealism was at its high point in the mid-1920s, attracting artists from both sides of the Atlantic, including the photographer, artist, and filmmaker Man Ray from the United States, Salvador Dalí and Luis Buñuel from Spain, and the French poet Paul Eluard and composer Erik Satie, but the movement had splintered by the early 1930s, with many, including Breton and Louis Aragon, shifting away from autonomous art toward an active engagement with Communism.

The history of the avant-garde cannot be traced easily through the development of specific movements. There was too much cross-pollination of ideas and techniques, and some practitioners do not easily fit into one or other "ism," with Man Ray producing some of his best work in the 1930s (such as *A l'Heure de l'Observatoire—Les Amoureux,* 1932–1934) and others such as Louis Guglielmi working toward a personal vision of social surrealism (evidenced in paintings such as *Phoenix,* 1935, which places a picture of Lenin within the rubble of modernity). Other influential figures moved between groupings, such as the American art guru and collector Peggy Guggenheim, who was instrumental in exhibiting experimental art from the 1920s (including Pablo Picasso, René Magritte, and Constantin Brancusi) through midcentury, when she championed the abstract expressionism of Jackson Pollock and Robert Motherwell. The experimental filmmaking of Alain Resnais in *L'Année dernière á Marienbad* (*Last Year at Marienbad,* 1961) and the *nouveau roman* of Alain Robbe-Grillet carried forward the spirit of the French avant-garde into the 1960s, while the visual experimentation of Kenneth Anger and Maya Deren, the musical minimalism of John Cage, the dissident writing of William Burroughs, and the Fluxus movement fed into the American counterculture of the mid- to late 1960s.

By the 1980s the transatlantic avant-garde had been thoroughly institutionalized, perhaps beginning as early as 1929 with the opening of the Museum of Modern Art in New York City. With the increasing corporate control of cultural production and exhibition (such as the Saatchi Gallery in London) and with the avant-garde seen now as the "official" face of modernism, it has lost much of its potential to irritate, annoy, and stimulate, as Gertrude Stein described its goals in 1926. But the vitality of outsider art, the relative newness of digital art forms, and the radicalization of aesthetic practices linked to protests about the global economy suggest that the spirit of an international avant-garde should certainly not be consigned to history.

Martin Halliwell

See also: Breton, André; Burroughs, William S.; Duchamp, Marcel; Music (Classical); Painting; Photography; Ray, Man; Sculpture; Soupault, Philippe; Stein, Gertrude; Surrealism; Theory; World War II.

References

Breton, André. *Manifestoes of Surrealism,* trans. Richard Seaver and Helen R. Lane. Ann Arbor: University of Michigan Press, 1972.

Crunden, Robert M. *American Salons: Encounters with European Modernism, 1885–1917.* New York: Oxford University Press, 1993.

Kolocotroni, Vassiliki, Jane Goldman, and Olga Taxidou, eds. *Modernism: An Anthology of Sources and Documents.* Edinburgh: Edinburgh University Press, 1998.

Lewis, Helena. *Dada Turns Red: The Politics of Surrealism.* Edinburgh: Edinburgh University Press, 1990.

Nicholls, Peter. *Modernisms: A Literary Guide.* London: Macmillan, 1995.

Richter, Hans. *Dada: Art and Anti-Art.* London: Thames and Hudson, 1997.

Tashjian, Dickran. *A Boatload of Madmen: Surrealism and the American Avant-Garde, 1920–1950.* London: Thames and Hudson, 1995.

AVIATION

The French aviation industry—considered as the whole range of technological, industrial, commercial, and transportation activities related to flight—has traditionally been a site of interaction between France and the United States. Such interaction has mostly assumed the form of competition—essentially over technology and industry—but since the replacement in the 1950s and 1960s of transatlantic liners by jet airplanes as the conveyors of travelers between eastern and western shores of the Atlantic, aviation has redefined the parameters of physical human exchange between France and the United States. The mid-twentieth-century heyday of the great transatlantic liners such as the SS *United States,* the *Normandie,* and the *France* and their competition for the Blue Riband Trophy rewarding the fastest crossing of the (North) Atlantic has given rise to much cultural chronicling; similarly, the contemporary crossings between Europe and the United States by Airbus and Concorde (or by Boeing 747) reflect complex sociopolitical, socioeconomic, and sociocultural relations across the French Atlantic. Military aviation has also been a field in which the United States and France have interacted—mostly along classic lines of competition—with American companies fighting French companies such as Dassault and Aérospatiale for lucrative markets throughout the world.

During the 1920s and 1930s, the Atlantic was often the locus of elements of the heroic age of aviation as American, British, and French pilots applied the improvements to flight technology gained during World War I to the conquest of new and ever longer routes and more frequent and faster crossings of the South and North

Atlantic. In 1927 a French Bréguet plane made the first crossing of the South Atlantic, and during the 1930s the exploits of Jean Mermoz and Henri Guillaumet (made legendary by the writer and flyer Antoine de Saint-Exupéry) in opening up new routes to and over South America caught the public imagination. In 1933 another Bréguet took the record for the longest nonstop crossing—4,500 miles—of the North Atlantic and the French Atlantic. The aviator Costes was as well known as Lindbergh.

The story of Concorde remains perhaps the most emblematic case study of aviation in the French Atlantic, combining as it does real technological, political, and commercial rivalries and the intangible cultural shrinkage of the North Atlantic reduced to a few hours' travel for the elites of Europe and the United States. From the launch of the Franco-British program in 1962 to the insistence of Air France and British Airways on prolonging Concorde's service as far into the twenty-first century as possible, Europe's supersonic transport plane has been a potent symbol of the ties that bind France and the United States. However, other symbolic airplanes reveal some of the complexities of the permanent "air lift" between Roissy-Charles-de-Gaulle airport in Paris and the no less emblematically named JFK airport in New York City.

Contemporary (mass) air travel across the Atlantic is dominated by the Boeing 747 and by the Airbus, two long-haul commercial jetliners whose development and exploitation reflect differing approaches to aviation and air transportation. In the post–World War II era, advances in jet technology made separately on both sides of the Atlantic led to the development and production of military jets and gradually to civilian jetliners capable of drastically shortening the distance separating Europe and the United States. The passenger planes that ushered in the age of more convenient transatlantic travel were the romantically named Caravelle (Air France) and Constellation (BOAC) and Boeing's 707. The Boeing 707 first carried passengers in 1958, and the Caravelle was part of the Air France fleet from 1959 until 1981, thus sharing airspace with the jumbo 747s that entered service in 1970 and the Airbus (1974).

Technological and industrial rivalry in aviation between France and the United States until the 1960s was replaced by competition between the United States and Europe from the 1970s on, as the costs of research and development forced the concentration of European aerospace companies, initially on a national level but increasingly internationally. A number of French aviation firms merged in 1970 to create the Société nationale de l'industrie aéronautique et spatiale (SNIAS), which was renamed Aérospatiale in 1984 and alongside Dassault formed the basis of France's expertise in aerospace. Aérospatiale undertakes civil and military activities, but Dassault—as the producer of the famous Mirage family of fighters and fighter-bombers—specializes in military aviation. France's strength in aviation, and particularly in military aircraft such as the Mirage, combined with the importance of arms sales to the French military-industrial complex, has often brought France into competition with the United States over lucrative military contracts in sensitive areas of the world. The bilateral collaboration of the Franco-British Concorde project led to the multilateral cooperation of Airbus, in which France, Britain, Germany, and others merged the expertise of their aviation industries to produce a series of civil jetliners capable of competing with U.S. aircraft for the prime transatlantic routes and short- and medium-haul services within Europe and the United States.

Airbus Industrie is now Boeing's major rival, selling the same number of planes annually worldwide. However, although such a parity of industrial and technological expertise might suggest a new modus vivendi over flights between the two sides of the Atlantic, U.S. economic liberalism still finds much to quarrel with in French approaches to aviation. Much of the expansion of the popularity of flight in the latter part of the twentieth century took place as a result of the U.S. government's Airline Deregulation Act (1978), which allowed new airline companies to propose new services both over long- and short-haul routes, such as Freddie Laker's "Skytrain" North Atlantic line. This deregulation threatened the dominant position of national carriers such as Air France, accustomed to near monopolies on prestigious international routes, and introduced competition (for example, from Air Inter) on domestic routes. In the 1990s, U.S. economic neoliberalism continued to challenge French industrial and business practices in the form of European Commission rulings on government subsidies to state companies. The Société nationale des chemins de fer français (SNCF), Renault, and Air France were criticized for the financial support they received from the French state. Air France is now apparently destined for privatization, thus removing another element of difference between different ways of flying across the Atlantic.

Hugh Dauncey

See also: Concorde; Gaulle, General Charles de; Saint-Exupéry, Antoine de; World War I; World War II.

References
Carlier, Claude. *Dassault aviation: 50 ans d'aventure aéronautique, 1945–1995.* Paris: Chêne, 1996.
———. *Chronologie aérospatiale, politique, militaire 1945–1995.* Paris: Economica, 1997.
Chadeau, Emmanuel, ed. *Airbus: Un Succès industriel européen.* Paris: Rive droite, 1995.

AZNAVOUR, CHARLES (CHARLES AZNAVOURIAN) (1924–)

Singer, born in Paris in 1924.

For many the epitome of the French romantic singer, Aznavour has enjoyed a long career touring France and the world. His appearance on the cover of the U.S. magazine *Billboard* (1996), unusual for a French artist, confirms the extent to which Aznavour, often regarded as the French Sinatra, has become an international star.

Following tours of North America at the end of the 1940s with the songwriter Pierre Roche, Aznavour returned to Paris, where he performed at the Alhambra and Olympia musical halls during the mid-1950s. His initial success in the United States may partly be attributed to his appearance in François Truffaut's successful 1960 film *Tirez sur le pianiste* (*Shoot the Piano Player*). Furthermore, his appearance at Carnegie Hall (1963), the prestigious New York concert hall, led to a world tour in 1966 that included Canada as well as Latin America, where his Spanish version of "Avec" (With, 1964) was a huge hit. Although audiences enjoyed the exoticism of the French language as well as Aznavour's French accent, he nonetheless made a conscious effort to sing many of his songs in the languages of the countries where he toured. The 1970s saw several of Aznavour's songs translated into English and covered by North American artists, including Ray Charles ("La Mamma" [For Mama]), Fred Astaire ("Les Plaisirs démodés" [The Old Fashioned Way]), and Bing Crosby ("Hier encore" [Yesterday When I Was Young]). Aznavour also wrote "Sailor Boys" [Les Marins, 1974] for Liza Minnelli, whom he had introduced to Paris as a young performer. Aznavour's 1970 U.S. tour featured several West Coast universities that had seen a surge in political activism. Indeed, his songwriting showed a greater interest in social questions during the 1970s, with titles such as "Le Temps des loups" ("Time of the Wolves," 1970), which dealt with violence, and "Comme ils disent" ("As They Say," 1971), which contributed to breaking taboos around homosexuality.

At the turn of the millennium, Aznavour decided at the age of seventy-five to stop touring, but to celebrate his eightieth birthday in 2004, he performed a series of concerts at the Palais des Congrès in Paris, as well as undertaking a European tour. In 2000 he produced the musical *Lautrec* about the life of the French artist, which ran in London before transferring to Broadway. In 2001 Aznavour, who is of Armenian descent, played the role of a film director in *Ararat*. The film, directed by the Armenian Canadian filmmaker Atom Egoyan, commemorates the Turkish massacre of Armenians (1915–1916).

Chris Tinker

See also: Music (Pop); Truffaut, François.
References
Hawkins, Peter. "Charles Aznavour: A Sentimental Realist." *Chanson: The French Singer-Songwriter from Aristide Bruant to the Present Day.* Aldershot: Ashgate, 2000.
Reval, Annie, and Bernard Reval. *Aznavour: Le roi de cœur.* Paris: France-Empire, 2000.

B

BAKER, JOSEPHINE (FREDA JOSEPHINE MCDONALD) (1906–1975)

American dance artiste.

At the height of her success in interwar Paris, Josephine Baker was a millionaire at the age of just twenty-four. Dubbed in the French press as *La Bakaire,* her roles on stage in *La Revue nègre/The Negro Revue* (1925) and *La Folie du jour/The Day's Madness* (1926) and in film in *La Sirène des tropiques/*The Siren of the Tropics (Nalpas/ Etiévant, 1927), *Zou Zou* (Marc Allégret, 1934), and *Princesse Tam Tam* (Gréville, 1935) made Baker one of the most publicly visible figures in French cultural life until her death in Paris in 1975, where she was given a full state funeral. Baker was variously figured as the incarnation of Charles Baudelaire's Jeanne Duval, the *danseuse de bananes/*the banana dancer and *la petite Tonkinoise/the Tonkin girl* who brought the Charleston and the Blackbottom to France, all performed against the backdrop of interwar France that was just entering its colonial golden age.

Born in 1906 to an impoverished family in the racially troubled city of Saint Louis, Baker received little formal education and was married at thirteen. She seemed destined for a life of poverty and drudgery in common with other African American women of her social class and education. However, a talent for performance at an early age took Baker into the potentially more lucrative world of the black musical revue, where she quickly recognized that she could use the performative value of the black female body to escape from domestic service and menial labor. Considered too dark for the traditional sexual appeal of the "high yallers" and the "sepia lovelies" in the chorus line, Baker attracted attention with her comic talent in a series of blackface comedy roles and soon became well known for her traditional "pickanniny" routines *Shuffle Along* (1923) and *Chocolate Dandies* (1924) in Harlem and on Broadway.

Baker first traveled to France as part of the *Revue nègre* brought over from the United States by entrepreneur Caroline Dudley Reagan, who had discovered Baker at the end of a Broadway chorus line sticking out "like an exclamation point" (Haney, p. 44). Along with twenty-five musicians and dancers, the clarinetist Sidney Bechet among them, Baker arrived in Paris in 1925, where the *Revue* was quickly transformed from traditional American vaudeville with tap dancing and gospel spirituals to a more modern spectacle of

Josephine Baker was the star attraction in the 1920s at the Folies Bergères in Paris. (Bettmann/Corbis)

licity by Paul Colin, who produced a set of striking black, white, and red lithographs for the *Revue* depicting Baker virtually naked in a series of poses. Colin wanted to represent the "soul of Harlem," and his sketches drew upon both typical American black vaudeville imagery of the saxophone, blues notes, and jazz band as well as the highly racialized aspects of Baker's unclothed black female body. The posters created a new visual language of primitivism that articulated the double appeal of Baker and the *Revue nègre,* a coalescence of the imagined antiquity of *l'art nègre* with its apparently untutored sensual energy and the modernity of American popular culture, both of which became inextricably linked to a particular vocabulary of modernist primitivism. Published in 1926 in a collection called *Le Tumulte noir,* Colin's prints are a fusion of cubism, fauvism, and an American jazz aesthetic that constructed a visual grammar of race and sexuality around the representation of the female black body. The imagery was at once new in its modernist cultural juxtaposition and yet historically embedded in much older colonial discourses of Otherness.

Significantly, Baker's allure in the *Revue nègre* was one that crossed both high and popular culture. As such, it can be read as a particularly decisive modernist event, comparable to Sergei Diaghilev's Ballets russes, in which Nijinsky danced in *Le Sacre du printemps* (*The Rite of Spring,* 1913) at the same theater. Her appearance on the stage of the Théâtre Champs-Elysées in the *Danse sauvage* caused a palpable stir among the eclectic audience, made up of members of the Académie Française, journalists, fashion designers, artists, and intellectuals. Baker performed the *danse* bare-breasted in a scanty cos-

black Americanism. Seeking a new angle for the show, the producers André Daven and Jacques Charles of the *Revue* were advised by the artist Fernand Léger, "Give them Negroes. Only the Negroes can excite Paris!" after he had attended the Exposition des Arts Décoratifs. Léger's advice recognized the new aesthetic appeal of *l'art nègre* that had just begun to permeate both high and popular culture in modernist Paris and would soon become known as *négrophilie,* a wave of cultural primitivism that reached its apogee in 1925–1927. Josephine Baker's role in the *Revue nègre* as part of the *Danse sauvage* framed her as the iconic figure of negrophile primitivism.

The opening night of the *Revue nègre* was sold out, due in part to advance pub-

tume of feathers and beads with collars around her wrists and ankles—echoes of slavery mediated as primitive music hall adornment. Her partner was Joe Alex, a dancer from Martinique, who was sufficiently dark-skinned and "African looking" to present a favorable aesthetic contrast with Baker's lighter, African American skin tones and fashionably cropped and lacquered hair. The highly erotic dance was a "savage" pas de deux offering the audience a display of modern primitivism that appealed to both the avant-garde set in its self-consciously mediated spectacle of Otherness but also had a more popular appeal as a rehearsal of the authentic, primitive Africanness located in France's colonial territories. In this way, the *danse* consolidated the colonial ideologies of a spectacle of absolute Otherness that implicitly invoked the Self's *mission civilisatrice* (civilizing mission) encountering the uncontrollable libidinous energies of the African Other.

Baker's role in the *danse* was reproduced several times over the next few years, each time with a new and more modern variant on the costumes. The feathers finally metamorphosed into a skirt of soft, plush bananas and then later into one of phallic metal spikes that only nominally resembled the iconically savage fruit that had come to stand for a primitivized world outside of Europe.

In 1985 the Paris Metro ran an advertising campaign using an image of a young black woman dressed only in a skirt made of a fringe of yellow Metro tickets. From a distance the tickets resemble playfully phallic bananas that are depicted in motion against her glossy, darkened skin. The woman's hair is plastered down in a brilliantined Eton crop, and her face is dis-

torted by a caricatured wide, thick-lipped smile. The Metro poster is a take on one of the many images of Josephine Baker that appeared around Paris in the 1920s. The metro advertisement, framed by the caption "Tickets Folies 2ème Voiture le Plus Célèbre Spectacle de Paris," is a reminder that Josephine Baker was one of the most celebrated "exotic" spectacles, both on and off the music hall stage. Although she subsequently reinvented herself as a *grande chanteuse* (great singer), distancing herself from her earlier primitive roles, it is the image of Baker half naked, dancing frenetically in a suggestively phallic girdle of bananas, that has persisted in French popular cultural memory. Baker went on to have a long career in entertainment and worked as a member of the French Resistance, for which she was awarded the Légion d'honneur and the Croix de guerre. However, it is her erotic *danse sauvage* that continues to resonate in French cultural memory, and the inclusion of her image in François Mitterrand's 1988 election video testifies to the endurance of her place in modern French culture.

Carole Sweeney

See also: Baudelaire, Charles-Pierre; Dance; Jazz; Mitterrand, François; Primitivism; Saint Louis; World War II.

References

Ezra, Elizabeth. *The Colonial Unconscious: Race and Culture in Interwar France.* Ithaca/London: Cornell University Press, 2000.

Gates, Henry Louis, and Karen C. C. Dalton. "Josephine Baker and Paul Colin: African American Dance Seen through Parisian Eyes." *Critical Inquiry* 24, no. 4 (1998): 903–934.

Haney, Lynn. *Naked at the Feast: A Biography of Josephine Baker.* New York: Dodd, Mead, 1981.

hooks, bell. *Black Looks: Race and Representation.* London: Turnaround, 1992.

O'Connor, Patrick, and Bryan Hammond, eds. *Josephine Baker.* London: Bullfinch, 1988.

Stovall, Tyler. *Paris Noir: African Americans in the City of Light.* New York: Houghton Mifflin, 1996.

BALDWIN, JAMES (1924–1987)

Novelist, essayist, playwright, and political activist, James Baldwin is one of the most important American writers of the twentieth century. His life is marked by a movement between France and the United States, by a consciously developed transatlantic "doubleness" that presents in binational terms the many other dualities that can be found in his biography.

Born in Harlem, New York, Baldwin was brought up by his mother and stepfather, a Baptist minister, both recent African American migrants from the South. A nervous and brilliantly articulate child, Baldwin channeled his passionate personality into an extraordinary early career as a boy preacher before losing his faith, exploring a developing homosexuality, and devoting his attention to writing. Managing to publish a few essays and a short story and also to secure the vague patronage of established writer Richard Wright, Baldwin set off in 1948 for Paris (as Wright had done the year before), having received a small writing fellowship.

Baldwin's period on the Left Bank was in many ways indicative of a wider phenomenon: many African American artists, musicians, and writers had come to Paris in an attempt to escape the systematic racism of the United States. Baldwin was, however, no darling of the existentialists, rejected the doctrines of "committed litera-ture," and had little interest in the poetic declarations of francophone négritude. Upon the publication of essays like "Equal in Paris" and "Encounter on the Seine: Black Meets Brown" (published in *Notes of a Native Son,* 1955) and his first two novels, *Go Tell It on the Mountain* (1953) and *Giovanni's Room* (1956), it was in the United States, not France, that Baldwin's star began to grow.

Remaining relatively obscure in Paris, Baldwin returned to the United States in 1957, desperate to engage actively with the major political problem—the nonexistent civil rights of American blacks—in his native land rather than fruitlessly chatter about the major problem—the anticolonial revolution in Algeria—in his country of adoption. Meanwhile, Baldwin's writing reached a peak with the monumental novel *Another Country* (1962). If the first novel had been an all-black (and relatively straight) American epic, and the second an all-white, gay European tragedy with Jamesian overtones, the third depicted a world of ceaseless fluctuation between black and white, between homo- and heterosexuality, and between France and the United States. Rufus, Vivaldo, Yves, and the rest of Baldwin's Balzacian cast of French and American characters illustrate their creator's reluctance to remain in one position, and they inhabit a narrative whose explosive and often painful energy results from precisely this tension. Interestingly, *Another Country,* as much as Baldwin's alliances with Malcolm X and other militants, helped to generate an enormous Federal Bureau of Investigation dossier on Baldwin.

Moving to the Provençal village of Saint-Paul de Vence in 1972, Baldwin spent the remaining years of his life commuting between France and the United

States, continuing to write. He was awarded the Légion d'honneur in 1986 and died in Saint-Paul de Vence in 1987.

Andrew Asibong

See also: Gay Movement; Literary Relations; Wright, Richard.

References

Campbell, James. *Talking at the Gates: A Life of James Baldwin.* London: Faber and Faber, 1991.

———. *Exiled in Paris: Richard Wright, James Baldwin, Samuel Beckett, and Others on the Left Bank.* New York: Scribner, 1995.

BALLOONING

Although the hot air balloon, invented in 1783 by the Montgolfier brothers and shortly followed by the invention of a hydrogen-filled balloon, is associated with Anglo-French relations or, more specifically, Anglo-French rivalry, the connections between France and the United States concerning balloons are numerous.

If 1783 is the year in which the balloon was invented, for Americans it is also significant as the year in which the peace treaty ending the American Revolution was signed. Benjamin Franklin is of course known as the diplomat who negotiated this treaty, but he was also a keen scientist, whose experiments into electricity led not only to the development of lightning rods but also to a complete reevaluation of the nature of electricity itself. Franklin, therefore, enthusiastically joined the Parisians to witness the launch of the first aerostat that the capital had seen, a hydrogen balloon designed by Mr. Charles and Mr. Robert that took off from Paris on August 27. A member of the Royal Society of London, Franklin sent copious reports to the society's chairman, Sir Joseph Banks, detailing the experiments that had taken Paris by storm and listing suggested uses of the vehicle as a means of preserving game in the cool regions of the sky, of collecting ice, or even as a form of sightseeing offering a bird's-eye view over the surrounding area. Following the first manned balloon flight on November 20, 1783, he developed the latter suggestion more seriously, prophetically imagining the use of balloons to observe enemy movements during a siege or even for communications between a besieged town and the outside world. Moreover, like many of his contemporaries, Franklin also imagined the horrors of a war waged from the sky by means of balloons and held out hope that the new invention might be able to convince rulers of the folly of war. Yet if Franklin dreamed of peace, he could not resist expressing a certain "mocking" surprise that the British were not involved in the development of flight and in a letter to Sir Joseph goes as far as identifying himself with the French when he talks about the national characteristics necessary to develop the invention.

Franklin's theory that the balloon would one day be used in warfare was put into practice in the Napoleonic era, when a military school of aeronautics was formed at Meudon. Used successfully for observations during the battle of Fleurus and on other occasions, the military school was closed in the early nineteenth century when Napoléon lost interest in balloons, and was not reestablished until the Franco-Prussian War and the siege of Paris in 1870, when balloons enabled important people and posts to escape from the encircled capital. Before this, however, the American Civil War had already proved the usefulness of a balloon corps for observation. Under the command of Professor Thaddeus Lowe,

A hot air balloon similar to the one in which the French political leader Léon Gambetta escaped from Paris in order to organize the resistance to the invading Prussians during the Franco-Prussian War is seen being inflated in the Place Saint-Pierre (ca. 1870). (Hulton-Deutsch Collection/Corbis)

information gathered from the balloons was sent to general headquarters via telegraph, which provided the Union generals with up-to-date information on enemy movements before, during, and after battles and enabled the soldiers to fire cannons accu-rately on targets that could not be physi-cally seen from the ground. The Confeder-ates also attempted to establish a balloon corps, first with a Montgolfier balloon and later with a hydrogen balloon constructed from multicolored patches of silk, the different colors and patchwork effect leading to the legend that it had been made from the material of silk dresses donated by the ladies of the Confederacy.

Jules Verne set the beginning of his novel, *L'Île mystérieuse* (The Mysterious Island, 1874), in the besieged city of Richmond, from which the principal characters who are prisoners of war escape by means of a balloon. The balloon is carried by a hurricane for five days and travels an amazing distance of 6,000 to 7,000 miles before finally coming down just short of the mysterious island. The balloon corps operational during the Civil War had had to cope with storms, but the inspiration for the long-distance balloon journey that awaits Verne's characters also came from his more recent acquaintance with the adventures of balloonists attempting to leave Paris during the Franco-Prussian War. In one incident the balloon was in danger of being blown out to sea, but the balloonists just managed to land on Belle Ile, and in another the balloon traveled more than 900 miles in fifteen hours to land in Norway. In Verne's text, the balloonists end up on an island that is not marked on any map, which they significantly baptize l'Ile Lincoln.

L'Île mystérieuse is not the only Vernian text to incorporate a balloon into its narrative. Indeed, his first successful novel, *Cinq Semaines en ballon* (Five Weeks in a Balloon, 1863), is, as its title suggests, centered around the adventures linked to a long balloon journey that takes the central characters, Dr. Samuel Fergusson, Dick Kennedy, and Fergusson's loyal servant Joe, over central Africa to discover the source of the Nile River and map previously uncharted territory. Although Verne's inspiration for this story came from diverse sources, it is beyond doubt that Edgar

Allan Poe's works, including *The Balloon Hoax* (1850) and *The Unparalleled Adventure of One Hans Pfaall* (1835), heavily influenced his writing. In the year following the publication of *Cinq Semaines en ballon*, Verne published a critical essay on Poe in which, although he openly admired the American's approach to fiction, he criticized the way in which the bounds of scientific credibility became mixed up with the bounds of the fantastic. Unlike Poe, Verne prided himself on the scientific realism of his work, and if he was inspired by the American author, he also set himself apart from him, defining his work as being all the better for not being a hoax. Often cited as one of the founding figures of science fiction whose works were translated into many languages, Verne had an influence on world literature that is without question. Among the authors that Verne's science fiction may have influenced is Mark Twain. The similarities between *Tom Sawyer Abroad* (in which Tom, Huck, and Jim accidentally get taken up in a balloon and cross the Atlantic for a series of adventures, published in 1894) and *Cinq Semaines en ballon* are too close to be pure coincidence.

Kate Turner

See also: American Civil War; Aviation; Baudelaire, Charles-Pierre; Bonaparte, Napoléon; Franklin, Benjamin; Poe, Edgar Allan; Twain, Mark; Verne, Jules.

References

Evans, Charles M. *The War of the Aeronauts: The History of Ballooning in the Civil War.* Mechanicsburg, PA: Stackpole Books, 2000.

Lopez, Claude-Anne. *Mon Cher Papa: Franklin and the Ladies of Paris.* New Haven: Yale University Press, 1990.

Mckeithan, D. M. "Mark Twain's *Tom Sawyer Abroad* and Jules Verne's *Five Weeks in a Balloon.*" *Studies in English* 28 (1949): 257–271.

BARDOT, BRIGITTE (1934–)

French actress, born in Paris in 1934.

Together with Betty Grable (1916–1973), Lana Turner (1921–1995), and Marilyn Monroe (1926–1962), Brigitte Bardot was one of the most beautiful and photogenic blondes ever to have graced the silver screen. However, whereas her American counterparts were sophisticated Hollywood studio creations destined for mass consumption, her naturalness and her unpredictability made her a unique and atypical movie star.

Bardot was born into a middle-class family. As a child, she trained as a ballet dancer and studied theater. She acted in her first films as a teenager in the early 1950s, but it was her work as a model that first generated interest and allowed her to ensure a fan base in Italy and Britain. In 1956, she starred in her first important feature film, *Et Dieu créa la femme* (*And God Created Woman*), directed by her first husband Roger Vadim. The film quickly became the symbol of a new youth culture. She embodied overt sexuality lacking artifice. It was less her acting skills than her astonishing physique that made her famous on both sides on the Atlantic: nude scenes and the portrayal of a natural and uncomplicated female sexuality marked the first controversy of a career that would include many. Her famous pout, her hairdos, and her impeccable sense of style turned her into a major fashion icon, influencing other female movie stars such as Julie Christie (b. 1941) and Jane Fonda (b. 1937).

Bardot's film career then took off but spanned only two decades. Although not a great dramatic actress, she gave credible performances in *Vie privée* (Malle, 1962) and *Le Mépris* (Godard, 1963), by far her best works. Her vitality and natural spon-

Brigitte Bardot leading a campaign against the culling of baby seals. (Brozeck Miroslaw/Corbis Sygma)

taneity worked better in comedies such as in *Viva Maria!* (Malle, 1965). Her costars included some of the major French actors of the time, such as Jean Gabin (1904–1976), Annie Girardot (b. 1931), Jeanne Moreau (b. 1928), and Michel Piccoli (b. 1925), to name but a few.

Bardot gave up acting in 1973 to dedicate herself to animal welfare (a rather unappreciated cause in France). In the late 1970s, she launched a violent attack against seal hunting in Canada. Many Canadians felt that her campaign ("Canadiens assassins") was an expression of culture bashing, repositioning issues of Canadian national identity in terms of colonialism.

In addition to her sculptural beauty, Bardot's private life attracted much attention from fans and the media alike. Her marriages to Roger Vadim, actor Jacques Charrier (b. 1936, the father of her only child, Nicolas), and millionaire Gunter Sachs (from whom she separated after two months); her three suicide attempts; and her often provocative statements all generated passion and fueled "Bardot-mania" ("bardolâtrie") that would never really abandon her. Indeed, even when out of the spotlight, controversy still followed her. Her marriage to Bernard Dormale, a *Front National* sympathizer, upset many. So too did her two autobiographical books, *Initiales B. B.* and *Un Cri dans le silence,* which were seen by many to contain regrettably politically incorrect comments on immigrants and homosexuals and which further damaged the credibility of her fight for animal welfare.

Florian Grandena

See also: Cinema, 1945 to the Present; Fonda, Jane; Godard, Jean-Luc; Malle, Louis; Vadim, Roger.

References

de Beauvoir, Simone Ortner. "Brigitte Bardot and the Lolita Syndrome." *Les Ecrits de Simone de Beauvoir.* Ed. Claude Francis and Fernande Gontier. Paris: Gallimard, 1970: 363–376.

French, Sean. *Bardot.* London: Pavillion Press, 1996.

Nadeau, C. "B. B. and the Beasts: Brigitte Bardot and the Canadian Seal Controversy." *Screen* 37, no. 3 (autumn 1996): 240–250.

BARNES, DJUNA (1892–1982)

American expatriate writer, poet, journalist, playwright, illustrator, and portrait painter, born at Cornwall-on-the-Hudson, New York, in 1892.

Barnes was a well-known figure between the wars in the literary scenes of New York, London, Berlin, and Paris, where she lived for nearly fifteen years. Although she never received a formal education in her youth, after her unconventional parents divorced, Barnes studied art at the Pratt Institute and the Arts Students League of New York. While living in Greenwich Village, she became a successful and financially independent journalist and a self-styled, self-fashioned woman, avant-garde and bisexual, renowned for her caustic wit, she lived a cultivated bohemian life in the company of other artists, photographers, and writers such as Marcel Duchamp and William Carlos Williams. She wrote several one-act plays that were produced by the Provincetown Players (1919–1920) and was an original member of the Theater Guild. At times using the pseudonym "Lydia Steptoe," she also began writing illustrated stories, articles, and theatrical reviews for New York newspapers and magazines.

Between 1913 and 1931, Barnes supported herself financially as a journalist by writing for mass periodicals and daily newspapers, although she thought of her popular journalism as "rubbish." Barnes's reputation as a writer, however, was established by the publication of *The Book of Repulsive Women* (1915), a collection of poetry and drawings; *A Book,* a second collection of stories and drawings (1923); *Ryder* (1928), a semiautobiographical novel written in Chaucerian style tracing family trauma (it was published in expurgated form in the United States after the illustrations were deemed too risqué and objections were made to passages suggesting religious irreverence or referring to bodily functions); and *Ladies Almanac,* a privately published, highly spirited satire of Natalie Barney's expatriate, lesbian literary salon in Paris (1928) that was also banned by U.S. Customs.

Sent to Paris on a journalist assignment by *McCalls* magazine in 1921, Barnes joined other American expatriate writers and artists who had taken up residence there, including Gertrude Stein and Ezra Pound. She was especially close friends with Mina Loy and Natalie Barney. In Paris, Barnes met and began a passionate love affair with Thelma Wood, a silverpoint artist who was later fictionalized as the elusive Robin Vote in Barnes's internationally known, experimental work, *Nightwood* (1936). Another semiautobiographical story, the novel is set mostly in Paris, and follows the disastrous relationships between Robin Vote, an American expatriate and bisexual woman, and those who are inexorably drawn to her, only to lose her. Shaped by Barnes during her stay at Peggy Guggenheim's Hayford Hall in southwestern England in 1932 following the breakup of her relationship to Thelma Wood, *Nightwood*—thought to be a profound meditation on women's relationships—is now considered a twentieth-century classic.

At the outbreak of World War II and following treatment for alcoholism, Barnes returned to New York. In 1941 she moved into a small apartment at Patchin Place in Greenwich Village, where she lived a very private life until her death in 1982. During her years there, Barnes published a few poems and a "bestiary" called *Creatures in an Alphabet.* In those years she was elected to the National Institute of Arts and Letters (1959) and published one more major work, *The Antiphon* (1958), a verse drama in the style of Jacobean dramatists that staged the conflict between a daughter and her mother over incestuous family relationships. In a letter, one of Barnes's brothers claimed that *The Antiphon* was written in a spirit of revenge against her family (Herring, pp. 280–281), but Djuna Barnes insisted that instead she was looking for justice.

Jodey Castricano

See also: Barney, Nat(h)alie Clifford; Duchamp, Marcel; Literary Relations; Pound, Ezra Loomis; Stein, Gertrude; Williams, William Carlos; World War II.

References

Benstock, Shari. *Women of the Left Bank: Paris, 1900–1940.* Austin: University of Texas Press, 1986.

Herring, Phillip. *Djuna: The Life and Work of Djuna Barnes.* New York: Viking, 1995.

O'Neal, Hank. *"Life Is Painful, Nasty and Short . . . in My Case It Has Only Been Painful and Nasty." Djuna Barnes, 1978–1981: An Informal Memoir.* New York: Paragon House, 1990.

BARNEY, NAT(H)ALIE CLIFFORD (1876–1972)

American writer Natalie Clifford Barney was born to a wealthy and socially distinguished family and is probably best remembered for living her life on a grand scale and being a prominent salonist of early twentieth-century expatriate Paris. Her parents came from wealthy Ohio families, and her mother Alice, an accomplished painter who studied in Paris with James Whistler, encouraged her daughter's interest in literature and the arts. Having been sent to a French boarding school at the age of eleven, Barney returned to the United States in 1889 and from then on frequently visited France before settling there permanently in 1902.

In 1909, Barney moved to 20, rue Jacob on the Parisian Left Bank, where she was soon hosting her famous Friday salons, which continued for almost sixty years. This artistic community included a wide range of cultural celebrities such as Auguste Rodin, Rainer Maria Rilke (1875–1926), Colette, James Joyce (1882–1941), Paul Valéry (1871–1945), Gertrude Stein, Alice B. Toklas, T. S. Eliot (1888–1965), Ezra Pound, Jean Cocteau, André Gide (1869–1951), Djuna Barnes, Sylvia Beach, Truman Capote (1924–1984), and Françoise Sagan (b. 1935).

Famously nicknamed "The Amazon" by poet Rémy de Gourmont, Natalie Barney lived as she chose and gracefully rebelled against Victorian mores and conventions, refusing to wear corsets, smoking cigarettes, and openly celebrating her love of women. She conducted affairs with such figures as the courtesan Liane de Pougy, poet Renée Vivien, painter Romaine Brooks, and Oscar Wilde's niece Dolly Wilde. Her scandalous *rive gauche* (Left Bank) lifestyle is depicted in literary works by the likes of Radclyffe Hall (1880–1943), Ezra Pound, and Djuna Barnes, who portray her as the rather thinly disguised heroine who defies society and tradition.

Natalie Barney published twelve books, all but one and a half written and published in French: *The One Who Is Legion, or A. D.'s After-Life,* her only novel, was written and published in English in 1930, and *Poems and Poèmes: Autres Alliances,* written half in English, half in French, was published simultaneously in Paris and New York in 1920. Barney's oeuvre includes poetry, fiction, drama, memoirs, and collections of *pensées* (thoughts), and it resists the societal norm, expressing her revolutionary and progressive attitudes toward life, sex, and womanhood. Her first book, *Quelques Portraits—sonnets de femmes* (1900), contains French love poems written to former and current lovers, whereas *Actes et entr'actes* (1910) is a strongly feminist collection of verse plays and poems. Barney published three collections of *pensées: Eparpillements* (1910), *Pensées d'une Amazone* (1920), and *Nouvelles Pensées de l'Amazone* (1939). Her most accessible book is probably *Aventures de l'esprit* (1929), a series of portraits of writers such as Stein, Colette, Barnes, and Marcel Proust (1871–1922). Barney's last book *Traits et portraits* (1963), containing literary sketches as well as essays, was published when she was eighty-seven.

Although her publications spanned more than six decades and both sides of the Atlantic, Barney's literary achievement is overshadowed by her prominent social position among French and American artists and intellectuals. She died in Paris in 1972.

Sandra Kaiser

See also: Barnes, Djuna; Beach, Sylvia;
Cocteau, Jean; Colette; Literary Relations;
Pound, Ezra Loomis; Stein, Gertrude;
Toklas, Alice B.; Whistler, James.

References

Benstock, Shari. *Women of the Left Bank:
Paris, 1900–1940*. London: Virago Press,
1987.

Rodriguez, Suzanne. *Wild Heart, A Life:
Natalie Clifford Barney's Journey from
Victorian America to the Literary Salons of
Paris*. New York: Ecco, 2002.

Weiss, Andrea. *Paris Was a Woman: Portraits
from the Left Bank*. London:
HarperCollins, 1995.

BARRIN DE LA GALISSONIÈRE, ROLAND-MICHEL, MARQUIS (1693–1756)

Born in Rochefort, France, La Galissonière became a midshipman in Rochefort in 1710. His life was spent mainly as a naval officer. In the years 1710–1746 he went through several promotions. Though mostly stationed at Rochefort, he served in various capacities in a number of locations, including several along the Atlantic coast—Ile Royale, Canada (later Cape Breton Island), the West Indies, the Mediterranean, and along the coasts of Spain, Africa, and Brazil. On May 1, 1747, he was appointed commandant general in New France. His position entitled him to all the duties and powers of a governor-general of New France, as well as the latter's salary, but he could not be appointed to that position because there already was a governor-general, Jacques-Pierre de Taffanel de La Jonquière, Marquis (1685–1752). The latter had been taken prisoner by the British during the War of the Austrian Succession (1740–1748). The minister of the navy, Jean-Frédéric Phélypeaux, comte de Maurepas (1701–1781), who had supported La Galissonière's appointment, appreciated the fact that he immediately accepted the post that he had not sought. In fact, he had just refused an offer for a similar post in Saint-Domingue.

La Galissonière arrived in Quebec on September 19, 1747, and stayed for two years. His mandate was characterized by the increasingly expansionist policy of the British continental provinces. With little support in terms of money and manpower on the part of the French Ministry of the Navy, which was responsible for the French colonies, he implemented a self-sufficient defensive strategy. He continued to rely on a system of alliances with the aboriginal nations; tried to keep the Americans at bay through the building of a line of fortified posts along the Ohio valley; and curbed the traditional profit-seeking attitude of the French officers toward their appointments as commanders in the western forts, which was often disadvantageous to the aboriginal peoples, who then turned to the British. Meanwhile, he tried to boost the demography of New France by favoring the arrival of new settlers and supporting the development of agriculture, livestock breeding, and industrial activities such as the Quebec shipyards and the Saint-Maurice ironworks (Forges Saint-Maurice) near Trois-Rivières. La Galissonière left Quebec for good on September 24, 1749, and North America a few weeks later, when he sailed from Louisbourg headed for France on or shortly before October 21, 1749.

After his return to France, which La Galissonière welcomed, he was appointed a member of the joint British-French North American boundary committee (1749) and later saw naval action in the early stages of the French and Indian War (1754–1763).

Before the official declaration of war, his capture of the British island of Minorca (June 29, 1756) was the military highlight of his career, although that episode in particular must be attributed more due to the British commander's lack of initiative than to the boldness of La Galissonière's own strategy. La Galissonière died in Montereau, France, in 1756.

Luca Codignola

See also: French and Indian War; Louisbourg; New France; Ohio; Quebec; Rochefort; Santo Domingo.

References

Groulx, Lionel-Adolphe. *Roland-Michel Barrin de La Galissonière, 1693–1756.* Toronto: University of Toronto Press, 1970.

Pritchard, James S. *Louis XIV's Navy 1748–1762: A Study of Organization and Administration.* Kingston/Montreal: McGill-Queen's University Press, 1987.

BARTHES, ROLAND (1915–1980)

French cultural theorist, semiotician, and essayist, Roland Barthes has had a considerable impact across the Atlantic, especially in the United States, Canada, and Brazil. The writers Susan Sontag and Paul de Man have been particularly influenced by his writing.

Throughout his career Barthes made regular visits to the United States, in the 1950s, 1960s, and 1970s, speaking at conferences (for example, on the avant-garde in New York in 1967) and publishing his famous article "The Death of the Author" in the avant-garde magazine *Aspen* in the same year. His writings on American cultural phenomena are numerous: from Billy Graham (b. 1918), Charlie Chaplin (1889–1977), and Edward Steichen's "The Family of Man" (1957) exhibition in *Mythologies*

(1957)—an acerbic collection of skits on contemporary media culture of the 1950s (with a faint hint of anti-Americanism typical of 1950s France)—to his appreciation of Bernard Buffet's paintings of New York, written on his own return from New York in 1959. He was also a close friend of the Cuban novelist Severo Sarduy, and Barthes's influence can be seen in the latter's writing.

But perhaps his most important and lasting impact on the transatlantic dialogue between France and the United States is his role in the avant-garde journal *Tel Quel.* Barthes participated in the vogue for American modern art (and poetry) in France led by Telquelian Marcelin Pleynet in the late 1960s and throughout the 1970s. Pleynet helped to sensitize a (hitherto suspicious) French audience to the work of artists such as Robert Motherwell and Cy Twombly, and to minimal art. Barthes wrote important pieces on Saul Steinberg (in 1976) and on Cy Twombly. Commissioned by the Whitney Museum of Modern Art for a retrospective on Twombly in 1979, Barthes's piece, "The Wisdom of Art," presents Twombly essentially as a symbolist, although, as Marjorie Wellish argues (1997, 209), "Europe, not America, remained more hospitable to art nurtured in the legacy of symbolism." Though not specifically on Atlantic matters, Barthes's catalog essay illustrates the visual and writerly links between American modernism and French poststructuralism.

In addition to writing on pop art and Andy Warhol in this late 1970s period, Barthes was also well acquainted with photographer Richard Avedon, writing about his portraits as well as Robert Mapplethorpe's in his famous *Camera Lucida* (1980).

Andy Stafford

See also: Painting; Photography; Sarduy, Severo; *Tel Quel;* Theory.
References
Knight, Diana, ed. *Critical Essays on Roland Barthes.* New York: G. K. Hall, 2000.
Sontag, Susan, ed. *A Barthes Reader.* New York: Hill and Wang, 1982.
Wellish, Marjorie. "The Art of Being Sparse, Porous, Scattered." *Writing the Image after Roland Barthes.* Ed. Jean-Michel Rabaté. Philadelphia: University of Pennsylvania Press, 1997: 201–216.

BARTHOLDI, FRÉDÉRIC-AUGUSTE (1834–1904)

French sculptor, born in Colmar.

Bartholdi's most famous work is his colossal *Liberty Enlightening the World,* better known now as the Statue of Liberty, installed in New York City harbor in 1886. A believer in the Republic, and a man of great ambitions, entrepreneurial skills, and energy, Bartholdi made the most of his modest talents by committing himself to patriotic, sometimes colossal public monuments. Besides the Statue of Liberty, which was as much a fund-raising diplomatic achievement as a technological sculptural innovation, Bartholdi created the colossal stone sculpture *The Lion of Belfort* (1880) to commemorate the bravery of his fellow Alsatians during the Franco-Prussian War (1870–1871), in which he himself had served in the National Guard. Commissioned by the French government in gratitude for American support during the Franco-Prussian War, Bartholdi's *Lafayette Arriving in America* was unveiled in 1876 in New York City's Union Square.

The idea of a monument to liberty, French-American friendship, and the centennial of U.S. independence was first conceived, according to Bartholdi, by the Republican Edouard de Laboulaye in 1865.

Nevertheless, in the 1860s, Bartholdi concentrated on the design of a colossal statue of an Egyptian fellah (peasant) woman that he hoped would serve as a lighthouse at the Suez Canal. *Egypt Bringing Light to Asia* was doubtlessly inspired by his own youthful voyage to Egypt in 1855–1856, during which he made several drawings of fellah women at the banks of the Nile and also 105 quite beautiful calotypes, not only of immense stone ruins like the *Colossi of Memnos* but also of empty, atmospheric landscapes. Bartholdi returned to Egypt in 1869, only months before the inauguration of the Suez Canal, to sell his lighthouse to the Egyptian leader Ismaïl Pasha, but he turned it down. Only after the Franco-Prussian War did Bartholdi shift his attention to Laboulaye's American project. Despite Bartholdi's later public protests to the contrary, the American statue was an adaptation of the earlier Suez Canal lighthouse. Bartholdi repeatedly traveled to the United States, first in 1871 to seek support for the plan and also to identify the best location. It was Bartholdi who selected Bedloe's Island in New York harbor. To promote his projects, he returned to the United States in 1876–1877, 1885, 1886, and again in 1893. The Statue of Liberty was erected in the outskirts of Paris between 1880 and 1884, where it became a tourist attraction; it was dismantled and transported to New York City in 1885 and officially unveiled on Bedloe's Island in 1886.

Typically determined to exploit every opportunity, Bartholdi in 1887 proposed yet another public sculpture commemorating French-American friendship to the newspaper magnate Joseph Pulitzer, who had decisively contributed to fund-raising efforts in the United States. Simply inverting the model provided by the success of

New York Public Library. *Liberty: The French-American Statue in Art and History.* New York: Harper and Row, 1986.

Statue of Liberty, sculpture of lion, and inset portrait of sculptor Frédéric Auguste Bartholdi. (Library of Congress)

the Statue of Liberty, Bartholdi asked Pulitzer to launch a subscription for a statue of George Washington and the Marquis de Lafayette to serve as a gift from the United States to France in honor of the centennial of France's revolution. Despite Pulitzer's unwillingness to pay the full cost, the sculptor ultimately made two versions, one now standing in Paris's Place des Etats-Unis (1895) and another placed at 114th Street and Morningside Drive in New York City (1900). Bartholdi died in Paris on October 4, 1904.

Darcy Grimaldo Grigsby

See also: Lafayette, Marquis de; Photography; Republicanism; Sculpture; Statue of Liberty, The; Washington, George.
References
Betz, Jacques. *Bartholdi.* Paris: Editions de Minuit, 1954.

BASQUES

The Basques of France and Spain have long been regarded as the "mystery people" of Europe. Although much debated, the origin of their ancestors is unknown; and their language, Euskera, is non-Indo-European and linguistically unusual. The discovery of certain distinctive biological features has also fostered a view of the Basques as unique among European populations. They have the highest rate of type O blood and the lowest frequency of type B blood in Europe. They also have the highest rate of Rh negative factor in the world. Although attempts have been made to link modern Basques to Stone Age ancestors in southwestern France and northwestern Spain, more conservative estimates trace the Basques' presence in the area from 5000 to 3000 B.C.

Straddling the western Pyrenees, "the Basque country" (*Euskal Herria,* in Basque) consists of three provinces in France and four in Spain. Created by the Statutes of Autonomy passed in 1979 in Spain, the Basque Autonomous Community includes the provinces of Gipuzkoa, Bizkaia, and Araba. The fourth Spanish Basque province, Nafarroa, has its own autonomous statutes. In France, the provinces of Lapurdi, Behe Nafarroa, and Xiberoa have a population of some 263,000 people. The total population of the Basque country is just under 3 million.

In the sixteenth century, the colonization of the Americas involved Basque expertise in maritime activities, including shipbuilding and navigation, as well as colonial administration. Pioneers in the Atlantic whaling industry, Basques fished off Labrador and the Grand Banks of Newfoundland from as early as 1550 until the late seventeenth century. Basques were also extensively involved in cod fishing in the Gulf of Saint Lawrence, an area dominated by French and Spanish Basque enterprise for roughly half of the sixteenth century. Their influence extended to trade in furs, beluga, whalebone, and walrus. Both Basques and Bretons regularly visited Cape Breton to trade furs and to fish. English explorers and entrepreneurs challenged the commercial dominance of the Basques in the period 1585 to 1603. Many Basque ships were targeted by English privateers. One of the most famous was the French Basque vessel, the *Catherine de Saint Vincent,* with its cargo of oil, fish, and furs. The sister of Henry IV, Catherine (Princess of Bourbon), threatened reprisals against English ships trading with Basque ports if the ship and its goods were not released intact.

Many factors underpinned Basque emigration to New World destinations. French and Spanish colonialism drew Basques into trade, the military, and the church. Several other factors encouraged their diaspora across the Atlantic over the centuries: the Basque system of inheritance that allows only one heir; the economic, social, and political upheaval caused by the Napoleonic and Carlist Wars and the Spanish civil war; and limited economic opportunities at home for a largely rural Basque population.

From the 1830s until the start of the twentieth century, the French Basque provinces lost a substantial portion of their population to New World destinations, notably to Uruguay and Argentina. Emigra-

tion to the United States also proved an attractive option for Basques who were economically and/or politically oppressed and seeking new opportunities abroad. Most sought their fortunes in the California gold rush of the 1850s. Initially supplying the mining communities of the American West, Basques entered the sheep- and cattle-raising industry in California, Arizona, western Nevada, and Wyoming. Some turned to dairy farming. From the 1850s, San Francisco served as the main port of entry for French Basques. One of the first Basque hotels there served as an important social and business center for those involved in the livestock industry. By 1900, there were some 120,000 French Basques in California. In Southern California, Basques in the livestock trade often worked alongside French emigrants from Béarn. Thus began a process of chain migration linking the American West to the *pays basque* (Basque country). That process included the secondary migration of many Basques to different parts of the New World, as well as their return migration to the homeland, for economic, political, and social reasons and for varying lengths of time.

During the Spanish civil war (1936–1939), the French Basque country sheltered Basques opposed to Franco and was an embarkation point for exiles seeking a safe haven in the Americas. In 1937, the Basque government went into exile after the bombing of Bilbao. In 1941, the headquarters of the Basque government in exile were moved to New York by its president, Jose Antonio de Aguirre. He lived in New York until 1946 and taught at Columbia University.

During the Nazi occupation of France and the French Basque country (1940–1944), many Basques were involved in underground resistance networks that enabled Allied intelligence and military personnel, as well as thousands of refugees, to escape into Spain.

Basques in the Americas have affirmed and maintained their ethnic identity through a range of social, educational, and cultural avenues. In the late nineteenth and early twentieth centuries, Basque boardinghouses and hotels were key sources of information and mutual aid and helped Basques adapt to their new sociocultural and economic surroundings. As their needs changed, many Basque Americans sought to renew or to create cultural ties with their homeland and Basque heritage, largely through the creation of Basque centers or clubs, the first of which were formed in New York and Los Angeles at the start of the twentieth century. These organizations underpin Basque diaspora identity and seek to preserve Basque traditions and heritage. They do so through commensality at dinners and festivals and through collective participation and instruction in Basque dance, music, language, cooking, and sports (such as handball, pelota, and jai alai). In 2003, there were thirty-seven officially registered Basque centers in the United States, with thirteen in California. A further six centers are located in Mexico and Central America. In South America, most of the centers are found in Uruguay (nine) and in Argentina (eighty-four). The three officially registered Basque centers in France are located in Paris, Bordeaux, and Jurançon, near the French Basque country.

In 1973–1974, the North American Association of Basque Organizations (NABO) was formed in an attempt to increase communication and collaboration between French and Spanish Basque Americans. In 2003, NABO was composed of thirty-three Basque centers across the United States. According to the U.S. census of 2000, 57,793 people claimed Basque ancestry, of whom 20,868 lived in California.

Among the most prominent contemporary members of the French Basque American community, the Laxalt family of Nevada traces its roots to the province of Xiberoa. Paul Laxalt was governor of Nevada from 1967 until 1971 and then served as a U.S. senator (1974–1987). Robert Laxalt (1923–2001) is widely regarded as the literary spokesman of Basque Americans and was a founder of the University of Nevada Press, which has a Basque book series.

Although the majority of Basque Americans avoid involvement in the politics of the Basque country itself, the Basque Autonomous Government in Spain fosters close ties between the Basque homeland and Basque communities throughout the world. It provides financial support for Basque cultural activities and, among other initiatives, funds programs for diaspora youth, potential leaders of the global Basque community.

Sandra Ott

See also: Argentina; Brittany; Fishing; Fur Trade; Language; Mexico; Newfoundland; Piracy and Privateers; Saint Lawrence River; Whaling; World War II.

References

Douglass, William, and Jon Bilbao. *Amerikanuak: Basques in the New World.* Reno: University of Nevada Press, 1975.

MacClancy, Jeremy. "Biological Basques, Sociologically Speaking." *Social and Biological Aspects of Ethnicity.* Ed. Malcolm Chapman. New York: Oxford University Press, 1993: 92–129.

Totoricagüena, Gloria. *Identity, Culture, and Politics in the Basque Diaspora.* Reno: University of Nevada Press, 2004.

BATAILLE, GEORGES (1897–1962)

One of the most influential French thinkers of the twentieth century.

Bataille was associated with the surrealists, was influential in returning Friedrich Nietzsche and G. W. F. Hegel to prominence in France, and was the author of pornographic novels, books on art, and texts of nihilistic mysticism and "sacred sociology." His most significant theory is that of "the accursed share," in which waste, loss, eroticism, expenditure (*dépense*), and transgression take priority over accumulation, reproductive sex, saving, rationality, and the law. This theory pits "archaic" customs against capitalism, using practices present in pre-Columbian America, as well as among the peoples of the northwest of North America, to oppose the world of capitalist rationality. Bataille refers to Marcel Mauss's theorization of the potlatch, where one group seeks to outbid the other, either in giving or destroying their own materials. The concept of property that underpins liberal capitalism is absent here and is challenged, and the endless recycling of gift and countergift offers a new way, for Bataille, of conceptualizing a world not limited to capitalist economics. This theory is further developed through an analysis of the role of sacrifice in Aztec society. The person to be sacrificed is "the accursed share"—that which must be sacrificed so that the rest may live. Both practices show an awareness of a "general economy" of waste and destruction, which is how he sees the universe fundamentally operating, despite modern society's qualms about what cannot be rationalized and subject to the restricted form of the economy.

Bataille was not afraid to romanticize these earlier societies. As early as 1928, he noted the high level of civilization enjoyed throughout pre-Columbian America and also asserted that sacrifice did not hinder the development of that civilization but gave those societies their specific character, as well as a better sense of death and how humanity related to the world. He also clearly distinguished between the recognizably (to European eyes) advanced Maya, the violent sacred underpinning of the Aztec world, and the hierarchical bureaucracy of the Inca. He did not, however, recommend a return to sacrifice but a reassessment of the distribution of wealth. Writing *The Accursed Share* just after World War II, Bataille suggested the Marshall Plan be extended and establish a principle of the gift, in order to diminish the possibility of war (because war is the outcome of having an unspent surplus). So although the modern United States was a paradigm, for Bataille, of the wrong sort of economy, its strength and growth meant that it must expend, both for its own good and that of everyone else.

Paul Hegarty

See also: Marshall Plan, The; Painting; Pornography; Theory; World War II.

References

Hegarty, Paul. *Georges Bataille*. London: Sage, 2000.

Richman, Michèle. *Reading Georges Bataille: Beyond the Gift*. Baltimore: Johns Hopkins University Press, 1982.

BATON ROUGE

Capital of Louisiana, named by French explorers in 1699.

In 1682, René Robert Cavelier, sieur de La Salle, claimed for France all the lands

The Battle of Baton Rouge, Louisiana, August 4, 1862. (Library of Congress)

drained by the Mississippi River and its tributaries, calling it "Louisiana" in honor of Louis XIV. In 1699, an exploration party under the command of Pierre Le Moyne, sieur d'Iberville, stopped on the east bank of the Mississippi River at the first high ground—approximately 100 miles from the coast and 175 miles up the river—where they found a vertical pole stained with animal blood that served as the boundary marker for two Indian tribes. They named the place Baton Rouge, "red stick." After receiving a land grant in 1718, Bernard Diron Dartaguette was the first to settle the area, but his small plantation failed by 1727. As a town, Baton Rouge dates from 1763, when, following their victory in the French and Indian War, the British established a military outpost under the name Fort New Richmond. Spain conquered the town in 1779 and renamed it

Fort San Carlos and the area West Florida. When by the Treaty of San Ildefonso in 1800 Napoléon Bonaparte compelled Spain to return much of Louisiana to France and then in 1803 sold it to the United States, West Florida was not included. U.S. settlers forced the issue by seizing Fort San Carlos in 1810 and raising the flag of the "West Florida Republic," which was quickly replaced by the U.S. flag. In 1812, when Louisiana became the eighteenth state, West Florida was included within it, and the town reverted to the name Baton Rouge. Until 1846 when it became the capital of Louisiana, Baton Rouge was known for little except for being the home of Zachary Taylor, elected president of the United States in 1848, and for a visit in 1825 from Gilbert, marquis de Lafayette. During the American Civil War, Louisiana was a secessionist state, and

Baton Rouge, by then a thriving river port, was occupied by Union forces in August 1862. Baton Rouge recovered slowly from the Civil War, its prosperity returning only with the decision in 1909 by Standard Oil (now Exxon) to construct a refinery. That began the petrochemical boom that, along with the deep-water port and the governmental operations attendant upon its status as state capital, sustained the city economically. Baton Rouge also became prominent in higher education. The Louisiana Seminary of Learning was established at Pineville in 1860, with William T. Sherman its first superintendent; it moved to Baton Rouge in 1869 and in 1877 was renamed Louisiana State University. Southern University, founded in 1879 at New Orleans to provide an undergraduate education for blacks and now the largest predominantly black university in the United States, moved in 1914 to Scotlandville, which was later incorporated into Baton Rouge. This combination of education, government, and industry has made the greater Baton Rouge area, which by the 2000 census had a population of 706,000, the most dynamic region in Louisiana.

Benjamin F. Martin

See also: Bonaparte, Napoléon; French and Indian War; Iberville, Pierre Le Moyne d'; La Salle, René-Robert Cavelier de, Sieur; Lafayette, Marquis de; Louisiana; Mississippi River.

References

Carleton, Mark T. *River Capital: An Illustrated History of Baton Rouge.* Woodland Hills, CA: Windsor Publications, 1981.

Davis, Edwin A. *Louisiana: The Pelican State.* Baton Rouge: Louisiana State University Press, 1985.

Meyers, Rose. *A History of Baton Rouge: 1699–1812.* Baton Rouge: Louisiana State University Press, 1976.

BAUDELAIRE, CHARLES-PIERRE (1821–1867)

French poet and translator, born in Paris, the son of François Baudelaire and his young wife Caroline Dufaÿs.

Caroline became a widow at the age of twenty-seven, when Baudelaire was only five. She then married General Aupick. At the age of twenty-one, Baudelaire received his father's inheritance, which he spent on clothes, books, expensive furniture, opium, and hashish. In 1841, in order to separate the young man from bad company, Aupick sent him under supervision to India, but he never arrived—a storm at sea forced his return to Paris. He told friends—even in letters—about his experience in Calcutta. Even though he did not go beyond the Mauritian islands, he often referred to India as a factual occurrence in his life, and as such, a permanent influence on his poetry. General Aupick was far from accepting the youngster's bohemian life or his relationship with Jeanne Duval, whom Baudelaire met in 1842 and who became his lifetime mistress. By that time, the prestigious Hotel Pimodan in Ile Saint-Louis was young Baudelaire's address.

After he had spent almost half his inheritance, in 1844 his family appointed a financial supervisor. His anguished letters show his difficulties in living on allowances. Most of the time he had creditors pursuing him. Despite these problems, Baudelaire worked hard as a literary and art critic and wrote poetry. His closest friends were artists and writers: Claude Monet, Eugène Delacroix, Théodore de Banville, Charles Asselineau, Félix Nadar, Théophile Gautier, Jean Courbet. In 1845 Baudelaire attempted suicide. Some believe the gesture was meant solely to move his mother.

Nothing changed: he continued to be shackled by his debts.

In 1857 Baudelaire published the first edition of *Les Fleurs du mal/The Flowers of Evil*, the most important European book of poetry of its time. In 1868 his *Prose Poems* proved to be even more innovative: his themes included time passing in split seconds, prostitution, and the ugly side of life. Undoubtedly, he was inspired by Edgar Allan Poe, whose writings he translated into French. It is rather difficult to determine Poe's exact influence on Baudelaire's poetry, however, because many of Baudelaire's poems were already written when he first read the American writer's works. Baudelaire himself acknowledges having been directly influenced by Poe when he wrote *Le Flambeau vivant/The Living Flame* for *Les Fleurs du mal*. He first published in 1852, in the *Paris Magazine, Edgar Allan Poe: Sa Vie et ses ouvrages* (Edgar Allan Poe: His Life and Works). During 1852 and 1853 Baudelaire translated several texts by Poe, which he published in various newspapers: *Histoires extraordinaires,* in 1857 *Nouvelles Histoires extraordinaires,* and in 1865 *Histoires grotesques et sérieuses.* Translation constituted the poet's only stable source of income. His admiration for the American writer was immense. He even mentioned their physical resemblance. For Baudelaire, Poe was a complete author: critic, poet, and novelist.

For Baudelaire, prosecution for *Les Fleurs du mal* for obscenity was a great sorrow. In 1867 Baudelaire died in his mother's arms in a bedroom the walls of which were covered with works by his friend Edouard Manet.

Raimunda Bedasee

See also: Literary Relations; Painting; Poe, Edgar Allan.

Reference
Marchi, Dudley M. "Baudelaire's America—Contrary Affinities." *Yearbook of General and Comparative Literature,* vol. 47: 37–52.

BAUDRILLARD, JEAN (1929–)

It is hard to match Baudrillard's influence in the world of contemporary culture and in the critique of that culture. He has been analyzing postmodernism since the early 1970s (although he rarely uses the word), has written highly controversial texts on war and terrorism, and brought the banal phenomena of today into the realm of theoretical discourse. Despite numerous visits to the United States in the early 1980s, Baudrillard's main connection to that country is through his texts, perhaps most notably in *America* (1988). To comment on contemporary politics and culture requires acknowledgement of America's centrality to the (globalized) world, and even though many European theorists did not pay substantial attention to the American role until the 1990s, Baudrillard has long maintained that the world we live in is driven and realized by America and phenomena that emanate from it. There are two standard ways of defining the American role, and Baudrillard does neither: for him, it is not a question either of political hegemony or of some sort of neocolonialism based on commercialized cultural exports. They are of course relevant but are secondary to the dominant state we are in: simulation.

According to Baudrillard, humans have always lived in a world of simulacra, but unlike Plato, his theory places no perfect form behind the things of this world that we perceive—there are only ever simulacra, or copies without an original. The modern world goes from simulacra based on production, where there is a gap between signifier and signified, such that meaning is produced (this occurs in tandem with capitalism), to full simulation, where there are only simulacra. Baudrillard also terms this condition "hyperreality," where there is an increased insistence on reality, which hastens its disappearance and the spread of simulation and the virtual. This is a historical, if necessarily ungrounded argument, based on the change in capitalism that flowed from the crash of 1929—consumer society and credit have to fill in the gaps. Speculative capitalism has to lose any link to real production, and finally, the crises of capitalism are seen to alter rather than remove capitalism. The effects of the Depression spread out from America, now clearly the economic capital of the world. The next key "moment" is the development of the mass media, and they find their complete form in America (this completion is still ongoing). The cold war replaces "real war," and Baudrillard writes of the spread of deterrence to all levels of culture such that nothing really happens anymore—even though something always *seems* to be happening. The end of the cold war confirms America's dominance, but not in the sense of victory—rather it is the dominance of a model that America itself has been caught up in—that is, simulation (there is no end of history, only the "illusion of the end").

Baudrillard is fascinated by celebrity but tends to analyze individuals (like Michael Jackson or Madonna) or individual events (Bill Clinton "not having sex"), rather than constructing a model for celebrity culture. Similarly, he does refer to

Hollywood, Disneyland, the strangeness (as he sees it) of California—but, in the case of Disneyland, for example, it is to argue that Disneyland covers up the fact of the unrealness of the rest of America. War, and America's role in it, whether during or after the cold war, is central to Baudrillard's presentation of the "world today": instead of emphasizing that reality is real because of its violence, war brings a further level of simulation. Vietnam, as the first televised war, undermined the realness of what was going on precisely as it was brought to the viewer in his or her home. It was a war that had no existence outside simulation, but—and this point is vital—it is still dangerous to be in or near one of these wars, possibly even more so, because the ends and actions of simulated war are less predictable and have less to do with concrete gains. The first Gulf War represented a heightening of the irreality of war for Baudrillard—it was a war that was not even happening as it was caught up in models of itself, the virtual reality of new technology, endless TV coverage, and the absence of much fighting. The Iraq War has only reiterated much of what Baudrillard said then.

More controversial still was Baudrillard's essay on the 2001 attack on the World Trade Center. Since the 1970s, this building had caught his attention—capitalism was exemplified in the Manhattan skyline, and that skyline was dominated by a symbol of dualistic monopoly. Furthermore, as he wrote in 2000, the World Trade Center expressed the drift into hyperreality of that same system. The September 11 attack on the building was an attack on the global system, but it also represented the violence of the global itself, turned back on itself. Baudrillard went on to say that "we" (presumably the

West) felt some sort of pleasure at the collapse, happy for "us" to be attacked. The towers then committed suicide, their collapse the only possible response to the extremity of the hijackers' suicides and murders. His point here is that the attack was a "symbolic exchange"—something that eludes rational calculation, and as he sees it, the "suicide" of the buildings is a reply rather than a weakness. He is on firmer ground when talking of Western or rather, in this case, American complicity at a practical level. Apart from conspiracy theories and the preventability of September 11, there is still the question of the perpetrators being based and trained in America, using American planes—illustrating for Baudrillard that the global is only ever attacking itself. More recently still (but before the second Gulf War), Baudrillard described the attack as a sort of credit card, allowing increased American violence in its "war on terrorism."

Like the essay on the September 11 attacks, *America* has also proved an awkward text, with its superficial reading of America as cinematic, shallow, idiotic, with its culture on the verge of becoming the desert that surrounds it. However, it has also been criticized for its praise of America, with its claim that America is a "realized utopia," a place of opportunity, cultural invention, and racial harmony. More interestingly, Baudrillard claims that America is the only truly modern society (and much of the book can be seen as a critique of French and European society) or a "primitive society of the future" (*America,* p. 7). Either way, it is to be seen as something different from Europe, and its banality or shedding of irony are markers of where culture is going (although the irony of ironic American comedy going global eludes him here).

His largest claim is that America is utopia: its founders believed that unlike other utopias, this one not only could exist, it already did, so America has always lived, as a result, as it if were utopia already. Baudrillard's point is not that it really is one but that it is one that has been made real, and it is all we will ever get as utopia—that is not an ideal society in reality but more the belief in it. Anyone who does not see it that way will be removed from positions of influence, and anyone who falls outside (like the ill or the homeless) will be forcibly excluded. The book as a whole tends to easy generalization, but its claims about utopia are nuanced and innovative.

Paul Hegarty

See also: Disneyland Paris; Iraq War; Madonna; 9/11: Political Perspectives; Theory; Television; Utopias; Vietnam War.

References
Baudrillard, Jean. *America.* London: Verso, 1988.
———. *The Spirit of Terrorism.* London: Verso, 2002.
Kellner, Douglas. *Jean Baudrillard: From Marxism to Postmodernism and Beyond.* Stanford: Stanford University Press, 1989.

BAZIN, ANDRÉ (1918–1958)

France's most influential film critic, celebrated for the importance he attributes to mise-en-scène (the way in which the world "out there" is framed and staged for the camera) and for his strong advocacy of a realist cinema.

To the dialectical and ideological use of montage by directors such as the Russian Marxist Sergei Eisenstein and to the stylization of the German expressionists, Bazin opposed a respect, deriving from his Catholic version of phenomenology, for the "world as it is," leading him to extol the openness—some might even say the messiness—of a Jean Renoir or a Roberto Rossellini as the quintessence of cinema. This in turn, along with his abiding interest in genre, meant that he more than any previous French or indeed European critic championed Hollywood cinema at its best. His first book dealt with Orson Welles, and the essays posthumously grouped as *What Is Cinema?* (1958–1962) address the Western or the film noir as eruditely and enthusiastically as they do the Italian neorealists or French auteurs such as Marcel Carné and Robert Bresson. Bazin's work can thus be understood as an important part of the postwar fascination with American culture. *Cahiers du cinéma,* which Bazin cofounded in 1951, was to continue this advocacy in a manner that profoundly influenced the future development of French cinema. Bazin's approach was less self-consciously auteurist than theirs (perhaps because, unlike the leading *Cahiers* writers, he never went on to direct films himself), placing more stress on cinema as process of production. The hitherto lowly cultural status of the Hollywood "dream factory" was for Bazin no obstacle to the access it provided to the essence of things as they are, in which respect it could be seen as the true heir to the poetic realism of the prewar French cinema.

Keith Reader

See also: *Cahiers du cinéma;* Catholic Church; Cinema, 1945 to the Present; Film Noir.
Referenece
Andrew, Dudley. *André Bazin.* Oxford/New York: Oxford University Press, 1978.

BEACH, SYLVIA (1887–1962)

The daughter of a New England Presbyterian minister, Sylvia Beach settled in Paris during World War I. In November 1919, together with her friend and partner, Adrienne Monnier, she set up a bookshop and lending library, Shakespeare and Company, which specialized in English and American books. In 1922, the shop moved to 12, rue de l'Odéon, across the street from Monnier's establishment, La Maison des Amis des Livres (The House of the Friends of Books). Shakespeare and Company soon became the favorite meeting place of American expatriates and French writers. Some of the early visitors included André Gide, André Maurois, Ezra Pound, and the American poet Robert McAlmon. During the 1920s, Gertrude Stein also became a regular visitor, alongside well-known French authors such as Paul Valéry. Shakespeare and Company contributed to establishing the European reputation of American writers, among them Ernest Hemingway and F. Scott Fitzgerald. Sylvia Beach famously financed the first edition of James Joyce's *Ulysses* (1922) at a time when the mainstream publishers rejected the book on account of its alleged pornography. Joyce's letters to Beach, published in 1987, bear witness to the invaluable role that Shakespeare and Company played for two decades in facilitating the intellectual exchanges between European and American writers. Only months after Joyce's untimely death in 1941, Beach had to remove all the books in the shop to the fourth floor of the building and paint out the sign, following the visit of a German officer who ordered the shop to be closed and threatened to confiscate the entire stock.

As described in Beach's compelling memoirs, the occupation ended with the arrival of American troops in 1944, when Hemingway himself "liberated" the bookshop and helped disperse snipers from the rooftop of Monnier's flat. Shakespeare and Company reopened on the Left Bank only in 1951, with a new name, Le Mistral, and under the management of another East Coast American bibliophile, George Whitman. With Sylvia Beach's agreement, Whitman resurrected the original name of the bookshop in 1964 and continued to provide shelter and support to struggling writers, who could live free of charge in the store and make use of its library. The first, censored, edition of Beach's memoirs came out in 1959, when the editors cut sections of her manuscript that dealt with "controversial" matters, such as the author's relationship with Adrienne Monnier. The same year, Beach played a significant part in the organization of the exhibition on American writers in Paris during the 1920s, which was held at the Centre Culturel Américain in Paris. A revised version of the same exhibition ("Paris of the Twenties: An Exhibition of Souvenirs of British, French, and American Writers at Shakespeare and Company") was hosted by the USIS (United States Information Service) gallery in London the following year. To this day, Sylvia Beach has remained one of the most prominent Americans in Paris, whose autobiographical work charts the evolution of famous anglophone writers (such as Samuel Beckett, Virginia Woolf, T. S. Eliot) and provides a vivid account of the interaction between the French and American cultural traditions from the early 1920s to the end of World War II.

Ramona Fotiade

See also: Fitzgerald, F. Scott; Hemingway, Ernest; Literary Relations; Pound, Ezra Loomis; Stein, Gertrude; World War I; World War II.

References

Banta, Melissa, and Oscar A. Silverman, eds. *James Joyce's Letters to Sylvia Beach, 1921–1940.* Bloomington: Indiana University Press, 1987.

Beach, Sylvia. *Shakespeare and Company.* London: Faber and Faber, 1960.

BEAU DOMMAGE

Quebec pop-folk music band.

Beau Dommage gained fame in the mid-1970s with melancholy ballads set in Montreal. Mixing the West Coast sound of melodic pop-folk with poetic lyrics and vocal harmonies, they became a successful and cross-generational band.

Beau Dommage was founded in 1972 by three Montreal university students, Pierre Huet (lyrics), Robert Léger (keyboards and flute), and Michel Rivard (guitar, vocals, lyrics, and composition). To this initial core were added Pierre Bertrand (guitar, bass, and voice; he replaced Huet in 1973), followed by Marie-Michèle Desrosiers (keyboards, vocals) and Réal Desrosiers (drums). In 1975, Michel Hinton (keyboards) succeeded Léger.

Influenced by the pop melodies of the Beatles and the West Coast sound of the late 1960s, Beau Dommage generally played pop-folk with an emphasis on acoustic guitars and vocal harmonies. The three singers often took turns for the lead or sang in chorus. They were received by the Quebec media and public as "true" Québécois artists who had managed to establish the first crossover between poetic lyrics in French and an Anglo-American pop style. Nearly all the artists wrote lyrics or composed melodies, but Michel Rivard did most of the songwriting.

Beau Dommage's songs are "realist" insofar as they are usually set in identifiable Montreal locales. They make reference to local districts ("Chinatown," 1974) and well-known streets (Rue Saint-Paul rhymes with "Le Blues d'la métropole," 1975). Their songs tend to describe the daily lives of recently uprooted city dwellers, setting compositions in a minor key to convey melancholy. Alluding to the illusory attraction of urban living for country folk, their song "La Complainte du phoque en Alaska" (1974) was an instant hit, which the "father" of Quebec popular music, Félix Leclerc, also recorded in an unprecedented gesture of encouragement.

Touring in France in the mid-1970s, Beau Dommage won the Best Foreign Act award for their second album in 1976 (*Où est passée la noce?/Where Did the Wedding Go?*). They produced four albums in the space of five years, but in 1978 the band split up after several members decided to try to lead solo careers. To mark their tenth anniversary, in 1984, the band reformed for two concerts in Quebec City and Montreal (later issued as two live recordings) and were awarded a Félix Leclerc prize by the Quebec recording association for their œuvre.

In 1992, the band once again reformed, this time to celebrate the 350th anniversary of the founding of Montreal, and appeared at Montreal's *Francofolies* festival. The rapturous response of their fans gave Beau Dommage the impetus to record a new album, which was released in 1994 and sold an incredible 200,000 copies in four weeks. Touring in Quebec in 1995, they sold over 50,000 tickets, which showed their loyal audience's support and their continuing commercial viability. This was followed in 1999 by the reissuance of a compilation album.

Barbara Lebrun

See also: Charlebois, Robert; *Francofolies, Les;* Leclerc, Félix; Montreal; Music (Folk); Music (Pop); Vigneault, Gilles.

References

Baillargeon, Richard, and Christian Côté. *Une Histoire de la musique populaire au Québec, Destination Ragou.* Montreal: Triptyque, 1991.

Thérien, Robert, and Isabelle d'Amours. *Dictionnaire de la musique populaire au Québec (1955–1992).* Quebec: IQRC, 1992.

BEAUCHEMIN, YVES (1941–)

Québécois author, born in Rouyn-Noranda, Quebec, in 1941.

In 1946, Beauchemin's parents decided to move to the small village of Clova. To occupy his time, Beauchemin would read for hours stories that took him to different worlds and made him appreciate writing his French essays at school. He then went to the University of Montreal, where he completed a degree in French and art history in 1965. Before becoming a full-time writer in 1983, he first taught literature at the Universities of Quebec and Montreal, wrote a humorous column for the magazine *Sept-jours* for three years, and then worked as musical adviser and researcher for Télé-Québec. Throughout this period, he continued to read his favorite classical authors, including Honoré de Balzac, Gustave Flaubert, Stendhal, Marcel Proust, and Jules Romains. His passion for reading led him to begin writing. He had already tried to write a novel by the time he was twelve years old, and later on he wrote a few short stories. Having published several short stories in magazines in the second half of the 1960s, he finally made a name for himself with his novel *L'Enfirouapé* (a Québécois word meaning to be manipulated or "had") in 1974, which won him the Prix France-Québec the following year. In 1981, his second novel *Le Matou* (*The Alley Cat*) brought him success, not only in Quebec but in France and many other countries as the novel was translated into seventeen languages. After receiving the Grand Prix Littéraire du Journal de Montréal and Prix de la Ville de Montréal in 1981, the book won the Prix du Livre de l'Eté in Cannes a year later. Ten years later, the same novel won the Grand Prix Littéraire des Lycéens d'Ile-de-France, voted for by secondary school students. In 1985, the adaptation of this novel for the cinema and television also became a great success.

Beauchemin's third novel, *Juliette Pomerleau/Juliette,* published in 1983, was also acclaimed in Quebec and in France, bringing him more prizes: the Prix du Grand Public du Salon du Livre de Montréal (1989), the Prix Jean-Giono (1990), the Prix des Lectrices de *Elle* (1990), and a nomination for the Prix Goncourt in 1989. A TV adaptation of *Juliette Pomerleau* was shown in Quebec in 1999. His fourth novel, *Les Emois d'un marchand de café/*The Emotions of a Coffee Seller, was first published in Paris in 1999 before being released in Montreal a year later. Beauchemin's other works include the novel *Le Deuxième Violon* (*The Second Fiddle,* 1996); a diary, *Du Sommet d'un arbre/*From the Top of a Tree (1986); and four novels for children, *Une Histoire à japper/*A Story That Yelps (1991), *Antoine et Alfred* (1992), *Alfred Sauve Antoine/*Alfred Saves Antoine (1996), and *Alfred et la lune cassée/*Alfred and the Broken Moon (1997). His novels are appreciated in France for their refreshing, humorous, and moving stories and characters.

Beauchemin also wrote the libretto for the opera *Le Prix* in 1992, which was composed by Jacques Hétu. In April 1993, he became a member of the Académie des Lettres du Québec. In 2000, the University of Bordeaux organized a conference on his work. Beauchemin is a passionate defender of the French language in Quebec and a member of both the Quebec writers' union and the Regroupement pour les droits politiques du Québec, a group for political rights in Quebec.

Marion Bernard

See also: Language; Quebec; Romains, Jules.
Reference
Piccione, Marie-Lyne, ed. *Rencontre autour d'Yves Beauchemin: Actes du colloque de Bordeaux, centre d'études canadiennes, Université Michel Montaigne Bordeaux III.* Paris: L'Harmattan, 2001.

BEAUVOIR, SIMONE DE (1908–1986)

French novelist, philosopher, and political activist.

Simone de Beauvoir is best known as the author of the groundbreaking existentialist analysis of a woman's social construction, *Le Deuxième Sexe* (*The Second Sex,* 1949). Despite often being overshadowed by the celebrity of her longtime companion Jean-Paul Sartre, Beauvoir's work is gaining increasing recognition, and she is now considered to be one of the most complex and original thinkers of her generation. She is linked to the Americas primarily through her travel and research in the United States

Existentialist writer Simone de Beauvoir (1908–1986) was well known for her feminist work The Second Sex *(1949). She studied at the Sorbonne with existentialist philosopher Sartre, later joining him as a professor in the 1940s. (Hulton-Deutsch Collection/Corbis)*

during the late 1940s and early 1950s, a connection strengthened by her personal relationship with the American writer Nelson Algren.

Born in Paris in 1908, Beauvoir grew up the eldest of two daughters in an upper-middle-class French family; she documents this childhood with sociological precision in the first volume of her acclaimed autobiography, *Mémoires d'une jeune fille rangée/Memoirs of a Dutiful Daughter* (1958). A student of philosophy at the Ecole Normale Supérieure, she came second (Sartre was first) in the *agrégation* of her year. Soon after becoming a high school philosophy teacher, she began to write essays and fiction exploring existentialist questions of freedom, anguish, and moral responsibility, issues that became increasingly pressing as World War II approached. She published her first novel,

L'Invitée/She Came to Stay, during the occupation in 1943, a roman-à-clef that yoked a philosophical exploration of the "Other" to the experiments in sexual liberty she and Sartre had undertaken since their meeting, all through the careful dissection of a contemporary Parisian ménage à trois. Emerging with Sartre at the end of the war as a star of the new French vogue for existentialism, Beauvoir continued to write novels, plays, philosophical tracts, and articles, eventually winning the Prix Goncourt in 1954 for her novel *Les Mandarins/The Mandarins.* From the 1950s onward Beauvoir became increasingly preoccupied with international politics, turning her work toward critical explorations of colonialism, patriarchy, and capitalist consumerism.

Beauvoir had been fascinated by the United States long before her first visit to the country for a series of lectures in 1947: not only were her literary influences frequently American (William Faulkner, John Dos Passos, Ernest Hemingway), but she also saw the United States as a country full of potential for the true realization of existentialist freedom and individuality. Her increasing ambivalence toward the United States, however, and her disgust at its economic inequalities, its worship of capitalism, and its antiblack racism is documented both in the third volume of her autobiography and in the analysis of her 1947 visit, published as *L'Amérique au jour le jour (America Day by Day,* 1948). A classic "French intellectual in America" text, it nevertheless reflects Beauvoir's fondness for the more personal aspects of her American experience. Treated with suspicion by the American authorities (Beauvoir would have to wait several months before being granted another visa), the text remains a vital and vibrant foreigner's analysis of a fascinating postwar United States in transition, a puzzling and contradictory country on its way to becoming the most powerful nation on Earth. The relationships she established with individual Americans during this trip ensured that the United States remained a central part of Beauvoir's life over the next decade. The writer Richard Wright and his wife became close friends of Beauvoir in both the United States and later France, Wright teaching Beauvoir much about racial oppression and its pertinence to her inquiries into the female condition in *Le Deuxième Sexe.* Even more important was the figure of Nelson Algren, a writer she met in Chicago and with whom she began an intellectual and romantic partnership that lasted for several years. Despite returning to France (and to Sartre), Beauvoir's relationship with Algren resulted in her existence being painfully divided between Paris and Chicago, both literally (she and Algren traveled back and forth between the two continents several times in order to maintain some semblance of continuity) and emotionally: Sartre may have been her intellectual partner for life, but with Algren, Beauvoir found her first truly passionate relationship with a man. Fantasizing about an eradicated Atlantic, Beauvoir allowed Algren and the United States to seep into her everyday existence in Paris, translating Algren's work for the journal she had set up with Sartre after the war, *Les Temps modernes,* and writing Algren the long, passionate letters (in English) documenting her life in Paris that would be published in 1999. This "doubleness" by which Beauvoir's life and work became characterized is reflected in the novel *Les Mandarins,* not only in the details of the psychiatrist heroine Anne's competing relationships with a Frenchman and an American, but at the very level of the book's structure, torn as it is between two different subjectivities, that of Anne and that of Henri, her husband's (Camus-inspired) friend.

Although Beauvoir's ultimate fidelity to her pact with Sartre precluded a final commitment to Algren and hastened the end of that particular Franco-American relationship, her increasingly active political and intellectual life perpetuated her connection to the Americas. Invited with Sartre in 1960 to visit postrevolutionary Cuba, she met with Fidel Castro and Che Guevara and gave several lectures to Cubans on the politics of existentialism and on the situation of women, performing a similar role in Brazil some months later. Also around this time, she and Sartre developed a relationship with the Martinican militant psychiatrist Frantz Fanon, and by signing the "Manifeste des 121," she made concrete her public opposition to French action in Algeria. Despite having written on "the woman question" as early as 1949 in *Le Deuxième Sexe,* Beauvoir did not officially embrace the feminist movement to the point of active militant action until the late 1960s, when she played a major role in the foundation of the women's liberation movement. *Le Deuxième Sexe,* however, a work maligned as pornographic by the likes of François Mauriac and misogynistic by many subsequent commentators, can be considered as her legacy to feminist thought. Ironically, the work is the cornerstone not of the body-centered "French feminism" that would gain academic popularity in the early 1970s, but rather of an overwhelmingly Anglo-American corpus of radically non-essentialist feminist texts far more preoccupied, as was Beauvoir, with the dismantling of purely discursive "feminine truths."

Completing her four-part autobiography in the 1970s, Beauvoir spent the latter part of her life with her adopted daughter Sylvie le Bon and died in Paris in 1986.

Andrew Asibong

See also: Dos Passos, John; Fanon, Frantz; Feminisms; Hemingway, Ernest; Sartre, Jean-Paul; Theory; World War II; Wright, Richard.

References

Bair, Deirdre. *Simone de Beauvoir: A Biography.* New York: Summit Books, 1990.

Beauvoir, Simone de. *America Day by Day.* Berkeley: University of California Press, 1999.

Moi, Toril. *Simone de Beauvoir: The Making of an Intellectual Woman.* Cambridge, MA: Blackwell, 1994.

BÉCAUD, GILBERT (FRANÇOIS SILLY) (1927–2001)

French singer, born in 1927 in Toulon; died in 2001 in Paris.

During the 1950s, Bécaud became one of the most successful French music hall singers, whose influence both as a composer and as a performer extended well beyond France. Working over the years with various lyricists, especially Louis Amade, Pierre Delanoë, and Maurice Vidalin, he was behind some of the most successful hit songs on both sides of the Atlantic.

A classically trained pianist, Bécaud accompanied the singer Jacques Pills on a tour of North and South America during 1950–1951. Changing his name from François Silly to Gilbert Bécaud, he returned to France to pursue his own career as a singer. Initially billed in France as a *vedette américaine* (American star), Bécaud appeared in 1954 at the newly opened Olympia music hall. His energetic performances, which earned him the nickname "Monsieur 100,000 volts," appealed to French and North American youth audiences alike. At the end of the 1950s, France saw the arrival of North American rock 'n' roll and its French equivalent, *la chanson yéyé.* Responding to new trends in popular music, Bécaud began to compose for the younger singers of the *yéyé* generation such as Richard Anthony and Hervé Vilar.

Across the Atlantic, Bécaud and his work achieved success, especially in Canada and in the United States. In 1961 he composed the music for Gilles Vigneault's song "Natashquan," whose text evoked the fishing village where the Québécois singer-songwriter had spent his childhood. Bécaud's English version of "Et maintenant" ("What Now, My Love," 1961) was a huge hit for Frank Sinatra, with whom he was often compared. In 1966 Bécaud performed a live television concert that was screened in the United States. He also cowrote the hugely successful "Je t'appartiens" ("I Belong to You," 1955), recorded in English toward the end of the 1960s as "Let It Be Me" by big names in North America such as James Brown, Bob Dylan, the Everly brothers, Nina Simone, and Sonny and Cher. Bécaud's songs were also covered by Sammy Davis Jr., Judy Garland, Liza Minnelli, Elvis Presley, and Barbra Streisand, to name but a few. Bécaud collaborated with Neil Diamond on two of his greatest hits, "Love on the Rocks" ("L'Amour est morte," 1981) and "September Morn" ("C'est en septembre," 1977). His marriage to an American in 1976 further strengthened his links with the United States, where he realized his ambition of writing and staging a musical. Collaborating with the English librettist Julian More, Bécaud produced *Madame Roza* (1986), based on the novel *La Vie devant soi* (*The Life before Us*) by Romain Gary. The show was performed initially in Baltimore and Los Angeles and also ran for a short period on Broadway, before transferring to Paris.

Chris Tinker

See also: Dylan, Bob; Gary, Romain; Music (Pop); Vigneault, Gilles.

References

Looseley, David. *Popular Music in Contemporary France: Authenticity, Politics, Debate.* Oxford: Berg, 2003.

Reval, Annie, and Bernard Reval. *Gilbert Bécaud: Mes jardins secrets.* Paris: France-Empire, 2001.

BEDAUX, CHARLES EUGÈNE (1886–1944)

Charles E. Bedaux was one of the most innovative and colorful persons among the founders of professional management consulting. He invented the "Bedaux system" and made it popular as a productivity strategy among the world's business leaders. He built the first global network of consulting companies and became one of the highest-earning citizens in the United States. Macroeconomic projects that he developed led indirectly to his still contentious death.

Parisian by birth, as a young man Bedaux migrated to the United States and became a naturalized citizen. He developed a method to measure professional labor. The basic principle of the system is that all human labor can be measured in time; adjusted for speed, effort, and efficiency; and augmented by a rest factor to allow for re-

covery from fatigue. The compound measurement results in an objective standard, the "B." Every qualified worker can perform 60 B's per hour as a normal performance and up to 80 B/h as an optimum performance. In combination with the time standards, an incentive system was introduced, wherein 60 B/h performance stands for the guaranteed base salary, and a linear premium is paid to the worker for performances over 60 B/h, up to a maximum of $33^1/3$ percent of the base salary at 80 B/h. This was called the "Bedaux system." Because the system forced both management and workers to focus on methods and performance, it often led to breakthrough performance leaps.

Bedaux established his first management consulting firm in Grand Rapids, Michigan, in 1916. Another in New York followed in 1921. In 1926 the British Bedaux Company was formed. International Bedaux was established in 1928 with head offices in Amsterdam. Other Bedaux companies opened all over Europe, Africa, Australia, and the East. Some of the leading management consulting firms of today have their roots with Bedaux.

Bedaux bought the Château de Candé in Monts, Indre-et-Loir, France, where he lived with his second American wife Fern Lombard and from where he undertook his countless business trips around the globe. It was in this castle that Charles and Fern Bedaux in 1937 hosted the wedding of the Duke of Windsor—the former King Edward VIII of England—and Mrs. Wallis Simpson.

Restless, adventurous, and not publicity shy, Bedaux undertook various expeditions. The best known is the "Champagne Safari," a 1,500-mile expedition through the northern mountains of British Columbia in 1934. On the geographical map today one can still find Mount Bedaux and Fern Lake. In 1995 the Canadian director George Ungar, using twelve reels of original film material, produced a documentary, *The Champagne Safari,* about this adventure, which had to be abandoned because of the conditions.

The first film reference to Bedaux came in *Modern Times,* produced, directed, written, and filmed by Charlie Chaplin between 1932 and 1936. In the movie, Charlie plays the poor Tramp, victimized by an industry run amok. The machines that battered Charlotte, his gamine (played by his wife Paulette Goddard), had been set into motion by the febrile brain of Mr. Beddoes, Charlie's caricature of Charles Bedaux.

Bedaux got mixed up with business dealings for both the Allied forces and the Germans before and at the beginning of World War II. He was flown to Florida for interrogations by the Department of Justice and died there in February 1944. The official cause of his death was suicide. Controversy continued after his death. In 1945 the *New Yorker* magazine devoted a series of three articles to him under the title "Annals of Collaboration." At the same time, the Charles de Gaulle government in France, after detailed scrutiny, posthumously granted Bedaux the Légion d'honneur.

Jurrian te Gussinklo Ohmann

See also: Gaulle, General Charles de; World War II.

References

Christy, Jim. *The Price of Power: A Biography of Charles Eugène Bedaux.* New York: Doubleday, 1984.

Goddard, John. "Bedaux's Crossing." *Canadian Geographic* 115, no. 5 (September–October 1995): 64–70.

BEGUINE

The word *beguine* is said to come from the English word "begin," which bandleaders used to mark the start of the music. Although the French and English spellings vary (*biguine* in French and *beguine* in English), the variation is mainly due to phonological transfer. *Biguine* in French is pronounced the same as *begin,* whereas *beguine* is an English pronunciation of the word *biguine.*

Beguine is a generic term used to define a certain type of music born from the fusion of French ballroom music and that of the African population of Martinique and Guadeloupe. By the end of the nineteenth century, there were three distinctive types of beguines in the Caribbean: *biguine de salon,* or chamber beguine; *biguine de bal,* or ballroom beguine; and *biguine de rue,* or street beguine.

Chamber beguine was much closer to the French musical tradition and included instruments such as piano, violin, and cello. Ballroom beguine used a wider range of instruments and combined music, songs, and dance. Street beguine was particularly prevalent among the lower classes and very popular during carnival time. The satirical lyrics served as political and social commentaries. In street beguine, the song and quality of the voice played a particularly important role.

The diversity of beguines also reflects their evolution and the diverse backgrounds of listeners and musicians. Chamber beguine was very much the arena of whites and mulattoes. Beguine involving songs and dance, more widespread among the black population, was condemned by the church as satanic music. After the 1902 eruption of the Montagne Pelée volcano and the submergence of Saint Pierre under the sea, beguine was banned in Martinique. The church attributed the catastrophe to those songs. Beguine was supplanted by the polka—enjoyed predominantly by the white and mulatto population in Martinique and Guadeloupe—but did not disappear.

Opportunities for beguine musicians in the Antilles were very limited. It was only in the 1930s, thanks to musicians such as clarinet player Alexandre Stellio (1885–1939), who took their music to Paris, that beguine started to gain wider recognition. Beguine won popularity in France through le Bal Nègre or le Bal Blomet, a dance hall at 33, rue Blomet in Paris. When Stellio arrived from Martinique in May 1929, he and other musicians from the Caribbean—including violonist Ernest Léardée, the trombonist Archange St. Hilaire, pianist, bassist, cellist Vic Torcals, and drummer and vocalist Orphelien—formed the Orchestre Antillais du Bal Blomet, which stayed in residence at the Bal Nègre for under a year.

Beguine music and dance became a symbol of the French Caribbean. The musical instrumentation was very similar to that of New Orleans orchestras, and instruments included clarinet, trumpet, and drum chest, piano, violin, saxophone, guitar, and bass. As beguine evolved, so did the rhythm and the variety of instruments played. Beguine quickly became popular outside the Caribbean, even in Anglo-Saxon countries. It owes part of its popularity to Cole Porter's 1935 song "Begin the Beguine," which became an international hit in 1938, even though the music itself was not a beguine but a bolero. Beguine remained popular until the 1970s and was progressively supplanted by another fusion of musical styles also born in the French Caribbean: zouk.

Marie-Annick Gournet

See also: Dance; Guadeloupe; Martinique; Porter, Cole.

References

Berrian, Brenda. *Awakening Spaces: French Caribbean Popular Song, Music, and Culture.* Chicago: University of Chicago Press, 2000.

Rosemain, Jacqueline. *La Musique dans la société antillaise (1635–1902).* Paris: L'Harmattan, 1988.

BEINEIX, JEAN-JACQUES (1946–)

A prominent French filmmaker, most often associated with the new *cinéma du look* generation (alongside Léos Carax and Luc Besson), Beineix was born in Paris in 1946 and started his career as an assistant to mainstream directors, such as Claude Zidi, René Clément, and Claude Berri. He first acquired an international reputation following the controversial release of *Diva* (1980). Severely criticized in France for its aesthetic emphasis on image at the expense of content, *Diva* was successfully distributed in the United States and went on to gain belated recognition at home, with massive box-office sales and the attribution of four Césars in 1982.

Having decried the perceived superficiality of Beineix's approach in relation to the realist narrative tradition, the French press gradually started to identify his distinctive visual style with the postmodern offensive of a new school of cinema, informed both by the Hollywood film industry and the *nouvelle vague*/New Wave. An adaptation of a crime series by Delacorta, *Diva* reaffirmed the New Wave *cinéastes'* admiration for American thrillers and the iconoclastic use of established genres as a springboard for the auteur's personal experimentation. Beineix's use of filters and saturated colors (which anticipated Besson's *Le Grand Bleu/The Big Blue,* 1988) and his refined treatment of sound and mise-en-scène at the expense of narrative became a trademark of the *cinéma du look.* In alternating between the story of a young postman's pirate recording of an opera singer and the police investigation of a vice ring that centers on a prostitute's taped confession, *Diva* foregrounded the postmodern blend of high-brow and popular cultural references. Beineix's caricature of the villains and the recurrent use of highly stylized derelict or fashionable interiors prompted comparisons with comic strips and advertising. In turn, Beineix's spell in advertising in the mid-1980s provoked debates concerning the visual aesthetics of the *cinéma du look.*

In 1982, commercial failure and critical rejection at Cannes marked Beineix's transition from independent filmmaking to big-budget production with *La Lune dans le caniveau/The Moon in the Gutter,* an adaptation of David Goodis's American thriller. However, Beineix's third adaptation of a thriller, *37°2' le Matin* (*Betty Blue,* 1986), based on a novel by Philippe Djian, became an instant public and critical success, consecrating the young charismatic couple of Béatrice Dalle and Jean-Hughes Anglade in a sensual and picaresque voyage of self-discovery reminiscent of Jean-Luc Godard's *Pierrot le fou.* The reflexive mood of Beineix's road movie starring Yves Montand, *IP5* (1992), which came after the largely ignored release of his lyrical exploration of the circus in *Roselyne and the Lions* (1988), made little impact and re-

mained defined by the lead actor's tragic death at the end of the shooting. A series of excellent documentaries, *The Children of Romania* (1992), *Otaku* (1993), and the moving account of Jean-Dominique Bauby's death in the television production, *Locked in Syndrome* (1997), passed almost unnoticed. More recently, *Mortal Transfer* (2001) and the TV documentary, *Loft Paradoxe* (2002), failed to persuade the critics and left the general audience divided over Beineix's evolution, despite his successful running of an independent production company, Cargo Films.

Ramona Fotiade

See also: Besson, Luc; Cinema, 1945 to the Present; Crime Fiction; Djian, Philippe; Godard, Jean-Luc; Montand, Yves.

References
Powrie, Phil. *French Cinema in the 1980s.* Oxford: Oxford University Press, 1997.
———. *Jean-Jacques Beineix.* Manchester/New York: Manchester University Press, 2001.

BENEZET, ANTHONY (1713–1784)

Educator and social reformer.

A French Huguenot by birth, Benezet immigrated to Philadelphia as a young man. He is best known for his abolitionist writings and his commitment to providing educational opportunities for women, German and French immigrants, and African Americans.

Benezet was born into an affluent mercantile family in Saint Quentin, Picardy. After his father's estate was confiscated in 1715, the family moved to Rotterdam, then to London, and ultimately, in 1731, to Philadelphia. Anthony Benezet was naturalized as a citizen of Pennsylvania in 1735 and married Quaker minister Joyce Marriott in 1736; neither of their children survived infancy.

Benezet's pedagogical career began with stints at the Germantown Academy (1739–1742) and the Philadelphia English School (1742–1754). As an educator, Benezet promoted gentle discipline, rigorous teacher training, and the extension of educational opportunities to youth of both genders and all races and ethnicities. In 1754, Benezet helped found a Quaker school for girls; in 1767, he founded a school for poor girls, where he taught until 1782. He befriended the Acadian refugees from Nova Scotia who arrived in Philadelphia from 1755 onward, raised funds for their maintenance and lodgings, and in 1762 sponsored some of the Acadian children's application to attend school in Philadelphia. Benezet began teaching black children and adults in his home around 1750 and encouraged the Philadelphia Quaker Meeting to open the Africans' School in 1770; he remained associated with the institution until his death. In 1778, Benezet published three textbooks that reflected his interest in broad elementary education.

Meanwhile, Benezet became increasingly active in the movement to abolish slavery. In 1754, he helped persuade the Philadelphia Meeting to condemn slaveholding. In succeeding years, Benezet published a series of pamphlets in which he urged a transatlantic audience to rethink its assumption of African inferiority. *A Short Account of That Part of Africa Inhabited by the Negroes* (1762) and *A Caution and Warning to Great Britain and Her Colonies* (1766) were followed by Benezet's most important work, *Some Historical Account of Guinea* (1772). Benezet was the first abolitionist writer to make extensive use of slave traders' records and journals to argue against the slave trade; his history had a profound impact on Thomas Clarkson and John Wesley in Britain and on Jacques-Pierre Brissot, Abbé Raynal, and the Marquis de Lafayette in France. Olaudah Equiano drew on Benezet's research in his autobiography. Benezet was a founding member of the first antislavery society in North America in 1775 and worked for the passage of Pennsylvania's gradual emancipation law in 1780. Benezet's writings also left a mark on his native country, where they helped inspire the formation of the abolitionist organization Les Amis des noirs a few years after his death.

Darcy R. Fryer

See also: Acadia; Antislavery Movements; Huguenots; Lafayette, Marquis de; Nova Scotia; Raynal, Guillaume-Thomas-François; Slavery.

References

Brookes, George S. *Friend Anthony Benezet.* Philadelphia: University of Pennsylvania Press, 1937.

Jackson, Maurice. "The Social and Intellectual Origins of Anthony Benezet's Antislavery Radicalism." *Pennsylvania History* 66, supplement (1999): 86–112.

Kashatus, William C. "A Reappraisal of Anthony Benezet's Activities in Educational Reform, 1754–1784." *Quaker History* 78, no. 1 (spring 1989): 24–36.

BENOÎT, JEAN (1922–)

Québécois artist, performer, designer, and sculptor.

Benoît joined the surrealist movement in 1959 and continues to produce surrealist art (despite the movement's official end in 1969) from Paris. He exhibited with the Paris surrealist group in 1959 and 1965, and his first solo exhibition was in the Galerie 1900–2000 in Paris in 1996.

Prior to his arrival in Paris in 1948, Benoît studied under the artist Alfred Pellan (1906–1988) at the Ecole des Beaux-Arts in Montreal, and in 1948 he was a founding member of the avant-garde group, the Prisme d'yeux. That year he also married fellow student artist Mimi Parent (b. 1924) and together they left Montreal to continue their careers in Paris.

Benoît's work is greatly influenced by Oceanic art, anthropology, and the libertine writings of the Marquis de Sade (1740–1814), especially Sade's notorious novel, *120 Days of Sodom*. Benoît's first major surrealist intervention in Paris in 1959, a performance entitled Exécution du Testament du Marquis de Sade, spoke to these influences. It launched both his membership in André Breton's surrealist group as well as the international surrealist exhibition dedicated to Eros. For the performance in the apartment of surrealist poet Joyce Mansour on the night of December 2, 1959 (the 145th anniversary of Sade's death), Benoît designed a fantastic costume, performed a striptease to the recorded sounds of city noise, and ended the event by branding his own chest with the name SADE. The purpose of his Testament was to protest, to declaim Sade's right to an atheistic burial. For the 1965 L'Ecart absolu international surrealist exhibition at the Galerie de l'Oeil in Paris, he continued his theater of effect with an eponymous performance and lavish costume dedicated to the renowned nineteenth-century necrophiliac Sergent Bertrand. His sculpture *Le Bouledogue de Maldoror*, also shown in 1965, was a life-sized bulldog, made of a patchwork of leather gloves, with glass spikes down its spine and a mirror underneath its stocky legs to expose its angry phallus.

In more recent years, Benoît has also produced luxuriously illustrated, handwritten love letters and "scrolls," often decorated with phallic drawings, wine labels, and feathers. It is not surprising that the artist took pride of place in Annie Le Brun's 1989 exhibition, Petits et grands théâtres du marquis de Sade. In the 1970s and 1980s he made a series of macabre sculptures (from 30 to 80 centimeters in height), usually in leather, of decayed skulls, ghoulish creatures, and erotically intertwined couples (*Adam and Eve*, 1984). Other works include wooden walking sticks carved with creatures that evoke medieval decoration in their fantastic bestiality and engorged genitalia; luxury, carved leather cases for rare book editions (André Breton and Philippe Soupault, *Champs magnétiques*, 1972–1973); and jewelry that seems to pay homage to Sadean heroines, including a choker made of leather with a fang-toothed, red-eyed bat as the centerpiece (1992). In his art, Benoît fuses performance, art, and craft, continuing the surrealists' engagement with design and fashion and exploiting the pornographic imagination.

Alyce Mahon

See also: Breton, André; Montreal; Painting; Parent, Mimi; Pornography; Sculpture; Soupault, Philippe; Surrealism.

References
Le Brun, Annie. *Jean Benoît*. Exhibition catalogue. Paris: Galerie 1900–2000, 1996.
Petits et grands théâtres du marquis de Sade. Exhibition catalogue. Paris: Paris Art Center, 1989.

BERNABÉ, JEAN (1942–)

One of the most recognized linguists of the Caribbean and a fervent defender of the Creole language.

Born in 1942 in Lorrain, Martinique, Bernabé is mostly known for his work promoting the recognition of the Creole spoken in the Lesser Antilles. His belief is that Creole, as a language, will be put at risk if it becomes less and less used for speech and writing. Therefore in March 1975, he set up the Groupe d'etude et de recherche en espace créolophone et francophone (GEREC-F), whose primary aim is to promote research into and activities supporting the development of the Creole language and the study of Caribbean civilization. The GEREC-F is now a well-established and respected organization with a membership drawn from scholars all over the world. It has lobbied for the creation of the "CAPES Créole" (the equivalent of a bachelor of education degree in Creole language and civilization), which was offered as a postgrad teaching diploma for the first time in 2002. GEREC-F has a range of publications, some of which are produced bimonthly, including *Espace créole,* which publishes a range of theoretical articles; *Mofwaz,* which features articles presenting a pedagogical approach to the linguistic situation in the French-speaking Caribbean islands; *Textes, Etudes et Documents,* which focuses on literary discourses and the diglossic situation in the Caribbean; and *Guide Capes,* which presents a series of texts that can be used to study for the "CAPES Créole." These publications have been published mostly by Ibis Rouge, one of the few successful Caribbean-based publishing companies. Bernabé is also known as an advocate of the *créolité* movement because of

his contribution to *Eloge de la créolité,* coauthored with Raphaël Confiant (another active member of the GEREC-F) and Patrick Chamoiseau. Bernabé's doctoral thesis, entitled *Fondal-Natal: Grammaire basilectale approchée des créoles guadeloupéens et martiniquais*/Fondal-Natal: A close basilectal grammar of Creole in Guadeloupe and Martinique and published in 1983 by L'Harmattan, the year of the viva (voce examination) for his doctorate, is the first work in a long list of publications on Creole vocabulary and grammar.

Bernabé has been working at the Schoelcher University campus in Martinique since 1973, fulfilling various key administrative and pedagogical roles, including that of deputy vice chancellor in charge of research and international cooperation. He is currently professor of Creole regional culture and language and coordinator of the research group GEREC-F.

Marie-Annick Gournet

See also: Chamoiseau, Patrick; Confiant, Raphaël; *Créolité;* Language; Martinique.
References
Chamoiseau, Patrick, and Raphaël Confiant. *Lettres créoles.* Paris: Gallimard, 1999.
Gallagher, Mary. "Whence and Whither the French Caribbean 'Créolité' Movement?" *ASCALF Bulletin* 9 (1994): 3–18.

BERNANOS, GEORGES (1888–1948)

One of France's greatest Catholic novelists, and a cultural critic of enormous talent, Bernanos was also a determined anti-American, part of a broad group of 1930s intellectuals who blamed American "modernity" for the collapse of civilization. Bernanos's disdain for the United States followed him throughout his many political transformations—moving easily across the spectrum from left to right. However, unlike most of the Catholic intelligentsia, Bernanos stood firmly against Nazism and for Free France. During his wartime exile in Brazil, he broadcast (via the BBC) scathing attacks on Vichy and penned patriotic defenses of French Jewry. Yet only a few years earlier, he had supported Francisco Franco and had written one of the most poisonous books of the interwar period, *La Grande Peur des bien-pensants* (1931), a truly bizarre tribute to his "genius mentor" Edouard Drumont, France's most accomplished anti-Semite. Bernanos's overall legacy remains controversial and complicated.

Georges Bernanos's encounters with the New World were all (save his Brazilian exile) theoretical. He never visited the United States, yet that country informed much of his life's work. He was born in Paris in 1888 into a reactionary Catholic family—his father read *La Libre Parole* to the family at breakfast—and matured into a promising Action Française (AF) militant, trusted with running one of their newspapers shortly after World War I. Literary fame and a very public break with AF came after the publication of his novel *Sous le soleil de Satan* (*Under Satan's Sun,* 1926) and later his enormously successful *Journal d'un curé de campagne* (*The Diary of a Country Priest,* 1936). These books were deeply religious meditations, attacking both the secular world and the hypocrisy of the Catholic Church. They gave few signs of Bernanos's political obsessions.

Those interests came to light in *La Grande Peur des bien-pensants,* in which he celebrated Drumont as a "magical" figure and adopted the terms of Drumont's anti-Americanism. Bernanos spoke contemptu-

ously of the United States as the place of Jewish triumph.

Although this book suggested the beginning of a career as a professional anti-Semite, Georges Bernanos had nothing further to say on the subject. Something fundamental changed after he visited Spain in 1936. The book he wrote on his return, *Les Grands Cimetières sous la lune* (1938), was a thorough rejection of rightwing Catholic politics. Outraged by what he had seen passing for "Christian civilization" in Franco's Spain, Bernanos never again supported any political movement, and when World War II broke out, Bernanos threw himself into the cause of resistance.

His anti-Americanism, however, became more and more explicit. Even during World War II, in his "Lettre aux Roosevelt," a chapter in *Lettre aux Anglais* (1942)—ostensibly a plea for American assistance—he thoroughly condemned American values. Bernanos devoted his short postwar career (he died in 1948) to an active campaign against America and Americanism. One of his last books, *La France contre les robots* (1947), went so far as to adopt the "Americans are Nazis" formula that was widespread among the cold war far left. Although sometimes consistent with the extremes of left and right, Bernanos's politics, therefore, ultimately defy classification.

Seth Armus

See also: Anti-Americanism; Brazil; Catholic Church; World War I; World War II.

References

Griffiths, Richard. *The Reactionary Revolution: The Catholic Revival in French Literature, 1870–1914.* New York: Ungar, 1965.

Speaight, Robert. *Georges Bernanos: A Study of the Man and the Writer.* New York: Liveright, 1974.

BESSON, LUC (1959–)

French film director, born in Paris in 1959.

Much of Besson's early life was spent traveling the globe with his scuba-diving-instructor parents. At the age of seventeen an injury left Besson unable to dive, and he returned to Paris and embarked upon a filmmaking career. However, as later films, notably *Le Grand Bleu* (*The Big Blue,* 1988) and *Atlantis* (1991), reveal, his early passion for the sea was to have a profound impact upon his cinematic work.

Besson served his apprenticeship working in advertising and music videos and as an assistant director. At the age of twenty-three he shot his first full-length feature, *Le Dernier Combat/ The Last Battle* (1983), a violent but witty reworking of the science fiction genre. The critical success of this film meant that Gaumont, the distribution and production company, made available a large budget and two leading French stars (Isabelle Adjani and Christophe Lambert) for his next feature, *Subway* (1985). Unlike *Le Dernier Combat,* this film was disliked by the vast majority of French critics but was a huge popular success. Indeed, it set the pattern for the reception of Besson's work from that point on.

Besson's work has typically been described in terms of the so-called *cinéma du look,* a style of filmmaking that emerged in France in the 1980s and was exemplified by the films of directors such as Besson, Jean-Jacques Beineix, and Léos Carax. Although clear distinctions can be made between the films of these directors, what they do share is an emphasis on visual style, an exploration of the alienation of youthful protagonists, and references to other cultural forms, notably advertising, music videos, and American genre cinema. The critical response to these concerns was to condemn the films as "superficial," "populist," and, from time to time, "too American."

This hostility, of course, speaks volumes about French constructions of cultural agendas and "national" cinemas. Besson's response revealed his own contempt for the critical establishment. Both *Le Grand Bleu* and *Nikita* (1990) continued his exploration of the themes and stylistic traits that had distinguished his earlier work, albeit via very different genres and narratives. *Le Grand Bleu* opened the Cannes film festival in 1988 and was panned by hostile critics. Nevertheless, it became a huge audience hit and remains one of the most popular French films of the last fifty years. *Nikita* also proved a critical failure but a popular success and received the questionable accolade of a Hollywood remake, *The Assassin* (a.k.a. *Point of No Return*), directed by John Badham in 1993, as well as a spin-off syndicated TV series made in Canada, *La Femme Nikita* (1997–2001).

This transatlantic connection is indeed central to Besson's career and filmography. His sixth and seventh features, *Léon* (1994) and *Le Cinquième Elément* (*The Fifth Element,* 1997), were entirely French productions, yet distribution rights were sold to American companies, and both were shot in English, featured British and American actors, and were set in a version of New York. Both films became major international successes. Although Besson's most recent film as a director, *Jeanne d'Arc* (1999), suggests a new interest in specifically French historical concerns, its visual and narrative style continues the reworking of Hollywood cinematic techniques that identified his earlier films. Moreover, his work as a scriptwriter and/or producer, notably on popular hits such as *Taxi* (Gérard Pirès, 1998), *Taxi 2* (Gérard Krawczyk, 2000), and *Yamakasi: Le Samouraï des temps modernes* (Ariel Zeitoun, 2001), reveals a continuing attempt to rejuvenate popular French cinema through a refusal to abide by the constraints of traditionally "French" cinema and an exploitation of the tropes of both French and American popular culture.

Lucy Mazdon

> *See also:* Beineix, Jean-Jacques; Cinema, 1945 to the Present; Joan of Arc; Lambert, Christophe; Remakes.
>
> **Reference**
> Hayward, Susan. *Luc Besson.* Manchester: Manchester University Press, 1998.

BIANCIOTTI, HECTOR (1930–)

Writer, born in 1930 near the Argentinean city of Córdoba.

Hector Bianciotti is the son of Italian immigrants from the Piedmont region who settled in the Pampas. As a child, he was forced to learn Spanish, since his parents, eager for their children to be as integrated as possible, forbade them from using Italian. He started his education at the religious (Salesian order) Villa del Rosario and at the age of twelve entered the seminary, where he took an interest in literature and music. Realizing at eighteen that the priesthood was not his vocation, he eventually moved to Buenos Aires, where he encountered the fear evoked by the regime of Juan Perón. At this point, helped by a friend who was also a police informer, he left Argentina for Europe and arrived in Rome, where he lived in poverty. He spent four years in Spain and then settled in France in 1961.

Bianciotti found work as a reader for the Gallimard publishing house and, in 1969, started to publish articles in *La Quinzaine littéraire.* These French-language articles led him to a post at the *Nouvel Observateur* as a journalist writing on literature. During this period, he wrote four novels in Spanish, which were then translated into French: *Les Desertos dorados* (*Les Déserts dorés*/The Golden Deserts, 1967), *Detrás del rostro que nos mira* (*Celle qui voyage la nuit*/She Who Travels at Night, 1969), *Ritual* (*Ce Moment qui s'achève*/This Moment That Ends, 1972), and *La Busca del jardín* (*Le Traité des saisons*/A Treatise on Seasons, 1977). Bianciotti's 1982 collection of short stories, *El Amor no es amado* (*L'Amour n'est pas aimé*/Love Is Not Loved), includes a tale originally written in French. It was in 1985, after his naturalization as a French citizen in 1981, that he abandoned Spanish and adopted the French language, publishing the prize-winning novel, *Sans la miséricorde du Christ*/Without Christ's Mercy. In 1989, he left Gallimard and joined the publishers Grasset as a reader. He then became a literary critic for *Le Monde des livres.* Bianciotti reflected on his youth in Argentina in his novel *Ce que la nuit raconte au jour*/What Night Tells the Day (1992). Other notable works include *Le Pas si lent de l'amour*/Love's Slow Step (1995), *Comme la trace de l'oiseau dans l'air*/Like a Bird's Trace in the Air (1999), and *Une Passion en toutes lettres*/A Great Passion (2001).

Bianciotti, an admirer of the work of Paul Valéry, was elected to the Académie Française in 1996. His literary works excel in their description of their heroes' crises of conscience, offering subtle and detailed psychological analysis. He often takes his own life as the inspiration for his stories, as, for instance, in *Ce que la nuit raconte,* in which he describes the simple life of his parents, his fascination with an old aunt, and his adolescent first loves, without forgetting his love of music that became a passion. His writing is reminiscent of that of Marcel Proust and other writers he admires, such as Paul Claudel or Marcel Jouhandeau.

Jérôme Ceccon

See also: Argentina.

References

Gasquet, Axel. "Hector Bianciotti." *L'Intelligentsia du bout du monde: les écrivains argentins à Paris.* Paris: Editions Kimé, "Détours littéraires," 2002.
Weiss, Jason. *The Lights of Home: A Century of Latin American Writers in Paris.* New York: Routledge, 2003.

Jean-Baptiste Le Moyne Bienville. (Library of Congress)

BIENVILLE, JEAN-BAPTISTE LE MOYNE, SIEUR DE (1680–1767)

A vital participant in the colonization of French Louisiana at the end of the seventeenth and during the first half of the eighteenth century.

Born in Montreal in 1680, Bienville was one of fourteen children. He joined the French navy as a young boy and was severely wounded aboard the *Pélican* off the coast of New England. His brother Pierre, sieur d'Iberville, then took him to France, where d'Iberville received orders to command an exploration and establishment of a colony in America. Bienville, who was younger by nineteen years, accompanied his brother to the New World. Before d'Iberville returned to France in May 1699, he appointed Bienville king's lieutenant, making him second in command to their brother François Marie, sieur de Sauvolle, who was in charge of the new colony.

In September 1701, d'Iberville instructed Bienville to move supplies and men from Fort Maurepas to Massacre Island, now known as Dauphin Island, in Mobile Bay. He traveled up the Mobile River approximately 38 miles, making notes and sketches. Upon seeing Bienville's notes, d'Iberville commanded him to establish a fort there, named Fort Louis de la Louisiane. The fort's construction was completed in March 1702. At twenty-two years old, Bienville became governor of the new colony.

The new fort faced many challenges, including diminishing food and supplies and a movement against Bienville led by the commissaire of the colony and its vicar-general. Jean-Baptiste Martin Dartaguiette arrived in 1708 to investigate and report on the accusations of fraud and incompetence against Bienville and his family. His report was inconclusive, and Bienville and the *commissaire* both remained in power, with

Dartaguiette as mediator. Extensive flooding and decomposing of Fort Louis's buildings forced Bienville to relocate the fort's settlement downriver in 1711, where Mobile is located today. In September 1712, Antoine Crozat leased the colony from a financially struggling France and appointed Antoine de la Mothe Cadillac as governor, demoting Bienville to lieutenant governor. Crozat returned the colony to France in 1717, and John Law then leased it. Bienville received the Cross of Saint Louis from L'Epinay, the new governor, who left the position the next year in the face of insubordination by Bienville's followers. In 1718, Bienville was once again named governor and established the city of New Orleans, which became the headquarters of the colony in 1720 upon Law's dismissal by France. Bienville himself was removed from office in 1724 due to accusations of illegal trade but in 1733 was returned to the governorship by France's Minister of Marine Jérôme Phélypeaux, comte de Pontchartrain. This was to be his last stint as governor. He led two major unsuccessful campaigns against the Chickasaw tribes because they were allied with both the British and the Natchez tribe, both of which harassed the new colony. These attempts to destroy them ended his political career in the Louisiana colony, and in 1743 he departed to live the rest of his life in France. He died in March 1767 and was buried in Montmartre with full military honors.

Amber Wingfield

See also: Cadillac, Antoine Laumet de la Mothe; Crozat, Antoine; Iberville, Pierre Le Moyne d'; Louisiana; Mobile; New Orleans; Saint Louis.

Reference

Thomason, Michael, ed. *Mobile: The New History of Alabama's First City.* Tuscaloosa: University of Alabama Press, 2001.

BIGELOW, JOHN (1817–1911)

American journalist, lawyer, statesman, and editor, John Bigelow contributed greatly to the preservation of the freedom and unity of the United States. A fervent defender of antislavery and free trade, he was very influential both in American public opinion and abroad. His diplomatic efforts in France did much to prevent the French from siding with the Confederacy during the Civil War.

Bigelow was born in Malden, New York, on November 25, 1817. He graduated from Union College in 1835 and practiced law in New York for several years after passing the bar exam in 1838. From 1848 to 1861 he shared with William Cullen Bryant the ownership and editorship of the New York *Evening Post.* His antislavery and free trade editorials were especially vigorous.

Abraham Lincoln appointed him consul at Paris in 1861, after which Bigelow progressed to chargé d'affaires, envoy extraordinary, and minister plenipotentiary to the court of Napoléon III in 1864. While consul, Bigelow wrote *Les Etats-Unis d'Amérique* (The United States of America) in 1863 to counteract the apparent desire of the French people for dissolution of the American Union, by showing them the relative importance of the commerce of the Northern and Southern states. This work was much credited with preventing French recognition of the Confederacy.

During that same year Bigelow discovered that a French shipbuilder, with the connivance of Napoléon III, was constructing two formidable ironclads and two corvettes for the use of the Confederacy; Bigelow devoted his energies to thwarting this scheme and succeeded in preventing

John Bigelow's diplomatic efforts in France did much to prevent the French from siding with the Confederacy during the Civil War. (Library of Congress)

ular biography, and historical or political discussion. However, his main literary achievements were the editions, between 1868 and 1888, of Benjamin Franklin's autobiography and autobiographical writings, which Bigelow annotated heavily, and of the complete works of Franklin, in ten octavo volumes (1887–1889). These editions were based in part upon the editor's personal investigations of manuscript sources found in France and elsewhere and supplanted the well-known, long serviceable, but less accurate edition of Jared Sparks (1836–1840).

Bigelow was a close friend of Samuel J. Tilden, governor of New York State and the Democratic candidate who ran against Rutherford B. Hayes for the U.S. presidential election of 1876. Bigelow became his literary executor, editing his speeches and other political writings, publishing a biography in 1895, and editing a two-volume collection of Tilden's letters and literary memorials (1908).

Claudia Wolosin

See also: American Civil War; Antislavery Movements; Franklin, Benjamin; Mexico; Panama Canal; Slavery.
References
Bigelow, John. *Retrospections of an Active Life.* New York: Baker and Taylor, 1909–1913.
Clapp, Margaret Antoinette. *Forgotten First Citizen: John Bigelow.* Boston: Little, Brown, 1947.

the delivery of all but one of these vessels to the Confederate agents. His book *France and the Confederate Navy* (1888) gives an account of this episode.

In 1865–1866, it devolved upon Bigelow, as minister to France, to represent his government in its delicate negotiations concerning the French occupation of Mexico, and he discharged this difficult task with credit. From 1875 to 1877, he served as secretary of state of New York, where he was instrumental in the development of the New York Public Library and was a staunch proponent of the development of the Panama Canal.

Bigelow was a prolific writer, and his many works included books of travel, pop-

BINOCHE, JULIETTE (1964–)

French actress, born in Paris in 1964, who began her career in theater and television in France.

Binoche's early cinematic work includes auteur films such as Jean-Luc

Godard's *Je vous salue Marie!* (*Hail Mary,* 1984) and André Téchiné's *Rendez-vous* (1985). She came to prominence in France with her roles in Léos Carax's *Mauvais Sang* (*Bad Blood,* 1986) and *Les Amants du Pont-Neuf* (*Lovers on the Bridge,* 1991) and went on to become one of the most prominent actors of her generation. Her leading role in *Le Hussard sur le toit* (*The Horseman on the Roof,* Rappeneau, 1995), a key French "heritage" film of the 1990s and France's most expensive film to date, bears witness to her important status in the national cinematic culture and her burgeoning international appeal. Roles in later costume dramas, Diane Kurys's *Les Enfants du siècle* (*The Children of the Century,* 1999) and Patrice Leconte's *La Veuve de Saint-Pierre* (*The Widow of Saint-Pierre,* 2000), suggest Binoche continues to be a star capable of carrying big-budget movies mobilized to boost both domestic box-office revenues and the prestige of French cinema overseas.

Binoche began to develop a European career from the late 1980s, notably in Philip Kaufman's *The Unbearable Lightness of Being* (1988), Louis Malle's *Damage* (1992), and Krzysztof Kieslowski's *Trois couleurs: Bleu* (*Three Colors: Blue,* 1993). Her physical appearance has always been central to her star persona. Her rather delicate, gamine beauty is reminiscent of actresses of the French New Wave, but in these European or international coproductions it became something non-French but always fragile and "other." This is particularly striking in *Damage,* where Binoche's appearance forms a marked contrast to Miranda Richardson's much more strained physical features. Roger Ebert, film critic for the *Chicago Sun-Times,* has described Binoche as "almost ethereal in her beauty and innocence," and it is arguably this perception of her appearance and performance style that has tended to inform many of her film roles.

Binoche's major break in Hollywood came with Anthony Minghella's *The English Patient* in 1996. She played Hana, the Canadian nurse who tends to Ralph Fienne's Count Almasy and whose own memories act as a counterpoint to his own tragic recollections. To the great surprise of much of the media, Binoche won an Oscar for best supporting actress for the role. Perhaps due to Binoche's relative obscurity in the United States at that point, it had been widely accepted that Lauren Bacall would win the award for her role in *The Mirror Has Two Faces* (Streisand, 1996). Binoche went on to further international success in Lasse Hallström's Anglo-American coproduction *Chocolat* (2000), based on the best-selling novel by Joanne Harris.

By 2002 Binoche had become the highest-paid actress in France, and although she has turned down a number of parts in Hollywood in favor of French or European films, her international presence has been confirmed by the work described and indeed by her role as the "face" of the Lancôme perfume "Poème" from 1995 to 2000.

Lucy Mazdon

See also: Cinema, 1945 to the Present; Cosmetics; Godard, Jean-Luc; Malle, Louis.

References

Austin, Guy. *Stars in Modern French Film.* London/New York: Arnold, 2003.

Vincendeau, Ginette. *Stars and Stardom in French Cinema.* London: Continuum, 2000.

BLAIS, MARIE-CLAIRE (1939–)

Marie-Claire Blais is one of a small number of Québécois authors to have a significant international readership, due partly to the fact that she has spent extended periods in France and the United States. Born in Quebec City to a working-class family, Blais did not complete her convent school education because she needed to earn money, but subsequently attended night classes at Laval University. She began writing at an early age and completed her first novel when she was seventeen. *La Belle Bête* (*Mad Shadows,* 1959) was well received by critics, as were *Tête blanche* (1960), and *Le Jour est noir* (*The Day Is Dark,* 1961). In 1961, Blais received a Canada Council Grant, which enabled her to undertake a year's study in Paris. Here, at the encouragement of the U.S. critic Edmund Wilson, she applied for a bursary from the Guggenheim Foundation and, in 1963, left Quebec again for Cambridge, Massachusetts. From 1964 until 1969, she lived in Wellfleet, on Cape Cod, with her lover, the artist Mary Meigs, and Meigs's long-term partner, the political activist Barbara Deming. During this time, Blais wrote her most famous work, the darkly humorous *Une Saison dans la vie d'Emmanuel* (*A Season in the Life of Emmanuel,* 1965). The novel, which charts a period in the life of a family in 1940s rural Quebec, made the writer an international star but was the object of a backlash two years later, when certain critics erroneously interpreted it as a realist and therefore unflattering portrayal of francophone Quebec society. Since living with Meigs in Brittany in the early 1970s, Blais has divided her time between Key West in Florida, Montreal, and Quebec's eastern townships. A prolific and highly successful author, she has written novels, short stories, poetry, plays, screenplays, and an autobiographical travelogue on her experiences in the United States, *Parcours d'un écrivain: Notes américaines* (*American Notebooks: A Writer's Journey,* 1993).

The carnivalesque *Une Saison dans la vie d'Emmanuel* is a playful yet satirical reworking of the novel of the land, a mainstay of Québécois literature from the middle of the nineteenth century until the emergence of social realism in the 1940s that celebrated the French-Canadian nationalist tenets of agriculturalism, Catholicism, and the revenge of the cradles—a high birth rate. Like Anne Hébert's *Kamouraska* (1970), the novel constitutes part of Quebec's feminine nationalist canon, since it carries out a subversion of the values rejected during the Quiet Revolution by those who embraced a modern vision of a secular, independent Quebec. From the mid-1960s onward, Blais's work has increasingly engaged with the theme of homosexuality—both female and male—as in *Le Loup* (*The Wolf,* 1972), *Les Nuits de l'Underground* (*Nights in the Underground: An Exploration of Love,* 1978), and the quasi-autobiographical trilogy, *Les Manuscrits de Pauline Archange* (*The Manuscripts of Pauline Archange,* 1968–1970). Blais's current trilogy, which includes *Soifs* (*These Festive Nights,* 1995) and *Dans la foudre et la lumière* (*Thunder and Light,* 2001), continues an experimentation with language that is typical of the writer.

Ceri Morgan

See also: Brittany; Gay Movement; Hébert, Anne; Quebec; Quiet Revolution.

References

Green, Mary Jean. *Marie-Claire Blais.* New York: Twayne, 1995.

Oore, Irène, and Oriel C. L. MaLennan, eds. *Marie-Claire Blais: An Annotated Bibliography.* Oakville, ON: ECW, 1998.

BLUM-BYRNES AGREEMENT

The Blum-Byrnes Agreement was first initiated to allow a complete penetration of U.S. imports (including films) into the postwar French market. However, it had a counterproductive effect, paradoxically contributing to the creation of a protectionist and defensive system of film production.

During World War II, French screens were almost uniquely dedicated to French film productions. Other national cinemas were very rarely shown: the only feature films available for release were pre-1940 foreign films as well as more recent American ones that had been imported and distributed in France with no release authorization. By the end of the war, French film professionals feared an invasion of foreign films that would directly threaten the industry and asked for the establishment of quotas. Film producers proposed the following regulation: of thirteen films on general release, eight had to be French. Instead, the Blum-Byrnes Agreement (named for the signatories: Léon Blum, one of France's leading veteran statesmen, and U.S. secretary of state James Francis Byrnes) came into force on May 28, 1946: the treaty proposed canceling a $2 billion debt against a $500 million loan and a complete opening of the French market to U.S. exports. As far as cinema was concerned, this meant guaranteed complete access for American films to French screens. Under this treaty, the French film industry was also offered a four-year protection plan in order to regain the strength that it had lost during the war and the occupation. However, only four weeks out of every four months were exclusively dedicated to French feature films.

Filmmakers, together with producers and many famous actors of the time, publicly and vehemently protested against the agreement, denouncing unfair and uncontrollable American domination. They set up the Comité de défense du cinéma français (Committee for the Defense of French Film) in December 1947, which proposed the idea that, as an art, cinema could not be bound by the laws of the market and mere commercial considerations but needed strict state regulation (an intense and still very pertinent debate now best known as the *exception culturelle*). The committee contributed to the creation of a temporary special fund on September 23, 1948, that imposed a new tax on entries. This fund became the main financing body of French cinema five years later, and since 1959 it has been the backbone of French film production.

Florian Grandena

See also: Cinema, 1945 to the Present; World War II.

References

Crisp, Colin. *The Classic French Cinema: 1930–1960.* London: Indiana University Press, 1993.

Regourd, Serge. *L'Exception culturelle.* Paris: PUF, 2002.

BLUTEAU, LOTHAIRE (1957–)

Born in Montreal on April 14, 1957, actor Lothaire Bluteau is widely known in Quebec because of his leading role in Denys

Arcand's celebrated film *Jésus de Montréal* (Jesus of Montreal, 1989), and he became known outside Canada for his participation in *Black Robe* (1991). Much like Jean-Pierre Léaud, another introspective actor, Bluteau's acting style is usually characterized by minimalism.

Bluteau began his acting career in Montreal with small parts in Brigitte Sauriol's films (*Bleu Brume*/Blue Mist in 1982; *Rien qu'un jeu*/Just a Game in the following year) and onstage with the help of Paul Buissonneau at his Théâtre de Quat'-Sous in Montreal. After many minor roles onscreen, Lothaire Bluteau was first recognized by critics for the part of an insane but gentle young man in Yves Simoneau's *Les Fous de Bassan* (*In the Shadow of the Wind*, 1987), based on a novel by Anne Hébert.

Director Denys Arcand often said he already had Bluteau in mind as he began writing the script for his film *Jésus de Montréal*, and he admitted that the project could not have materialized without the actor. Bluteau personifies with great intensity a rebellious young actor in search of truth, who plays the role of Jesus in an annual passion play in Montreal and progressively identifies with him.

For many, Bluteau gained worldwide celebrity with another spiritual role when he played Father Laforgue in *Black Robe* (1991), an international coproduction directed by the Australian Bruce Beresford. Here, he is a "Black Robe," the Algonquin Indians' nickname for one of the French Jesuit missionaries who went to New France. The script of *Black Robe* was written by novelist Brian Moore, who in fact based it on the seventeenth-century chronicle *The Jesuit Relations*.

Back in Quebec, Bluteau played the leading role in Robert Lepage's first feature film, *Le Confessionnal* (*The Confessional*, 1995). (Bluteau and Lepage had both acted in *Jésus de Montréal*.) Here, Bluteau plays a young man from Quebec City, Pierre Lamontagne, who is seeking to discover his roots and his true identity.

Since then, Bluteau has acted more outside Quebec, establishing a successful international career, mainly in the United States and Britain. He appeared in *I Shot Andy Warhol* (Harron, 1996), *Bent* (Mathias, 1997), *Other Voices, Other Rooms* (Rocksavage, 1995), *Senso unico* (Bhattacharya, 1999), *Solitude* (Schlaht, 2001), *Dead Heat* (produced in Germany, Malone, 2002), and *Disappearances* (Craven, 2004), and he played a villain in the third season of *24* (2004), starring his fellow Canadian Kiefer Sutherland.

Yves Laberge

See also: Arcand, Denys; Catholic Church; Jesuits; Lepage, Robert; Montreal; New France; Quebec.

References

Coulombe, Michel. *Denys Arcand: La vraie nature du cinéaste. Entretiens*. Montreal: Boréal, 1993.

Coulombe, Michel, and Marcel Jean, eds. *Dictionnaire du cinéma québécois*. 3rd ed. Montreal: Boréal, 1999.

BOILEAU-NARCEJAC

Boileau-Narcejac were two writers who constituted one author. This tandem created an original current in French crime fiction: they were much translated, and many of their novels were filmed, most noteworthy among them *D'Entre les morts* (*The Living and the Dead*, 1954; retitled *Sueurs froides*), which became Hitchcock's *Vertigo* (1958).

Pierre Louis Boileau (1906–1989) began writing crime fiction in the 1930s and published his first full-length crime novel, *La Pierre qui tremble* (The Trembling Stone), in 1934. Pierre Robert Ayraud (1908–1998) embarked on a career as a high school teacher of literature and philosophy; he began to experiment with the detective genre as a school exercise, went on to compose pastiches of famous authors, and published his first crime novel, *L'Assassin de minuit* (The Midnight Assassin), in 1946, using the pen name "Thomas Narcejac" to keep his two activities separate. He also cowrote with another author under the pseudonym John Silver Lee, and he published an essay "Esthétique du roman policier" (Aesthetics of the Detective Novel) in 1947.

Boileau and Narcejac read each other's work and corresponded before they met in 1948. Their first joint work, *L'Ombre et la proie* (The Shadow of the Prey), was serialized in 1951, and they continued writing crime novels, stories, and films, as well as plays for radio and television, until 1989. Theorists and *pasticheurs* of crime fiction, their joint aim as authors was to create a distinctive French approach that fell between the translations of detective puzzles typical of the old established Le Masque collection and the hard-boiled American novels that were beginning to appear in the Série noire. In their work, "Whodunit?" is less important than what in fact was (or is being, or will be) done. Their novels are built of layers of intrigue, psychological tension, and implacable situations in which victims, often would-be assassins, figure more than detectives, and the awaited crime comes from an unexpected angle.

In *Maléfices* (Evil Spells, 1961), the narrator believes his mistress is attempting to kill his wife, but in fact the attempts on her life are stage-managed by the wife herself to persuade her husband back to her. When the mistress dies in an accident, the narrator believes himself responsible. The final scene shows the wife happy to have her husband back just as he is going to give himself up to the police. *Carte Vermeil* (1979) is set in an old folks' home on the Riviera. The narrator, Michel Herboise, falls in love with Lucile, a new inmate. Thinking her to be responsible for the deaths of her former husband, her present husband, and another resident who had surprised her embracing Herboise, he believes himself an accessory to the murders. However, it turns out that the husband's death was an accident and the other two were killed by one of the nurses on behalf of relatives impatient to inherit. The last chapter reveals that Herboise is her next victim.

Stephen F. Noreiko

See also: Crime Fiction; Film Noir.
References
Boileau-Narcejac. *Tandem ou 35 ans de suspense.* Paris: Denoël, 1986.
———. *Le Roman policier.* Paris: PUF, 1988.
Colin, Jean-Paul. *Boileau-Narcejac: Le Parcours d'une oeuvre.* Paris: Encrage, 1999.

BOLÍVAR, SIMÓN (1783–1830)

The *Libertador* (Liberator), one of the most important figures of the Latin American independentist movements, born in Caracas in present-day Venezuela. He drew his inspiration, as did many others at the time, from French republican ideals.

Bolívar lived in Europe for only a few years, from 1799 to 1807, mainly in Bilbao, Madrid, Paris, and Rome, but also in Bordeaux and Vienna. During this period he stayed in Paris on three occasions: for the first two months of 1802, from April 1804 to April 1805, and finally from April to November 1806.

The first stay, although brief, left its mark on the young Bolívar. It was at the time of the Treaty of Amiens, which brought an end to a decade of war, and Paris was jubilant. Upon his return to Spain, he wrote to his friend Alexandre Dehollain: "Should I tell you what happened to me in Paris? It is certainly a place where one can amuse oneself endlessly without ever becoming bored. I did not know sadness during my stay in this delicious capital. . . . I can say that Spain seemed to me a country of savages, when I compared it to France; thus, you can be sure that, if I come to live in Europe, it will not be anywhere but Paris."

In 1802, Bolívar married a Spanish woman, Teresa del Toro, and left for Caracas, but his wife died a few months later, in January 1803. At the end of the year, the young widower returned to Europe.

During his second stay in Paris, Bolívar met Alexander von Humboldt and Aimé Bompland, two scientists who had settled there after their voyages of exploration in the Americas, particularly to Venezuela. Bolívar lived in the rue Vivienne, near the Palais Royal, in the very heart of the capital, and he frequented the salons. He also witnessed Napoléon's coronation, and although Bolívar had previously admired the clever strategist and consul of the republic, his enthronement was a disappointment. He even considered Napoléon's decision to take the crown as "despotic" or "tyrannical." Later, he saw Napoléon again, in Milan, while accompanied by his mentor Simón Rodríguez.

It was in Paris that Bolívar acquired his political education. He was an avid reader of Voltaire and Jean-Jacques Rousseau, but also of Montesquieu, René Descartes, Socrates, Niccolò Machiavelli, Miguel Cervantes, John Milton, Plutarch, and John Locke, all of whom he referred to in his correspondence. Evidence of his immersion in the political life of the period can be found in the fact that, like numerous famous Americans of the period, Bolívar became a Freemason. While in Paris in November 1805, he was awarded the grade of companion by the Saint Alexander lodge in Scotland.

Upon his return to Venezuela in 1807 after a trip to the United States, Bolívar began his struggle for the independence of the Spanish colonies of the Americas. His participation was first political in nature, but he very quickly excelled as a military leader. After a decade of war, Bolívar succeeded in liberating several Latin American countries from Spanish control. In 1819, he suggested the union of Venezuela, Nueva Granada (present-day Colombia), and Ecuador in a single nation: the Republic of Gran Colombia. The independence movement continued southward until 1824, with the liberation of Peru and the creation of Bolivia. However, internal divisions finally brought the dreams of a Hispano-American union to an end. Bolívar died in Santa Marta, Colombia, on December 17, 1830.

Pablo Aiquel

See also: Bonaparte, Napoléon; Republicanism; Venezuela; Voltaire, François.

References

Falcón, Briceño, et al. *Bolívar en France.* Caracas: Comité Ejecutivo des Bicentenario de Simón Bolívar, 1984.

Frank, Waldo David. *Birth of a World: Bolívar in Terms of His Peoples.* Boston: Houghton Mifflin, 1951.

Trend, J.B. *Bolívar and the Independence of Spanish America.* Bolivarian Society of Venezuela, 1951.

BOMBARDIER

Montreal-based aerospace and rail equipment group and the world's third-largest aircraft maker.

Bombardier's revenues for the fiscal year ending January 31, 2004, were $15.4 billion, and its shares are traded on the Toronto, Brussels, and Frankfurt stock exchanges. The company employs over 64,000 employees and operates on five continents, with a high concentration of activity in North America and Europe. More than 95 percent of its revenues are derived from markets outside Canada.

The company's origins were modest. It was founded as L'Auto-Neige Bombardier Limitée in 1942 in rural Quebec by J.-Armand Bombardier, to manufacture tracked vehicles for transportation on snow-covered terrain. As a result, Bombardier is now commonly called the father of snowmobiling.

In 1974 the company diversified into the transit equipment industry, with a contract to build rolling stock for the Montreal subway system. And in December 1986 its acquisition of Canadair, the leading Canadian aircraft manufacturer, took it into aerospace. Another notable move into this sector came in October 1989, when the company bought Short Brothers, the Northern Ireland manufacturer of civil and military aircraft that was founded in 1901 and is famous for receiving the first aircraft production contract in history from the Wright brothers in 1909.

The 1990s saw expansion by multiple additional acquisitions in rail and aerospace, such as the assets and operations of Learjet Corporation, builder of the famous Learjet business aircraft. Diversification continued, too: in 1990 the subsidiary Bombardier Real Estate was created, with responsibility for the management of Bombardier's real estate assets. Shorts Missile Systems was founded in 1993, a 50-50 joint venture company between Short Brothers and Thomson-CSF of France, to make very short-range surface-to-air defense systems.

The start of the new millennium established Bombardier as the industry leader in all activities related to the production of rail vehicles, when it acquired DaimlerChrysler Rail Systems. However, the company's fortunes began to turn down in 2003, signaled by the appointment as chief executive officer of Paul Tellier, who initiated a radical program of divestiture because of the downturn in the aircraft manufacturing industry.

In 2004–2005, Bombardier was still under pressure, not just because it is responsible for the biggest-ever transportation supply contract, worth $7.9 billion for the London Underground, but as a result of widespread stress in the global aviation sector. At the start of 2004, the company also restructured its lagging rail division, Bombardier Transportation, as the last major piece in Tellier's campaign to revive the company that had included management changes, paring down Bombardier Aerospace and Bombardier Capital, the financing arm, and selling its recreational products segment. Time will tell whether Tellier has done enough.

Mark Vernon

See also: Aviation; Montreal; Quebec.
References
Macdonald, Larry. *The Bombardier Story: Planes, Trains, and Snowmobiles.* London: John Wiley and Sons, 2003.
Webb, M. *Armand Bombardier, Inventor of the Snowmobile.* Toronto: Copp Clark Pitman, 1991.

BOMBARDIER, DENISE (1941–)

Denise Bombardier is a familiar figure on Canadian television and has been a recognizable voice on the airwaves of Radio Canada for four decades. A multitalented person, she has hosted countless programs on culture, public affairs, health, and politics and has interviewed hundreds of personalities on radio and television. From the 1960s onward, she traveled often to Paris, where she was foreign correspondent for Radio Canada.

After gaining her masters in political science at the University of Montreal in 1971 (with *Les "cent jours" du gouvernement Sauvé/The 100 Days of the Sauvé Government*), Bombardier defended her Ph.D. in sociology at the Sorbonne in 1974. As a journalist, she is a polemicist who writes provocative essays on contemporary French civilization from a North American perspective. Her first book, on French public television, was titled *La Voix de la France: Essai sur la France vue à travers sa télévision* (The Voice of France: Essay on France Seen through Its Television, 1975). She also wrote a book on Quebec that was published in France just before the first sovereignty referendum: *Dossier Québec* (1980).

In the 1980s, Bombardier began publishing novels with Les Editions du Seuil in France. They include an autobiographical novel about her childhood and teenage years, *Une Enfance à l'eau bénite* (A Holy Water Childhood, 1985), which remains her most famous work, but also more or less autobiographical novels about a passionate female character, such as *Tremblement de coeur* (Heart Murmur, 1990), *Nos Hommes* (Our Men, 1995), *Aimez-moi les uns les autres* (Love Me Everyone, 1999), and *Ouf!* (2002). Bombardier's novels greatly contributed to her fame outside Quebec. She was a guest on the very select French TV show *Apostrophes* during the 1980s and later on *Bouillon de culture,* both hosted by Bernard Pivot.

Bombardier has also written a corrosive essay about the social representation of the "Other," entitled *Lettre ouverte aux Français qui se croient le nombril du monde* (Open Letter to the French Who Think They Are the Center of the World, 2000). In addition to her extensive publications on French culture, she wrote a critical essay on human values in contemporary Quebec titled *Propos d'une moraliste* (A Moralist's Remarks, 2003).

During her career, Bombardier was occasionally a freelance journalist for various magazines such as *L'Express, Le Point, Télérama,* and *Géo* in France; in Quebec, she sometimes served as columnist for the newspaper *Le Devoir* and for the most popular magazines such as *Châtelaine* and *L'Actualité.* She also appeared on television in Switzerland on the Radio Suisse Romande, and she was a producer and host for a TV show titled *A Boulets rouges,* which aired on a cultural network, La Cinq, in France.

Bombardier remains the model of a journalist who can succeed at many levels in more than one country. She even had a small part in Michel Brault's film, *Entre la mer et l'eau douce (Between Sweet and Salt*

Water, 1967). She was awarded the Chevalier de la Légion d'honneur in France in 1993. Similarly, she became Chevalier de l'Ordre national du Québec in 2000.

Yves Laberge

See also: Brault, Michel; Quebec; Television.
Reference
Maisonneuve, Pierre. *Denise Bombardier: Tête froide, coeur tendre.* Ottawa: Novalis, 1998.

BONAPARTE, ELIZABETH PATTERSON (1785–1879)

"The belle of Baltimore," "Betsy" was born to William Patterson, a wealthy merchant, and Dorcus Spear Patterson in Baltimore and was educated at home and at a local French school. Considered one of the most beautiful women in the United States and known for her wit and willfulness, Betsy's marriage secured her place in history.

Napoléon's youngest brother, Jérôme, landed in New York in 1802 and traveled to Baltimore, where he met Betsy. According to private letters, the attraction was immediate and mutual. Baltimore County issued the couple a marriage license on October 29, 1803. Hoping to forestall the marriage, the Patterson family sent Betsy to Virginia. She returned a few weeks later; newspapers published notice of the impending nuptials in November. At the request of the Pattersons, Alexander J. Dallas (later secretary of the U.S. treasury) drew up a marriage contract, and the wedding, officiated by John Carroll, the bishop of Baltimore, took place on December 24, 1803. The bride was eighteen and the groom twenty. Shortly before the nuptials, the French consul, Louis A. Pichon, wrote to William Patterson to inform him that although such a marriage was legal in the

United States, French marriage law required parental consent for those under the age of twenty-five.

As the Bonapartes toured the East Coast (newspapers described Betsy's revealing clothing and the couple's habit of receiving visitors while in bed), Napoléon published notice that "Miss Patterson" was not welcome in France. The Patterson family dispatched Betsy's brother Robert to meet with Napoléon. U.S. secretary of state James Madison and U.S. minister to France William Livingston explored diplomatic solutions. Jérôme and Betsy departed for France later that year, determined to win Napoléon's approval. Once in Europe, the couple found all French ports closed to her. Jérôme proceeded to France and a pregnant Betsy to England. Napoléon would not yield. After Pope Pius VII refused to annul the marriage, the emperor used his legal and secular power to annul the union.

Jérôme Napoléon Bonaparte was born in England on July 7, 1805. Betsy and her son returned to Baltimore in September 1805. At Napoléon's behest, Jérôme married Princess Catherine of Württemberg in August 1807. In return for leaving Europe, Napoléon granted Betsy a 60,000-franc yearly allowance, which she received until his exile.

Newspapers chronicled Betsy's plight while she lived in Washington and Baltimore from 1805 to 1815. Unrest in France moved her to legally end her marriage; in 1813, the Maryland state legislature granted her petition for divorce. After Napoléon abdicated, Betsy returned to Europe, where she lived until her father's death in 1834; she never remarried. Betsy died in a Baltimore boardinghouse on April 4, 1879.

The Patterson-Bonaparte romance captivated the imagination of the American republic. For contemporaries, this moral, cautionary tale was an omen for those with aristocratic ambitions. During the late nineteenth century and the twentieth century, the story became fodder for romance novels.

Cynthia D. Earman

See also: Bonaparte, Jérôme; Bonaparte, Napoléon; Catholic Church.

References

Dider, Eugene L. *The Life and Letters of Madame Bonaparte.* New York: Charles Scribner's Sons, 1879.

Langdon, Harper I. "The Career of a Baltimore Girl." *The Ladies' Home Journal* 12, no. 7 (June 1895): 11.

BONAPARTE, JÉRÔME (1784–1860)

The youngest of eight surviving children was born to Maria Letizia (Ramolino) Buonaparte in Ajaccio, Corsica, a few weeks before the death of her husband Carlo Buonaparte. From 1794 to 1795, Jérôme lived in Marseilles, and in 1797 he enrolled in the College of Juilly. With the 1800 ascension of Napoléon to First Consul, Jérôme moved to the Tuileries Palace, where he enjoyed court life. Following a duel, Napoléon sent Jérôme to sea with the French navy. The youngest Bonaparte sailed first to Egypt and then to Santo Domingo, where he earned a promotion to ensign. For his second tour, the young officer sailed to the Antilles. Promoted to lieutenant, Jérôme took command of his first ship in 1802. In Saint Lucia, he contracted yellow fever and was ordered back to France.

Trying to evade capture by the British, Jérôme landed in New York in 1802. He was considered handsome, headstrong, and spoiled, and reports of his dalliances preceded him as he toured the East Coast. In Baltimore, Jérôme met and became enamored of Elizabeth "Betsy" Patterson. Over the objections of the French consul, the couple married. Outraged by his brother's insolence at marrying without permission, Napoléon insisted that Jérôme return alone to France. Despite Napoléon's public refusal to acknowledge the marriage, Jérôme and his pregnant wife left for France in 1805. Napoléon's officers refused to allow Betsy to land, and as she retreated to England, Jérôme proceeded alone to meet with his brother. Elizabeth Patterson Bonaparte gave birth to a son, Jérôme Napoléon, on July 7, 1805. Napoléon refused to yield and had the Patterson-Bonaparte marriage dissolved; Jérôme returned to the navy, where he rose to the rank of *capitaine de vaisseau* after negotiating the release of 231 captives from the Barbary pirates. As commander of the *Veteran,* Jérôme's next tour took him past the Cape of Good Hope and also to Martinique. Jérôme distinguished himself during this cruise by capturing eighty enemy ships and losing only five men, and he was promoted to rear admiral, named prince of the empire, and awarded the Légion d'honneur.

Even though Jérôme's naval service was over, his military career continued. Napoléon appointed Jérôme a brigadier general and placed him in command of the Army of the Allies. In August 1807 Jérôme married Princess Catherine of Württemberg (1783–1835) at Napoléon's behest, and Napoléon appointed Jérôme king of Westphalia. Jérôme and Catherine had two children: Mathilde Bonaparte (1820–1904) and Napoléon Joseph Charles Paul Bonaparte (1822–1891). Jérôme ruled

Westphalia for six years. He returned to France in 1815 and commanded troops at Quatre-Bras and Waterloo, where Napoléon was finally defeated that same year. When the exile of the Bonapartes ended in 1847, Jérôme returned to France. As president of France, Louis Napoléon Bonaparte appointed Jérôme governor des Invalides in 1849. Jérôme Bonaparte died in 1860 in Paris and was interred at the Hôtel des Invalides.

Cynthia D. Earman

See also: Bonaparte, Elizabeth Patterson; Bonaparte, Napoléon; Martinique; Piracy and Privateers; Saint Lucia; Santo Domingo.

References

Aronson, Theo. *The Golden Bees: The Story of the Bonapartes.* Greenwich, CT: New York Graphic Society, 1964.
Lamar, Glenn J. "The Military and Political Career of Jerome Bonaparte, 1800–1815." Ph.D. dissertation, Florida State University, 1994.

BONAPARTE, JOSEPHINE TASCHER DE LA PAGEIER DE BEAUHARNAIS (1763–1814)

Marie-Joseph-Rose, "Empress Josephine," "La Américaine," was born to Joseph-Gaspard and Rose-Claire (des Vergers de Sannois) Tascher de la Pageier in Martinique. Raised in genteel poverty, "Rose" (as she was known until her marriage to Napoléon) attended convent school on the island.

In 1779, Rose and her father set off for France. Désirée Renaudin, Rose's aunt, hoping to secure her own fortune, arranged a marriage between Rose and Alexandre de Beauharnais. This marriage of convenience begot two children: Eugène-Rose (1781–1824) and Hortense Eugènie (1783–

1837). The couple separated in 1785. During the Reign of Terror, both Rose and Beauharnais were imprisoned; Beauharnais was executed and Rose released. The newly widowed Rose survived on loans, credit, and the generosity of lovers, including Generals Lazare Hoche and Paul Barras.

Napoléon Bonaparte first encountered Rose Beauharnais in the salons of Paris. The widow's sweetness and charm captivated him. The young, rough Corsican did not at first impress her, but eventually his passion overrode her reservations, and when he proposed, Rose accepted. They married in a civil ceremony on March 9, 1796. Neither family approved of the marriage. Napoléon was dismayed to discover that his new wife brought more debts than funds to the union. Over the ensuing years, the couple became closer; Napoléon ascribed his military successes to Josephine and treated her children as his own. Tension arose when she failed to produce an heir, and rumors of affairs, encouraged by Napoléon's brothers and sisters, surrounded her. Nevertheless, Napoléon and Josephine reaffirmed their marriage vows in a religious ceremony prior to their coronation as emperor and empress of France on December 2, 1804.

Josephine took an active interest in gardens and flowers. In 1804 she appointed the artist Pierre-Joseph Redouté "Painter to Josephine, Empress of the French." Redouté's watercolors hung on the walls of Malmaison, Josephine's house outside of Paris, and Redouté's books, *Jardin de Malmaison* (Malmaison Garden), *Les Liliacées,* and *Les Roses* (Roses) immortalize the blossoms that Josephine cultivated.

Napoléon's siblings continued to press for a divorce. Following the conception of two sons, Léon Denuelle (1806–1881) and Alexandre-Florian, Comte Walewski (1810–1868) with two different mistresses, Napoléon followed through on his threat to divorce Josephine. In 1809, Napoléon's civil and ecclesiastical courts dissolved the marriage, and Josephine retired to Malmaison.

On May 27, 1814, Josephine died from complications of a cold.

Cynthia D. Earman

See also: Bonaparte, Napoléon; French Revolution; Martinique.

References

Bruce, Evangeline. *Napoléon and Josephine: An Improbable Marriage.* New York: Scribner, 1995.

Erickson, Carolly. *Josephine: A Life of the Empress.* New York: St. Martin's Press, 1998.

Stuart, Andrea. *The Rose of Martinique: A Life of Napoléon's Josephine.* London: Macmillan, 2003.

As emperor after 1804, Napoléon initiated an embargo policy intended to strangle the British economy. The worst sufferer, however, was the United States. (Library of Congress)

BONAPARTE, NAPOLÉON (1769–1821)

Revolutionary First Consul and, from 1804 to 1815, first emperor of the French.

Bonaparte possessed a variegated genius and had a phenomenal career as ruler, military leader, legal reformer, artistic director, and scientific patron of France. His military successes allowed him to impose the reforms of the French Revolution, to greater or lesser degree, on much of the rest of Europe, and military necessity forced other nations (notably Prussia and, briefly, the United States) to adopt military and other policies thought to be fit for the international environment he made. From his accession to the First Consulship in 1799 to his defeat at Waterloo in 1815, his foreign policy as leader of one of Europe's—and thus the world's—two greatest powers had a significant and lasting effect upon the United States.

Prominent Americans such as Thomas Jefferson held out hope that Bonaparte, as First Consul, would adopt a pro-American foreign policy, which would have been especially welcome in the wake of the 1798–1800 undeclared quasi war between the United States and France. In this hope, francophiles were to be disappointed.

Most prominent of those Napoleonic initiatives regarding the United States was his decision in 1803 to sell the Louisiana Territory to the fledgling North American nation. In response to a request for a far more circumscribed land sale, Bonaparte offered an area including much of today's western United States, plus part of what is now Canada, for $15 million. It was the greatest land sale in history, and it cemented Thomas Jefferson's Republican Party in the affections of Jefferson's countrymen. Bonaparte had intended to reestablish France's Caribbean empire after the loss of Haiti, but the evident impracticability of doing so led him to sell his mainland empire for what he could get rather than see Britain capture it by force.

As emperor after 1804, Napoléon, still preoccupied by his life-and-death struggle with Great Britain and increasingly dominant on the continent of Europe, initiated an embargo policy intended to strangle the British economy. The worst sufferer, however, was the United States. In response to the British Orders in Council of 1806, France adopted the Berlin and Milan Decrees of 1806 and 1807, which banned British ships from continental ports and announced that any ship that submitted to British search or regulation would be seized by the French navy. In sum, American ships had been banned from all territory controlled by France and Britain.

President Jefferson's response was his feckless embargo, the most unpopular measure by far of his administration. Adopted by Congress in 1807 and strengthened thereafter, this policy said that the United States would trade with no foreign nation. It brought little positive response from the major powers, and difficulty in enforcing it led to severe sectional strains on the new U.S. Constitution. The British had no real alternative to draconian naval policy, and Napoléon's contempt for the United States was such that he at one point referred to the American flag as "star-spangled bunting." In fact, however, the great preponderance of U.S. foreign trade at the time was with Britain, so the embargo could be seen as practically aiding the French.

In 1810, Nathaniel Macon's Bill Number 2 became U.S. policy. Revoking the embargo, it pledged to reimpose it against one of the major powers as soon as the other lifted its anti-American policies.

Napoléon's disastrous Russian campaign of 1812 and his armies' defeat in Iberia freed British forces for operations in the New World during the War of 1812. For that reason alone, some Americans lamented at least the timing of his defeats.

Kevin Gutzman

See also: Foreign Policy, 1776–1945; French Revolution; Haiti; Jefferson, Thomas; Louisiana Purchase.

References

Perkins, Bradford. *The Cambridge History of American Foreign Relations.* Vol. I: *The Creation of a Republican Empire, 1776–1865.* Cambridge: Cambridge University Press, 1993.

Tucker, Robert W., and David C. Hendrickson. *Empire of Liberty: The Statecraft of Thomas Jefferson.* New York: Oxford University Press, 1990.

BORDEAUX

In the eighteenth century Bordeaux was France's most prosperous Atlantic port. Though the city had a long history as the administrative and judicial capital of Guienne, home to a royal intendant and to a provincial *parlement* (parliament), its economy was increasingly dominated by trade, especially with the Caribbean. Contemporaries described the years before the French Revolution as a golden age, when ships lined the quays along the Garonne and merchants rivaled established legal families as the leaders of urban society. Huge profits were made from the West Indies, from trade with Martinique, Guadeloupe, and especially Saint-Domingue, where Bordeaux men went as colonists and whence Bordeaux ships brought back rich cargoes of coffee, indigo, and rum. Colonial produce was reexported throughout continental Europe as Bordeaux became rich on an entrepôt trade that complemented the city's other main staple, the sale of fine wines from its hinterland in the Médoc. In the course of the century the balance of this trade changed dramatically, and the city's prosperity became dangerously dependent on the Antilles. Though wine exports tripled in value, their part in Bordeaux's trade fell to under 30 percent, and the city's links to its rural hinterland were weakened. And if Bordeaux never became as reliant on the slave trade as its great Atlantic rival, Nantes, slave ships made up an increasing percentage of the city's commercial activity, with some of Bordeaux's most prominent merchants pursuing the triangular trade with West Africa and the Caribbean or the American South. Black servants and freed slaves were a common sight around the port, adding to Bordeaux's claims to be a cosmopolitan city, a melting pot of different cultures.

Bordeaux's commercial wealth was there for all to see. During the eighteenth century, trade grew at a rate of more than 4 percent annually, far outstripping the French economy as a whole. The tonnage of the ships sailing from the port more than doubled in the years between 1720 and 1789, and the value of their cargoes increased twentyfold. It was a period of high investment and conspicuous consumption, with rich *négociants* reinvesting the profits of trade in handsome suburbs and lavish town houses. Bordeaux took pride in its status as a regional capital and, particularly while Tourny occupied the post of intendant from 1743 to 1758, was endowed with elegant boulevards and gracious public buildings. Its provincial academy, the *musée* where lawyers and merchants congregated, and its active cultural and theatrical life all helped turn it into one of the focal points of the French Enlightenment. Bordeaux was also a major draw for immigrants throughout the century, attracting the young and ambitious from across the Southwest; it was perceived as a place where fortunes were made, a city open to all men of talent, where foreigners settled freely and Protestants and Jews were integrated into the urban elite. For the rural poor, too, Bordeaux offered work and opportunity; they found jobs on merchant vessels, as porters or stevedores along the waterfront, or as laborers on the city's many building sites. Many came from the immediate hinterland, from the Agenais and Périgord, but others were lured from further afield, with large numbers from the foothills of the Pyrenees and from the Limousin. The population rose from around 66,000 at the time of Tourny's census in 1747 to over 100,000 by 1790. Bordeaux's future, it seemed, was secure, thanks to the city's privileged relations with the West Indies and especially with Saint-Domingue, which, on the eve of the French Revolution, accounted for three-quarters of the city's colonial trade.

The revolution spelled disaster for Bordeaux's commercial prosperity, though this effect had less to do with its ideology than with the long years of war that it unleashed. The merchant community largely welcomed the revolution in 1789, which opposed privilege and opened careers to talent. The majority of the deputies

Bordeaux sent to the National Assembly were progressives who favored civil equality and the rights of man. Many went further, indeed, supporting the creation of the republic in 1792. Thereafter, however, things went badly wrong for the Bordelais. Their most prominent deputies distrusted the extreme radicalism of the Jacobins and the Paris sections. They provided many of the Girondin leaders like Marguerite-Elie Guadet and Pierre Vergniaud—the term *Girondin* was taken from the name of Bordeaux's department, the Gironde—who would be overthrown in the violent Jacobin coup of June 1793 and then tried and executed. The city's reputation was tarnished by the federalist revolt against the convention during the months that followed, which cast doubt on the loyalty of the merchant community. The Terror also hit the city's merchants hard. More than 200 were arrested; many suffered heavy fines, and fifteen were among those guillotined on the Place de la République in the center of Bordeaux.

More serious still for the Atlantic trade were the effects of the revolutionary wars, especially after hostilities began with Britain, the greatest naval power in Europe, in the spring of 1793. Bordeaux's merchants and shipowners had been able to continue trading during the early years of the revolution, but now their very livelihood was at stake. For Britain, this was a war about wealth and colonies as much as about military power on the European continent, and the wealth of France's West Indian islands evoked covetousness and envy. Bordeaux's merchant community did not foresee the disaster that awaited them. They had, after all, survived a series of maritime conflicts during the eighteenth century and had evolved their own strategies

to counter the threat. But this war was different, lasting for twenty years and attacking basic commercial freedoms. The revolutionaries themselves imposed strict controls on the movement of shipping. Imported goods were requisitioned by the state and paid for in devalued paper currency. French vessels suffered attacks on the long and hazardous journey back from the Antilles; their cargoes were plundered and the ships seized. A naval blockade was imposed that prevented neutral shipping from trading in French ports and destroyed the entrepôt trade. Insurance rates spiraled, and shipowners were forced to take desperate risks, with the consequence that many respectable trading firms were forced out of business. For others, often younger men willing to arm their vessels and accept the risk of loss, the war provided the opportunity to make a quick fortune out of smuggling and privateering. But that could not compensate for the huge decline in legitimate trade. Ships and docks lay idle, unemployment rose, and Bordeaux's population started to fall.

There was a partial recovery after the fall of the radical Jacobin leader Maximilien Robespierre in 1794, but Bordeaux's golden age was over. From 1795 some foreign, and especially U.S., ships returned to the Garonne with colonial imports, but the momentum experienced in the later eighteenth century was not recovered. The prosperity of the port was undermined by the abolition of the slave trade and even more by the loss of Saint-Domingue, which became an independent state, Haiti, in 1804. And though Napoléon tried to restore slavery, Atlantic trade enjoyed only a partial recovery. Bordeaux's position, in particular, was fatally weakened. Saint-Domingue, the key to its fortune, was lost forever; Britain had taken control of the trade in colonial produce with northern Europe; and Le Havre, closer to Paris and to the textile industry of Normandy, was better placed to exploit the new commercial opportunities in the United States. Nineteenth-century Bordeaux was condemned to long decades of commercial and demographic decline in a France whose economic epicenter had swung violently away from the Atlantic seaboard.

Alan Forrest

See also: Bonaparte, Napoléon; Coffee; French Revolution; Guadeloupe; Haiti; Le Havre; Martinique; Nantes; Piracy and Privateers; Santo Domingo; Slavery; Wine.

References

Butel, Paul. *The Atlantic*. Seas in History. London: Routledge, 1999.

Forrest, Alan. *The Revolution in Provincial France: Aquitaine, 1789–1799*. Oxford/New York: Clarendon Press, 1996.

Pariset, François-Georges, ed. *Bordeaux au dix-huitième siècle*. Bordeaux: Fédération historique du sud-ouest, 1968.

BORDUAS, PAUL-EMILE (1905–1960)

Québécois painter and writer, born in Saint-Hilaire in 1905.

Together with the painter Ozias Leduc, Borduas worked on numerous projects decorating churches throughout Quebec and later in France and the United States. In was on Leduc's advice that Borduas enrolled at the Montreal Ecole des Beaux-Arts in 1923. It was again on Leduc's advice that he went to finish his training as a religious painter in Paris where, in 1928, he attended the Ateliers d'Art Sacré.

When the economic crisis of the 1930s forced the Catholic Church to suspend its restoration work, Borduas held a number of teaching posts in primary schools. The number of paintings he produced during this period was thus limited. It was his post at the School of Furniture in 1937 that gave his career a new lease on life. In 1939, he collaborated with John Lyman on the creation of the Contemporary Arts Society, whose aim was to encourage exhibitions of contemporary art. In the years that followed, Borduas played a role in many exhibitions, including his own first one-man show, Peintures surrealistes (Surrealist Paintings), in 1942.

Borduas challenged the standardization and conformism that hindered his students' personal and artistic development. He brought together a number of students for discussions of art and the future of society, and together they laid the foundations for the Quebec automatist movement. In 1945, they developed a plan for an exhibition to be held in a working-class area. Held in 1946, the exhibition brought together works by Borduas, Marcel Barbeau, Roger Fauteux, Pierre Gauvreau, Jean-Paul Mousseau, and Jean-Paul Riopelle. It was the first automatist exhibition and outraged bourgeois critics.

In 1947, Borduas wrote a manifesto, *Refus global* (*Global Refusal*), which shook Quebec conservatism in its period of "grande noirceur" (great darkness) and denounced the joint control, not to say censorship, exercised by the Union nationale and the clergy on the population of Quebec. This text, in demonstrating an audacity previously unseen, invited the collective to recognize that God does not exist and to embrace modernity. It constituted a plea for freedom of expression and creation, as well as for freedom of choice.

The publication of *Refus global* provoked a scandal, and Quebec would have to wait more than a decade for the profound change it called for to take place. In this way, Borduas turned out to have been a visionary, since he felt that he had been born too early, in a country that was too young.

The importance of *Refus global* for the cultural evolution of Quebec, even in Borduas's life, cannot be denied. Because the critics were particularly virulent toward him, he had to take on almost single-handedly the burden of the manifesto, although it had been signed by fifteen other artists. He lost his post at the Ecole du meuble. Hurt, he wrote *Projections délibérantes* (*Deliberating Projections*), an autobiographical pamphlet in which he explains his actions and makes his own defense. However, the press at the time paid no attention to it, and Borduas lived through the darkest years of his life, as is reflected in his work. His departure for the United States in 1953 brought a certain depth to his painting. In 1955, he exiled himself in France, where he remained until his death in Paris in 1960. It was only posthumously that he gained recognition and that his status was confirmed by a number of exhibitions throughout the world. In 1977, the Quebec government created the Prix Paul-Emile Borduas, which is awarded for contributions to the field of the visual arts.

Sonia Lebel

See also: Catholic Church; Duplessis, Maurice Le Noblet; Painting; Quebec; Quiet Revolution; Surrealism.

References

Gagnon, François-Marc. *Paul-Emile Borduas.* Ottawa: Galerie nationale du Canada, 1976.

———. *Paul-Emile Borduas (1905–1960): Biographie critique et analyse de l'œuvre.* Montreal: Fides, 1978.

Robert, Guy. *Borduas.* Montreal: Presses de l'Université du Québec, 1972.

BORGES, JORGE LUIS (1899–1986)

Argentine essayist, storyteller, and poet with a profound influence on major twentieth-century writers and thinkers on both sides of the Atlantic.

Borges was born in Buenos Aires, where he experienced a sheltered childhood, developing at an early age interests in philosophy and literature. He spent part of his youth in Geneva during World War I, where he completed his schooling, and in Spain, where he started to write avant-garde poetry. When he returned from Europe, his writing sought to reflect the transformations of urban life in Buenos Aires, and he abandoned both Latin American regionalist writing and Spanish avant-garde *ultraísmo* (*ultraism*). From the 1930s onward Borges wrote short stories and essays whose blend of metaphysical, aesthetic, and mystical questions would give his work its particular flavor. His most memorable stories are published in works such as *Ficciones* (*Fictions,* 1944) and *El Aleph* (1949), although he continued to publish until the time of his death. He was completely blind for the last thirty years of his life.

Against a background in which Latin American writing was still conceptualized in terms of its passive reflection or total rejection of European culture, Borges claimed for Latin Americans the task of *appropriating* European culture and refashioning it "with irreverence." It is in this encounter between different times, spaces, and cultures that Borges's writing finds its true expression and where it germinated many contemporary ideas about culture, ideas about literary influence and authorship, originality, and textuality that have become central to French-identified cultural theories. Thus, in one story an imaginary French symbolist, Pierre Menard, becomes the "author" of *Don Quixote,* not by rewriting the great work but simply by reading it 300 years later. In another, the universe is represented as a library of infinite design, inhabited by librarians whose life is governed by an endless search for the "catalogue of catalogues." Borges has been appropriated by many as a postmodern *avant-la-lettre* and has influenced numerous major French thinkers from Michel Foucault and Roland Barthes to Jacques Derrida and Jean Baudrillard. He also set trends for innumerable Latin American writers, replacing land with the labyrinth as the foundation for reflections on cultural identity.

Borges did not think much of Paris and had a particular dislike for the modishness of French literary culture. Nevertheless, much of Borges's popularity outside Latin America is due to the French, who were the first to translate and circulate his works. Furthermore, his thought itself is also strongly influenced by Baudelaire, Stéphane Mallarmé, and Paul Verlaine, among others, influences that are felt in his preoccupation with dreams, mythology, and language. Yet, as the story about Pierre Menard demonstrates, the notion of influence is for Borges something of a misnomer. Even the copy becomes a singular event that cannot be reduced to original intentions and that

Jorge Luis Borges. 1962. Much of Borges's popularity outside Latin America is due to the French, who were the first to translate and circulate his works. (Library of Congress)

transcends literary-historical monumentalization. As for encyclopedias, along with mirrors and atlases, their foundations are as much rhetorical as factual.

Rory O'Bryen

See also: Argentina; Avant-Gardes; Barthes, Roland; Baudelaire, Charles-Pierre; Baudrillard, Jean; Derrida, Jacques; Foucault, Michel; Literary Relations; Theory; World War I.

References

Bloom, Harold, ed. *Jorge Luis Borges.* New York: Chelsea House, 1986.
Sarlo, Beatriz. *Borges: A Writer on the Edge.* London: Verso, 1993.

BOSSU, JEAN-BERNARD (1720–1792)

French sailor and explorer, born in a village southwest of Dijon in 1720.

Bossu's career as an officer in the French navy took him on three different occasions to the French colony of Louisiana. The account of his first two journeys (1751–1757 and 1757–1762), to the Mississippi valley and to what now is Alabama, was published in Paris in 1768 with the title *Nouveaux Voyages aux Indes occidentales; Contenant une Rélation des differens Peuples qui habitent les environs du grand Fleuve Saint-Louis, appellé vulgairement le Mississipi; leur Religion; leur gouvernement; leurs mæurs, leurs guerres et leur commerce,* and was translated into English in 1771.

Bossu was a keen observer, and his description of eighteenth-century New Orleans is particularly acute. He speaks of the diverse population of the city, made up of Europeans, Indians, Africans, and half bloods of European and native descent. He describes the American-born offspring of French settlers as "brave, tall, well-built," with a natural inclination toward the arts and sciences, adding that it was the usual practice to send the sons to France for further education. Bossu goes on to mention the increasing use of slave labor to clear the land in order to grow indigo, tobacco, rice, corn, and sugarcane and describes the life of the planter aristocracy as one affording the opportunity for hunting, fishing, and other pleasures of life. One of Bossu's own hunting expeditions nearly ended tragically, when he was awakened one night by a 20-foot alligator that was attempting to drag away his sleeping bag, to which he had incautiously attached his catch of cat-

fish. He mentions that the Acolapissas and the Washas (Ouachitas) north of New Orleans wrestled alligators for sport and describes their technique of jamming a piece of hardwood or iron bar into the mouth of the alligator.

A particularly interesting letter in Bossu's collection is related to ways to conserve and prolong life in America. He mentions a dish consisting of "dried and smoked game, roasted or boiled with corn ground in a hardwood mortar," called chili, which he describes as very tasty and healthful. Bossu goes on to advise a life of moderation, stating that "voluptuousness and intemperance in eating and drinking" have proved to be deadly to settlers (Bossu 1962). He suggests that settlers should allow themselves time to get accustomed to the climate, avoiding fruit and liquor until their bodies adjust. In addition, he advocates periodic bleeding to prevent apoplexy and the occasional use of "gentle laxatives." Bossu comments on the excellent health of the natives of Louisiana and concludes that it is because of their work and exercise that they are not plagued with gout, kidney stones, and other ailments to which the European settlers in Louisiana were prone.

Susan Castillo

See also: Cuisine; Louisiana; Mississippi River; New Orleans; Slavery; Tobacco.

References

Bossu, Jean-Bernard. *Travels in the Interior of North America, 1751–1762.* Trans. and ed. S. Feiler. Norman: University of Oklahoma Press, 1962.

Sayre, Gordon M. *Les Sauvages Américains: Representations of Native Americans in French and English Colonial Texts.* Chapel Hill: UNC Press, 1997.

BOUCHARD, LUCIEN (1938–)

Lawyer, diplomat, politician, and administrator, born in Saint-Coeur-de-Marie (Lac-Saint-Jean) on December 22, 1938.

Lucien Bouchard is one of the few Canadian politicians to have had a double career, holding the highest positions at both the federal and provincial levels. He was also leader of the opposition of the Canadian parliament (1993–1996) and premier of Quebec from 1996 to 2001.

Bouchard lived in Paris while he was Canada's ambassador to France from July 1985 to March 1988. While in Paris, he represented Canada at the first Sommet de la francophonie (1986) and presided over the International Preparation Committee for the second francophone summit, which was to take place in Quebec City in September 1987. Bouchard truly believed in *la francophonie* and felt attached to France; he also called Switzerland "a magnificent country."

Just before ending his term as ambassador, Bouchard was made secretary of state for Canada by the prime minister, Brian Mulroney, on March 31, 1988; he was elected a member of the Canadian parliament for Lac-Saint-Jean on June 20, 1988, and later became minister of the environment in Ottawa. But Bouchard's long career culminated when he founded a new political party, the Bloc Québécois, in July 1990. Only three years later, that young party became the official opposition on the federal scene in Ottawa, even though all its voters and deputies were exclusively from Quebec. Although he had tried to obtain a fair place for Quebec in the federal government during the 1980s, Bouchard's move toward separatism was a reaction toward English Canada's refusal to recognize Quebec as a distinct society within Canada after the constitutional crisis of 1990 (the collapse of the Meech Lake Accord). Bouchard often said that the time for discussion between federal and provincial deputies over the status of Quebec was over; it was time for a definitive separation. His book *A Visage découvert* (1992; translated as *On the Record,* 1994) gives the clearest account of the Quebec separatist movement.

In 1995, Bouchard nearly led his supporters to victory in a Quebec referendum for independence that gave 49 percent to the "yes" campaign. As premier of Quebec following Jacques Parizeau's resignation, he went back to France on a regular basis to meet French politicians and allies, such as President Jacques Chirac. At the 1997 Sommet de la francophonie in Hanoi (Vietnam), Bouchard caused a commotion when he asked all members of the Organisation internationale de la francophonie to respect human rights (he was singling out certain African countries). Chirac tried to limit these comments by saying that all African nations had to progress toward democracy at their own pace. Bouchard's resignation as premier was partly provoked by hard-line nationalists in the Parti Québécois. He was succeeded by Bernard Landry.

In 2002 the French government made Bouchard a Commandeur de l'Ordre de la Légion d'honneur.

Yves Laberge

See also: Chirac, Jacques; *Francophonie, La;* Ottawa; Quebec; Quebec City.

References

Maillard, Rémi, ed. *Lucien Bouchard mot à mot.* Montreal: Stanké, 1996.

Vastel, Michel. *Lucien Bouchard: En attendant la suite.* Outremont: Lanctôt, 1996.

BOUCHARD, MICHEL MARC (1958–)

Québécois playwright, born in 1958 in Lac Saint-Jean, a region that would later feature prominently in his writing.

Michel Marc Bouchard wrote and mounted his first play at only fourteen years of age. Later, while studying tourism at CEGEP (between high school and university in the Quebec system), he authored and produced two more plays, an experience that eventually led him to enroll in theater at the University of Ottawa. Subsequently, Bouchard became very involved as an actor, author, and producer with several Ottawa theater companies. From 1988 to 1990 he was artistic director of the Théâtre du Trillium, also in Ottawa, and from 1994 to 1995 he held the position of writer in residence at the Théâtre du Nouveau Monde in Montreal.

Bouchard's intimate knowledge of stagecraft complemented a fast-growing body of original writing. His first published work, *La Contre-nature de Chrysippe Tanguay, écologiste* (Chrysippe Tanguay, the Unnatural Ecologist, 1984), relates the story of a gay couple, Louis and Jean, who wish to adopt a child. Louis is an actor playing the role of Chrysippe, and this play within a play is used to expose the profound psychological struggles he faces in terms of gender and sexuality. This play forms part of the Tanguay series, in which the author uses mythology to explore the affective dimensions of human relationships. Beginning with *Dans les bras de Morphée Tanguay* (In the Arms of Morphée Tanguay, unpublished), this cycle also includes *La Poupée de Pélopia* (Pelopia's Doll, 1985), a play about a woman who confronts her father with his crime of incest, and *Les Muses orphelines* (*The Orphan Muses,* 1989), which tells the story of three siblings abandoned as children by their mother, who come together to rectify the "truth" about their past.

The theme of the adult revisiting a painful childhood occurs repeatedly in Bouchard's work, as witnessed by *L'Histoire de l'oie* (*Teeka's Tale,* 1991), an internationally acclaimed children's play denouncing physical abuse, and *Le Chemin des Passes-dangereuses* (*Down Dangerous Passes Road,* 1998), an eerie story of fate about three brothers reunited for a wedding who find themselves, after a deadly car accident, at the very place their father "accidentally" met his death. Bouchard's most famous play remains *Les Feluettes* (*Lilies,* 1987). Set in a prison in 1952, the play relates the story of Simon, an inmate wrongly imprisoned for the murder of Vallier who sequesters Bilodeau, now a bishop, and forces him to witness events from their youth as played out by other prisoners. The inmate actors take us back to 1912, revealing the love between Simon and Vallier, expressed through the roles they play in the parish priest's production of Gabriele D'Annunzio's *Martyrdom of Saint Sebastian. Les Feluettes* experiments with layers of theater and language to express identity, fidelity, and courage. A screen version, produced by Toronto filmmaker John Greyson, has also met with critical success and opened the door to a larger audience, both in English Canada and in the United States.

Bouchard's audience extends to Europe as well, where the French adaptation of *Les Muses orphelines* (1994) showed the international appeal of "local" theater. His other published plays include *Rock pour un faux bourdon* (Rock for a Faux Bourdon, 1987), *Les Grandes Chaleurs* (*Heatwave,*

1993), *Le Voyage du couronnement* (*The Coronation Journey,* 1995), *Les Papillons de nuit* (*The Night Butterflies,* 1999), *Sous le regard des mouches* (Under the Gaze of Flies, 2000), and *Les Manuscrits du déluge* (*Written on Water,* 2003), as well as a number of one-act plays, including *Du haut de ses vingt ans* (Looking Down from Twenty, 1987) and *Le Jade et l'ébène* (Jade and Ebony, 1997).

Shawn Huffman

See also: Gay Movement; Theater.

Reference

Godin, Jean Cléo, and Dominique Lafon. *Dramaturgies québécoises des années quatre-vingt: Michel Marc Bouchard, Normand Chaurette, René-Daniel Dubois, Marie Laberge.* Montreal: Leméac, 1999.

French travel writer Louis Antoine de Bougainville. Bougainville's American journals offer fascinating insights into the politics and military policies of New France in the eighteenth century. (Library of Congress)

BOUGAINVILLE, LOUIS ANTOINE DE (1729–1811)

French travel writer.

Although Louis Antoine de Bougainville is known primarily for his scientific expedition to the South Pacific, from which he brought back the flower (bougainvillea) that bears his name, his American journals offer fascinating insights into the politics and military policies of New France in the eighteenth century. Bougainville's early education was in law, but later he went on to become a distinguished mathematician (with two books on integral calculus) and soldier. During the French and Indian War (1754–1763), he went to Canada as an aide to General Louis Joseph de Montcalm, commanding troops at the siege of Quebec in 1759.

Bougainville's American journals offer intriguing insights into the reactions of a French philosopher confronted by Menominee captives, whom he describes as "man in conditions closest to nature" and depicts as physically robust and eloquent of speech. He is particularly impressed by the natives' facility in finding and following tracks in the forest. He attributes it to their capacity to read the inclination of the sun, the inclination of trees and leaves, and what he regards as a "perfection of the instinct," adding that the natives are capable of determining "the number that have passed, whether they are Indians or Europeans, if the tracks are fresh or old, if they are healthy or sick people" (Castillo and Schweitzer, p. 455).

Bougainville was disillusioned by profligacy and lack of discipline among French soldiers, which he viewed as the consequence of excessively high salaries; he expresses the fear that the climate of insubordination and indolence existing among the troops in New France may spread across the Atlantic to the mother country. He describes the prevalence of money changing at ruinous rates in Quebec (comparing it to the extortionate practices of the moneylenders on the rue Quimcampoix in Paris) along with widespread hunger caused by disastrous wheat harvests. Bougainville's American journals are often elegiac in tone, contrasting the simpler life of the colony's earlier years with the climate of greed, avarice, and economic speculation existing in 1758. He died in 1811.

Susan Castillo

See also: French and Indian War; Montcalm, Louis Joseph de; New France.

References

de Bougainville, Louis Antoine. *Adventure in the Wilderness: The American Journals of Louis Antoine de Bougainville, 1756–1760.* Ed. and trans. E. P. Hamilton. Norman: University of Oklahoma Press, 1964.

Castillo, Susan, and Ivy Schweitzer. *The Literatures of Colonial America: An Anthology.* Oxford: Blackwell, 2001.

Okon, Luzian. *"Nature" and "Civilisation" dans le Supplément au voyage de Bougainville de Denis Diderot.* Frankfurt: Peter Lang, 1980.

Pagden, Anthony. "The Savage Critic: Some European Images of the Primitive." *Yearbook of English Studies* 13 (1983): 32–45.

BOUKMAN, DANIEL (DANIEL BLÉRALD) (1936–)

Prominent Martinican playwright who, following in the footsteps of Frantz Fanon, abandoned the Caribbean to settle in Algeria, taking up antiracist and political liberation issues across the Atlantic and as far away as Palestine.

His best-known play, *Les Négriers* (*The Slave Ships*, 1971), likened the contemporary exilic relocation of black West Indians to France to the slave trade. Other plays have taken up the themes of racism, money, and power, such as *Ventres pleins, ventres creux* (Full Bellies, Empty Bellies, 1971) and *Orphée nègre* (Negro Orpheus), a dramatic poem, which was not only a Marxist critique of négritude parodying Sartre's 1947 essay "Orphée noir," but was also, according to Bridget Jones, a "savage and explicit" attack on Aimé Césaire. This connection is significant because Boukman was clearly influenced by Césaire's turn toward drama in the late 1960s.

Boukman was no stranger to polemic in these plays or in his life. He had refused to fight for France in Algeria in 1961, deserting and changing his name to Boukman in respect of the heroic historical figure who died fighting to liberate Haiti from slavery in 1791. Thus, Boukman established his Atlantic credentials: a Caribbean with an antislavery hero's name writing theater to denounce racism and exploitation on both sides of the Atlantic, in France and in the Caribbean. Indeed, *Les Négriers* was first performed in Paris, and the Mauritanian avant-garde filmmaker, Med Hondo, made the screen version, *West Indies* (1979). Boukman's main aim was to denounce the "genocide by substitution" taking place in the French Caribbean, whereby blacks are shipped to work in low-paid jobs in France and replaced by white French settlers and administrative workers from France. He takes no prisoners in his satirical broadsides against Charles de Gaulle, Léopold Senghor (then president of Senegal), Gaston Monnerville, and even Edouard Glissant.

Inspired by the Palestinian struggle against Israeli occupation, Boukman wrote a homage and critique of the situation in 1976, *Et jusqu'à la dernière pulsation de nos veines . . .* (And Until the Last Throbbing of Our Veins . . .), attacking the Jordanian army for the 1970 massacre as much as praising Jews fighting on the side of Palestinians. More recently, he has shifted his focus back to considering the role of the Creole langauge in the Caribbean.

Andy Stafford

See also: Antislavery Movements; Césaire, Aimé; Fanon, Frantz; Gaulle, General Charles de; Glissant, Edouard; Language; Martinique; Slavery.

References

Boukman, Daniel. *Les Négriers.* Paris: L'Harmattan, 1978 [1971].

Jones, Bridget. "Theater and Resistance?" *An Introduction to Caribbean Francophone Writing: Guadeloupe and Martinique.* Ed. Sam Haigh. Oxford: Berg, 1999.

BOULLE, PIERRE (1912–1994)

A contemporary mainstream author, Pierre Boulle's best-remembered works are without a doubt *Bridge over the River Kwai* and *Planet of the Apes,* both of which were made into full-length feature films. Boulle blended his personal experiences into fictitious worlds where the human condition was often depicted in a way that was both pessimistic and absurd.

Boulle was born in Avignon and studied electrical engineering at the Ecole Supérieure d'Electricité in Paris. After working in France as an engineer, he moved to Malaysia in 1938 and worked as an overseer in a rubber plantation near Kuala Lumpur.

At the outbreak of World War II, Boulle joined the army in Indochina. When German troops occupied France, he joined the Free French Mission in Singapore. During that time he served as a secret agent under the name Peter John Rule and helped the resistance movement in China, Burma, and Indochina.

In 1943, Boulle was captured by the Vichy French loyalists on the Mekong River and sentenced to a life of hard labor. He escaped in 1944 from imprisonment in Saigon and served until the end of the war in British Special Forces. Before returning to France and becoming a writer, Boulle continued his work at the plantation in Malaysia; he also spent some time in Cameroon. He had started to keep a diary in prison, and in 1950 Boulle published his first novel, *William Conrad.*

A very mainstream writer, Boulle turned his six years in Southeast Asia in World War II into a major work, *The Bridge over the River Kwai.* The novel was awarded the Prix Sainte-Beuve in France in 1952 and was made into a full-length motion picture in 1957. It won eight Academy Awards, including Best Picture. Boulle combined in his works a captivating story with a pessimistic view of human endeavors and absurdities. Another of his novels, *Planet of the Apes* (1963), which was made into a film in 1968 and has since inspired several film adaptations, is an ironic tale about the relationship between men and animals. It transferred the basic relationship between the Japanese soldiers and Allied prisoners—the repression of a weaker group by a stronger and its moral effect on both sides—into the distant future. Boulle depicted a world where humankind had lost its position as the dominant species and apes ruled over human savages.

Other books by Boulle include *Face of a Hero* (1953), *The Executioner* (1954), *Not the Glory* (1955), *The Test* (1955), and *A Noble Profession* (1960). Among Boulle's later works are *The Photographer* (1967), in which an Algerian war veteran sees an opportunity to take the ultimate photograph when he discovers that his friend wants to murder the president; *The Whale of the Victoria Cross* (1983), a story of naval warfare and marine mammals; and *Because It Is Absurd (on Earth as in Heaven)*, a collection of short stories. *L'Ilon* (1990) was a story about his childhood. The last book he wrote was entitled *A Nous Deux, Satan!* (1992).

Boulle was made an officier de la Légion d'honneur and a recipient of the Croix de guerre and the Medal of the Resistance. He died in Paris on January 30, 1994.

Claudia Wolosin

> *See also:* Cinema, 1945 to the Present; Rubber; World War II.
> **References**
> Culture SF. "Pierre Boulle."
>   http://www.culture-sf.com/biblios/
>   boulle.php (cited February 20, 2004).
> Frackman Becker, Lucille. *Pierre Boulle.* New York: Twayne, 1996.

BOURASSA, ROBERT (1933–1996)

Premier of Quebec from 1970 to 1976 (two terms) and again from 1985 until 1994 (two terms).

A strong believer in federalism, Bourassa was the youngest politician to occupy the position of premier when he became head of the Quebec government in March 1970. After his reelection in October 1973, Bourassa passed the much contested Bill 22 in July 1974, a law that made bilingualism official in a province where bilingualism was already the key problem and the cause of social conflicts between the dominant anglophone minor-

ity and the francophone majority. At the end of its second term, his Liberal Party was accused of corruption and was beaten by René Lévesque's Parti Québécois by a large majority.

After his defeat in November 1976, Bourassa temporarily retired from politics and went to Europe for a year, where he became a visiting scholar at the Institut des affaires européennes in Brussels and at the Institut européen d'administration des affaires in Fontainebleau, France. Between 1978 and 1982, he was also visiting professor in international relations for many universities in the United States (the School of Advanced International Studies at Johns Hopkins, Yale University, the University of Southern California at Los Angeles) and Quebec (Université Laval, Université du Québec à Montréal). Although Pierre Trudeau openly disdained Robert Bourassa, the latter helped Trudeau in the "no" campaign for the 1980 referendum on Quebec sovereignty.

Presented as a resourceful, renewed man, Bourassa was reelected again for two terms as premier of Quebec, from 1985 to 1994. During that period, when asked about the possibility of giving French citizenship automatically to all Québécois, Bourassa simply answered that France could take the first step of not asking for visas for tourists from Canada. It was the time when France temporarily required non–European Union visitors to obtain visas because of problems related to immigration and terrorism. Robert Bourassa shared with President François Mitterrand a vision of Quebec as a part of Canada.

As premier of Quebec, Robert Bourassa made relatively few official trips to France, in 1974, 1989, and 1991. President Mitterrand came twice to Quebec in 1987, and

Prime Minister Jacques Chirac came the same year to sign a fiscal agreement.

Bourassa is also remembered as the premier who was prepared to accept Canadian federalism at any cost, even during the Meech Lake negotiations about the place of Quebec in the Canadian federation, as shown in Jacques Godbout's documentary, *Le Mouton noir* (1992). A best-selling book in two volumes about Bourassa's attitudes was released in Quebec in 1994 by journalist Jean-François Lisée. Bourassa had to fight cancer and left politics in 1994. Among many distinctions, Bourassa received an honorary doctorate from Tel Aviv University and the Légion d'honneur from France (posthumously, in 1997).

Yves Laberge

See also: Chirac, Jacques; Godbout, Jacques; Language; Lévesque, René; Mitterrand, François; Quebec; Quebec City.

References

Comeau, Paul-André. "Son exil bruxellois: Les répercussions sur ses hypothèses constitutionnelles." *Robert Bourassa: Un bâtisseur tranquille.* Ed. Guy Lachapelle, Valéry Colas, and Robert Comeau. Sainte-Foy: Presses de l'Université Laval, 2003.

Lisée, Jean-François. *Robert Bourassa et les Québécois.* Montreal: Boréal, 1994.

Poirier, Georges. "Robert Bourassa en France." *France-Québec* 72 (March–April 1989): 13.

BOURDIEU, PIERRE (1930–2002)

French sociologist Pierre Bourdieu is probably the best known among foreign contemporary social scientists in U.S. universities. In 1982, Bourdieu was elected as professor at the prestigious Collège de France, where Emile Durkheim was chair of sociology almost a century before. Bourdieu wrote about a wide variety of sociological topics and especially on social theory, the sociology of culture, and fine arts; he created sociological concepts such as "symbolic capital," "doxa," "field," and "habitus."

Bourdieu's numerous works have influenced scholars not only in the social sciences but also in literary theory and cultural studies. Along with Jean Baudrillard and Michel Foucault, Bourdieu was recognized as a leading intellectual in France, particularly in the 1970s and 1980s, and became famous in Anglo-Saxon countries by the 1980s as his books began to be translated into English. Academics in cultural studies recognized in Bourdieu's thoughts a theoretical framework that could be used to understand power, class, and processes of domination. The relationship among class, culture, and taste in individuals is best exemplified in one of Bourdieu's most respected books, *Distinction* (1979, published in English in 1990). Oddly, as Bourdieu's reputation declined in France in the mid-1990s, U.S. scholars began adopting his early theoretical frameworks during the same period, even though Bourdieu was always opposed to the U.S. sociological tradition and often rejected ethnomethodology. Selections from Bourdieu's writings are often included in anthologies and readers on cultural studies published by U.S. scholars. But a skeptical Bourdieu found too much theoretical discussion and not enough data analysis in cultural studies. Bourdieu's works have also been used in Canadian universities (mostly in Quebec) and in Latin American countries such as Brazil.

A sometimes controversial and often provocative figure, Bourdieu was much criticized in France by the mid-1990s because of his attacks on French journalists, whom he considered as "reproducing the dominant system and its ideology" without being fully aware of the process in which they participated (quoted in a documentary by Pierre Carles, *La Sociologie est un sport de combat/Sociology Is a Combat Sport,* 2001). Bourdieu was also opposed to the neoliberalist globalization trend and even sent a video message of support to protestors during demonstrations against the World Summit held in Quebec City on April 4, 2001.

Yves Laberge

See also: Baudrillard, Jean; Foucault, Michel; Theory.
References
Lane, Jeremy F. *Pierre Bourdieu.* London: Pluto Press, 2000.
Swartz, David. *Culture and Power: The Sociology of Pierre Bourdieu.* Chicago: University of Chicago Press, 1997.

BOURGEOIS, LOUISE (1911–)

Louise Bourgeois is considered a leader in twentieth-century sculpture. Her works have been greatly influenced by the surrealists, and her dominant themes include her childhood, her relationship with her parents, sexuality, betrayal, guilt, and power.

Bourgeois was born on December 25, 1911, in Paris, the second daughter of Joséphine Fauriaux and Louis Bourgeois. She first experienced the artistic world while helping her parents restore tapestries in their studio. Bourgeois drew designs for the damaged areas of the tapestries, while her mother toned down the more elaborate designs for the conservative American art collectors who purchased them. These early experiences introduced Bourgeois to cutting, sewing, and, most important, creating.

After high school, Bourgeois enrolled in the Sorbonne to study geometry but soon decided to dedicate herself to art. She attended the Ecole des Beaux-Arts for a short period of time and also studied at the Ecole du Louvre, the Académie Julian, and the Atelier Fernand Léger. Bourgeois considered Léger to be her best teacher; it was Léger who suggested that she devote herself to sculpture.

In 1938, Bourgeois married the American art historian Robert Goldwater and emigrated to the United States, becoming a naturalized citizen in 1951. Bourgeois and Goldwater had three sons: Michel, Jean-Louis, and Alain. Upon her arrival in New York, Bourgeois enrolled in the Art Student League, studied painting in Vaclav Vytlacil's studio for two years, and also began to produce engravings. Her first participation in a group show took place at the Brooklyn Museum.

In June 1945, Bourgeois had her first solo show, "Paintings by Louise," at the Bertha Shaefer Gallery, which included her paintings *Natural History, Mr. Follett,* and *Connecticutiana.* Two years later, she had her second solo show at the Norlyst Gallery, where she exhibited *Conversation Piece, Jeffersonian Court House,* and *Roof Song,* among others.

In 1949, Bourgeois debuted her sculptures at a show held by the Peridot Gallery. Among the works included in this first show were *Portrait of C. Y., Woman in the Shape of a Shuttle,* and *The Blind Leading the Blind.* She held two other shows at the Peridot Gallery in the 1950s, which included the pieces *Sleeping Figure, Spring,* and *Forêt/Garden at Night.*

Although she is a highly prolific artist, Louise Bourgeois did not receive full international recognition until 1978, when she created her first public commission, *Facets to the Sun,* for the Norris Cotton Federal Building in Manchester, New Hampshire. Also in 1978, Bourgeois showed her *Confrontation* piece, which was combined with the performance piece *A Banquet/A Fashion Show of Body Parts.* This performance piece parodied fashion shows by showing latex dresses covered in breasts.

The main symbolism in Bourgeois's work originates in her childhood and her sexuality's role in her early family life as the means through which she could understand and re-create that history. Her work also depends on public interaction, despite its highly personal nature. For example, in *Maman 1999,* three 30-foot-high towers provide meeting areas, while a 35-foot-high spider, representing her mother's role as protector, looks on.

Stephanie Longo

See also: Painting; Sculpture.
References
Bernadac, Marie-Laure. *Louise Bourgeois.* Paris: Flammarion, 1996.
Wye, Deborah, and Carol Smith. *The Prints of Louise Bourgeois.* New York: Museum of Modern Art, 1994.

BOURGET, PAUL (1852–1935)

Conservative novelist, essayist, and poet, whose 1895 *Outre-mer (Notes sur l'Amérique)* praised the dynamism and the religious and ethnic eclecticism of the United States.

Born in Amiens (Somme) on September 2, 1852, Bourget began his literary career writing for the magazines *La Revue des Deux Mondes, La Nouvelle Revue,* and *L'Illustration* and for various newspapers. When he turned to novels, his studies of

medicine as well as the humanities led him to reject the prevailing scientific determinism that characterized naturalist writers like Emile Zola and critics like Ernest Renan. In *Le Disciple* (1889), Bourget manifested this assertion of free will and his conservative attitudes through a plot in which moral values overcome deterministic materialism. Acclaimed as the defender of traditional virtues, he was elected to the Académie Française in 1894. He converted to Roman Catholicism in 1901 and thereafter produced a series of novels depicting the corrupting influence of modern life, most notably in *L'Etape* (1902), about social mobility, *Un Divorce* (1904), about marriage, and *L'Emigré* (1907), about the decline of the aristocracy. Conservative but never reactionary, he is best described as *bien pensant,* "right thinking," like the bourgeois, moralistic politics of his friend Raymond Poincaré. When Bourget died in Paris on December 25, 1935, his writings filled ninety volumes.

Bourget published *Outre-mer* after an eight-month (August 1893–March 1894) trip to the United States, during which he traveled as far north as Boston, as far west as Chicago, and as far south as Florida. He claimed his intention was to discover the "American soul" and his method to observe behavior. He was especially interested in how the forces of democracy, science, and race were shaping the United States. Inevitably, he became a cataloger of superficial particulars, but from them he deduced certain generalizations. He recognized that although Americans were sometimes philistine and unsophisticated, there was enormous creative energy beneath the rude exterior. He praised public schools and universities and especially coeducation but criticized the tendency to make learning overly utilitarian. He declared the United States vigorous while describing France as increasingly decadent. Two years later, the famously francophobe Mark Twain wrote a witty, tendentious reply, "What Paul Bourget Thinks of Us," published in his *How to Tell a Story and Other Essays* (1897), unfairly accusing Bourget of having been overly critical and questioning the capacity of anyone from France to judge Americans. In fact, few French visitors have ever written more positively about the United States.

Benjamin F. Martin

See also: Twain, Mark; Zola, Emile.
References
Bowman, Edgar M. *The Early Novels of Paul Bourget.* New York: Carranza and Company, 1925.
Feuillerat, Albert. *Paul Bourget.* Paris: Plon, 1937.
Singer, Armand E. *Paul Bourget.* Boston: Twayne, 1976.

BOYER, CHARLES (1897–1978)

French screen actor, born in Figeac in the Lot département (equivalent of county), whose international career spanned five decades.

Despite his French origins, Charles Boyer was a Hollywood star of the classic era. He studied drama at the Conservatoire in Paris, making his stage and screen debut in 1920 in the silent era of film. Having worked on multilanguage versions of films in France and Germany, Boyer was soon invited by MGM to join the small community of French filmmakers reunited in Hollywood to make French-language versions of American films. This early stage in Boyer's career (1929–1939) was character-ized by constant transatlantic travel between the United States and Europe. Despite marrying British actress Pat Patterson in 1934 and settling in Hollywood, Boyer initially struggled to find interesting work in the United States, while France offered him leading roles and originals (Marcel L'Herbier's *L'Epervier* (The Hawk); *La Bataille* (The Battle), both 1933; Fritz Lang's *Liliom* or L'Herbier's *Le Bonheur* (Happiness), both 1934; Anatole Litvak's *Mayerling,* 1936, opposite Danielle Darrieux). Ending his contract with MGM, Boyer chose independent producer Walter Wanger in the hopes of getting more substantial roles, which indeed materialized with *Private Worlds* (La Cava), opposite French-born Hollywood star Claudette Colbert; *Break of Hearts* (Moeller), with Katharine Hepburn; and *Shanghai* (Flood), with Loretta Young, all in 1935. These productions established Boyer as a powerful romantic lead, seducing his screen partners as much as female audiences. From then on, Boyer became the ultimate Latin lover, the talking Valentino with a smooth, soothing voice that would turn any woman's head in an instant (Marlene Dietrich in Boleslwaki's *The Garden of Allah* and Hathaway's *I Loved a Soldier,* both in 1936; Greta Garbo in Brown's *Conquest* and Claudette Colbert in Litvak's *Tovarich,* both 1937, to name but a few). With his dark good looks, sophistication, and acting range, Boyer could be more than just a Frenchman, like Maurice Chevalier was before him. He was often a "European," Russian, Polish, German, and so on, or sometimes an Arab or oriental, but always exotic. Yet Boyer always remained faithful to France and French cinema, crossing the Atlantic regularly up to 1939, when World War II forced him to choose for a while between the two countries and the two cinemas. During the war years, Boyer set up the French Research Foundation, helping many compatriots in exile, for which he won a special Oscar in 1942. The Boyers were indeed central to the expatriate, exile, and refugee community in Hollywood, both on a social and professional level. This close-knit community often worked together, as evidenced in the cast and crew lists, and Boyer was a regular feature on these lists. The star also carried on playing romantic leads until the end of the 1940s (*All This and Heaven Too,* Litvak, 1940, opposite Bette Davis; *Gaslight,* Cukor, 1944, and *Arch of Triumph,* Milestone, 1948, both opposite Ingrid Bergman). Boyer's transatlantic career remained as prolific and successful until the mid-1970s, maturing well on the screen. After his son committed suicide in 1965, Boyer himself ended his life shortly after his wife's death, reinforcing the myth of the ultimate romantic.

Catherine Hellegouarc'h

See also: Chevalier, Maurice; Cinema, 1895–1945; Cinema, 1945 to the Present; Colbert, Claudette; Darrieux, Danielle; World War II.

References

Chassagnard, Guy. *Charles Boyer Acteur: Un Enfant de Figeac.* Figeac: Guy Chassagnard et Segnat Editions, 1999.

Swindell, Larry. *Charles Boyer: The Reluctant Lover.* New York: Doubleday, 1983.

BOYER, JEAN-PIERRE (1776–1850)

Haitian politician, born a free mulatto on February 28, 1776, in Port-au-Prince, in the French colony of Saint-Domingue. After independence in 1804, Boyer was president of Haiti from 1818 to 1843,

when he was forced into exile, first to Jamaica and then to Paris, where he had received his early education and where he was also to die on July 9, 1850. The assassination in 1806 of Jean-Jacques Dessalines, emperor of Haiti (1804–1806), led to civil war (1807–1820) between the black kingdom in the North, governed by Henri Christophe, and the mulatto republic of the South, led by Alexandre Sabès Pétion (1770–1818). Following Pétion's death in 1818, Boyer, his successor, succeeded in unifying the country and establishing a period of relative political stability, the latter badly shaken by the revolt in 1791 of black slaves against their French overlords.

Prior to the 1820s, when Boyer took up the cudgel, emigration schemes to transport emancipated slaves from the United States to Haiti, largely supported by the abolitionists Thomas Clarkson (1760–1846) and William Wilberforce (1759–1833), had met with little success. Boyer believed that the valuable agricultural expertise gained by slaves on U.S. plantations could help reestablish Haiti's formerly strong agricultural base and thus a strong economy and therefore was receptive to overtures from advocates of emigration within the United States. On April 30, 1824, in a letter designed to encourage prospective emigrants, Boyer responded reassuringly to Loring D. Dewey, the general agent of the Society for African Colonization, who sought clarifications on the defraying of emigrants' travel expenses, the distribution and stocking of land, education, and tolerance of different religions and laws. Although Boyer would not permit the society to establish a colony within Haiti with its own laws and courts, comparable to one of the states of the United

States yet answerable to a central government, he did promise land, religious tolerance, and citizenship to all who set foot on Haitian soil.

Boyer's support for the emigration scheme was given in the form of a considerable weight of coffee, the proceeds of which, when sold, would help finance the voyages from the United States to Haiti. His emigration drive of the 1820s, to a country that for many symbolized black liberation and equality, failed, however, when many emigrants, faced with insurmountable difficulties arising from linguistic, cultural, and religious differences, chose to return to the United States as early as the late 1820s. Boyer's questionable foreign policies brought further financial setbacks to Haiti in 1825, when a settlement of 150 million francs with France, designed to buy French recognition of Haitian independence, proved to be financially devastating. His 1826 Rural Code of Haiti, a draconian vagrancy bill that sought to limit free movement and thus freedom of enterprise among rural laborers, served only to hold him further in disfavor. Jean-Pierre Boyer's presidency, marked both by an evident material and monetary gap between the rural blacks and the mulattoes of the towns and a stagnant economy, finally led to a rebellion in 1843 in which he was ousted.

Janette McLeman-Carnie

See also: Antislavery Movements; Christophe, Henri; Coffee; Dessalines, Jean-Jacques; Haiti; Santo Domingo; Slavery.

References

Dixon, Chris. *African America and Haiti: Emigration and Black Nationalism in the Nineteenth Century.* Westport, CT: Greenwood Press, 2000.

Nicholls, David. *From Dessalines to Duvalier: Race, Colour and National Independence in Haiti.* Cambridge: Cambridge University Press, 1979.

BRAULT, MICHEL (1928–)

Québécois cinematographer and film director.

Born in Montreal in 1928, Brault is a pivotal figure in the emergence and the history of Quebec cinema, as much if not more for his role as cinematographer and as codirector than for his own directorial output. Coming to cinema from photography, he was part of a wave of francophone technicians who entered the National Film Board of Canada (NFB) after it moved to Montreal in the mid-1950s. Associated at an early stage with the direct cinema tendency that eschewed the authoritative, neutral, and script-led NFB documentary orthodoxy, in 1958 he codirected with Gilles Groulx an influential short documentary, *Les Raquetteurs* (*The Snowshoers*), about a snowshoe festival in the Quebec provincial town of Sherbrooke. One enthusiastic viewer of the film was the French documentary director Jean Rouch, whom Brault met at a seminar in California on the ethnographic filmmaker Robert Flaherty in 1959. On his invitation, Brault worked as cinematographer on the cinéma-vérité film Rouch directed in Paris in 1961 with Edgar Morin, *Chronique d'un été/ Chronicle of a Summer.* Brault went on to work in the 1960s with other documentary filmmakers in France, including William Klein (*Eldridge Cleaver, Black Panther,* 1969; *Festival panafricain d'Alger/Algiers Panafrican Festival,* 1970).

In Quebec, Brault's work is associated with the development of direct cinema in the service of the emerging cultural assertiveness and exploration of the new cinema of the 1960s, most notably in his work with Pierre Perrault, with whom he codirected *Pour la suite du monde/Moontrap* (1963). This film, with its subtle media-tions between filmmakers and rural inhabitants, its fabulating reenactments of old traditions, and its breathtaking cinematography of the Saint Lawrence, nonetheless leaves itself open to the accusation of traditionalism. Brault's 1967 fictional feature, *Entre la mer et l'eau douce,* with its portrait of a rural *arriviste* finding musical success in Montreal, to an extent revisits the territory of the earlier film, providing a more nuanced ethnic and modernizing portrayal of Quebec society.

While Brault continued to make contributions to some of the most significant Quebec films of the 1970s and 1980s as a cinematographer, he also enjoyed directorial success with *Les Ordres* (1974), which won the director's prize at Cannes. The film successfully adapts the direct cinema tradition, putting it in hybrid, fictionalized form as it follows the fates of individuals caught up in mass arrests following the Canadian federal government's invocation of the War Measures Act during the October crisis of 1970. This political and social dimension to Brault's filmmaking also appeared in subtle ways in films made initially for television from the late 1980s. *Les Noces de papier* (1989), released theatrically after its acclaim at the Berlin Film Festival of 1990 but suffering from its simultaneous release with the similarly themed Hollywood production *Green Card* (Peter Weir, 1990), stars Geneviève Bujold as an academic who agrees to an arranged marriage with a Latin American refugee. *Shabbat Shalom* (1994) also explores the ethnic diversity of Quebec identity in relation to Jewish minorities. Brault returned to Quebec history with *Quand je serai parti . . . vous vivrez encore* (1999), set in 1838 at the time of the Patriots' Revolt against colonial rule.

Bill Marshall

See also: Bujold, Geneviève; Jutra, Claude; Klein, William; Morin, Edgar; Perrault, Pierre; Quebec; Rouch, Jean; Saint Lawrence River.
Reference
Marshall, Bill. *Quebec National Cinema.* Montreal: McGill-Queen's University Press, 2001.

BRAZIL

The French have had contact with Brazil for almost as long as the Portuguese. After the failure of French attempts to establish settlements (1555–1560, 1612–1615), known in Luso-Brazilian historiography as "the French invasions," Portuguese Brazil remained relatively closed and unknown to the French. However, this situation began changing in the years preceding Brazil's declaration of independence (1822). Especially over the next century, the influence of French culture and ideology in Brazil was enormous, out of all proportion to French influence in economic relations (where Britain dominated) or to the tiny scale of actual French immigration when measured against the traditional components of the population (Indian, African, Portuguese, and especially people descended from all three) or against the new immigration (from Germany, Italy, Spain, and Japan). French cultural hegemony was increasingly challenged by assertions of Brazilian distinctiveness. Brazil in turn influenced major twentieth-century French artists and intellectuals, though the modern French popular stereotype of Brazil is of a quasi Eden dominated by carnival, mulatto women, and soccer.

Following the first Portuguese sighting and exploration of mainland South America (1500–1502), French ships were soon regularly loading up along the coast with

Map of Brazil. (MAPS.com/Corbis)

brazilwood (*pau-brasil*), a source of red dye in great demand among European textile manufacturers, for example, in Rouen. Then the monarchy became interested in Brazil: the 1550 entry of Henri II and Catherine de Medici into Rouen featured a mock Tupinambá village and about fifty Indians. In November 1555, Nicolas Durand de Villegagnon, leading 600 men in two ships, took control of the bay known as Guanabara to the Indians and as Rio de Janeiro to the Portuguese, who had earlier been ousted from there by the Tamoio, a federation of Tupinambá tribes. The French expedition was sponsored by Henri II and, like the unsuccessful venture in Florida, by Gaspard de Coligny, admiral of France. The aims probably included establishing effective occupation of a potentially lucrative territory, protecting French commerce, and perhaps—though this is disputed—founding a potential refuge for Huguenots persecuted in France. The French settled on an island at the mouth of the bay, where they built Fort Coligny. The

Tupinambá sold them slaves, captured from enemy tribes such as the Maracajá Temimino. The French decimated their Tupinambá allies with imported diseases.

Villegagnon, who later became anti-Protestant but at this stage had Lutheran and perhaps even Calvinist sympathies, had problems enforcing his code of sexual conduct on the Norman interpreters, whom he found living among the Indians. He (or possibly Coligny) invited Calvin to send moral reinforcements: fourteen Calvinists from Geneva, including Jean de Léry, were among the ninety or so people to arrive in March 1557, including five young women. However, the relation between Villegagnon and the Calvinists soon deteriorated because of theological disagreements about the Eucharist. In October Villegagnon banished the dissenters from Coligny Island. They took refuge among the Tupinambá until January 1558, when some, including Léry, embarked on a famine-ridden voyage to France, whereas five preferred to return to Villegagnon, only for him to drown three of them for refusing to recant. In 1560 twelve ships sent by the Portuguese governor-general captured Fort Coligny. "Antarctic France," as it was called, was over. It lived on in memory thanks to the conflicting, partly eyewitness accounts of Léry and André Thevet, through whose mediation readers ranging from Montaigne to Lévi-Strauss encountered the Tupinambá.

The next French colonial attempt in Brazil was "Equinoxial France" (1612–1615), founded in the Bay of Maranhão by Daniel de la Ravardière and the Razilly brothers, accompanied by some Capuchin missionaries. The settlement, Saint-Louis-du-Maragnon, to the north of Portuguese possessions, was handed over to the Portuguese. Later incursions were made by Jean-François Duclerc (1710) and René Duguay-Trouin (1711), the latter managing to capture and ransom Rio de Janeiro. In 1767 Louis Antoine de Bougainville's voyage round the world took him along the coast of Brazil: he eyed Rio jealously, expressing nostalgia for the days of Ville-gagnon. French eyewitness reports of the interior remained rare, but in 1745 Charles-Marie de La Condamine reported back to the Académie des sciences on the nine years he had spent there with other astronomers measuring degrees of latitide and longitude. French relative ignorance about Brazilian Indians helped foster the pre-romantic ideal of the noble savage, as in the utopian novel by Bernardin de Saint-Pierre, *L'Amazone,* written between 1800 and 1803.

Ideology associated with the French Revolution reached Brazil in the late eighteenth and early nineteenth centuries, when it reinforced various attempts to achieve liberation from the Portuguese. After the emancipation of slaves in French colonies (1848), there was a campaign in France against slavery in Brazil until its abolition (1888). Progressive, republican Brazilian intellectuals often quoted Victor Hugo on democracy and Auguste Comte on positivism, which played a part in the formation of a national, multiethnic, specifically Brazilian identity in the writings of Euclides da Cunha (1866–1909) and others. Also in a spirit of science and progress, the French study of nature in Brazil intensified when several naturalists and geographers visited, among them the botanist Augustin César Prouvençal de Saint-Hilaire, whose six years of trekking on the back of a mule started in 1816. Jules Verne set a geographical novel in Brazil: *Jangada, huit cents lieues sur l'Amazonie* (1881). Some of the naturalists painted what they saw, such as the self-educated Hercule Florence (who arrived in 1825) or Charles de Clarac (b. 1777), responsible for a famous engraving, *Forêt vierge du Brésil.* Foremost among these French painters was Jean-Baptiste Debret: the lithographs in his album *Voyage pittoresque et historique au Brésil* (1834–1839) were based on his sketches and watercolors. More fleetingly, the visit that Edouard Manet made to Rio and its carnival, in 1849 when he was seventeen, had an impact on his art. In 1818 a delegation of French artists arrived with a view to founding an Académie des Beaux-Arts, which was inaugurated in 1826. The French studied Brazilian culture as well as nature: the naturalist Ferdinand Denis, the founder of Brazilian and Portuguese studies in France, published a literary history of Brazil (1825).

Throughout the belle époque, the elite of Rio prized Paris (which many Brazilian intellectuals visited), French culture, language, and even fashion, despite the climate. A French lycée was established in 1916, and in 1934 the University of São Paulo was founded by a French mission headed by Georges Dumas. Its first teachers included the anthropologist Claude Lévi-Strauss, who until 1938 conducted fieldwork—among the Caduveo, Bororo, Nambikwara, and Tupi-Kawahib—upon which he drew for decades to come; the celebrated historian Fernand Braudel; and the sociologists Paul Arbousse Bastide and Roger Bastide, who spent much of his life in Brazil.

French cultural hegemony was resisted, however. Nísia Floresta Brasileira Augusta, a rare female émigrée from Brazil and the author of many works, including *Le Brésil* (1871), denounced European ethnocentrism, although she loved France. The early twentieth-century writer Monteiro Lobato was more straightforwardly francophobic. The modernist reportage on Paris of António de Alcântara Machado (1901–1935) reversed the usual ethnographic perspective. Brazilian modernism often had an assertively nationalist dimension, culminating in a 1922 São Paulo exhibition of painting, sculpture, and music (including works by the composer Heitor Villa-Lobos).

The relation between Brazilian and French modernism was often reciprocal. The poet Blaise Cendrars stayed in Brazil in 1924, 1926, and 1927–1928, interacting with avant-garde poets such as Oswald de Andrade. The Brazilian influence on Cendrars's poetry was long-lasting, though largely within the framework of the traditional French construction of the Americas as exotic. Cendrars lured to Brazil his friend Le Corbusier, who gave lectures at Rio and influenced architects such as Lúcio Costa and Oscar Niemeyer. The composer Darius Milhaud, having been Paul Claudel's secretary in Rio for the diplomatic mission in 1917, incorporated Brazilian popular music into his *Bœuf sur le toit* (1920). Brazil had a profound effect not only on modernists but also on the novelist Georges Bernanos, who lived there from 1937 to 1945, and on the philosopher and sociologist Roger Caillois, who first entered the country in 1939.

Neil Kenny

See also: Architecture; Bernanos, Georges; Caillois, Roger; Cendrars, Blaise; Claudel, Paul; Florida; French Revolution; Huguenots; La Condamine, Charles-Marie de; Le Corbusier; Lévi-Strauss, Claude; Montaigne, Michel de; Music (Classical); Noble Savage; Verne, Jules.

References
Carelli, Mario. *Cultures croisées: Histoire des échanges culturels entre la France et le Brésil de la découverte aux temps modernes.* Paris: Nathan, 1993.
Lestringant, Frank. *Cannibals: The Discovery and Representation of the Cannibal from Columbus to Jules Verne.* Trans. R. Morris. Cambridge: Polity Press, 1997.
McGrath, John. "Polemic and History in French Brazil, 1555–1560." *Sixteenth Century Journal* 27, no. 2 (summer 1996): 385–397.
Needell, Jeffrey D. *A Tropical Belle Epoque: Elite Culture and Society in Turn-of-the-Century Rio de Janeiro.* Cambridge: Cambridge University Press, 1987.

BREL, JACQUES (1929–1978)

Belgian-born singer-songerwriter, born in 1929 in Brussels.

Brel epitomizes the golden age of French *chanson,* or song, in the 1950s and 1960s. Although he was well received during his U.S. tours, particularly in his concerts at the prestigious Carnegie Hall in New York in 1964 and in 1967, he reached a wider audience in the United States through English-language adaptations of his songs.

It was while on Broadway in 1967 that Brel saw the musical about the life of Miguel Cervantes's Don Quixote, *Man of La Mancha,* written by Dale Wasserman, Mitch Leigh, and Joe Darion. In 1968 Brel brought his own version of this musical, *L'Homme de la Mancha,* to Brussels, playing the lead role. Around the same time, Brel himself became the subject of a North American tribute musical, *Jacques Brel Is Alive and Well and Living in Paris* (1968). For Eric Blau and Mort Shuman, a personal friend of Brel, the musical fulfilled their ambition to translate and bring Brel's songs to a U.S. audience using theater. Initially staged at the Village Gate in New York in 1968, the revue still retains a cult following and continues to this day to run in small theaters and cabarets throughout the English-speaking world. Brel's songs, interspersed with fragments of his own commentary, presented the main concerns of his work. Although Brel dealt largely with universal themes such as love and death, the musical has a more contemporary edge while still remaining largely faithful to the spirit of Brel's originals.

Eric Blau turned his scenario into a screenplay for Denis Héroux's 1975 film version of the musical, which was shot in the south of France. Brel lent his support to the film and appeared in it, performing one of his best-known songs, "Ne me quitte pas" (If You Go Away, 1959). Although Héroux's film also attempts to express the personal and social themes of Brel's work and nostalgically evokes the world of the French cabaret, it is nonetheless geared toward a contemporary North American audience and may be compared to the fantasy/hippie musicals of the 1970s.

Brel's songs have since been covered in many countries by many non-French-speaking artists. One of the most successful and popular English-language cover versions of Brel to date is "Seasons in the Sun," whose original title was "Le Moribond" (The Dying Man, 1961). A huge chart hit in 1974 for the Canadian singer Terry Jacks, the somewhat sugary English lyrics and vocal delivery unfortunately retain little of the acerbic wit of Brel's original version. Brel died in 1978 in Paris.

Chris Tinker

See also: Héroux, Denis; Music (Pop); Shuman, Mort.

References

Blau, Eric. *Jacques Brel Is Alive and Well and Living in Paris.* New York: E. P. Dutton, 1971.

Todd, Olivier. *Jacques Brel, une vie.* Paris: 10/18, 2001.

BRESDIN, RODOLPHE (1822–1885)

French artist who created magical prints that were admired for their rich detail.

Two lithographs, *La Comédie de la mort* (1854) and *Le Bon Samaritain* (1861), are perhaps his most famous works. However, for most of his life Bresdin lived in poverty and was well known only among a small circle of intellectuals and artists. Part of his fame was based on his curious lifestyle, which served as a model for the tragic, solitary artist in Jules Champfleury's novel *Chien-Caillou* (1845). The title derived from a corrupted form of Chingachgook, the Indian chief and hero of James Fenimore Cooper's *The Last of the Mohicans* (1926). Bresdin admired the American Indian and romanticized the New World in letters to his friends, in which he described a "new country where one might gain one's freedom through hard work" (quoted in Van Gelder, p. 11). Fantasies about America's virgin forests may have inspired the densely overgrown landscape settings in many of his works. Unfortunately for Bresdin, when he was finally able to go to America—leaving Le Havre for Canada in 1873—he did not find financial or artistic success. Not much is known about this trip, and much of what has been written is fantasy—including the notion that Bresdin's winning design for a U.S. banknote helped to pay for the artist, his wife, and six children to travel across

Etching by Rodolphe Bresdin, 1822–1885, "Flight into Egypt." Bresdin's magical prints were admired for their rich detail. (Library of Congress)

the Atlantic. All that remains from the trip are a few designs he made while in Montreal for journals that were never actually published. He returned to Paris in 1877.

Bresdin was born in Montrelais, France, on August 13, 1822, the son of a tanner. In 1861 twelve of his etchings were published in the *Revue Fantaisiste*. Other contributors included Charles Baudelaire, Théodore de Banville, Alphonse Daudet, Théophile Gautier, and Champfleury. In the same journal, Banville wrote a glowing review of Bresdin's contributions to the Salon of 1861, especially praising *Le Bon Samaritain*. Bresdin spent a fair amount of time in the south of France. One legend suggests that he walked from Paris to Toulouse (sometime around 1848 or 1851). Shortly after his Parisian success of 1861, he moved back to Bordeaux and lived on the rue Fosse-aux-lions (Lion's

den), sometimes even signing his prints with this name. It was there that he was visited by Odilon Redon (1840–1916), who became his student. In 1863 Bresdin's works were exhibited in the office of the newspaper *La Gironde*. In 1864 he became a member of the Société des amis des arts de Bordeaux and exhibited his works with that group. Bresdin married in 1865, but by 1870 he had become ill with rheumatism and eye trouble and spent time in the Hôpital Necker. However, his illness did not seem to prevent him from participating in the uprising of the Paris Commune in 1871. Bresdin died of congestion in Sèvres on January 11, 1885.

Leslie Stewart Curtis

See also: Bordeaux; Le Havre; Montreal; Painting.

References

Bibliothèque nationale de France, Paris. *Rodolphe Bresdin (1822–1885), Robinson graveur.* Catalogue by Maxime Préaud. Catalogue of exhibition held May 30 to August 27, 2000.

Redon, Odilon. "Rodolphe Bresdin, dessins sur pierre, eux-fortes, dessins originaux." *La Gironde,* January 10, 1869.

Van Gelder, Dirk. *Rodolphe Bresdin: Monographie en trois parties. Catalogue raisonné de l'œuvre gravée.* 2 vols. The Hague/Paris: M. Nijhoff/Le Chêne, 1976.

BRETON, ANDRÉ (1896–1966)

The leader of the surrealist movement and one of the most influential writers of the French avant-garde, André Breton was born in Tichenbray (Orne) and spent his childhood on the Brittany coast. His first poems, among them a sonnet dedicated to Paul Valéry, were published in 1914. Breton had started studying medicine the previous year, and during World War I he served in the neurological ward in Nantes and then in 1917 was posted to the psychiatric centre at Saint-Dizier, where his early interest in Freudian psychoanalysis led to the discovery of the artistic potential of methods used in the observation and treatment of mental illness. Guillaume Apollinaire, with whom he corresponded during the war, introduced Breton to Philippe Soupault and Louis Aragon in Adrienne Monnier's Parisian bookshop. Breton's debut volume *Mont de piété* (Pawnshop, 1919) came out the same year as the inaugural issue of *Littérature,* the magazine he founded with Soupault and Aragon, which became affiliated with the dada movement, before the official break with Tristan Tzara in 1922. The publication of the first *Surrealist Manifesto* and the launch of the magazine *La Révolution surréaliste* in 1924 marked the birth of the new movement and defined its ideology, as well as its distinctive exploration of the unconscious through "automatic" techniques (inspired by Breton's experience with psychiatric and psychoanalytical methods). *Les Champs magnétiques* (*Magnetic Fields,* 1920), the first example of "automatic" writing, produced by Breton in collaboration with Soupault, provided the basis for a wide range of language-based and visual experiments aimed at uncovering the "true functioning of thought," "in the absence of all control by reason, excluding any aesthetic or moral preoccupation" (as stated in the manifesto's definition of surrealism). For almost two decades, until the outbreak of World War II and his exile to New York, Breton's works outlined the major concepts of surrealism and shaped the evolution of the movement. From the early formulation of the idea of "convulsive beauty" in *Nadja* (1928) to the political debates and purges

of the mid-1920s leading up to the *Second Surrealist Manifesto* (1930), from the dialectical interpretation of dream and reality in *Les Vases communicants* (*Communicating Vessels,* 1932) to the theory of objective chance and "mad love" in *L'Amour fou* (1937), Breton remained the catalyst and driving force behind the transformations that earned surrealism its unparalleled prestige among competing avant-garde trends and ultimately established its international reputation. In 1938, Breton traveled to Mexico and met Leon Trotsky, with whom he wrote the manifesto entitled *Pour un art révolutionnaire indépendant* (For an Independent Revolutionary Art). Breton had joined the Communist Party in 1927 but broke with it in 1935 during the Congress

André Breton was the leader of the surrealist movement and one of the most influential writers of the French avant-garde. (Library of Congress)

for the Defense of Culture. During World War II, Breton left occupied Paris and was initially hosted in Marseilles by the American Emergency Rescue Committee, alongside Victor Brauner, Max Ernst, André Masson, and Benjamin Péret. His exile in New York occasioned the surrealist exhibition of 1942 (*First Papers of Surrealism*) and the launch of the magazine *VVV,* in which Breton published *Prolegomena to a Third Manifesto of Surrealism or Else.* Breton returned to Paris in 1946 with his wife Elisa, whom he had met in New York and who inspired his last meditation on love, dreams, and objective chance, *Arcane 17* (first published in 1944 in the United States).

Ramona Fotiade

See also: Brittany; Ernst, Max; Masson, André; Mexico; Nantes; Painting; Péret, Benjamin; Sculpture; Surrealism; Theory; World War I; World War II.

References

Balakian, Ana, and Rudolf E. Kuenzli. *André Breton.* London: Willis Locker and Owen, 1998.

Polizzotti, Mark. *Revolution of the Mind: The Life of André Breton.* London: Bloomsbury, 1995.

BRITTANY

The interaction of the land and the sea has profoundly affected the historic development of Brittany. The Atlantic has provided the Bretons with wealth, work, and adventure, but it has also formed the entry points for hostile invasions and epidemics.

The Romans named the peninsula "Armorica," meaning the land facing the sea. Its coastline was the site of Julius Caesar's most famous naval battle, against the Veneti in 56 B.C. Following Roman occupation, the peninsula's Celtic cultures and languages were reaffirmed by groups of Celts fleeing southward across the English Channel from Saxon (or possibly Irish) invasions of the British Isles in the fifth and sixth centuries. These same groups contributed significantly to the spread of Christianity throughout the region.

During the Middle Ages, Brittany's coastal position provided it with a privileged position on trade routes and also allowed it to preserve a substantial diplomatic and political autonomy from the more powerful French monarchy. Genoese galleys sailed to the region in 1293, thus establishing maritime trade links from the Mediterranean to the North Sea, and Breton ships began to sail regularly to the Mediterranean in the mid-fifteenth century. In the fifteenth century, its shipbuilders made use of the *carvel* nail (enabling the use of flush rather than overlapping planks of wood) to develop a new type of oceangoing vessel, the three-masted caravel, which became a common and successful design across Europe. Breton rulers cultivated connections with the English kings and attempted to stay neutral during the Hundred Years' War (1337–1453). At the same time, however, the region's easy maritime access allowed Vikings to sack Nantes in 843 and 853 and to terrorize neighboring towns.

Brittany was formally annexed to the French Crown in 1532. In the succeeding decades, however, it developed into a fair-sized maritime power, retaining a degree of autonomy from the French state. Specialist forms of shipbuilding developed: it seems probable that the use of portholes was pioneered by Bretons in 1531. Fishing evolved into a substantial occupation along the coastal towns. Even within Brittany, industries such as rope making and sailmaking provided employment for rural dwellers. Commercial and trade links with England were vital for the region's economy: butter, salt, paper, and linen were exported from Brittany, and herring, tin, lead, and wool were imported.

This happy semi-independence ended in the seventeenth century, as the French state imposed increasingly high trade tariffs. The Atlantic was no longer an open highway for Breton vessels. Instead, as the French state developed aggressive, imperialist policies in the eighteenth century, the Breton seascape was militarized and regulated. Ships from Nantes sailed to Africa and the West Indies, participating in the slave trade. New ports were built: Lorient, on the southern coast, was the base for French expeditions to the East. Brest, on the western tip of the peninsula, was one of the French navy's most important ports. Although the cod-fishing port of Saint-Malo, to the north, was not developed by the French state to the same extent, it was the site for one of Sébastien Vauban's most impressive coastal fortifications. At various points during the seventeenth and eighteenth centuries, Breton piracy was encouraged by the French state. Along the coast, adult males were conscripted to serve in a coastal militia, and peasants were required to perform corvées (labor services) to build defenses and communications. Although the sea certainly provided employment for many Bretons, its presence was never simply advantageous: in 1733, 1741, and 1757–1758, oceangoing ships carried typhus epidemics to Brittany.

This heavy state intervention had dramatic effects on Breton society. Firstly, it created advanced cities of French-speaking bureaucrats, merchants, and naval officials in areas in which the Breton language had

previously been dominant. Secondly, these new policies significantly distorted the Breton economy, ruining the old trade across the English Channel and forcing Breton manufacturing into a dependency on French state policies. As older industries declined, more people left the Breton countryside, initiating a tradition of emigration and travel and—eventually—creating a worldwide Breton "diaspora." Breton merchants were divided in their assessment of state policies. On the eve of the French Revolution, some called for the free market and growing competition and others for protection for Breton manufacturers against British imports.

The sociocultural gap between the French-speaking ports and the Breton-speaking villages, now largely concentrated in the west of the region, grew in the nineteenth century, when a romantic revival rediscovered the Breton peasantry as exotic and primitive creatures, possible links to a dimly understood ancient Celtic past. Novels such as Pierre Loti's astonishingly successful *Le Pêcheur d'Islande* (*The Icelandic Fisherman*), published in 1886, popularized similar images of Breton primitivism, simplicity, and religiosity. Some of the region's northern ports, such as Dinan, developed as tourist sites. However, in the industrial port of Brest, Fernand Pelloutier devised the militant creed of anarcho-syndicalism.

During World War II, Brittany's unique geographic position was once again of vital importance. German U-boats operated from Brest and Saint-Nazaire, and following the liberation in 1944, a pocket of German soldiers held out for months near Saint-Nazaire. It was also in this period that a significant number of Americans were first present in Brittany, working with the Departmental Committees of Liberation. The tensions between the U.S. forces and the French authorities are neatly evoked in Louis Guilloux's narrative *O.K., Joe* (1976). Much of the ports of Brest and Saint-Nazaire was destroyed in 1944, and many of their inhabitants were housed in temporary prefabricated houses while the towns and their suburbs were rebuilt.

Today, Brittany remains a naval and maritime region. Approximately half of all French fishermen and fishing boats are based in the region. Saint-Nazaire survives as a world center of commercial shipbuilding and Brest as a major naval port. As a tourist center, Brittany is the third most popular destination in France, beaten only by Paris and the Mediterranean coast, and attracts significant numbers from Germany, the Netherlands, and even Eastern Europe. The distinctive characteristics of the Breton coastline—sunny, but also windy and "fresh"—feature prominently in tourist literature, differentiating this "Celtic" region from its urban and Mediterranean rivals. Recently the image of the ocean as a healing, nurturing presence has been exploited by new centers of "thalassotherapy," which offer maritime spa treatments. There are approximately fifty such centers in France: one-third of them, including the largest, are located in Brittany.

The region's uneasy relationship with the ocean continues. At the western tip of Brittany, the *Rail d'Ouessant* is one of the busiest sealanes in the world, with approximately 140 ships passing through it each day. As a result, the region has been the victim of six major oil slicks from oil tankers sinking near its coastline since 1970. The latest of these was the *Erika,* which sank to the south of the *Rail d'Ouessant* in Decem-

ber 1999. In 2000, tourist visits to the whole of Brittany, including inland regions and the northern coastline, which were completely untouched by the oil slick, declined by approximately 30 to 40 percent.

Sharif Gemie

See also: Fishing; French Revolution; Language; Nantes; Saint-Malo; Slavery; Tourism; World War II.

References
Cassard, Jean-Christophe. *Les Bretons et la mer au Moyen Age: Des origines au milieu du XIVe siècle.* Rennes: Presses Universitaires de Rennes, 1998.
Josse, Charles. "Quel avenir pour la pêche bretonne?" *Ar Men* 117 (December 2000): 2–13.
Nières, Claude. "Rivalités France-Angleterre vue de Bretagne au XVIIIe siècle." *La Révolution française.* Ed. Robert Chagny. Grenoble: Presses Universitaires de Grenoble, 2002: 21–34.
Stoll, Stéphanie. "Le spectaculaire réveil de Saint-Nazaire." *Ar Men* 118 (February 2001): 2–15.

BROSSARD, NICOLE (1943–)
Québécois writer, born in Montreal.

Nicole Brossard is one of Quebec's leading proponents of *l'écriture au féminin* (writing in the feminine), a radical writing practice that draws on so-called French feminism as well as on feminist traditions from the United States. As its name suggests, *l'écriture au féminin* is informed by *l'écriture féminine* (feminine writing), associated primarily with the post-Lacanian feminists Julia Kristeva, Hélène Cixous, and Luce Irigaray. However, it also retains an emphasis on the experiential realities of being a woman and on the material female body, as found in the work of U.S. feminists Adrienne Rich and Mary Daly.

Brossard began her writing career as an avant-garde practitioner and cofounded the literary journal *La Barre du jour* in 1965. From 1974, however, she began to write as a feminist and lesbian, a shift that she attributes to having become a mother and falling in love with another woman at the same time. The mother-daughter relationship and lesbian desire are central to *L'Amèr, ou le chapitre effrité: fiction théorique* (*These Our Mothers; or, The Disintegrating Chapter: Fiction Theory,* 1977) and are key themes within the writer's oeuvre. Brossard has written poetry, theory, fiction, autobiography, and autofiction, as well as drama and cinema to a lesser extent. In conjunction with Luce Guilbeault and Margaret Wescott, Brossard made the film *Quelques Féministes américaines* (*Some American Feminists,* 1977), and she collaborated on the canonical Québécois feminist play, *La Nef des sorcières* (*A Clash of Symbols,* 1976). Besides her seminal collection of essays, *La Lettre aérienne* (*The Aerial Letter,* 1985), Brossard is best known for her poetry—notably *Mécanique jongleuse* (*Daydream Mechanics,* 1973), *Amantes* (*Lovhers,* 1980), and *Musée de l'os et de l'eau* (*Museum of Bone and Water,* 1999) and fiction. Her intertextual and theoretically informed novels, such as *French Kiss* (1974), and *Picture Theory* (1982), disrupt traditional literary conventions and are considered challenging to readers, although the publication of the feminist-postmodern, *Le Désert mauve* (*Mauve Desert,* 1987), and its sister text, *Baroque d'aube* (*Baroque at Dawn,* 1995), saw Brossard's fiction become more accessible.

Brossard is one of a number of Québécois women writers to engage in intellectual and creative dialogue with anglophone feminists in Quebec and elsewhere in Canada, as well as in the United States. A cofounder of the bilingual feminist journal

Tessera, she has also collaborated with the Vancouver-based writer Daphne Marlatt. Important themes in Brossard's work include the coming together of writing and the female body, the subversion of masculinist discourse, women's oppression, the city—especially the writer's native Montreal—North America, translation, feminine collaboration, and technology. Particularly important is the metaphor of the hologram, with the holographic woman functioning as a utopian figure who, of necessity, is imaginary within patriarchy but who nevertheless offers the potential for challenging the oppressive roles this position assigns to women. Brossard's work has been translated into English, Spanish, and German, confirming her status as a major feminist writer of our times.

Ceri Morgan

See also: Feminisms; Gay Movement; Montreal; Theory.

References

Knutson, Susan. *Narrative in the Feminine: Daphne Marlatt and Nicole Brossard.* Waterloo, ON: Wilfred Laurier University Press, 2000.
Parker, Alice A. *Liminal Visions of Nicole Brossard.* New York: Peter Lang, 1998.

BRÛLÉ, ETIENNE (C. 1592–1633)

Etienne Brûlé traveled with Samuel de Champlain on the voyage to Canada in 1608, a voyage that is remembered for the founding of Quebec, and subsequently explored vast expanses of the North American landscape. He was the first European to visit and explore four of the five Great Lakes, he carried out much exploration in the Quebec area, and he visited Pennsylvania and Maine.

Born near Paris around 1592, Brûlé was a young man at the time of the 1608 voyage. He was taken as a servant to Champlain and was chosen to take part in an exchange with the local Huron people. As a result of the exchange, Brûlé lived among the Huron tribe, learning their language, their customs, and their way of life. Brûlé took to the Huron life very quickly and shocked his fellow Frenchmen, including Champlain, when he visited them some months after the initial exchange. During his time with the Huron people, Brûlé undertook a great deal of exploration of the area surrounding Quebec and further afield. He returned to the French colony in July 1618, where he was used as an interpreter.

While living with the Huron people, Brûlé quickly became assimilated into their way of life, so much so that when Champlain saw him for the first time after he had been living with them, he described his appearance and manner as *sauvage* (savage), exactly like the indigenous people. Jesuit missionaries also found his way of life unacceptable. When Quebec was taken by English forces in 1629, Brûlé was denounced by some as a traitor, and when his fellow colonists returned to France, he decided to retire and live among the Huron tribe. However, events conspired against him, and he was killed by his Huron hosts in 1633.

Brûlé's accomplishments are many. He traveled from Quebec to Lake Huron by way of the Ottawa River. He visited not only Lake Huron but also Lake Superior, Lake Erie, and Lake Ontario. He followed the course of the Susquehanna River to its junction with the sea and thus traversed large areas of New York, Pennsylvania, and Maine. Most important, he was the first European to accomplish these feats in almost all cases. However, he did not write a narrative of his experiences, and thus details about his life and his deeds have to be pieced together from a number of different accounts, some unfavorable to his way of life.

Jo Edwards

See also: Champlain, Samuel de; Hurons; Maine; Quebec.

References

Bishop, Morris. *White Men Came to the Saint Lawrence: The French and the Land They Found.* Montreal: McGill University Press, 1961.

Cranston, James Herbert. *Etienne Brûlé: Immortal Scoundrel.* Toronto: Ryerson Press, 1969.

Parkman, Francis. *France and England in North America.* Vol. 1, *Pioneers of France in the New World.* New York: Frederick Ungar, 1965.

BRYCE ECHENIQUE, ALFREDO (1939–)

Of the numerous Latin American authors who have lived in France, with his burlesque and autobiographical style, Bryce Echenique was among the first to demystify Paris, which had been considered to be the El Dorado of artists.

Born in Lima, Peru, on February 19, 1939, Bryce Echenique lived in France from 1964 to 1984, first and mainly in Paris and then for the final three years in Montpellier; since 1984, he has lived in Spain. The son of a bourgeois family, grandson of the president of the Republic, and a descendant of the last viceroy, with a father of British origin and a mother who descended from the local Spanish nobility, Bryce Echenique left Lima after studying law. It was in France that he became a writer.

A master of the "entertainment narrative," Bryce Echenique had an international success with his first novel, *Un Mundo para Julius* (*Un Monde pour Julius,* 1970). Three of his works were set exclusively in France. The first, *La vida exagerada de Martín Romaña* (*Vie exagérée de Martin Romaña,* 1981), recounts the tribulations of a Peruvian in Paris. The second, *Reo de nocturnidad* (*Noctambulisme aggravé,* 1997), is set in Montpellier and features a university professor, like Bryce Echenique himself, as the central character. The third book, a collection of short stories, is titled *Guía triste de París* (*Guide triste de París,* 1999).

In Peru, Bryce Echenique had been raised very strictly by his father, a banker, who enrolled him in an English-language school (*No me esperen en abril* [*Ne m'attendez pas en avril*], 1995), made him study law, and intended to send him to Cambridge University. However, the young Bryce Echenique wanted to become a writer and was able to rely on the support of his mother, a francophile and such a fan of Marcel Proust that she baptized her son Alfredo Marcelo. This influence was crucial. Even if Bryce Echenique mocks in his novels the figure of his mother, who would later take him to visit Proust's grave, *Julius* has a child as a central character and develops a number of Proustian themes.

The demystification of Paris and of France distinguish Bryce Echenique from other great Peruvian writers, such as the poet Cesar Vallejos and the author Mario Vargas Llosa, who for their part followed the path taken by the poet Rubén Darío ("France is the country of our dreams"). It is no coincidence that Darío was the subject of their university theses.

Bryce Echenique's disillusioned take on France and Paris is not only literary. In *Guide triste de Paris,* which has a deeply South American tone, he criticizes and is amused by the barricades of May 1968, an event that he witnessed firsthand.

Pablo Aiquel

See also: Darío, Rubén; Literary Relations.
Reference
Weiss, Jason. *The Lights of Home: A Century of Latin American Writers in Paris.* New York: Routledge, 2003.

BUGNET, GEORGES (1879–1981)
French-born writer.

Early academic promise, followed by study at the University of Dijon, suggested a career in universities, but Bugnet abandoned his studies to take up a career in journalism (at the newspaper *La Croix de Haute Savoie*). Soon after his marriage (1904) he emigrated to Canada, where, filled with enthusiasm for life in the wilderness, he settled in Alberta to experience the extreme hardship of subsistence farming in a remote part of the province. In his early forties he returned to writing during a particularly hard winter after twenty years of unremitting physical labor on his holding.

Bugnet's two best-known works, *Nipsya* (1924) and the much more pessimistic *La Forêt* (*The Forest,* 1934), use his experience of life in Alberta. Nipsya is a beautiful Métisse, half Cree, half Irish, raised by her Cree grandmother, who attracts the interest of three men: Mahigan, a Cree; her Métis cousin Vital Lajeunesse, more French than Cree; and the young Scot Monsieur Alec, owner of the local trading post. Nipsya's hesitation among the three suitors is set against the rising of Louis

Riel, of which Vital is a leader. The tragedy of the rising is minimized because the story is seen through the eyes of Nipsya, who is far removed from the actual fighting. Bugnet concentrates on the journey of Nipsya from adherence to the Cree traditions of her grandmother to acceptance of Christianity to please the ardently Catholic Vital (who reflects Bugnet's own views). Despite his admiration and sympathy for the Crees, Bugnet believed that the only way forward for them was to accept the civilization represented by Monsieur Alec and the Catholicism urged at length by Vital. The book, as we have it today, is less didactic than in its original version. Constance Woodrow translated it into English to some critical acclaim, making the book more readable by eliminating some speeches of Vital. Bugnet readily admitted that the result was an improvement.

La Forêt is the story of Roger and Louise, a young French couple who, like the Bugnets, settle in a remote part of Alberta and for three years wage a losing battle against the encircling forest. Louise in particular grows to hate the implacable Nature that surrounds them, and as their marriage is increasingly threatened after the death of their child, the couple abandon the struggle and withdraw to the city.

Bugnet's other works are Le Lys de sang (The Lily of Blood, 1923, subsequently rewritten), in which a hero based on the author escapes in his imagination from the Canadian winter to Africa; Siraf (1934), a philosophical dialogue between the spirit of the forest and a man from this world; and Les Voix de la solitude (The Voices of Solitude, 1938), a collection of short texts. In later life, Bugnet was active in francophone journalism in Alberta and a distinguished horticulturalist. Bugnet is little known outside western Canada despite the early success of the English translation of Nipsya. His two major novels repay reading for the beauty of much of his writing and the insights that he offers into Albertan history experienced firsthand (La Forêt) or through the reminiscences of eyewitnesses (Nipsya). Bugnet died in Saint Albert, Alberta, in 1981.

Peter Noble

See also: Alberta; Catholic Church; Métis; Riel, Louis.

References

Carpenter, David C. "Georges Bugnet: An Introduction." *Journal of Canadian Fiction* 1, no. 4 (1972): 72–78.

Papen, Jean. *Georges Bugnet: Homme de lettres canadien.* Saint Boniface, Man.: Edition des Plaines, 1985.

BUJOLD, GENEVIÈVE (1942–)

Québécois film actress.

The Quebec film industry that emerged in the early 1960s typically produced celebrities, in the sense of familiar, televisual figures more appropriate to the cinema of a small country, rather than stars. Geneviève Bujold was the first to acquire a career outside these boundaries, gaining a place in the French star system in the 1960s but then becoming an important figure in films associated with the more independent end of American cinema.

In Quebec, the narrative of Bujold's star persona begins with her as a typical Quiet Revolution figure, the daughter of a Montreal bus driver, educated like most of her generation at convent school but then rebelling against this in the form of 1960s autonomy and individualism. Early experience hosting a TV pop music show and appearing onstage and in short National Film

Board productions was followed by her "discovery," as legend has it, by Alain Resnais's mother while Bujold was part of a visiting theatrical troupe in France. Resnais cast her opposite Yves Montand in his meditation on memory and the Spanish civil war, *La Guerre est finie* (*The War Is Over,* 1966). She followed this with French films directed by Philippe de Broca (*Le Roi de coeur* [*King of Hearts*], 1966) and Louis Malle (*Le Voleur* [The Thief of Paris], 1967), before returning to Quebec to star as the waitress who breaks off a relationship with the central character in Michel Brault's *Entre la mer et l'eau douce* (*Between Sweet and Salt Water,* 1967). This period also marks the beginning of her collaboration with her English-Canadian husband Paul Almond, who directed her in *Isabel* (1968), *The Act of the Heart* (1970), and *Journey* (1972).

Bujold's American breakthrough began with her Oscar nomination for *Anne of the Thousand Days* (Charles Jarrot, 1969) opposite Richard Burton, and although she continued to make films in France (and with Almond), and her status enabled the financing of *Kamouraska* (Claude Jutra, 1973), the failure of the latter film meant that most of her films in the next two decades were American, usually in genre cinema (*Earthquake,* Robson, 1974; *Obsession,* de Palma, 1976; *Coma,* Crichton, 1978; opposite Clint Eastwood in *Tightrope,* Tuggle, 1984). The mature Bujold's combination of authority, anticonformism, and vulnerability, along with her subtle and enigmatic performances, meant that she was again favored by more noncommercial directors, notably Alan Rudolph (*Choose Me,* 1984; *Trouble in Mind,* 1985; *The Moderns,* 1988), and, returning to Canada, David Cronenberg (*Dead Ringers,* 1988).

The return to Quebec cinema and to Michel Brault, began with *Les Noces de papier* (1989), in which she plays an academic who enters into a marriage of convenience with a Latin American refugee. Brault also directed her in *Mon Amie Max* (1994) as a mother seeking her son. Although Bujold's roles became more secondary in the latter half of the 1990s, fans can only speculate as to what might have been had she not abandoned the role of Captain Janeway after the first day of filming the TV series *Star Trek Voyager* in 1994. (Her scenes are available on DVD.)

Bujold is both a Quebec nationalist and an international figure, especially within Quebec itself. Although her origins tended not to play a significant role in her American work, save as an extra patina of sophistication more associated with Frenchness than with Quebecness, she remains an interesting example of the malleability and mobility of star construction, depending on age, audience, and which national cinema is being embodied.

Bill Marshall

See also: Brault, Michel; Jutra, Claude; Lévesque, René; Malle, Louis; Montand, Yves; Quebec; Quiet Revolution; Resnais, Alain.

Reference
Marshall, Bill. *Quebec National Cinema.* Montreal: McGill-Queen's University Press, 2001.

BURROUGHS, WILLIAM S. (1914–1997)

American writer.

Even in a century of experimental art, Burroughs's writing stands out as extreme, in terms of both content and form. His controversial books include the autobiographical *Junky* (1953, originally *Junkie*) and *Queer* (1987, but written at the same time as *Junky*), but it is *Naked Lunch* (1959) that took stream-of-consciousness writing into new realms with its graphic and fantastical take on modern society. His texts offer a nihilistic and withering critique of a nihilistic, power-crazed society. Burroughs's time in Tangier (in 1954 and on and off until 1964) was pivotal. There he filled his room with what would later become novels, in between consuming large amounts of whatever drugs were available. From there, he went to Paris, where the famous "Beat Hotel" (9, rue Gît-le-Coeur) reunited an entire generation of more or less stateless writers. It is at this point that Burroughs actually became a writer, in the sense of being taken seriously and also on his own terms. Allen Ginsberg brought *Naked Lunch* to Maurice Girodias, the proprietor of Olympia Press (known for its pornography but also home to Samuel Beckett's novels and Vladimir Nabokov's *Lolita*), who suggested it be taken away and edited properly. After editing, the Olympia Press published the first edition of *Naked Lunch*. Burroughs saw his literary reputation soar on the back of that novel and the ensuing prosecution for obscenity in the United States. He also received a particularly French confirmation of this status, when his being a writer helped him get off a drugs charge in Paris in 1958.

Burroughs's work owes more to France than the superficial biographical connection—the style and the misanthropic satire flow from the writing of Arthur Rimbaud, Paul Verlaine, Louis-Ferdinand Céline, and Jean Genet. He also, curiously, claimed Marcel Proust as an inspiration, writing

William Burroughs at his typewriter in Paris, 1962. (Bettmann/Corbis)

that they shared a profound interest in character and what happened to people. In what is generally seen as a key moment in the "postmodernizing" of literature, he actually used other people's texts, along with newspaper cuttings and a host of other documents, in his "cut-ups," which formed the basis for entire novels through the 1960s and featured strongly in later works. This technique of "citation" is supposed to reveal true, hidden messages from within texts and works as a sort of magical form of intertextuality (or, perhaps, a form of Stéphane Mallarmé's ultimate book). Burroughs took the idea from Brion Gysin, with whom he wrote *The Third Mind* (1978) as a vehicle for the new technique, which was also highly visual, drawing attention to "the word" itself. He imagined language as a virus, something that was dangerous psychologically and at the biological level, and saw his writing as a way out, some sort of cure.

Paul Hegarty

See also: Céline, Louis-Ferdinand; Genet, Jean; Literary Relations.

References

Burroughs, William. *The Adding Machine: Selected Essays.* New York: Arcade, 1993.

Sobieszek, Robert A. *Ports of Entry: Willam S. Burroughs and the Arts.* London/New York: Thames and Hudson, 1996.

BUTOR, MICHEL (1926–)

French novelist, essayist, critic, and author of travel literature.

Butor gained prominence with two early novels, *L'Emploi du temps* (1956) and *La Modification* (1957), as a result of which he is customarily associated with the *nouveau roman* movement. His early novels were written, however, against a background of traveling and working outside France, and it was contact with the United States in the 1960s (and subsequent periods spent traveling or working there) that triggered a series of erudite works experimenting with genre and combining travel writing with elements of fiction and essayism.

A member of a generation of young French people attracted to postwar North America as a result of the country's potential for cultural and economic renewal, Butor first traveled there in 1960 to work as a visiting professor at Bryn Mawr College in Philadelphia. He held a series of subsequent posts—at the University of Buffalo (1962–1963), Northwestern University (1965), the University of New Mexico (1969–1970 and 1973–1974), and the University of Montreal (1992)—and ad-

dressed his experiences in a series of texts, including *Où/*Where (*Le Génie du lieu/* Spirit of the Place, 2; 1971) and *Improvisations sur Michel Butor* (1993). The United States in the 1960s was a source of major culture shock. Struck by phenomena such as supermarkets, freeways, and regular domestic air travel, Butor developed a poetics of space and place to account for his journeys around the continent. The principal example of this is *Mobile* (1962), a typographically experimental and generically indeterminate text dedicated to Jackson Pollock. With a persistently nonlinear structure, *Mobile* is a provisional, fragmented account of a journey through the fifty-two states of the United States whose structure is essentially alphabetical (although doubly disorientating for anglophone readers because the author uses toponyms in French). Mixing perspectives—historical and contemporary, individual and collective—and incorporating transcribed texts from signs, catalogs, and prospectuses, *Mobile* juxtaposes geographically distinct places in a text that is also a work of satirical social commentary. He focuses especially on racial tension, the plight of Native Americans, and, in references to an imaginary theme park called "Freedomland," a sense of the stage management of history. With its combination of celebration, admiration, and critique, *Mobile* reflects the ambivalent attitude of 1960s French intellectuals toward the United States; ultimately, however, it rejects any clear-cut division between the two countries and emphasizes elements of their shared (revolutionary) histories as well as the European roots of many of the social issues that underpin the text.

Racial disharmony is also addressed in the second major text inspired by Butor's

American experiences, *6,810,000 Litres d'eau par seconde: Etude stéréophonique* (6,810,000 Liters a Second: A Stereophonic Study, 1965). This account of Niagara Falls, combining history, myth, and the imagined reactions of contemporary tourists, is made up of a pattern of different voices—including two different descriptions of the falls by François-René de Chateaubriand—that create a polyphonous effect. A major contribution to French representations of Niagara, it contrasts the romantic view of the falls with a more decadent contemporary version of the tourist site, reduced to a honeymooners' resort. The text describes a journey from spring to winter and is an account of fading love, disintegrating dialogues, and the fallibility of memory. These two major texts and the shorter fragments on North American subjects published subsequently (including *Transit,* 1992, with its passages on British Columbia and northwest Canada) reveal Butor's intense engagement with North American geography, history, and culture, as well as his sustained endeavor to explore, challenge, and reinvent understandings of North America in the French imagination.

Charles Forsdick

See also: Chateaubriand, François-Auguste René de, Vicomte; Mobile; Niagara Falls.
References
Calle-Gruber, Mireille, ed. *Butor et l'Amérique.* Paris: L'Harmattan, 1998.
Spencer, Michael. *Michel Butor.* New York: Twayne, 1974.

C

CABET, ETIENNE (1788–1856)

Etienne Cabet was born in 1788 to a Dijon, France, cooper family. Educated as a lawyer, in 1831 he joined the Chamber of Deputies by election; but dejected by King Louis-Philippe's lack of interest in equality and his regime's habit of condescension, Cabet lasted only a couple of years in office. Accused of sedition because of articles and editorials he had written and overseen as editor of the newspaper *Le Populaire* (the shareholders of which included its audience, artisans, from Paris and Lyon mainly), Cabet avoided detention by fleeing to England in 1834. There—awaiting his amnesty, which came in 1839—Cabet wrote a history of the 1789 revolution; he had already produced a poison-pen account of the revolution of 1830. While across the English Channel, he also became immersed in the work of Robert Owen, the Communist founder of the factory reform movement in New Lanark, Scotland. In *Voyage in Icaria* (1840), applying what he had learned, Cabet presented his own vision of an ideal cooperative society.

Voyage in Icaria recommends a classless and cashless world, in which all production and distribution of goods and services are ruled jointly by government and the family

for the benefit of each and every member. The text (before turning to designs for housing and suggestions for diet) argues that such a system of mutual give-and-take, administered by vote, would ensure the abolition of poverty. It casts private enterprise as its principal villain (not the institution of Christianity, as in Thomas More's *Utopia* of 1516)—as the fount of greed, or competition, and the antithesis of art. Unlike Karl Marx and Friedrich Engels, however, Cabet rejects violence as a means of change. Instead he urges a kind of exile, or refusal to participate in capitalism. Yet like them Cabet did not advise a return to an artisanal and agricultural world. Despite his fascination with scriptural Christianity (see his *Le Vrai Christianisme suivant Jésus-Christ* [1846]) and wariness of mechanization, he understood that industry had arrived to stay.

Cabet's ideas met with success, encouraging a following of "Icarians" that would number in the hundreds of thousands. In 1848 a fraction of them, ready to surrender theory for practice, seeking peace and quiet, departed Europe to establish a camp in Fanin, Texas. In the United States, they soon endured challenges of one kind and another, including a contract swindle that forced a retreat to New Orleans, Louisiana.

Cabet himself arrived in 1849 and decided to move the colony to Nauvoo, Illinois, a place established by Mormons. Despite dissension from within, there a version of "Icaria" existed until shortly after Cabet's death in St Louis in 1856. Elsewhere, in Cheltenham and Corning, villages in Iowa, variants of this community survived longer, but feebly. Because of the advance of industrial and financial capitalism, repression, and their avoidance of conflict—a form of escapism according to Cabet's critics—none of these societies remained at the turn of the century. Their contradictory emphasis on hierarchy (Cabet had a tendency to be authoritarian) also made them fail.

Johan Åhr

> See also: Bonaparte, Napoléon; French
> Revolution; Illinois Country; Iowa;
> Jefferson, Thomas; Louisiana; Louisiana
> Purchase; New Orleans; Texas; Utopias.
> **References**
> Johnson, Christoper H. *Utopian Communism
> in France: Cabet and the Icarians,
> 1839–1851.* Ithaca, NY: Cornell University
> Press, 1974.
> Sutton, Robert P. *Les Icariens: The Utopian
> Dream in Europe and America.* Urbana:
> University of Illinois Press, 1994.

CADILLAC, ANTOINE LAUMET DE LA MOTHE (1658–1730)

Founder of the French trading outpost Fort Pontchartrain du De Troit in 1701, Antoine Laumet de la Mothe Cadillac began his long career in New France in 1683 as a simple soldier in the Port Royal garrison. He soon advanced in rank and status and in 1694 was appointed commandant of Michilimackinac, where he remained until 1697. There his mission consisted of consolidating the ties between New France and native tribes in the Great Lakes region. Relations deteriorated, however, as the natives began to increase trade with the British. Cadillac also took advantage of his position to engage in illegal trafficking.

Following his mission at Michilimackinac, Cadillac returned to France, where he presented his plans for a settlement that would keep the British and their native allies out of the Great Lakes. On July 24, 1701, Cadillac arrived with about 100 men at the site that would become Detroit. When he was recalled to France in 1710, Detroit's native population numbered in the thousands, but it was home to only a handful of French Canadians.

Cadillac's next appointment was in 1711 as governor of Louisiana, where he remained until 1716, at which time he was deposed, tried, and sentenced to the Bastille. Restored to favor in 1718, he obtained a decree in 1722 allowing him to regain possession of his Detroit property which he in turn sold to the Canadian Jacques Baudry de la Marche. The proceeds of the sale allowed him to acquire the office of governor of Castelsarrasin in his native province of Gascony, where he died October 16, 1730.

In 1902, Henry Martin Leland and General Motors created the prestigious Cadillac automobile, which bears Cadillac's name and coat of arms in honor of Detroit's founder.

Maureen Waters

> See also: Automobiles; Detroit; Louisiana; New
> France.
> **References**
> Brown, Henry D. *Cadillac and the Founding
> of Detroit.* Detroit: Wayne State University
> Press, 1976.

Dunnigan, Brian Leigh. *Frontier Metropolis: Picturing Early Detroit, 1701–1838.* Detroit: Wayne State University Press, 2001.

CAHIERS DU CINÉMA

One of the key journals, along with *Positif,* in the burgeoning writing about film in postwar France.

Founded in 1951, *Cahiers du cinéma* (*cahiers* means "notebooks") has exerted an important influence to the present day. French cinema in the years of postliberation Reconstruction had been dominated by what was known as the *tradition de qualité*—often adaptations of literary works directed by such figures as Claude Autant-Lara and René Clément, relying heavily on star actors and adhering to a closely written script. *Cahiers* mercilessly lampooned these films and championed the Hollywood cinema of the 1940s and 1950s, which had of course been inaccessible in France under the occupation and threatened to flood the national market thereafter. A character in Jean-Pierre Melville's Resistance drama *L'Armée des ombres* (*Army in the Shadows,* 1969) speaks of how the French will know that they are free when it becomes possible to see *Gone with the Wind* (Fleming, 1939). *Cahiers* can in one sense be said to have treated Hollywood films much as European art films had always been treated—as texts with an author/auteur in the person of the director. Howard Hawks, Alfred Hitchcock, and Billy Wilder benefited from the same kind of serious critical appraisal that the likes of F. W. Murnau and Jean Renoir had always received. This was particularly marked in the case of Hitchcock, frequently dismissed as a talented prankster until Claude Chabrol and Eric Rohmer drew attention to the importance of philosophical and theological themes, such as the transference of guilt, in his work.

Chabrol and Rohmer, of course, went on to distinguished careers as directors, and that is likewise true of other *Cahiers* writers such as Jacques Rivette, Jean-Luc Godard, and François Truffaut, all of whose work in varying degrees bears the imprint of the *Cahiers* embrace of auteurism and the low-budget style of Hollywood B-movie making. Myth has it that these five key figures first met at Henri Langlois's Cinémathèque on the Left Bank of Paris, where it was possible to spend entire afternoons and evenings watching vintage Hollywood (and other) films. The *ciné-club* movement, fostered by André Bazin, a cofounder of *Cahiers,* was also propitious terrain for the development of an informed film culture, in which the journal's part was crucial.

All this changed dramatically in the aftermath of the May 1968 uprising, which saw *Cahiers* take a strongly, and often forbiddingly, politicized stance. The political practice of Maoism, in alliance with the cultural theories of Louis Althusser and Jacques Lacan, led the journal to turn its back on the broad range of filmmakers and readings that had characterized it before and to embrace an often sectarian hagiography in which the post-1968 films of Godard or the political aesthetics of Bertolt Brecht all but displaced any consideration of Hollywood or other popular cinema. The collapse of revolutionary hopes and the journal's dwindling circulation caused this line to be abandoned in the early 1970s, since which time the journal has catered to an educated cinephile readership and remains the most widely read film journal in France and one of the most important in the world.

Keith Reader

See also: Bazin, André; Chabrol, Claude; Cinema, 1945 to the Present; Godard, Jean-Luc; Lacan, Jacques; Melville, Jean-Pierre; *Positif;* Truffaut, François; World War II.

References
Forbes, Jill. *The Cinema in France: After the New Wave.* London: BFI/Macmillan, 1992.
Hillier, Jim, ed. *Cahiers du cinéma: Four Volumes of Translated Essays.* London: Routledge and Kegan Paul, 1985–2000.

CAILLOIS, ROGER (1913–1978)

French poet and essayist.

Roger Caillois began his literary career on the margins of the surrealist movement between 1932 and 1934. Following a fundamental disagreement with André Breton concerning what he regarded as the idealistic implications of the movement, Caillois distanced himself from it. A brilliant student of Marcel Mauss and Georges Dumézil at the Ecole Pratique des Hautes Etudes en Sciences Sociales (1933), *agrégé* (postgraduate diploma) in grammar (1936), Caillois drew close to Georges Bataille and founded the Collège de Sociologie (1937–1939) with him and Michel Leiris. Their aim was to study the social phenomena of the sacred. The myth and the sacred, and the attraction and repulsion provoked by the latter, became Caillois's favored areas of research.

Caillois attempted to understand the origin and the motivations behind the construction of human myths. In *La Mante religieuse* (The Praying Mantis, 1934), he took as his point of departure a meditation on the sexual mores of the mantis, developing a thesis highlighting the continuity of a biological link between nutrition and sexuality that exists in both the animal and in the human worlds. His aim was to underline how the instinctive behavior of the mantis (with the female of the species eating the male after the sexual act) engenders in humans the development of myths around the notion of fatal female powers of seduction. It was, for him, proof that the origin of some myths lies in the material universe.

It was also during the Collège de Sociologie years that Caillois published the essay *L'Homme et le sacré* (*Man and the Sacred,* 1939), in which he developed his analyses of the polarity of the sacred. His writings from this period also show his conviction that the sacred alone could serve to bind together human communities, a belief that was to lead him to study the function of myth in literature and in society. By bringing his meditations into the political domain, he tried to demonstrate that new myths capable of replacing the old ones could allow for a renewal of European societies, which were visibly in crisis. The analyses and ideas formulated during this period would not often be understood and would often be labeled as cryptofascist (see the elitism and the Nietzschean tone in *Le Vent d'hiver* (Winter Wind, 1937). More recently, however, critics have suggested that the texts from the Collège de Sociologie period should be read as a left-wing response to the national-socialist utilization of myth and rituals and of the communitarian energy that results from them.

On the eve of World War II, Caillois was invited to Argentina by Victoria Ocampo. He was introduced to South

American literary circles and met Jorge Luis Borges, Pablo Neruda, and several other great writers. Upon his return to France in 1945, he played the role of go-between by publishing their work in the *La Croix de Sud* collection, which he launched and directed for Gallimard.

The war and his stay in Argentina brought about many changes in Caillois's political and intellectual position. From this period onward, he sought, above all, to offer an ethical contribution, a proposal to reelaborate civic values that had been erased by Hitlerism, the war, and the defeat in 1940. With the support of Ocampo, he created the review *Lettres françaises* in Buenos Aires in order to maintain contact between French writers throughout the world.

When Caillois returned to France in 1945, he joined the United Nations Education, Scientific, and Cultural Organization, where he became director of the journal *Diogène*. His career as a senior civil servant enabled him to combine his broad cultural interests and his love of travel.

Four main directions characterize Caillois's thought. The first concerns his aesthetic position. Caillois refused literary idealism (*Procès intellectuel de l'art*/Art on Intellectual Trial, 1934). He demanded, in the literary domain as in any other, strict rules (*Les Impostures de la poésie*/The Impostures of Poetry, 1944). He defended the encyclopedic poetry of Saint-John Perse (*Poétique de Saint-John Perse*/Poetics of Saint-John Perse, 1954), which excludes no information from the real. He admires the "magic" element found in Latin American literature, which seems, to him, to stem from the depths of the earth and to allow for access to a "natural" fantastic.

In the postwar years, Caillois developed a rigorous meditation on poetics and aesthetics (*Vocabulaire esthétique*/Aesthetic Vocabulary, 1946; *Babel,* 1948; *Art poétique*/Art of Poetry, 1958; *Esthétique généralisée*/General Aesthetics, 1965), returned with renewed attention to the fantastic (*Au Coeur du fantastique*/To the Heart of the Fantastic, 1965), and wrote tales (*Ponce-Pilate*/Pontius Pilate, 1961, and *Guide du XVème arrondissement à l'usage des fantômes*/A Ghost's Guide to the 15th District of Paris, 1977).

The second direction taken by his research led him to classify, organize, and rationally explain the multiple correspondences that, in his view, wove together the strands of a universe seen as unitary. The isomorphisms and secret analogies of an exclusively material (and thus antiromantic) nature, which connected the different realms, remained constantly at the heart of his investigations. He had deciphered them in his essay on the praying mantis and continued to reveal them in *Méduse et Cie,* (Medusa and Co., 1960) and in *Le Mimétisme animal* (Animal Mimetism, 1963). To study the causes and the functioning of their recurrent manifestations, Caillois relied on Dimitri Mendeleev's periodic table (*Cases d'un échiquier,* 1970) and appealed for the establishment of "diagonal sciences" that alone would be able to question what he called, in the development of his meditations, "adventurous coherences" (*Cohérences aventureuses,* 1976) and "hidden recurrences" (*Récurrences dérobées,* 1978).

His third orientation led him, as sociologist and ethnologist, to examine the phenomena that demonstrate the human need for vertigo, the upheaval of the senses, or ecstasy. The appendix to *L'Homme et le sacré,* dealing as it did with sex, games, war, and their relationship as much with debauchery as with the sacred, had prepared the sociological analyses he developed in *Les Jeux et les hommes* (*Man, Play and Games,* 1958), a work in which Caillois finds "vertigo" to be one of the fundamental categories that help to classify play activity. Further meditations on the same subject were collected in *Instincts et sociétés* (1964) and in *Bellone ou la pente de la guerre* (1963).

Caillois's stay in Argentina gave him another subject for moral and poetic meditation. His discovery of the arid and deserted expanses of the American continent led him to reflect on the relationship between nature and civilization (*Patagonie*/ Patagonia, 1942; *Espace américain*/American Space, 1949). In relation to these works and based on the contents of his intellectual autobiography (*Le Fleuve Alphée*/ The River Alph, 1978), a "moralist" Caillois has been spoken of, meditating on questions of virtue, civilization, and human effort in order to escape the decline that cyclically strikes humanity. It was in the continuation of these reflections that Caillois finally turned his output toward the form of the prose poem centered on the observation of minerals. Caillois dedicated several collections to this topic (*Pierres*/ Stones, 1966; *L'Ecriture des pierres*/The Writing of Stones, 1970; *Pierres réfléchies*/ Reflected Stones, 1975; *Trois Leçons des ténèbres*/Three Lessons from Darkness, 1978), all to critical acclaim.

Agnese Silvestri

See also: Argentina; Bataille, Georges; Borges, Jorge Luis; Breton, André; Leiris, Michel; Neruda; Pablo; Ocampo, Victoria; Surrealism; Theory; World War II.

References

Felgine, Odile. *Roger Caillois.* Paris: Stock, 1994.

Jenny, Laurent, ed. *Roger Caillois: La pensée aventurée.* Luçon: Editions Belin, 1992.

Massonnet, Stéphane. *Les Labyrinthes de l'imaginaire dans l'œuvre de Roger Caillois.* Paris: L'Harmattan, 1998.

CAJUNS

Acadians who settled in Louisiana and their descendants.

Cajun is the English version of *Cadien,* shortened from *Acadien.* The British began deporting Acadians who refused to swear allegiance to the throne in 1755, and the resulting upheaval is known as the *grand dérangement* (Great Upheaval or Expulsion). Acadians relocated to Louisiana as early as 1757, with a major influx occurring in 1785. Cajun country, or Acadiana, consists of an upright triangular area in southern Louisiana, home to approximately 400,000 Cajuns, according to the 1990 census. Accounts of Cajuns' isolation from outside influences (supposedly the cause of their cultural resilience) have been exaggerated, for they have absorbed elements from Native American, Spanish, German, African, and Anglo-American cultures. Though French has been disappearing as a day-to-day language, it remains important in music, which (like dancing and cuisine) is one of the most recognizable aspects of Cajun culture and identity for Cajuns and non-Cajuns alike.

Misconceptions about Cajuns can be found as early as Longfellow's *Evangeline* (1847). Often thought to be characterized by strong kinship ties, an attachment to their Catholic religion (in spite of anticlerical tendencies), and their skill for navigating swampy areas in canoelike pirogues, Acadians quickly adapted to their new environment and forged a new agricultural lifestyle on the prairies and bayous. Although negative stereotypes have held that Cajuns are an uneducated rural folk, Acadiana has undergone considerable urbanization and industrialization, particularly with the incursion of the oil industry, which provided new jobs until the mid-1980s. Other often-cited aspects of Cajun culture include a cohesive collective spirit, a distinctive folk architecture, and a rich folklore and folk practices. During the surge of international interest in the Cajuns in the 1970s and 1980s, Cajun music, dancing, and cuisine became more popular outside of Acadiana. Most frequently associated with black Louisianans, zydeco has both influenced and been influenced by Cajun music.

Likewise, Cajun French has exchanged elements with Afro-Louisiana Creole (along with other languages). After 1922, speaking French in school was outlawed and punished in Louisiana. Though Cajuns had retained French as their mother tongue until that point, this official assault took its toll as parents began to discourage speaking French, and a distinctively Cajun English increasingly became the primary vehicle for Cajun identity. An attempt to reverse this process occurred in 1968 with the founding of the Council for the Development of French in Louisiana (CODOFIL), which favored standard French over the Cajun vernacular and thus has not recovered from its elitist reputation. This renewed interest in French coincided with a Cajun pride movement that began as early as the 1960s and intensified in the 1980s, when many repudiated negative labels and stereotypes held by Anglo-Americans. As part of this reaffirmation of Cajun identity, a number of writers began to forge a literary French heavily inflected with the Cajun vernacular in the 1970s, with poetry as their privileged genre. This literary renaissance has fostered and been fostered by cultural links with other regions of the Acadian diaspora, which have provided educational and publishing opportunities.

Jarrod Hayes

See also: Acadia; Catholic Church; Dance; *Evangeline; Francophonie, La;* Fur Trade; Language; Louisiana; Louisiana Purchase; Mississippi River; New Orleans; Slavery.

References

Ancelet, Barry Jean, Jay D. Edwards, and Glen Pitre. *Cajun Country.* Jackson: University Press of Mississippi, 1991.

Bernard, Shane K. *The Cajuns: Americanization of a People.* Jackson: University Press of Mississippi, 2003.

Brasseaux, Carl A. *The Founding of New Acadia: The Beginnings of Acadian Life in Louisiana, 1765–1803.* Baton Rouge: Louisiana State University Press, 1987.

Stivale, Charles J. *Disenchanting Les Bons temps: Identity and Authenticity in Cajun Music and Dance.* Durham: Duke University Press, 2003.

CAMUS, ALBERT (1913–1960)

Born in Mondori, Algeria, of French and Spanish parents, Camus was shaped by his early experiences and sense of place. A sensual engagement with life (sun and sea, love and sports) coexisted with deep alienation (arising from early poverty, tuberculosis, being French in an Arab nation, and later being a provincial in France). During World War II, Camus edited *Combat,* the leading paper of the Resistance forces. In novels such as *L'Etranger* (*The Stranger,* 1942), *La Peste* (*The Plague,* 1947), and *La Chute* (*The Fall,* 1956); plays such as

Caligula (1945); and in philosophical essays such as *Le Mythe de Sisyphe* (*The Myth of Sisyphus,* 1942) and *L'Homme révolté* (*The Rebel,* 1951), Camus recognized the contingent and absurd nature of the human condition. Against despair, he argued for a passionate commitment to the world, tinged with moral responsibility. Camus appeared as a voice of restraint, opposing the execution of French collaborators with the Nazis and refusing, contrary to most of his fellow intellectuals, to sanction the violence of Algerian rebels against French colonial rule. Camus always felt most comfortable understanding issues in concrete terms rather than as abstractions.

Although he preferred not to be labeled an existentialist, Camus's philosophical concerns placed him in that camp, along with Jean-Paul Sartre and Simone de Beauvoir. Camus's greater literary gifts, appealing personality, and humanistic orientation won him a large audience in the United States after World War II. He visited the United States briefly in 1946, dismissing Americans as unduly cheerful and hence unable to deal adequately with the complexities of life, despite Camus's deep identification with American writers such as Herman Melville and James M. Cain, both of whom stressed a tragic sensibility. Camus actually modeled his *L'Etranger* on Cain's clipped prose style.

At Columbia University, Camus lectured on "The Human Crisis," stressing individual and collective responsibility for evil in the world. Camus called for a revolt against the inhumanity of torture and totalitarianism, while avoiding self-righteousness. Camus's moderation and commitment struck a positive note with an emerging sense among American intellectuals of a strenuous anti-Communist liberalism. Dwight Macdonald's brooding essay, "The Root Is Man" (1946), arose out of his conversations with Camus. Both Macdonald and Camus rejected rigid ideologies of the right and left in favor of an almost anarchistic sense of moral commitment to humane values.

Camus's work was also influential in postwar Latin America, and in 1949 he did a lecture tour of Brazil and Chile via Argentina, where the exiled Catalan producer Margarita Xirgu's production of his play *Le Malentendu* (*The Misunderstanding*) had been banned by the Peronist government. Camus's short story "La Pierre qui pousse" ("The Growing Stone") in the collection *L'Exil et le royaume* (*Exile and the Kingdom,* 1957) features a French engineer, alienated from European society, faced with the class and racial hierarchies and religious sensibilities of a Brazilian village.

In the late 1950s and early 1960s, Camus's influence in the United States spread. Writers and intellectuals wanted to engage with Camus, hence Hayden Carruth's novel *After the Stranger* (1965) and Arthur Miller's play *After the Fall* (1964). Camus's novel, *L'Etranger,* with its accessible prose, was commonly assigned for translation in high school and college French courses. After this initial introduction to Camus, many young Americans who were in the process of becoming involved in the emerging civil rights and antiwar movements of the 1960s looked to Camus for guidance. Tom Hayden, a leader of the antiwar movement, also respected Camus's counsel to practice revolt in moderation. In looking back on his more radical actions, Hayden regretted that he had not followed Camus's strictures more closely. Camus's reputation in the United States faded in the 1980s, as Rea-

Albert Camus, Nobel Prize winner. 1957. (Library of Congress)

gan conservatism and postmodernism pushed aside liberal humanism. In recent years, however, publication of new monographs suggest renewed attention to Camus.

George Cotkin

See also: Beauvoir, Simone de; Sartre, Jean-Paul; Theory; World War II.

References

Cotkin, George. *Existential America.* Baltimore/London: Johns Hopkins University Press, 2002.

Lottman, Herbert R. *Albert Camus: A Biography.* Garden City, NY: Doubleday and Co., 1979.

Todd, Olivier. *Albert Camus: A Life.* Trans. Benjamin Ivry. New York: Alfred A. Knopf, 1997.

CAPUCINE (GERMAINE LEFEBVRE) (1931–1990)

Born in Toulon, France, Capucine was a 1950s fashion model and Hollywood star of the early to mid-1960s. Although Capucine appeared in a few French movies in the late 1940s, it was only in the late 1950s, after having worked as a model for French couturier Hubert de Givenchy, that her film career took off. Bearing some resemblance to two other famous Givenchy muses and inspirations, Audrey Hepburn and Jacqueline Kennedy, Capucine embodied the beauty ideal of the 1960s, and in her films she epitomized cosmopolitan chic and glamour. Her androgynously slim physique; classic facial features dominated by large, melancholy eyes and high cheekbones; and cool, aristocratic demeanor all contributed to a striking and vaguely exotic presence onscreen. As an actress, however, she was often perceived as lacking in emotional warmth and possessing a limited range of expression.

In Hollywood from 1958, her studio Columbia launched her in the costume biopic *Song without End* (Cukor/Vidor, 1960), in which she played a princess opposite Dirk Bogarde's Franz Liszt. In the following years Capucine acted alongside established Hollywood stars such as John Wayne (*North to Alaska,* Hathaway, 1960) and William Holden (*The Lion,* Cardiff, 1962; *The 7th Dawn,* Gilbert, 1964), but none of these films significantly advanced her career. Indeed, most of her roles tended to be largely decorative and rarely gave her the opportunity to prove her acting abilities. Even in her best-remembered film, the comedy *The Pink Panther* (Edwards, 1963), her nominal status as the film's leading lady is overshadowed by the performances of most of her costars. Her arguably most interesting role was in Edward Dmytryk's *Walk on the Wild Side* (1962), a bizarre melodrama set in New Orleans and now considered a camp classic, in which she played a depressive sculptress pursued by a lesbian brothel madam (Barbara Stanwyck) and a sadistic drifter (Laurence Harvey). Although her appearance as an upper-class nymphomaniac in the Woody Allen–scripted *What's New, Pussycat?* (Donner, 1965) cemented Capucine's place in the pantheon of swinging sixties icons, few of her other films during the decade have stood the test of time, even though her performance in the Italian portmanteau production *Le Fate* (Bolognini/Monicelli, 1966), in which she parodied her established screen persona, proved that she could be an able comedienne when given the chance. By the late 1960s, Capucine had relocated to Europe, where Federico Fellini cast her in *Satyricon* (1969), her last major film appearance of note. From the 1970s onward, her screen roles became increasingly sporadic and consisted mainly of supporting characters and cameo parts in French, Italian, and multinational European productions; TV series; and two sequels to *The Pink Panther* in the early 1980s, *The Trail of the Pink Panther* (Edwards, 1982) and *Curse of the Pink Panther* (Edwards, 1983). After suffering from manic depression for most of her life, Capucine committed suicide in 1990 by throwing herself out of the window of her eighth-floor apartment in Lausanne.

Tim Bergfelder

See also: Allen, Woody; Cinema, 1945 to the Present; Fashion; Inspector Clouseau; New Orleans.

References

Barrios, Richard. *Screened Out: Playing Gay in Hollywood from Edison to Stonewall.* London: Routledge, 2003.

Hadleigh, Boze. *Hollywood Lesbians.* New York: Barricade Books, 1994.

Liaut, Jean-Noël. *Hubert de Givenchy: Entre vies et légendes.* Paris: Grasset, 2000.

Palmer, Alexandra. *Couture and Commerce: The Transatlantic Fashion Trade in the 1950s.* Vancouver: University of British Columbia Press, 2001.

CARLE, GILLES (1928–)

Québécois film director.

Born in 1928, in Maniwaki near an Algonquin reservation and partly of native descent, Carle had an upbringing that included the plural and hybrid elements of Quebec culture: Catholicism, American popular culture such as country and western via the radio, and the multiculturalism of the Abitibi region, recently opened up for internal "colonization" and immigration from abroad. Indeed, in his prolific output of fifteen features, notably in those films he scripted himself, Carle tended to take ideas and run with them, skimming a multitude of surfaces. His place in Quebec film history is assured first of all by his role in the emergence of a Quebec popular cinema in the 1960s.

An early interest in poetry led to filmmaking and entry into the National Film Board (NFB) of Canada. In 1965 Carle surreptitiously turned an NFB documentary project on snow clearing in Montreal into a fictional feature, a comedy about a quintessential Québécois "little man," *La Vie heureuse de Léopold Z.* (The Merry World of Leopold Z.). Taking advantage of the relaxation of censorship and increased resources for the private sector, he followed with *Le Viol d'une jeune fille douce* (*In Trouble* in the U.S., 1968), which set a pattern for most of his subsequent features in its baroque and satirical portrait of Quebec identity and mores, but in typical 1960s fashion centered on male heterosexual desire and the spectacle of female bodies, a new "popular-erotic" in Quebec cinema. It is this which prevents his 1969 film *Red* from fulfilling its promise of investigating the native dimension of Quebec identity. In this vein and supported by the production company he founded with Pierre Lamy in 1971, Carle made several highly successful films in the 1970s, five with his then partner Carole Laure. Two of these, *La Mort d'un bûcheron* (The Death of a Lumberjack, 1973) and *Fantastica* (1980), along with the macho countercultural comedy *Les Mâles* (*The Men,* 1970) and *La Vraie Nature de Bernadette* (*The True Nature of Bernadette,* 1972), which explores the reversibility and ambiguity of Catholic notions of sainthood and the contemporary vogue for a "return to nature," figure among the top twenty box-office successes for Québécois films in France. This success has been explained by Carle's presentational skills, his assiduous promotion in person of his films in France, his niche marketing of himself to certain sections of the French media as a "left-wing" director, and his courtship of the *ciné-club* network and its journals *Cinéma* and *Revue du cinéma,* which sought to distinguish themselves from *Positif* and *Cahiers du cinéma,* which ignored Carle altogether.

Carle's fame in France meant he was an appropriate choice for two lavish Franco-Québécois coproductions of the early 1980s based on literary best-sellers. *Les Plouffe* (*The Plouffe Family,* 1981), based on the novel by Roger Lemelin about a working-class family in Quebec City on the eve of World War II, was an effective piece of cinematic storytelling and spectacle, with accents adjusted and references to

the hexagon (and a fleeting appearance by French actress Stéphane Audran) added for the French audience. *Maria Chapdelaine* (1983), based on the novel by Frenchman Louis Hémon set in rural Quebec at the beginning of the century, again starred Carole Laure in the lead role. Since then Carle has made several documentaries and also fictional features (such as *La Postière*/The Postmistress, 1992) starring his wife Chloé Sainte-Marie but has failed to repeat his successes of the 1970s and early 1980s.

Bill Marshall

See also: *Cahiers du cinéma;* Catholic Church; Hémon, Louis; Laure, Carole; *Maria Chapdelaine; Positif;* Quebec; World War II.

References

Coulombe, Michel. *Gilles Carle: Le chemin secret du cinéma.* Montreal: Liber, 1995.

Marshall, Bill. *Quebec National Cinema.* Montreal: McGill-Queen's University Press, 2001.

Prédal, René. "La Vie heureuse, ou la vraie nature de Gilles Carle." *L'Aventure du cinéma québécois en France.* Ed. Michel Larouche. Montreal: XYZ, 1996.

CARLSON, CAROLYN (1943–)

Appointed director, star dancer, and head of an experimental dance group at the Paris Opera in 1974, Carolyn Carlson became the first modern American dancer to reign at the opera, defying a centuries-old tradition.

Born in Fresno, California, to parents of Finnish origin, Carlson began her dance career with studies at the University of Utah and the San Francisco School of Ballet. She toured six years with Alwin Nikolais, modern dance multimedia pioneer, and served as his emblem figure between 1964 and 1971. While she was a member of the Nikolais company, she received the

Meilleur Danseur award at the International Dance Festival in Paris in 1968. After moving to Paris in 1971, she briefly joined the company of Anne Béranger, with whom she performed until 1973, and there Carlson created her first choreographies: *Rituel pour un rêve mort* (*Ritual for a Dead Dream*), *Aux quatre coins* (*To the Four Corners*), and *Verfangen*. During this period she worked with the Mudra School run by Maurice Béjart in Brussels, as well as the London School of Contemporary Dance. In 1974, she met Rolf Lieberman, director of the Paris Opera, and was appointed as the first modern choreographer in residence at the opera, with duties to perform modern dance and to head the Group of Theater Research for the Paris Opera House (GRTOP).

From 1974 to 1980, Carlson held the title of *etoile-chorégraphe* (star choreographer) of the opera and collaborated with lighting designer John Davis on a series of unique works for GRTOP that she has termed "visual poetry." Such works as *X-Land*, a solo for dancer Paolo Bortaluzzi based on improvisation, featured new aesthetic and plastic qualities for dance by portraying in static poses the development of everyday gestures. Other works, such as *L'Or des fous*, created less than a year after Carlson's arrival, contained elements blended from American modern dance, including acoustic effects, the human voice communicating inarticulate sounds and stammering, and movement. Carlson herself appeared as a dancer, making use of stark, enigmatic movements to evoke a white-masked, estranged heroine, unaware of her fellow dancers' goings-on.

Carlson performed at the Teatro Danza La Fenice in Venice between 1980 and 1984, choreographing such works as *Chalk Work* to music by Wakevitch and *Blue Lady* to music by René Aubry, a work that blended choreography with a religious serenity and has been performed in forty countries. Believing that choreography is not limited to steps, Carlson has never stopped revolutionizing her dance. From 1985 to 1991 she returned to Paris, creating at the Théâtre de la Ville such works as *Shamrock*, set to music by Gabriel Yared, and *Steppe* and *Going Home*, set to music by Aubry, and collaborating with Robert Wilson on the jazz opera *Cosmopolitan Greeting*.

In 1994, Carlson and Pierre Barnier formed L'Atelier de Paris Carolyn Carlson in the Cartoucherie near the Bois de Vincennes. *Spiritual Warriors*, a collection of solo works, was choreographed and performed by Carlson and contemporaries at the L'Atelier in 2000. She simultaneously served as director of dance for the Venice Biennale from 1999 to 2002 and has received the title of Chevalier de la Légion d'honneur (2000), preceded by that of Chevalier des Arts et Lettres (1985) by the French government. In 2002, she received the Médaille de Vermeil de la Ville de Paris.

Pamela Gay-White

See also: Dance; Jazz; Music (Classical).
References
Bremser, Martha. "Carolyn Carlson." *Fifty Contemporary Choreographers*. Veronica Turnbull. London: Gale, 1999: 55–58.
Macaire, Alain. *Interview with Carolyn Carlson*. Paris: Théâtre de la Ville, 1986.
Schneider, Katja. "Carolyn Carlson." *Ballettanz*. (September 2002): 200.

CARMEN

An opera (1875) by Georges Bizet (based on a 1845 novella by Prosper Mérimée)

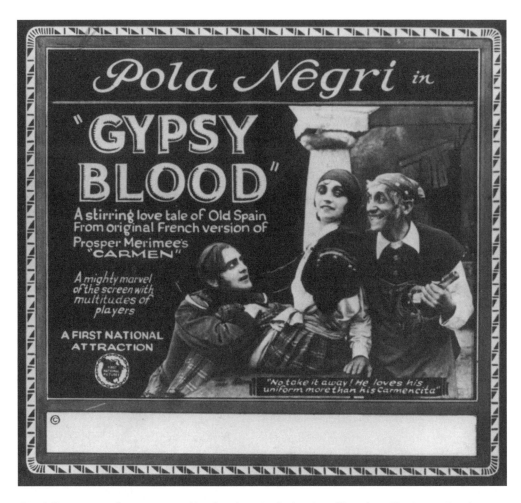

Bizet's Carmen *proved an attractive subject for adaptation by American filmmakers. Here is a motion picture scene from 1921 of Pola Negri in "Gypsy Blood." (Library of Congress)*

that has been frequently adapted by American filmmakers. It proved particularly popular in the silent era, with six adaptations: later film and TV versions married Bizet's tunes to contemporary American styles.

In its tale of the fatal love of a bourgeois soldier from the north of Spain (which in turn implied its close neighbor France) for a Gypsy woman from the oriental South, Bizet's *Carmen* popularized the fascination expressed by the French romantics for Spanish exoticism and primitivism. In the burgeoning film industry of the early twentieth century, *Carmen* fitted the need for familiar stories and also the desire to attract more upmarket audiences into the cinema. U.S. film companies seized the opportunity to make some of the best-known versions of *Carmen* in silent film. Since the opera remained in copyright, however, filmmakers usually cited Mérimée's novella as the main source in order to avoid legal problems, even while drawing on Bizet for plot, character, and accompanying music. Most notable among the early American film versions is Cecil B. DeMille's *Carmen* (1915), which used an opera star (Geraldine Farrar) rather than a film star to give the film greater highbrow impact. Other versions included Raoul Walsh's *Carmen* (1915), which came out at the same time as the DeMille (with film vamp Theda Bara in the title role); Charlie Chaplin's parody of DeMille in *Burlesque on Carmen* (1916); Walsh's second attempt at the story with *The Loves of Carmen* (1927, with Dolores del Río); and a Max Sennett comedy, *The Campus Carmen* (Goulding, 1928). Even Disney made a version in 1930, *Chile con Carmen* (Lantz/Nolan).

In 1948 Charles Vidor's *The Loves of Carmen* became a star vehicle for Rita Hayworth and the focus of a heavy merchandising campaign to tie in with the film. Publicity emphasized that the film was *not* based on the opera, and the film's stress on Gypsy customs points to the ethnological final chapter of Mérimée's novella. Otto Preminger's 1954 film adaptation of Oscar Hammerstein II's musical *Carmen Jones,* with an all-black cast (including star Dorothy Dandridge), caused controversy in France. Hammerstein used Bizet's music but with lyrics sung in a supposedly black style, which some sectors of the French press felt debased the original. Their debate assumed that the film could only be valued in terms of French cultural heritage rather than on its own, American terms. The Bizet estate banned the film from being shown in France (at Cannes in 1955 it could only be shown out of competition), and only with the lapse of copyright in 1981 did the film receive a general French release.

Later American Carmen films dipped into soft porn (Radley Metzger's *Carmen,* *Baby,* 1967) or lesbianism (Juliet Bashore's *Kamikaze Hearts,* 1986, which makes a nod to the opera). *Carmen* also made its way into TV cartoon fare, as in the Tom and Jerry cartoon *Carmen Get It!* (Deitch, 1962), in which the cat chases the mouse around an opera house during a performance of Bizet; or in the cartoon show *The Simpsons,* where the Simpsons go to the opera in an attempt to imbibe high culture. The most recent American film version to date is the MTV film *Carmen: A Hip-Hopera* (Townsend, 2001), starring Beyoncé Knowles of the band Destiny's Child in the leading role. The film uses rap lyrics set to Bizet's melodies.

Ann Davies

See also: Cinema, 1895–1945; Cinema, 1945 to the Present; Hip-Hop Music and Culture; Mérimée, Prosper; Music (Classical); Pornography; Primitivism; Remakes.

References

Baldwin, James. "Life Straight in De Eye." *Commentary* 19, no. 1 (January 1955): 74–77.

Batchelor, Jennifer. "From *Aida* to *Zauberflöte*." *Screen* 25, no. 3 (May–June 1984): 26–38.

McClary, Susan. *Georges Bizet: Carmen.* Cambridge: Cambridge University Press, 1992.

CARON, LESLIE (1931–)

Born in Boulogne-Billancourt, just outside Paris, Leslie Caron made her name as a Hollywood star in Hollywood musicals playing French ingenues. A classically trained ballerina, she was introduced to Gene Kelly, who had seen her dancing in the Champs Elysées Ballet and was seeking a replacement for the pregnant Cyd Charisse for his next film, *An American in*

Paris. This film was to make Caron a star in 1951, and she repeated her success in *Lili* (Walters, 1953), with Fred Astaire in *Daddy Long Legs* (Negulesco, 1955), and in *Gigi* (Minnelli, 1958). These roles fixed Caron's star image as emblematic of a waif-like French femininity. Less overtly erotic than Bardot (who trained as a ballet dancer with Caron and who took America by storm in 1957), she nonetheless offered the sexual promise of the *femme-enfant*. This was a type of youthful femininity that chimed with the times on both sides of the Atlantic: the gamine incarnated by stars such as Audrey Hepburn in Hollywood and Françoise Arnoul and Bardot in France.

Caron's transatlantic connections also extend to her private life. Her mother, also a ballet dancer, was American. Caron cites her mother's ambition as the motivating force behind her success: she was sent to ballet school from the age of nine. Caron's first husband was also American: she married George Hormel, the heir to the Spam fortune, at the age of twenty, but the marriage lasted only a short time, and they were divorced in 1954. Later on, the press cited her affair with Warren Beatty as the cause of her divorce from Peter Hall in 1966, but Caron herself refers to her frustration at the limitations her marriage placed on her career.

Caron's star persona was so closely identified with the gamine of her early musical roles that when she decided to give up dancing for health reasons in the late 1950s, she struggled to break into nonmusical dramatic roles. She did succeed, however, and her career has comprised many different kinds of roles and has succeeded in continuing her acting career well into middle age and beyond, in films including *Father Goose,* with Cary Grant (Nelson, 1964), and the gangster film, *Chandler* (Magwood, 1971). Caron has been nominated for two Academy Awards, the first for *Lili* and the second for her role as an unmarried pregnant woman in the British film, *The L-Shaped Room* (Forbes, 1962). Most recently, she has played roles in the British-American coproductions *Funny Bones,* with Jerry Lewis (Chelsom, 1995) and *Chocolat* (Hallström, 2000), with Juliette Binoche and Johnny Depp, and in the Franco-American *Le Divorce* (Ivory, 2003). Caron has also had a considerable career in television in the United States and in France, including a recent adaptation of *Murder on the Orient Express* (2001). It is perhaps emblematic of cinematic constructions of femininity that in spite of the diversity of her roles and the fact that she continues to work today, Caron is still best known on both sides of the Atlantic as Gigi.

Sarah Leahy

See also: Bardot, Brigitte; Binoche, Juliette; Cinema, 1945 to the Present; Dance; Kelly, Gene.

References

Altman, Rick. *The American Film Musical.* Bloomington/Indianapolis: Indiana University Press, 1987.

Parish, James Robert, and Ronald L. Bowers. *The MGM Stock Company: The Golden Era.* New Rochelle, NY: Arlington House, 1973.

CARPENTIER, ALEJO (1904–1980)

Writer, historian, and musicologist, Alejo Carpentier is best known for novels such as *El Reino de este mundo* (*The Kingdom of This World,* 1949) and *Los Pasos perdidos*

(*The Lost Steps,* 1952). A Cuban national who wrote in Spanish, Carpentier is linked to France through ancestry, through long sections of his life spent in Paris, and through the recurring analysis in his novels of France's historical presence in the Caribbean.

Born in Havana in 1904, the son of a French father and a Russian (Swiss-educated) mother, Carpentier spent most of his childhood in Cuba, growing up to work as a journalist for the left-wing antigovernment paper *Carteles,* an activity that culminated in eventual exile in 1928. Carpentier spent the next eleven years in Paris, where he began to explore his dual cultural heritage, not only frequenting the French surrealists but also becoming increasingly preoccupied with the question of how a progressive Latin American identity might be expressed on both an individual and collective level. His first novel, *¡Ecue-Yamba-O!* (1933), reflects an idealized vision of the Americas, his (Afro) Cuban protagonist representing the vitality, optimism, and hybridity that Carpentier and other *indigenista* writers felt were fundamentally lacking in an increasingly desperate and decadent Europe.

The outbreak of war and his claim that French culture had completely stopped influencing him led Carpentier to return to Cuba in 1939. (He would leave again for political reasons in 1945, living in Venezuela for the next thirteen years.) His literary project at this point can be described as an investigation into the inadequacy of European thought, ideology, and practice in the *essentially magical* context of the Americas, from the eighteenth century to the present day. Thus *El Reino de este mundo* analyzes, from the point of view of the fantastically metamorphosing

slave Ti Noel, the nefarious presence of the French plantation owners in prerevolutionary Saint-Domingue, their eradication by the *Vodun*-inspired new Haitian Republic, and their lingering destructive influence in the shape of new black dictators like King Henri Christophe. *Los Pasos perdidos* observes the wretchedness of both twentieth-century U.S. capitalism and French existentialism in the face of the nonsystematized timelessness of the Latin American jungle. The historical epic *El Siglo de las luces* (*Explosion in a Cathedral,* 1959) attacks the utter failure of the French to be faithful to their revolution in the context of the Caribbean, focusing in particular on the hypocritical actions of eighteenth-century French political charlatan Victor Hugues, first abolishing slavery in the Antilles and then reinstigating it when Bonaparte commanded.

Carpentier returned to Cuba in 1959 upon the revolution's victory, becoming Cuban cultural ambassador in Paris. His writing increasingly explored Latin American identity as a fragmented or "baroque" experience, in which any concept of *origins* becomes impossible to sustain, an idea explored through the metaphor of music in the short novel *Concierto barroco* (*Baroque Concert,* 1974). Carpentier died in Paris in 1980.

Andrew Asibong

See also: Bonaparte, Napoléon; Christophe, Henri; French Revolution; Haiti; Santo Domingo; Slavery; Venezuela; *Vodun;* World War II.

References

González Echevarría, Roberto. *Alejo Carpentier: The Pilgrim at Home.* Ithaca, NY: Cornell University Press, 1977.

Harvey, Sally. *Carpentier's Proustian Fiction: The Influence of Marcel Proust on Alejo Carpentier.* London: Tamesis, 1994.

CARREFOUR

For the latter years of the Third Republic, France was the classic land of the small shopkeeper. This sector thrived in the interwar and then the immediate postwar years, but the *trente glorieuses* years of economic expansion after 1945 put paid to what was a marginal sector of the economy, though not without considerable political upheaval. Discontent at the difficulties faced by small shopkeepers was expressed through the Poujade movement, but also the various shopkeepers' representatives (like Gérard Nicoud) had substantial political weight. The upshot was that planning laws prevented the rapid development of supermarket retailing in France, and it lagged behind other European countries until the late 1960s.

The first into the breach was Edouard Leclerc's chain of supermarkets that sold to the public at a discount. They were very successful because of their competitive prices, and Leclerc was soon followed by other retailers. Thus in the 1970s the French retail sector developed the massive American-style *hypermarché* (hypermarket) that could be as large as 22,000 square meters, led by the Carrefour chain, which dominates the sector but is far from alone. Carrefour, through huge turnover (shifting lots of goods), kept prices low, but their shops were at once gigantic and attractive, designed for areas where driving rather than walking was the primary mode of transportation and located strategically on the periphery of the major towns.

Carrefour was founded in 1959 by Marcel Fournier and Defforey, who opened their first shop in Annecy in Haute-Savoie. Their first *hypermarché,* with twelve checkouts and 400 parking places, opened in 1963 in Sainte-Geneviève-des-Bains. In 1975 it started to sell "generic" unbranded goods at a discount, and it expanded, taking over other retailers and branching out, as well as setting up more stores in France and abroad. In 2002 it was the first retailer in Europe and the second worldwide, with 9,632 outlets in some thirty countries (in seven of which it was the leading retailer), and there were 45 *hypermarchés* in the French group by the year 2000. In 1982 Carrefour opened in Argentina and then Brazil, and by 2002 it also had stores in Chile, Mexico, and Colombia, giving it 154 outlets in the Americas as a whole. To a certain extent the mass-market supermarket has developed further in France than in other European countries, and many British citizens use the Eurostar or the Channel Tunnel to shop at the Carrefour in Lille. However, the standardization and homogenization (sometimes called "Americanization") of this type of retail has not materialized, and variety and distinctiveness have been retained, even as the small local shop has died out.

David Bell

See also: Argentina; Chile; Mexico; World War II.
Reference
Ardagh, John. *France Today.* London: Penguin, 1990: 380–382.

CARTIER, JACQUES (1491–1557)

French explorer.

Cartier was not the first Frenchman to sail to what is now called Canada, but the royal expeditions he led there (1534–1542), the third notionally under the command of Jean-François de la Roque, seigneur de Roberval, included the first French attempt at American colonization.

It failed, like those that followed in Brazil and Florida. Not until 1608, with Samuel de Champlain's foundation of Quebec, was a lasting French colony established.

François I was determined not to let the Spanish and Portuguese monopolize the New World. In the 1530s he persuaded Pope Clement VIII to concede that the 1493 "Papal Donation" of that world to those two powers applied only to lands that were already known and effectively occupied. Giovanni da Verrazzano had sent François I a report of his 1524 voyage along the eastern coast of the American continent as far north as Newfoundland. Bretons from Saint-Malo had been fishing off Newfoundland since at least the late fifteenth century.

In 1534 François I sent Cartier with two ships to explore the hinterland of Newfoundland: they sailed on April 20. Cartier, born in 1491, was a master mariner from Saint-Malo who had already visited Newfoundland and possibly Brazil. The aim at this stage was not colonial settlement but the discovery of gold, other precious materials, and the northwest passage to the Orient that Europeans had sought since Columbus's voyages. Cartier sailed into the Strait of Belle Isle and soon turned south, charting the west coast of Newfoundland and the Gulf of Saint Lawrence, which he then crossed westward, skirting round the Magdalens and Prince Edward Island. Turning north along the coast of New Brunswick, he entered Chaleur Bay, thinking for a while that it might be the northwest passage. Having reached the Gaspé Peninsula but having missed the mouth of the Saint Lawrence River, he arrived back in France on September 5. During this 1534 expedition, the first recorded encounters between Euro-peans and Iroquoian-speaking people took place. On the north shore of Chaleur Bay, the French encountered some Micmac, with whom they traded ironware for furs. Then, in Gaspé Harbor, they came across an approximately 300-strong fishing party from the group of Saint Lawrence Iroquoians who have come to be known as Stadaconans, since they were based in and around Stadacona (the site of present-day Quebec City). Cartier compelled the two sons (Taignoagny and Domagaya) of the Stadaconan headman (Donnacona) to return with him to France so that they could become interpreters and informants. Donnacona seemed to consent, whether because he had no choice or because he wished to secure a trading alliance with the French.

Cartier reported back to François I, and although no gold or northwest passage had been found, the king instructed Cartier to continue trying, partly enticed by the captives' accounts of the native copper trade. A second, better-resourced expedition left Saint-Malo on May 19, 1535. Entering the Gulf of Saint Lawrence in the same place as in 1534, they charted its north coast as far as Anticosti Island, and this time, guided by Taignoagny and Domagaya, sailed into the Saint Lawrence River, where they were reunited with Donnacona and then reached Stadacona. They had reached the region that Cartier understood as "Canada": it stretched along the Saint Lawrence from roughly where the freshwater begins (at Grosse Ile) to halfway between present-day Quebec City and Trois-Rivières. The French noted that the term "Canada," meaning "village," was part of the Saint Lawrence Iroquoians' vocabulary. The safe return of Donnacona's sons was welcomed, but the Stadaconans

Jacques Cartier's first interview with the Indians at Hochelaga, now Montreal, in 1535. (Library of Congress)

seem to have become more mistrustful once Taignoagny and Domagaya told them about France, and especially when they revealed Cartier's intention of sailing further up the Saint Lawrence to contact the other group of Iroquoians in the region, based in the large town of Hochelaga (present-day Montreal). Although Cartier thought that the Stadaconans were subjects of the Hochelagans, in fact the two were probably just distinct, hostile tribes or groups of villages.

Donnacona tried at length to dissuade Cartier from going to Hochelaga: this is the first recorded example of an Indian group in eastern North America trying to secure the lucrative position of middleman in the trading of European goods with the interior. Cartier, uncomprehending of Iroquoian diplomacy, unwittingly rejected the alliance offered and continued to Hochelaga, arriving on October 2 (Octo-

ber 13, modern calendar), on the southern shore of present-day Montreal Island. Aspects of his brief visit, such as his ascent of Mount Royal or his reading the Gospel to Indians, have become legendary. He returned to his base on the Saint Charles River near Stadacona. In December, almost all the French got scurvy; twenty-five died, but the rest were cured by a brew that two women, sent by Domagaya, showed them how to prepare. In May 1536 Cartier kidnapped Donnacona, his two sons, and others, returning to France with them and two young Iroquoian girls whom he had received as tokens of alliance. None of the ten taken ever returned to Canada. By about 1541, all but one were dead.

Donnacona had told Cartier about a "Kingdom of the Saguenay" in the interior, full of gold and rubies. He said he had seen one-legged peoples, plus others who lacked anuses and ate no solids. Perhaps hoping that this would help their chances of re- turning, Donnacona and his fellow captives talked up all of this to an impressed François I, who sponsored a third voyage, this time with the intent of establishing a colonial settlement. The king hoped to find spices and gold and silver mines and to profit from the nascent fur trade. The search for the northwest passage had now been displaced by greater focus on the interior. With one eye on the Pope and on Iberian hostility to his plans, François I made the conversion of Indians to Christianity an official aim. Command of the expedition was given to Roberval, with Cartier as second in command. Cartier left first, on May 23, 1541, with five ships, this time including women; the men ranged from felons to nobles. They admitted to the Stadaconans that Donnacona was dead but claimed that the other nine were all living the life of lords in France. From his subsequent actions, it seems that Agona, the new headman, did not believe them. Cartier built a fortified settlement 9 miles upstream from Stadacona, calling it Charlesbourg-Royal. Crops were planted and cattle unloaded from the ships. The surrounding Indians experienced this behavior as a provocation, since no permission had been requested for this use of the land. They ceased bartering and started a war of attrition against the French, picking them off when they ventured outside the settlement, killing some thirty-five over the winter. The Hochelagans became hostile too. By June 1542, with still no sign of Roberval, the colonists gave up, sailing to Saint John's Harbor in Newfoundland, where Cartier encountered Roberval but, disobeying the latter's orders, continued back to France. The "diamonds" and "gold" that he thought he was bringing

back with him turned out to be quartz and iron pyrite. Cartier died in 1557.

Firsthand accounts of all three voyages exist, probably composed wholly or partly by Cartier himself. They are ship journals and reports to the king on topography and natural resources: their descriptions of "savages" are overtly instrumental rather than aiming at any ideal of ethnographic objectivity. Only the account of the second voyage was printed in French in Cartier's lifetime, in 1545, once the enterprise's failure meant that there was no point in secrecy. The account of the first voyage was first published in Italian translation in 1556; that of the third voyage is known only in a truncated English version (1600).

Neil Kenny

See also: Brazil; Champlain, Samuel de; Florida; François I, King of France; Fur Trade; Montreal; Quebec; Roberval, Jean-François de la Roque, Seigneur de; Saint Lawrence River; Saint-Malo; Verrazzano, Giovanni da.

References

Cartier, Jacques. *The Voyages.* Trans. H. P. Biggar, intro. Ramsay Cook. Toronto/Buffalo/London: University of Toronto Press, 1993.

Hoffman, Bernard G. *Cabot to Cartier: Sources for a Historical Ethnography of Northeastern North America, 1497–1550.* Toronto: University of Toronto Press, 1961.

Trudel, Marcel. *The Beginnings of New France, 1524–1663.* Trans. P. Claxton. Toronto: Clelland and Stewart, 1973, chaps. 2–3.

CARTIER-BRESSON, HENRI (1908–2004)

Artist and photographer.

Henri Cartier-Bresson began his artistic life as a student of painting and surrealism. Born in Chanteloup, France, he was first attracted by the ideas of the surrealist

Henri Cartier-Bresson photographs the streets of Brooklyn from beneath the Brooklyn Bridge (1946). His work in Brooklyn was chronicled in a photographic essay for Harper's Bazaar *magazine. (Genevieve Naylor/Corbis)*

movement at its very beginnings, in the early 1920s. He studied for a time under the painter and sculptor André Lhote (1885–1962) and always maintained his practice of drawing. It was in 1931 in Africa that he first took up photography as a medium for his images, adopting in 1932 his trademark Leica, an unobtrusive 35mm rangefinder camera. It was the beginning of a long and productive relationship of man and machine.

Cartier-Bresson is perhaps best known for a style of reportage photography for which he coined the phrase "The Decisive Moment" in a publication by that name in 1952. He accomplished, however, much more. After his first exhibition of photographs in 1933, he traveled to North America, first to Mexico, where he exhibited with photographer Manuel Alvarez Bravo. Cartier-Bresson then traveled to New York, where he learned filmmaking with Paul Strand (1890–1976), already famous for his early modernist film *Manna-hatta* (1921) with painter Charles Scheeler and his proletariat film *The Wave* (1933).

Cartier-Bresson returned to Europe, where he began to make films even while he continued to photograph for news agencies and picture magazines like *Verve* and *Life*. He spent three years of World War II in captivity (1940–1943), escaping finally on his third attempt. Work began immediately on a new set of portraits, this time of French luminaries like Georges Braque, Pablo Picasso, Pierre Bonnard, and Henri Matisse, even while he joined the resistance movement and helped other escaped prisoners. He again spent a year in the United States in 1946, traveling, photographing, and working for a large exhibition at the Modern Museum of Art in New York. At the time, it was widely believed to be a posthumous exhibition and that Cartier-Bresson had died in captivity. Rumors of his death notwithstanding, he founded, together with Robert Capa (1913–1954), David "Chim" Seymour (1911–1956), William Vandivert, and George Rodger (1908–1995), the Magnum photographic cooperative in 1947—the only international cooperative of freelance photographers.

Cartier-Bresson's artistic life burgeoned as he traveled the world, documenting the death of Mohandas Gandhi and the birth of the People's Republic of China, as well as street life at home in Paris. In 1970 he married photographer Martine Franck and began to devote more time to his drawing. He retired from photography in 1975, the same year of his first exhibition of drawings, to turn wholly to his self-proclaimed first love of drawing.

Kelley Wilder

See also: Mexico; Photography; World War II.
References

Cartier-Bresson, Henri. *The Decisive Moment: Photography by Henri Cartier-Bresson*. New York: Simon and Schuster, 1952.
Montier, Jean-Pierre. *Henri Cartier-Bresson and the Artless Art*. London: Thames and Hudson, 1996.

CASSATT, MARY (1844–1926)
American painter.

The second half of the nineteenth and first half of the twentieth centuries saw a huge influx of American artists and writers to Paris. They built on a tradition of "returning to cultural sources" popular since the late eighteenth century, and this in turn was based on the "grand tour" of earlier times. Mary Cassatt is one of the more notable artists who went from the United States to Paris. Her painting career really took off in the 1870s. After periods spent in Spain and Italy, she returned to Paris and joined the "independents," better known to us now as the impressionists (later on, she would play a crucial part in encouraging the collection of impressionism in the United States). Art history has had scant place for women artists before the twentieth century, and her exceptionality (along with that of Berthe Morisot) covers the occlusion of a great number of women artists notable in their day.

Cassatt almost invariably portrayed women of the period (1870s to 1900, principally) and showed them in domestic settings or, more accurately, in the spaces women were actually occupying at the time. Art history has tended to reduce her work to a variant of genre painting, but since feminist art historians' work in the 1970s, her more formal and "social-

At the Opera *by Mary Cassatt. Cassatt was one of the more notable American painters who went to Paris. (Burstein Collection/ Corbis)*

critical" practices have been readdressed. Cassatt shows women as subjects rather than as objects of painting, or even as exemplifying a particular social group. This is done through the peculiar proximity of the scenes shown, which position the artist and viewer as female (in contrast to Edouard Manet's critical use of male positioning). Her work shows experimentation in content and form, in the use of color as a formal tool but also in terms of the realization of the depiction. Cassatt, argues Griselda Pollock, does not simply show us women (she was scathing about "lady's art" while being part of the suffrage movement) but the women of modernity—where they were, how they dressed, how they relate to one another. Her scenes of mothers and children could be misread as representing something timeless, but could better be read as statements about communication,

feminine sociality, and class (as we see women from all classes and how they relate to the interior spaces). One work often cited is *Little Girl in an Armchair* (1878), wherein a small child slumps sullenly on a blue chair, in a still room filled with blue chairs. Such a picture is not just a depiction of a class milieu but offers a formalized *modernist* take on that milieu. Similarly, *At the Opera* (1878) ties in with the modernist radicalization of vision. Rather than being the object of the male gaze, the central female figure looks intently through binoculars, away from the viewer. The theater and opera represented a form of public space accessible to women, and Cassatt shows, in this and a range of pictures set in the theater, but with varying representational and formal strategies, the possibilities of occupying that space as a subject.

Paul Hegarty

See also: Feminisms; Painting.
References
Garb, Tamar. "Gender and Representation." *Modernity and Modernism.* Ed. Francis Frascina et al. New Haven/London: Yale University Press/Open University, 1993.
Pollock, Griselda. *Mary Cassatt: Painter of Modern Women.* London: Thames and Hudson, 1998.

CATHER, WILLA (1873–1947)

American writer, born near Winchester, Virginia, who wrote about the European immigrant pioneer and French religion and culture in North America. Cather's move from Virginia to Nebraska marks her early pioneer novels (*O Pioneers!* and *My Ántonia*) and short stories about life on the American Divide, where Cather's subjects suffer from economic hardship and cultural deprivation.

Willa Sibert Cather (1873–1947), American novelist and Pulitzer Prize winner. Cather wrote about the European immigrant pioneer, French religion, and culture in North America. (Bettmann/Corbis)

Cather grew up a Methodist, believing fundamentally that art was a temple and community builder. A descendant of two Southern families that fought each other in the American Civil War, Cather recounts the same struggle among European families during World War I in *One of Ours* (1922), just as she laments family and social division over emancipation in *Sapphira and the Slave Girl* (1940).

Cather began writing and editing drama and theater criticism at college, where she read William Shakespeare, Ralph Waldo Emerson, Walt Whitman, and Henry James, after whom she modeled her early works. Cather worked as a journalist and teacher in Pittsburgh and then was editor for *McClure's* magazine and Alfred Knopf in New York. There, she enjoyed Wagnerian opera, which influenced her most autobiographical novel, *The Song of the Lark* (1915).

Other celebrated works include meditations on art and religion, such as her collection, *Youth and the Bright Medusa* (a.k.a. *The Troll Garden,* 1905); *Death Comes for the Archbishop* (1927), recounting the journeys of French missionaries in North America; and her Quebec novel, *Shadows on the Rock* (1931), exploring the civilizing effect of Catholicism. In the Pulitzer Prize–winning novel *One of Ours,* an American fights in the Battle of Verdun and both dies for mankind and lives out his own version of the Christian martyrs' sacrifices. On the verge of death, Cather's alter ego finds himself as much enraptured by the landscape and music as by the loss of human life. The work remains an elegy for Provence, with which Cather had a lifelong, long-distance love affair. On her first journey there, Cather decided to quit journalism for the life of an author, and an early work, written in Avignon, about medieval heroism there inspired this love of France and last work, destroyed posthumously by her forty-year companion, Edith Lewis.

The French and European influence on Cather's work is vast and various. Early stories discuss poor youth ("Paul's Case") yearning for the music of a European past, such as that of Jules Massenet's "repetitions of the *Blue Danube*" and Pietro Mascagni's "Intermezzo" from *Cavalleria Rusticana.* American immigrants from Sweden, France, Norway, and Bohemia live and die for their art, and Thea Kronborg, the artistic heroine of *The Song of the Lark,* sings Richard Wagner and Gustav Mahler (*Lohengrin* and *Woglinde*).

Cather died at her home in New York City from a cerebral hemorrhage in 1947.

Four volumes of short stories and two volumes of Cather's critical essays were collected posthumously in *The Kingdom of Art* (1966).

Erna Cooper

See also: American Civil War; Catholic Church; James, Henry; World War I.

References

O'Brien, Sharon. *Cather: Stories, Poems and Other Writings.* New York: Library of America, 1992.

Porter, David H. "Cather on Cather II: Two Recent Acquisitions at Drew University." *Willa Cather Pioneer Memorial and Educational Foundation Newsletter and Review* 46, no. 3 (2003): 53–58.

CATHOLIC CHURCH

Catholicism, an export of the Spanish and French colonial governments, had a definitive role in the formation and creation of the religious, cultural, and political life of the colonies and subsequent nations in the Americas. Spanish colonies in the Americas were dominated by the Catholic Church. Roman Catholicism was the only faith tolerated, and large numbers of missionaries and regular clergy went to the colonies with the primary mission of converting the native population. Unlike Catholic dominance in South and Central America, in North America Catholic influence was mainly concentrated in the North, where French explorers and traders settled much of eastern Canada and the United States, bringing with them the Catholic faith.

From 1535, when Jacques Cartier explored the valley of the Saint Lawrence River, through the seventeenth and eighteenth centuries, the region was colonized by French Catholics. By the mid-eighteenth century, the Catholic population in Canada numbered more than 60,000. The dominance of the Catholic Church was particularly evident in its control over the colonies' cultural and social life. One of the defining aspects of New French settlements was the ongoing battle for control between the French Jesuits and the French colonial government, although the French court supported the church missionary effort. In seventeenth-century France, the state gave the Catholic Church responsibility for education and health care. Therefore, the Catholic Church had a central role in establishing the institutional framework in New France. Before New France had a parish, it had schools, hospitals, and a college run by the church. Founded in 1635, the Jesuits College at Quebec City was the first postsecondary educational institution north of Mexico.

However, French colonial efforts were aimed at organizing trade more than settlement. The lack of desire among colonists to settle land, as well as the fact that colonizers were mainly single males (primarily trappers) who often intermarried with the natives, reduced conflicts with the latter. Some French trappers adopted native beliefs, customs, and practices once they married in, but the French government was more tolerant than the Spanish government of non-Catholic and native practices. Although Quebec City, the largest settlement, was founded in 1608 as a missionary town, from the beginning the more secular governmental authorities fought with the Catholic Church for control. The arrival in 1659 of Bishop François de Laval increased the tension between civil and religious officials, particularly over the brandy trade.

By the end of the 1750s, Britain or Spain took over all the French territories in North America. In the main French cities—Quebec, Montreal, New Orleans, and Detroit—French Catholics, wary of foreigners, retreated into their communities. Church and family were at the center of social life. The destruction of New France by British colonization and subsequent attempts to overrun the Roman Catholic population meant that Catholicism was integrated into cultural and national identity. To keep the French Canadians onside as the American colonies headed toward revolution, in 1774 the British parliament passed the Quebec Act, which guaranteed the preservation of the French Civil Code and the Roman Catholic Church in Quebec.

Before the British conquest of Quebec, there was no printing press in French Canada, and all public and social activities (theater was often censored) were closely controlled by the Catholic Church. However, writing about New France was abundant, and substantial amounts of colonial literature, mainly concerning exploration and travel, were published in France for European readers. Well into the twentieth century, imported cultural "products" (music, literature, theater, artistic styles, fashion, and social habits) from France inhabited the cultural space of French Canada. The Catholic Church supported this position of hegemony.

In contrast to the conflicts between state and religion in the French colonies, religious motivation was one of the reasons the English founded colonies. William Penn founded Pennsylvania as a refuge for Quakers, and Lord Baltimore founded Maryland as a refuge for Catholics. John Carroll, a representative of a notable colonial Catholic family, was the first Roman Catholic bishop in the United States and the first archbishop of Baltimore. Under his leadership, the Roman Catholic Church became firmly established in the United States. Carroll was a pioneer in exploring positive relations between Catholic religionists and their fellow citizens. In New Orleans the Cathedral of Saint Louis, king of France, rededicated in 1794 after the fire of 1788, is the oldest continuously active Roman Catholic cathedral in the United States.

Even more than churches as institutions, educational institutions, including the parish schools, were an important factor in preserving and spreading Catholicism in North America. In the United States, elementary and secondary schools were formed late in the nineteenth century because Catholic leaders feared Protestant influences in public schools. These Catholic agencies helped reconcile the civic (acceptance of the United States as a state) and the religious (belonging to Rome as a religious center). During the latter half of the nineteenth century, the Catholic Church increased the number of missions among the native peoples of both the United States and Canada and extended the already strong Catholic presence established through French colonial governance in Haiti and the French Caribbean. At the end of the seventeenth century, France took Haiti from Spain and developed it as a thriving slave trade colony. Catholicism was the official religion there, but voodoo was a widely accepted practice.

In the nineteenth century, the Catholic Church in French Canada struggled with British attempts to convert their parishioners to Protestantism and the British political doctrine of assimilating the French nation, which they considered "inferior." The Catholic Church played an important role in preserving the French nation in Canada. In 1834 the Saint Jean Baptiste

Society, a French Canadian patriotic association, was founded with the mission of defending the linguistic and cultural heritage of French Catholics. From the 1960s onward, the society was primarily concerned with Quebec separatism. The rebellions of 1837 in Lower Canada (Quebec) were a response to attempts at the cultural elimination of the French nation and Roman Catholic Church from Canada. From the 1840s onward, the Catholic Church slowly started to regain control, and the clergy assumed considerable power. By using education and the press to reach people, the Catholic Church became the driving force behind French Canadian nationalism. For the clerical and professional elite, the acceptable social order was regulated by the Roman Catholic Church. Agriculture was the foundation of social and material life, and the family was the central social institution, whereas commercial endeavors were held in contempt. The contrast between the Protestant idea of acquiring money and wealth through work and Catholicism's emphasis on the religious mission remained an important social, cultural, and political division between anglophone and francophone communities.

Henri Bourassa, one of the key leaders of the Quebec nationalist movement at the beginning of the twentieth century, sought to find a way for bilingual coexistence to develop within the confederation of French and English in Canada. Bourassa believed that the province of Quebec by its origin and tradition was home to the idea of social Catholicism and as such could continue to preserve and spread the Catholic faith throughout Canada and America. This idea of Quebec as a bastion of Catholicism having an impact on other Catholic communities in the Americas reflects a colonial past where religious and cultural protectionism was an outcome of conflict with other religions and nations over land and power.

A crisis in the institutions of the Catholic Church in Quebec occurred when Maurice Duplessis was leader of Quebec's conservative Union nationale and premier of the province for most of the period 1936–1960. He and his party were vehicles for clerical nationalism, a conservative ideology that emphasized agriculture and traditional values that profoundly marked twentieth-century Quebec. During that period, children born to unmarried parents were left in the care of Catholic religious orders that operated orphanages, and during Duplessis's premiership, a child abuse scandal broke. The "Duplessis orphans" case was widely recognized as the largest case of institution-based child abuse (in many cases sexual abuse) in Canadian history.

The Catholic Church lost significant power and followers during the period of the Quiet Revolution in the 1960s. Quebec's inherited suspicion regarding the real desire of English Canada to assimilate Catholics into the Protestant anglophone majority was later complemented by new criticism of the French colonial legacy. Moreover, Quebec's need to have its own culture replaced the traditional concern about the possible disappearance of French culture. The role of the Catholic Church as a provider of the social narrative that helps the French nation in Canada to cohere was replaced by a national identity founded on space and territory. Catholic concerns about the preservation of a religious-national identity were replaced or rather merged with the ideology of the political Left, which led to the emergence of Quebec separatist movements that strove for the formation of a new nation in Quebec. This factor led to a shift in the 1980s and 1990s from protectionism to internationalism.

Aleksandar Dundjerovic

See also: Cartier, Jacques; Duplessis, Maurice; Fur Trade; Guadeloupe; Haiti; Jesuits; Laval, François de Montmorency; Mexico; New France; New Orleans; Quebec; Quebec City; Quiet Revolution; Saint Lawrence River; Saint Martin.

References

Boland, Raymond J. "The French Connection: The Contribution of French Catholicism to the Church in North America." http://www.diocese-kcsj.org/Bishop/French%20Connection.htm (cited April 26, 2004).

Dickinson, John, and Brian J. Young. *A Short History of Quebec*. Montreal: McGill-Queen's University Press; 2nd ed., 2000.

Grescoe, Taras. *Sacré Blues: An Unsentimental Journey through Quebec*. Toronto: Macfarlane Walter and Ross, 2001.

Lippy, Charles, Robert Choquette, and Stafford Poole. *Christianity Comes to the Americas: 1492–1776*. New York: Paragon House, 1992.

CÉLINE, LOUIS-FERDINAND (1894–1961)

Pseudonym of Louis-Ferdinand Destouches, a physician and writer whose novels combined searingly iconoclastic and dismal views of humanity with street slang and later anti-Semitism.

Born in Courbevoie, a Paris suburb, Destouches was sent abroad to study German and English for a business career. Invalided out of the army with arm injuries, headaches, and a ringing in his head that never left him, he worked in 1916 in Cameroon, where he contracted malaria and dysentery. Returning to France, he received a medical degree from the Univer-

sity of Paris in 1924, ultimately becoming a specialist in public health. In 1925, he left to work for the League of Nations, for whom he traveled to Switzerland, Africa, the United States, Cuba, and Canada. He returned to France to open a medical practice in 1928 and three years later joined the Clichy municipal clinic staff in Paris. While there, Destouches published the critically acclaimed journal *Voyage,* using his maternal grandmother's first name, Céline, as a nom-de-plume.

Céline's first novel, *Voyage au bout de la nuit* (*Journey to the End of Night,* 1932), recalled his injuries suffered at Ypres with the French army during World War I, his subsequent work for a lumber company in Africa, followed by the study of social medical practice in Ford factories in Detroit, and his return to medical practice in Paris. He later wrote of New York's urban impersonality and the alienation among Ford assembly-line workers in Detroit.

His equally acclaimed second novel, *Mort à Crédit* (*Death on the Installment Plan,* 1936), recalled a violent father and a mother stricken with polio who helped support the family by working as a saleswoman. In 1936, Céline met Lucette Almanzor, a dancer eighteen years his junior, who became his third wife and constant companion for the rest of his life. Convinced in late 1937 that an international Jewish conspiracy was plotting another world war, Céline published *Bagatelles pour un massacre* (*Trifles for a Massacre*), a lengthy pamphlet that, along with *Ecole des cadavres* (*School of Corpses,* 1938) and *Les Beaux Draps* (*The Fine Mess,* 1941), established him as a prominent anti-Semitic polemicist.

During the 1940–1944 occupation of France, Céline worked at a dispensary in suburban Bezons and continued to write. *Guignol's Band,* the last of his autobiographical novels, appeared in 1944. He gave interviews for and published letters in the collaborationist press in Paris. Denounced as a traitor, he fled in 1944 with remnants of the Vichy government to Sigmaringen in Germany and, again, in the spring of 1945 across a devastated Germany to Denmark. Following amnesties of collaborators, Céline returned in 1951 to suburban Paris, where he spent the remainder of his years writing novels, in his disjointed and jaundiced style, about his travels and exile.

Céline's denunciations of war and colonialism and his evocation of the seamier sides of urban life influenced writers such as Henry Miller, Kurt Vonnegut Jr., and William Burroughs. Critics have tried to reconcile his literary talent and stylistic innovations with his unrelenting pessimism about humanity and his blistering racism. In addition to denouncing Jews during the occupation, he also publicly criticized—at some personal risk—"Aryan stupidity."

Bertram F. Gordon

See also: Burroughs, William S.; World War II.
References
Buckley, William K., ed. *Critical Essays on Louis-Ferdinand Céline.* Boston: G. K. Hall, 1989.
Hewitt, Nicholas. *The Golden Age of Louis-Ferdinand Céline.* Leamington Spa, UK/New York: Berg Publishers, 1987.
Vitoux, Frédéric. *Céline: A Biography.* Trans. J. Browner. New York: Paragon House, 1992.

CÉLORON DE BLAINVILLE, PIERRE-JOSEPH (1693–1759)

Born in Montreal, grandson of a member of the Canadian nobility, Céloron de Blainville joined the colonial regulars (*troupes de la marine*) at age thirteen (1707) and spent most of his life and career with the force. In 1738 he was appointed commander at Michilimackinac. While serving in that capacity, in 1739–1740 he led an expeditionary force of 200 Canadians and thirty aboriginal peoples against the Chickasaw of Upper Louisiana. For his military merits, in 1741 he was awarded the cross of Saint-Louis, the highest military distinction. In 1742 he was transferred to Detroit and from there in 1744 to Fort Niagara. In both instances he was praised by the leaders of the aboriginal nations, but the fur traders accused him of inhibiting their commercial ventures. Recalled from Fort Niagara in 1745, in 1747 he was given command of Fort Saint-Frédéric on Lake Champlain, but soon thereafter, in 1748, he was returned to Detroit to quell an insurrection of the western aboriginal nations.

Meanwhile, the Ohio valley was the center stage of the new expansionist policy of the British continental colonies. The area was theoretically under French control, but in practice the British were succeeding in winning over several aboriginal nations through a policy of providing cheaper goods. The French Crown began to envisage the building of a line of fortified posts along the Ohio valley meant to curb British expansion. Céloron de Blainville was given the command of an expeditionary force of 213 men, mostly Canadians, accompanied by a few aboriginal peoples. They left Montreal on June 15, 1749, and for five and a half months they traveled for 3,000 miles toward the west and the south, going as far as the mouth of the Great Miami River (Rivière-à-la-Roche). Céloron de Blainville buried several lead plates claiming the land for France but discovered that a number of powerful Indian nations, such as the Mingo, Shawnee, and Miami, had been won over by the British. In 1750 Céloron de Blainville was sent back to Detroit as town major, only to be recalled to Montreal in 1751 to serve in the same capacity. Overall, he proved to be better as a soldier than as a civil administrator. His activities during the French and Indian War (1754–1763) are not known. He died in Montreal.

Luca Codignola

See also: Detroit; French and Indian War; Fur Trade; Lake Champlain; Louisiana; Montreal; Ohio.

References

McConnell, Michael Norman. *A Country Between: The Upper Ohio Valley and Its Peoples, 1724–1774.* Lincoln/London: University of Nebraska Press, 1992.

White, Richard. *The Middle Ground: Indians, Empires, and Republics in the Great Lakes Region, 1650–1815.* Cambridge: Cambridge University Press, 1991.

CENDRARS, BLAISE (FRÉDÉRIC-LOUIS SAUSER) (1887–1961)

Swiss-French poet, writer, and adventurer.

Known for his quasi-autobiographical and mythopoetic writing, Cendrars (born in La Chaux-de Fonds, Switzerland) populated his picaresque novels and poems with the historic figures, types, and sites of the Americas. It was his trip to the United States in 1911 that resulted in his literary debut with the poem, "Les Pâques à New York" ("Easter in New York," 1911), his rebirth as Blaise Cendrars, and a new style of writing that critics have called the birth of modern poetry. *Le Panama; ou les Aventures de mes sept oncles* (*Panama and the Adventures of My Seven Uncles,* 1918), considered Cendrars's most original poem, interweaves

adventures in Alaska and Panama with tales from uncles in the New World: a butcher in Galveston, Texas; a chef in Denver, Colorado; and a guide in Patagonia.

In 1923, Cendrars met the Brazilian writer Oswaldo de Andrade and his wife, the artist Tarsila do Amaral. At their invitation, he traveled to Brazil in 1924, returning again in 1926 and 1927 and possibly a fourth time in 1928. These trips produced numerous works about the Americas: *Kodak (Documentaire)* (*Kodak [Documentary],* 1924), poems about North America; *Feuilles de routes* (*Ocean Letters,* 1924), poems about South America originally illustrated by Tarsila; *L'Or* (*Sutter's Gold,* 1925), a novel about the California gold rush; *Moravagine* (1926), a novel in which half of the adventures occur in the Americas; *Dan Yack* (1929), a two-part adventure with stops in Antarctica; and *Rhum* (*Rum,* 1930), a novel about Jean Galmot in French Guiana.

In the 1930s, Cendrars turned to journalism and traveled several more times to New York, including a trip in 1935 during which he gave daily radio reports to French listeners. In 1936, *Paris Soir* sent him to Hollywood for the Universal Studios premier of *Sutter's Gold,* a movie based on his book, after which he returned via the Panama Canal. Cendrars's long-standing interest in film and in visual conceptions of writing resulted in two books about Hollywood. *L'ABC du cinéma* (*The ABC of Cinema,* 1926) and *Hollywood: La Mecque du cinéma* (*Hollywood: Mecca of the Movies,* 1936) provide vignettes of the era's stars and their haunts as well as his critique of the studio system. In other works, he claimed meetings with Charlie Chaplin, wrote about Al Capone, and planned projects on John Paul Jones, the U.S. naval commodore during the Revolutionary War, and "Admiral" Jim Fisk, the Erie Railroad tycoon.

Cendrars sustained forty-five years of correspondence with Henry Miller, whom he met in 1934, and John Dos Passos, who called Cendrars the "Homer of the Transsiberian," was an early translator. Cendrars in turn translated Al Jennings's *Through the Shadows with O. Henry* and Ferreira de Castro's *A Selva* (*Virgin Forest*). In two late works, Cendrars returned to the subjects of his early travels: *Brésil* (*Brazil,* 1952), a poem originally sent to Tarsila in 1926, and *Noël aux quatre coins du monde* (*Christmas at the Four Corners of the Earth,* 1953), with stories about a New York rabbi slaughtering chickens in assembly-line fashion on Christmas Day, New Mexican Indians celebrating with peyote, a Mass of the Cock in Bahia, Brazil, and a mystical countess in Rio de Janeiro. Cendrars died in Paris in 1961.

Maureen Shanahan

See also: Brazil; Dos Passos, John; Guiana; Miller, Henry Valentine.

References

Bochner, Jay. *Blaise Cendrars: Discovery and Re-creation.* 2nd ed. Toronto: University of Toronto Press, 1996.

Cendrars, Blaise. *Complete Poems.* Trans. Ron Padgett. Berkeley: University of California Press, 1992.

Leamon, Amanda. *Shades of Sexuality: Color and Sexual Identity in the Novels of Blaise Cendrars.* Amsterdam: Rodopi, 1997.

CERTEAU, MICHEL DE (1925–1986)

French philosopher and cultural theorist who was spurred by the uprisings of May 1968 into undertaking a philosophy informed by anthropology and sociology as they relate to the quotidian. Certeau's epistemology of alterity in modernity is exemplary of the turn that both cultural studies and philosophy took after the events of May 1968.

Born in Chambéry, Certeau entered the Society of Jesus after studying at the Universities of Grenoble and Lyon. After being ordained in 1956 and completing his doctorate at the Sorbonne in 1960, Certeau's academic interest centered on the study of mysticism, the works of Bienheureux Pierre Favre and Jean-Joseph Surin in particular. His interest in the early period of the Jesuits and in the forces that combine to create the collective human sense of history and knowledge in general were complemented by works of contemporary Jesuit philosophy, such as those of Pierre Teilhard de Chardin, and also by an interest in Jacques Lacan.

Profoundly affected by May 1968, Certeau secured a grant from the Délégation générale à la recherche scientifique et technique (Office for Scientific and Technical research [DGRST]) for a study into how members of a culture exist within its rules yet in resistance to or engagement with them: a reality demonstrated in the attacks on the establishment by the student riots but also in the academic critiques of Michel Foucault, Jean-François Lyotard, Jacques Derrida, and Gilles Deleuze. To effect this study involved the use of approaches brought from the human sciences, especially sociology and anthropology, as well as the epistemology of belief. This massive project was eventually published in part as *L'Invention du quotidien,* with a later second volume. Translated as *The Practice of Everyday Life* in 1984, the study is the dominant text for most people working on Certeau in English, particularly in connection with other post-1968 philosophers. The influence of this school, especially that of Deleuze and Félix Guattari as well as Foucault, is discernible in his approach to the quotidian and to everyday practices as Other to the systems and discipline of the status quo. This is a recognition that the operational logic of culture defines the subject, but that the subject often resists or evades definition through alternative uses ("strategies," "tactics") of space and practice, such as those of the workplace or in spectacular culture.

The popularity of Certeau's philosophy is evident in the interest taken by recent philosophers such as Brian Massumi and more widely in a general interest in cultures and practices of alterity in contemporary life. It is not surprising to find that this interest has located itself in the study of Western, and specifically American, politics and culture and its effect on the reality of everyday life (Certeau himself lived in California for six years). One of the most famous and influential passages of *L'Invention du quotidien* opens with Certeau on the 107th floor of the World Trade Center in New York, beginning his analysis of representation and behavior in modernity by starting with a panoramic view of its spatial metaphor (the city) from its symbolic center.

Damian Sutton

See also: Deleuze, Gilles; Derrida, Jacques; Foucault, Michel; Guattari, Félix; Jesuits; Lacan, Jacques; Lyotard, Jean-François; Theory.

References

Ahearne, Jeremy. *Michel de Certeau: Interpretation and the Other.* Cambridge: Polity Press, 1995.
Buchanan, Ian. *Michel de Certeau: Cultural Theorist.* London: Sage, 2000.

CÉSAIRE, AIMÉ (1913–)

Major Martinican poet, dramatist, and politician whose writing posits the relationship between Africa and the Caribbean, mediated by France and Europe.

Césaire's credentials as an Atlantic figure are impeccable. He was cofounder in 1947 of the Paris-based journal and publisher of books on African and Caribbean affairs, *Présence africaine,* and a key theorist of négritude, a political and cultural movement and theory of black solidarity and antiracism first developed in the 1930s and 1940s. Négritude attempted to unite all black peoples in the world subjugated by European colonialism and Western racism, but it insisted on the centrality of Africa (and hence slavery) in determining black pride. Inspired by the Harlem Renaissance and theorized often via poetry, it was renowned for its lack of a coherent and agreed definition. It is, however, a crucial component in the black Atlantic, given its historical horizons of slavery and antislavery. Négritude's poetic manifesto is undoubtedly Césaire's *Cahier d'un retour au pays natal* (*Notebook of a Return to the Native Land,* 1939). Having met Césaire with Lévi-Strauss in 1942, André Breton described this epic poem as "the greatest lyric monument of our time." Mixing Caribbean, African, and European poetic traditions into a multivoiced and troubling narrative, the *Cahier* is a now a classic of francophone Caribbean literature, still taught across the Atlantic in Africa. Inspiration for the poem was Césaire's return to Martinique in 1935 to find a downtrodden people, who, through discovering their African and slave-revolt roots, are shown to stand up and demand dignity and freedom. Césaire's Atlantic is nevertheless a resolutely triangular one.

Educated in France in the 1930s, and a member of France's parliament (elected in 1945 to represent Martinique in the new Constituent Assembly in Paris), Césaire had also cofounded in 1930s Paris the journal *L'Etudiant noir* (Black Student). As a member of France's elite education system, he assimilated the greats of French literature—Charles Baudelaire, Arthur Rimbaud, Stéphane Mallarmé. His 1950 speech, *Discours sur le colonialisme* (Discourse on Colonialism), was an indictment of European colonialism and a Communist tirade against U.S. imperialism (but he left the Communist Party over the 1956 invasion of Hungary). His main focus was, nevertheless, Africa and the Caribbean and the history of antislavery. He wrote a biography of Haitian revolutionary and antislavery leader Toussaint L'Ouverture (1961) and then a series of plays, the most famous of which—*Une Saison au Congo* (*A Season in the Congo*, 1967)—deals with murdered Congolese leader Patrice Lumumba. Though Césaire was not a regular visitor to Africa, his work is saturated by references to it and its echoes across the Atlantic, in both the Caribbean and France.

Andy Stafford

See also: Breton, André; Fanon, Frantz; Lévi-Strauss, Claude; Martinique; Slavery; Toussaint L'Ouverture, François.

References

Confiant, Raphaël. *Aimé Césaire: Une traversée paradoxale du siècle.* Paris: Stock, 1993.

Stafford, Andy. "Travel in the French Black Atlantic: Dialoguing and Diverging, between Aimé Césaire and Edouard Glissant." *ASCALF Critical Studies in Postcolonial Literature and Culture* 1 (2001): 15–30.

CHABROL, CLAUDE (1930–)

Born in Paris, Claude Chabrol is one of the most important French film directors of the past forty years. A critic at *Cahiers du cinéma* and one of the founders of the New Wave (considered by many to begin with his film *Le Beau Serge/Handsome Serge* of 1958; he was also an art supervisor and a consultant on Jean-Luc Godard's *Breathless*), Chabrol's prolific output of over fifty films has included many styles and genres but is especially characterized by obsessional murder mystery plots set in a bourgeois (and often provincial and familial) milieu. The protagonists' culture is then dissected in psychologically ambiguous ways, according to varying emphases on (Catholic) guilt and a class politics from which the workers are paradoxically absent.

Chabrol's New Wave credentials are underlined in his first films by the location shooting, direct style, and emphasis on the director/screenwriter as chief creator of his artistic work. In addition, Chabrol's impeccable cinephile credentials included an interest in identifying with visionary Hollywood author-directors, hence his passion, from his film club youth onward, for Fritz Lang's German but also American periods (he paid homage to Lang in the Berlin-shot international coproduction *Docteur M* in 1990) and for Alfred Hitchcock, on whom Chabrol wrote the first full-length book study—along with then fellow-Catholic Eric Rohmer—in 1957. After other important films such as *Les Cousins* (1958) and *Les Bonnes Femmes/The Girls* (1960), Chabrol spent some years in genre (war, spy) cinema, until he hit a successful middle period in the late 1960s and early 1970s with the so-called "Hélène cycle" (his then wife Stéphane Audran played various characters by that name): *Les Biches* (*Bad Girls,* 1967), *La Femme infidèle* (*The Unfaithful Wife,* 1968), *Le Boucher* (*The Butcher,* 1969), *La Rupture* (*The Break Up,* 1970), and *Juste avant la nuit* (*Just before Nightfall,* 1971). Since *Violette Nozière* in 1978, Chabrol has often worked with Isabelle Huppert, in films such as *Une Affaire de femmes* (*Story of Women,* 1988, in which she plays an abortionist executed under the wartime Vichy regime), an adaptation of *Madame Bovary* (1991), *La Cérémonie* (*A Judgment in Stone,* 1995, a version of the 1930s Papin sisters case, in which servants murdered their employers), *Rien ne va plus* (*The Swindle,* 1997), and *Merci pour le chocolat* (*Nightcap,* 2000). Other successes of this period include the pair of films he made with Jean Poiret as the eponymous *Poulet au vinaigre* (1985, infelicitously translated as *Cop au vin*) and *Inspecteur Lavardin* (1986).

The ups and downs of Chabrol's career have included brief forays into English-speaking or transatlantic cinema. These films, often neglected or forgotten but many deserving of attention, include *Ten Days' Wonder* (1972, based on an Ellery Queen novel), a quasi-metaphysical study of patriarchal authority embodied by Orson Welles and played out in an oedipal relationship with his son Anthony Perkins; the self-parodic *Folies bourgeoises* (*The Twist,* 1976), starring Bruce Dern and Ann-Margret; and *Blood Relatives* (1978), based on a novel by Ed McBain and shot in Montreal, starring Donald Sutherland as the policeman involved in an incestuous intrigue. In the same city Chabrol shot a Brian Moore adaptation of Simone de Beauvoir's *Le Sang des autres* (*The Blood of Others,* 1984, starring Jodie Foster). His adaptation of Henry Miller's *Quiet Days in*

Clichy (1990) was one of his least successful films critically and commercially.

Chabrol's eclecticism and prolific output ensure that his work is characterized by paradoxical combinations of the local and global, the historical and the generic, a close engagement with French culture and politics (in 1993 he made a documentary about wartime propaganda films titled *L'Oeil de Vichy/The Eye of Vichy*), but also an ability to roam across the film culture of the Atlantic world.

Bill Marshall

See also: Beauvoir, Simone de; Cinema, 1945 to the Present; Godard, Jean-Luc; *Madame Bovary;* Miller, Henry Valentine.

References

Austin, Guy. *Claude Chabrol.* Manchester University Press, 1999.
Blanchet, Christian. *Claude Chabrol.* Paris: Rivages, 1989.
Wood, Robin. *Claude Chabrol.* London: Studio Vista, 1970.

CHALLE, ROBERT (1659–1720)

For a long time Robert Challe's connections with Canada were as obscure as almost everything else about him. In the last quarter century, scholars such as Jean Mesnard and Frédéric Deloffre have brought to light more and more aspects of his life and work, including his Canadian experiences. He now emerges as one of the most fascinating figures of eighteenth-century French literature. Born into a Parisian middle-class family, Challe received a good education and saw some military service. He decided to leave France after a family quarrel, with a share his mother's family had bought him in a new company aimed at developing the Acadian fishing industry (Compagnie des pêches sédentaires d'Acadie). He sailed for

Canada in 1682, along with Jean Bergier, the company's manager. Challe made five voyages in all to Acadia, the last in 1687 or 1688.

In 1683 he endured a grueling overland journey from Cape Canso to Quebec to plead the new company's cause to the French authorities in the face of opposition from existing settlers. His reports for the minister Jean-Baptiste Colbert, marquis de Seignelay, on the company's affairs stressed the ever-present threat of English competition. When Bergier stood down in 1685, Challe hoped to replace him but was set aside in favor of Duret de La Boulaye, a relative of the principal shareholder. Challe blamed La Boulaye's negligence for the English capture and looting of the company's headquarters at Chedabucto—a disaster for the company and for Challe himself, who was wounded and captured. Returning to France on his release, he joined an expedition of the French East India Company, which set sail for Pondicherry in 1690, returning to France via the West Indies in 1691. In 1692 he was present at the lost naval battle of La Hougue.

Challe seems to have traveled also in the Mediterranean but increasingly devoted himself to writing. *Les Illustres françaises* (*The Illustrious French Lovers,* 1713) is now recognized as arguably the most important French novel between *La Princesse de Clèves* (The Princess of Cleves) and *Manon Lescaut*. More recently, Challe has been identified (partly because of the Canadian references in the text) as the author of *Difficultés sur la religion proposées au Père Malebranche*, an original and powerful statement of deism. His *Mémoires* provide fascinating, if not always reliable, accounts of his Canadian experiences. He bitterly laments the loss to France of the resources of Acadia and prophesies that Quebec will soon fall to Britain as well. While criticizing the French government's failure to sustain the colonies and the ignorant authoritarianism of the governors, he offers thoughtful analyses of how a colony should be run and shows respect and concern for the indigenous peoples. He reports a powerful anticolonial speech by the Iroquois chief he calls "Arouïmtesche" (Otreouti, or "Grand Gueule"), but he may be projecting his own loathing of the Jesuits onto the speaker. His Canadian disappointments seem to have sharpened his critical and pessimistic outlook on life. In any case, his failure as a colonist was certainly a gain to French literature.

Michael Moriarty

See also: Acadia; Fishing; Jesuits; Quebec.
References
Challe, Robert. *Mémoires, Correspondance complète, Rapports sur l'Acadie et autres pièces*. Ed. Frédéric Deloffre and Jacques Popin. Geneva: Droz, 1996.
Deloffre, Frédéric, ed. *Un Destin, une œuvre: Robert Challe: Textes et documents inédits*. Paris: SEDES, 1992.

CHAMOISEAU, PATRICK (1953–)

Born in 1953 in Fort-de-France, Martinique, Patrick Chamoiseau is one of the most successful and acclaimed francophone Caribbean writers living today. Author of numerous works of fiction (including *Solibo magnifique/Solibo Magnificent*, 1988, and *Texaco*, 1992, for which he won the Prix Goncourt), autobiography (*Une Enfance créole/Childhood*), and theory (notably *Eloge de la créolité/In Praise of Creoleness*, cowritten with Jean Bernabé and

Raphaël Confiant), his writing project can perhaps be summed up as an exercise in cultural, mental, and material emancipation of the Caribbean from the grip of "Frenchness" in all its repressive guises, an experiment in a new postcolonial subjectivity based on hybridity or *créolité*.

Chamoiseau trained as a lawyer in Martinique and in Paris but currently resides (working as a probation officer) in Martinique. Despite a professed affinity for such writers as François Rabelais and Emile Zola, Chamoiseau refuses to consider himself a French novelist, preferring to draw comparisons with the likes of Spanish-speaking Alejo Carpentier, whose cultural complexity he sees as more pertinent to his own situation than the French language he shares with the writers of the Hexagon. Calling for a new, nonhierarchical relation between France and the Antilles, starting with the destruction of the current "departmental" status of Guadeloupe and Martinique (which he considers as an insidious continuation of French colonialism), Chamoiseau's work proposes instead an unstable and unreadable "Creole" identity, one represented neither by white France nor by Césairean négritude. In *Texaco,* the contemporary Martinican heroine Marie-Sophie comes to realize that enslavement by the racist and capitalist "modernizing" forces of the "En-Ville" can only be escaped by a combination of active political resistance and a refusal of all coherent and "recuperable" labels, practices, timescales, identities, and discourses. She finds her place *between* the oral and the written, the magical and the real, the present and the past. Similarly, the aged maroon, the eponymous hero of *L'Esclave vieil homme et le molosse* (*The Old Man Slave and the Mastiff,* 1997) will attain subjectivity liberated from the nineteenth-century colonial plantation once he has been reborn into a realm of mental dissolution within the forest. Chamoiseau's fictitious texts are themselves linguistic warriors against French domination, written in a French imbued with the rhythms, vocabulary, and idiosyncrasies of Creole, a weirdly "possessed" literary language, less definable and more resistant to categorization even than Creole itself.

Publishing the epic novel *Biblique des derniers gestes* (*Scripture of Last Acts*) in 2002, Chamoiseau continued his experiment in the subversion of both French and Frenchness, reasserting as strongly as ever through his work the need to accept *créolité*—and all the potential disorder, confusion, and chaos it can imply—as a way of life infinitely preferable to the sterility of metropolitan control.

Andrew Asibong

See also: Bernabé, Jean; Carpentier, Alejo; Césaire, Aimé; Confiant, Raphaël; *Créolité;* Guadeloupe; Martinique, Zola, Emile.

References

Chamoiseau, Patrick. *Ecrire en pays dominé.* Paris: Gallimard, 1997.

Condé, Maryse, and Madeleine Cottenet-Hage, eds. *Penser la créolité.* Paris: Karthala, 1995.

Lewis, Shireen K. *Race, Culture, and Identity: Francophone West African and Caribbean Literature from Négritude to Créolité.* New York: Peter Lang, 2001.

CHAMPLAIN, SAMUEL DE (CA. 1570–1635)

Traditionally called the "Father of New France." From 1603 until his death, he devoted himself to trade, exploration, and colonization in what is now called Canada, becoming the dominant Frenchman in these enterprises. In 1608 he founded the first lasting French colony, at Quebec on the Saint Lawrence River.

Born in Brouage (Saintonge) in the Bay of Biscay, Champlain was initially a soldier in the French Wars of Religion on the side of Henri de Navarre. In 1598, Champlain, whose father was a sea captain, probably enlisted in a Spanish expedition to the West Indies and Central America that lasted over two years. In 1603, his mapmaking or painting skills may have been what got him onto an expedition sent by Aymar de Chaste to the Saint Lawrence River to trade and to find a site for a new, trade-based colony. Aymar de Chaste held the controversial monopoly over the fur trade of New France. After the failed Cartier/Roberval expedition of 1541–1543, French free trade had continued to develop in Nova Scotia, New Brunswick, and the Gulf of Saint Lawrence, but only from the 1580s—following the emergence of a professional fur trade on the Saint Lawrence in about 1581—had French prospects for a trade-based colony reappeared. Colonies at Sable Island (1598–1603) and Tadoussac (1599–1600) were short-lived, although Tadoussac continued to be the main trading station on the Saint Lawrence. The 1603 expedition convinced Champlain that Acadia might be better than the Saint Lawrence for a colony. He probably helped sway Pierre Du Gua de Mons—to whom the monopoly passed in 1603—in that direction too. Champlain was prominent in a longer expedition (1604–1607) that charted the coastline as far south as Cape Cod and founded a colony on the mouth of the Sainte Croix River (New Brunswick), from where it soon moved to Port Royal on the Bay of Fundy (Nova Scotia), lasting until it was destroyed by the Virginians in 1613.

Referred to as the Father of New France, Champlain founded the first lasting French colony, at Quebec on the Saint Lawrence. (Library of Congress)

However, by 1607, when Champlain returned to France, it was clear that the winding Maritimes coastline made it impossible to enforce the monopoly against the free traders. He persuaded de Mons to revert his focus to the Saint Lawrence and was put in command of one of two vessels sent out in 1608. On July 3, Champlain established a colony on the Saint Lawrence, choosing the narrows of Quebec (previously Stadacona) because they enabled illicit river trade to be policed. Unlike Cartier before him, Champlain secured the consent of the local Indians, now the Montagnais, who were the middlemen in the fur trade between the French and the Algonquin, through whom in turn Champlain soon acquired (in

1611) a direct trade link to the Huron. The Iroquoian-speaking Stadaconans and Hochelagans encountered by Cartier and Roberval had disappeared. Because the Algonquin-speaking tribes north of the Saint Lawrence supplied better and more numerous furs than the Iroquois to the south, the French were allied with the former against the latter. Champlain now implemented a new policy devised by him and/or de Mons's deputy (Gravé du Pont): instead of just arming the Montagnais and others against the Iroquois, the French would fight alongside them. This decision strengthened the alliance with the Montagnais, helped create one with the Huron too (lasting until 1649), and thereby also enabled the French to explore the interior. In 1609 Champlain and two other Frenchmen fought in a Montagnais, Algonquin, and Arendarhonon (Huron) raid against the Mohawk (Iroquois), whom they defeated on July 29, south of present-day Lake Champlain. The French muskets gave an enormous advantage.

Having returned to France in 1609, Champlain was back in Quebec in 1610, leaving it on June 14 to go upriver and participate alongside Montagnais, Algonquin, and Huron in killing almost all the occupants of an Iroquois fort at the Battle of Richelieu River, where he sustained an injury. In a three-way diplomatic exchange, Champlain left the young Etienne Brûlé with the Algonquin for a while and in return received a Huron headman's brother (Savignon), whom he took to France in 1610 and brought back to Canada on his next voyage (1611), when Champlain also built a wall, two gardens, and a square on Montreal island, to see if the clay used would withstand the winter.

Between 1608 and 1613 free trade had been winning out: the fur monopoly had been suspended, much to the frustration of Champlain, who proposed grander colonizing plans than those of de Mons, based on a diversified economy exporting not only fur but also timber, tar, fish, and much else. In proposals that he wrote up in 1618, he advocated establishing a new town on the Saint Lawrence called Ludovica (in honor of Louis XIII), in the valley of the Saint Charles River. Champlain's vision involved assimilating Indians to French culture, converting them to Christianity, and getting them to live like the French. A monopoly on the fur trade west of Quebec was restored, and in 1612 Champlain was invested with wide-ranging powers as the lieutenant of his new patron, the Prince de Condé, viceroy of New France. Champlain's next voyage there, in 1613, was an unsuccessful attempt to find the rumored northern ocean (Hudson Bay) that one Nicolas de Vignau, whose testimony turned out to be probably false, claimed to have seen. In 1613, the Company of Canada was founded, mostly with Rouen and Saint-Malo merchants as shareholders and with Champlain guaranteed a large salary.

In 1615 Champlain brought four missionaries (Recollet friars) with him from France. The Huron, having obtained Champlain's agreement to fight the Iroquois with them, took him on what turned out to be an enormous journey into the interior, some of it against his will: up the Ottawa River, into Georgian Bay, past Muskoka, into Huron country near Lake Simcoe, and then to somewhere in present-day New York State, where they inconclusively attacked the Iroquois, after which Champlain, injured again, had to be carried back to Huron country, where he wintered, not returning to Quebec until July 1616. His desire to explore the interior for himself seems to have faded thereafter. He devoted himself to administering Quebec. In 1627 Cardinal Richelieu began expanding colonization, taking direct control of New France and founding the Company of the Hundred Associates. However, in 1627 war broke out between the French and the English. Champlain, hampered by deteriorated relations with the Montagnais, who resented many of his actions as well as the French monopoly, which deflated fur prices, surrendered the small, starving colony of Quebec to the British in 1629. He was repatriated via England, but following Quebec's restoration to the French in 1632, he returned in 1633 as commander of New France and Richelieu's representative. He died in 1635, unaware that the decision had already been taken to replace him the following year by an ally of the Jesuits (who had displaced the Recollet friars in New France). He left a wife, Hélène, who was not yet twelve when they married in 1610 and who now became a nun. She had tried to leave him earlier but had been brought back by force.

Evaluations of Champlain vary. He was adventurous, courageous, ambitious, egotistical, at times astute. When his Indian allies tortured prisoners after battles or forced them to eat their comrade's heart, he sometimes (unlike some later Europeans) strongly objected, perhaps less out of abhorrence for violence in itself than because they were prisoners rather than criminals. When in 1608 a locksmith (Jean Duval) led a conspiracy to murder Champlain in Quebec in the hope of obtaining a reward from the Basque free traders, Champlain had Duval's

severed head prominently displayed. Although Champlain gained long experience in dealing with indigenous peoples, he also remained blind to much in their culture, at least partly because he saw them essentially as means to French ends. He chronicled his experiences in a series of books printed in France between 1604 and 1632.

Neil Kenny

See also: Acadia; Basques; Brûlé, Etienne; Cartier, Jacques; Fur Trade; Jesuits; Montreal; New Brunswick; New France; Nova Scotia; Quebec; Richelieu, Cardinal Armand Jean du Plessis de; Roberval, Jean-François de la Rocque, Seigneur de; Saint Lawrence River; Saint-Malo; Tadoussac.

References

Armstrong, Joe C. W. *Champlain.* Toronto: Macmillan, 1987.

Heldenreich, Conrad E. *Explorations and Mapping of Samuel de Champlain, 1603–1632.* Toronto: York University, 1976.

Trigger, Bruce G. *The Children of Aataentsic I: A History of the Huron People to 1660.* 2 vols. Montreal: McGill-Queen's University Press, 1976.

CHANUTE, OCTAVE (1832–1910)

Civil engineer, businessman, and aviation enthusiast. Chanute's chief contribution to the invention of the airplane lay in his developing a two-wing glider that became the model for the Wright brothers' invention.

Born in Paris in 1832, Chanute emigrated to the United States with his father in 1838 and was educated in private schools in New York City. Although he had no formal training as a civil engineer, he nevertheless progressed through employment with various railroad companies to become the chief engineer of the Chicago and Alton Railroad in 1863. After the Civil

French civil engineer, businessman, and aviation enthusiast, Chanute's chief contribution to the invention of the airplane lay in his developing a two-wing glider that became the model for the Wright brothers' invention. (Library of Congress)

War he designed and supervised the construction of the first railroad bridge over the Missouri River at Kansas City. In the 1870s and 1880s he served as an engineering consultant to the railroads that were expanding across the American West. In 1890, he went into the business of railroad tie preservation, a successful enterprise that gave him the financial security to pursue his studies in aeronautics.

In 1894 Chanute published *Progress in Flying Machines,* a compendium of articles in a book that quickly became an invaluable reference for aviation experimenters worldwide. He had been researching and experimenting since the 1850s, and his library in Chicago was probably one of the most complete on the subject of aeronautics in the world. In 1896 he engaged in two experiments on the south

shore of Lake Michigan, testing a multi-wing machine called the *Katy-Did* as well as developing a two-wing glider. This glider, 16 feet long, with two arched wings held rigid by wires, weighed 23 pounds. It was flown with a "pilot" hanging off a bar below the wings who directed the machine off a sand dune into a strong wind. On September 4, 1896, a number of flights, the longest of which was 253 feet, convinced Chanute that he was on the right track. A flight of 359 feet into a strong north wind on September 11 was the most successful. Following more experiments in 1897, he presented his findings to the Western Society of Engineers in October of that year. In the following years, a number of lectures and articles by Chanute convinced many engineers that the problem of successful heavier-than-air flight was one that could be taken seriously by professionals, and was not simply the domain of crackpot experimenters.

When the Wright brothers became interested in the challenge of heavier-than-air flight, Chanute was the first person they contacted. Over 500 letters between Chanute and the brothers provide one of the best historical sources of the progress of the Wright brothers in their struggle to develop the airplane. Chanute offered advice and encouragement as well as visiting them at Kitty Hawk. Although he remained skeptical of the viability of the airplane until he died in 1910, his contribution was recognized by Wilbur Wright, who wrote in 1911, "I think I was fully justified in saying that if he [Chanute] had not lived the history of human flight would have been quite different from what it has been" (quoted in McFarland, pp. 1018–1019).

Steve Spicer

See also: Aviation.
References
Crouch, Tom. *A Dream of Wings.* London,
New York: W. W. Norton, 1981.
McFarland, Marvin D. *The Papers of Wilbur
and Orville Wright. Vol II.* New York:
McGraw-Hill, 1953.
Spicer, Steve. *The Octave Chanute Pages.*
March 1996. (cited February 21, 2004,
http://spicerweb.org/chanute/chan_ind
.html).

CHARLEBOIS, ROBERT (1944–)

Psychedelic, anticonformist, and nationalist, Charlebois was the leading light of Quebec rock music and counterculture until the mid-1970s. Born in Montreal on June 24, 1944, he succeeded in creating and exporting to France a repertoire that combined Quebec and wider North American references. Specialists of music of the period tend to talk of a before-Charlebois era and an after-Charlebois era. Even though his mass popularity is in the past, he nonetheless is an undeniable source of influence in Quebec music.

Charlebois's early career augured little of what was to come, since his first album in 1965 straightforwardly followed the path laid out by the hugely prominent folk music of the time. However, a trip to California in 1967 opened up the horizons of flower power and boosted his creativity. At the time, music in Quebec meant either folksingers with their audience of intellectuals and students or "yéyé" singers happy to provide French-language versions of American hits. Transformed by his journey, Charlebois created a francophone rock music combining European and American influences.

He offered a kind of cultural revolution, singing about continental North American realities but in *joual* (a mixture of Quebec slang, English, and standard French). At the end of 1968, this process reached its culmination with *L'Osstidcho* (*L'hostie de show,* or *This Fucking Show*), a sort of antispectacle combining music, humor, improvisation, and all kinds of performance. Its scandalous reception contributed to the Charlebois legend. The sociologist Jacques Julien wrote of Charlebois as a prophet for his generation. In 1972, Charlebois achieved the old Quebec ambition of triumphing in Paris, shattering as he did so the rustic image of Quebec that had existed in France since the success there of Félix Leclerc in the 1950s. Charlebois was worlds apart from that image: onstage, the characters he invented (Garou, Superfrog) and his extravagant costumes put him in the same vein as glam rock and David Bowie's Ziggy Stardust.

Success, however, was relatively short-lived. At the end of the 1970s, Charlebois abandoned his characters, became more conventional, and saw his popularity erode. The cover of his 1977 album *Swing Charlebois Swing* had him playing golf, dressed in light blue trousers and a canary yellow polo neck. Did this mean Garou was dead and the bourgeoisie had been embraced? Many of his fans saw this transformation as a betrayal. A few years later he enjoyed more hit singles, but in a middle-of-the-road style. His output since 1990 has been sporadic.

Frédéric Demers

See also: Counterculture; Garou; Language;
Leclerc, Félix; Music (Pop).
References
Gagnon, Claude. *Robert Charlebois déchiffré.*
Montreal: Leméac, 1974.

Julien, Jacques. *Robert Charlebois: L'enjeu d'
"Ordinaire."* Montreal: Tryptique, 1987.
Rioux, Lucien. *Robert Charlebois.* Paris:
Seghers, 1973.

CHARLEVOIX, PIERRE-FRANÇOIS-XAVIER DE (1682–1761)

Father Pierre-Francois-Xavier de Charlevoix began to write about the New World because of his discontent with existing narratives that purportedly described the landscapes and peoples of New France. He was not along in his feeling of dissatisfaction. At the end of the seventeenth century, the French traveler Dièreville complained of the difference he had encountered between the New France he had observed firsthand and the descriptions of it he had found in books, particularly that of Baron Lahontan. Years later, Father Charlevoix, a Jesuit priest sent to Canada in 1705, would echo this criticism, deploring the runaway success of Lahontan's *New Voyages to North America* and characterizing it as "a monstrous hodgepodge of fables." He was particularly outraged by Lahontan's anticlericalism and what he saw as the book's libertine tendencies. In 1719, Charlevoix was officially asked to study the question of the boundaries of Acadia, then a source of conflict between the French and the British. Shortly thereafter, from 1720 to 1723, he carried out at the orders of the king an extensive journey into the interior of the American continent to gather information about the Western Sea.

After returning to France, Charlevoix dedicated himself to writing his own account of his experiences in New France. His *Journal of a Voyage to North America,* published in 1744, is notable for its vivid

Peter Francis Xavier de Charlevoix. Charlevoix dedicated himself to writing his own account of his experiences in New France. His Journal of a Voyage to North America, *published in 1744, is notable for its vivid descriptions of not only the topography but the social structures of colonial Quebec. (Library of Congress)*

descriptions of not only the topography but the social structures of colonial Quebec. Charlevoix depicts the Creoles of Canada as healthy, vivacious, and obsessed with sartorial elegance to the point of being willing to go without food in order to appear well dressed. He adds that nowhere else is the French language spoken with greater purity. Charlevoix's narrative is also noteworthy for its detailed discussions of the rituals and social structure of native groups (particularly the Yasous and the Natchez) of the lower Mississippi valley and New Orleans, which have provided invaluable historical and anthropological information about these tribes in the eighteenth century to later ethnographers.

Charlevoix describes New Orleans as a precarious settlement consisting of warehouses, barracks, and a few houses but imagines the day when its geographical situation and climate will help it become the capital of a large, rich colony.

Susan Castillo

See also: Lahontan, Louis Armand de Lom d'Arce, Baron de; Mississippi River; New France; New Orleans.

References

Amat, Christian. "Un Missionaire philosophe face à l'Amérique: Le R. P. Charlevoix." *L'Amérique des Lumières.* Ed. Jean Balcou and René Pomeau. Geneva: Droz, 1997.

Marouby, Christian. "From Early Anthropology to the Literature of the Savage: The Naturalization of the Primitive." *Studies in Eighteenth-Century Culture* (1985): 289–298.

CHARNAY, CLAUDE-JOSEPH-DÉSIRÉ (1828–1915)

French archaeologist.

A key figure in the history of archaeology in nineteenth-century Mexico, Charnay was the author of the first widely known publication of photographs of Mexico's ancient monuments. Made during his first voyage to Mexico between 1857 and 1859, the forty-seven prints featured in *Cités et ruines américaines: Mitla, Palenqué, Izamal, Chichen-Itza, Uxmal, recueillies et photographiées par Désiré Charnay avec un texte par M. Viollet-le-Duc* (American Cities and Ruins: Mitla, Palenqué, Izamal, Chichen-Itza, Uxmal, Collected and Photographed by Désiré Charnay with a text by M. Viollet-le-Duc, Paris, 1862–1863) introduced French viewers to Mexico's extraordinary architectural and sculptural ruins. Charnay's extremely beautiful, large-scale photographs were a remarkable achievement given the cumbersome nature of the wet collodion process, which required not only the coating of a glass plate with a fast-drying emulsion just prior to exposure but also the processing of prints immediately thereafter. In his accompanying text, Charnay cast himself as an intrepid explorer conquering extreme temperatures, strangling overgrowth, murderous insects, humidity, inadequate supplies, and also civil war. Officially sanctioned by France's minister of public instruction, Charnay's first voyage coincided with intensifying French interest in the occupation of Mexico. In 1864, Charnay returned to Mexico with French troops sent to support Emperor Maximilian, who had been installed by Napoleon III. If the French government proved ambivalent about extending the empire, Charnay himself was explicitly imperialistic and declared it "France's duty to rouse Mexico from its numbness" (Davis, p. 21).

After the execution of Maximilian in 1867, Charnay left Mexico but returned for a third visit from 1880 to 1882. Regretting his ignorance during his first voyage, an ignorance that had led to his reliance on photography, Charnay now took himself seriously as a professional archaeologist and excavator. He arrived in Mexico determined to prove that all Central American monuments were of "Toltec" origin and also quite modern. Charnay's archaeological ambitions and unfounded theories were mocked during his lifetime; his self-fashioning as an explorer-archaeologist sharply contrasted with the methodical, scholarly excavations of his English counterpart, the archaeologist Alfred Maudslay. Despite being awarded the Logerot Prize by the French Geographic Society in 1884 and appointed officer in the Legion of Honor in 1888, Charnay suffered a steady decline in his reputation at the century's close. His superb collodion prints, by contrast, secured his reputation as a photographer. He was also the author of voyage accounts and popular fiction and the translator and editor of pre-contact and colonial manuscripts. He returned to Mexico for a fourth and final time in 1886 and also made voyages to Madagascar (1863), Chile and Argentina (1875), Java (1878), Australia (1878–1879), and Yemen (1897) and repeatedly to the United States.

Darcy Grimaldo Grigsby

See also: Argentina; Chile; Mexico; Photography.

References

Charnay, Désiré. *Voyage au Mexique, 1858–1861*. Ed. Pascal Mongne. Paris: Gingko, 2001.

Davis, Keith F. *Désiré Charnay, Expeditionary Photographer*. Albuquerque: University of New Mexico Press, 1981.

CHARRIÈRE, HENRI (1906–1973)

French criminal and prisoner in French Guiana, Henri Charrière depicted a lively career of imprisonment, adventures, and escapes in an autobiography, *Papillon* (1969).

The son of a country schoolteacher, Charrière was born in 1906, in the central French department of Ardèche. His mother died when he was eleven. Charrière's youth was anything but uneventful, and, after a number of years of committing misdemeanors and petty crime, he had established a solid reputation among the French underworld as a first-rate safecracker and thief.

In October 1931 he was convicted of murder—a murder he did not commit, as was later proved—and sentenced to a life of hard labor. Led to the *Conciergerie*—the jailhouse located on the banks of the Seine in central Paris—he met his fellow inmates Degas and Julot, with whom he sailed for the hard labor camp in the Pénitencier de Saint Laurent in French Guiana, South America. The three of them spent the first weeks of their imprisonment at the hospital for inmates, from where Julot escaped and was never heard from again.

In Cayenne, Charrière—alias Papillon, or "Butterfly," a nickname given to him because of the butterfly tattoo he wore on his chest—met Clousiot and Maturette, two other inmates, and soon after, the three of them escaped from the labor camp with the help of other inmates. Degas had been given the opportunity to escape as well but preferred to stay behind. This was the beginning of Papillon's life on the run, full of encounters with many generous people.

The three convicts were arrested in Rio Hacha, where Papillon, with the help of another convict, escaped yet a second time. He was taken in by a tribe of South American Indians, with whom he spent seven months before returning to Rio Hacha, where he was then captured once again. Along with Clousiot and Maturette, Papillon was sentenced to two years of solitary confinement in appalling conditions on Devil's Island, so appalling that Clousiot was unable to bear this burden and died soon after his release.

Thus began true prison life for Papillon. Following another escape attempt, which unfortunately failed, he was sentenced to eight years of solitary confinement, but served only nineteen months in all. With another inmate, he escaped by sea to Venezuela, and this time for good. Charrière finally found himself to be a free man at the age of thirty-seven, in 1944.

Charrière later became a Venezuelan citizen and lived in Caracas. His most famous autobiographical novel, *Papillon,* was followed by several other works depicting his adventures and hardships during these years.

Henri Charrière died in Madrid, Spain, on July 29, 1973.

Claudia Wolosin

See also: Devil's Island; Guiana; Venezuela.
Reference
Armelle, Pierre, and Georges Psuquey. *Le Dieu de Papillon: Essai.* Tours: Mame, 1970.

CHATEAUBRIAND, FRANÇOIS-AUGUSTE RENÉ DE, VICOMTE (1768–1848)

French author, born in Saint-Malo.

Portrait of François-Auguste René de Chateaubriand (1768–1848), French writer and statesman. On April 8, 1791, Chateaubriand embarked upon his first and only voyage to North America. (Library of Congress)

On April 8, 1791, seeking new and firsthand inspiration for an epic poem in prose, *Les Natchez* (*The Natchez: An Indian Tale*), Chateaubriand embarked upon his first and only voyage to North America. In keeping with popular interests in eighteenth-century France, *Les Natchez* embraces American exoticism, the riches of natural history, the customs of the indigenous peoples, and especially man in his natural state (*l'homme de la nature*). Traveling along the northeastern Atlantic coast and New England, into Upper Ohio, and to the Great Lakes of Canada, Chateaubriand sought to study nature, in its broadest meaning, in a pure, unsullied state.

Returning to France on January 2, 1792, armed with copious notes and replete with recollections and ideas, he first wrote *Atala,* published in 1801. In addition to his own primary sources of information for *Atala, René,* and *Les Natchez* (1826) gleaned during his travels, he had a wealth of secondary material at his disposal: Bernardin de Saint-Pierre's *La Chaumière indienne* (*The Indian Cottage,* 1790), Jean-François Marmontel's *Les Incas* (*The Incas,* 1778), François de Salignac de La Mothe Fénélon's *Les Aventures de Télémaque* (*The Adventures of Telemachus,* 1699), the Jesuit missionary Pierre-François-Xavier de Charlevoix's *Histoire et description générale de la Nouvelle France* (*History and General Description of New France,* 1744), and Joseph-François Lafitau's *Les Moeurs des sauvages américains comparées aux moeurs des premiers temps* (*Customs of the American Indians Compared with the Customs of Primitive Times,* 1724), to name but a few. *Atala,* at once a geographic and human tableau, opens with a magnificent description of the Mississippi—although it is unlikely that Chateaubriand visited the region—before turning to a first-person retrospective on a tragic tale of conflict between natural aspirations and religious laws as told by Chactas, the blind Natchez, to René, a young European living with the tribe. In moving, lyrical passages, Chateaubriand describes the customs of America's indigenous peoples, funeral rites, marriage ceremonies, ethnic dances, and hunting techniques, concluding in the epilogue with a spectacular tableau of Niagara Falls.

René, the sequel to *Atala,* is a study of the *vague des passions,* an excess of human emotions, in René's case, the result of an unconsummated, incestuous relationship with his sister, Amélie. René comes to epitomize the *mal du siècle*—metaphysical anguish, revolt, a strong inclination to solitude, a love of nature, and reverie—of a generation trying to find a useful function and identity in postrevolutionary France. Set in Louisiana, the story covers René's travels to Italy, Greece, and England before returning to the peaceful bosom of the "happy savage" (*heureux sauvage*) in America. Through horrific scenes of rape, murder, and suicide worthy of a *roman noir,* Chateaubriand argues in *Les Natchez,* even while taking liberties with historical events, that both civilizations, the French and the Natchez, are capable of profoundly disturbing atrocities.

Le Voyage en Amérique/Journey to America (1827) encompasses motivation for the voyage, descriptions of places visited, the study of flora and fauna, the customs and language of the indigenous peoples, and topics previously dealt with in *Atala* and *Les Natchez.* Interesting comparisons are made between the indigenous peoples of Florida, Louisiana, and Canada. While reflecting on the myths surrounding the "savage state" (*état sauvage*), Chateaubriand muses over the future of the United States, symbol of freedom and a republic he admires, although sometimes with reservation. His optimism is repeated again in *Mémoires d'outre-tombe* (*Memoirs from Beyond the Tomb,* vol. 1), the complete version published posthumously between October 1848 and July 1850. In the richness of detail expressed in poetic and lyrical passages, Chateaubriand, precursor of French romanticism, both instructs and seduces by the harmony among the content, rhyme, and musicality of his descriptive and dramatic prose. A visionary of the first order, he foresaw the forging and modernization of all future societies (vol. 4).

Janette McLeman-Carnie

See also: Charlevoix, Pierre-François-Xavier de; Florida; Louisiana; Mississippi; New France; Noble Savage; Ohio.

References

Chinard, Gilbert. *L'Exotisme américain dans l'œuvre de Chateaubriand.* Geneva: Slatkine Reprints, 1970 [1918].

Painter, George. *Chateaubriand: A Biography.* London: Chatto and Windus, 1977.

CHAUVET, MARIE (1916–1973)

A native of Haiti born in 1916 into the Port-au-Prince bourgeoisie, Marie Chauvet was a playwright and novelist. She began her literary career in 1947 with the play *La Légende des fleurs* (Legend of the Flowers, published under the pseudonym "Colibri") and went on to publish four novels: *Fille d'Haïti* (Haitian Girl, 1954), *La Danse sur le volcan* (*Dance on the Volcano,* 1957), *Fonds des nègres* (1961), *Les Rapaces* (*Birds of Prey,* 1986), and a collection of novellas titled *Amour, colère, folie* (Love, Anger, Madness, 1968).

Amour, colère, folie, her best-known work, is a damning indictment of the regime of Haitian president-for-life François Duvalier. It was published by Gallimard, apparently with the assistance of Simone de Beauvoir. In Haiti, the collection's depiction of dictatorship and black nationalism instigated much controversy: Chauvet's husband, apparently fearing reprisals from the Duvalier government, eventually bought the rights to the novel and stored any published copies in a Port-au-Prince warehouse, where they languished for twelve years. Following this incident, Chauvet divorced her husband and fled to New York, where she died in 1973.

One of the few women writers to publish in Haiti prior to the 1970s, Chauvet was virtually ignored by Haiti's literary establishment, as well as by critics abroad, until *Amour, colère, folie* was "rediscovered" in 1980. From that time on, critics of French Caribbean literature, especially those writing from a feminist perspective, have extolled Chauvet's later works for their subversive depictions of gender, race, and class and for their challenging of Haiti's male-dominated literary tradition, with its masculinist depictions of race, nation, and political change.

Initially a writer of sentimental historical fiction (*La Danse sur le volcan* and *Fille d'Haïti*), Chauvet moved into more experimental directions with *Amour, colère, folie* and *Les Rapaces.* Written in diary form by a self-confessed "old-maid" whose dark skin is the embarrassment of her light-skinned bourgeois family, the tale of sexual obsession in "Amour" unfolds against the background of a fictionalized account of a massacre that took place under Duvalier in the town of Jérémie. While women are being tortured in the nearby prison by Calédu, the black general sent to "tame" the town's recalcitrant and racist bourgeoisie, the protagonist Claire fantasizes scenes of sadomasochistic sexual liaisons, a fantasy life that gradually inspires her participation in the growing resistance to Calédu and her eventual liberation of the town. In the Kafkaesque "Colère," a middle-class family loses its lands to an armed group reminiscent of Duvalier's *Tontons Macoutes.* The daughter Rose, a virgin, gives her body to the group's sadistic leader in exchange for the restitution of the lands, a choice that eventually allows her a kind of political agency. Finally, "Folie" delves into the psyches of three mad poets hiding out in a garret and awaiting the arrival of the black nationalist military commander and their certain execution.

Chauvet's subversive textual politics have gained her the reputation as one of Haiti's first postmodern novelists. Her craft and her daring criticism of the Duvalier regime make her today one of Haiti's most discussed writers.

Valerie Kaussen

See also: Beauvoir, Simone de; Feminisms; Haiti.

References

Chancy, Myriam. *Framing Silence: Revolutionary Novels by Haitian Women.* New Brunswick: Rutgers University Press, 1997.

Dayan, Joan. "Reading Women in the Caribbean: Marie Chauvet's *Love, Anger, and Madness.*" *Displacements: Women, Tradition, Literatures in French.* Ed. Joan Dejean and Nancy K. Miller. Baltimore: Johns Hopkins University Press, 1991.

Duffey, Carolyn. "In Flight from the Borderlines: Roses, Rivers, and Missing Haitian History in Marie Chauvet's *Colère* and Edwidge Danticat's *Krik? Krak!* and *The Farming of Bones.*" *The Journal of Caribbean Literatures* 3, no. 1 (2000): 77–91.

Scharfman, Ronnie. "Theorizing Terror: The Discourse of Violence in Marie Chauvet's *Amour, colère, folie.*" *Postcolonial Subjects: Francophone Women Writers.* Ed. Mary Jean Green et al. Minneapolis: University of Minnesota Press, 1996.

CHERBOURG

The history of Cherbourg is closely linked to that of Normandy. The town and seaport are located in Manche *département* (the equivalent of "county"), Basse-Normandie *région,* in northwestern France. Cherbourg lies on the English Channel, at the northern tip of the Cotentin Peninsula and at the mouth of the small Divette River. The port benefits from a well-sheltered harbor.

Cherbourg's jetty, completed in the 1850s after several decades of intermittent effort, converted the town into a major military and commercial port. Its value as a port made Cherbourg the first objective of the U.S. 1st Army after landing at the beaches of Normandy on D day (June 6, 1944) during World War II. The closest landing took place at Utah Beach, located just a few miles southeast of the town.

Supported by amphibious tanks, the first assault waves of the 8th Regiment of General Raymond Barton's 4th U.S. Infantry Division landed on the beach at 6.30 A.M. Due to a navigational error, they ended up roughly 2 kilometers south of their planned destination. This turned out to be providential, as the German defenses

D day landing on the coast of Normandy, June 6, 1944. (National Archives)

were far weaker here. During the battles that ensued, the city was stubbornly defended by its German occupiers, who systematically destroyed the port installations before surrendering to the Allied forces on June 27. The Allied troops rapidly rebuilt a temporary port to handle the vast quantity of weapons and other supplies needed until the hostilities ended.

Although the port's cargo traffic is now light, there is much ferry traffic between Cherbourg and the British Isles, and yachts and commercial fishing boats use the harbor. In 2003, nearly 1.5 million ferry passengers transited through the Cherbourg harbor. For nearly a century the harbor has been a port of call to the world's most luxurious "floating palaces," or transatlantic ocean liners, from the Queen Mary I in 1937 to the Queen Mary II in 2004. Gateway to the Americas for more than a century, Cherbourg remains faithful to its tradition of welcoming the greatest cruise liners and is the only French port where the Queen Elizabeth 2, jewel in the crown of the Cunard fleet, regularly stops over en route to New York.

Shipbuilding (including nuclear submarines), ship repair, and other industries depending on the port (such as electronics and metallurgy) are economically important in the area. Nearby, the nuclear power plant at La Hague reprocesses nuclear waste.

The town is the terminus of a railway line from Paris. Cherbourg's cultural offerings include the Thomas Henry Museum, which exhibits French paintings of the seventeenth to the nineteenth century, as well as Flemish and Italian works. At the nineteenth-century Fort du Roule, overlooking the town, is the Liberation Museum, commemorating the 1944 invasion of the Allied troops.

Claudia Wolosin

See also: Nuclear Technology; Painting; World War II.

References

Gibory, Eric. *Normandie.* Paris: Hachette, 2003.

Herval, René. *Normandie.* Grenoble: Arthaud, 1971.

CHEVALIER, MAURICE (1888–1972)

French-born international music star, who still embodies French culture and identity around the world to this day.

Chevalier, who came from a large, poverty-stricken family in a working-class suburb of Paris, started working at eleven in odd apprentice jobs before discovering show business and developing a very personal singing comedy act in local cabarets. He became a highly popular music hall performer in famous venues such as the Empire, the Casino de Paris, and the Folies Bergère. He worked with the music hall star Mistinguett and eventually led stage revues himself with hit songs in the 1920s. Pioneers of the emerging medium of film, such as Max Linder, Louis Gasnier, and Henri Diamant-Berger, started hiring Chevalier for shorts toward the end of the 1910s.

The advent of sound made the musical genre extremely popular for a while, and the U.S. studios MGM and Paramount, constantly on the lookout for stars and talent, fought over the French music hall superstar. Chevalier finally settled first for Paramount, leaving for Hollywood in 1928. Despite learning English in a German POW camp with a fellow prisoner during World War I, Chevalier always retained his characteristically heavy French accent. His stardom was such before he came to Hollywood that his arrival was highly publicized, with French director Robert Florey recording his transatlantic voyage in *Skyscraper Symphony* (1929). Richard Wallace's *Innocents in Paris* (1929) was Chevalier's first Hollywood film and became a hit largely due to his performance, which established his screen persona for the rest of his long career as a frivolous, roguish seducer. Some twenty musicals followed, in both American and French versions, most of them directed by Ernst Lubitsch (*The Love Parade*, French and American versions, 1930; *The Smiling Lieutenant*, French and American versions, opposite Claudette Colbert, 1931; *One Hour with You*, French and American versions, 1932; *The Merry Widow*, French and American versions, 1934). Many of these Viennese-style operettas teamed him with Jeanette MacDonald, making them one of the golden screen couples of Hollywood. For the period 1928–1935, Chevalier was one of Hollywood's highest-paid, top-billed stars despite his humble beginnings and heavy French accent, making him somewhat the personification of the American dream.

Despite his huge success, Chevalier eventually fell out with Irving Thalberg at MGM about his billing and returned to France in 1935. In the buildup to World War II, French cinema was entering a dark, pessimistic phase that Chevalier's persona did not fit, but he was nevertheless offered a few parts in some important films of the period (Julien Duvivier's *L'Homme du Jour*, Maurice Tourneur's *Avec le Sourire*, both 1936; Robert Siodmak's *Pièges*, 1939). Chevalier also starred in René Clair's *Break the News*, shot in the United Kingdom in 1938. Chevalier carried on performing in France but resumed his Hollywood career at the end of the 1950s with box-office hits such as Vicente Minnelli's *Gigi* (1958), with Leslie Caron and Louis Jourdan. Chevalier's American films of the 1930s and 1960s, extremely rich in French actors and personnel, have made a lasting impact on Hollywood's representation of Paris and France.

Catherine Hellegouarc'h

See also: Boyer, Charles; Caron, Leslie; Cinema, 1895–1945; Cinema, 1945 to the Present; Clair, René; Colbert, Claudette; Duvivier, Julien; Florey, Robert; Gasnier, Louis J.; Hollywood's Paris; Jourdan, Louis; Pepe Le Pew; Rosay, Françoise; Tourneur, Maurice; World War I; World War II.

References

Freedland, Michael. *Maurice Chevalier.* London: Arthur Barker, 1981.

Ringgold, Gene, and Bodeen De Witt. *Chevalier: The Films and Career of Maurice Chevalier.* Secaucus, NJ: Citadel Press, 1973.

CHICAGO

Eschikagou, Algonquian for "a foul-smelling place," was located at the portage of southwestern Lake Michigan to the Des Plaines River, which eventually ran to the Mississippi River. French explorer Louis Joliet recommended Chicago in 1674 as the site for a canal linking the Great Lakes to the Mississippi River watershed. Nothing came of Joliet's suggestion, but the site was important enough for the French to build a small fort there in 1680. From the beginning, Chicago sat at the center of a regional transportation network.

Besides being a portage, Chicago in 1680 was a Miami Indian village and of some importance in the Great Lakes Indian trade. The Iroquois of New York massacred many of the Miamis at Chicago in 1687 in their effort to control the western Indians' trade with Europeans. The French ministry closed all western forts save one in 1696 because of a lack of funds, a glutted European fur market, and Jesuit complaints that soldiers and traders hampered efforts at converting Indians to Christianity.

The Miamis did not return, but in their place came the Potawatomis, Ojibwes, Ottawas, and Sauks. The French opened a trading post at Chicago around 1716, and it remained until the end of the French and Indian War. The Chicago Indians, however, maintained their affinity for France after the Treaty of Paris of 1763 and were among the leaders in the Indian uprising of 1763–1764, which tried to push the British out of the frontier posts and encourage the French to return.

The French eventually came back, but too late for the Indians and not in the manner they anticipated. In 1779 Jean-Baptiste Point du Sable from San Marc, Haiti, built a house and store at the portage, marking the return of western settlement to Chicago.

Du Sable (c. 1745–1818) was the son of a French sea captain and an African slave. Apparently his father gave him free status, for he was educated in France. He later worked as a seaman aboard one of his father's ships, which sank en route to New Orleans around 1764. Injured, du Sable nevertheless made it ashore, but without his identity papers. A French Jesuit mission nursed him back to health and hid him from Spanish authorities who would have seized him as a fugitive slave. At the mission, he met an Indian from the Illinois Country who convinced du Sable to go north, where he met his wife, a Potawatomi. He eventually arrived in Chicago in 1779, building the first permanent house there.

Enigmatic and enterprising, du Sable brokered peace treaties between tribes and was in quick succession a French partisan, British informant, and American Indian agent in the 1770s. In 1782, he established a trading post near his house and carried on a prosperous trade with Indians, traders, military contractors, other trading posts, and the region's few settlers. In 1800 he sold his business to an employee and moved near Saint Louis. He died there in 1818.

Jim Fisher

See also: French and Indian War; Fur Trade; Haiti; Illinois Country; Jesuits; Joliet, Louis; Mississippi River; New Orleans; Saint Louis; Slavery; Treaty of Paris.

References

Edmonds, R. David. *The Potawatomis: Keepers of the Fire.* Norman: University of Oklahoma Press, 1978.

Meehan, Thomas. "Jean-Baptiste Point du Sable, the First Chicagoan." *Journal of the Illinois State Historical Society* 56 (1963): 439–453.

Tanner, Helen H., ed. *Atlas of Great Lakes Indian History.* Norman: University of Oklahoma Press, 1987.

CHILE

France had an enduring influence on Chilean social, political, and cultural life in the nineteenth century. This influence, which principally affected the political and intellectual elites, was particularly decisive during the period surrounding the country's independence. The first constitutions, the first civil code, and the restructuring of the education system in the 1820s and

Map of Chile. France had an enduring influence on Chilean social, political, and cultural life in the nineteenth century. (MAPS.com/Corbis)

1830s owed much to the French model. After 1920, when the political elites started to look toward Germany and the United States, French cultural influence went into sharp decline. France, for its part, turned toward Chile when Salvador Allende was elected president in 1970.

As early as the independence period of the 1800s and 1810s, Chilean elites were interested in French Enlightenment thought. In an attempt to counteract the Spanish colonial authorities, such notions as "nation," the "social contract," "separation of powers," "republic," and "sovereignty of the people" were emphasized. The French Revolution, however, and in particular its laicism, did not receive much support from the future fathers of Chilean independence. During the 1840s, thanks to a liberalization of trade, books from France became more widely distributed in Chile. It was in this context that Alphonse de Lamartine's *Histoire des Girondins* (History of the Girondins) met with great success among the Chilean student population. Having taken part in the 1848 revolution, Francisco Bilbao, militant and essayist and admirer of Lamartine, criticized upon his return to Chile the lack of social reform and the influence of the clergy. The political actions of Santiago Arcos had a longer-term effect. Educated in France, a reader of the utopians (Henri de Saint-Simon, Charles Fourier, Robert Owen), he was one of the first defenders of Socialism in Chile. In 1850, he founded the Society of Equality, a political group that rapidly became the home of protest against the government of President Manuel Bulnes. The society preached the primacy of reason, the sovereignty of the people, and universal fraternity. In the field of literature, writers of the 1842 generation, like José Victorino Lastarria, were greatly influenced by the pre-romantics (Chateaubriand and Jean-Jacques Rousseau) and the Romantics (Lamartine and Victor Hugo). Andrés Bello, lawyer and reformer of the Chilean education system and an admirer of the Enlightenment philosophers, established a civil code that served as a model for the entire continent of Latin America. In academic spheres, throughout the last three decades of the nineteenth century, the brothers Jorge and Luis Lagarrigue contributed to the popularization of Auguste Comte's positivism.

At the start of the twentieth century, large numbers of French immigrants moved to Chile to specialize in the tanning industry, open department stores, and work in viticulture. Various French religious communities ran prestigious education establishments, while, under the impulse of a dynamic cultural policy, France opened a number of Alliances françaises in major cities. Nevertheless, at the end of World War I, the Chilean education system turned more toward the German community, which was more established, and toward the U.S. model, whose universities were more and more involved in the education of the elites. Chilean writers, for their part, kept their eyes trained on the avant-garde period in France, as is proved by the case of the poet Vicente Huidobro, a great figure of modern Latin American poetry, who not only lived in France for almost ten years but also chose to write both in French and in Spanish. At the start of the 1970s, it was France's turn to look to Chile, notably to the politically committed poetry of Pablo Neruda, and (through the influence of such figures as Alain Touraine and Régis Debray) to Salvador Allende, the democratically elected Socialist president. Following the assassination of Allende in 1973, many Chileans, such as the filmmaker Raúl Ruiz, the *chansonnier* Angel Parra, and the musical group Quilapayún, sought exile in France. Ruiz has made numerous films in France, taking on all kinds of projects and following the path he has made his own, that of a cinema both surreal and experimental (*Les Trois Couronnes du matelot,* 1982; *Trois Vies et une seule mort,* 1996).

Mauricio Segura

See also: Avant-Gardes; Cinema, 1945 to the Present; Debray, Régis; French Revolution; Huidobro, Vicente; Neruda, Pablo; Ruiz, Raúl; Surrealism; World War I.

References

Contreras, Francisco. *Pour l'élargissement de l'influence française dans l'Amérique du Sud.* Paris: Bossard, 1919.

Matthieu, Gilles. *Une Ambition sud-américaine: Politique culturelle de la France (1914–1940).* Paris: L'Harmattan, 1991.

CHIRAC, JACQUES (1932–)

French politician, born in Paris on November 29, 1932.

Chirac worked and studied in the United States (picking up excellent English). He almost got married there but returned and graduated from the ENA (Ecole Nationale d'administration) in 1959. In 1962 he joined the ministerial staff at the Commissariat du Plan and then moved to Prime Minister Georges Pompidou's staff before he began aggressively cultivating the left-wing Corrèze constituency, which he won in 1967.

Chirac's attention to constituency business was famous and his ministerial rise was rapid, with eight posts of increasing seniority until 1976. Chirac's first coup came in the 1974 presidential elections, when, as the minister of the interior, he organized the declaration by forty-three Gaullist deputies that they would support Giscard d'Estaing and not their own candidate.

French President Jacques Chirac, who opposed the American military intervention in Iraq in 2003. (Embassy of France)

When Giscard d'Estaing won the presidency, Chirac was made prime minister. In August 1976 he resigned, declaring that he did not have the means to do the job properly, and he reestablished the Gaullist Party in November 1976 as the Rassemblement pour la République/Rally for the Republic (RPR). Chirac won Paris city hall in 1976, which provided a world stage, enabling him to promote his own people up through the ranks and constitute a sort of government in exile.

But Chirac's RPR felt undervalued, especially after the 1978 election, and the party began a long harassment of the government. In 1981 Chirac's first presidential campaign proved to be as much against President Giscard d'Estaing as the Left and was a major contributory factor in the de-

feat of the incumbent. Chirac emerged as the principal figure on the Right and his RPR the Right's largest party. When a conservative victory appeared inevitable in the general elections of 1986, Chirac's decision, as a Gaullist, to work with an opposition president legitimized the "cohabitation." As prime minister from 1986 to 1988, he held all the power, but President François Mitterrand had already established Gaullist foreign policy priorities. Both president and premier agreed to refuse overflight rights to the United States so that it could bomb Libya in 1986, and France's independence within the West was reaffirmed. However, ill-advised education reforms brought students onto the streets in demonstrations reminiscent of 1968 and caused the withdrawal of the measures. A number of high profile "events" failed to win the 1988 election for him—the result was a resounding defeat (he polled only 46 percent).

Chirac allowed his former finance minister and friend Edouard Balladur to take the post of prime minister in 1993. Chirac developed a left-leaning presidential program that exploited the disarray on the Left, and although failing to top the first round, he won the presidential election of 1995 in the runoff.

There then began a fraught two years, starting with the resumption of nuclear testing in the Pacific to general protests. At this time a move back toward the North Atlantic Treaty Organization (NATO) was anticipated, but France's demand for leadership of the Mediterranean sector could not have been accepted, and the formal reintegration never took place. Prime Minister Alain Juppé ditched the presidential platform, which fomented discontent. He followed it up with a series of policy mistakes that undermined the government's credibility. President Chirac decided to hold a snap election a year before schedule, in May–June 1997, but the upshot was a narrow victory for the Left, and Chirac had to invite his former Socialist opponent Lionel Jospin to form a government.

This "cohabitation" from 1997 to 2002 was the longest of the Fifth Republic, but Chirac started it in poor shape. However, he rebuilt his position and reestablished his control over the opposition and the RPR by 2000. In 2002, therefore, Chirac was by no means a shoo-in candidate, and the Left had changed the electoral calendar to place the presidential elections before the general elections. Chirac had rebuilt his presidential stature as a paternal figure and had used the disaster of September 11 to emphasize his preeminence in foreign affairs. In this he was aided by a prearranged visit to the United States shortly after the disaster, at which he was able to affirm his solidarity with the Americans. At the first ballot of the presidential elections Chirac did prove to be a weak candidate and polled only 19.88 percent, a result that, in other circumstances, would have been a humiliation. However, the Left's candidate (Prime Minister Jospin) polled only 16.18 percent, and the Front National's Jean-Marie Le Pen polled 16.86 percent, taking him into the runoff to face Chirac. In the runoff Chirac polled 82.21 percent to Le Pen's 17.79 percent in the biggest victory of the Fifth Republic. In the subsequent general elections Chirac's supporters took 365 of the 577 seats in the new assembly.

Thus in 2002 Jacques Chirac was elected for a further five-year presidential term, backed by a massive majority in the assembly but on only the most general and vague of campaigns. In 2003, whether by calculation or inadvertence, the French government appeared to be the main obstacle to an agreement on Iraq in the UN Security Council. France was skeptical of the need to invade Iraq and jealous of its independent position in the Middle East but was ultimately powerless to prevent U.S. and coalition action. Chirac's stature as a president willing to stand up to the United States was undermined, however, by his brusque dismissal of those Europeans who did support the invasion of Iraq. After Saddam Hussein was overthrown, Chirac argued for a bigger UN role in the rebuilding of Iraq.

David Bell

See also: Gaulle, General Charles de; Giscard d'Estaing, Valéry; Iraq War; Mitterrand, François; NATO; 9/11: Political Perspectives; Pompidou, Georges.

References

Keeler, John T., and Martin Schain, eds. *Chirac's Challenge*. New York: St. Martin's Press, 1996.
Knapp, Andrew. *Gaullism since de Gaulle*. Aldershot: Dartmouth, 1994.

CHOPIN, KATE (KATHERINE O'FLAHERTY) (1850–1904)

U.S. writer of short fiction and two published novels, profoundly influenced by and responsive to French writing and culture.

Born in 1850 of an Irish immigrant father and French Creole mother, Katherine O'Flaherty married a Creole businessman, Oscar Chopin, and moved from her home city of Saint Louis, Missouri, to New Orleans, Louisiana, and then (after her husband's financial disasters in the 1870s) to Cloutierville, a small town in the rural Cane River area of the state. In both areas she was observing southern life at a time of considerable gender and racial tension and upheaval. Her fictional and poetic writing reflects those tensions, especially viewed from the perspective of the French Creole community of New Orleans and the French Acadian rural groups on Cane River. Her interest in these French-speaking people among whom she lived was part of a lifelong engagement with French culture. She visited Paris on her honeymoon (at the very moment of the imperial government's collapse and the Garde National's assumption of power) and read widely in French literature, even when—as a young widow—she returned to Saint Louis in 1883 and began to write fiction about French Louisiana at a geographical and emotional distance.

Chopin's biographer, Emily Toth, believes the writer met French painter Edgar Degas in New Orleans, during the five months of 1872 that he spent in the city, exploring his own troubled mixed-race identity and painting French Creole women thrown into shadow during and after the great upheaval of the Civil War. Toth attributes to Degas two names and a possible narrative thread in Chopin's most controversial and daring novel (now regarded as her masterpiece), *The Awakening* (1899). His intimate, painter Berthe Morisot, had an unhappily married friend, Edma Pontillon, a name extraordinarily similar to Edna Pontellier, the chosen name of Chopin's unsatisfactorily married and frustrated artist heroine. Furthermore, Degas's New Orleans neighbor, Léonce Olivier, had a wife América, who eloped suddenly to Paris with his brother René de Gas—and never returned. This scandal was the talk of the town, especially as Léonce was a decent if dull husband. In Chopin's novel, the abandoned husband is called Léonce Pontellier.

Like Degas, Kate Chopin was living in New Orleans at a time when racial unease and violence simmered beneath the surface, in a city recovering slowly and bitterly from a civil war it was still waging—not only between Union and Confederate factions but also between the dying French Creole order and the U.S. political and economic forces that sought to homogenize the city. Chopin gathered material for a novel that would reflect the divided houses, waning Creole power bases, and radically shifting nature of class, gender, and race relations in the postbellum city. And she did this by an insistent ironic reference to the Frenchness of her city and adopted community—a Frenchness that was no longer dominant or at ease in a postcolonial, postbellum U.S. city.

A recorder of two key Louisiana French cultures, as a half-French writer Chopin uses French names, literary works, and phrases throughout her writing. France is an imaginary and exotic site of nostalgia, yearning, and aspiration. Frenchness signifies desire, the illicit, and sexual pleasure in stories such as "A Point at Issue" and "Lilacs," as well as in her first published novel, *At Fault,* and her second, destroyed novel, which began with a Parisian scene and was reputedly explicit. In *The Awakening,* there are clear intertextual references to Guy de Maupassant and other French writers in terms of a feminized version of city streetwalking, the main character Edna transformed into a female flaneur. However, unlike Charles Baudelaire's classic anonymous and marginal Parisian man, Edna Pontellier can only masquerade as a flaneur. She walks through the city, but never with that relaxation or easy openness to erotic encounter of her lover Arobin or the city dweller celebrated by Walter Benjamin.

Helen Taylor

See also: Acadia; American Civil War; Degas, Hilaire Germain Edgar; Louisiana; New Orleans.

References

Taylor, Helen. *Gender, Race, and Region in the Writings of Grace King, Ruth McEnery Stuart, and Kate Chopin.* Baton Rouge: Louisiana State University Press, 1989.

———. "Walking through New Orleans: Kate Chopin and the Female Flâneur." *Symbiosis: A Journal of Anglo-American Literary Relations* 1, no. 1 (April 1997): 69–85.

Toth, Emily. *Unveiling Kate Chopin.* Jackson: University Press of Mississippi, 1999.

CHOQUETTE, ROBERT (1905–1991)

Poet, novelist, radio and television scriptwriter, journalist, and diplomat, born on April 22, 1905, in Manchester, New Hampshire.

Through his writings, his diplomatic functions, and his active participation in the literary life of Quebec, Robert Choquette played an important role in the promotion and spread of French Canadian culture abroad. Born to Québécois parents who had emigrated to the United States, Choquette moved to Montreal with his family in 1913. In 1917, he began his studies at the Collège Saint-Laurent and went on to obtain an English-language baccalaureate at Loyola College. His literary career began in 1925, when he published his prize-winning first collection of poetry, *A travers les vents* (Through Winds). Following a period of work at the Montreal English-language daily *The Gazette,* from 1927 to 1930 he was director of *La Revue moderne.* At the same time, he was vice president and secretary of the French section of the Association of Canadian Authors. In 1932, inspired by a trip to New York, he published his second collection of poems, *Metropolitan Museum,* which again won the David prize, tied with his good friend the poet Alfred DesRochers. This collection introduced the notion of urban life and, more broadly, the modernity of metropolitan centers to French Canadian poetry. His fourth collection of poetry, *Suite marine,* published in 1953, garnered a third David prize as well as prizes in France. From 1927 to 1975, Choquette also published five novels, a play, a collection of legends, and six essays, as well as contributions to journals and newspapers.

The development of French radio in Quebec at the end of the 1920s marked a shift in Choquette's career. In addition to his literary and poetic works, he created numerous radio programs from 1930 to the 1970s, as well as writing the script for some 5,500 episodes of radio and TV serials, genres in which he was to become a pioneer. His radio and television work ably mixed rural and urban themes, a duality that coincided with changes in the society and imagination of Quebec.

Choquette spent many periods abroad: in France, from 1961 to 1963, he gave several interviews and participated in conferences focusing on his work and on French Canadian cultural life. In 1964, he was made consul general of Canada in Bordeaux and built many ties between Quebec and French institutions. From 1968 to 1970, he was Canadian ambassador to Argentina. He became president of the Société des écrivains canadiens in 1971 and president of the Académie canadienne-française from 1973, an institution he had helped to create in 1944.

As well as three David prizes, Robert Choquette received numerous distinctions, including companion of the Order of Canada in 1969. Today, a prize for literary creation awarded annually by Radio Canada carries his name.

Although it is the aesthetic value of his work that has been recognized by Quebec literary history, Choquette's role in the development of popular media culture and the spread of French Canadian literature abroad, especially in France, has also been recognized. Choquette died in Montreal on January 22, 1991.

Daniel Chartier and Dominic Marcil

See also: Argentina; Bordeaux; Literary Relations; Quebec.

References

Beausoleil, Claude. "Robert Choquette: A Neo-Romantic with Modernist Tones." *Eclipse,* no. 41 (1989): 10–54.

Legris, Renée. *Robert Choquette.* Montreal: Fides, 1972.

———. *Robert Choquette: Romancier et dramaturge de la radio-télévision.* Montreal: Fides, 1977.

CHRISTOPHE, HENRI (1767–1820)

Haitian revolutionary leader.

Following the assassination of Jean-Jacques Dessalines on October 17, 1806, Henri Christophe was declared provisional chief of government of the nascent Republic of Haiti. Probably Grenadian by birth, Christophe had spent time in the United States and had worked as a waiter, manager, and innkeeper before becoming a general in the Haitian slave insurrection. Christophe served first under the command of François Toussaint L'Ouverture and then, after Toussaint's deportation to France, of Dessalines himself as he led the combined mulatto and black forces to their final, decisive victory. Christophe was soon drawn into a civil war with Alexandre Sabès Pétion, one that lasted until 1820.

Like his predecessors, Toussaint L'Ouverture and Dessalines, Christophe pursued a cautious foreign policy: although he supported Thomas Clarkson, William Wilberforce, and the abolitionists, he assured the regional colonial powers that he would not interfere in the slave trade. In common with Pétion, King Christophe (he had himself crowned on June 2, 1811) refused to negotiate with France over Haiti's independence and sought the recognition of "the first black republic" by all world powers. His constitutions of 1807 and 1811 omitted Dessalines's prohibition of foreign ownership of Haitian property, and in general he encouraged free trade and foreign investment, particularly with Britain, which Christophe saw as a potential ally in resisting French attempts to recolonize Haiti. Christophe's anglophilia was such that he invited English schoolteachers to settle in Haiti and stated that he would make English Haiti's official language.

Internally, however, Christophe's autocratic policies became increasingly unpopular. He pursued Toussaint L'Ouverture and Dessalines's policy of reinvigorating the sugar, coffee, and cotton plantations by placing military and state officers in charge of strictly controlled laborers. Economically, this policy was something of a success, and the surplus generated was used on defense, most famously on the construction of the formidable Citadelle Laferrière. Politically, however, it was a deeply unpopular policy that led to an uprising, in the midst of which Christophe committed suicide in 1820. Christophe's tragic demise has attracted the attention of the major Caribbean writers of the twentieth century: Aimé Césaire, Edouard Glissant, and Derek Walcott have all written on this contradictory, enigmatic figure, and on the way Christophe, like the other major figures of the revolution, ultimately overturned the colonial rulers only to replace them with their own privileged cliques.

Martin Munro

See also: Césaire, Aimé; Dessalines, Jean-Jacques; Glissant, Edouard; Haiti; Slavery; Toussaint L'Ouverture, François.

References

Cole, Hubert. *Christophe: King of Haiti.* London: Eyre and Spottiswoode, 1967.

Geggus, David P., and David B. Gaspar, eds. *A Turbulent Time: The French Revolution and the Greater Caribbean.* Bloomington: Indiana University Press, 1997.

CINEMA, 1895–1945

Making an Atlantic comparison between France and the United States with regard to film is challenging, since both countries (and their respective film historians) claim to have invented motion pictures. In 1893, Thomas Edison created an imperfect machine, the Kinetograph, that simulated movement with a loop film, but without any projection system and no screen. The viewer had to look inside the lenses in a small hole in order to see the illusion of the movement of the images. However, in 1894, in France, the Lumière brothers (Auguste and Louis) invented a way to show motion pictures on a screen, and their first public (and paying) screening of the *Cinématographe* was held at the Grand Café, in Paris, on December 28, 1895. They presented some ten films, including *La Sortie des usines Lumière* (1894) and *L'Arroseur arrosé* (1895).

From the early days of motion pictures, the Lumière brothers conceived their invention as a way to educate the masses and show documentary images from all countries and cultures. They hired many cameramen to shoot images on all continents. In 1898, their catalog already had some 1,000 titles, most of them less than a minute long. Among the many locations in the Americas where the Lumière operators (especially Félix Mesguisch) presented French-made films in 1896 were Boston, Brooklyn, Buenos Aires, Caracas, Chicago, New York, Philadelphia, Rio de Janeiro, São Paulo, and Washington, D.C., but also Guadeloupe, Guatemala, Chile, and Mexico. From then on, many famous settings in the Americas were filmed by the Lumière operators, mostly where they presented their own movie programs, such as in New York City, Boston, Chicago, and Mexico. They also went to Canada to film an "Indian Dance" near Montreal in 1898.

In the early twentieth century, French cinema was dominant worldwide at a time when Hollywood studios as we now know them were not yet established. French director Jean Durand tried to imitate the western genre with *Arizona Bill* (1909) and *Attaque d'un train* (*Attack on a Train,* 1910). Another French director, Victorin Jasset, adapted a popular serial story for the screen, from a U.S.-style hero named Nick Carter, in 1908.

French cinema was quite influential during the 1910s. For instance, Charlie Chaplin copied his tramp character from French actor Max Linder, a comic director who created numerous films inspired by the style of the Parisian *théâtre de boulevard* from the nineteenth century. In fact, Chaplin's assembly line in *Modern Times* (1935) was also copied from a very similar scene in René Clair's earlier film, *A nous la Liberté* (*Liberty for Us*, 1931).

It was only by the late 1910s that the major U.S. studios took control from most nations in terms of distribution networks, especially when France was defending its own border during World War I. Many good French directors from that era, like Léonce Perret, Maurice Tourneur, and his son Jacques Tourneur, all went to the United States in 1914. There, Perret directed almost twenty films that sometimes included references to France, including *La Fayette, We Come!* (1918). When Perret went back to France, he managed to initiate some coproductions such as *Madame Sans-Gène* (1923) with Gloria Swanson. Maurice Tourneur stayed in the United States until 1927 and afterward returned to France, staying even during World War II. In the same way, two brothers from Paris, director Albert Capellani and actor Paul Capellani, simultaneously emigrated to Hollywood from 1915 to 1922 after making a fine debut in France.

The end of the 1920s saw the coming of the talkies, which changed everything because the ease of reediting subtitles in silent films was replaced by the problem of dubbing. Experimental films gained a select audience during that period. Philadelphia-born photographic artist Man Ray had met Marcel Duchamp in New York City in 1915; Man Ray emigrated to Paris in 1921 and directed an avant-garde short film, *Retour à la raison* (1923), followed by *Emak Bakia* (1927) and *L'Etoile de mer* (1928), illustrating an animation based on a surrealist poem by Robert Desnos. Man Ray returned to the United States from 1940 to 1951 and went back to Paris until his death in 1976. Spanish-born Luis Buñuel, also a member of the Groupe Sur-

réaliste, directed his first movies in France (*Un Chien andalou*, 1929; *L'Age d'or*, 1930) before going to the United States and Mexico in the early 1930s. In fact, Buñuel received Mexican citizenship even though he is known and remembered for his French films.

The talkies prompted some producers (MGM, Paramount, Tobis) to shoot new movies in two or three versions (English, French, and sometimes German) in the early 1930s. At that time, it appeared easier to shoot films in many versions instead of dubbing them.

Jacques Tourneur began his career as his father's Maurice's assistant and directed his first films in France, such as *Tout ça ne vaut pas l'amour* (All That Is Not Worth Love, 1931). But Parisian-born Tourneur directed his most important movies in Hollywood, where he returned on his own in 1935, specializing in fantastic, gothic films like *Cat People* (1942) and *I Walked with a Zombie* (1943), both produced by RKO. Tourneur stayed in Hollywood for many decades, much longer than his father, and worked a little in England in the 1950s; he later returned to France to retire.

Some French directors went to the United States before the Nazi era. Jacques Feyder went to Hollywood from 1929 to 1931 after making ten films in France, Austria, Switzerland, and Germany. He was the first director to adapt the legendary story of Atlantis in 1921. In the United States, Feyder directed a silent film with Greta Garbo, *The Kiss* (MGM, 1929), and a few talkies before going back to France (although Feyder remained in Switzerland during World War II).

One of the most respected directors in France, René Clair, first tried a new career in England after the failure of his comedy

Le Dernier Milliardaire (*The Last Billionaire,* 1934); he later went to the United States in 1940. Clair directed Marlene Dietrich in *The Flame of New Orleans* (1941), and carried on with comedies such as *I Married a Witch* (1942) and drama in *And Then There Were None* (1945). He went back to France in 1946 to pursue his career and to become the first film director to be elected as a member of the Académie Française.

Another important French director, Julien Duvivier, began a brilliant career in France in 1919 and did some double versions (in French and German) of his films from 1931. He had much success with *Maria Chapdelaine* (1934), the first of three feature films adapted from the Louis Hémon novel and partly shot in Saguenay, Canada. French actor Jean Gabin played the role of lumberjack François Paradis and tried to imitate the Quebec accent. Four years later, Duvivier went to Hollywood to direct *The Great Waltz* (1938), went back to France afterward, and then returned to Hollywood in 1941 to do *Tales of Manhattan* (1942), *Flesh and Fantasy* (1943), and *The Impostor* (1944). The last film Duvivier directed in France before the war, a patriotic fresco titled *Untel père et fils* shot in 1940, opened first in 1943 in the United States, not France, where it would have been banned by the Nazis. The French première of that film came only in 1945.

After 1933 many German directors, actors, and technicians left their country to settle down in France, where they pursued their creative work, and later emigrated to the United States. The German directors who made at least one movie in France before going to Hollywood are numerous: Fritz Lang, Robert Siodmak, Billy Wilder, Max Ophuls, and G. W. Pabst. In 1932 the latter directed a wonderful remake of Pierre Benoit's novel *L'Atlantide,* set in Morocco but filmed in Berlin, in French, German, and English versions.

When the Nazis invaded France in 1940, the new political situation changed two elements in terms of the motion picture industry. First, many good directors and actors left France to go to the United States. The best French actors, such as Jean Gabin, Jean-Pierre Aumont, and Michèle Morgan, also emigrated to the United States from 1940. Second, since U.S. films were forbidden in France, movie theaters that were often full because they were warm and safe presented mainly bad German films from the 1940s and very good French films. The 1940–1944 years were a very prosperous era for French cinema in terms of artistic content and commercial success, even though most of these films were not exported to the United States before the end of the war. The lack of competition allowed French films to get the best audiences, thus encouraging producers to make more films in France. Emerging French directors included Henri-Georges Clouzot (*Le Corbeau/The Raven,* 1943) and Marcel Carné (*Les Enfants du paradis/Children of Paradise,* 1945); scripts by Jacques Prévert, Jean Giraudoux, and Jean Cocteau were successful. The hiatus in film trade between France and the United States went on for five years. It was only in 1945 that French audiences discovered for the first time the most important Hollywood movies made since the beginning of the decade, such as *Gone with the Wind* (1939), Chaplin's *The Great Dictator* (1940), Orson Welles's *Citizen Kane* (1941), and *Casablanca* (1942). But from 1945, the U.S. authorities made sure they could always count on the French audiences in the future by pushing the controversial Blum-Byrnes Agreement, which strove to eliminate the French quotas on film imports.

In some cases, emigration had durable consequences, as some European directors decided to stay in the United States even after the end of World War II. Strongly influenced by the Hollywood films of Erich von Stroheim, French director Jean Renoir was already famous in Europe during the 1930s, when he directed *La Chienne/The Bitch* (1931) and *La Bête humaine/The Human Beast* (1938), two movies that inspired Fritz Lang to produce remakes of them in Hollywood during the 1950s. After the failure of his film *La Règle du jeu/The Rules of the Game* (1939), Renoir went to Italy for a short while in 1940 and then left to go to Hollywood that same year in order to gain an international audience. During that period, Renoir alternated between conventional adaptations such as *Swamp Water* (1941) and *The Southerner* (1945) with propaganda films made for the free zone in Europe: *Vivre libre* (*This Land Is Mine,* 1943) and *Salut à la France* (*Salute to France,* 1944). Even though he would later work again in France (in the 1950s), Renoir went on living in Beverly Hills and even took U.S. citizenship. Jean Benoit-Lévy, another French director who went to the United States during World War II, wrote the first book about film ethics, which was in fact first published in Montreal: *Les Grandes Missions du cinéma* (Editions Léo Parizeau, 1945).

As European directors went to the United States, some U.S.-born artists made the reverse journey. Born in Middleton, Connecticut, in 1911, director Jules Dassin studied in France during the 1930s and made a few spy films in Hollywood in the early 1940s, including *Nazi Agent* (1942); he was later blacklisted during the McCarthy era and went to France to pursue his career, like Joseph Losey.

During World War II, some U.S. films mentioned the political situation in Europe, and many sympathized with France during the occupation. Perhaps the cult movie par excellence, Michael Curtiz's *Casablanca* included some talented European actors (the Londonian Claude Rains, the Swede Ingrid Bergman) and some émigré German actors from the expressionist era (Conrad Veidt, from *The Cabinet of Dr. Caligari;* Peter Lorre, from Fritz Lang's famous *M*). All these characters were cast around Humphrey Bogart. Set in North Africa while Morocco was still a colony of occupied France, *Casablanca* illustrated perfectly the specific alliances and tensions in the Atlantic triangle during World War II. The same winning ingredients were mixed again in 1944 into another film, *A Passage to Marseilles.*

As his own war effort, Alfred Hitchcock (who was fluent in French) directed two short films in French: *Bon voyage* (1944) and *Aventure malgache* (1944). After directing *The Negro Soldier* (1943), a tribute to the African roots of the African American soldiers, Frank Capra supervised another propaganda documentary titled *Tunisian Victory* (1943), about the Allies' campaign in North Africa during World War II. But as Suzanne Langlois (2001) explains, most of the strongest images from World War II were seen after 1944, when people in liberated France viewed the illicit documentary images that were shot in the occupied zone since 1940, for instance in *La Libération de Paris* (1944), showing the Allies in France.

In Quebec, the shortage of films from occupied France became a problem when audiences tired of always seeing reruns of the same pre-war movies from Marcel Pagnol and others. U.S. films presented in their original version without any dubbing or subtitles were everywhere. The solution was the creation of a new film industry. Some Canadian producers established companies dedicated to cinema, and they made some of the first Canadian films; some were in fact directed by filmmakers who came mostly from France, such as Jean-Marie Poitevin (*A La Croisée des chemins*/At the Crossroads, 1943) and René Delacroix. With the exclusive help of a Canadian producer, France-Film, Delacroix went to France to codirect a religious film, *Notre-Dame de la Mouïse* (1941) and later a co-production between France and Canada titled *Docteur Louise* (1949). Fedor Ozep, who left Russia for France in the mid-1930s, emigrated to Quebec for a few years, where he directed films in French such as *Le Père Chopin* (1944), known in France under the title *L'Oncle du Canada,* followed by French and English versions of *La Forteresse/Whispering City* (1949), shot in Quebec City.

The years after World War II saw the emergence of francophone films in Montreal and the growing omnipresence of Hollywood in Europe.

Yves Laberge

See also: Blum-Byrnes Agreement; Chile; Cinema, 1945 to the Present; Cocteau, Jean; Dassin, Jules; Duchamp, Marcel; Duvivier, Julien; Hémon, Louis; Language; Losey, Joseph; *Maria Chapdelaine;* Mexico; Montreal; Morgan, Michèle; Quebec; Ray, Man; Surrealism; Tourneur, Jacques; Tourneur, Maurice; World War I; World War II.

References

Barnier, Martin, and Raphaëlle Moine, eds. *France/Hollywood: Echanges cinématographiques et identités nationales.* Paris: L'Harmattan, 2002.

Langlois, Suzanne. *La Résistance dans le cinéma français 1944–1994: De La Libération de Paris à Lebera me.* Paris: L'Harmattan, 2001.

Legrand, Jacques, ed. *Chronique du cinéma.* Bassillac: Editions Chronique et Jacques Legrand, 1996.

Lévy, Jean-Benoit. *Les Grandes Missions du cinéma.* Montreal: Editions Léo Parizeau, 1945.

Rittaud-Hutinet, Jacques. *Auguste et Louis Lumière: Les 1000 premiers films.* Paris: Philippe Sers éditeur, 1990.

CINEMA, 1945 TO THE PRESENT

The history of Franco-American cinematic relations is highly complex and yet only too frequently is reduced to a simplistic story of Hollywood's cultural imperialism and valiant French attempts to defend domestic cinema. Prior to the outbreak of World War I, French films represented around 60 percent of the global market and dominated the U.S. market. However, the industry was badly hit by the war years and never fully recovered. The rapidly expanding and increasingly powerful Hollywood industry gradually increased its hold on world markets, and the advent of sound technology in the 1930s and the heyday of U.S. studio production up until the end of the 1940s meant that French cinema never managed to regain its former authority. A love-hate relationship was established. Admiration for the foreign product in both countries was matched by fears of U.S. economic might (in France) and criticism of

French protectionism and elitism (in the United States).

A number of events and statements provide ample illustration of this relationship. At the world conference for ministers of culture organized by the United Nations Educational, Scientific, and Cultural Organization (UNESCO) and held in Mexico in July 1982, Jack Lang, then France's minister of culture, made an infamous speech in which he decried the invasion of American cultural products, calling for a true program of cultural resistance. Lang was explicit in his condemnation, describing this American influx as cultural and financial imperialism and stressing the need to reinforce France's cultural position in the world economy. At the heart of this cultural crusade were the audiovisual media, particularly film and television. Lang envisaged a new European cultural order, led by France, that would provide a counterbalance to the economic might of the dominant culture industries, specifically those of the United States.

These discourses continued to be voiced by various French commentators throughout the 1980s and reached a head in the early 1990s with the reactions to the negotiations of the Uruguay Round of the General Agreement on Tariffs and Trade (GATT) and French calls for a "cultural exception." Attempts to deregulate the audiovisual market revealed the apparent incommensurability of European (specifically French) and North American conceptions of commerce and culture. U.S. executives proposed a trade agreement that would provide equal opportunities for American intellectual services (including the audiovisual industry). They sought curbs on public funding for audiovisual production through European subsidies and objected to levies imposed on foreign films shown in France. Moreover, they argued that European quota systems inhibited equal access to markets and thus contravened the ethos of GATT.

In marked contrast, the French government called for *l'exception culturelle,* the exclusion of the audiovisual industries from the GATT agreement. France claimed that the loss of a form of protection for indigenous cinema and television industries would signal the end of European production and mean total dominance of the European markets by the United States. The negotiations became a clash of ideologies, between a French tradition of state cultural policy and aid for the audiovisual industries and a U.S. rejection of any form of public regulation of culture and a total commitment to free trade.

It is important to stress that the European position was largely a reaction to French governmental pressure. Indeed, in many European states, particularly Britain, the debate was perceived as being between the United States and France alone. The outcome of the negotiations in the form of a decision to exclude the audiovisual industries from GATT was hailed as a great victory by the French government.

Lang's speech and the GATT discussions may well be just two incidents in a long and complex history, but they merit mention here because they clearly demonstrate the rift that separates French and U.S. conceptions of the audiovisual industries. For the U.S. negotiators, audiovisual production was no more than an industry and should be treated in the same way as any other form of material production. As an industry, film and television should be entirely deregulated, and according to hegemonic U.S. free-market ideologies, this would lead to diversity and consumer choice. Attitudes in France were quite different. There existed a wide consensus that deregulation of the audiovisual industries would lead to a standardization dominated by Hollywood. Above all, there was a widespread insistence in France upon the cultural importance of audiovisual production and the necessity of separating this practice from other forms of industrial production. Cultural production was placed at the center of national identity; to forgo protection of the film and television industries would mean an end to French *différence* and an attendant U.S. hegemony. Such convictions were widespread and were voiced by politicians, journalists, intellectuals, and members of the industry from across the political spectrum. In December 1993, Jacques Toubon, minister of culture for the incumbent right-wing government, echoed the remarks made by his left-wing predecessor in Mexico, calling for a more active international cultural policy that would enter into direct combat with U.S. production and the threat of cultural uniformity. To show that he meant business, Toubon went on to finance ninety supplementary copies of Claude Berri's *Germinal* (1993) in order to prevent Spielberg's *Jurassic Park* (1993) from dominating French cinemas as it had dominated those of other countries.

These discourses can be seen as part of an enduring articulation in France of the threat of American culture, particularly Hollywood cinema. The Blum-Byrnes Agreement of 1946, for example, gave rise to reactions very similar to those mobilized around the GATT. Both agreements involved a whole set of economic measures between France and the United States, but they have typically been reduced in France to the cinema measures, which, it was claimed, very nearly brought about the end of French cinema. This claim itself is extremely simplistic, but the outcry caused by both these agreements and the resistance to the GATT both serve to underline the enduring nature of French fears about the impact of Hollywood cinema on the domestic industry.

French cinema does indeed exist in a global cinematic economy dominated by Hollywood and is dependent upon various forms of protection and subsidy in order to retain a space in both the domestic and foreign markets. Moreover, despite the attempts at deregulation described above, Hollywood does indeed practice a number of forms of protectionism, notably the very limited distribution of foreign films in the U.S. market.

However, to describe Hollywood production as a straightforward threat to French cinema is to deny the sheer complexity of the various processes of influence and exchange between the two industries and moreover the difficulties inherent in attempting to categorize films as straightforwardly French or American. Since the very early days of film production, the relations between French cinema and Hollywood and the ways in which they have responded to one another have had a profound impact on these apparently distinct cinemas. The remaking of French films in Hollywood and the presence of French émigré personnel in the U.S. market are but two examples of this interaction. Examples of intertextuality and exchange at the level of film style and narrative are plentiful. Perhaps the best-known examples are the films of the French *nouvelle vague* and their deliberate and self-conscious quoting of U.S. cinema. Jean-Luc Godard's *A bout de souffle* (*Breathless,* 1959) pays explicit homage to U.S.

cinema via its referencing of Hollywood B-movies and Humphrey Bogart, while simultaneously challenging the rather turgid conventions of contemporary French production. More recently, directors such as Luc Besson have turned to the aesthetics of Hollywood and given them a distinctly French twist in an attempt to revivify French popular cinema. Examples include recent domestic box-office successes such as *Taxi* (Gérard Pirès, 1998) and its sequel *Taxi 2* (Gérard Krawczyk, 2000), both scripted by Luc Besson, which transfer the decidedly American car-chase movie to the streets of Marseilles and Paris. Tellingly, and despite French anxieties about Hollywood, the government-sponsored agency Unifrance, dedicated to the promotion of French cinema overseas, has played an active role in selling remake rights to U.S. producers and has long been a presence at the annual Sarasota French Film Festival in the United States.

Ultimately, it may be vital to retain some degree of support for French attempts to protect indigenous cinema. If Hollywood production typically represents around 70 percent of box-office takings in France, as opposed to between 80 and 90 percent in Britain, it is largely due to various forms of government support and subsidy. However, we should also remember that if, as these figures suggest, Hollywood films have a very forceful presence in French cinemas, then they clearly become an integral part of French cultural life. It is worth pointing out that the U.S. films that do well in France are not *necessarily* the same films that do well elsewhere, and they are not *necessarily* consumed and received in the same way. Finally, any consideration of Franco-American cinematic relations

should recall that Hollywood films contribute sizable sums of money to the *compte de soutien* (support account), via a levy on box-office receipts and as a result, albeit in a roundabout way, play a key role in the continuation of fresh and innovative French cinema.

Lucy Mazdon

See also: Anti-Americanism; Besson, Luc; Blum-Byrnes Agreement; GATT; Godard, Jean-Luc; Lang, Jack.

References

Austin, Guy. *Contemporary French Cinema.* Manchester: Manchester University Press, 1996.

Forbes, Jill. *The Cinema in France.* London: Macmillan, 1992.

Hayward, Susan. *French National Cinema.* London: Routledge, 1993.

Mazdon, Lucy, ed. *France on Film: Reflections on Popular French Cinema.* London: Wallflower, 2001.

CIRQUE DU SOLEIL

The first circus of Québécois origin to have gained international recognition.

Cirque du Soleil is a modern circus that breaks with tradition by banning animals from the ring in favor of human talent, costumes, colored lighting effects, and magical music. It was created in 1984 by young street artists under the leadership of Guy Laliberté, himself an accordionist, stilt walker, and fire-eater, during the Fête foraine de Baie-Saint-Paul, a festival in Baie Saint Paul that brought together many public entertainers. This event led the Quebec government to ask the group, known at the time as Le Club des talons hauts, to put on a show for the celebration of the 450th anniversary of the voyage to Canada by Jacques Cartier. Cirque du Soleil was thus born with the financial support of the Quebec government, and it toured in Quebec and the following year in Ontario.

This commission was the beginning of a great adventure that continues through the creation of high-quality, creative, and diverse shows staged for all audiences, as well as through the spread of a whole variety of connected activities. Although continuing to specialize in the creation of shows in the big top or in theaters (such as, for example, the Bellagio in Las Vegas or the Walt Disney Resort in Orlando), Cirque du Soleil has created its own multimedia division, which produces films, videos, music, DVDs, and television programs for which Cirque has received numerous prizes.

Cirque du Soleil is recognized for the cultural diversity of its artists and artisans, as well as for its blending of artistic and acrobatic disciplines. It has become a true cultural business. Its headquarters in Montreal employ more than 2,700 people, of which approximately one-quarter are artists, the primary sources of Cirque's rich success. Since 1984, Cirque has produced fifteen creations, including such classics as *Saltimbanco, Alegria, Quidam, Dralion,* and *Varekai.* Now set up in the United States for four permanent shows, the Cirque took a new tack in 1998 with *"O,"* a show that was staged entirely in water and was presented at the Bellagio in Las Vegas. More controversial, the 2003 creation *Zumanity* was an adults-only show.

Since Cirque first started, more than 40 million spectators in ninety cities across five continents have watched the Cirque du Soleil's magical performances. Cirque has received numerous prizes and awards: Emmy, Drama Desk, Bambi, and Ace Awards; Gémeaux, Gemini, and Félix

Members of Cirque du Soleil performed at a benefit concert called Quebec/New York, in Montreal September 28, 2001. The benefit concert contained over 100 Quebec artists, including singer Céline Dion, to help raise funds for the victims of the suicide hijackings in New York City on September 11. (Reuters/Corbis)

prizes; and the Golden Rose at the Montreux Comedy Festival in Switzerland. It also won the Prix du Centre national des arts du gouverneur general du Canada in 2000, as well as being given its own star on the Canadian Walk of Fame in Toronto.

Sonia Lebel

See also: Cartier, Jacques; Ontario; Quebec.
References
Boudreault, Julie. *Le Cirque du Soleil: La création d'un spectacle: Saltimbanco.* Quebec: Nuit blanche, 1996.
Harvie, Jennifer, and Erin Hurley. "States of Play: Locating Quebec in the Performances of Robert Lepage, Ex Machina, and the Cirque du Soleil." *Theater Journal* 51, no. 3 (1999): 299.

CITROËN (AUTOMOBILES CITROËN)

Citroën was one of the world's first automobile manufacturers and, as part of the PSA Peugeot Citroën group, is now the largest private car manufacturer in France. It has plants in twelve countries and sales in eighty-five countries.

The company was founded in 1913 by André Citroën as the Citroën Gear Company, developing gearing technology that resembled the chevrons that today form its logo. Citroën was key to the importing of modern industrial working practices into France, and its Type A was the first mass-produced car in Europe, made starting in 1919 at the Quai de Javel factory in Paris.

Citroën first became known in foreign markets in 1921, a year in which it exported around 3,000 cars, though arguably its first transatlantic claim to fame came when Charles Lindbergh used the lights of the Citroën logo, shining the full length of the Eiffel Tower from 1925 to 1934, as a navigation beacon for his solo flight across the Atlantic in 1927. Then began a long expansion through a network of subsidiaries. Other corporate landmarks include the introduction of the 5CV Type C in 1922, the so-called democratized car, also dubbed the first lady's car and painted yellow, earning it the nickname "Petite Citron."

After the 1929 stock market crash, Citroën entered a financial crisis that ended with the government asking Michelin, the company's chief creditor, to bail it out in 1934 in return for financial control. André Citroën died in 1935.

In 1936, morale began to return with the start of work on the 2CV, or *deux chevaux* (2 horesepower), first conceived of as an umbrella on four wheels, though production was delayed until 1948 because of World War II (the *New York Times* called it a cross between a frog and a camel). In 1943 Citroën produced no cars at all and refused to comply with the Vichy government.

In 1962, during a decade of international expansion, Citroën established a sales subsidiary in Montreal. An increase in exports to 55 percent of the total sales volume helped the company recover from the 1973 oil crisis.

Peugeot's share in the company had risen to 90 percent by 1976, when the PSA holding company was created, and in the mid-1980s Citroën underwent a complete brand overhaul, with advertising that included a herd of thoroughbred horses and a change in color for the dealership network from blue and yellow to red and white. The last 2CV rolled off the assembly line in 1990.

At the time of writing, PSA's operations in the Americas include two plants in Argentina and one in Brazil. PSA Peugeot Citroën's sales of 30,000 vehicles are up from 18,000 in 1998 but are dwarfed by the more than 1 million vehicles sold in Western Europe.

Mark Vernon

See also: Argentina; Automobiles; Brazil; Michelin; World War II.

References
Ducorray, R. *Dates.* 1991.
"Valiant Little Champion of the Road, Au Revoir." *New York Times,* March 9, 1988.
"Why a Little Car Won a Big Place in Europe's Heart." *Wall Street Journal,* July 11, 1984.

CLAIR, RENÉ (RENÉ-LUCIEN CHOMETTE) (1898–1981)

One of the greatest French film directors of the classic era, born in Neuilly, near Paris, who also wrote extensively about the medium of cinema.

Despite being classified among the top five French directors of the 1930s, alongside Jean Renoir, Julien Duvivier, Jacques Feyder, and Marcel Carné, and also displaying populism in his work, Clair made films quite apart in tone from the pessimistic "poetic realism" of his peers. Clair started in the film business as an actor and critic before moving to directing as an assistant to Jacques de Baroncelli in the mid-1920s and joining the avant-garde. His first notable silents were *Entracte* (1924), *Un Chapeau de paille d'Italie* (*An Italian Straw Hat*, 1928), an international success, and *Les Deux Timides* (1928), already showing his light, witty, satirical style with a lot of movement and apt comic timing. In the many articles and essays Clair wrote on film aesthetics and techniques, he always emphasized the importance of motion and rhythm, which were indeed characteristic of his films (*Cinema Yesterday and Today*, 1972; *Reflections on the Cinema*, 1953). Not hampered by the advent of sound, Clair in fact studied its possibilities carefully, using it creatively as a means to further and complement the meaning of images, as in *A nous la Liberté/Liberty for Us* or *Le Million* (both 1931). Like his contemporaries, Clair's favorite subject in the 1930s was working-class Paris and its people, yet he was more interested in showing the comical absurdity of urban life than its alienating or threatening nature. In that respect, Clair's representation of the modern city was closer to Charlie Chaplin's than Carné's. Russian émigré Lazare Meerson designed the sets on *Un Chapeau de paille, Les Deux Timides, Sous les toits de Paris* (Under the Roofs of Paris, 1930), *A nous la Liberté, Le Million,* and *Quatorze Juillet/14 July* (1933), contributing to Clair's representation of Paris. Clair left for Great Britain in 1936 and directed the whimsical comedy *The Ghost Goes West* (1936) and *Break the News* (1938) with Maurice Chevalier, before spending the war years in Hollywood. Of the French directors exiled in Hollywood, Clair is probably the one who enjoyed the most success, with *The Flame of New Orleans* (1941), starring Marlene Dietrich, *I Married a Witch* (1942) with Veronica Lake, *Forever and a Day* (codirector, 1943), *It Happened Tomorrow* (1944) with Dick Powell and Linda Darnell, and *And Then There Were None* (1945). Returning to France after the war, Clair directed Chevalier again, but this time in French, in *Le Silence est d'or* (1947), an interesting and underrated film about the days of silent cinema. Despite some success with films starring Gérard Philipe (*La Beauté du diable*, 1950; *Les Belles de nuit*, 1952; *Les Grandes Manoeuvres*, 1955), Clair's postwar films did not revive the interest he had inspired in the 1920s and 1930s.

Catherine Hellegouarc'h

See also: Chevalier, Maurice; Cinema, 1895–1945; Cinema, 1945 to the Present; Duvivier, Julien; Renoir, Jean; World War II.

References

Billard, Pierre. *Le Mystère René Clair.* Paris: Plon, 1998.

Dale, R. C. *The Films of René Clair.* Metuchen, NJ: Scarecrow Press, 1986.

McGerr, Celia. *René Clair.* Boston: Twayne, 1980.

CLAUDEL, PAUL-LOUIS-CHARLES-MARIE (1868–1955)

French author, born in Villeneuve-sur-Fère.

Paul Claudel had a fascinating and durable relationship with the United States. Beginning in the late nineteenth century and extending well into the post–World War II period, he was that oddest of creatures—a poet-ambassador. Outside of his contribution to French letters, Claudel is remembered for comments on U.S. affairs in three different stages of his life; first, as a deeply impressed observer (and critic) of U.S. capitalism in the 1890s, second as the French ambassador in Washington during the tense years 1927–1933, and finally, as a pro-American who was nonetheless cynical about U.S. policy at the end of World War II—a stance somewhat compromised by Claudel's less-than-sterling Resistance credentials.

Claudel is one of modern France's greatest playwrights and poets, a symbolist who dissented from his cohort in his strong devotion to Christianity. His odd, biblically influenced prose has been called "psalmlike," and his religious dedication is evident everywhere in his work. Like his contemporary Charles Péguy, Claudel adhered to a Catholic worldview that, although extremely conservative, was never reactionary, and his second career as a diplomat suggests the extent to which this man of God was engaged with mundane worldly concerns.

After graduating from Lycée Louis le Grand, Claudel entered the Ecole Libre de Sciences Politiques, where his interest in Edgar Allan Poe, complemented by his admiration for Eugène Lavasseur (an economist convinced of the link between true

French author Paul Claudel is remembered for favorable—and critical—comments on American affairs. (Library of Congress)

spiritual freedom and a free-market economy), convinced him to seek an appointment in the United States. In 1893, aged twenty-seven, he accepted a position in the young Third Republic's diplomatic corps as a vice consul in New York and later consul general to Boston. Fascinated and repelled by U.S. dynamism, Claudel began a lifelong association with the New World—his interest in the United States also always being part of his personal struggle with modernity.

A half-forgotten play survives from Claudel's writing in this era, *L'Echange*. It is the overblown story of a part American Indian forced to "sell" his French wife to a U.S. capitalist because of his debts. These thinly veiled symbols capture Claudel's mood—romantic Native Americans; good, simple French Catholics; and practical but morally dubious U.S. capitalists, all struggling on the American frontier. It remains an intriguing play, not least because Claudel makes the U.S. capitalist a mouthpiece for economic ideas he himself shared.

This play would have been of little interest had Claudel not been appointed, to the surprise of many, French ambassador to Washington in 1927. Although an unremarkable official, Claudel nonetheless won over the Washington establishment. Officially, he conformed to the pro-Americanism of André Tardieu rather than the Americanophobia of Georges Duhamel, yet his letters and private correspondence show a man still struggling with his ambivalence toward U.S. capitalism, as well as an increasing contempt for Protestantism.

At the end of World War II and approaching eighty years of age, private citizen Paul Claudel again accepted public positions, speaking out in favor of the Atlantic Charter. But he had also, however, made some famously anti-American remarks in his diaries, including some comparisons to Nazi Germany. The impressions formed by his youth remained unreconciled, and for all his public pro-Americanism, the issue of whether the United States was a model or a warning for France seems never to have been settled for Paul Claudel.

Seth Armus

See also: Anti-Americanism; Catholic Church; Duhamel, Georges; Poe, Edgar Allan; World War II.

References

Humes, Joy Nachod. *Two against Time: A Study of the Very Present Worlds of Paul Claudel and Charles Péguy.* Chapel Hill: University of North Carolina Press, 1978.

Knapp, Bettina. *Paul Claudel.* New York: Ungar, 1982.

Mathy, Jean-Philippe. *Extrême Occident: French Intellectuals and America.* Chicago: University of Chicago Press, 1993.

COCA-COLA COMPANY

Coca-Cola enjoys 51 percent of the worldwide soft drinks market, with 160 products distributed in over 200 countries, and is arguably the best-known global brand. North America represents about one-third of its sales, where it also owns the Minute Maid Company and Schweppes Beverages, including the Canada Dry brand.

The company's proficiency is widely admired and said to be based upon four excellences: consumer marketing, infrastructure (production and distribution), product packaging, and customer marketing (including to vendors).

But the founder, Dr. John Styth Pemberton, knew none of this success. In 1869, he came to Atlanta, and by 1886 he had invented a mixture of sugar, water, coca extracts, and kola nut, adding caffeine so that it could be marketed as a headache cure. A label in 1887 read: "Makes not only a delicious and invigorating beverage but a valuable Brain Tonic and cure for all nervous afflictions."

He died the next year, when the company was owned by Asa G. Chandler. Chandler's philanthropic zeal led to success. By 1895, the drink could be bought all over the United States, and sales were growing in Canadian cities. The first bottling franchise was established in 1899, a key to speeding up expansion, and by 1911 the marketing budget had reached a massive $1 million (by which time all references to medicinal benefits had been dropped). In 1916, the curved shape of the Coke bottle could be seen in the shops.

In 1923, Winship Woodruff became president, and he stabilized the company financially, as well as introducing such innovations as the six-pack, the suggestion that the drink was good for home consumption,

Coca-Cola advertisement, late nineteenth century. By 1895, Coca-Cola could be bought all over America, and sales were growing in Canadian cities. (Library of Congress)

and vending machines. By 1930 a quality control program ensured that Coca-Cola tasted the same wherever it was bought.

World War II put Coke firmly on the road to global domination. The company committed to providing any person in uniform with a bottle for five cents regardless of where they were stationed. Coca-Cola became identified with the American way of life, and plants were set up in Europe and North Africa. In the 1950s the company opened up to twenty plants a year as expansion continued, and by 1969, 6 billion gallons of the drink had been sold.

The "It's the Real Thing" advertising campaign was launched in the 1960s to combat the appearance of rival Pepsi Cola. In the 1980s, Coca-Cola enjoyed the most successful brand extension in history, with

the launch of Diet Coke, now the number three soft drink in the world, and committed one of its biggest blunders when it tried to change the original drink.

Introduction to France did not at first go smoothly. The Communist Party teamed up with vineyard owners in resistance. But their efforts were futile, and the first bottling plant opened in 1919. Another difficult period in France came in 1997, when the company tried to buy Orangina from Pernod Ricard. The government blocked the sale, citing anticompetitive practices. The purchase of the Schweppes brand was similarly resisted, although it went through in 1999. Coca-Cola now faces other difficulties, notably the launch of a French Islamic version of the drink, Mecca Cola. For now, though, Coca-Cola's dominance seems secure: although country sales are kept secret, the scale of its presence is indicated by the fact that it operates five production facilities, two distribution warehouses, and seven sales centers in France and is responsible for 14,000 direct and indirect jobs.

Mark Vernon

See also: Mineral Water; World War II.

References
Hays, Constance L. *Pop: Truth and Power at the Coca-Cola Company.* London: Hutchinson, 2004.
Oliver, Thomas. *The Real Coke: The Real Story.* London: Macmillan, 1987.
Pendergast, Mark. *For God, Country, and Coca-Cola.* New York: Texere Publishing, 1993.

COCTEAU, JEAN (1889–1963)

One of the most versatile, prolific authors of the twentieth century, Jean Cocteau elaborated a personal conception of total art, which he defined in terms of the overarching notion of "poetry" and which found expression in a variety of fields, ranging from fiction to graphic art, from filmmaking to drama, and from couture to postage stamp design and mural painting. Cocteau was born into a middle-class family and became very early on associated with avant-garde circles in Paris. In 1915, he met Pablo Picasso, who had a lasting influence on his work. Only two years later, he collaborated with Picasso, the composer Erik Satie, and the director of the *Ballets russes,* Serge de Diaghilev, in the creation of a highly controversial ballet *Parade,* which propelled Cocteau to instant fame. His first book of poems, *Aladdin's Lamp* (1919), further established the iconoclastic reputation of an artist already known as the "Frivolous Prince" in Parisian bohemian circles. Cocteau turned this nickname into the title of another collection of poems he published at the age of twenty-one. By this time he had befriended and inspired the Group of Six (which gathered the representatives of the new musical avant-garde, such as Darius Milhaud, Francis Poulenc, and Georges Auric). During the 1920s, Cocteau published two novels: *Thomas l'imposteur* (*Imposter,* 1923) and *Les Enfants terribles* (1929), as well as a major work of criticism, *Le Rappel à l'ordre* (Return to Order, 1926). Apart from his landmark adaptation of *Beauty and the Beast* (1946), released in the United States in 1947, Cocteau's best-known cinematic work was his "Orphic Trilogy," which he started in 1930, with *The Blood of a Poet,* and continued with *Orpheus* (1949) and the *Testament of Orpheus* (1959). A quintessential exploration of the author's conception of poetic creation and of his personal

Jean Cocteau, standing on ladder, putting the finishing touches on his wall sketches of the life of Saint Peter in Saint Peter's Chapel, Villefranche, France, 1956. (Library of Congress)

mythology, based on the ancient myth of the poet who descended into the world of the dead in search of his lost love, the "Orphic Trilogy" ingeniously blends autobiographical and fictional elements into a self-reflexive, loosely structured meditation on human mortality and the timeless condition of art.

In December 1948, Cocteau traveled to the United States, where he met such figures as Greta Garbo, Charlie Chaplin, and Marlene Dietrich. He returned to France in January 1949 and during the flight home wrote the *Lettre aux Américains,* a critique of the lack of experimentation and creativity in American culture. His U.S. experiences formed the basis of part of Robert Lepage's play *Needles and Opium,* which also offers an account of Miles Davis's almost simultaneous trip to

Paris and encounter with French singer Juliette Greco. Following Cocteau's trip, the U.S. actor Yul Brynner made a cameo appearance (alongside Picasso and Cocteau's lifelong partner, Jean Marais) in the *Testament of Orpheus.* Cocteau became a Chevalier de la Légion d'Honneur in 1949, despite his earlier misguided salute to a fascist artist, Arno Becker. The exhibition of Cocteau's drawings that opened in November 2000 at the Andy Warhol Museum celebrated the influence of the charismatic French author on the work of the U.S. pop artist, while reminding the general audience and the critics of their shared aestheticization of the male body and their shared iconic status in the gay world.

Ramona Fotiade

See also: Avant-Gardes; Cinema, 1945 to the Present; Dance; Gay Movement; Lepage, Robert; Music (Classical); Painting; Surrealism.

References

Andra, Jean. "The Myth of the American Experience: Observations by Two Frenchmen, De Tocqueville and Cocteau." *Weber Studies: An Interdisciplinary Humanities Journal* 3 (spring 1986): 28–33.

Cocteau, Jean. *Professional Secrets: An Autobiography of Jean Cocteau.* New York: Harper and Row, 1972.

Evans, A. B. *Jean Cocteau and His Films of Orphic Identity.* Philadelphia: Art Alliance Press, 1977.

COFFEE

Coffee, today the second most valuable commodity traded legally around the world, has played a large role in spreading French culture, cuisine, and habits across the Atlantic. Until well into the nineteenth century, both a good deal of writing about the drink and copious amounts of the beans themselves reached the United States through French hands.

The coffee plant, *Coffea arabica,* originally grew as an understory shrub in the high forests of what is today Ethiopia. Coffee fruit and beans were initially used as a kind of energy food or stimulant by travelers, warriors, and Sufi monks. Exported first to Yemen and from there in stages around the center of the globe to locales warm and high enough to permit its cultivation, coffee was made into a beverage by the sixteenth century at the latest.

Street vendors sold coffee in Venice beginning in the 1630s, and the drink reached Marseilles by 1644, accompanied there by Turkish utensils for its preparation. The first recorded Western coffeehouse opened in Oxford, England, in 1650. Coffee appeared in Paris by 1657 and Versailles by 1664. The Café de Procope, opened in 1686, was perhaps not the first establishment to sell the drink in Paris but quickly became the best-known early French café, especially for its elegant use of marble, elaborate chandeliers, and tall mirrors. Imbibing coffee thus became a new public act in which all classes could hope to participate.

Thus the coffeehouses created an important new social niche between home and mosque or church. Here it was possible to exchange news, views, and gossip. Although some rulers appear not to have worried overly about the political implications of such interchange, others attempted to suppress the incipient public life of the coffeehouses by ordering their closure, for example, in edicts issued by the governor of Mecca in 1511 and by Charles II in 1675. Neither order served its purpose, as the Turkish houses quickly revived, and the

English king was forced to rescind his decree within weeks.

By 1721 some 300 cafes existed in Paris; possibly 2,000 dotted the city on the eve of the French Revolution of 1789. During the eighteenth century, coffee and later tea began to replace the beer soup that had long served as Europeans' breakfast, especially among the lower classes. In 1782 a French commentator remarked that every shopgirl and cook drank coffee and that it had reached even the bottom rungs of society.

The drink quickly jumped the Atlantic. The Dutch brought coffee to New Amsterdam by 1668 but apparently did not set up a regular shop to sell the beverage. Records of businesses in the early English colonies are scanty and sometimes tainted by the Boston–New York rivalry; in any event, a Mrs. Jones reportedly sold "Coffee and Chuchaletto" from a store in the former city by 1671, and the King's Arms coffeehouse appeared in the latter in 1696.

In the interim, coffee had become not merely a transatlantic but a global attraction. Following their nose for spices, well developed by the High Middle Ages, Western Europeans avidly pursued the new beverage and its exotic accoutrements. Coffee, tea, and chocolate were revolutionary in their role as the first nonalcoholic hot drinks served in Europe. Besides altering dietary patterns, coffee and tea facilitated the grinding labor required in factories by providing physical stimulation and at least the semblance of an occasional hot meal. For the better-off classes, coffee brought with it new forms of dress, furniture design and use, taste and sophistication, and objects of everyday use.

An Ottoman ambassador to the French court, Soliman Aga, arrived in Versailles to considerable enthusiasm in 1669. One of the most appealing items the ambassador brought with him was coffee. By virtue of his exalted rank, Soliman could limit his guests, and the coffee he offered, to the top ranks of the French nobility. Thus his visitors could properly distance themselves in their consumption and taste from would-be social climbers among the bourgeoisie. By the late 1690s the Duchess of Lesdiguières and her chambermaids dressed in Turkish costume whenever they served her coffee.

Tales of Turkey and Turkish style had captured the French imagination in a powerful way, manifested in plays by Molière and Racine, a travelogue by the Chevalier d'Arvieux, and the translation by Antoine Galland in 1704 of *The Arabian Nights' Entertainments*. But coffee, now an object of desire as well as a pleasant drink, would never have reached many members of the French elite, let alone the shopgirls, if it had not made a circuit across the Atlantic and back to the Old World. Once again, the Dutch led the way. Their skill at seafaring, organizing merchants and fighters, and utilizing capital allowed their conquest of the Spice Islands (the Moluccas) from Portugal in 1605. From spices it was an easy step to be thinking about the profit to be made in coffee. The Dutch East India Company came to dominate the coffee trade at Mocha (Yemen) in 1696, and in the same year the Dutch introduced the cultivation of coffee in Java and Surinam.

Having trees to spare, the Dutch gave one to the French government in 1714, which installed it in a Paris greenhouse. Although its distant relatives could already be found across the globe, this particular specimen might be called the mother tree. In 1723 a French naval officer took one of its offspring on a legendary voyage to Martinique, during which he reportedly shared his meager water ration with the plant. The shrub flourished in its new environment, and in turn its descendants spread throughout Latin America and ultimately back through Asia and the Pacific to replace diseased stock in the nineteenth century.

Although Martinique was coffee's first stop in the Caribbean, its major home in that region quickly became Haiti. Across Latin America, sugar and slavery grew simultaneously, with coffee only a short distance behind. From the tree's arrival in Haiti in the 1730s until the slave rebellion of 1791, the French colony supplied perhaps 50 percent of the world's coffee and 40 percent of its sugar. The two crops became voracious devourers of men and women even as they produced wealth and pleasure for Europeans.

The major works of avid coffee drinkers such as Denis Diderot, Immanuel Kant, Jean-Jacques Rousseau, and Voltaire quickly appeared in English and traversed the Atlantic; Voltaire's comedy *Le Café, ou l'Ecossaise,* which takes place entirely in a coffeehouse/inn, premiered in 1760. The play was translated into English in the same year as *The Coffee House, or Fair Fugitive.* It was convenient for the Americans to have French thought, style, and literature—in English translations—at hand as tension built in the eighteenth century between the British colonies south of Canada and the home country. The French, for all their ancien régime faults, could be elevated by the Americans in contrast to the increasingly irritating British. It was equally fortunate that the consumers of rebellious North America were situated so close to the French coffee-producing islands of the Caribbean. When colonists vented their anger at British taxes and monopolies by dumping tea into Boston Harbor in 1773, coffee could rise to the occasion. The Continental Congress soon passed a resolution condemning tea, making it almost a patriotic duty to drink coffee. Thomas Jefferson, surely owing in some measure to his stay in France from 1784 to 1789, seconded Americans' preference when he declared coffee "the favorite drink of the civilized world."

The French connection across the Atlantic through the medium of coffee grew stronger as time went on. By 1815 the word "café" began to replace "coffeehouse" in the United States, partly as a result of the young country's acquisition of New Orleans. As with most things related to the table, French terms dominated American notions of what coffee should be for many years, even if on the western shores of the Atlantic no one could make a cup worth drinking. It was not until a few American writers, notably Ernest Hemingway, and a few hundred thousand soldiers in two world wars tasted the European product that the desire for fine coffee began to gain ground in the United States.

Robert Thurston

See also: French Revolution; Haiti; Hemingway, Ernest; Jefferson, Thomas; Martinique; Molière; New Orleans; Sugar; Voltaire, François.

References

Pendergrast, Mark. *Uncommon Grounds: The History of Coffee and How It Transformed Our World.* New York: Basic Books, 1999.

Schivelbusch, Wolfgang. *Tastes of Paradise: A Social History of Spices, Stimulants, and Intoxicants.* Trans. David Jacobson. New York: Vintage Books, 1992.

Ukers, William H. *All About Coffee.* 2nd ed. New York: Tea and Coffee Trade Journal Company, 1935.

COHEN, GUSTAVE DAVID (1879–1958)

A French medievalist, born in Saint-Josse-ten-Noode, Belgium, Cohen was a refugee scholar in New York. He received doctorates in law, romance philology, and literature and, in addition to producing editions, adaptations, and translations, also published widely in fields related to French literary history, romance linguistics, folklore, pedagogy, and criticism. A frequent contributor on literature, culture, and politics to wireless and print media in France and the United States, Cohen was recognized by fellow academics and the public of his day as an authority on the performance history of early French theater.

While a professor at the Sorbonne in 1933, Cohen created the Groupe de théâtre médiéval (GTM), a student group known as the Théophiliens and considered part of a revivalist project. His previous faculty posts had included universities in Leipzig and Amsterdam, as well as Strasbourg in 1919, where Cohen saw himself defending the sovereignty of the French university from incursions across the Rhine. Seriously wounded in combat at Vauquois-en-Argonne in 1915, he implemented a program to educate refugee children in the Netherlands. His war service and the course of Franco-German relations helped shape Cohen's professional life and his public calls to protect France against perceived threats from Germany. In October 1940, he fell victim to Vichy's anti-Semitic statutes; suspended from university teaching, he sought exile in the United States.

Cohen's classicist friend Henri Grégoire contacted the New School's Alvin Johnson in New York, who coordinated an American campaign to secure funding from the Rockefeller Foundation for a nonquota visa and a position at Yale University. Cohen arrived in New York in August 1941. When the Comité français de libération nationale (CFLN) called Cohen to Algiers in 1943, he left New York as one of the most prominent Gaullist activists in the city.

He had worked with Alvin Johnson and Jacques Maritain to establish the Ecole Libre des Hautes Etudes on Fifth Avenue, assembling exiled French and Belgian scholars in a faculty of letters (administered by Cohen), a faculty of law and political science, a section of sciences, and satellite institutes. The governing council split over a proposition to affiliate the accredited school with the CFLN, echoing political divisions in the émigré community. The dispute that saw Maritain resign his presidency in 1944 pitted his principle of institutional autonomy against overt support for Charles de Gaulle of the kind embodied by Claude Lévi-Strauss and, by cable from Algiers, Cohen.

With Maritain's support, Cohen had organized the first of three consecutive summer encounters at Mount Holyoke College in 1942 and began to assemble an intercontinental list of participants, including Jean Wahl (a veteran of the intellectual gatherings known as "Décades de Pontigny"), Roman Jakobson (of the Ecole Libre), Lee Simonson, George Santayana, Wallace Stevens, and Katherine Anne Porter. Cohen devised a Joan of Arc commemoration in New York in 1943 featuring Shaw's *Saint Joan*. He staged the *Miracle de Théophile* at Yale with Wallace Fowlie as lead. Cohen visited Montreal in 1942 and 1943 to introduce two of his adaptations of Old French plays performed by Père Legault's Compagnons de saint Laurent, spoke to Canadian community groups about the war effort, and appeared on radio in Montreal promoting the plays. His war-related writings were collected in *Lettres aux Américains* (1942 and 1943).

Stephen Steele

See also: Gaulle, General Charles de; Joan of Arc; Lévi-Strauss, Claude; Maritain, Jacques; Stevens, Wallace; World War I; World War II.

References

Mehlman, Jeffrey. *Emigré New York: French Intellectuals in Wartime Manhattan (1940–1944).* Baltimore: Johns Hopkins University Press, 2000.

Solterer, Helen. "The Waking of Medieval Theatricality: Paris, 1935–1995." *New Literary History* 27, no. 3 (summer 1996): 357–390.

COLBERT, CLAUDETTE (LILY CLAUDETTE CHAUCHION) (1903–1996)

One of the most capable light comediennes in Hollywood history. Colbert was born on September 13, 1903, in Paris, the daughter of a banker, and arrived in the United States as a child. A chance meeting at a party in 1923 led to a string of ingenue roles on Broadway. She debuted onscreen in *For the Love of Mike* (Capra) in 1927. But it was as Poppaea, lounging nude in a bath of asses' milk in Cecil B. DeMille's *The Sign of the Cross* (1932), that Colbert got noticed. After another delectable turn in DeMille's salacious *Cleopatra* (1934), Colbert found her niche in the screwball comedy *It Happened One Night* (Capra, 1934). This cross-country caper was literate and sexy, earning Colbert an Academy Award as the spoilt heiress pursued by Clark Gable's cynical reporter in a genre that she would make her own. So indelible

was the mark Ellie Andrews made on the national psychology that when an admirer in *Since You Went Away* (Cromwell, 1944) concocts a recruiting poster in which Colbert hitches her skirt up, audiences could congratulate themselves for recalling a certain ruse to stop a passing car.

With her round, slightly feline face, plucked eyebrows, compact deportment, and velvety voice, Colbert exuded a combination of Gallic hauteur and chorus girl sauce that epitomized the "Continental" depression comedies at which she and her studio, Paramount, excelled. *Bluebeard's Eighth Wife* (Lubitsch, 1938) had Colbert purchasing a pair of pajama bottoms in a Nice haberdashers while Gary Cooper searched for a pair of tops. In *Midnight* (Leisen, 1939), Indiana chorine Eve Peabody masquerades at a Parisian society gathering as the Baroness Czerny, borrowing her name from the cabbie. In 1942, *The Palm Beach Story* (Sturges) knowingly traded on the characteristically Colbertian theme of opportunistic gold digger ritzing gullible millionaire. Marshaling herself for wartime solidarity, in 1944 Colbert earned an Academy Award nomination for her beleaguered midwestern housewife in *Since You Went Away*, a melodrama that blithely recalled *Imitation of Life* (Stahl), the 1934 soap opera in which Colbert's genteel white lady befriends her sassy black housekeeper. To such wartime vehicles as *So Proudly We Hail* (Sandrich, 1943), she brought a compassionate steadfastness that recalled a Paris valiantly awaiting liberation.

Colbert originally wanted to design clothes, and her sense of haute couture brought elegance to her every appearance. Appreciating that getting in costume

Claudette Colbert and Clark Gable hitchhiking in a scene from It Happened One Night. *Movie still. (Bettmann/Corbis)*

meant getting in character, she also did all her own makeup. Never late, always knowing her lines, she famously preferred her left profile and could be as particular as any leading lady. But she had worked with the finest directors of the classical period and remained popular through the 1950s, occasionally returning to the stage and making two films in France. In later life she lived in retired splendor in Barbados. Colbert's first husband was actor-director Norman Foster (1928–1935). In 1935 she married Dr. Joel Pressman, who died in 1968. She died after a series of strokes in 1996.

Richard Armstrong

See also: Cinema, 1895–1945; Cinema, 1945 to the Present.

References

DiBattista, Maria. *Fast-Talking Dames.* New Haven: Yale University Press, 2001.

Sarris, Andrew. *You Ain't Heard Nothin' Yet: The American Talking Film: History and Memory, 1927–1949.* New York: Oxford University Press, 1998.

COLBERT, JEAN-BAPTISTE (1619–1683)

French statesman.

Jean-Baptiste Colbert is remembered for his role in the downfall of his rival Nicolas Fouquet; his efforts to reform the French system of taxation and scale down national debt; his vigorous programs for constructing roads, shipyards, and harbors such as Brest and Rochefort; and his policies supporting commerce and colonization.

Colbert began his career as private secretary to Cardinal Mazarin, who recommended him to Louis XIV. In 1665, the French king appointed Colbert general comptroller of finances. He was then designated secretary of state for naval affairs in 1669 and set about revamping French naval administration, recruitment, and shipbuilding in hopes of increasing France's naval capacity and strength. As a practitioner of mercantilism, Colbert encouraged the growth of industry and agriculture, sought to break down trade barriers within France, and challenged Dutch and British commercial strength. Among his methods for establishing French marine and trade supremacy, Colbert privileged the establishment of trading companies and founded the West India Company (1664). He demonstrated a particular interest in the development of New France and demanded that it become self-sufficient and no longer exist at the mercy of maritime disasters. The colony quickly benefited from the implementation of a series of incentives to stimulate emigration through the prospects of owning tax-free land and engaging in hunting and fishing. Additionally, Colbert increased the labor supply for the colony by sending hundreds of indentured workers, settlers, and marriageable girls there annually. It is estimated that as a result of his emigration policy, the population of French-speaking Canada grew from 2,500 to more than 10,000. Other incentives included bonuses for men who married at age twenty or younger; colonists were also encouraged to marry native women who had converted to Catholicism. Parents in New France who failed to marry their sons before age twenty and their daughters before age sixteen were fined. The lure of the lucrative fur trade, however, shifted colonists' interests away from Colbert's vision of settlement. He tried in vain through various methods to regulate the fur trade.

A patron of the arts and sciences, Colbert is also remembered as founder of the Academy of Sciences and the Paris Observatory. His economic doctrine based upon the principles of mercantilism, nationalism, and state intervention has commonly come to be known as Colbertisme. Jean-Baptiste Colbert died in September 1683.

Maureen Waters

See also: Catholic Church; Fur Trade; New France; Rochefort.
References
Eccles, W. J. *The French in North America, 1500–1783.* Markham, ON: Fitzhenry and Whiteside, 1998.
Trout, Andrew. *Jean Baptiste Colbert.* Boston: Twayne, 1978.

COLETTE (SIDONIE-GABRIELLE COLETTE) (1873–1954)

One of the most celebrated French writers of the twentieth century, born in Saint-Sauveur-en-Puisaye, France, in 1873.

Colette's novels, journalism, and autofiction are characterized by a lyrical attentiveness to people, nature, and animals; a

French writer Colette, author of Gigi. *Colette made her first and only visit to the United States in 1935. (Library of Congress)*

wry irreverent humor; and great stylistic originality. She has been exceptionally well translated into English, notably by Enid McLeod, Roger Senhouse, and David le Vay. Colette claimed transatlantic blood connections, made a single well-publicized trip to the United States, and saw one of her stories adapted to become a hugely successful MGM musical.

It is probable, though unproven, that Colette's ancestry included a West Indian female forebear. In the auto-fictional *La Maison de Claudine* (*My Mother's House,* 1922), Colette recalls her mother, Sido (née Landoy), speaking of her father (hence Colette's maternal grandfather) as "Le Gorille." A daguerreotype of "the Gorilla" that

hangs on the wall explains the sobriquet: it shows "the head and shoulders of a 'colored man'—a quadroon, I believe—wearing a high white cravat, with pale, contemptuous eyes, and a long nose above the thick Negro lips that had inspired his nickname" (Colette 1966, p. 69). Claude Pichois and Alain Brunet, in their authoritative biography of Colette, agree with earlier biographers that at some point between the mid-seventeenth and eighteenth centuries members of the Landoy family emigrated to the West Indies and then returned to France, so that Henri Marie Landoy (1792–1854) may well have been the descendant of a white Landoy and a black "Antillaise." No precise genealogical records have ever been discovered to prove this claim.

Colette made her first and only visit to the United States in 1935, as *Le Journal*'s reporter aboard the *Normandie,* the new French luxury liner that was competing with British ships to make the fastest Atlantic crossing. She broadcast her impressions of the liner and of New York on French radio, as well as publishing them in the newspaper. What seems to have impressed her most was the warmth of her American welcome, which made her feel ashamed of French inhospitality, and her visit to Harlem and its jazz clubs, especially the music and the casual grace of the women dancers.

The novella *Gigi* (1945) was adapted in 1948 for the Broadway stage, with a little-known Audrey Hepburn, recommended by Colette herself, in the title role. Then in 1958 the play was adapted for the screen as a musical: Vincente Minnelli directed; Alan Jay Lerner and Frederick Loewe wrote the award-winning songs; Cecil Beaton was art director; and Leslie Caron, Maurice Chevalier, and Louis Jourdan starred. The story of a girl schooled from childhood to be a high-class prostitute, but whose emotional honesty wins the hero's heart and hand rather than just his financial protection, *Gigi* was splendidly filmed on location in Paris, in carefully restored belle époque interiors. The decorum demanded in 1950s Hollywood meant that the sex-for-money transactions underlying Colette's plot were discreetly veiled, but the film makes effective use of costumes, decor, and performance to convey the gap between the era's glittering surface and the emotions of those it exploits. *Gigi* introduced a small part of Colette's

work to a mass transatlantic audience. Colette died in Paris in 1954.

Diana Holmes

See also: Caron, Leslie; Chevalier, Maurice; Jazz; Jourdan, Louis.

References

Colette. *My Mother's House* and *Sido.* Trans. Una Vincenzo Troubridge and Enid McLeod. Harmondsworth: Penguin, 1966.

Holmes, Diana. *Colette.* Basingstoke/London: Macmillan, 1991.

Pichois, Claude, and Alain Brunet. *Colette.* Paris: Editions de Fallois, 1999.

COMIC STRIPS

The francophone comic strip, or *bande dessinée* (BD), is revered in France under the title of Ninth Art (*Neuvième Art*), thus standing on a par with the likes of poetry, architecture, painting, or, more recently, cinema. Charles de Gaulle famously once compared himself with Tintin, and the World Cup–winning football team of 1998 was likened to the unconquerable Gauls of the *Astérix* strips. Sales of *bandes dessinées* regularly reach six figures, and the genre has its own section in the bibliographical review *Livres de France.* The national center for the *bande dessinée* in the southwest city of Angoulême (Centre National de la Bande Dessinée et de l'Image, or CNBDI) formed part of François Mitterrand's Grands Travaux of prestige building projects, and its Belgian counterpart, the Centre Belge de la Bande Dessinée (CBBD), occupies a centrally located art nouveau building as part of an urban regeneration scheme for Brussels. By comparison, comics in the United States are generally viewed as being outside the establishment, often associated with subversive subcultures or the purely infantile. Despite such apparent differences, the francophone and North American traditions are closely linked and interdependent, both in terms of historical development and current exchanges.

The centenary of R. F. Outcault's *Yellow Kid* in 1995 sparked a fierce debate as to who invented the comic strip. Although the Sunday supplements of turn-of-the-century U.S. newspapers launched a tradition of early serial strips, including the much-celebrated dreamland adventures of Little Nemo (Winsor McCay, 1905), French scholars have pointed to the Swiss schoolmaster Rodolphe Töpffer as providing the first *bandes dessinées.* In the 1830s Töpffer created a series of sequential narrative images based on the eccentric mishaps of characters such as M. Pencil or M. Cryptogram, with an explanatory text beneath each box. One might argue, however, that a defining element, the speech bubble or *bulle,* although present in U.S. cartoons, did not regularly appear in France until Alain Saint-Ogan's *Zig et Puce* (1925), the comic adventures of the two eponymous boys, later to be joined by their penguin friend Alfred.

The nineteenth- and early twentieth-century forerunners of the modern BD were generally single images (cf. today's cartoon) or sequential boxes, each surmounting several lines of text. In illustrated publications aimed at an adult audience (e.g., *Le Charivari,* 1832; then *Le Courrier Français,* 1884; *Le Sourire,* 1891; *Le Rire,* 1894), these BDs could be political, satirical of everyday life, or overtly erotic. In children's journals the *histoires en images,* as they were known, were relatively rare and generally lighthearted in tone. Emile-Joseph Pinchon's adventures of Bé-

cassine (from 1905 onward), the dim-witted Breton maid, center on the comic and absurd mishaps that result from her misunderstandings. Bécassine was perhaps the first illustrated character to embrace stardom in early Hollywood fashion, with *La Semaine de Suzette* (Suzette's Week), the girls' journal in which she appeared, eventually offering a range of spin-off products such as dolls, tea sets, or board games.

The birth of the modern *bande dessinée* can be attributed to American parents with the launch of the *Journal de Mickey* (*Mickey Mouse's Journal*) in 1934. This was the first publication to reach mass circulation figures, approximately 400,000 a week as compared with 50,000 for previous bestsellers. The formula found by the journal's owner, Paul Winckler (with the silent backing of the publisher Hachette), was simple but effective. He created a syndication system for France under the name of Opera Mundi, thereby giving journals cheap access to U.S. strips. To these he added a French context through the journal itself: textual stories based on elements of French culture; information sections; and above all, reader participation via games, letters, and the now famous Club Mickey. The strips and characters may have been foreign, but the context Winckler gave them brought them into French culture.

In addition to translations of the best-known Disney strips, Winckler introduced a wide range of favorites from what was to become known as the golden age of U.S. comics: *Jungle Jim* (*Jim la Jungle*), *Brick Bradford, Pete the Tramp* (*Père Lacloche*), and Little Annie Rooney (*Les Malheurs d'Annie*). Sister or rival publications such as *Robinson, Hurrah!* or *Tarzan* followed the same model or even provided imports alone, with the result that superheroes such as Buck Rogers, Flash Gordon ("Guy l'éclair"), or Prince Valiant became household names in France.

The success of Winckler's system is apparent from the influence it had on the homegrown tradition that followed. It became the norm for *bande dessinée* journals to contextualize the strips with elements that presented the publication's particular stance. In the case of the period of wartime occupation, the pro-Nazi *Téméraire* created a circle of friends akin to the Hitler Youth Movement, to be juxtaposed with strips such as *Vers des mondes inconnus* (To Unknown Lands) by Auguste Liquois and Raymond Poïvet, in which Aryan figures were the "goodies" and the "baddies" had Semitic features. After the war the same formula held good, but now the two main publications—both for boys—were the Communist *Vaillant* (Valiant) and the Catholic *Coeurs Vaillants* (Valiant Hearts). Ironically, the majority of the former *Téméraire* artists became pillars of these journals: Liquois and Poïvet, for example, produced strips telling of the deeds of Resistance heroes (e.g., *Fifi, gars du maquis*) for *Vaillant*.

Coeurs Vaillants is also worthy of note as the publication that introduced *Tintin* to France from 1931 onward. Hergé (the pen name of Georges Remi) had originally published the adventures of the boy scout/detective in *Le Petit Vingtième,* the children's supplement of the Brussels-based Catholic newspaper, *XXe Siècle.* Their popularity and ability to evolve with time led to nineteen complete stories from 1929 to 1976. In hindsight some of the early adventures, such as the colonialist *Tintin au Congo* (1930) or the anti-Semitic *L'Etoile mystérieuse* (*The Shooting Star,* 1942), seem uncomfortably close to the fashions of their times. In other cases, such as the start of Tintin's trip to the Moon (*On a marché sur la lune/Destination Moon,* 1950), nineteen years before Neil Armstrong's expedition, the innovation is admirable. In terms of style, Hergé is seen as father of the *ligne claire* school, whereby clearly defined outlines form the backbone of the image. Tintin is also one of the rare *bande dessinée* creations to have engendered an industry of critical studies, starting with Pol Vandromme's *Le Monde de Tintin* (The World of Tintin) in 1959.

Hergé is the best-known author of a rich tradition of *bande dessinée* in Belgium. The journal *Spirou,* launched in 1938, is one of the longest-running successes in the world of comics and was the launchpad of the *Ecole de Marcinelle,* named after the district in Charleroi from which Dupuis, its publishers, operate. Successes have included Morris's *Lucky Luke,* André Franquin's *Gaston Lagaffe,* and Peyo's *Les Schtroumpfs* (*The Smurfs*). A comparison of the French and Belgian BD traditions is a study that remains to be done.

In France it was the Catholic and Communist lobbies that provided the inspiration for a milestone of the BD's development, the 1949 law on children's publications (Loi du 16 juillet 1949 sur les publications destinées à la jeunesse). Although *bande dessinée* theory as we now know it was nonexistent, the 1930s and 1940s had seen an array of tracts condemning illustrated stories as an incitement to illiteracy and violence, as a result of their supposedly antieducational, antireligious, or even pornographic nature. The law made illegal most scenes of violence or undress and the depiction of victory by evil forces. Above all, under the Communist influence, the law drastically reduced the percentage of foreign (thus principally U.S.) strips that a children's journal could publish. Around the same time in the United States Dr. Frederic Wertham's *Seduction of the Innocent* (1954) led to a Senate committee investigation—with anti-Communist undertones—and thereafter heavy censorship of comics.

The U.S. influence was nonetheless still heavy, with the law resulting in French artists taking over in the style of their transatlantic counterparts. Pierre Nicolas, for example, told the story of Mickey Mouse's travels through French history, meeting such characters as François I and Napoléon. Furthermore, it was *Mad* magazine (founded in 1952) that inspired René Goscinny and Jean-Michel Charlier in the creation of *Pilote* (1959–1989), the magazine that took the *bande dessinée* into adulthood in the late aftermath of the 1949 law. Although *Pilote* is best known for introducing Albert Uderzo and René Goscinny's *Astérix* series, the list of its artists reads like a Who's Who of the modern *bande dessinée:* Claire Bretécher, Cabu, Philippe Druillet, Jean-Claude Forest, F'murr, Jean Gir/Moebius, Marcel Gotlib, Greg, Morris, Raymond Poïvet, Jacques Tardi, and so on.

Strips such as Jean-Claude Forest's *Barbarella* (1962), later to be made into a feature film starring Jane Fonda (1968), made it clear that the *bande dessinée* was no longer for children. Under the influence of U.S. underground comix, new journals (*Echo des Savanes,* 1972; *Fluide Glaciale,* 1975; *Métal Hurlant,* 1975) continued this trend, mixing eroticism, humor, and/or science fiction. In the case of *Charlie Hebdo* (1970), social satire appeared side by side with U.S. imports—the journal's title is in reference to Charlie Brown of Charles Schulz's *Peanuts*—often introduced to a French audience for the first time. Since the 1980s the journal format has given way to that of album (hardback edition) production and spin-off products, a reflection in itself of the "grown-up" buying power the industry now attracts. With the new content also came adult reaction, and from the mid-1960s there has been an ever-increasing industry of BD criticism, exhibitions, and festivals. In particular the annual festival in Angoulême, held over the last weekend of January, attracts national media attention and hundreds of thousands of visitors.

The influence of North America has thus been felt at all stages of the *bande dessinée's* historical development, but it has also been a subject of inspiration in itself. Many a French speaker feels acquainted with the values of the Wild West through Morris's *Lucky Luke,* or with the adversities facing a trapper in colonial North America via the adventures of Blek le Roc, first chronicled in 1954. Frank Margerin's 1990s comic adventures of the *banlieue*-based Ricky show the influence of American culture—pinball, music, cinema, comics—on French life and have culminated in the hero crossing the Atlantic for one album (*Ricky chez les Ricains,* 1998). The Astérix albums are peppered with pastiches of Hollywood stars—Laurel and Hardy, Kirk Douglas, and Sean Connery all make appearances—and *Astérix et Cléopâtre* (1965) derives much of its humor from its parody of the Elizabeth Taylor and Richard Burton blockbuster. Astérix also makes the transatlantic trip (*La Grande Traversée,* 1975) and mimics the Statue of Liberty in one of the album's central scenes.

For the collector, Hergé's third Tintin adventure, *Tintin en Amérique* (1932), remains a milestone. Hergé used a number of anti-American sourcebooks to document a story that centers on organized crime in Chicago, with Al Capone as the chief villain. But the album includes much of the wonders of the United States in the 1930s, as Tintin climbs the skyscrapers, as well as raising social questions—the status and treatment of the Native American population, the economic importance of oil—that are still relevant today. Some original editions of *Tintin en Amérique* are currently valued at 5,000 euros.

The French-language comic strip is also alive and well in Quebec, where the form has its distinct identity while remaining close to the French tradition. In addition to boasting associations, distributors, and regular festivals, Montreal and Quebec have produced a number of artists of note. Serge Gaboury, for example, is known for the caricatures that have adorned magazines (e.g., *Croc*) and daily newspapers since the 1980s. More recently, Julie Doucet's stark and often shocking autobiographical portrayal of Montreal life (e.g., *Ciboire de Criss,* 1996) has been acclaimed on both sides of the Atlantic. Taking inspiration from Robert Crumb, Doucet gives an intimate female viewpoint to the visualization of fantasies and obsessions that are hers, but also those of modern life.

The tradition of exchange between French-speaking Europe and North America continues to underpin the world of comics and *bandes dessinées.* U.S. superheroes and well-established favorites such as *Peanuts* continue to fare well in France, as do less traditional productions: the works of Scott McCloud, Art Spiegelman (*Maus*), and Robert Crumb are all available in French translation, and these artists have been honored guests at mainstream festivals, including Angoulême. The exchange is less marked in the opposite direction, although both Tintin and Astérix have met with reasonable success. One noteworthy case is that of Moebius, whose science fiction fantasy creations have exported well. Not only are his albums available in North America, his *Métal Hurlant* journal has spawned the spin-off *Heavy Metal,* and his *bande dessinée* work has inspired (with his collaboration) large-scale Hollywood productions such as *Dune* (1975), *Alien* (1977), and Luc Besson's *The Fifth Element* (1997).

The increasingly vibrant world of animation provides further overlap between BD and the moving image. In addition to adapting successful preexisting strips (*Astérix, Tintin, Lucky Luke*), the form also has a clear tradition of original creations with a French–North American interconnection: best known is Warner Brothers' Pepé Le Pew, the romantic skunk with a French touch that makes reference to the country's perfume industry.

Like jazz and the detective novel, the comic strip is a form of popular culture that has seen a rise in status when imported to France. The *bande dessinée,* however, is unique as an area in which the Gauls have beaten off the transatlantic invader (or believe they have) to make the tradition their own.

Laurence Grove

See also: Besson, Luc; Bonaparte, Napoléon; Catholic Church; Chicago; Cinema, 1945 to the Present; Fonda, Jane; François I, King of France; Gaulle, General Charles de; Language; Lucky Luke; Mitterrand, François; Pepé Le Pew; Quebec; Space Technology; Sport; Statue of Liberty, The; Westerns; World War II.

References

Dierick, Charles, and Pascal Lefèvre, eds. *Forging a New Medium: The Comic Strip in the Nineteenth Century.* Brussels: VUB University Press, 1998.

Forsdick, Charles, Laurence Grove, and Elizabeth McQuillan, eds. *The Francophone Bande Dessinée.* Amsterdam: Rodopi, 2004.

Gaumer, Patrick, and Claude Moliterni. *Dictionnaire mondial de la bande dessinée.* Paris: Larousse, 1998.

Horn, Maurice, ed. *The World Encyclopedia of Comics.* Philadelphia: Chelsea House, 1999.

Morgan, Harry, and Manuel Hirtz. *Le Petit Critique illustré: Guide des ouvrages de langue française consacrés à la bande dessinée.* Montrouge: PLG, 1997.

Sabin, Roger. *Comics, Comix, and Graphic Novels: A History of Comic Art.* London: Phaidon, 1996.

COMPAGNIE D'OCCIDENT

The Compagnie d'Occident (also known as the Compagnie du Mississippi), which was established in 1717 by the Scottish financier John Law and changed its name to the Compagnie des Indes in May 1719, had a monopoly over trade in Louisiana from 1717 to 1731, as well as a monopoly over Canadian beaver exports from 1718 to 1760.

As early as 1715, John Law had put to the Regent a plan for the economic and financial recovery of France, the "Système," which was at first refused but which the Scot finally succeeded in putting into place progressively. After founding the Banque générale in 1716, he created the Compagnie d'Occident, which received its letters patent in August 1717 and was granted a monopoly over trade in Louisiana. The area covered by the company included the whole of the Mississippi valley, the Illinois Country becoming part of Louisiana through a decree in September 1717. The company's obligations were vast: it was to transport 6,000 colons and 3,000 black slaves over twenty-five years; it was also responsible for expenditure related to religion and defense.

Over the following years, the Compagnie d'Occident took over all the other large French trading companies, as well as all large sources of state revenue. Farms were to have brought the company the financial support necessary for the exploitation of its immense colonial domain. Nevertheless, these purchases initially forced it to issue new shares, which the general public bought with banknotes. The Banque générale had been turned into a Banque royale in December 1718; in August 1719, an edict was issued according to which the state's debt would be written off through the refunding of loans and offices in banknotes. Because the investment market was too rigid, the new holders of banknotes invested them by buying shares in the Compagnie des Indes. From May 1719, the share value began to increase, and this feverish period of investment, fueled by intense propaganda, continued to grow, while the bank continued to issue banknotes that did not correspond to a metal standard. The "Système" thus found itself at the mercy of a shift in public opinion that took place in the first months of 1720. The inability to refund all investors led to bankruptcy.

After July 1720, the "Système" was liquidated: the bank was closed, the original financial and fiscal organization was reintroduced, and the Compagnie des Indes was henceforth only responsible for any trade activity under the tight control of the monarchy. While its actions in Louisiana between 1717 and 1720 had helped to give the colony stability, the company then imposed destructive cuts. Eventually, after the massacre of the Natchez in 1729, the company returned Louisiana to the Crown in 1731. It retained the monopoly over exports of Canadian beaver products until the fall of New France.

Cécile Vidal

See also: Fur Trade; Illinois Country; Louisiana; Mississippi River; New France; Slavery.

References

Giraud, Marcel. *Histoire de la Louisiane française.* 5 vols. Paris: PUF, 1966.

Haudrère, Philippe. *La Compagnie française des Indes au XVIIIe siècle (1719–1795).* Paris: Librairie de l'Inde, 1989.

COMPAGNIE DU SÉNÉGAL

French slave trading company.

The Compagnie du Sénégal is intimately linked with French participation in the triangular Atlantic slave trade, and it also laid the foundations for the colonization of francophone West Africa. However, the compagnie was not a monolithic institution, and its history was extremely turbulent and unsettled. Its first incarnation was under the name of Compagnie du Sénégal et de Gambie, established in 1624 by merchants from Dieppe and Rouen. In 1634, it became the Compagnie du Cap Vert et du Sénégal, under the patronage of Cardinal Richelieu, and was awarded a monopoly on the nascent slave trade.

Control of France's African and Asian trading posts soon passed to the Compagnie des Indes Occidentales, which went bankrupt in 1672, and a new Compagnie du Sénégal emerged, buying the failed company's Senegal *comptoir.* The Compagnie du Sénégal sought to strengthen its position on the coast of Africa, taking control of the island of Gorée (off the coast of Dakar) from the Dutch in October 1677. Over the next two years, the Dutch would also be forced out of their coastal positions on the mainland. The compagnie then set about imposing by force its "right" to trade in the region, carrying out a series of violent raids on the Senegalese kingdoms of Baol, Sine, and Kajoor, after local monarchs had attempted to resist its presence.

On March 21, 1679, the Compagnie du Sénégal signed a treaty with the Directeurs généraux du domaine royal d'Occident to provide slaves and goods to the French islands of the Caribbean, and it also began to provide slaves for galley ships in France. Originally, it was awarded this monopoly on the slave trade for an eight-year period, for which it had to guarantee a supply of 8,000 slaves per annum. In June 1679, the seal was set on the compagnie's fortunes when it received *lettres patentes* from Louis XIV, according it slaving and other trading rights for all of Africa until 1704.

However, the compagnie was unable to fulfill the terms of its treaties, and the number of slaves sent to the Caribbean and to French galley ships fell well below the levels promised. Such failings are not surprising as the company had been expected to establish a smooth-running slave operation almost from nothing. Nor was its position helped by France's entry into war with Spain and Holland, with the company losing many ships to enemy naval attacks. By 1681, it had gone bankrupt, its goods were sold off, and yet another company of the same name was launched. In subsequent decades, the compagnie (in various incarnations) fared little better in meeting the growing demand for slaves in the Caribbean, but it nonetheless helped to establish the slave trade on the Senegalese coast, a trade that would go from strength to strength as the eighteenth century progressed. The final incarnation of the compagnie was eventually absorbed into John Law's Compagnie des Indes in 1719.

David Murphy

See also: Richelieu, Cardinal Armand Jean du Plessis de; Slavery.

References

Ly, Abdoulaye. *La Compagnie du Sénégal.* Paris: Présence Africaine, 1958.

Searing, James F. *West African Slavery and Atlantic Commerce: The Senegal River Valley.* Cambridge: Cambridge University Press, 1993.

COMPUTER TECHNOLOGY

Computing technology has—in various ways—been an issue between France and the United States. Since the beginning of the nuclear age in the 1940s, "supercomputing" technological ability has been a requirement for nations with independent nuclear deterrents, and France has therefore been anxious to develop and maintain such ability. In general industrial and commercial terms, computers have become crucial instruments in almost all sectors of economic activity, but additionally, as computing has become a tool of information and communication—most vividly demonstrated by the Internet in the 1990s—the French state has developed concerns over U.S. domination of cyberculture. Both as an underpinning of military applications and strategy and as the medium of cultural communication, computing technology has engaged with the re-

lationship between France/Europe and the United States.

French governments in the mid-1960s were more than ever preoccupied by the perceived "technology gap" between France (and Europe) and the United States; the sectors that seemed most undeveloped were nuclear and space technologies and computing. Although each of these sectors was crucial in its own right to France's much-prized military, technical, or industrial independence, computing technology was deemed a field of expertise that was core to French activities in all high-tech sectors, and the weakness of France's domestic computer industry was thus all the more a cause for concern. The link between technological independence and military/political independence was underlined heavily when the United States refused to allow France the use of the Control Data supercomputer needed to facilitate the final preparation of the nuclear deterrent. State support for the French computer industry was an element—under the heading "Plan Calcul"—of French national planning from 1966 until 1981, as French governments attempted to negotiate a French-European-Atlantic resolution to the U.S. domination of advanced computing technology.

Of all France's attempts to define transatlantic technological and industrial relations on the basis of equality or parity in technical and commercial terms, the field of computing is perhaps where French "technological Colbertism" (to use Elie Cohen's description of French government policy) has been the least successful. Although in aviation, the Concorde and Airbus projects asserted French and European capabilities and in nuclear technology, France created its own deterrent force and civil nuclear power industry (albeit with much U.S. technology), in computing, French industry has remained weak. French strategy for computer technology was first to develop a domestic industry capable of competing in France with U.S. products, and then, through European cooperation (led by France's "national champion") to match U.S. companies.

The first Plan Calcul descended into confusion in the late 1960s as the leading French computer firm La Compagnie des Machines Bull (CMB)—whose difficulties in competing with IBM had drawn the sector's problems to the attention of government in the first place—failed to conclude partnerships with French companies such as CGE or CSF and collaborated with the U.S. General Electric. What followed was a saga of complex mergers and takeovers that left the French computer industry weakened rather than strengthened. During the early 1970s the state-supported company CII competed in the French market with Bull–General Electric and IBM before being taken over (with Bull) by the U.S. firm Honeywell to become CII-HB.

In 1979, CGE sold its participation in CII-HB to Saint-Gobain, which then assumed control of the computing firm while simultaneously acquiring an interest in Olivetti's computing-related activities. This apparent new departure—a French firm with a strong basis in computers—was then sabotaged, when the new Socialist administration nationalized Saint-Gobain and instructed it to withdraw from computing technology. Attempts to forge a European dimension to French computer expertise likewise failed during the 1970s, as the Unidata project between CII, Siemens, and Philips lasted only two years (1973–1975).

The 1960s and 1970s were the main period during which France attempted to encourage a domestic computer industry through a dirigiste approach. The failure of French attempts to develop an independent industrial base in computer technology was—somewhat surprisingly—accompanied by something of a success in the field of software, computer consulting, and computing-related services. French awareness of the dangers of the technology gap and forward thinking along the lines of the celebrated 1978 Nora-Minc government report *The Computerization of Society* seemed to push France into thinking about the ways in which a country without a strong foothold in computing hardware could still participate in the information and communications revolution—the cyberculture—that computers were bringing into existence. During the 1990s in particular, the French state put into operation programs of technological development intended to drag France forward into the Internet information age.

Hugh Dauncey

See also: Aviation; Concorde; Cyberculture; Nuclear Technology; Space Technology.

References

Nora, Simon, and Alain Minc. *The Computerization of Society: A Report to the President of France.* Cambridge, MA: MIT Press, 1980.

Servan-Schreiber, Jean-Jacques. *Le Défi américain.* Paris: Denoël, 1967.

CONCORDE

The Franco-British supersonic passenger transport plane Concorde is arguably the most famous plane in the world, despite the fact that only sixteen planes were ever produced and that its commercial exploita-

A crowd watches as the last of the British Airways Concordes lands at Heathrow Airport in London. On the fence in the background a sign in French reads, "Concorde, we love you." (Eva-Lotta Jansson/Corbis)

tion was limited both in terms of the routes it served and the small numbers of travelers it carried. The crash of an Air France Concorde near Paris in June 2000—killing all 100 passengers and crew—almost ended the dream of Concorde's story, but such was the strength of the fame and symbolic significance of the plane in relations between the United States and Europe that Concorde rose Phoenix-like from the flames and in late 2001 was rescheduled for service as long as was deemed technically feasible. However, Air France and British Airways jointly decided after less than eighteen months of flying that in the face of falling revenue and rising maintenance costs, the plane would have to be definitively withdrawn from service by autumn 2003 and thus brought the story of Con-

corde to a conclusion. The conception, birth, development, and exploitation of Concorde have all been intimately influenced by relations between the United States, France, and the United Kingdom; the practical role for the aircraft has always been to shrink the French Atlantic by bringing New York closer to Paris and London, but the symbolism of Concorde has been principally to widen divisions between Europe and the United States.

The French and British governments agreed to develop Concorde in late 1962. Both the United Kingdom and Gaullist France were eager to demonstrate to the United States that European technology, industry, and commerce were capable of creating the world's first supersonic transport plane and that the much-discussed "technology gap" between the United States and Europe could be bridged by a collaborative project involving Europe's main aviation champions. Concorde was intended to bridge the Atlantic in a way no U.S. plane could, and the project stimulated the U.S. government and Boeing to launch their own supersonic transport (SST) program in 1963, but ambitious U.S. technical choices (Mach 3 rather than Concorde's Mach 2) led to the cancellation of the SST in 1971.

Initially, as Concorde was developed during the 1960s by BOAC (later British Airways) and Air France, U.S. airlines such as Pan Am expressed interest in purchasing the aircraft, in anticipation of the new era of supersonic air travel to be fully ushered in by Boeing's larger, faster SST. But after the successful testing of Concorde prototypes in 1969 and the cancellation of the SST, only Air France and BOAC confirmed orders for the plane (1972). U.S. airlines canceled their interest in 1973 as the oil crisis threatened the viability of supersonic air travel, and that, added to U.S. resentment at Europe's SST, created opposition to Concorde in the United States, which included a ban on supersonic flights in and out of New York.

When Concorde inaugurated the world's first supersonic commercial flights in January 1976, they significantly avoided the North Atlantic, reflecting other traditional French and British geopolitical interests and new tensions the Franco-British SST had created between the United States and Europe. Air France's Paris-Dakar-Rio and British Airway's London-Bahrain routes were eventually complemented by services to New York, but throughout its development and operation, Concorde has exemplified the distance (geographical and cultural) as well as the proximity (commercial and industrial) of relations spanning the French Atlantic.

Hugh Dauncey

See also: Aviation.
References
Costello, John. *Concorde: The International Race for a Supersonic Passenger Transport.* London: Angus and Robertson, 1976.
Turcat, André. *Concorde: Essais d'hier, batailles d'aujourd'hui.* Paris: Le Cherche Midi, 2000.

CONDÉ, MARYSE (1937–)

Guadeloupean writer and academic.

Condé's work reflects the tensions and the freedoms of a life spent traveling between three continents. She left Guadeloupe in 1953 and would not live there again for over thirty years. After studying at the Sorbonne, she went to live in Guinea in 1960, and spent over a decade teaching there and in Ghana and Senegal before returning to France in 1973, where she earned her doctorate at the Sorbonne and started writing novels. In 1986 she went back to live in Guadeloupe but soon began teaching at universities in the United States: the University of California at Berkeley, Harvard University, the University of Virginia, the University of Maryland, and, since 1995, Columbia University, where she remained until her retirement in December 2002. From the 1970s onward, she has written a great deal: not only the thirteen novels for which she is best known but also plays, short stories, children's books, and many articles and essays on Caribbean literature. She has played an important role in popularizing Antillean literature through her own publications (notably *La*

Poésie antillaise/West Indian Poetry, 1977; *Le Roman antillais*/The West Indian Novel, 1977; *La Civilisation du bossale,* 1978; *La Parole des femmes*/Women's Speech, 1979) and through the Center for French and Francophone Studies, which she established at Columbia University.

Condé's writing is characterized by a refusal to conform to conventions; ironic and unsentimental, she exposes the myths of exoticism, of racial stereotyping, and of the cultivation of a racial identity based on a nostalgic and in her view mistaken insistence on belonging to a particular community (satirized in *Les Derniers Rois mages/ The Last of the African Kings,* 1992). Her critical attitude toward Antillean identity politics has brought her into conflict with fellow writers, in particular the *créolité* group led by Patrick Chamoiseau and Raphaël Confiant. Condé dislikes their fetishization of the Creole language and their phallocentrism; this latter is part of a wider feminist dimension of her fiction, in which the oppression of women by men is a recurring theme. Her ambivalence toward Guadeloupe is motivated by the stifling narrow-minded intolerance that is too often found in small societies, depicted in *Traversée de la Mangrove/Crossing the Mangrove* (1989). But, equally, the Caribbean fantasy of self-realization in Africa is treated with skepticism in several of her novels—especially *Heremakhonon/Here- makhonon; A Novel* (1976) and *Une Saison à Rihata/Season in Rihata* (1981), whose heroines discover that their idealized view of traditional African society blinds them to the political turmoil of postindependence African states. Nor does life in France or the United States offer any simple solution to the problems of the rootless Caribbean subject (*La Vie scélérate/Tree of Life,* 1987; *Desirada,* 1997). Her protagonists move between islands and between continents, creating for themselves an existence that is neither idyllic nor tragic but complicated; they have a kind of nomadic energy and determination to resist being confined to one place or one social milieu. For Condé, the Caribbean is not a geographical entity but a migratory transatlantic culture that crosses borders and interacts with others all over the Americas, Europe, and Africa.

Celia Britton

See also: Chamoiseau, Patrick; Confiant, Raphaël; *Créolité;* Guadeloupe.

References

Callaloo. "Maryse Condé: A Special Issue." 18.3 (summer 1995).

Pfaff, Françoise. *Conversations with Maryse Condé.* Lincoln: University of Nebraska Press, 1996.

CONFIANT, RAPHAËL (1951–)

Born in 1951, in Martinique, Raphaël Confiant belongs to the first generation of writers from the postdepartmentalization era. The small islands of the Antilles have for long belonged administratively and economically to France, despite being situated within the Americas. As a result, in both his fictional and theoretical work, Confiant has had to negotiate this complex and often paradoxical French Atlantic relationship. Along with fellow Martinicans, the linguist Jean Bernabé and author and essayist Patrick Chamoiseau, Confiant is a founding member of the *créolité* movement. The principles of this movement stem from the violence and brutality of the rupture from Africa and the profound and complex impact of the colonial process.

For Confiant and his colleagues, the journey across the Atlantic is therefore seen as the birthplace of contemporary Creole identity.

The turn of the twenty-first century finds Confiant in a difficult position, expressed once again in the relationship between his role as a fictional author and as a Creole militant. He is an extremely prolific writer and has won several literary prizes in France—most notably the Prix Antigone for his first novel in French, *Le Nègre et l'amiral* (The Negro and the Admiral, 1988) and the Prix Novembre for *Eau de café* (1991). Confiant sets most of his novels in Martinique, drawing on the specificity of the Antillean surroundings while highlighting differences from metropolitan France. He caricatures and exaggerates events and characters, constructing a grotesque world that appears to stem directly from the madness of the ongoing colonial process (cf. *L'Allée des soupirs*/The Lane of Sighs, 1994; or *Nuée ardente*/Ardent Cloud, 2002).

Although he began writing novels in Creole (all of which have now been translated into French), a limited readership eventually led Confiant to write in French. He refers to the impossibility of either language to express fully his Antillean reality and thus follows Chamoiseau in his endeavors to construct a language in which both French and Creole are interwoven to reflect the plural, mosaic identity that he believes is Antillean—neither French nor American. The uniqueness of the islands' history and geography, the brutal confrontation of so many cultures, and the evolution of the Creole language has resulted in a creolization process that Confiant believes will define tomorrow's world.

Confiant's writing can be seen to embody the French Atlantic—representing the continual movement between Europe and the Americas, beginning with the violence of the Middle Passage. However, his perception of the absurdity of the current sociolinguistic and political situation seems to mark the beginning of a realization that the role he wants to accord to the Creole language is not possible through fiction. As his profile as a passionate advocate of Creole linguistic policy continues to rise (cf. *Le Dictionnaire des néologismes créoles*/The Dictionary of Creole Neologisms, 2001), the danger of stagnation looms, as he is increasingly entrapped in the internal struggles of Antillean politics.

Catriona Cunningham

See also: Bernabé, Jean; Chamoiseau, Patrick; Créolité; Language; Martinique.

References

Cecatty, René de. "La Bicyclette créole ou la voiture française: Un entretien avec l'écrivain antillais Raphaël Confiant." *Le Monde*, November 6, 1992.

Ludwig, Ralph, ed. *Ecrire la parole de la nuit: La nouvelle littérature antillaise.* Paris: Folio, 1994.

CONSTANT, PAULE (1944–)

French writer, born at Gan, France.

Constant spent her childhood in French Guiana and Cameroon and her adolescence in Djibouti, Laos, and Cambodia before returning to France, where she earned her doctorate at the Sorbonne. She lived another eight years in the Ivory Coast before settling at Aix-en-Provence in 1975, where she is a professor of French literature at the Institut d'Etudes Françaises pour Etudiants Etrangers, University of Aix-Marseilles. Constant published her first novel in 1980 and is the author of a total of eight works of fiction and one essay, almost all of which have received prestigious literary honors, as well as numerous articles in journals. In 2000, in Aix, Constant created the Centre des Ecrivains du Sud–Jean Giono, over which she presides, to promote contemporary literature by writers living in the south of France, through interviews, literary days, and conferences.

Constant's work is deeply disturbing and demands particular participation on the part of the reader. In spite of a powerfully oppressive pessimism and an abiding sense of infinite loss, a suggestion of resistance that presupposes the possibility of reparation and rehabilitation emerges in the face of otherwise appalling and virtually unending violence. Constant uses her characters' failures to expose a primitive and fragile humanity underlying a veneer of civilized sophistication and in so doing poses questions that signal widespread commonalities in pre- and postcolonial worlds. Although her settings are always distant, temporally or spatially, she critiques a pervasive loss of consciousness of the nature of the self and the accompanying loss of collective responsibility for identity construction in contemporary culture. The care and education of girls and the condition of women are themes that are always present in her work, enlarging the broadly anticolonial message to allow female characters to represent human existence. Her work is also profoundly Catholic yet filled with biting (and sometimes hilarious) criticism of hypocrisy within the church.

In terms of style, Constant's oeuvre is intentionally Balzacian; characters and personalities reappear from novel to novel, and there are, so far, three trilogies: the "Tiffany" trilogy includes *Ouregano* (1980; Prix Valéry Larbaud, 1981), *Propriété privée*/Private Property (1981), and *Balta* (1983). The African trilogy includes *Ouregano*, *White Spirit* (1989; Prix François-Mauriac, Prix Lutèce, Prix du Sud Jean-Baumel, Grand Prix du Roman de l'Académie Française), and *Balta*. The U.S. trilogy, of which only the first two are published to date, includes *Confidence pour confidence*/Trading Secrets (1998; Prix du Roman France-Télévision, Prix Goncourt, 1998) and *Sucre et Secret*/Sugar and Secret (2003; Prix Amnesty des droits de l'homme, 2003). The first critiques postmodern U.S. sensibilities, and the latter is highly critical of the use of the death penalty in the United States. Constant's other works of fiction are *Le Grand Ghâpal*, a comic tale (1991; Prix Gabrielle d'Estrées, 1992), and *La Fille du Gobernator*/The Governor's Daughter (1994). The latter is set in a prison colony in Guiana, where Constant lived briefly as a child. It works well as a perfect metaphor for Hell. Her essay on the education of privileged girls in the seventeenth century is entitled *Un Monde à l'usage des demoiselles*/A World for Young Ladies (Grand Prix de l'Essai de l'Académie Française, 1987). Her works have been translated into twenty-two languages.

Margot Miller

See also: Catholic Church; Guiana.
References
Miller, Margot. *In Search of Shelter: Subjectivity and Spaces of Loss in the Fiction of Paule Constant.* Lanham MD: Lexington Books/Roman and Littlefield, 2003.
Rye, Gill. *Reading for Change: Interactions between Text and Identity in Contemporary French Women's Writing (Baroche, Cixous, Constant).* Bern: Peter Lang, 2001.

CONSTANTINE, EDDIE (1917–1993)

U.S. actor best known for his embodiment of the hard-boiled FBI agent, Lemmy Caution, in a series of French films made in the 1950s and early 1960s.

Constantine is the first American to have become a star working in French cinema. Constantine was born in Los Angeles in 1917 and trained as a dancer and singer. He moved to France in 1947 with his first wife, Hélène Musel, a ballet dancer. Constantine was discovered by Edith Piaf, who launched his singing career. His first French film, *La Môme vert-de-gris* (*Poison Ivy*, Borderie), was released in 1953 when he made his mark as Lemmy Caution. His success in the French film industry during the 1950s and 1960s was such that his only substantial U.S. role saw him cast as a French pilot (*Raid on Entebbe,* 1977).

Constantine's star persona can be seen as emblematic of French postwar attitudes toward the United States: a fascination for U.S. culture tempered by fear of U.S. dominance, engendered partly by the huge influx of U.S. films, which had been banned during the war. This fascination led to many film adaptations, such as the eight Lemmy Caution films based on British writer Peter Cheyney's novels, including *Les Femmes s'en balancent* (*Dames Don't Care,* Borderie, 1953) and *Cet Homme est dangereux* (*Dangerous Agent,* Sacha, 1953). Constantine/Caution was just one of the screen versions of tough, hard-drinking, womanizing masculinity, but his particularity lay in his U.S. roots, emphasized in the films, especially through his accent. This characterization was continued across many different "private-eye" figures played by Constantine, including Johnny Jordan in *Ça va barder* (*Give 'em Hell,* Berry, 1955), Barney Morgan in *Je suis un sentimental* (*Headlines of Destruction,* Berry, 1955), and Nick Carter in *Nick Carter va tout casser* (*License to Kill,* Decoin, 1964) and *Nick Carter et le trèfle rouge* (*Nick Carter and the Red Club,* Savignac, 1965).

Constantine is also credited with bringing humor to his roles, creating almost a parody of the private-eye character. Many of his films played knowingly on this, flaunting his character's outrageous drinking capacity and prowess with women. This self-reflexivity was taken to new heights with his last appearance as Caution in Jean-Luc Godard's *Alphaville: Une étrange aventure de Lemmy Caution* (*Alphaville: A Strange Adventure of Lemmy Caution,* 1965). *Alphaville* displaced the familiar character into a dystopian future city, combining elements of the science fiction and crime genres. The film deliberately parodied not only Constantine's star persona but also U.S. film culture.

Ironically, given that *Alphaville* is now possibly the only film that Constantine is known for internationally, his French film career did not survive Godard's mythologizing of his most famous role—and the films he made during the late 1960s did not enjoy the success of his earlier thrillers. He moved to Germany in the 1970s and worked with young directors such as Rainer Werner Fassbinder and, in the 1990s, in European art films—*Europa* (von Trier) and *Allemagne 90 neuf zéro* (*Germany Year 90 Nine Zero,* Godard), both 1991. Arguably, Constantine was hugely successful in 1950s France, as Ginette Vincendeau has pointed out, because his gentle mockery of the "ultramasculine" American hero made over the U.S.

private eye into a French national icon in a way that chimed perfectly with French ambivalence toward the United States at that time.

Sarah Leahy

See also: Cinema, 1945 to the Present; Film Noir; Godard, Jean-Luc.

References

Buss, Robin. *French Film Noir.* London/New York: Marion Boyars, 1994.

Vincendeau, Ginette. "France 1945–1965 and Hollywood: The *Policier* as Inter-National Text." *Screen* 33, no. 1 (spring 1992): 50–80.

COPI (RAOUL DAMONTE) (1939–1987)

Cartoonist, playwright, and novelist, born in Buenos Aires in 1939.

Copi grew up in Uruguay (his novel *L'Uruguayen* [1972] is a homage to his lost childhood in Montevideo), where his upper-middle-class parents had sought exile from the Peronist regime in 1945, educating their children in U.S. and European culture and encouraging Copi to write plays for pocket money. They emigrated to Paris in the early 1950s and then returned to Buenos Aires to fight to overthrow Peron in 1955. Copi settled permanently in Paris in 1962, where he made ends meet by street painting, eventually getting a break at the magazine *Le Nouvel Observateur,* to which he contributed a series of acerbic cartoons (*La Femme assise*) depicting the eponymous seated woman who blithely comments on the absurdities of life—a satirical take on the political immobility and conservatism of mid-1960s France. Copi's later cartoons *Libérett,* some of which were criticized as racially offen-

sive, were eventually deemed too outrageous for *Libération* in the late 1970s.

Copi's major plays include *Eva Peron* (1969), with its risqué jokes about the heroine's fatal cancer, cutting down the Santa Evita myth to a cunning career plan. In a final twist, Evita slaughters her nurse, then passes off the body as her own, while escaping with the loot. The first production, directed by fellow Argentinean exile Alfredo Arias, crossed-dressed Evita and was condemned by Buenos Aires, the theater trashed by far-right extremists. Copi's subsequent meditation on gender identity, *L'Homosexuel, ou la difficulté de s'exprimer* (1971), functionally translated into English as *Sex Changes in Siberia,* showed a group of Russian bourgeois unwrapping each other's layers of transformation— male actors playing girls who were boys who were girls and so forth. Gay identity based on object choice was secondary to Copi, whose interest was in gender deviance. *Le Frigo* (1983) is a one-man show, a satire on class pretensions and gay lifestyle—Copi himself played all the parts—a "lady-doctor" Freud, an SM clone, and a Garbo look-alike. Copi is perhaps best known for his television commercials in the 1980s for Perrier water, in which he often appeared as a soubrette, or maid, exuberantly flaunting the product as madness, in a wonderful moment of high camp, proclaiming Perrier to be mad—*fou* the masculine for *folle.*

The novel *Le Bal des Folles* (*The Queens' Ball,* 1977) weaves the life of his gadfly character into the more substantial web of the homosexual subculture of Saint Germain-des-Près in the 1950s and 1960s. Copi's narrator situates his project less as a "homosexual novel" than as a "queen's novel." But Copi was keen to mark his distance from the institution of French literature: he admitted that he took part in the literary TV program of the 1980s (*Apostrophes*) only because of his national status as a Latin American outsider. The transparent characters of his novels and plays are designed as cartoon sketches of people on the sexual margins of society. To change sex, the Latino Pierre is shown to reject his ethnic origins, viewing other Latinos as vulgar. The narrator follows the transition with a degree of sadness, as he literally *loses* his lover. This theme of loss later set the tone for his last work, *Une Visite inopportune* (1988), a play as cruel and witty as ever, making black humor out of his imminent death. Copi died from an AIDS-related illness in Paris in 1987.

Nick Rees Roberts

See also: AIDS; Argentina; Gay Movement; Hocquenghem, Guy; Mineral Water; Williams, Tennessee.

References

Copi. *Textes rassemblés par Jorge Damonte.* Paris: Editions Christian Bourgeois, 1990.

Hocquenghem, Guy. *La Dérive homosexuelle.* Paris: Editions universitaires Jean-Pierre Delarge, 1977.

Weiss, Jason. *The Lights of Home: A Century of Latin American Writers in Paris.* New York: Routledge, 2003.

CORTÁZAR, JULIO (1914–1984)

Born in Brussels in 1914 to Argentinean parents, writer, musician, and left-wing activist Julio Cortázar became internationally famous in the 1960s for his fantastical short stories and experimental novels, notably the epic *Rayuela* (*Hopscotch,* 1963), a work that led Carlos Fuentes to describe him as the Latin American Marcel Proust.

Cortázar was a key player in the so-called "Boom" phenomenon of trailblazing writers (including Gabriel García Márquez) emerging from Latin America during the decade of the 1960s.

Cortázar grew up in Argentina, where his mother fostered his growing love for French literature (he would later cite Lautréamont as a particularly powerful influence) and fluency in the French language. Cortázar's first collection of stories, *Bestiario,* was published in Argentina in 1951, but he left his country the same year, unhappy with Juan Perón's arrival to power, and settling definitively in Paris. An experienced translator of such French authors as André Gide, Marguerite Yourcenar, and Jean Giono, Cortázar continued to translate in France (for the United Nations Educational, Scientific, and Cultural Organization) and to develop his own writing. Indeed, translation itself is often one of the central themes in his texts, encapsulating as it does some of his major preoccupations: alterity, transformation, and the radical movement between different subject positions.

Many of Cortázar's stories and novels take place in a Paris beneath the surface of which lurks some repressed element that could at any moment tip the protagonists into the unknown realm of the fantastic. Since his characters are frequently Latin Americans resident in Paris, it is often a totally unresolved—and irresolvable—interpenetration of (American) past and (French) present that will showcase the fragility within these subjects of any sense of a coherent and unified self. It is in the traumatic gap *between* identities that the Cortázarian fantastic (ghosts, possessions, metamorphoses, etc.) will take root and grow. Characters are always prone to dis-

Julio Cortázar, author of Hopscotch *(Pantheon)/ José Gelabert, 1965. (Library of Congress)*

Fascinated by all the fluctuating, unbalanced human products of the French/American experience, Cortázar does not limit himself to Argentine protagonists: one of his most successful creations is Johnny (a thinly disguised Charlie Parker), the protagonist of the novella *El Perseguidor* (The Pursuer), an African American in Paris whose inability to be comprehended by those around him will aggravate an already anguished relationship with time, order, and reality and will culminate in his death. Cortázar himself died in Paris on February 12, 1984, having been finally accorded French citizenship by President François Mitterrand in 1981.

Andrew Asibong

See also: Argentina; Fuentes, Carlos; García Márquez, Gabriel; Lautréamont, Comte de; Mitterrand, François; Yourcenar, Marguerite.

References

Carter, E. D. *Julio Cortázar: Life, Work and Criticism.* Fredericton, NB: York Press, 1986.

Standish, Peter. *Understanding Julio Cortázar.* Columbia: University of South Carolina Press, 2001.

solve into somebody else, something else, or into some other era. In addition to these commonplaces of fantastic literature, however, in Cortázar's world, geography itself becomes equally ungraspable. Thus in the short story "El otro cielo" (The Other Heaven), the Lautréamont-inspired protagonist, a South American serial killer living in nineteenth-century Paris, walks between the second arrondissement and central Buenos Aires by means of a mysterious passage, a phenomenon he has apparently come to terms with. In *Hopscotch* the two halves of the book, one set in Argentina and the other in Paris, but both concerning the character Horacio Oliveira, often seem to be taking place at the same time.

COSMETICS

The social and economic significance of cosmetics and makeup has changed in pivotal ways throughout Western history. For the French, the use of cosmetics was emblematic of a life of privileges and sophistication symbolized by the court. When Catherine de Médici married the future king Henri II in 1533, she brought Florentine refinement to the court in the form of unguents, fragrances, and various powders and lipsticks, forming the elementary basis of contemporary makeup. Catherine's political intentions were, nevertheless, hardly

Chanel cosmetics counter. (Les Stone/Corbis Sygma)

concealed by the gloss of novelty she brought to sixteenth-century courtly life. She also used cosmetics in ruthless and calculating ways, murdering undesirable enemies and family members and therefore turning makeup into a deceiving, poisonous, and often lethal statement of political power.

The influence of Italian *Barocco,* or baroque style, over all aspects of French culture led to the exuberance of Versailles, which was built between 1660 and 1685 by Louis LeVau and Jules Hardouin-Mansart. When Louis XIV moved the court there in 1677, the plays, festivities, concerts, and operas performed for the king meant that makeup had become de rigueur for any self-respecting courtesan, regardless of age and gender. The rapidly

changing fashions of elaborate hairstyles, intricate adornment, and luxurious attire complemented exuberant and often extreme makeup that signified belonging to the exclusive sphere of courtly pleasures. Men wore white powder and bright lipstick often made from natural pigments and animal substances. The significance of the *mouche,* a black dot resembling a beauty mark worn by courtesans, varied according to its location on a woman's face. Courtly makeup rapidly became a complex and intricate form of communication. The very act of making oneself up and using cosmetics therefore stood for one's entry into the world and acted as a significant step toward social and cultural recognition.

The prestigious—and somewhat illusory—connotations of cosmetics were instrumental in the expansion of what is now known as one of the most profitable industries across both sides of the Atlantic, generating billions of dollars in profit each year. Elizabeth Arden was one of the first women to turn the cosmetic industry into a highly lucrative and international business. Born Florence Nightingale Graham in Canada in 1878, she initially trained as a nurse. She soon started seeing beauty potential in the skin salves and burn creams she used on her patients. Her kitchen became a laboratory where she began to experiment with different ingredients in order to come up with the perfect cream formula. Despite several initial failures, she stuck to her goals and moved to New York at age thirty. She opened her own beauty salon in 1910 on Fifth Avenue and changed her name to Elizabeth Arden. By selling a range of treatments and products to a growing customer base, she became highly successful, and her credibility grew within the U.S. and Canadian markets. Her genius was to understand that North American women were longing for prettiness and glamour after experiencing the puritanical restraint of post-Victorian society. Her name was soon associated with leading Hollywood stars, who used her innovative products such as Eight-Hour Cream. Arden was a pioneer in marketing and was selling over 100 products by the 1920s. Elizabeth Arden became a global brand, leading the way for other twentieth-century cosmetics empires such as Estée Lauder, Helena Rubinstein, and Bobbi Brown.

Arden's success inspired French houses who were originally famous for their fragrances or clothes to enter the cosmetics business. Guerlain, Chanel, and Dior all introduced skin care and makeup products, realizing the potential for such markets.

The French beauty business developed in the 1960s and quickly became a powerful industry.

Companies such as Clarins were established in the United States at the beginning of the 1980s. The company is still renowned for producing beauty products and fragrances whose formulations are exclusively based on plants and natural extracts. The family business is now an international group licensing designer fragrances and beauty lines for the likes of Loris Azzaro and Thierry Mugler. The Clarins Group currently employs more than 5,000 people and had global earnings of more than $1 billion in 2002. Other companies such as Lancôme, Sisley, and L'Oréal have enjoyed similar successes in both fragrance and beauty developments.

The makeup artist also plays a crucial role in the maintenance and growth of the cosmetics industry. Several makeup artists whose work was initially limited to fashion photography and runway presentations now have their own cosmetics lines. François Nars and Stéphane Marais are the most recent examples of a generation of French makeup artists gaining momentum on both sides of the Atlantic. The key relationship existing between such brands as Elizabeth Arden, Lancôme, and L'Oréal and Hollywood actresses such as Catherine Zeta-Jones, Uma Thurman, and Milla Jovovich means that the industry will always rely on film and style as key marketing tools. "Finding a face" to launch a new product or fragrance is therefore a necessity for international beauty conglomerates. The trend, however, tends to work both ways. Using her name and fame as a singer and actress, Jennifer Lopez recently launched successful fragrances and cosmetics lines.

The ultimate taboo seems to be makeup for men. Although the male cosmetics industry is a highly successful and profitable one, men in makeup still have a subversive and scandalous appeal. Jean-Paul Gaultier, who put men in skirts in the early 1980s, recently launched a makeup line for men, predicting a change in attitude toward such products. Commercial success is, however, far from being guaranteed, as "male makeup" remains the ultimate challenge for the beauty industry.

Philippe Pourhashemi

See also: Cinema, 1945 to the Present; Fashion; L'Oréal.

References

Corson, Richard. *Fashions in Makeup, from Ancient to Modern Times.* New York: Universe Books, 1972.

Gavenas, Mary Lisa. *Color Stories: Behind the Scenes of America's Billion-Dollar Beauty Industry.* New York: Simon and Schuster, 2002.

Woodhead, Lindy. *War Paint: Madame Helena Rubinstein and Miss Elizabeth Arden, Their Lives, Their Times, Their Rivalry.* New York: John Wiley, 2004.

COSTA-GAVRAS (CONSTANTINOS GAVRAS) (1933–)

A French film director and screenwriter of Greek origin, born in Loutra-Iraias, Costa-Gavras is associated with political cinema. In more than a dozen films in France and in Hollywood, he has developed the popular genre of the political thriller, combining compelling narratives, real-life events, and international stars.

Costa-Gavras arrived in France in 1949 after being refused a visa to the United States. He studied at the Sorbonne and the IDHEC (Institut des Hautes Etudes Cinématographiques) cinema school before starting his career in 1958 as assistant to established directors such as René Clair, Henri Verneuil, Yves Allegret, and Jacques Demy. His first film, *Compartiment tueurs* (*The Sleeping Car Murders,* 1965), a successful detective thriller, featured Yves Montand, with whom he worked in several subsequent films. This film, partly financed by the actors, enabled Costa-Gavras to try out a visual style inspired by *cinéma vérité* documentary techniques.

Z (1969), starring Montand, cowritten with Jorge Semprun, and set in the period leading to the 1966 military coup in Greece, was a critical and popular success, marking the international recognition of his talent with an Oscar and prizes at Cannes, and it remains a landmark in French cinema. It defined Costa-Gavras's style as a director, namely the combination of a popular genre with serious themes like political oppression, imperialism, tyranny, justice, and guilt.

Z was followed by other successful political films, such as *L'Aveu* (*The Confession,* 1970), denouncing the excesses of Stalinism in Czechoslovakia, and *Etat de siège* (*State of Siege,* 1973), criticizing the political role of the United States in Latin America. *Section spéciale* (*Special Section,* 1975), one of several films on World War II, examines collaboration within the French Vichy government.

When he failed to find money for his films in France, Costa-Gavras moved to Hollywood. His first film in English, *Missing* (1982), starring Jack Lemmon and Sissy Spacek and based on a true story, the kidnapping and murder of an American journalist in Chile, was an uncompromising film and a commercial success. It won an Oscar and a joint Palme d'or in Cannes, possibly because it was accessible and hewed closely to the familiar American thriller conventions. *Betrayed* (1988), starring Debra Winger and Tom Berenger, explored racism in rural America. In *Music Box* (1989), a melodrama that won the Golden Bear at the Berlin Festival, Jessica Lange plays a daughter questioning her father's Nazi war criminal past.

Costa-Gavras's career has been uneven, and some of his more psychological dramas have not been well received. After the failure of *Mad City* (1997), he directed *Amen* (2002), a much-discussed film about the passivity of the Catholic Church during the Holocaust.

Costa-Gavras promotes the cause of political justice through films based on historical situations. He is considered a major international political filmmaker, and his films, unsurprisingly, tend to be controversial. While he takes clear stands and questions human conscience, Costa-Gavras uses the dramatic power of the film medium to expose mainstream audiences to important issues. He has always been actively involved in the debates of the cinema profession and was in charge of the Cinémathèque française in the 1980s.

Isabelle Vanderschelden

See also: Catholic Church; Chile; Cinema, 1945 to the Present; Montand, Yves; World War II.

References

Buss, Robin. *French Film Noir.* New York/London: Marion Boyars, 1994.

Michalczyk, J. *Costa-Gavras: Political Fiction Film.* Philadelphia: Art Alliance Press, 1984.

Prédal, René, ed. *Le Cinéma de Costa-Gavras.* Paris: Cerf, 1985.

COTTON

When things go well in Quebec, people say "ça file bien" (it spins well), but when they are fed up, they are "au coton" (in cotton). For better and for worse, cotton defined the industrial experience of French Canadians and Franco-Americans. Yet this primacy of cotton is historical rather than empirical. Time and place accorded it an importance that mere numbers never could.

As residents of British colonies, both *Canadiens* and *Acadiens* were exposed to large-scale importation of cotton goods as soon as the Napoleonic wars ended in 1815. By both value and volume, cotton goods remained until the late nineteenth century the most important British export to what would become Canada. In the major ports of British North America, dry goods merchants made up a quarter to a third of all mercantile firms. Settlement of the Canadas fed this trade, as the first cash crop of most pioneering peasants on the forested fringe of settlement was potash. Made by leaching the cinders of hardwood trees cut down in land clearance, potash was the principal bleaching agent used in British textiles prior to the development of the modern chemical industry.

Most French-speaking residents of British North America, however, continued to wear homespun woolen goods. Indeed, the wearing of this *étoffe du pays* (homespun woolen goods) became a symbol of political liberties, when in response to the Russell Resolutions of 1836 the Patriote movement launched a boycott of British textiles. (The iconic symbol made famous by the Front de liberation du Québec during the October Crisis of 1970 was of an armed peasant wearing homespun.) The expanding production of homespun by peasant women, particularly in the foothills of the Laurentians and along the Lower South Shore of the Saint Lawrence, reached commercial quantities by the third quarter of the nineteenth century.

The Cajun population of Louisiana was marginal to the development of King Cotton in the early nineteenth century, but the same could not be said of the wealthy French planter families displaced by the revolution in Saint-Domingue (now Haiti) and of French citizens expelled from the Spanish Caribbean in 1810, some 2,700 of whom chose to take refuge in New Orleans. Over the ensuing decades they were joined by a further 8,500 French immigrants to this booming capital of the New South. This period coincided with the development in northern France of a large cotton industry, where 368 mills employed 100 hands or more by 1845. So it is not surprising that there were commercial and financial ties, but this nascent industry had in Napoleonic France relied on Italian cotton and then, after the restoration of the monarchy, largely on Egyptian cotton. During the American Civil War, France maintained diplomatic relations with the Confederacy, more in hope of support for its Mexican adventure than out of any dependence on Southern cotton.

Direct participation in the manufacture of cotton goods by French Canadians first took place in New England. Although an estimated 70,000 people emigrated to the United States from Canada during the 1850s, the largest migratory waves followed the end of the Civil War and appear to have been linked to the growing indebtedness of French Canadian farming families. From 37,000 in 1860, the French Canadian population in New England grew to 208,000 in 1880 and 573,000 by 1900. These census figures capture perhaps half of what was a continuous large-scale movement back and forth across the border.

Initially, nationalist members of the French Canadian intelligentsia considered these popular class economic migrants to be *traîtres* (traitors), and Georges Etienne Cartier reputedly dismissed them as *la canaille* (trash). By the 1880s, however, these textile factory workers were increasingly seen as the future of the French in North America. Honoré Mercier went as far as to predict that a century's continued growth would see 100 million Franco-Americans by 1989.

These French Canadian migrants found work in textile mills throughout New England, where they displaced a second-generation Irish workforce that dated from the 1850s. Work in the mills was a family affair, with boys and girls as young as thirteen and fourteen working up to seventy-two hours a week, often under the supervision of one of their parents. No clear gender division of labor then characterized the industry, although in all mills the lowest-paid tasks were reserved for women and children. The close relationship between family time and industrial time in Manchester, New Hampshire, went so far by the early twentieth century that two-thirds of married women worked in the mills between pregnancies. This appears to have been the major difference between the lived experiences of female textile workers in the United States and Canada. Women worked after their marriage in the mills in the United States between their pregnancies. This was not the case in Canada, where after marriage women effectively withdrew from the paid labor force. Their husbands, however, shared more than just a varied relationship to the work process: patriarchal privileges and a shared masculine sporting culture. Before the Great War annual baseball tournaments linked Fall River, Massachusetts, to Valleyfield, Quebec.

In Canada, the cotton industry dates from 1874, when both the Hudon mill in Hochelaga, just east of Montreal, and Montreal Cotton in Valleyfield opened. Following the adoption of a strongly protectionist trade policy by the Canadian government in 1879, leading dry goods wholesalers moved into cotton production, opening seventeen new plants by 1885. From the industry's inception, most workers were Québécois. Indeed, the principal textile town in English Canada was Cornwall, Ontario, a largely French Canadian city just west of the Quebec provincial border on the Saint Lawrence River. The binational character of the industry was, therefore, from its inception a defining feature: an overwhelmingly French Canadian workforce labored in mills managed and owned by English Canadians.

During the early decades of the cotton industry in Quebec the lack of a clearly defined gendered division of labor facilitated collective action by what was still a predominantly female workforce. Between 1880 and 1913, French Canadian textile workers struck fifty times. The key moments of mass mobilization were 1900 and 1906–1907, with six and nineteen strikes, respectively.

Organized as the 7,500-strong Federation of Textile Workers of Canada, the workers in 1906–1907 failed in their attempt to protect wages and piece rates in an industry in the midst of dramatic restructuring. In 1905, under the auspices of the Bank of Montreal, four of the largest Canadian producers merged to create Dominion Textile, which then secretly purchased a controlling interest in Montreal Cotton and, in 1907, established a price cartel with the three remaining independent companies that was to last thirty-one years.

This shift from competition to oligopoly financed a dramatic increase in workload along more clearly defined gender lines. In the relatively unskilled carding rooms, where cotton is cleaned and prepared for spinning, wage differentials rose to three to one. With Charles Gordon, the company president, serving as vice chair of the Imperial Munitions Board, World War I proved exceptionally profitable; in 1919 alone, Dominion Textile returned after-tax profits of 87 percent on preferred shares and 31 percent on common equity. Through the 1920s, Dominion Textile's unchallenged control permitted regional specialization, as the company became the leading private employer throughout the heartland of Quebec.

Wage cuts combined with reduced work hours to hit workers hard in the 1930s, particularly in the mills in smaller towns, where company policy, supported by the local Catholic clergy, discouraged women from working after marriage. Strikes in 1937 halted the downward trend and under pressure from the Confederation of Catholic Trade Unions led to a royal commission into the state of the textile industry. Known as the Turgeon Commission, it uncovered the price cartel and revealed a rapacious, unilingual corporate structure.

Most workers remained unorganized. In 1943, led by Madeleine Parent, the largely female workforce at the Merchants plant in Saint-Henri, described in Gabrielle Roy's classic *Bonheur d'occasion* (*The Tin Flute*), succeeded in establishing a trade union independent from the Catholic Church. In the most important of the immediate postwar strikes in Quebec, Madeleine Parent and Kent Rowley successfully unionized the Valleyfield operations, before falling victim to the Red Scare purges of the late 1940s.

New single-floor, continuous-process plant design to accommodate European (largely Swiss) technologies transformed the work environment in the 1950s and early 1960s. Tensions in the older plants over control of the work process led to a major strike in 1964. The degree of worker dissatisfaction was dramatically captured in Denys Arcand's National Film Board production *On est au coton* (*Cotton Mill, Treadmill*), but Dominion Textile was powerful enough to block release of the film for six years. In the late 1960s the company successfully engineered a secession from the increasingly militant Confederation of National Trade Unions. The resultant Confederation of Democratic Unions blocked rank-and-file attempts to oppose the new corporate strategy of shifting production to the southern United States through the 1970s and 1980s, symbolized by the purchase of the denim producer DHJ. Ironically, it was the success of this denim strategy that ultimately led to the collapse of the industry. In 1993, a Wall Street syndicate purchased control of the company, closed down the Canadian operations, and in a reverse takeover sold the denim factories to the major American producer Burlington. Au coton is now merely the name of a chain of clothing stores.

Robert C. H. Sweeny

See also: American Civil War; Arcand, Denys; Catholic Church; Denim; Fashion; Montreal; Quebec; Roy, Gabrielle; Saint Lawrence River; Sport; World War I.

References

Brandt, Gail Cuthbert. "Weaving It Together: Life Cycle and the Industrial Experience of Female Cotton Workers in Quebec, 1910–1950." *Labour/Le Travail* 7 (spring 1981): 113–125.

Chassagne, Serge. *Le Coton et ses patrons, France, 1760–1840.* Paris: Editions de l'Ecole des hautes études en sciences sociales, 1991.

Dominion Textile Inc. *Fonds.* National Archives of Canada, Ottawa.

Dumont, Fernand. *Récit d'une émigration: Mémoires.* Montreal: Boréal, 1997.

Ingersoll, Thomas N. *Mammon and Manon in Early New Orleans: The First Slave Society in the Deep South, 1718–1819.* Knoxville: University of Tennessee Press, 1997.

COUNTERCULTURE

The creation of lifestyles and cultural practices alternative to those established has for long been a feature of American life, and a projection of Europeans onto a myth of "America." Taking utopian and religious forms from the seventeenth century, in the rapidly modernizing and emerging consumer societies of the Western world following World War II countercultural movements were associated with new cultures of youth, music, narcotics, and sexuality. As the advanced form of consumer culture, American society has heavily influenced these trends in Europe, whether through figures such as James Dean in the 1950s or those of the late 1960s who emerged in a country in turmoil over race and the Vietnam War.

In France, the hegemony of Marxist thought in intellectual and student circles for much of the 1960s meant that American countercultural tendencies were downgraded. However, in the wake of the events of May 1968—a confused and complex mixture of older revolutionary politics, cultural and ideological upheaval, media event,

A group of protesters kneel in front of riot police during confrontations outside the Summit of the Americas in Quebec City, April 20, 2001. (Reuters/Corbis)

and libidinous carnival that nevertheless mobilized millions over genuine social, economic, and political grievances—elements on the French Left did begin to look at the new American countercultures for inspiration and for a way of disengaging from some of the more puritan Marxist-inspired ideologies in order to address questions of desire. The magazine *Actuel* (1970–1975), cofounded by Jean-François Bizot, Michel-Antoine Burnier, Bernard Kouchner, and Patrick Rambaud, was a crucial conduit in these years. American counterculture also influenced Michel Foucault and Guy Hocquenghem, who in 1968–1970 belonged, along with others from the 1968 generation such as the architect Roland Castro, to a group called "Vive la révolution," which

was seeking this kind of dialogue. In April 1970, for example, Hocquenghem wrote an article titled "Changer la vie," in which figures such as Jimi Hendrix and Janis Joplin are defended in the name of creativity, for the "revolution" must not subordinate or replace "life." For Hocquenghem, these evolutions were part of a transition taking him to the founding of a "modern" gay movement in France, itself a reworking in that context of an American development with its roots in black civil rights and the counterculture. But they also expressed a concern that if the post-1968 revolutionaries did not engage with the counterculture, the bourgeoisie would get there first. Indeed, much analysis in France of May 1968 from the tenth anniversary onward argues that it was the foundation of the new phase in French capitalism characterized by personalization, individualism, fluidity, and hedonism (Debray, Lipovetsky) and that events have proven the victory of the *babas* (hippies) over the Marxists (Joffrin).

With the appropriation by contemporary capitalism of countercultural agendas from the 1960s, attention since the 1990s has been on the emergence of "anticapitalist" or antiglobalization movements. The demonstrations in Quebec City in April 2001 were seen all over the world and even received approbation from Pierre Bourdieu, via a satellite letter sent from Paris. Mobilizing around issues of trade policy at an international level and helped by the Internet, these coalitions are oppositional to the current order, but like those in the 1960s contain a complex array of residual (traditional) and also alternative ideologies whose future place inside or outside the system remains uncertain.

Bill Marshall

See also: Avant-Gardes; Bourdieu, Pierre; Breton, André; Debray, Régis; Foucault, Michel; Hocquenghem, Guy; Surrealism; Vietnam War; World War II.

References

Bizot, Jean-François, ed. *Underground: L'histoire.* Paris: Denoël, 2001.

Debray, Régis. "A Modest Contribution to the Rules and Ceremonies of the Tenth Anniversary." *New Left Review* 115 (May–June 1979): 45–65.

Hocquenghem, Guy. *L'Après-mai des faunes.* Paris: Grasset, 1974.

Joffrin, Laurent. *Un Coup de jeune: Portrait d'une génération morale.* Paris: Arlea, 1987.

Lipovetsky, Gilles. *L'Ere du vide: Essais sur l'individualisme contemporain.* Paris: Gallimard, 1983.

Moore, Marie France. "Contre-culture et culture politique au Québec: Une analyse de contenu de la revue Mainmise." M.A. Thesis, Département de science politique. Montreal: Université du Québec à Montréal, 1975.

COUREURS DE BOIS

Name given to itinerant French or French Canadian fur traders in New France and Louisiana during the seventeenth and eighteenth centuries.

In New France and Louisiana, coureurs de bois was the name given to young French and French Canadian men who traded furs with Indians in their distant villages without official authorization. In exchange for furs, coureurs de bois delivered metal tools, textiles, muskets, alcohol, and other European manufactured goods to their Indian suppliers. Traveling vast distances on foot and by canoe and acquainted with Indian languages and customs, the coureurs de bois played an important role in the French exploration of the continent and in securing military and commercial alliances with Indians. During the last decades of the seventeenth century, the metropolitan government's willingness to diversify the colonial economy, as well as growing concerns about the disorderliness and "immorality" of the coureurs de bois reported by New France missionaries and officials, prompted authorities to restrict and control fur trading expeditions by setting up a trading permit system (*régime de congés*) in 1681. This permit system created a "respectable" class of traders known as voyageurs. By contrast, the term *coureurs de bois* was mostly used to designate illicit traders and carried some pejorative connotation. Despite subsequent prohibitions, hundreds of coureurs de bois continued to travel to Indian country in search of furs. In the eighteenth century, coureurs de bois could be found trading in the Great Lakes region and in the upper and lower Mississippi valley. Even though their knowledge of Indian languages and customs made them valuable intermediaries between

French officials and Indian communities, especially in regions of New France and Louisiana where the French colonial presence was limited or nonexistent, their adoption of Indian ways and their unions with Indian women often drew the ire of civil and church authorities. Formidable agents of cross-cultural interactions, the coureurs de bois would continue to exert their influence over the course of American history well beyond the demise of French North American colonies. Their marriages with Indian women gave rise to the Métis communities of Canada, and a number of traders of French Canadian ancestry would serve as guides and interpreters for U.S. explorers of the American West during the nineteenth century.

The precursors of the coureurs de bois in French North America were young Frenchmen who, during the early years of French exploration and settlement, were placed in welcoming Indian communities to learn Indian languages and customs and thus facilitate relations between natives and newcomers. Know as *truchements,* these young men developed a strong taste for the liberty and fraternity they found among their Indian hosts. Their embrace of Indian life and abandonment of Christian morals and behavior often scandalized missionaries, who accused them of undermining their evangelizing efforts. In 1635, the authorities of New France attempted to recall all the *truchements,* but the appeal of the Indian world was too strong; many returned to Indian country as coureurs de bois and inspired other young Frenchmen to follow their example. One such *truchement* turned coureur de bois was Etienne Brûlé. In 1608, the founder of New France, Samuel de Champlain, sent Brûlé to live among the Hurons. When Brûlé came back the next year to Quebec with a Huron delegation, he reportedly spoke fluent Algonquin, sported face paint, and had adopted Huron dress and hairstyle. Brûlé had no desire to resume his French life and returned to Huronia with those who accepted him as one of their own. For the rest of his life, Brûlé became the archetypal coureur de bois, a Frenchman turned Indian whose life choice disturbed French officials, all the while remaining an indispensable intermediary between French merchants and Indians and a source of valuable geographical and geopolitical information.

In the seventeenth and eighteenth centuries, the coureurs de bois played a crucial economic role in French North America. In New France and Louisiana, the pelts and furs they traded with Indians constituted a substantial proportion of colonial exports. Despite the increasing importance of other Atlantic-bound colonial products such as wheat, rice, wood, or fish, by the mid-eighteenth century, furs still made up 50 percent of New France exports, while peltry accounted for about one-third of the total value of the French Louisiana export trade. The European manufactured goods the coureurs de bois took to Indian communities in exchange for pelts also transformed the economy, material culture, and geopolitics of Indian America. The growing dependence of Indians on the metal goods, muskets, and alcohol the coureurs de bois brought them furthered competition between Indian groups for access to these goods and in turn shaped the dynamics of European-Indian commercial and military alliances.

The importance of the coureurs de bois in helping colonial governments secure these alliances cannot be underestimated. Their linguistic skills, their intimate knowledge of Indian diplomacy and warfare, and the strong ties they had established in Indian communities often prompted both French and British colonial governments to seek their services. The coureurs de bois's knowledge of the peoples and landscape of North America also made them valuable sources of information and guides for the exploration of the American interior during the eighteenth century. If colonial authorities often denounced the "savage ways" of the coureurs de bois, they nevertheless heavily relied on them to stake their imperial claims on the continent.

Agents of the now much celebrated process of *métissage,* or cross-cultural borrowings and transformations characteristic of French colonialism in North America, the coureurs de bois led a life that often baffled contemporary commentators. Their adoption of Indian dress, customs, and languages and the intimate relations they formed with Indian women (a practice vigorously denounced by French civil and church authorities by the turn of the eighteenth century) signified a rejection of their "civilized" background. Indeed, some coureurs de bois assimilated so thoroughly into Indian communities that it was sometimes difficult for European observers to distinguish them from their Indian kin. In most cases, the children they had with their Indian wives were raised among Indians and never integrated into French colonial society.

The coureur de bois as historical figure contributed to the development of Métis identity and culture in Canada. But the coureur de bois as cultural figure still resonates in contemporary Canadian society and is often invoked to express notions of hardiness, virility, and independence associated with Canadian and Québécois identity. The moniker has been adopted by a number of outdoor clubs and tourist businesses in Ontario and Quebec, and the business travel section of the government of Quebec's official tourist website promises incentive travelers a holiday "filled with high emotions and unexpected adventures" for "the modern coureur de bois."

Guillaume Aubert

See also: Brûlé, Etienne; Champlain, Samuel de; Fur Trade; Hurons; Louisiana; Manitoba; Métis; Mississippi River; New France; Quebec; Riel, Louis.

References

Brown, Jennifer S. H., and Jacqueline Peterson, eds. *The New Peoples: Being and Becoming Métis in North America.* Saint Paul: Minnesota Historical Society Press, 2001.

"Business Travel." Bonjour Quebec: Quebec Government Official Tourist Site. http://www.bonjourquebec.com/anglais/ affaires/index.html (cited May 30, 2004).

Eccles, W. J. *The French in North America, 1500–1783.* East Lansing: Michigan State University Press, 2000.

Germain, Georges-Hébert. *Les Coureurs de bois: La saga des Indiens blancs.* Outremont, Quebec: Libre Expression, 2003.

Jacquin, Philippe. *Les Indiens blancs: Français et Indiens en Amérique du Nord, XVIe- XVIIIe siècles.* Paris: Payot, 1987.

Vaugeois, Denis. *America: L'Expédition de Lewis and Clark et la naissance d'une nouvelle puissance.* Sillery, Quebec: Septentrion, 2002.

COURNAND, ANDRÉ FRÉDÉRIC (1895–1988)

French-trained physician whose medical career in the United States culminated in a Nobel Prize for physiology and medicine.

André Frédéric Cournand was born in Paris on September 24, 1895. He studied physics, chemistry, and biology at the Faculté des Sciences in Paris, graduating in 1913. The following year, he began his medical studies, but upon the outbreak of World War I he volunteered for the French army, where he served as a battalion surgeon until the end of the conflict. On leaving the army, he resumed his medical studies and became an intern at the Hôpitaux de Paris in 1925. During the next few years he gained clinical experience, especially in internal medicine, under Professor Robert Debré, head of the pediatric service of the Children's Hospital in Paris.

In the 1930s, anxious to study and work in the United States, Cournand secured a residency in the tuberculosis (later chest) service of Columbia University at Bellevue Hospital in New York. He became chief resident of this service and conducted research on the physiology and physiopathology of respiration under the guidance of D. W. Richards. Cournand also began his own work on the development of physiologic methods of exploration of the cardiopulmonary system. By using the catheter technique developed by W. Forsmann, Cournand and D. R. Richard Jr. succeeded in measuring the blood pressure in the lung artery. This discovery was crucial for the surgery of patients affected by silicosis, and eventually it was recognized by the 1956 Nobel Prize. During World War II Cournand was an investigator for the U.S. Office of Scientific and Research Development, working in the Chemical Warfare Service.

Although Cournand became a U.S. citizen in 1941, he never cut his ties with his home country. Throughout his career, he stayed in close contact with his former teacher, Robert Debré. In the spring of 1945, as the war was ending in Europe, Cournand proposed a plan to the Rockefeller Foundation to assist French medical research. In 1947, with the support of the French government and the Rockefeller Foundation, a Medical and Surgery Relief Committee (MSRC) was established in New York to provide grants to French clinicians eager to learn the new techniques of biomedicine then in use in North America. The MSRC also provided scientific equipment (centrifuges) and new medicines (cortisone) to Louis Bugnard, director of the French Institut National d'Hygiène. In 1950, Debré attempted to lure Cournand back to France, where he could help with the renewal of medical research. When Debré suggested Cournand for a chair at the Collège de France, however, his candidature was blocked by academic rivalries. Cournand decided to stay in New York, where he was appointed professor at Columbia University's College of Physicians and Surgeons in 1951. A few years later, when Cournand was awarded the Nobel Prize as a U.S. citizen, Debré characterized this as "a severe warning for French medical research." Professor André F. Cournand died in 1988.

Jean-François Picard

See also: World War I; World War II.
References
Centre National de la Recherche Scientifique. "Histoire de la recherche médicale en France au vingtième siècle." http://picardp1.ivry.cnrs.fr/histrecmed .html (cited March 26, 2004).
Schneider, William H., ed. *Rockefeller Philanthropy and Modern Biomedicine: International Initiatives from World War I to the Cold War.* Indiana University Press, 2002.

COURRIER DES ETATS-UNIS, LE (1828–1939)

The longest-running French-language newspaper in the United States was founded in New York in 1828. *Le Courrier des Etats-Unis* (CEU) ceased publication when World War II began in 1939, after a difficult period during the Great Depression. As a tribute, a later French-language U.S. newspaper, *France-Amérique,* revived the name *Le Courrier des Etats-Unis,* and since 1966 has incorporated it as its regional (U.S.) news section heading. *France-Amérique* was started in New York in 1943 and became an international edition of *Le Figaro* (Paris); published weekly, its current circulation is around 20,000. It is interesting to note that a similar political impetus was present at the origins of CEU and *France-Amérique.* The founders of both newspapers sought to provide a New World voice for civil and religious freedom in France. CEU promoted republican and Bonapartist ideals over the ancien régime views perpetuated by Charles X, and it deplored Louis Philippe's July Monarchy after 1830; *France-Amérique* supported General Charles de Gaulle in his opposition to the fascist Vichy government of the 1940s.

The original slogan of CEU was "Journal politique et littéraire." The paper's early period pre-dated the steamship era and the creation of the Cunard line in 1840, which improved the transatlantic supply of news. So, at first, the CEU relied more heavily on literary features, miscellany, and local stories. It appeared on eight pages on Saturdays; an annual subscription cost $8. On November 18, 1829, a Wednesday edition was added. Depending on the news supply, the midweek edition ran between four and eight pages, and an extra weekday edition would occasionally appear. Beginning on February 25, 1838, there were two weekday editions (Tuesdays and Thursdays) instead of one, the Saturday edition grew to sixteen pages, and the slogan was changed to "L'Organe des populations de langue française." From June 11, 1847, the CEU was published daily (except Sundays) and continued to increase its popularity by appealing to a general readership. In the bookstore it operated on its premises, La Librairie du Courrier des Etats-Unis, back issues of French newspapers could be purchased along with books and magazines. CEU was not illustrated, but one notable exception was a special Sunday edition of October 24, 1886. On the front page, a four-column engraving accompanied an article celebrating the unveiling, in New York Harbor later that week, of Frédéric-Auguste Bartholdi's famous statue, "Liberty Lighting the World."

H. P. Sampers, the CEU's greatest owner-editor (from 1879 until 1908) saw the paper as a vital link not only between Franco-Americans and France, but one that promoted understanding between all French and American populations. Indeed, earlier in the nineteenth century, it had been an important information and cultural channel between France and readers in Lower Canada (early Quebec) and, later, between francophone communities as remote as Newfoundland and Louisiana. It printed articles and letters contributed by French Canadians; items from the CEU were also reprinted in French Canadian and other North American French-language periodicals.

Shelley Beal

See also: Bartholdi, Frédéric-Auguste; Louisiana; Newfoundland; Statue of Liberty, The; World War II.

References

Bélisle, Alexandre. *Histoire de la presse franco-américaine.* Worcester, MA: Ateliers typographiques de *L'Opinion publique,* 1911.

Habert, Jacques, and Jean-Louis Turlin. "Cinquantenaire" (fiftieth anniversary edition). *France-Amérique* (May 22–28, 1993).

Lamonde, Yvan. "Le Bas-Canada et le *Courrier des Etats-Unis* de New York (1828–1840)." *Cahier des Dix* 56 (2002): 217–233.

COUTURIER, MARIE-ALAIN, O. P. (1897–1954)

French cleric and art critic.

Father Marie-Alain Couturier played a vital role in the twentieth-century transatlantic debate over the sacred in art. As coeditor of the French journal *L'Art sacré,* he campaigned against the mass-produced, sentimental church decor known as "L'art de Saint-Sulpice." He called on the church to enlist the talents of the greatest artists of the time, as had been done in earlier epochs. In the twentieth century, this would necessarily mean working with non-Catholics and even with nonbelievers.

Born in Montrison (Loire) on November 15, 1897, Couturier moved to Paris in 1919 to study art at the Académie de La Grande Chaumière. He joined the Ateliers d'art sacré later that year, where his training focused on painting, fresco, and stained glass. A supporter of Les Camelots du roi, the youth wing of Charles Maurras's monarchist Action française, Couturier withdrew from political activism upon choosing to become a Dominican in 1926. He would soon denounce the spirit of conformity and clericalism in the church and would even come to see the anticlerical laws of the Third Republic as the guarantor of the church's spiritual liberty.

In 1940 Couturier traveled to New York to preach the Lenten season and remained in North America until 1945. He frequented other prominent exiles in New York, speaking and writing in support of the Gaullist *France libre,* invoking the art of the School of Paris as the symbol of the liberty that Vichy and Adolf Hitler had suppressed. He introduced Dominique and Jean de Ménil to the city's galleries, helping them begin one of the world's great private collections, now housed at the Ménil Museum in Houston. Couturier also lectured and taught in Montreal, where he sponsored groundbreaking exhibitions of young, antiacademic French Canadian artists favorable to nonfiguration and abstraction, which he now concluded was most suited to conveying the sacred and the spiritual in art. As a cleric who condemned the Vichy regime's collaboration and anti-Semitic laws, Couturier also won credibility for *la France libre* in Quebec.

Upon his return to France, Couturier assembled a group of artists, including Marc Chagall, Jacques Lipschitz, and Georges Braque, to decorate a new church on the Plateau d'Assy in the Alps. He also convinced Fernand Léger to execute a series of stained glass windows for a new workers' church in Audincourt, helped Le Corbusier secure a commission for the Dominican convent at L'Arbresle, and served as stained glass consultant and model for Saint Dominic at Henri Matisse's Chapel of the Rosary in Vence.

Father Couturier's writings include *Art et Catholicisme* (1941) (republished in 1945 with an additional "Note sur l'abstraction"); *Chroniques* (1947); and the posthumous compilations *Art et liberté spirituelle* (1958), *Dieu et l'Art dans une vie* (1965), *Art sacré* (1983), *La Vérité blessée* (1984), and *Vence Chapel: The Archive of a Creation* (1999), a record of Couturier's and Henri Matisse's conversations on art and faith.

Robert Schwartzwald

See also: Catholic Church; Gaulle, General Charles de; Le Corbusier; Painting; World War II.

References

Schwartzwald, Robert. "The 'Civic Presence' of Father Marie-Alain Couturier, O. P. in Québec." *Québec Studies* 10 (spring–summer 1990): 133–152.

Weber, Joanna M. "Marie-Alain Couturier, O. P. on Art and the Church in the Twentieth Century." M.A. thesis, Yale University, 1989.

CRÉOLITÉ

The word *créolité* (Creoleness) appears in writing for the first time in 1975, in the subtitle of the second edition of the magazine *Mouchach,* published by the Guadeloupean linguist Hector Poullet. The word was coined in reaction to comments by the secretary of state of the départements d'outre mer, territoires d'outre mer (DOM-TOM) on the Frenchness (*francité*) of Creoles. The magazine, *Mouchach: Bulletin de la créolité,* focused on the study of Creole but did not bring a theoretical approach to the term *créolité.* It was only in 1989, with the publication of *Eloge de la créolité* (*In Praise of Creoleness*) by Jean Bernabé, Patrick Chamoiseau, and Raphael Confiant, that the word was put in a theoretical framework. Bernabé, Chamoiseau, and Confiant define *créolité* as "the interactional or transnational aggregate of Caribbean, European, African, Asian, and Levantine cultural elements, united on the same soil by the yoke of history" (1993, p. 87).

The *créolité* movement is often presented as an antithesis to the négritude movement because it clearly rejects some of its key features, such as universalism and the purity of the black race, in favor of diversity and cultural hybridization. However, despite these apparent contradictions, the advocates of the *créolité* movement do not see négritude and *créolité* as opposites. They recognize that they are indebted to Aimé Césaire, father of négritude in the Caribbean, for linking the experience of the black diaspora to its African roots and enabling the black population to rediscover pride in their color and heritage. *Créolité* is a continuation of the quest for identity explored in both preceding literary movements in the French Caribbean, négritude and *antillanité.* However, it goes further than these movements by opening a wider field, focusing on the Creole population rather than the Antillean population. *Créolité* highlights the harmonious cohabitation of the diverse civilizations living in the Caribbean as a result of slavery, indentured servantship, exile, or migration. Writing in a *créolité* style implies a rewriting of the history of the Caribbean with neither a Franco-centric perspective nor one focused on Africa, but rather celebrating the diverse origins of the population and the cultural mix resulting from the cohabitation. *Créolité* valorizes the Creole language as a unifying force and a key element of popular identity. The advocates of the *créolité* movement recognize the limitation of Creole as a language for literature and therefore suggest overcoming this difficulty by creating new vocabulary through, for example, the creolization of

French words or French transformations of Creole.

The paradox is that the recognition of this literary movement, through the awarding of the Prix Goncourt to Chamoiseau for his novel *Texaco,* has encouraged a proliferation of novels written in the *créolité* style rather than in Creole. Confiant, Bernabé, and other advocates of *créolité* work for the promotion of the Creole language through the publication of Creole dictionaries, stories, grammar books, and articles on Creole. Many of these are specifically designed for the teaching of the Creole CAPES (certificat d'aptitude pédagogique à l'enseignement secondaire, France's high school teaching qualification), set up in 2001. There is still, however, an ongoing debate between some créolistes and some advocates of *créolité* as to the writer's role: to use or to serve the language.

Marie-Annick Gournet

See also: Bernabé, Jean; Césaire, Aimé; Chamoiseau, Patrick; Confiant, Raphaël; Language; Poullet, Hector.

References

Bernabé, Jean, Patrick Chamoiseau, and Raphael Confiant. *Eloge de la Créolité.* Paris: Gallimard, 1993.

Condé, Maryse, and Madeleine Cottenet-Hage. *Penser la créolité.* Paris: Karthala, 1995.

Perret, Delphine. *La Créolité: Espace de création.* Martinique: Ibis Rouge, 2001.

CRÈVECOEUR, MICHEL-GUILLAUME-JEAN DE (1735–1813)

Born in Caen, France, as "Michel-Guillaume-Jean Saint-Jean," he died in Sarcelles, near Paris, France. "Hector St. John" was his adopted pen name. At sixteen he migrated to England, and in 1754 he went to North America as an officer in the French army (1754–1763). After traveling extensively in the British colonies from Niagara to Florida, around 1769 Crèvecoeur settled in Orange County in New York State, on the northern side of the Hudson Highlands, where he lived with his U.S. wife, Mehetable Tippet, of Yonkers, New York. During the American Revolution, he took the Loyalist side, was arrested on suspicion of being a spy (1780), and eventually returned to France. After three years in his native Normandy, he served as French consul in New York from 1784 to 1790. There, in 1787, he established the Société Gallo-Américaine with fellow Frenchmen Jacques-Pierre Brissot de Warville (1754–1793) and Nicolas Bergasse and Swiss republican Etienne Clavière (1735–1793). Crèvecoeur then returned to France for good.

Crèvecoeur is best known for his writings. His most influential book was *Letters from an American Farmer,* which was published in London in 1782 under the name "Hector St. John de Crèvecoeur." It was followed by the three-volume *Voyage dans la haute Pennsylvanie et dans l'état de New York* (1801). *Letters* is a fictional account of life in the United States narrated through twelve letters purportedly written by James, an innocent colonial farmer, to a friend in London. A sort of philosophical novel in the accepted style of the times, *Letters* praises the new American man, the product of a synthesis between his many original ethnicities and his experience in a new country (Americans are "a mixture of English, Scotch, Irish, French, Dutch, Germans and Swedes" who bred "that race now called American"). American values such as industry, self-reliance, and democracy were extolled throughout the book. Rural reality, however, was honestly depicted. Crèvecoeur also contributed to several U.S. newspapers under the pen name "Agricola." A 1925 collection, *Sketches of the Eighteenth-Century America,* included unpublished papers discovered in the twentieth century.

Luca Codignola

See also: Florida.
References
Alvarez Saar, Doreen. "The Heritage of American Ethnicity in Crèvecoeur's *Letters from an American Farmer.*" *A Mixed Race: Ethnicity in Early America.* Ed. Frank Shuffelton. New York/Oxford: Oxford University Press, 1993: 241–256.
Regis, Pamela. *Describing Early America. Bartram, Jefferson, Crèvecoeur, and the Rhetoric of Natural History.* De Kalb: Northern Illinois University Press, 1992.

CRIME FICTION

More than any other genre of French literature, crime fiction has been transformed by influences emanating from the United States. Moreover, in France today crime fiction is a conspicuous example of the way in which boundaries demarcating high and low cultural forms have been blurred. Contemporary novelists such as Patrick Modiano and Jean Echenoz are attracted to structural and psychological motifs associated with crime stories, but unlike their many predecessors who borrowed elements of the crime narrative with a view to parody or pastiche, this generation delivers no such value judgment. Conversely, the work of popular crime writers like Daniel Pennac and Fred Vargas has prompted serious discussion within the conservative French academy. Renewed interest has also been shown in the canonical figures of Georges Simenon, Arthur Conan Doyle, Agatha Christie, and Frédéric Dard, whereas writers groomed in the Série Noire—France's most illustrious stable of crime writing—are forging reputations in the wider literary world beyond the mean streets.

The unrivaled position of Commissaire Maigret as France's most successful export in the field of crime fiction is anomalous, at odds with the new identity that French crime literature has acquired over the latter half of the twentieth century. Maigret's creator, Georges Simenon, was Belgian, a skilled writer who wrote prolifically to make money. His idle sleuth employs a simple method of detection: he waits and watches until the crime solves itself. Simenon represents France as a geographical entity. Maigret takes us to the dockers' bars on the banks of the Seine or to the canal systems, but he mostly visits small provincial towns. This is a world of country doctors, lonely widows, traveling salesmen, the prefect and the subprefect, occasionally disturbed by other, less appealing stereotypes. History, politics, and literary ambition are by and large evacuated from the Simenon oeuvre.

The evolution of a modern crime fiction in France—one in tune with the ideas, issues, and anxieties of its day—began in the United States of the 1920s with the publication of "hard-boiled" crime stories in cheap "pulp" magazines like *Black Mask.* Translations of the hard-boiled classics reached France in the 1930s, establishing a fertile cultural exchange that perhaps illustrated the ambivalence of a country dazzled and repulsed in equal measure by American modernity. In 1945 the former surrealist Marcel Duhamel founded the Série

Noire (literally, "black [or dark] series") in the basement of the Gallimard building, France's most prestigious publishing house. It proved to be a watershed. Ostensibly set up to provide translations of U.S. and English crime literature, the Série Noire soon began to foster homegrown talent. Other successful ventures into crime publishing, such as the Fleuve noir, Rivages, and Viviane Hamy's Chemins nocturnes, followed in its wake, but with more than 2,500 titles to its name, the Série Noire remains at the forefront of the industry.

Duhamel promised sensationalism, in other words, sordid sex and graphic violence, but in 1944 Raymond Chandler had alluded to a different aesthetic when he wrote of how Dashiell Hammett "took murder out of the Venetian vase and dropped it into the alley" ("The Simple Art of Murder"). Crime had been returned to people "who do it for a reason," and it was this ideological impetus that helped to consolidate a distinctively "French" variant on the hard-boiled U.S. model, which became known as the *roman noir.* The first three French-authored novels published in the Série Noire—Terry Stewart's *La Mort et l'ange*/Death and the Angel (1948) and *La Belle Vie*/The Beautiful Life (1950) and John Amila's *Y a pas de bon dieu!*/There Is No God! (1950)—are all set in the United States, or what the authors imagined to be the United States, yet by this time Léo Malet had published *120, rue de la Gare* (1943), a novel that, though its plot owes much to Hammett's *The Maltese Falcon* (1929), is clearly set in France and, what is more, in the France of the German occupation of 1940–1944.

Malet is better known for his "nouveaux mystères de Paris" series of the 1950s, in which private eye Nestor Burma investigates crimes perpetrated within various arrondissements or districts of the French capital. The author's dedication to the individual qualities of each arrondissement visited in the course of the series is such that students of architecture in Paris are even now advised to read selected passages from the novels in order to enhance their appreciation of line, plane, and contour. However, Malet's most accomplished work is his "Trilogie Noire," published over a twenty-year period, and especially the first installment, *La Vie est dégueulasse*/Life Is Disgusting (1948). The story is narrated in the authentic vernacular of a young criminal, whose preoccupation with sex and death echoes the surrealist ecstasies of Malet's pre-war poetry. Having participated in the holdup of a wages' van and subsequent murder of a security guard, he eludes the authorities for a time until he perishes in a hail of police bullets. *La Vie est dégueulasse* dispenses with the baggage of the traditional detective or gangster novel. There is no investigation, no compliant moll to comfort the fugitive, and no honor among thieves; instead, we are afforded a perspective on a brief existence of rare intensity in which violence, cruelty, the exaltation of power over death, and the pain of hunger hold sway.

André Héléna, a near contemporary of Malet, has been plucked from obscurity by crime-writing devotees. Héléna wrote a handful of scintillating novels that engage more directly with the historical realities of his day. They include *Les Salauds ont la vie dure*/Once a Bastard, Always a Bastard (1949)—the first of a planned trilogy that was never completed—and his swan song, *Les Clients du Central Hôtel*/The Guests at the Central Hotel (1959), both of which send his reader on a journey back in time to the *années noires* of Vichy France. Héléna's skill and originality lie in his ability to put his reader in a situation that has yet to happen, to write in such a way that we willingly suspend our knowledge of the a posteriori, of the debates, controversies, and discoveries that orientate our perception of the war years.

In *Les Salauds ont la vie dure*, our perspective is reduced to that of Maurice, a small-time crook from Montmartre, who avenges the infidelity of his girlfriend by killing her, her lover who is an officer in the Gestapo, and his driver. At no point are we given an external perspective on Maurice; rather he speaks through the narrative in the rich slang of the underworld. Whereas much occupation literature is overlaid with a retrospective discourse in which ethical choices are justified or beaten down and the Gaullist myth of a united France in silent opposition to Vichy and the German dictator is exposed, the reader of *Les Salauds ont la vie dure* clings to the coattails of Maurice as he tracks across the country ahead of his pursuers, improvising an existence as a professional killer en route. This is a story of reflexes and the instinct to survive in a world of food scarcities, informants, and double agents. Héléna, himself an ex-*maquisard* (resistance fighter), gives a vivid insight to life in occupied France that ends on a surprisingly upbeat note, as the criminal outlaw is readmitted into a community fighting for its freedom. The subtle point of this epic tale is that the extraordinary phenomenon of the German occupation of France compelled ordinary people to embrace the world of the gangster or hoodlum, a world of lies, betrayals, and summary death.

Likewise, in *Les Clients du Central Hôtel*, the routine of life in a Perpignan hotel shortly before and after the liberation functions as a microcosm of occupied France. The institutions that support civil society have evaporated, and bourgeois conventions have peeled away to expose a curious hedonism, as characters pursue fleeting pleasures in an all-encompassing climate of fear. The banality of hotel management contrasts with the precarious existences of the guests for whom a chance remark or encounter could spell oblivion. *Les Clients du Central Hôtel* brings both the instability of life in France immediately prior to the liberation and a philosophical sense of the absurd into sharp focus.

The language of Héléna and Malet's fiction, incorporating street dialect, criminal slang, and an extravagant use of metaphor, demonstrates the extent to which the French *roman noir* of the 1940s and 1950s broke with traditional concerns of storytelling. However, as the 1960s erupted in a frenzy of political activism, the genre was hijacked by literary pirates who used it to write stories attacking the vested interests of the ruling classes and state-sponsored violence. Seldom has the gap between fiction and reality been so narrow. In 1972 a novel by Jean Amila entitled *La Vierge et le taureau*/The Virgin and the Bull, which was inspired by the author's covert, solo operation to delay the testing of nuclear bombs in the Pacific, came out. Within days it had been withdrawn from sale. Two years later, following numerous death threats, Amila was beaten to within an inch of his life. He suffered a total amnesia but somehow relearned to read and write and made a triumphant comeback in 1982 with *Le Boucher des hurlus*/The Butcher of Les Hurlus, a novel based on his experience as the orphaned child of a World War I deserter. In the vanguard of the "néo-polar"—as this latest school of crime writing became known—were polemicists from both wings of the political spectrum. From the Right, in novels tinged with nostalgia for a lost rural idyll such as *La Nuit des grands chiens malades*/The Night of the Big Sick Dogs and *Je Suis un Roman noir*/I Am a Dark Novel (both published in 1971), A. D. G. attacks the decadence of modern urban life and the hypocrisy of those who would sooner blame the ills of society than the individual who commits the crime. From the Left, Jean Vautrin's stylized portrayals of the violence, deprivation, and hopelessness of life in the outlying suburban estates surrounding France's major cities in novels like *Billy-ze-kick* (1972) and *A Bulletins rouges* (1974) resonate thirty years later. However, the most influential figure was undoubtedly Jean-Patrick Manchette, a Communist former teacher who had strong links with the radical situationist movement. Aesthetically and politically, Manchette took his cue from Dashiell Hammett. Paul Madvig, the confident fixer in Hammett's masterpiece, *The Glass Key* (1931), a story of political maneuvering in a corrupt eastern city, thinks he can force entry to the political elite by wooing the senator's daughter, but the aristocracy slams the door in his face, and his key shatters in the lock. Money cannot buy social standing. The glass key alludes both to Madvig's fate and to the identity of the killer. It is a solitary symbol in a fictional rhetoric that has been ruthlessly purged of unnecessary adjectives, adverbs, and metaphor. Over the course of several novels, including *Nada* (1972), *Le Petit Bleu de la côte ouest*/Singing the West Coast Blues (1976), and *La Position du tireur couché*/ *The Prone Gunman* (1981), Manchette

fine-tuned a similarly unadorned prose style that encapsulated the alienation of the individual in the late twentieth century, enslaved by market forces and the class system.

Crime writers have since continued to take up causes. The villain of Didier Daeninckx's seminal novel, *Meurtres pour mémoire*/Murder in Memoriam (1984), is a dead ringer for Maurice Papon, the indicted war criminal and former budget minister during the Giscard d'Estaing presidency. In a brilliant demonstration of the way that the novel form can bring history to life, Daeninckx shows that Papon should also have been implicated for his role in the massacre of hundreds of peaceful Algerian demonstrators that took place in Paris on the night of October 17, 1961, and lasted for several days. Papon was, at the time, prefect of police in the capital. Jean-Claude Izzo wrote three elegiac *romans noirs* published in the latter years of the 1990s that celebrate the Mediterranean culture of Marseilles while at the same time exposing the extent to which political and business leaders in the South and beyond are in the pay of the Mafia. And, most fascinating, in 1995 Jean-Bernard Pouy instigated the "Le Poulpe (Octopus)" series, whereby different writers were invited to contribute stories starring "Le Poulpe," otherwise known as Gabriel Lecouvreur, a freelance investigator who takes on cases suspected of having a far-right involvement. However, although contemporary French crime fiction is a significant vector of social and political anxiety, it would be wrong to characterize it as exclusively political and interventionist, just as it would be misleading to talk of it as essentially urban and macho. Some commentators argue that the influence of Hammett and more widely of a modernist American style of writing associated with William Faulkner and Ernest Hemingway has been exaggerated. They point to the centrality of the narrative or plot and to the rational powers of observation and deduction embodied in the figure of the Great Detective as robust, resilient archetypes hailing from the nineteenth century. Even the term *roman noir* is rooted in the gothic tradition. The "Le Poulpe" series is a case in point. Not only does it confound the popular prejudice that sees crime fiction as tacky and disposable, but it also challenges the prevailing literary culture in France, which many people see as an elitist enterprise producing expensive books that are little more than exercises in introspection. Against this backcloth of perceived sterility crime fiction has flourished, with successful series for children like La Souris noire, more comic strip adaptations, and a myriad of new writing talents. The accent is on invention. Two of the most gifted novelists of the current generation are Fred Vargas and Daniel Pennac.

Vargas, an archaeologist by trade, describes enigmas, strange happenings that only begin to unravel when specialist historians are called to assist the enquiry. In *Pars vite et reviens tard/Have Mercy on Us All* (2001), she revives the medieval tradition of *la criée,* when what we now think of as the *petites annonces,* or small ads, were recited publicly in the local marketplace. Her plots are beautifully composed, her character portraits are exquisite, and her observations, whether on the nature of public hysteria in the face of inexplicable events or on the work of human memory and the connections between images, are acute. Daniel Pennac is the most widely read contempo-

rary novelist in France. His ongoing "Malaussène" saga, which numbers six novels to date, is infused with an irrepressible exuberance. Pennac's imagination, like that of his erstwhile friend, photographer Robert Doisneau, works in black and white. The dark side of institutional corruption, social exclusion, rampant consumerism, and a profound reflection on the ancient myth of the scapegoat is juxtaposed with a fantastic evocation of life in the Parisian suburb of Belleville, a veneration of itinerant storytellers, and the construction of an alternative society around the indomitable Malaussène family, or tribe, which is in itself an anthropological enigma. Both Vargas and Pennac have added considerably to what might be regarded as the stock features or residual elements of the modern crime story: a strong narrative, an ear for dialogue, and an eye for detail. They are original voices in their own right; what they share with other equally estimable contemporaries like Tonino Benacquista, Maurice G. Dantec, and Thierry Jonquet is an artistic freedom that they have found through bending the rules of a popular genre.

David Platten

See also: Film Noir; Giscard d'Estaing, Valéry; Hemingway, Ernest; Maigret; Surrealism.

References

Atack, Margaret, ed. "Crime and Punishment: Narratives of Order and Disorder." *French Cultural Studies* 12, no. 36 (October 2001).

Deleuse, Robert. *Les Maîtres du roman policier.* Paris: Bordas, 1991.

Lacassin, François. *Mythologies du roman policier.* 2 vols. Paris: UGE/10x18, 1974.

Lits, Marc. *Le Roman policier: Introduction à la théorie et à l'histoire d'un genre littéraire.* Liège: Editions du Céfal, 1999.

Mandel, Ernest. *Delightful Murder: A Social History of the Crime Story.* London: Pluto Press, 1984.

Mesplède, Claude. *Les Années "Série Noire."* 4 vols. Amiens: Encrage, 1997.

"Le Polar: entre critique sociale et désenchantement." *Mouvements,* nos. 15–16 (May–August 2001): 5–117.

Pons, Jean, ed. "Roman Noir: Pas d'Orchidées pour les *Temps Modernes." Les Temps Modernes* 595 (August–September–October 1997).

"The Simple Art of Murder." *Atlantic Monthly* (December 1944).

Symons, Julian. *Bloody Murder: From the Detective Story to the Crime Novel.* Harmondsworth: Penguin, 1985.

CROZAT, ANTOINE (1655–1738)

French financier, born in Toulouse, who held the monopoly for trade in Louisiana from 1712 to 1717.

The early years of the colony had been difficult due to the War of the Spanish Succession, which started a few years after the colony's creation in 1699. When the armistice was signed in 1712, the Crown, almost bankrupt after half a century of wars under Louis XIV, decided to hand Louisiana over to a trading company. Since the merchants of the Atlantic ports had shown little haste in participating in such an undertaking, the minister for the navy placed his trust in Antoine Crozat, king's counsel and secretary of finances. This son of a banker and Toulouse magistrate had married Marie-Marguerite Le Gendre d'Armeny, daughter of a rich farmer in 1690. He found himself in possession of a considerable fortune, which he had earned in financial offices and maritime operations. He was one of the shareholders of the Compagnie des Indes orientales and a director of the Compagnies de Guinée, de l'Assiente et de Saint-Domingue.

On September 14, 1712, patents were signed that handed the commercial monopoly in Louisiana, excluding the Illinois Country, to the company founded by Crozat for fifteen years. In exchange for its privileges, the company only had to send two ships a year to the colony, with twenty young people of both sexes on board, and twenty-five barrels of merchandise for the king's use. The financier quickly realized that he would not be able to develop trade in Louisiana with such an unambitious migration policy. However, he considered that this was the responsibility of the monarchy, which, financially ruined, refused all his suggestions. As a result, Crozat persisted with commercial policies that were highly damaging for some colons, sending ships on an irregular basis and selling his goods at prohibitively expensive prices. Furthermore, his commercial operations were quickly limited by the sums of money he paid out in the king's name from 1714 onward. The establishment of the regency and the navy council in 1715 did not bring any major changes to the situation.

In January 1717, Crozat submitted his letter of resignation to the royal authorities. The previous year, a court that was supposed to pursue financiers who were accused of defrauding public funds had imposed a fine of 6,600,000 livres upon Crozat. He immediately decided to give up the colony and suggested to the regent that he should deduct his fine from the capital that he had frozen for the monarchy. In the end, Crozat lost nothing as a result of the Louisiana investment, thanks to his commercial profits and to the compensation paid to him by the Crown for the remaining ten years before the monopoly was due to end in 1727. The colony developed only slightly under his control.

Cécile Vidal

See also: Illinois Country; Louisiana; Louisiana Purchase.

References

Giraud, Marcel. *A History of French Louisiana.* Volume 1, *The Reign of Louis XIV (1698–1715).* Trans. Joseph C. Lambert. Baton Rouge: Louisiana State University Press, 1974.

———. *A History of French Louisiana.* Volume 2, *Years of Transition (1715–1717).* Trans. Brian Pearce. Baton Rouge: Louisiana State University Press, 1993.

CUBAN REVOLUTION

A philosophy of exporting revolution and a desire to counter the dominance of the United States characterized the Cuban-French relationship during an era of cold war diplomacy that was profoundly influenced by the 1959 Cuban Revolution. The initial reluctance of France to go against the U.S. policy of isolating the Cuban government in the early 1960s was short-lived, and during the cold war, France became Cuba's most important European trading partner after Spain. In the post–cold war world the relationship has become less important for both nations, as other countries, unwilling to abide by the U.S. economic embargo of Cuba, have invested in the Cuban economy, focusing on the tourist industry. France continues to support the "constructive engagement" approach adopted by the European Union (EU), and although French interests still seek to counter U.S. hegemony, the strategy now centers on strengthening the EU rather than seeking a particular leadership role in the Third World, as was the case in the 1960s. In addition, the myth of the Cuban Revolution was extremely influential on the French Left of the 1960s and 1970s, as encouraged by writers such as Régis Debray and publishers such as François Maspero. (As an example of the evolution of that generation, the latter's return to Cuba is recounted in a series of articles in *Le Monde* in July 1999.)

The bipolarity of the superpower conflict encouraged Cuban and French governments to diversify their diplomatic relations. After the humiliations of World War II, France sought to develop a leadership role in the Third World, particularly in Africa. Although a sense of nationalism and anti-imperialism characterized Cuban independence and revolutionary struggles, the need to diversify economic relations began to define Cuban foreign policy as the country shifted from overdependence on U.S. trade to overdependence on Soviet financial assistance.

Following the revolution, the White House secured virtual diplomatic and economic isolation of Cuba, with most Latin American nations breaking diplomatic ties. Economic ties had also degenerated following the U.S. embargo initiated as a response to the seizure of U.S. assets by the Cuban government the previous year. The years following the revolution were characterized by the Cuban government's support of liberation fighters across Latin America and Africa, in an attempt to avoid isolation and establish allies with which to trade in order to offset dependency on the Soviet Union, as trade with the United States, previously some 80 percent of total trade, evaporated with the embargo.

Despite U.S. policy, seen by many as serving only to push the island into the Soviet sphere, many European nations continued to trade with Cuba, helping consolidate the revolution at a critical juncture. During the period from the revolution until late 1963, however, French-Cuban relations were decidedly cool. In March 1960, French banks formed part of a European consortium withdrawing an offer of a $100 million loan to Cuba, and Charles de Gaulle's government refused to offer credit guarantees to French firms seeking business on the island. Diplomatically, Algeria had become a particularly contentious issue, as Cuba saw the African country's struggle for independence as a cause célèbre in the region. France, seeking to ensure the subordination of Algeria to French needs, was also desperate to make concessions to adopt a popular stance among Third World leaders. The response of the Evian Accords, granting Algerian independence in 1962, were therefore met with skepticism in Havana. France's anti-Soviet posture during the Berlin crisis of 1961 and its instantaneous support of the United States during the Cuban missile crisis of 1962 further engendered a spirit of mistrust between the countries.

Seeking to position France favorably with Third World countries and the Eastern Bloc, de Gaulle began to follow a course of rapprochement with China and the Soviet Union, lending state support with credit guarantees to French exporters to Cuba, a concession not afforded to other Latin American countries. Trade with the island was further diversified as sugar imports were complemented with other agreements for plant construction, and France imported almost a third of all Cuban nickel exports by the end of the decade. Following the failure of Che Guevara's Bolivian expedition, Cuban attention further shifted to Africa with the hope of rejuvenating domestic enthusiasm for revolutionary ideals, particularly among Cuba's Afro-Cuban community. Castro's involvement in Africa brought Cuba into further conflict with France, which was seeking to establish a series of client states under a process of gradual decolonization. Emphasizing Afro-Cuban culture and a connection between French interventions and neocolonialism, Cuban and French African policy clashed in the Belgian Congo (Democratic Republic of Congo), Algeria, Zimbabwe, Namibia, South Africa, Mozambique, Angola, Ethiopia, and Guinea-Bissau throughout the 1960s and 1970s.

With a moderation of de Gaulle's foreign policy by the late 1960s and Georges Pompidou's curtailment of nickel imports in April 1972, the intensity of the French-Cuban relationship waned. French intellectual enthusiasm for the Cuban Revolution declined too, following the "Padilla affair" in 1971, when many important European writers who had previously supported the revolution wrote a letter of criticism to the Cuban government, attacking its "Stalinist" tendencies and poor human rights record. Both the Cuban government's inward-looking obsession with producing a 10-million-ton sugar harvest by 1970 and the normalization of relations with Chile, Peru, Argentina, and the former British Caribbean states served to shift Cuban attention back toward Latin America.

Although the Reagan administration sought to further restrict other nations' economic relations with Cuba, trade with Europe increased between 1980 and 1988. France had bought some 446 million pesos of exports and was surpassed only by Spain in the European Economic Community (EEC) as an important trading partner in the West. Seeking further sources of hard currency, Cuba expanded its tourist industry, encouraging joint ventures between the Cuban National Institute of Tourism and foreign corporations. One of the first, although ultimately unsuccessful, major contracts being discussed in 1986 was with the French Novotel chain to manage high-class Cuban hotels. The collapse of the Soviet Union in 1989–1991 sent the Cuban economy into crisis because almost three-quarters of Cuba's import and export market depended on the USSR. Investment since has concentrated on joint ventures with Canadian, Mexican, Spanish, and Italian, rather than French, companies in the tourist industry, now the predominant source of hard currency for Cuba.

The United States responded to Cuba's economic crisis by further tightening the embargo, prohibiting subsidiaries of U.S. corporations in Third World countries from trading with the island. Before the French company Pernod Ricard launched the Cuban trademark rum, Havana Club, onto the international market in 1992, the dominant rum trader, Bacardi, had promoted itself as the "best Cuban rum," capitalizing on the lack of any authentic Cuban rum being sold on the international market. Once this image was threatened, Bacardi gave financial backing to the Helms-Burton bill in 1996, which supported lawsuits against any foreign company "trafficking" in property previously owned by the United States. In addition, section 211 of the Helms-Burton bill was implemented in 1999, prohibiting the registration in the United States of trademarks that belonged to Cubans before they went into exile. Some critics have argued that this was a measure to support Bacardi in its case against Havana Club. The French company Pernod Ricard took the U.S. ruling to block Havana Club sales to the World Trade Organization and subsequently won its case.

Karen Leimdorfer and Adrian Davies

See also: Argentina; Chile; Debray, Régis; Florida; Foreign Policy, 1945–Present; Gaulle, General Charles de.

References

Chomsky, Aviva, Barry Carr, and Pamela Maria Smorkaloff. *The Cuba Reader: History, Culture, Politics.* Durham/London: Duke University Press, 2004.

Domínguez, Jorge I. *To Make a World Safe for Revolution: Cuba's Foreign Policy.* Cambridge, MA: Harvard University Press, 1989.

Erisman, Michael H. *Cuba's Foreign Relations in a Post-Soviet World.* Miami: University Press of Florida, 2000.

Hennessy, Alistair, and George Lambie, eds. *The Fractured Blockade: West European-Cuban Relations during the Revolution.* London/Basingstoke: Macmillan Press, 1993.

Verdès-Leroux, Jeannine. *La Lune et le caudillo: Le rêve des intellectuels et le régime cubain (1959–1971).* Paris: L'Arpenteur, 1989.

CUISINE

Cuisine refers to the style or quality of cooking for human consumption. The oldest and most essential of the arts and crafts, it involves a variety of primary techniques such as the application of dry heat and immersion in or contact with heated liquids or fats.

Cooking has evolved considerably over the centuries, from the use of just local ingredients to today's globalized food distribution. In France, food and wine are still major topics of conversation, and gastronomy is seriously respected and considered an art. France has had a lasting influence on the cooking and eating habits of many other countries. In fact, all over the world, French cooking and cuisine have become synonymous. France is also the only country that has an entire flock of institutes devoted to the serious study of food and wine. For example, the term *cordon bleu,* now associated with a cooking school in Paris, refers to members of a sixteenth-century French social club who wore crosses hung from blue ribbons around their necks and were famous for their lavish banquets. The nineteenth century was very productive in the domain of gastronomic literature. Among the best known and most quoted is *L'Art de la cuisine française au XIXème siècle/The Art of 19th-Century French Cuisine* (1833) by Marie-Antonin Carême. It is the first work to present culinary preparations as a system of interconnected parts that are built on fundamental principles and supports the belief that French cuisine is "universal." Another is *La Physiologie du goût/The Physiology of Taste* (1825) by the world-renowned author Jean-Anthelme Brillat Savarin (1755–1826), who was among the first to write seriously about eating and the art of the table. In 1955, the 200th anniversary of his birth, L'Académie de gastronomie Brillat Savarin came into being in France. The purpose of the new organization was to uphold and popularize regional cuisines, encourage gastronomic literature, and support young culinarians through contests and awards.

Even though everyone eats, culinary rules and customs are an intrinsic and variable part of a society or culture. For example, some foods are appreciated in some countries and totally rejected in others: in France, horse meat, rabbits, frog legs, and many very odiferous cheeses; in China,

dogs and rats; and in Japan, durian, a fruit that is known to have a peculiar fecal smell. The French have taken great pride in their food, and the rest of the world has recognized French cuisine as the most refined and sought after in the world.

In France the notion of *terroir* has to do with the land or, more specifically, the region in which certain food traditions have been established due to climate or the availability of food ingredients such as butter, olive oil, and certain fish or vegetables. Consequently, because most dishes are identified with a specific area of France, most French cookbooks are divided according to regions such as Brittany, Normandy, the Southwest, or the Southeast. Different areas yield different livestock feed, thereby giving the milk a different taste and the cheese its own personality. However, not all foods that are now accepted as indigenous had their origins in France.

For example, the potato was first introduced to England from South America, where it was cultivated by the Incas. Peasant agriculture of seventeenth- and eighteenth-century France was a delicate mechanism, and years of prolific yields could be followed by a sharp drop, depending on storms and the amount of summer rain. The potato, a new plant that thrived in wet weather and was hardier than grain, presented a solution. The agronomist Oliver de Serres (1539–1619) had written about it and had given it a name, *cartoufle,* which became *kartoffel* and its variants in Russian, Polish, and many other tongues. Unfortunately, the expansion of potato cultivation was unwelcome to some. The upper-class diet revolved around meat, bread, cheese, pastries, and wine. The rich also ate salads and vegetables such as endive, carrots, onions, roasted leeks, cabbages, and turnips. The poor enjoyed no such luxuries. Grain was their staple, and when the crop failed, they starved. So the potato was labeled peasant, undignified, insipid, starchy food. An irate man in Normandy had insisted that the tuber was dangerous because water used to make potato bread turned dark, proving that it contained putrefaction. Also, it belonged to the nightshade species, which was considered poisonous by many. The conflict was finally resolved by Antoine-Augustin Parmentier, a French army officer during the French and Indian War (1756–1763), who while a prisoner in Hamburg became used to potatoes, which were part of the prison diet. After his release he brought Louis XVI round to his way of thinking. The potato finally became fashionable and part of French cuisine. To this day, dishes containing potato are styled *parmentier.* The practice of deep-frying strips of potato—"french fries"—probably originated in France in the eighteenth century, and they are said to have been a common street food in Paris in the 1840s, hence one of their French appellations, *pommes pont neuf.* Whether or not Thomas Jefferson's French cook is the source of their spread to the United States remains open to speculation, but it is clear that, like so many aspects of daily life, their popularity at home spread with the tastes and habits acquired by U.S. soldiers in northern France in World War I.

Another example of a food making a double translatlantic crossing is the tomato. Originating in Peru and domesticated in Central America, it made its way after the Spanish Conquest to Naples and then to Provence. For long largely disregarded in northern Europe, where it had a reputation for being poisonous, its spread to northern France is said to be due to its consumption by Marseillais republican troops during the French revolutionary period; its common use in North America from the mid-nineteenth century is thus due to both French and Italian influence.

In France, cuisine has been divided into two categories: on the one hand, a popular form, home cooking, linked to the soil and therefore able to exploit the products of various regions and different seasons in accordance with nature. This cuisine is based on skills that are transmitted through generations by way of imitation and habit. It is traditional and not really exportable. On the other hand, the erudite cuisine known as haute cuisine is seen as a refined art form. Haute cuisine, or "grande cuisine," has always been the province of the well-off classes in every era. This is a cuisine of professionals that only chefs (mostly men) practice as an art based on invention and experimentation. Women have their place in the kitchen as long as they practice bourgeois or home cooking—but where the creations of grand cuisine are concerned, the French tradition agreed with Louis XIV, who liked to have women at his table but preferred men in his kitchen. However, both popular cuisine and haute cuisine are essentially regional. Geography dictates the ingredients—not least the cooking fat. For example, the Northwest uses butter and the Southwest lard, but the Southeast cooks with olive oil. Even though cuisine in France has evolved and has incorporated foreign influences such as North African couscous or Asian ingredients and techniques, there still remains a cuisine known as classical French cooking. This classical French cooking is what most "French" restaurants outside France aspire to emulate.

In the United States, haute cuisine embodies high cultural capital. It is chefs trained in one of France's culinary schools who can prepare dishes of this caliber. Ingredients are sometimes shipped to the United States from France, or similar ingredients are grown locally in order to achieve a reasonable facsimile. Restaurants serving French fare in the United States also intentionally modify recipes or avoid certain foods to accommodate local tastes and customs. For example, a lot of offal is consumed in France, for example, kidneys and sweetbreads, whereas it is almost never served in the United States. Steak tartare, basically raw hamburger, is rarely or never seen on a menu in the United States. French cuisine in the United States is the province of the well-to-do or those aspiring to a higher social level, with much emphasis placed on the importance of the relationship between the food and the wine. The influence of French culinary terms and attitudes has also become more prominent recently in the U.S. restaurant industry. Many establishments are now called bistros or cafés, and the chef is revered as an artist. The words *baguette, vinaigrette,* and *croissant* have entered everyday vocabulary.

In contrast, the cuisine of Quebec reflects its French heritage, in what is available both in food stores and on restaurant menus. There are a few typical Quebec dishes that have evolved as a result of the harsh climate or the available ingredients, such as poutine, a mixture of potatoes, cheese, and gravy that is also served in McDonald's in Quebec. The traditional working-class French Canadian cuisine was characterized by heavy protein and fat-rich dishes such as bacon, baked beans, and pies (the *tourtière*); the extensive use of maple syrup; and to a certain extent game. However, in contemporary Montreal, the influence is overwhelmingly French. The table d'hôte, a fixed-price menu, is featured in many restaurants and includes three courses, as is the custom in most French restaurants in France. Montreal restaurants' repertoire is more extensive than that of their counterparts in the United States. Pâtés, steak tartare, rabbit, and many French cheeses are readily available and consumed by the Québécois.

In the early eighteenth century, the French arrived in Louisiana, bringing with them their penchant for elegant, fastidiously prepared food—a quality that survives to this day in restaurants such as Arnaud's and Galatoire's in New Orleans. The thickening of soups and sauces was very important to them; the rich feel of French food would not exist without great thickening techniques. Their chief method of thickening was making a roux, a combination of butter and flour that is briefly cooked before adding a liquid. But they were intrigued by the Choctaw Indian's use of the sassafras leaf as a thickening agent, and they called the sassafras powder "filé": they noticed filé forms long threads if cooked too long in the soup as it thickens it, so they named it for the French verb "to make threads" (filaments).

A little later in the eighteenth century, slaves were brought from Africa to work on the local plantations, and with them they brought okra seeds. It was discovered that the mucilaginous nature of okra pods would also turn a thin broth into a thick one. Okra not only went into this evolving soup called gumbo but also gave it its name; the Bantu word for okra is *gombo,* and the Umbundu word for okra is *ochinggombo.* An international dish was born and christened. Traditionally, then, all gumbos start with a roux. Louisiana roux differs from French roux in that butter is rarely used in Louisiana; they use oil instead. Where the French cook roux for about two minutes, Louisianans may cook it for half an hour. The longer it is cooked, the darker and more flavorful it becomes, but it loses some of its thickening power, leading to a somewhat thinner gumbo. Louisianans like seafood gumbos that are thinner than most gumbos. Though gumbo is named for okra, a modern gumbo does not necessarily contain it. It is not necessary to use filé, but it adds a very nice texture. If overcooked, it becomes stringy and gummy.

In 1762 France gave up New Orleans and the French Caribbean islands to Spain, whereupon the Spaniards arrived in Louisiana, bringing a fourth culinary influence to the melting pot. This Spanish influence was manifest in the widespread use of rice and in the growing popularity of combining meat and fish in the same dish (as in the Spanish paella). Many of the Spanish married into Louisiana French families, and their children were known as Creoles (from a Spanish verb meaning "to create, to be born"). This is the original definition of Creole: a light-skinned person born in the New World whose recent ancestors came from Spain and France. And the Creoles of Louisiana were very strict about this definition.

It became an issue because some years later French people living in Canada began migrating to Louisiana from Acadia, today's Nova Scotia. With their French heritage and New World birth, they assumed they were Creoles. But the Creoles of Louisiana disagreed, saying, "You are from Canada and you don't have Spanish blood. You are Acadians." The word *Acadians* changed over time, and these people began to be called Cajuns. These transplanted Canadians, denied access to Creole society, exerted the fifth culinary influence on local cuisine, a very powerful one. They took up residence in the bayous of southern Louisiana, developing a rustic cuisine based on the local fish, game, fruits, and vegetables abundant in the bayous.

One more culinary element enters the picture. In the latter part of the eighteenth century, a group of Creoles left to live in the Caribbean. However, violent slave revolts forced them to leave Haiti and Martinique and return to New Orleans. Happily, they brought something back with them, the spices of the Caribbean, particularly hot red pepper. Seeds from these peppers were planted on Avery Island, Louisiana, by Thomas McIlhenny and today provide the world's largest source of Tabasco sauce.

Gumbo has become synonymous with the history of Louisiana. The spice of the Creole refugees is there, as well as the Spanish penchant for meat and fish. The Cajun predilection for shellfish is also present, as are the Choctaw, French, and African ideas about thickening. With gumbo ingredients, it is generally agreed that anything goes, as long as the thickening is done properly.

French cuisine has had a lasting influence on the cooking and eating habits of the Americas, and indeed, French cuisine has become synonymous with good cooking. It has undergone many changes in the past century. Meals have become smaller and less lavish, but good eating is simply a way of life in France, as well as in French Canada. Every large city in the United States features one or several French restaurants, and many markets sell French cheeses, bread, and wines. French cuisine remains dynamic. It is a professional cuisine that belongs to the chefs, but also a distinctive regional cuisine associated with the French provinces.

Edith Stetser and Richard Stetser

See also: Acadia; Brittany; Cajuns; Catholic Church; French and Indian War; Haiti; Jefferson, Thomas; Louisiana; Martinique; McDonald's; Montreal; New Orleans; Nova Scotia; Quebec; Slavery; Wine; World War I.

References

Ferguson, Priscilla Parkhurst. *Accounting for Taste: The Triumph of French Cuisine.* Chicago: University of Chicago Press, 2004.

Revel, Jean-François. *Culture and Cuisine.* New York: Doubleday, 1982.

Root, Waverly, and Richard de Rochemont. *Eating in America.* New York: Ecco Press, 1989.

Rosengarten, David. *Taste.* New York: Random House, 1998.

Trubek, Amy B. *Haute Cuisine: How the French Invented the Culinary Profession.* Philadelphia: University of Pennsylvania Press, 2000.

West-Sooby, John, ed. *Consuming Culture: The Arts of the French Table.* Newark: University of Delaware Press (Monash Romance Studies), 2004.

Zuckerman, Larry. *The Potato.* London: Macmillan, 1998.

CUMMINGS, E.E. (1894–1962)

The American Edward Estlin Cummings, better known by his legally changed and lower-cased name e.e. cummings, wrote rich, dense U.S. poetry but was too long dismissed as a sentimental traditionalist hiding behind the surface pyrotechnics of typography. While serving as volunteer ambulance drivers in World War I, he and a friend were interned in a French concentration camp for three months in 1917 for violating censorship laws in a letter they sent home. These events furnished the subject of *The Enormous Room* (1922), where Cummings's more or less eponymous protagonist KEW-MANGZ (for so French jailers pronounced his name) recounts how he refused to respond affirmatively to the question "Do you hate the Huns?" and insisted only that "I like the French very much." Cummings wrote his mother that his stay *en prison* at La Ferté Macé was the time of his life, and infinitely superior to his job at Collier's in New York. On this first, not-so-ill-fated trip to France, Cummings learned a lifelong commitment to saving the underdog and freeing the common man.

After the war and some time spent in New York, he returned to France in 1921–1923. On a spring night in Paris, in the company of fellow wartime ambulance driver John Dos Passos, Cummings was arrested again, this time only for three hours, for relieving himself in the street near the Place Saint Michel. He returned again in 1924, living in Paris intermittently throughout the 1920s and traveling abroad at least five times thereafter. In "Conflicting Aspects of Paris" and elsewhere, Cummings sang the praises of "Paname over Paree," a popular and genuine Paris rather than the artificial destination of the tourists, again promoting life over plumbing, that is, the enduring spirit of the city instead of the modern conveniences it lacked.

Cummings has been translated into over a dozen languages, from Arabic to Yiddish. In at least two he has enjoyed the special attention of devout fellow poets. Like William Faulkner and Richard Wright, Cummings won an appreciative audience in France, where fellow Harvardian D. Jon Grossman (1922–1990) would later see to his faithful transcription into

e.e. cummings (from a self-portrait in oils). (Library of Congress)

French. But Grossman did not confer so closely with Cummings and did not deliberately choose the difficult poems, as would Augusto de Campos, a Brazilian concretist poet who embraces formal constraints in his own poetry and in those poets whom he translates, such as the troubadour Arnaut Daniel. Genuinely remarkable is Campos's devotion in translating those most "perilous" poems of Cummings, beginning with "l(a," under their author's scrutiny from 1956 until his death and ever since in his devoted translator's own style, *Campos mentis,* that is, supremely attentive to the original but equally innovative, in what Campos has labeled his poetic transcreations ("transçriacões"). The result is a delicate testimonial to the international viability of Cummings's humanitarian poetics, admirably transposed into Portuguese. The infamous

"manunkind" of Cummings's poem "pity this busy monster" is appropriately and cleverly rendered "humanimaldade": that is, "humanimality."

Roy Rosenstein

See also: Dos Passos, John; Literary Relations; World War I.
References
cummings, e.e. "Conflicting Aspects of Paris." *E. E. Cummings: A Miscellany Revisited.* New York: October House, 1965: 154–158.
Friedman, Norman. *e.e.cummings: The Growth of a Writer.* Carbondale: Southern Illinois University, 1964.
Rosenstein, Roy. "Letter on Cummings in Brazil." *Spring: The Journal of the e.e. cummings Society,* N.S. 2 (1993): 96–97.

CYBERCULTURE

The Internet—and the cyberculture that it generates—provoke mixed feelings in France. Fundamentally, the French state holds two interrelated views: on the one hand, the World Wide Web is seen as yet another American/Anglophone threat to French language and culture and industry and commerce; on the other hand, the benefits of electronic communication and information give rise to hope that the web may yet be an arena in which French culture can resist the Coca-Colonization of U.S.-led globalization. Another reaction of the French state to the web and cyberculture has been that of concern that its anarchic freedom fits ill with practices of regulation and control of media technologies traditional in France.

On a more industrial/technical level, the irresistible rise of the Internet since the 1990s has been all the more galling to France because of the way in which it has undermined the Minitel—a successful

French technical and sociocultural video-text experiment launched in the early 1980s. In public policy, "what to do about the Internet" questions French traditions of dirigiste industrial policy as well as offering a technological and sociocultural opportunity to reinforce the claimed equality and meritocracy of French society through equalized access to knowledge for all. Culturally and politically, these are important issues, since the high visibility of the Internet in public opinion focuses attention on changing French practices in industry and business (privatizing France Telecom, respecting European Union rulings about competition), and the "democratic" (i.e., liberal/free-market) nature of Internet services has initially magnified existing inequalities of access to knowledge between France's information-rich and information-poor. The potential usefulness of the Internet in equalizing information access in France's still highly centralized society (where cultural and educational facilities are heavily concentrated in Paris) has been seized upon by successive governments anxious to include cyberculture in the Republican toolbox for maintaining liberty, equality, and fraternity. France has been conscious of its backwardness in computer technology since the 1950s and 1960s. In 1967, a major element of Jean-Jacques Servan-Schreiber's seminal analysis of the *défi américain* ("American challenge") was the way in which he saw U.S. computer hardware and software and the social and commercial use of computing changing the nature of U.S. society and business and leaving France behind. French thinking on the links between computing, culture, and society was further spurred by Simon Nora and Alain Minc's famous report, *The Computerization of Society*, which emphasized

the fundamental changes that would be wrought by the information age and how countries that did not master new technologies and practices would suffer.

France got its first taste of cyberculture in the 1980s with the Minitel. These terminals give French homes and businesses access to France's videotext network. Since 1980, when it was introduced experimentally in Saint-Malo, the Minitel has grown steadily in both popularity and use and now connects 20 million users with approximately 25,000 online services of all kinds. Minitel/Teletel has been a major element in modernizing the French public's attitudes toward telecommunications and information technologies. During the 1980s the Minitel was a symbol of France's industrial and social vision, demonstrating national ability in the techniques necessary for a wired society and familiarizing sometimes reluctant users with machines more complicated than the telephone for communication and transactions. The most famous Minitel service is the "electronic phone book," first introduced in 1985. But the extent of the other 25,000 services is enormous, ranging from weather information and train timetables, through distance banking and mail order, to the sending of telexes and exchanging of messages (some pornographic or erotic, as in the "Minitel rose"). After a decade of use, the Minitel sector was deemed to have reached maturity at a level of 1.5 billion connections and 100 million hours of communication.

During the 1990s the Minitel industry's turnover continued to grow, and although the total number of calls also continued to rise, faster data transfer and the familiarity of users with the technology led to shorter connections and a slowdown in sector growth. Between a quarter and a third of French households regularly consult Minitel services, representing a remarkable national cultural practice of some 14 million individual users, but beginning in the mid-1990s, Minitel faced competition from newer, faster systems, typified by the Internet. Although Minitel was symbolic of France's technological expertise and social modernity in the 1980s, this national experiment in videotext culture may soon become a symbol of France's declining independence vis-à-vis U.S. colonialism, technologically and culturally. Minitel is an intensely French technology—attempts to export the concept abroad have met with little success—and its replacement with U.S. cybertechnologies, together with the perceived redoubled onslaught of the English language via the Internet, undermines both France's technological base and its cultural homogeneity. As the use of the Internet gradually increased in France during the late 1990s, software enabling personal computers to emulate the Minitel became available in a neat example of how the videotext experiment had both established a useful familiarity with new communication/information technologies and at the same time constituted a brake on the French public's espousal of the web. France's reluctance to abandon Minitel has been a clear example of a persistent mistrust of what is often referred to as the *réseau américain* ("American network"). Only in 1996 did France Telecom finally resolve to enter the Internet market as a provider of services, thus establishing a positive strategy toward the Internet.

For many French commentators on cyberculture, the web (like film in the 1950s or Disneyland Paris in the 1990s) is considered to be a Trojan horse of American cultural imperialism, whose direct appeal to individuals via uncontrolled and unregulated channels (unlike the state-led Minitel) dupes French citizens into capitulation to the hegemony of "Anglo-Saxon" language and culture. Unlike in cinema, television, and radio, where the French state has erected defenses against Hollywood films and English-language pop songs, no quotas exist to stem the tide of U.S. influence. Jean Baudrillard has suggested that Disneyland Paris is an example of France "dreaming herself American," and if that is indeed the case, how will a France where homes and families are wired to U.S. and worldwide English-language websites protect its cultural and linguistic sovereignty? At the height of mid-1990s debates on how France should respond to the "American challenge" of the web, in 1996 the French minister of culture Jacques Toubon called for firm action by the state: the defense of France's "exception" would rely first on protecting French culture (because culture would guarantee the survival of the French language) and second on legal and regulatory controls limiting the pernicious effects of free-enterprise new technologies.

Telematics, the Internet, and the move toward multimedia superhighway services pose challenges to French culture and society at the domestic level, as well as potentially threatening the place of French culture and language in the world. The French state hopes to use the new technologies to defend traditional Republican principles of liberty, equality, and fraternity (in contradistinction to "Anglo-Saxon" "free-market" democracy) for the ordering of society. The modernization of telecommunications has been used in the past as a means of modernizing French society (the telephone system, cable), and a major attraction of cyberculture for the French state is its potential contribution to a more harmonious France through improved access to knowledge for all. As well as this "civic" function, many analysts see cybertechnologies and cyberculture/practices as instruments of empowerment and self-expression representative of a postindustrial, postmodern age in which liberty and equality are synonymous with access to information and in which fraternity is fostered by empowering citizens to both express their differences and tolerate differences in others. "Universal access"—guaranteed by state regulation of information superhighways—to the new technologies is seen as the solution to France's considerable current concern over *la fracture sociale* between the "haves" and "have-nots" of French society. "Equality of access" to knowledge, culture, and education brings its own benefits in France's theoretically highly meritocratic system of schooling, and the "quality of life" is to be improved by new work patterns allowing more efficient and flexible employment distribution across the country. Equal chances for all in the best traditions of the Republican state will thus be guaranteed by the new technologies. A new freedom of access to information will therefore come to the rescue of the old value of equality, increasingly considered threatened by the dysfunctionings of the modern economy. The new media technologies bring with them, of course, precisely the risk of creating a dual society of the information-rich and the information-poor, both in terms of areas devoid of culture and in terms of inequalities of social class, level of income, and education.

France's traditional suspicion of the culturally hegemonic tendencies of U.S. industry and finance and French sensitivity to the linguistic encroachment of English coalesce in the country's reaction to the Internet and the information superhighway. The Internet is prompting France to develop its own approaches to providing and regulating services, but it is unfortunate for France that such a challenge to its remaining "exceptionalism" is occurring in a political and economic context unfavorable to France's usual mechanisms of defense—the nationally led technological *grand programme* and European Union strictures on the provision of services. The current international triumph of economic liberalism and France's leading role in the drive to European union are leaving the French state bereft of its traditional weapons of economic, technological, and cultural nationalism. However, as with many issues in France, the question of "rights" is fundamental in the technical and cultural evolution of the Internet. Thus the "freedom," "individualism," and "anarchy" of the Internet perhaps pose more problems for France than for other societies less prone to obsessive constitutional definition of liberties and rights and to the complex legal regulation of audiovisual activities. The intensity of debate over the claimed "legal vacuum" in which the Internet has developed in France has revealed the state's anxiety over the autonomy of electronic information, echoing both traditional fears of U.S. cultural/linguistic imperialism and the disquiet of regulators at the anarchic proliferation of websites and services. While asserting the importance of solidarity, equality, and fraternity, France simultaneously defends the individual's right to privacy in domestic life and the duty of the state to regulate activities in the best interests of society. The French Internet is indeed fast becoming a symbolic medium and cultural resource, providing a means of resistance to U.S. influences and a means of combating communication problems in French society itself, but cyberculture and its organization are particularly problematic for the French state.

Hugh Dauncey

See also: Baudrillard, Jean; Computer Technology; Disneyland Paris; Servan-Schreiber, Jean-Jacques; Television.

References
Breton, Thierry. *Les Téléservices en France: Quels marchés pour les autoroutes de l'information?* Paris: La Documentation française, 1994.
Jacobs, Gabriel. "Cyberculture." *French Popular Culture: An Introduction.* Ed. Hugh Dauncey. London: Arnold, 2003: 77–89.
Nora, Simon, and Alain Minc. *The Computerization of Society: A Report to the President of France.* Cambridge, MA: MIT Press, 1980.

CYRANO DE BERGERAC

French theatrical character and French historical personage, born on March 6, 1619, and died on July 28, 1655, in Paris.

Despite the fact that he was a real person, a French satirist and dramatist who inspired a number of later writers, his name is mostly known as the fictional hero from Edmond Rostand's play *Cyrano de Bergerac* (1897). However, the unfortunate romantic lover from Rostand's play, who became one of the most popular characters of French theater and a world symbol of generosity and beauty of soul, has little to do with the real Savinien de Cyrano de Bergerac. The cause of Cyrano's real death was a banal accident: a piece of plank dropped on his head. This event was fictionalized in Rostand's play into assassination by his enemies. The real Cyrano enlisted in the army but had problems with discipline: a

bohemian and duelist, he gave up his military career. He went to study under the philosopher and mathematician Pierre Gassendi, whose scientific theories and liberal philosophies influenced Bergerac's own writing. His two best-known works, *Histoire comique des états et empires de la lune* and *Histoire comique des états et empires du soleil* (*A Voyage to the Moon: With Some Account of the Solar World,* 1754), reflect Gassendi's teachings.

Cyrano's writing did popularize new scientific theories; however, his principal aim was not to be scientific but to ridicule authority, particularly religious authority. Although his works point to new theories (he "predicted" the atomic structure of matter), they are rather a reflection of poetic imagination. His approach also mocks René Descartes's ideas, pointing to relativity and abstract concepts of what constitutes being and thinking. For example, in Cyrano's book *A Voyage to the Moon,* in order to get to the moon, the main character travels in a body machine ornamented with firecrackers and ends up in Canada.

The dissemination of "Cyrano de Bergerac" in the Americas occurred through the film versions. The charismatic character of the fictional Cyrano appeals to American popular culture mainly because of his selflessness, his ugly appearance yet poetic nature, and his honesty and richness of soul. Rostand's play first became influential through Italian filmmaker Augusto Genina's adaptation of it for silent film in 1925. Until then, Rostand's play was virtually unseen in the United States. The film features magnificent acting from Pierre Magnier as Cyrano. As a European film full of rich emotions and visual extravagance, it rivals the best of U.S. silent films. Three years (starting in 1922) were devoted to the hand coloring by the Pathe Stencil Color process.

The play thrived as a theater piece regularly performed in American repertoire. After World War II, the actor José Ferrer in the title role of Cyrano greatly popularized the play in the United States. After a successful Broadway production, for which Ferrer won a Tony Award, United Artists purchased the rights to the film and recast Ferrer as Cyrano (Michael Gordon, 1950). He won an Oscar and Golden Globe Award for this role. Ferrer also appeared on television as Cyrano, adding to the mass media popularity of this text. However, most people today know Rostand's play through Steve Martin's 1987 contemporary comedy version *Roxanne* (Schepisi) and through Jean-Paul Rappeneau's 1990 version with Gérard Depardieu in the title role.

Aleksandar Dundjerovic

See also: Cinema, 1895–1945; Cinema, 1945 to the Present; Depardieu, Gérard; Theater.

References

Brockett, Oscar G. *Century of Innovation: A History of European and American Theater and Drama since 1870.* Englewood Cliffs, NJ: Prentice Hall, 1973.

Fort, Alice, and Herbert S. Kates. "Cyrano de Bergerac." *Minute History of the Drama.* New York: Grosset and Dunlap, 1935.

Freeman, Edward. *Rostand: "Cyrano De Bergerac"* (Glasgow Introductory Guides to French Literature). Glasgow: University of Glasgow French and German Publications, 1995.

D

DAGUERRE, LOUIS JACQUES MANDÉ (1787–1851)

Artist, proprietor of the Diorama, and inventor of the daguerreotype.

Born at Cormeilles-en-Parisis to Louis Jacques Daguerre and his wife, Anne Antoinette (née Hauterre), Daguerre was raised after 1791 at Orléans. He was apprenticed at age thirteen to an architect, and later accepted as a pupil of Ignace Eugène Marie Degotti, scene painter to the Paris Opera, where he exhibited an aptitude for the creation of realistic illusions. In 1807, he began working for Pierre Prévost, the French patent holder of the process, in the production of large panorama paintings. These highly realistic depictions of cities and scenes of historic importance were displayed in rotundas carefully lit from above to enhance the illusion of reality. They appear to have been the basis from which Daguerre and Charles Marie Bouton, another of Prévost's assistants, launched their own business venture by creating the Diorama. Combining the scale of the panorama with technical details of the diapanorama, the Diorama offered a new and popular form of public entertainment that bore a striking resemblance to modern cinema.

Daguerre and Bouton opened the Diorama in 1822 on the rue de Marais in Paris, earning themselves instant celebrity for the lifelike paintings that appeared to change and move as carefully controlled lighting was applied to translucent canvas. Just two years later, Daguerre began his experiments on the chemical fixation of images in a laboratory on the top floor of the Diorama building. He was unsuccessful in his early work, but his experiments led him to contact Joseph Nicéphore Niépce, with whom he formed a partnership in 1829. Together, until Niépce's untimely death in 1833, they invented the chemical and technical foundations for the process that would become the daguerreotype, a negative rendered on a polished silver plate, viewed as a positive when reflected against a dark cloth.

The January 7, 1839, announcement signaling the beginning of public awareness of the daguerreotype was nowhere received more enthusiastically than in the United States. Excited by imagination and Samuel Morse's firsthand account of the beautiful images, an account printed April 20, 1839, in the *New York Observer*, the U.S. scientific and artistic communities anxiously awaited the revelation of

Daquerre. From a daguerreotype taken at his château, Brie-Sur-Marne, France, 1848. By Meade & Brother, Albany, New York. (Library of Congress)

Daguerre's working process, in August of the same year, and quickly imported daguerreotype cameras and manuals, adopting the French invention as an art all their own. The art of daguerreotype, both in portraiture and landscape, flourished in the United States and France for twenty years, until it was gradually replaced by less expensive and faster methods of photography.

Kelley Wilder

See also: Niépce, Joseph Nicéphore; Photography.
References
Gernsheim, Helmut, and Alison Gernsheim. *LJM Daguerre: The History of the Diorama and the Daguerreotype.* London: Secker and Warburg, 1956.
Rinhart, Floyd, and Marion Rinhart. *The American Daguerreotype.* Athens: University of Georgia Press, 1981.

DALIO, MARCEL (ISRAEL MOSHE BLAUSCHILD) (1899–1983)

Highly prolific French character actor, whose transatlantic career of some 150 films spanned almost fifty years.

Despite an unpromising background, starting his life in the Jewish ghetto around the rue des Rosiers in Paris, Dalio reinvented himself as an actor and started in films in the early 1930s. The depth and range of his acting won him the respect of the film profession, and he worked with the greatest directors of the period, such as Robert Bresson (*Les Affaires publiques/ Public Affairs,* 1934), Julien Duvivier (*Le Golem/The Golem,* 1936; *Pépé le Moko,* 1937), Jean Renoir (*La Grande Illusion/ Grand Illusion,* 1937; *La Règle du jeu* [*The Rules of the Game*], 1939), Pierre Chenal, Abel Gance, Robert Siodmak, and Marc Allégret. The actor thus enjoyed a flourishing career up to the time when the right-wing press targeted him viciously, publishing his picture as an example of the "typical Jew." Although well respected by his peers, Dalio's small stature and strong Semitic looks had often relegated him to roles of villains and cowards or seedy, louche characters, often Jewish. The first release of *La Règle du jeu* in 1939 was notoriously panned by audiences and most critics, and Dalio's portrayal of the Duc De La Chesnaye became an excuse for the press to unleash all their anti-Semitic venom. The forty-one-year-old actor was forced into exile with his wife, the actress Madeleine Lebeau, and sought refuge in Hollywood.

After a long, difficult journey through Portugal, Mexico, and Canada, Dalio arrived in Hollywood in 1940, and with some help from the émigré and exile colony, above all the actor Charles Boyer, he eventually landed a contract with Twentieth Century Fox. Dalio was not exactly stranded in the States, however, since many of the film artists he had worked with in France before the war were also in exile in Hollywood (Jean Gabin, Jean Renoir, Duvivier, René Clair, Michèle Morgan, and Jean-Pierre Aumont, to take the most famous). The exile community was very close-knit, and many worked together while in Hollywood. Indeed most of the films directed by French war exiles include a numerous French cast and crew, and Dalio was in Duvivier's *Tales of Manhattan* (1942) and *Flesh and Fantasy* (1943), both also featuring Boyer. This was also true of war propaganda films directed by U.S. citizens or exiles from other countries.

Fox did not really know how to employ the actor, who was typically given minor supporting roles as a token Frenchman. Often uncredited for his parts, Dalio was nevertheless cast in many Hollywood classics, such as Sternberg's *The Shanghai Gesture* (1941), starring Gene Tierney and Victor Mature, Michael Curtiz's *Casablanca* (1942), alongside Ingrid Bergman and Humphrey Bogart, and Howard Hawks's *To Have and Have Not* (1944) with Bogart and Lauren Bacall. After the war, Dalio went on to lead a transatlantic career, providing memorable supporting roles in both French and U.S. films (*The Snows of Kilimanjaro,* King, 1952; *Gentlemen Prefer Blondes,* Hawks, 1953; *Sabrina,* Wilder, 1954; *Razzia sur la Chnouf* [*Razzia*], Decoin, 1955; *Tendre Voyou* [*Tender Scoundrel*], Becker, 1966; *Les Aventures de Rabbi Jacob* [*The Adventures of Rabbi Jacob*], Oury, 1973; *L'Aile ou la Cuisse* [*Wing or Thigh*], Zidi, 1976).

Catherine Hellegouarc'h

See also: Boyer, Charles; Cinema, 1895–1945; Cinema, 1945 to the Present; Clair, René; Darrieux, Danielle; Duvivier, Julien; Florey, Robert; Hollywood's French Caribbean; Hollywood's Paris; Jourdan, Louis; Morgan, Michèle; Renoir, Jean; Simon, Simone; World War II.

Reference
Dalio, Marcel. *Mes années folles.* Paris: Lattès, 1976.

DAMAS, LÉON-GONTRAN (1912–1978)

Although of mixed race, Damas was one of the founding members, with Aimé Césaire and Léopold Sédar Senghor, of the négritude movement in the 1930s.

He was born in Cayenne (French Guiana) and educated at the Lycée Victor Schoelcher in Fort-de-France (Martinique) and the Collège de Meaux in France. He moved to Paris in 1929 and enrolled briefly at the Ecole des Langues Orientales, in addition to attending classes in law and literature. His subsequent studies at the Institut d'Ethnologie de Paris were more fruitful. He worked successively for the *La Revue du monde noir* (The Review of the Black World), *Légitime Défense,* and *L'Etudiant noir* (The Black Student), little reviews brought out by African and Caribbean students.

He was first and foremost a poet and was described by Aimé Césaire as the first modern negro poet in the francophone world. He was influenced by the Harlem Renaissance, especially Langston Hughes, Sterling Brown, and Claude McKay. His first collection, *Pigments* (1937), was a trenchant, racy, anticlerical, and anticolonial cry of revolt. Although Damas abandoned traditional French prosody, with its focus on syllable counting, these poems have a strong rhythm and often feature a wry, self-deprecating humor. The short texts of *Graffiti* (1952) are marked by a very personal angst and the theme of lost love (for an unnamed beautiful coquette); they come across as sad, sincere, and spontaneous. Damas himself regarded *Black-Label* (1956) as his best poetry: its four cantos renew the theme of revolt, but they are also lyrical songs of exile, suffused with love. Somewhat reminiscent of Césaire's poetry, *Black-Label* relies heavily on anaphora and alliteration; more importantly it paints a very positive picture of "les Nègres."

His first important prose writing was *Retour de Guyane* ("Return from Guiana," 1938), a virulent ethnological report on colonial rule, which criticizes the Eurocentric educational system, corrects the metropolitan view of French Guiana as a penal colony, and highlights its enormous agricultural and industrial potential. *Veillées noires* (1943) is a collection of Guianese folktales, transcribed from Creole: Damas's antiassimilation message continues in these fables peopled by animals, humans, and supernatural beings.

He was involved in the Resistance during World War II and represented Guiana in the National Assembly from 1948 to 1951, even though he had originally opposed its elevation to departmental status. He held various international cultural positions, traveled widely, not just in Africa and South America, and gave numerous lectures, especially on topics relating to négritude. In his later years he carved out a distinguished academic career, holding teaching posts at Federal City College and Howard University. His circle of friends included Louis Armstrong, the African American diplomat and educator Mercer Cook, the French writers Robert Desnos and Michel Leiris, the Senegalese editors Christiane and Alioune Diop, the Belgian poet and jazz writer Robert Goffin, and many African statesmen and diplomats.

Keith Aspley

See also: Césaire, Aimé; Guiana; Leiris, Michel; Martinique; McKay, Claude; *Revue du monde noir, La;* World War II.

References

Kesteloot, Lilyan. *Black Writers in French: A Literary History of Negritude.* Washington, DC: Howard University Press, 1991.

Racine, Daniel. *Léon-Gontran Damas: l'homme et l'œuvre.* Paris: Présence Africaine, 1983.

DANCE

France was the birthplace of ballet, as well as many of the court and social dances that pervaded Europe from medieval times. Ballet was a theatricalization of such dances, while the dances themselves survived in the fledgling United States in variants from the genteel cotillion to the more boisterous square dance. In the twentieth century, France also became an important crossroads for the dissemination of dance, primarily in hosting Sergey Diaghilev's Ballets russes (1909–1929), but it was also the gateway for the importation of popular Latin American dances like the habanera, the tango, and the maxixe. Because of the primacy of classical ballet, modern dance was relatively slow to catch on in France, but by the end of the twentieth century, France was home to a number of leading companies representing the full range of theatrical dance.

Social Dance

The genesis of all dance is in social dancing. Circle and line dances frequently form part of rituals, particularly those surrounding fertility—planting, harvest, or wedding celebrations. Village dances were gradually "refined" into court dances, often retaining in their names their regional distinctions (pavane [Paduana], allemande [German dance], even later the habanera [Havana dance]). As court dances became more intricate, the emphasis moved from participation to spectatorship; dance was institutionalized first in France when Louis XIV founded the Académie Royale de Danse in 1661. Meanwhile, social dances emigrated across the channel—French dancing masters were very popular for those English who could afford them—and then across the Atlantic. Understandably, given the puritan foundations of the northern colonies, the dances flourished most prosperously in the South. The landed gentry participated in cotillions—originally a sort of complicated social dance, similar to a quadrille, the word later came to mean a formal dance party, dense with social ritual; this lasted well into the twentieth century as occasions at which young ladies of certain status made their debuts and were courted by prospective husbands. At the opposite end of the class spectrum—though serving almost identical social purposes—was the square dance (an almost literal translation of *quadrille*) in which four couples form a square and perform complex maneuvers prompted by a "caller." A number of French terms have been retained: promenade, allemande, do-si-do (*dos à dos,* "back to back"), and sashay (*chassez*).

As a colonial power, France became a portal into Europe for a number of popular dances from the Americas. One of the earliest, and most important, was the nineteenth-century habanera, with its distinctive 3+3+2 rhythm. The habanera was immortalized in Bizet's tremendously popular opera *Carmen,* but it was also disseminated to South America, contributing to the development of the tango. Through trade connections with Argentina, the tango and its sister the maxixe were reimported to France in the first decade of the twentieth century. France also became a refuge for a number of African American musicians and dancers in the 1920s.

Theatrical Dance

After the founding of the Académie Royale de Danse (1661), noted opera composer Jean-Baptiste Lully created the Académie Royale de Musique in 1672, with Pierre Beauchamp as ballet master. Over the next century, ballet became a far more integral part of French opera than its Italian counterpart. Although based in social dance, the technique of professional dancers soon outstripped amateur abilities. Several forms of dance notation suggest that the patterns traced on the floor were still more important than the ornamental steps, although leaps, hops, pirouettes, and beats entered the language. In the eighteenth century, Jean-Georges Noverre (1727–1810) advocated the integration of dance with drama; working from his principles, Beethoven wrote his only ballet, *Die Geschöpfe des Prometheus* ("The Creatures of Prometheus," 1801). By this time, dance had begun separating itself from opera.

Ballet reached its peak in France during the romantic period; the earliest preserved full-length ballets date from the first half of the nineteenth century, centering in Paris even though most of the famous dancers were foreign, with the female dancer assuming greatest prominence during this period. Marie Taglioni introduced pointe shoes, and her ethereal movement enhanced her performance as the leader of the ghostly nuns in Giacomo Meyerbeer's opera *Robert le Diable* ("Robert the Devil," 1831). The chorus of female dancers on pointe in the long, bell-shaped romantic tutu was the genesis of the "white ballet," purely choreographic interludes in narrative ballets, usually representing supernatural spirits or nonhuman "characters." Similar choruses appeared in *La Sylphide* (Auguste Bournonville's 1836 choreography was not the first, but the oldest surviving example) and *Giselle* (Jules Perrot-Jean Coralli, 1841), one of the staples of the ballet repertoire. Choreographers trained in France disseminated the burgeoning style to Denmark (Bournonville) and Russia, where the close cultural connections with France led a number of dancers and choreographers to tour. As romantic ballet declined during the latter part of the century, French ballet master Marius Petipa almost single-handedly created classical ballet in Saint Petersburg. His ballets include Tchaikovsky's three "great" ballets, *Swan Lake* (1877), *The Sleeping Beauty* (1890), and *The Nutcracker* (1892), as well as *Don Quixote* (1869) and *La Bayadère* (1877); Petipa's original choreography has degenerated through oral transmission, but his clear-cut movement style and act structure was a dominating influence.

Ballet was reimported to Paris by Russian impresario Sergey Diaghilev with his Ballets russes, offering seasons in Paris from 1909 to 1929, the year of Diaghilev's death. The Ballets russes was undoubtedly the most important dance troupe of the twentieth century, perhaps ever; its impact spread far beyond the world of dance. Fashion, music, and even cinema (particularly the Hollywood musical of such directors as Vincente Minnelli and Gene Kelly)

Diaghilev's Ballets russes—exhibition organized by Serge Lifar. Poster by Jean Cocteau, 1939. (Library of Congress)

owe a tremendous debt to the aesthetic of the troupe, which was deeply collaborative—the best artists (Pablo Picasso, Léon Bakst, Jean Cocteau), composers (Igor Stravinsky, Maurice Ravel, Claude Debussy, Richard Strauss, Francis Poulenc), and choreographers (Michel Fokine, Vaslav Nijinsky, Bronislava Nijinska, Léonide Massine) worked together on ballets that tended to be short and "high concept." Early on, the Ballets russes was renowned for the exotic (*Polovtsian Dances*, *Cléopâtre*, *The Firebird*, *The Rite of Spring*, *Le Dieu bleu* [The Blue God]); it passed through cubism (*Parade, Pulcinella*), constructivism (*Pas d'acier, Le Chat* [The Cat]), and Chanel chic (*Les Biches, Les Matelots* [The Sailors]), and was entering a neoclassical phase with its last ballet master, the young George Balanchine, and his earliest surviving works *The Prodigal Son* and *Apollo*. Balanchine emigrated to the United States in 1933 and, building on Petipa and Diaghilev, revolutionized twentieth-century ballet, particularly with his development of the swift, athletic, plotless U.S. style.

Other Ballets russes alumni and alumnae spread ballet over most of the Western Hemisphere. The 1920s also saw a flourishing of other dance in France, with the Ballets Russes–inspired Ballet Suédois, which staged Darius Milhaud's *La Création du monde* (The Creation of the World, 1923) and *Le Bœuf sur le toit* (*The Cow on the Roof,* 1919), as well as a little-known ballet (*Within the Quota,* 1923) by Cole Porter; meanwhile at the Folies Bergère, African American dancer Josephine Baker was a huge sensation with her eccentric, highly sexual "primitive" dances.

After World War II, Diaghilev's protégé Serge Lifar led the Paris Opéra-Ballet, though its preeminence was eclipsed by Roland Petit's company in Marseilles; his ballerinas "Zizi" Jeanmaire and Leslie Caron both starred in Hollywood musicals. Modern dance influenced choreographers like Maurice Béjart and Maguy Marin. In the 1980s, Rudolf Nureyev revived the Paris Opéra-Ballet and mentored one of the most celebrated dancers of the late twentieth century, Sylvie Guillem. Their production of Prokofiev's *Cinderella* (1986) was a fitting culmination of the century's tripartite dance trade between Russia, America, and France: Guillem was

the ingenue, plucked from obscurity by a Groucho Marx look-alike studio head (Nureyev); she met her leading man on a set resembling the back lot from *Singin' in the Rain* (Donen and Kelly, 1952), populated by King Kong and a giant statue of Betty Grable.

Robynn Stilwell

See also: Argentina; Baker, Josephine; *Carmen;* Caron, Leslie; Cocteau, Jean; Fashion; Jazz; Jeanmaire, Zizi; Kelly, Gene; Music (Classical); Porter, Cole.
References
Garafola, Lynn, and Nancy Van Norman Baer, eds. *The Ballets Russes and Its World.* New Haven: Yale University Press, 1999.
Harris-Warrick, Rebecca, Noël Goodwin, and John Percival. "Ballet." *The New Grove Dictionary of Music Online.* Ed. L. Macy. http://www.grovemusic.com (accessed August 15, 2003).
Kirstein, Lincoln. *Dance: A Short History of Theatrical Dancing.* New York: Putnam's, 1935.
Sadie, Stanley, and John Tyrrell, eds. *The New Grove Dictionary of Music and Musicians,* 2nd ed. London: Grove Dictionaries, 2001.
Wiley, Roland John. *Tchaikovsky's Ballets.* Oxford: Clarendon, 1985.

DANGEROUS LIAISONS

Written by Choderlos de Laclos in 1782, the French epistolary novel *Les Liaisons dangereuses* has emerged as one of the most analyzed works of its time and has in recent years given rise to several cinematic adaptations. The story of the sadistic sexual and psychological manipulations of two perverse French aristocrats and ex-lovers, the Marquise de Merteuil and the Vicomte de Valmont, has been reconfigured in highly different screen versions, each of which has injected into the original ancien régime setting certain Americanized elements, the end result being a string of films that defy categorization as purely French or purely American cultural artifacts, but instead combine the two influences in varying proportions.

Roger Vadim's 1959 version, *Les Liaisons dangereuses,* starring Jeanne Moreau and Gérard Philippe, is a French production with French actors, but its temporal transposition of the eighteenth century intrigue to 1950s Paris results, bizarrely, in an intensely transatlantic text. The American jazz soundtrack and the numerous ornamental black American musicians the film relies on to convey the "decadence" of this postwar French existentialist milieu evokes a modern France soaked in American culture. Stephen Frears's *Dangerous Liaisons* (based on Christopher Hampton's 1985 theatrical adaptation of Laclos's novel), made in 1988 and starring Glenn Close and John Malkovich, is the most famous of the various film versions, and it combines Paris and Hollywood in quite a different manner. Retaining Laclos's pre-revolutionary French setting (the film was shot largely in and around the châteaux of Champs-sur-Marne), Frears presents Hollywood stars (including Michelle Pfeiffer, Uma Thurman, and Keanu Reeves) who perform comfortably in modern American accents despite inhabiting the garb of French nobles, actors happy to exploit their established screen images in the service of giving certain twentieth-century dimensions to the aristocratic protagonists. Milos Forman's less successful 1989 *Valmont,* with Annette Bening and Colin Firth, follows the same formula—English-speaking stars performing within the original French historical setting—but is an altogether less grandiose affair, its lesser-known stars failing to imbue the Marquise and the Vi-

comte with the quasi-royal arrogance of the earlier film's Hollywood elite cast. The most thoroughly Americanized of the screen versions of *Les Liaisons dangereuses* is also by far the most removed from the source novel: *Cruel Intentions* (Kumble, 1999) changes setting, actors, and characters from 1780s France to 1990s United States. Retaining Laclos's plot structure, the film settles, however, for a New York high school backdrop against which to paint the puzzlingly jaded teen passions now at stake.

The latest adaptation of *Les Liaisons dangereuses* continues to mix French and Anglo-American elements: starring Catherine Deneuve and Rupert Everett, Josée Dayan's Quebec-produced 2002 version is a television vehicle, screened both in Canada and on France's main channel TF1.

Andrew Asibong

See also: Deneuve, Catherine; Hollywood's Paris; Jazz; Remakes; Vadim, Roger.

References

Humbert, Brigitte E. *De la lettre à l'écran: Les Liaisons Dangereuses.* Amsterdam/Atlanta, GA: Rodopi, 2000.

Marvier, Marie. "Les Adaptations dangereuses." *Synopsis,* no. 25 (May/June 2003): 42–45.

DANTICAT, EDWIDGE (1967–)

Haitian-born novelist Edwidge Danticat grew up in Brooklyn and writes in English. As a young short story writer emerging from American university writers' workshops, she met with immediate success, to the extent that she was labeled a younger version of the greatest living African American author, Toni Morrison. Her works were almost simultaneously translated into

French, and the success of her short stories and two novels has been such that no one, not even francophiles themselves, can refuse her affiliation to *la francophonie* (the French-speaking world). Between two cultures, between contemporary American life and the past of Haiti, between English and either the French or the Creole of her mother and aunts, between the rich and dominant superpower and the poorer island, which has been mistreated for more than two centuries by colonialists and dictators, Danticat combines magic realism and a poetic form of journalism, history (the historical novel) and memory (*The Farming of Bones,* 1998), travel writing (*After the Dance, A Walk through Jacmel, Haiti,* 2002), and the short story (*Krik? Krak!* 1995).

The lineage of *commères* ("godmothers," literally, "co-mothers," like Spanish *compadre* and *commadre;* it also means "gossips"), daughters and mothers, aunts and neighbors, often women mistreated and viewed as witches, irrational, even mad, is central to her work. Danticat draws ample inspiration from cosmology and *Vodun* symbolism, and accords great importance to the mother-daughter dyad, to divisions between rural and urban living, and to problems of communication and understanding between first-, second-, and third-generation exiles. Filled with *marassa* (the *Vodun* term for "twins") symbolism, her work illustrates the numerous dualities inherent in the postcolonial condition: a device that is at once thematic (mother and daughter are "twins"), stylistic (Creole and French are the two sides of one language), and structural (a story entitled "New York Day Woman" makes a pair with one entitled "New York Night Woman"). Her orig-

inal writing combines tradition and modernity, Creole folklore, and the myths of New York (post-)modernity. Taboo subjects such as the boat people ("Children of the Sea," in *Krik? Krak!*), AIDS, and an examination of virginity in a rural setting where matri-focality goes hand in hand with feminine authority (*Breath, Eyes, Memory,* 1994) prove her engagement with generations of Haitian émigrés and the people of Haiti who struggle for a better life, in dignity and freedom.

Unlike a number of Haitian-Québécois authors, Danticat has fully reterritorialized herself in North American society. Belonging to the post-Duvalierist generation, she suffers less from nostalgia for the lost country, while sharing the pain and heartbreak of the first and second generations. The desire to return home has ceded its place to the urgency to begin a new life on the other shore, to the insertion into a new universe. As editor, Danticat has brought together testimonies on the Haitian diaspora in *The Butterfly's Way* (2001) and *The Magic Orange Tree (and Other Haitian Folktales)* (1997). In her most recent novel, *The Dew Breaker* (2004), the stories are linked by the fact that all of the characters involved know one former Haitian torturer who has moved to New York and started a new life with his wife and daughter, and has carefully tried to erase his past. When he is finally unmasked, he is rejected and unforgiven by his daughter, who narrates the opening story. In this novel, Danticat returns to the theme of memory and the dilemma of trying to forget or forgive in a republic where blood is still visible on the hands of many former servants of its "présidents à vie" (presidents for life).

Kathleen Gyssels

See also: Francophonie, La; Haiti; Language; *Vodun.*

References

Gyssels, Kathleen. "Une littérature haïtienne doublement exilée: *Krik? Krak!* d'Edwidge Danticat." *Ruptures. La Revue des 3 Amériques.* 13 (October 1997/March 1998): 195–202.

Gyssels, Kathleen. "Haitians in the City: Two Modern Day Trickster Stories." *JOUBERT. Journal for Postcolonial Studies* 7, no. 1 (autumn 2002).

DARÍO, RUBÉN (1867–1916)

Rubén Darío remains Latin America's most beloved, influential, and studied poet. He gave *modernismo* its name in 1888, though he had not initiated the movement. After Darío met the great Cuban poet and statesman, José Martí, in New York in 1893, Darío became standard-bearer of the school and the first world-class Latin American poet.

A mestizo of African, Indian, and Spanish blood, Darío left his native Nicaragua early, where he published poetry at age thirteen, already preoccupied with the "distant azure." Before his arrival in El Salvador in 1882, and then Chile in 1886, he was reading the Parnassian poets, especially Théophile Gautier and Victor Hugo, who said "L'art, c'est l'azur" (Art is the azure). That same aspiration toward an ethereal ideal had been evoked by Stéphane Mallarmé's poem "Azur" in the *Parnasse Contemporain* ("Contemporary Parnassus," 1866). Darío's *Azul* appeared in 1888 in Chile, making him famous across South America. By the early 1890s he was visiting Europe, especially Paris and Madrid, as inveterate traveler, diplomat, and cultural ambassador. His last trip was a third visit to New York in 1914, for a lecture series his health would not permit. When he suc-cumbed to cirrhosis in Nicaragua in 1916, he was mourned internationally.

Also from age thirteen, Darío read voraciously in the National Library in Managua. Everything was assimilated, from biblical, classical, and medieval texts to his contemporaries. More important for Darío and subsequent Nicaraguan poets than pre-modern sources or the span of Spanish literature were French and U.S. models. *Modernismo* meant not servile imitation but the integration of innovations from France and later the United States within the context of native Hispanic themes and inspirations. His first ambition in *Azul* was to replace Spanish ponderousness by applying lessons learned from French: harmony, shading, suggestiveness.

Darío's improbable dream had been to write in French. Failing that, he renewed Spanish vocabulary with deliberate gallicisms and other foreign words, as French writers since the nineteenth-century poet Charles Baudelaire have renewed French vocabulary with their anglicisms. In addition to the poets, Darío also knew well the novelists Alexandre Dumas and Emile Zola, as well as other writers. In Paris he saw the poet Paul Verlaine and met the Irish playwright and poet Oscar Wilde, whom he cited between 1893 and 1896, then eulogized warmly in 1900.

On landing in New York the first time, Rubén imagined himself in the solitary company of "the divine Edgar," Edgar Allan Poe. Like Baudelaire, he shared Poe's attraction to the strange and his fear of death, and he played among Spanish speakers a role comparable to the French poet's in popularizing "the great Yankee." Darío also read the senior contemporary poet of the United States with enthusiasm and saluted him in "Walt Whitman." The anti-imperialist "To Roosevelt" is probably his best political poem.

In *Los raros* (1896), Darío acknowledged strong nineteenth-century figures like Poe, Verlaine, and Martí who had marked him. Yet he himself remained independent, steeped in French and North American authors but a slave to no figure or school, not even *modernismo*. Indeed, his *modernismo* rejected any dogma, religious, political, and literary, whether from France or the United States.

Roy Rosenstein

See also: Baudelaire, Charles-Pierre; Chile; Literary Relations; Poe, Edgar Allan; Zola, Emile.

References

Faurié, Marie-Josephe. *Le Modernisme hispano-américain et ses sources françaises*. Paris: Instutut d'Etudes Hispaniques, 1966: 48–69.

Mapes, Erwin K. *L'Influence française dans l'oeuvre de Rubén Darío*. Paris: Champion, 1925.

Molloy, Silvia. *La Diffusion de la littérature hispano-américaine en France au XXe siècle*. Paris: PUF, 1972.

Rosenstein, Roy. "Re(dis)covering Wilde for Latin America: Martí, Darío, Borges, Lispector." *Rediscovering Oscar Wilde*. Ed. George C. Sandulescu. Gerrards Cross, UK: Smythe, 1994: 348–361.

DARRIEUX, DANIELLE (1917–)

Very few actresses can pride themselves on having a career as exceptionally long and rich as Danielle Darrieux's. Her natural beauty and elegance, her excellent comic timing, and her work with legendary filmmakers have contributed to make Darrieux one of the most respected and emblematic icons of French cinema.

Darrieux was born in Bordeaux in 1917. She studied the cello as a teenager but quickly turned to acting. At the age of fourteen, she got her first movie part in *Le Bal* (Thiele, 1931). It was her first success, and she was noticed by high-profile directors such as the U.S. filmmaker Billy Wilder (*Bad Blood,* 1934, shot in France) and the German-born Robert Siodmak (*The Depression Is Over,* 1934). She then met her first husband, Henri Decoin, a French filmmaker, who offered her the leading role in *Le Domino vert* (*The Green Domino,* 1935). She became Decoin's muse and showed great comic abilities in works such as *Mademoiselle ma mère* (1936) and *Abus de confiance* (*Abused Confidence,* 1938), the latter arguably her first mature performance.

It was with *Mayerling* (Litvak, 1936) that international recognition came, resulting in a seven-year contract with the U.S. Universal Studios. Her first Hollywood film was *The Rage of Paris* (Koster, 1938), but her career in the United States did not take off. Her contract with Universal allowed her to keep working with her husband, but despite a creatively productive relationship with Decoin, she separated from him in 1941. The war interrupted her career in America. She worked in occupied France and starred in such films as André Cayatte's *La Fausse Maîtresse* (*Twisted Mistress,* 1942).

After the war, Darrieux concentrated on melodramas: Max Ophuls offered her mature roles in *La Ronde* (*Roundabout,* 1950), *Le Plaisir* (*Pleasure,* 1951), and *Madame de . . .* (*The Earrings of Madame de,* 1952). Hollywood wanted her back: together with James Mason, she starred in Joseph L. Mankiewicz's *Five Fingers* (1953). She also had the opportunity to work with some of the greatest French film directors of the time, Marc Allégret,

Claude Chabrol, Julien Duvivier, and Claude Sautet, to name a few. She worked in Spain, Japan, and Germany, but her popularity was on the wane in France. Darrieux eventually renewed with success with Jacques Demy's exhilarating musical *Les Demoiselles de Rochefort* (*The Young Girls of Rochefort*, 1966). She worked again with Demy in 1982 (*Une Chambre en ville/A Room in Town*), but between these two films, her film career was irregular. However, she had considerable success in the theater.

Darrieux went back to America in the early 1970s when Broadway asked her to replace Katharine Hepburn in the musical *Coco* (based on the life of the French fashion designer Coco Chanel). The ferocious New York press praised her singing voice and her live stage performance. Although she did not manage to attract as many admirers as Hepburn, Darrieux gave the musical another chance and kept it afloat until the end of the season.

Since the 1990s, Darrieux has made frequent appearances in TV dramas. She has not abandoned her work for the cinema, as her work with young French film directors such as Jeanne Labrune and François Ozon shows.

Florian Grandena

See also: Chabrol, Claude; Cinema, 1945 to the Present; Demy, Jacques; Fashion.

References

Darrieux, Danielle, and Jean-Pierre Ferrière. *Danielle Darrieux*. Paris: Ramsay. 2003.

Sellier, Geneviève. "European Actors in Hollywood—Danielle Darrieux, Michèle Morgan and Micheline Presle in Hollywood: The Threat to French Identity." *Screen: The Journal of the Society for Education in Film and Television* 43, no. 2 (2002).

Dassin, Jules (1911–)

U.S. film director and screenwriter Jules Dassin was one of the most defiantly visible survivors of the Hollywood blacklist period in the late 1940s.

Born on December 18, 1911, in Middletown, Connecticut, Dassin was raised in the Bronx, before paying his own way through drama school in Europe. Upon his return to the United States, he gained experience in radio and theater, making his stage debut at the Yiddish Theatre in New York at the age of twenty-five.

In 1940 Dassin moved to Hollywood, where he was first employed at RKO Studios as an assistant director, and soon worked his way up to a directorial spot at MGM's short subjects unit, where he handled a twenty-minute adaptation of Edgar Allan Poe's *The Tell-Tale Heart* (1941). This led to a promotion to full-length feature films like *Nazi Agent* (1942), *Reunion in France* (1942), and *The Canterville Ghost* (1944).

From MGM, Dassin went to work for producer Mark Hellinger at Universal Studios, where he directed two crime classics, *Brute Force* (1947) and *The Naked City* (1948), which both clearly showed his growing penchant for the film noir genre.

The late 1940s gave rise to strong anti-Communist sentiments in the United States, and Hollywood celebrities were among those who were scrutinized for leftist tendencies. Just as he was gaining recognition as a director, Dassin was blacklisted in Hollywood as a result of the House Un-American Activities Committee hearings, led by Senator Eugene McCarthy, in which he was one of the people the HUAC forced Edward Dmytryk to identify as Communist.

Forced into exile in Europe, Dassin's last 1950s film for a major studio was Twentieth Century Fox's *Night and the City*, which was shot in London. He then moved to France, where he directed one of the most influential crime movies ever made, *Rififi* (1955). So successful was it that it earned him the Best Director prize at Cannes (1955) and set the standard for heist movies for decades to come.

By the late 1950s Dassin had moved to Greece, and it was there that he directed his second wife Melina Mercouri in *Never on Sunday* (1960), a scandalous comedy—at that time—about a merry prostitute. Mercouri performed superbly, forming a perfect contrast to Dassin, who played the role of a stuffy American moralist.

At the end of the McCarthy era, Dassin was allowed to return to Hollywood, and in the mid-1960s he directed *Uptight* (1968), a remake with a black cast of John Ford's 1935 film, *The Informer;* it clearly portrayed Dassin's alleged communistic tendencies as being a thing of the past. Not many of Jules Dassin's later, more personal films (the best known of which was an indictment of the Greek junta leaders, *The Rehearsal,* in 1974) were seen in America, even though the director's reputation, so unfairly tarnished in the early 1950s, had been completely restored so far as Hollywood was concerned. Dassin, however, never quite forgave the United States for what he had endured, and so chose to go into self-imposed exile in Switzerland.

Claudia Wolosin

See also: Cinema, 1895–1945; Cinema, 1945 to the Present; Film Noir; Poe, Edgar Allan.

Reference

Siclier, Fabien. *Jules Dassin.* Paris: Edilig, 1986.

DAVIS, MILES (1926–1991)

Jazz trumpeter and composer Miles Davis was born in 1926, growing up in Alton and East Saint Louis, Illinois, where the precocious and ambitious young man blew harmonies for Eddie Randall's band. In 1944 Davis departed for New York City to attend the Institute of Musical Art, but the youngster soon dropped out to play with "Bird," Charlie Parker.

In 1959 Davis made his name everywhere with *Kind of Blue.* The album's wide popularity was a function of its unpredictability. *Kind of Blue*'s emphasis on unrehearsed, improvised group performance gave it a novel and exciting edge. The Davis that directed its completion was not only a soloist with a knack for timing or spacing, capable of turning pristine note clusters into languid and wispy yet dynamic moods. (Playing fast or high was not his style, but that of his mentor Dizzy Gillespie.) This Davis was likewise a director capable of placing before his own ego the good of the ensemble, which included alto saxophonist Julian "Cannonball" Adderley, bassist Paul Chambers, and drummer Jimmy Cobb. Davis was not some capricious, introverted genius of the kind portrayed by the African American novelist Ralph Ellison: he mentored the young, impressionable John Coltrane with care on tenor saxophone, as well as many another future leader. And for all that was avant-garde about *Kind of Blue* it also, to ease its acceptance, contained a touch of the familiar. "Freddie Freeloader," titled after a Philadelphia bartender who survived on charity, quotes a hit by bluesman Junior Parker. Similar allusions, including a reference to Leonard Bernstein's "On the Town," inform other grooves.

For relief from the racism he fought at home, Miles Davis liked to visit Paris, France. He is pictured here with French actress Jeanne Moreau in 1957. (Bettmann/Corbis)

Read in the context of its era, *Kind of Blue* is also, notwithstanding the presence of pianist Bill Evans, a tribute to "black" creativity, an attempt to make visible the "Invisible Man." The album celebrates Africa: witness its contrast between open modal rhythms and Western chordal harmonies, especially in "Flamenco Sketches," which relies on Andalusian scales, originally from Morocco. In its attention to the magnificence of "otherness," there is additionally a way of hearing on *Kind of Blue* an outcry against the developing war in Vietnam. And in its glorification of team play it suggests that collective action can make a difference.

For relief from the racism he fought at home Davis liked to visit Paris. Here in 1949 he met Jean-Paul Sartre, as well as Juliette Greco, with whom he fell in love; the pair enjoyed strolling along the river Seine. In honor of a nation he cherished for its tolerance, accent on leisure, and beauty,

in 1957 Davis (with René Urtreger on piano) wrote and played the score for Louis Malle's film *L'Ascenseur pour l'échafaud* (*Lift to the Scaffold*). Yet Davis warned that, because of the serenity it offered, a place like the "City of Light," as Paris has often been called, could be a graveyard for art: it had robbed his friend Bud Powell, the pianist, of his anger and energy.

In the 1960s and 1970s the ever probing and imaginative Davis, first with Herbie Hancock and Wayne Shorter, then with Chick Corea and John McLaughlin, abandoned his "cool," or relaxed, version of bebop for "free" and "rock" jazz, incorporating electric guitars and keyboards, even an amplified trumpet, complete with wah-wah pedal. Just before his death in 1991, Davis was experimenting with rap, or "Doo Bop."

Johan Åhr

See also: Hip-Hop Music and Culture; Jazz; Malle, Louis.

References
Carr, Ian. *Miles Davis: The Definitive Biography.* New York: Thunder's Mouth, 1998.
Davis, Miles, with Quincy Troupe. *Miles: The Autobiography.* New York: Simon and Schuster, 1989.
Kahn, Ashley. *Kind of Blue: The Making of the Miles Davis Masterpiece.* New York: Da Capo, 2001.

DEANE, SILAS (1737–1789)

Patriot, spy, and diplomat, Silas Deane played an important role in bringing France to the aid of the American colonies during the Revolutionary War, and suffered for it.

Born December 24, 1737, in Groton, Connecticut, Deane received a classical education, studying law and graduating from

Yale College in New Haven, before being admitted to the bar in 1761. Practicing in Wethersfield, Connecticut, Deane also engaged in mercantile pursuits, building up a thriving business in Connecticut as merchant of timber, lead, and copper, goods that were sold to England. Between 1774 and 1776 he became deputy of the General Assembly and member of the Continental Congress, before being ordered by Congress to France in 1776 as secret political and financial agent.

As "agent of the American Colonies," Deane was accorded a status more powerful than that of secret agent, yet less than that of ambassador, since none was officially recognized. Serving with Benjamin Franklin and Arthur Lee, a young Philadelphia law student transported to London, Deane recruited a group of foreign officers, among them the Marquis de Lafayette, Johann De Kalb, and Baron Von Steuben, who together, by 1778, had arranged a military and commercial alliance between France and the colonies. Dean met in secret with Pierre Caron de Beaumarchais, the radical author of *Le Barbier de Seville* (*The Barber of Seville*) and *Le Mariage de Figaro* (*The Marriage of Figaro*), to secure arms. Beaumarchais obtained from the American Congress a contract guaranteeing payment. He wrote to Deane that he would send 200 bronze four-pounders, 200,000 rounds of ammunition, 20,000 excellent muskets, a few bronze mortars, in addition to cannonballs, sheets, tents, and gunlock plates. The terms of the agreement between the two men were based on the flimsiest of understandings, hindered by Beaumarchais's broken English, which hardly rivaled Deane's command of French, faulty as that was. Disparaging any need for long-term credit on the part of the

Baron De Kalb introducing Lafayette to Silas Deane. (Bettmann/Corbis)

American Congress, Deane assured Beaumarchais in 1776 that commodities of tobacco from Virginia and Maryland would readily be shipped as repayment within six months' time. Despite Deane's many attempts to persuade the American Congress on his behalf, Beaumarchais never received payment for the shipment of arms. The uncommitted Congress preferred to acknowledge the shipment of arms as "a gift from France," a misunderstanding that resulted in Deane's being recalled to America in 1778 and charged with profiteering. Accused as a traitor following the publication of private letters, Deane lived the rest of his life in exile. He returned to Europe to secure documents for his defense. It was not until 1842 that the American Congress voted to pay restitution to his heirs. Deane died on board a ship, sailing from Gravesend to Boston on September 23, 1789.

Pamela Gay-White

See also: American Revolution; Franklin, Benjamin; Lafayette, Marquis de; Tobacco.

References

Central Intelligence Agency, http://www.odci. gov/csi/books/warindep/intellopos.html (accessed February 5, 2004).

James, Coy Hilton. *Silas Deane: Patriot or Traitor?* East Lansing: Michigan State University Press, 1975.

Manceron, Claude. *Twilight of the Old Order.* New York: Knopf, 1977.

DEBRAY, RÉGIS (1940–)

One of the most prominent living French intellectuals, known to a wider public primarily for his firsthand involvement with struggles in Latin America in the 1960s, and later prominent for his work in mediology—the effect of technologies of transmission on what is transmitted—and as a defender of French Republican values and the nation-state against the encroachment of globalization. A brilliant philosophy student of Louis Althusser's at the Ecole Normale Supérieure, he left for Latin America on graduation to fight alongside Fidel Castro and Che Guevara. He was captured in Bolivia and sentenced to thirty years in prison in 1967, which focused attention on his theoretical justification of guerrilla warfare, *Révolution dans la révolution?/ Revolution in the Revolution?* Worldwide protests led to his release in 1970. He came to renewed prominence in 1979 with *Le Pouvoir intellectuel en France* (Intellectual Power in France)/ *Teachers, Writers, Celebrities,* a polemic against the corrosive influence exercised by the media over French intellectual life. This text marked the beginning of an unceasing investigation of how the medium profoundly affects the message, an investigation imbued at once with fascination for the visual image and with nostalgia for the "graphosphere," in which the written word was dominant. Debray oversees the publication of the journal *Cahiers de médiologie,* the major institutional expression of what he has termed *mediology,* distinguished from what an Anglo-American audience would recognize as *media studies* by its longer historical and philosophical perspective rather than by a specific focus on this or that text. In his more recent work, such as *I.f. (intellectuel français,* "French intellectual"): *suite et fin* ("concluded," 2000), he suggests that the dominance of intellectuals in French public life has come to an inevitable end.

Debray's public life and interventions would appear at least in part to give the lie to that conclusion. He served as François Mitterrand's Third World policy adviser in the early years of his presidency, though disillusionment with Mitterrand's second term of office, as for a great many others, rapidly set in. More recently he has been identified with positions close to the "national Republicanism" of former Socialist minister Jean-Pierre Chevènement—skeptical about the cultural and symbolic credibility of the European Union, stalwart in defense of the French nation-state and of the Republican values it supposedly though decreasingly embodies, harshly critical of the United States and of the forces of globalization, with their tendency to turn citizens into consumers. He earned notoriety in 1999 for what many saw as ill-judged criticism of the NATO intervention in Kosovo. *A demain de Gaulle!/ Charles de Gaulle: Futurist of the Nation?* extols de Gaulle's commitment to the nation-state and his devotion to the written word—values clearly at the antipodes from the federal interventionism and culture of the image, or "videosphere," characteristic of de Gaulle's old adversary, the United States. From his commitment to the emancipation of Latin America from U.S. control, through his enthusiasm for civic and state-centered values as against those of the virtually omnipresent market, to his recognition of the need to maintain a critical distance from the "eternal present" of the videosphere, Debray's life and work can be seen as articulating a sustained and consistent opposition to U.S. political and cultural hegemony in a distinctively French style and context.

Keith Reader

See also: Gaulle, General Charles de; Mitterrand, François; NATO; Republicanism.

References

Dagognet, François, Robert Damien, and Robery Dumas. *Faut-il brûler Regis Debray?* Champ Vallon: Seyssel, 1999.

Reader, Keith. *Régis Debray : A Critical Introduction.* London/East Haven, CT: Pluto, 1995.

DEGAS, HILAIRE GERMAIN EDGAR (1834–1917)

Born in Paris, Degas was one of the most important French artists of the nineteenth century. A member of the impressionist group, he was a notable draftsman who challenged conventions of painting, drawing, print-making, and sculpture by introducing new techniques and methods. After study at the Ecole des Beaux-Arts, an extended stay in Italy, and early history paintings, Degas's representations of modern life and his treatment of the figure from the late 1860s in his pictures of the ballet, the racecourse, and other scenes introduced new standards for these subjects as did the many portraits that he drew and painted.

Degas's mother, who died when he was thirteen, was born in New Orleans. In 1869 Degas's brother René married his cousin Estelle, a widow who fled to France after her husband was killed in the American Civil War. In October 1872 Degas accompanied René back to New Orleans, where he stayed until March the following year. There he painted *A Cotton Office in New Orleans* (1873, Musée des Beaux-Arts, Pau), a compelling study of fourteen men engaged in the family business there.

Possibly it was these U.S. connections that encouraged Degas to take an interest in U.S. artists in Paris. He tried to persuade Whistler to exhibit in the first impressionist exhibition in 1874, and continued to see him when he visited Paris from his new home in London. Degas also counted the American artist Mary Cassatt as a friend. In 1877 he invited her to show in the impressionist exhibition that year, an offer she took up in 1879. They collaborated on their printmaking, and Cassatt posed for Degas on many occasions. She appears in the pastel *At the Louvre* (c. 1879, private collection) and posed for several of the pastel studies of milliners of 1882, including *At the Milliners* (1882, Metropolitan Museum of Art, New York).

By the 1880s, Degas's difficulties with his eyesight, which eventually left him blind, increasingly led him to turn to pastel and sculpture. Treating the themes of the dancer, the bather, and the woman at her toilet, he created a startling group of late works.

By 1882 Cassatt's friendship with Degas had cooled slightly, but she continued to

A Cotton Office in New Orleans, *1873. (Erich Lessing/Art Resource, NY)*

encourage her family and several American friends to purchase work by Degas. These purchasers included Louisine Havemeyer, whose extraordinary collection is now in the Metropolitan Museum of Art, New York.

Anna Gruetzner Robins

See also: American Civil War; Cassatt, Mary; New Orleans; Painting; Whistler, James Abbott McNeill.

References

Benfey, Christopher F. *Degas in New Orleans: Encounters in the Creole World of Kate Chopin and George Washington Cable.* Berkeley: University of California Press, 1999.

Dumas, Ann, and David A. Bienneman. *Degas and America: The Early Collectors.* Minneapolis: High Museum of Art, 2000.

Feigenbaum, Gail, et al. *Degas and New Orleans. A French Impressionist in America.* New Orleans: New Orleans Museum of Art, 1999.

DELEUZE, GILLES (1925–1995)

French thinker, born in Paris in 1925. Although he traveled little in his career, a conception of the United States— influenced primarily by literary sources, but also drawing on the tradition of U.S.

pragmatism—is developed in his work. Deleuze conceives of literature as something like a diagram or "machine" that, rather than revealing the political or social unconscious, constitutes a dynamic "cartography" of the ways in which challenging ways of thinking might unfold. In this way, he presents not an idealized United States, but rather an abstract United States of variable speeds and intensities. The fact that the U.S. "pragmatic" revolution, based upon the ideal of universal emigration, has failed should not detract from the visionary potential of U.S. literature.

In *A Thousand Plateaus* (1980), Deleuze and the psychoanalyst Félix Guattari draw on Leslie Fiedler's analysis of the role of geography in U.S. mythology and literature. They outline various forms of "cartography" established by significant American writers. The West, for example, establishes a "line of flight" that combines travel, hallucination, madness, and the shifting of frontiers. Such cartographies avoid the private and the autobiographical in favor of the public, the political, and the popular.

In *Dialogues* (1987), Deleuze talks in more general terms about what he calls the "superiority" of "Anglo-American" literature. He claims that to escape or to trace a line of flight—what he calls elsewhere "deterritorialization"—is the highest aim of literature. The French literary tradition, Deleuze claims, is either overly psychological or overly historical. The American tradition is characterized in terms of the "rhizome," in that it establishes a proliferating network with multiple and unpredictable connections. The French tradition, on the other hand, is primarily "arborescent," since it is based on the search for roots and the analysis of hierarchy. In short, the abstract machine of American literature works on a horizontal axis, whereas the French, or "European" model, works on a vertical axis. Rather than searching for origins, "Anglo-American" literature is a necessarily collective project that is always starting again "in the middle."

Essays Critical and Clinical (1997) contains significant short pieces on Walt Whitman and Herman Melville. Here, he talks of the revolutionary American dream of a "society of comrades," a society "without fathers," and a pragmatic "unionism" of spontaneous fragments, as opposed to the European search for origins. He acknowledges that this dream was betrayed, but claims that it remains the "reality" of American literature, in which the fragmentary "self" of the "Anglo-Saxons" is opposed to the solipsistic "I" of the Europeans. Deleuze consistently argues in favor of experimentation rather than interpretation, and it is for this reason that he admires American pragmatism's affirmation that the world is always "in process." The discrete, knowing subject is replaced by a nomadic community of explorers, who replace knowledge of the world with "belief" and "confidence." Pragmatism should be thought of, Deleuze claims, as an attempt to transform the world, in that it eschews both particularity and universality in favor of the search for "originality."

Deleuze committed suicide by jumping from the window of his Paris apartment in 1995.

John Marks

See also: Guattari, Félix; Theory.

References

Khalfa, Jean. ed. *An Introduction to the Thought of Gilles Deleuze*. London: Continuum, 2002.

Lotringer, Sylvère, and Sande Cohen, eds. *French Theory in America.* London: Routledge, 2001.

Rajchman, John. *The Deleuze Connections.* London: MIT Press, 2000.

Stivale, Charles J. *The Two-Fold Thought of Deleuze and Guattari.* New York: Guilford, 1998.

DELSARTE, FRANÇOIS (1811–1871)

Founder of a system of vocal and physical expression, which significantly influenced the development of dance in the United States and acting in Russia and Europe during the modernist period.

Delsarte was born in Solesmes, France. Though he was orphaned and impoverished at an early age, his aptitude for music enabled him to undertake training as a singer and actor at the Paris Conservatoire from 1825. Unfortunately this training ruined his voice. He began a study of voice and gesture and from the 1840s began teaching a Cours d'Esthétique Appliqué (Course of Applied Aesthetics), also lecturing and giving demonstrations. He gained great acclaim and taught singers, actors, visual artists, clergymen, and politicians. He wrote little. Some notes, charts, and the beginnings of a book are extant, as well as notes on lessons and from lectures by pupils such as Angélique Arnaud and L'Abbé Delaumosne. His son Gustave and daughter Marie Delsarte-Géraldy continued to teach the system after Delsarte's death, Géraldy in America in 1892.

Delsarte claimed a scientific basis for his work in his systematic observations of living people in activity and also of corpses. He deduced from this a series of laws determining the natural expressiveness of human beings. The law of trinity affirmed the threefold nature of all things (reflecting the Holy Trinity), such as life, soul, and mind, with vital, spiritual, and intellectual functions. The nature of God was revealed through beauty, goodness, and truth; art was the demonstration of these sublime virtues. Music's trinity was rhythm, harmony, and melody. Movement is excentric or concentric (away from or toward the center), or normal, the center itself. The law of correspondence asserted that a function of the body corresponded to each spiritual function. A spiritual act corresponded to each grand function of the body: that is, thought or emotion always had a physical expression, and any gesture or movement would convey inner meaning. There were three aspects of gesture: static, dynamic, and semiotic, and nine of motion: altitude, force, motion, sequence, direction, form, velocity, reaction, and extension. With these laws, Delsarte developed a lexicon of gestures and their inner content. He sought also to define the mechanisms of breathing and the characteristics of speech and song similarly.

The system spread to America largely through man of the theater Steel Mackaye (1842–1894), who worked with Delsarte daily in Paris from 1869 to 1870. Mackaye lectured from 1871 on Delsarte in America and developed Harmonic Gymnastics, a movement training system on Delsartean principles, which he taught in New York from 1875. Genevieve Stebbins (1857–1915) studied with Mackaye and developed American Delsartism further, extending its theoretical base and introducing yoga and Swedish gymnastics into its practice, as well as teaching statue posing, pantomime, and drills. From 1870 to 1920 the Delsarte System of Oratory was the most popular single method of speech training in the United States.

American Delsartism had a significant influence on the development of modern dance. Isadora Duncan (1827–1927), Ruth St. Denis (1877–1968), and Ted Shawn (1891–1972) found in Delsartism new ways of thinking about movement as an alternative to ballet.

Abbé Delaumosne was instrumental in bringing American Delsartism back to Europe in the 1920s; it had already reached Russia and enjoyed popularity, influencing the acting experiments of Konstantin Stanislavsky and Vesevolod Meyerhold (largely through the work of Sergei Volkonsky) over the revolutionary period. Delsarte died in Paris in 1871.

Rose Whyman

See also: Dance.
References
Delaumosne, Abbé. *Delsarte System of Oratory.* New York: Werner, 1893.

Ruyter, Nancy Lee Chalfa. *The Cultivation of Body and Mind in Nineteenth-Century American Delsartism.* Westport, CT/London: Greenwood, 1999.

Shawn, Ted. *Every Little Movement.* New York: Dance Horizons, 1963.

DEMY, JACQUES (1931–1990)

Since René Clair's work in the early days of sound cinema, Demy is the only major French film director to have directed a significant number of musicals. The big-screen spectacle and bright colors of *Les Parapluies de Cherbourg/ The Umbrellas of Cherbourg* (1964)—which gave Catherine Deneuve her first major role—and *Les Demoiselles de Rochefort/The Young Girls of Rochefort* (1967) are a worthy match for the Hollywood classics of Vincente Minnelli or Robert Wise. Demy's close work-ing relationship with the composer Michel Legrand—paralleled in postwar European cinema only by Fellini's with Nino Rota—accounts for much of the appeal of his oeuvre, which has a more serious sociocultural dimension than may at first appear. The nonmusical *Lola* (1961), starring Anouk Aimée, ends with her former lover's returning to carry her off in a spectacularly large white Cadillac—a tongue-in-cheek homage to the modernization and Americanization of France evoked by Kristin Ross in *Fast Cars, Clean Bodies*. *Les Parapluies de Cherbourg*, set against the background of the Algerian war, likewise figures major changes in France through the contrast between the burgeoning fortunes of a car mechanic who comes to run his own garage and the decline of an old-fashioned umbrella shop in one of France's rainiest towns. Gene Kelly—epitome of the Hollywood musical—appears as an American pianist in *Les Demoiselles de Rochefort*. Demy's work nevertheless retains a distinctly French quality, partly through the use of Legrand's music, partly because so many of his films are set in the western French seaports—Nantes (*Lola*), Cherbourg, Rochefort—that he filmed with evident affection. He worked with many of France's leading stars—Jeanne Moreau in *La Baie des anges/Bay of Angels* (1963), Deneuve and her sister Françoise Dorléac in *Les Demoiselles de Rochefort*, Delphine Seyrig and Deneuve again in *Peau d'âne/Donkey Skin* (1970), Yves Montand in *Trois places pour le 26/Three Places for the 26th* (1988)—and was movingly profiled by his widow Agnès Varda in *Jacquot de Nantes*, released in the United States as *Jacquot*, of 1991. At once a regionalist poet of the cinema and France's outstanding exponent of a genre surprisingly rare in Europe, he remains an important figure in French film history.

Keith Reader

See also: Cherbourg; Cinema, 1945 to the Present; Deneuve, Catherine; Kelly, Gene; Legrand, Michel; Montand, Yves; Nantes; Rochefort.

References
Berthomé, Jean-Pierre. *Jacques Demy: Les racines du rêve.* Nantes: L'Atalante, 1996.
Ross, Kristin. *Fast Cars, Clean Bodies: Decolonization and the Reordering of French Culture.* Cambridge/London: MIT Press, 1995.
Stilwell, Robyn J. "Le Demy-monde: The Bewitched, Betwixt and Between French Musical." *Popular Music in France from Chanson to Techno.* Eds. Hugh Dauncey and Steve Cannon. Aldershot, UK/Burlington, VT: Ashgate, 2003: 123–138.

DENEUVE, CATHERINE (1943–)

French film actress, born in Paris in 1943.

Catherine Deneuve remains, at the beginning of the twenty-first century, France's most celebrated and respected film actress. Much of her cinematic importance stems from a consistently daring and unorthodox selection of French and American film projects that she has rendered unexpectedly marketable.

From early interpretations of wide-eyed singing maidens (in Jacques Demy's musicals) or neurotic Buñuelian antiheroines in *Belle de jour* (1966) and *Tristana* (1971) to recent turns as a gay university lecturer in André Téchiné's *Les Voleurs/Thieves* (1996) and as Odette Swann in Raúl Ruiz's adaptation of *Le Temps retrouvé/Time Regained* (2000), Deneuve has continued, well into her fifties, to in-

spire the most experimental directors of the age, lending their ambitiously avant-garde projects a quasi-aristocratic star appeal. Despite, or perhaps because of, Deneuve's indisputably French iconic status, she has functioned as a significant link between the European and the U.S. cinematic traditions. She is considered in the United States as the Parisian actress par excellence; her early forays into Hollywood were memorable exercises in a new kind of French feminine stereotype. Whether in 1969's comedy *The April Fools* (Rosenberg, with Jack Lemmon) or in 1983's vampire story *The Hunger* (Tony Scott, with David Bowie and Susan Sarandon), Deneuve brought a disturbing Old World sexuality to the modern, wholesome American backdrop of the film in question. Hitchcock was keen to exploit this highly fetishized aspect of Deneuve's Frenchness, but died before his plans to turn her into a new Continental "ice blonde" could be realized.

More recently, Deneuve has starred in several French-American or international projects, the most recent being Tonie Marshall's Paris–New York love story *Au Plus Près du Paradis/Nearest to Heaven* (with William Hurt, 2002). She is drawn to cinematic experiments with intertextuality, especially involving the French-American cultural relationship; this can be most clearly perceived in her increasingly bizarre connection to the contemporary musical. In Demy's *Les Demoiselles de Rochefort/The Young Girls of Rochefort* (1966), a joyous cross between Hollywood cabaret and quirky French melodrama, complete with a dancing Gene Kelly singing in French, Deneuve and her late sister Françoise Dorléac are a bewildering blend of Gallic damsel and Americanized Monroe and Russell clones. Deneuve's association with this type of perplexing crossbreed genre is persistent. In Lars von Trier's *Dancer in the Dark* (2001), she (playing a character originally conceived as African American) and Icelandic icon Björk are immigrant workers in a 1950s America that is the all-singing, all-dancing world of both the electric chair and *The Sound of Music;* in *8 Femmes* (2002), François Ozon's musical pastiche of the films of George Cukor, Douglas Sirk, and John Ford, she heads a cast of French actresses who veer constantly between parodies of their own famous personas and those of such American legends as Rita Hayworth, Lana Turner, and Madonna. In 2003 Deneuve appeared as the Marquise de Merteuil in a Franco-Canadian television production of *Dangerous Liaisons.*

Andrew Asibong

See also: *Dangerous Liaisons;* Demy, Jacques; Kelly, Gene; Madonna; Ruiz, Raúl.

References

Vadim, Roger. *The Memoirs of Roger Vadim: Bardot, Deneuve and Fonda.* Trans. Melinda Porter. London: Weidenfeld and Nicolson, 1986.

Vincendeau, Ginette. "Fire and Ice. An Icon of French Chic and Perverse Sexuality, Catherine Deneuve Tells Us a Great Deal about French Cinema and Culture." *Sight and Sound* 3, no. 4 (April 1993): 20.

———. *Stars and Stardom in French Cinema.* London: Continuum, 2000.

DENIM

Spearhead of the American commercial empire, uniform of the counterculture, sartorial must of the 1950s rebel, emblem of working-class functionalism, icon of the West, image of equality, fetishized commodity par excellence, denim also has a place in the circular economic and cultural currents of the French Atlantic. Since Lévi-Strauss arrived in San Francisco in the mid-nineteenth century, myths have abounded about the origin of denim jeans. According to one version, Lévi-Strauss and Company ordered the fabric for their celebrated trousers from the French city of Nîmes, hence "denim," and the ships carrying bolts of this *serge de Nîmes* were manned by sailors wearing pants made of a blue cotton cloth from Genoa. The truth is probably more prosaic. Jean, a cotton and wool blend, does indeed get its name from Genoa, the Italian city reputed to be at the origin of this cloth, but as early as the seventeenth century jean was mainly produced in England. So too with denim. Fashion historian Pascale Gorguet-Ballesteros has shown that as early as the eighteenth century the main centers of production of *serge de Nîmes* were located in England and the eastern United States, where the term early on designated a cotton, rather than silk and wool, twill. Furthermore, Lévi-Strauss's first pair of riveted blue jeans—called "waist overalls"—were made from denim shipped to San Francisco from New Hampshire and not from France.

A cotton twill was routinely used in France in the nineteenth and twentieth centuries to make overalls for workers—called *salopettes* and *bleus de travail* (work blues)—but it was not until after World War II that denim in the form of blue jeans became a polyvalent garment in France. Dictionaries attest to the usage of the word *jean* in France as early as 1948, and then *blue-jean,* occasionally spelled *bloudgine,* several years later, while denim, for its part, entered the French language as an anglicism in 1973. One of the iconic images of the early 1960s shows Brigitte

Denim advertising label showing boy on rigging of ship, ca. 1858. Myths have abounded about the origin of denim jeans. According to one version, Lévi-Strauss and Company ordered the fabric for their celebrated trousers from the French city of Nîmes, hence "denim," and the ships carrying bolts of this serge de Nîmes were manned by sailors wearing pants made of a blue cotton cloth from Genoa. (Library of Congress)

Bardot wearing jeans on the deck of a cutter off the coast of Saint Tropez, and since then consumers in France have bought millions of pairs of denim trousers. Through it all, denim in France has been made to stand both as the sign of an eager Americanization and as an icon of anti-Americanism. According to the writer Alison Lurie, postwar French teenagers wore jeans as a way of magically absorbing the power and virtue of the United States. In 2001, however, black denim was the garb of choice for the critics of transnational capitalism demonstrating in the streets of Genoa. Denim has become the marker of

an inevitable proximity and the badge of an irrevocable distance between the two sides of the French Atlantic. This simultaneous proximity and distance are echoed in an anecdote recounted by Europe's most celebrated anthropologist of the Americas. In a book of interviews, Claude Lévi-Strauss tells of a dinner in a crowded San Francisco restaurant. Asked to make a reservation, Lévi-Strauss left his name, upon which the waiter asked: "The pants or the books?" (Eribon, p. 30).

Phil Watts

See also: Bardot, Brigitte; Fashion; Lévi-Strauss, Claude; World War II.

References

Downey, Lynn. "A History of Denim."
www.levistrauss.com/about/history/denim.
htm (accessed May 6, 2004).

Eribon, Didier, and Claude Lévi-Strauss.
Conversations with Claude Lévi-Strauss.
Trans. Paula Wissing. Chicago: University
of Chicago Press.

Join-Dieterle, Catherine, et al. *Histoires du
jeans, 1750–1994.* Paris: Paris Musées,
1994.

Lurie, Alison. *The Language of Clothes.* New
York: Random House, 1981.

Quinn, Carin C. "The Jeaning of America—
And the World." *American Heritage,* May
1978.

DEPARDIEU, GÉRARD (1948–)

Depardieu is arguably the most prominent star in French cinema of the last thirty years. He was born in working-class Châteauroux in 1948, and throughout his career has made frequent reference to his humble origins and violent, marginalized youth. He began his acting career in the Parisian *café-théâtres* in the 1960s and early 1970s. The libertarian, frequently anti-establishment credentials of this kind of theater reinforced his status as an outsider, and this status was further reinforced in his early film roles, notably *Les Valseuses/Going Places* (Bertrand Blier, 1973), which turned him and his costar, Patrick Dewaere, into much-sought-after young actors.

A paradox lay at the heart of Depardieu's star persona and performance style until the late 1970s. In many of his major roles, the combination of violence and tenderness—for example, the softness of his voice—suggested a kind of sexual ambivalence. Then Depardieu's persona softened, and he took on much lighter, less threatening roles. He straddled a number of different genres and filmic styles, yet increasingly he played comic or romantic heroes in films such as *Préparez vos mouchoirs/Get Out Your Handkerchiefs* (Blier, 1978) and *Inspecteur La Bavure/Inspector Blunder* (Zidi, 1980).

By the 1980s Depardieu had become a major French star and a huge box-office draw. The early violence had given way to the lighthearted comedy of the Francis Veber hits, *La Chèvre/The Goat* (1981), *Les Compères/ComDads* (1983), and *Les Fugitifs/The Fugitives* (1986), and, perhaps most tellingly, to leading roles in a vast number of historical, or "heritage," dramas. Indeed, his presence in heritage hits such as *Jean de Florette* (Berri, 1986), *Cyrano de Bergerac* (Rappeneau, 1990), and *Germinal* (Berri, 1993) made him synonymous with the genre. This association with the heritage genre underlines Depardieu's identity as the primary French star of recent years. The combination of huge popularity films, quality filmmaking, and cultural authority lent by their literary sources have made these films a key factor in ongoing attempts to reinforce French cultural heritage. Depardieu's roles in these films have positioned him as another element of the same process.

The actor's career outside France has been both less complex and less successful. Depardieu's first attempt at conquering the international market was in Peter Weir's *Green Card* (1990), in which he plays a stereotypical Frenchman. This kind of role is continued in later English-language films such as Ridley Scott's *1492 Conquest of Paradise* (1992) and Steve Miner's remake *My Father the Hero* (1994). Although in Scott's film the clichéd Frenchness becomes a clichéd Europeanness, in each of these works the ambiguities and thus the forcefulness of Depardieu's French persona are effaced. It is perhaps telling that revelations about Depardieu's past in *Time* in 1991 caused a furor in Hollywood, and many believed that it cost him an Oscar for his role in *Cyrano*. It seems that the very complexities that ensured his early success in France, the combination of tenderness and violence, could lead only to disaster in the global market and as a result had to be removed.

Lucy Mazdon

See also: Cinema, 1945 to the Present; Cyrano de Bergerac; Veber, Francis.

References

Austin, Guy. *Stars in Modern French Cinema.* London: Arnold, 2000.

Chutkow, Paul. *Gérard Depardieu.* New York: Random House, 1994.

Vincendeau, Ginette. "Gérard Depardieu, the Axiom of Contemporary French Cinema." *Screen* 34, no. 4 (1993): 343–361.

———. *Stars and Stardom in French Cinema.* London: Continuum, 2000.

DEPESTRE, RENÉ (1926–)

Haitian intellectual and writer.

Of all the young militants of the *La Ruche* group who came to prominence following Jacques Roumain's death in 1945, René Depestre has proved to be the most enduring and influential.

Unlike Roumain and Jacques Stephen Alexis, Depestre was not born into the Haitian elite, but into a lower-middle-class family in the port of Jacmel. A prodigious talent, Depestre published his first poetry collection, *Etincelles*/Sparks, in 1945, and this was quickly followed by the surrealist-tinged *Gerbe de sang*/Wreath of Blood in 1946, the year in which he first left Haiti. His studies at the Sorbonne brought him into contact with the key literary and cultural figures of the metropole (metropolitan France), and also with the négritude group. Ever wary of racial absolutism, Depestre has tended to prioritize class conflict over race as the most significant point of tension in colonial and postcolonial societies. In 1951, his militant activities led to his expulsion from France, and thereafter he spent short periods of time in Prague, Havana, Vienna, Chile, Argentina, and Brazil, before returning to Paris in 1956. The following year he returned to Haiti, but was forced to leave after refusing to cooperate with Duvalier. On the invitation of Che Guevara, he went once more to Cuba, and lived there until his growing disillusionment with the revolution forced him to leave in 1978. Eight years working with UNESCO in Paris followed, before he finally retired to live in the Aude region of France. In 1991, he and his family obtained French citizenship.

Although Depestre has returned to Haiti only once in over fifty years, the island has remained his imaginary center. Following the early poetic expressions of the pain of exile, Depestre has gradually given up the hope and the desire to return, and his later work celebrates exile as a highly creative situation. Similarly, his early radical politics have mellowed, and, in a way that mirrors wider movements in Caribbean literature, the concern with collective issues has given way to the world of the personal and the particular. He has remained primarily a poet, though he has enjoyed most commercial success with his prose fiction works, notably *Le Mât de cocagne*/*The Festival of the Greasy Pole* (1979), a parody of Duvalier's Haiti, and *Hadriana dans tous mes rêves* (Hadriana in My Dreams, 1988), a magical realist, erotically charged evocation of the Haiti of childhood, narrated by means of an exilic reconstruction of the protagonist's fragmented memory. His prose essays, in particular 1980's *Bonjour et adieu à la négritude* (Hello and Goodbye to Négritude), track his own very particular path through négritude, surrealism, and Marxism, and as such are important documents of the major movements and debates in twentieth-century Caribbean literature. The self-styled *nomade enraciné* (rooted nomad) continues to be an important presence in French and Caribbean writing.

Martin Munro

See also: Alexis, Jacques-Stephen; Haiti; Roumain, Jacques; Surrealism.

References

Couffon, Claude. *René Depestre*. Paris: Seghers, 1986.

Dash, J. Michael. *Literature and Ideology in Haiti, 1915–1961*. London/Basingstoke, UK: Macmillan, 1981.

Munro, Martin. *Shaping and Reshaping the Caribbean: The Work of Aimé Césaire and René Depestre*. Leeds, UK: Maney Publishing for the Modern Humanities Research Association, 2000.

DERRIDA, JACQUES (1930–2004)

One of the internationally most renowned philosophers of the twentieth and early twenty-first centuries.

Derrida was one of the most celebrated and reviled French thinkers in the humanities in the United States. His work first attracted widespread attention in America from the late 1960s onward, in the wake of a 1966 conference at Johns Hopkins University, "The Languages of Criticism and the Sciences of Man." This conference marked the arrival of French structuralism in America, and Derrida's own work was si-

multaneously heralded as representing the inception of poststructuralism. The reception of his work in the American context was marked by a series of misappropriations, which can be broadly grouped into two stages: firstly, its annexation as a literary critical methodology, and subsequently, its conflation with, and reduction to, loosely defined variants of postmodern relativism.

Derrida was born in El-Biar, Algeria, on July 15, 1930. He studied at the Ecole normale supérieure (ENS) in Paris, as well as at Harvard for a year, and taught at the ENS for twenty years from 1964 to 1984. In 1983, he was elected to the Ecole des Hautes Etudes en Sciences Sociales and was among the founders of the Collège International de Philosophie in Paris, becoming its first director in 1984. From 1975 onward, he pursued a joint career, teaching for part of each year in the United States, principally within literature departments: first at Yale, then starting in 1987 at the University of California at Irvine, and from 1992 at the Cardozo School of Law, New York City.

The reception of Derrida's work in America is well known and has become problematic in its own right, in terms of both intellectual and institutional and cultural/linguistic displacements. The early impact of his work was exclusively within comparative literature and modern language departments rather than philosophy departments, which in turn had a determining influence on the mode of appropriation of his work. This reception was staged throughout the 1970s and early 1980s through the work of the "Yale critics," most notably Paul de Man, but also Geoffrey Hartman, Hillis Miller, and Harold Bloom. In 1979, the German-American translator and scholar Rodolphe Gasché accused these critics of turning Derrida's deconstruction of the Western philosophical tradition into a recast form of New Criticism, a reapplicable method of close reading of texts. Subsequent attacks accused Hartman and the others of instituting a "wild" literary Derrida at the expense of the major philosophical themes and import of his work. Jonathan Culler, himself instrumental in the wider reception of Derrida's work in the United States as an early and successful expositor, argued that the radical potential of deconstruction can only be tamed and defused by *any* institutionalization. Nonetheless, deconstruction has reemerged in America within a series of contexts from architecture and postcolonial studies to education, critical legal studies, and ethics. From this period also date the first attacks by American scholars and philosophers on Derrida's work as the source of apolitical textualism (Frank Lentricchia), nihilism (M. H. Abrams), bad or false philosophy (John Searle), and all the ills of U.S. higher education (Allan Bloom). Academic philosophy in the United States has taken an interest in Derrida in terms of the influential expositions of Richard Rorty, who divides early from late work in order to valorize the latter. More recently, Stanley Cavell has sought to relate Derrida's work to the ordinary language philosophy of J. L. Austin, on which Derrida himself wrote, and Wittgenstein.

Vivienne Orchard

See also: Theory.

References

Arac, Jonathan, ed. *The Yale Critics: Deconstruction in America.* Minneapolis: University of Minnesota, 1983.

Cavell, Stanley. *A Pitch of Philosophy: Autobiographical Exercises.* Cambridge, MA: Harvard University Press, 1994.

Culler, Jonathan. *On Deconstruction: Theory and Criticism after Structuralism.* London: Routledge and Kegan Paul, 1983.

Rapaport, Herman. *The Theory Mess: Deconstruction in Eclipse.* New York: Columbia University Press, 2001.

DES ROSIERS, JOËL (1951–)

Born in the town of Cayes, Haiti, on October 26, 1951, Joël Des Rosiers belongs to a generation of Haitian-Canadian poets (which also includes Robert Berrouët-Oriol, St. Valentine Kauss, and St. John Kauss) who were either born in Montreal or who went there at a young age, and whose work has been shaped by this double sense of belonging.

Leaving Haiti at the age of ten, Des Rosiers spent his adolescence in Montreal, before moving to study in Strasbourg in the early seventies, where he became involved with the situationist movement. Physician, prize-winning poet, and essayist, he has published four poetry collections and one essay collection with Editions Triptyque in Montreal: *Métropolis Opéra* (1987), *Tribu* (Tribe, 1990), *Savanes* (Savannahs, 1993), *Théories caraïbes* ("Caribbean Theories," 1996), and *Vétiver* (*Vetiver,* 1999). Des Rosiers has traveled widely, notably to Mexico, Israel, and the Sahel region of Morocco, where he spent several weeks with Touaregs. His work reflects the wide itinerary of his life: questions of roots, belonging, and sense of place are persistent concerns.

In contrast to his antecedents in Haitian and Caribbean writing (Jacques Roumain, Jacques-Stephen Alexis, Aimé Césaire), Des Rosiers does not romanticize Africanness and traditional culture in any straightforward nationalistic or racial way.

His work is concerned with the relationship between tradition and modernity, with conceptualizing an alternative modernity in which cultural traditions are reinterpreted and revalorized, without what he sees as the negative, ultimately futile pull of nostalgia and mourning for that which is lost. In this sense, his work has a timeless feel: he insists on creating and living now a future free from tradition, while at the same time he reinvokes humankind's deepest cultural mythologies as unchanging, necessary markers of our "tribal" identity.

Des Rosiers similarly eschews the great ideological discourses of his predecessors (Marxism, indigenism, and négritude), and his work, influenced by young Québécois poets such as François Charron and Jean-Paul Daoust, sketches an introspective movement to the personal and the intimate in Haitian-Canadian exiled writing. Unlike, say, his contemporary and compatriot, Dany Laferrière, Des Rosiers embraces *la francophonie* (the French-speaking world), and its inherent possibilities of intercultural communication and cross-fertilization. Although he at times infuses his restrained, sparse, lyrical poetry with creolisms, Des Rosiers generally employs French language as a neutral tool, and does not see it as a "trap," or means of potential cultural assimilation. In his celebration of exile and displacement from Haiti as sources of enriching cultural hybridization and as avenues to inspiring encounters with otherness, Des Rosiers's vision is ultimately influenced by postmodern conceptions of identity and belonging as fluid and multiple entities. His work at once describes and shapes the contemporary reconfigurations of Haitian identity in North America and beyond.

Martin Munro

See also: Alexis, Jacques-Stephen; Césaire, Aimé; Haiti; Laferrière, Dany; Montreal; Roumain, Jacques.

References

Des Rosiers, Joël. "Poems and Interview." *Callaloo* 15, no. 2 (1992): 407–430.

Gyssels, Kathleen. "Encre et ancrage: les recueils de Joël Des Rosiers." *Théories caraïbes: Poétique du déracinement.* Joël Des Rosiers. Montreal: Triptyque, 1996: xvii–xxx.

DESJARDINS, RICHARD (1948–)

Québécois singer-songwriter. Desjardins is one of Quebec's most celebrated singer-songwriters of the 1990s, accompanying carefully crafted lyrics with his evocative piano or bluesy ballads with the guitar.

Desjardins was born in Abitibi, in the northwest of Quebec, the son of a middle-class francophone forester. He joined the band Abbittibbi in the mid-1970s, playing piano as well as singing and writing, and toured the province in small-scale festivals, mostly playing covers of U.S. rock hits. Unable to carve out an original niche, the band split in 1982, their initial promise unfulfilled.

In 1988, however, Desjardins managed to produce his first solo album (*Les Derniers Humains* [The Last Human Beings]), funding it through a system of advanced subscription from his old fans and friends. This album set the tone for his subsequent work, with his smoky voice changing abruptly from velvet softness to gravelly attack, to the accompaniment of a melancholy piano or guitar. Lately, his music has also been peppered with Mediterranean influences, and the overall effect is one of intimacy and subtle eroticism.

Desjardins has consciously attempted to give a certain timelessness to his lyrics by referring to solitude, despair, or passionate love, and his most famous song is probably the love ballad "Quand j'aime une fois j'aime pour toujours" ("When I Love Once I Love Forever," 1990), adapted from a Cajun blues melody and popularized in France by the singer-songwriter Francis Cabrel (1992, reissued in 2000). Nonetheless, Desjardins has also anchored his songs in a specifically contemporary context, alluding for instance to anti-immigrant discrimination ("Miami," 1988), or using black humor to depict a stubborn clerk ("La caissière populaire/Cashier of the People," 1998).

Desjardins has also composed some curious historical pieces, tracing the violent foundation of Quebec ("Les Yankees," 1988), a mysterious journey through an icy night ("Akinisi," 1988), or a homosexual relationship in fifteenth-century France ("Lomer," 1998). Following his solo success, especially after his second album *Tu m'aimes-tu* (You Love Me? 1990), the band Abbittibbi regrouped in 1994–1997 and finally achieved a degree of success.

A versatile artist (he has composed film music and codirected two films), Desjardins is strongly committed to left-wing causes, campaigning for Native Indian rights in Mexico and green issues such as antideforestation. In 1999, he codirected *L'Erreur boréale/Forest Alert* with Robert Monderie, a documentary showing how the beloved forest of his childhood was being savagely destroyed by logging corporations. Critics of the government enthused about the film and helped establish Desjardins's image as an "authentic" and "rebellious" artist involved in concrete politics.

Since his first appearance at the 1992 Francofolies festival of La Rochelle in France, Desjardins has gathered a faithful audience on both sides of the Atlantic, receiving a string of prizes in Quebec and regular coverage from the mainstream French media. In 2001, after a yearlong stay in France, he was elected Man of the Year by the Canadian newspaper *L'Actualité,* thanks to his artistic skills and political credibility.

Barbara Lebrun

See also: Cajuns; Dion, Céline; *Francofolies, Les;* Leclerc, Félix; Mexico; Music (Pop); Quebec; Timber.

References
Baillargeon, Richard, and Christian Côté. *Une Histoire de la musique populaire au Québec, Destination Ragou.* Montreal: Triptyque, 1991.
Desjardins, Richard. *Paroles de chansons.* Montreal: VLB, 1991.
Thérien, Robert, and Isabelle d'Amours. *Dictionnaire de la musique populaire au Québec (1955–1992).* Quebec: IQRC, 1992.

DESSALINES, JEAN-JACQUES (1758–1806)

Haitian general and revolutionary leader. On January 1, 1804, Jean-Jacques Dessalines formally proclaimed the independence of the former French colony of Saint-Domingue, and returned the newly declared first black republic to its Arawak name, Haiti. This black general had been born on the Cormiers plantation, in the modern-day parish of Grande Rivière du Nord. He was first owned by a brutal white planter named Duclos, and later sold to a black master. Dessalines had fought since the earliest days of the slave insurrection with Georges Biassou and, in 1794, had become Toussaint L'Ouverture's guide in Grande Rivière du Nord. After the deportation of Toussaint L'Ouverture to France in June 1802, the remaining generals, including Dessalines, had been forced to make peace with Napoléon's general, Leclerc. By mid-October, however, Pétion had instigated a new rebellion, and Dessalines became the leader in this final, successful push for independence.

Dessalines stands apart from the two other members of Haiti's black trinity, Toussaint and Henri Christophe, in his unremitting hatred of all things French, a hatred he would justify to people by showing his deeply scarred back. Whereas most of the postrevolution Haitian elite, perhaps paradoxically, continued to identify with French customs, language, and principles, Dessalines rejected European "civilization," seeing in the adoption of its values a danger of imitating colonial structures and of instigating a new servitude in Haiti. Such was his resistance to "civilized" values that he refused to live in the colonial cities, instead establishing himself at Marchand, close to the Cahos hills. Also, whereas Toussaint and Christophe suppressed *Vodun* adherents, Dessalines was deeply involved with the *houngans,* the *Vodun* priests. His Haitian constitution did not permit one dominant religion, and thereby simultaneously weakened Catholicism's hold on religious power and legitimized *Vodun.*

The 1804 Proclamation of Independence clearly expressed Dessalines's francophobia, stating "Peace to our neighbors, but damn the French. Eternal hatred of France shall be our cry," and imploring the Haitian people to, "Swear to the whole world, to prosperity, to ourselves, to renounce France forever and to die rather

than live under domination." Dessalines's rejection of all things "white" was also apparent in the 1805 constitution's declaration that no white, of any nationality, could own property in Haiti. Certain whites—those Germans and Poles who had deserted Leclerc's army in 1802–1803—could consider themselves Haitian, though all Haitians, whatever their color, would henceforth be known as "blacks," a term that sought to replace the colonial "pigmentocracy," the sliding scale of color and class identity, and to bring racial cohesion and equality to Haiti.

The new republic faced many pressing problems, most notably the postindependence relationship with the foreign powers in the region, especially Britain, Spain, and the United States. Dessalines's first speech as head of state sought to reassure these powers that Haiti posed no threat to their colonies. Although the constitution forbade foreign ownership of Haitian property (a law that would not be lifted until the U.S. occupation of 1915–1934), Dessalines was sensitive to the importance of trade, and actively sought to forge links with Britain and the United States. The Americans cooperated until French pressure led them to impose an embargo on Haiti in 1806. Dessalines controlled trade closely, applying taxes on all imported goods and on some exports, including coffee.

Internally, too, Dessalines was beset by problems: the country was in ruins, and production was caught in a downward spiral. Also, despite his designation of all Haitians as blacks in the constitution, Dessalines was concerned about the perpetuation of the inherited colonial racial hegemony in the color and class conflicts between the predominantly mulatto *anciens libres* (literally, "old freedmen") and the mainly black *nouveaux libres* (new freedmen). Dessalines wished to eliminate this division, and unlike Toussaint, sought to unify black and mulatto into one larger, racially equal whole. He faced resistance, however, from the *anciens libres,* who were unwilling to give up their newly acquired lands and to lose the social advantages that they had inherited due to their lighter skin. The land issue was particularly delicate: many mulattoes had taken or been given lands owned by their fleeing white fathers. In 1804, Dessalines repealed all land transfers made after October 1802, effectively annulling mulatto claims to rich plantation lands. Although twentieth-century intellectuals like Jacques-Stephen Alexis and René Depestre later interpreted Dessalines's policy as an attempt to democratize land ownership, literally to give the land back to the people, disinherited mulattoes resented the move, and it was this issue above all that led to his final demise.

In addition, Dessalines was setting up his administration in a political void; the ruling white elite had been eliminated, and the new leaders of Haiti were essentially military generals, not politicians. Inevitably, therefore, the administration took on a military and authoritarian shape. There was a fine line between authoritarianism and autocracy, and Dessalines often crossed that line, alienating his fellow generals, as well as influential groups such as the mulattoes and the rich merchants. In 1806, an insurrection began in the South, with the support of most of the black and mulatto generals. On October 17, 1806, the Haitian emperor, as he had become known, was shot dead at Pont Rouge near Port-au-Prince. The order to assassinate Dessalines had come from a group of mulattoes and blacks in the South and West, a group that included his close friend General Alexandre Pétion; moreover, Christophe, Dessalines's successor, was aware of the plot. The brutality of Dessalines's murder has passed into Haitian folklore: some accounts tell of how, when his body reached Port-au-Prince, his head was shattered, and his feet, ears, and hands severed, and scraps of his body were thrown to the crowd.

A subsequent inspiration for many Haitian folktales, Dessalines was the only revolutionary leader to be made into a *loa,* a *Vodun* god, image, or spirit. The state, too, has propagated a cult of Dessalines: on the centenary of the Proclamation of Independence, the Haitian national anthem, the "Dessalinienne," was sung for the first time, and *noiriste,* or black nationalist, writers throughout the postindependence era have sought to rehabilitate Dessalines as a champion of the black masses. Duvalier proposed that Dessalines was "the first Haitian socialist," assassinated by the mulattoes due to his egalitarian policies. Unlike Christophe or Toussaint, however, Dessalines has not been the subject of biographies written in English, nor has he been widely celebrated by modern Caribbean authors; Derek Walcott, well-known West Indian poet, presented him as a bloodthirsty butcher in his first published work, *Henri Christophe,* and later, in "What the Twilight Says," called Dessalines and Christophe "squalid fascists who chained their own people." Ultimately, it seems that Dessalines's violent excesses, contradictions, and incoherences, in short his unalloyed, unrepentant "Otherness," are less easily accommodated into humanistic or rational literary or historical discourse than into the realms of *noiriste* propaganda, or of the oral baroque and the popular fantastic.

Martin Munro

See also: Alexis, Jacques-Stephen; Bonaparte, Napoléon; Christophe, Henri; Depestre, René; Haiti; Slavery; Toussaint L'Ouverture, François; *Vodun.*

References

Arthur, Charles, and J. Michael Dash, eds. *Libete: A Haiti Anthology.* London: Latin American Bureau (Research and Action), 1999.

Dayan, Joan. *Haiti, History, and the Gods.* Berkeley/Los Angeles/London: University of California Press, 1995.

Nicholls, David. *From Dessalines to Duvalier: Race, Colour, and National Independence in Haiti.* Cambridge: Cambridge University Press, 1979.

DETROIT

Founded by French soldier and colonialist Antoine de la Mothe, Sieur de Cadillac, in 1701, Fort Pontchartrain du De Troit, soon known simply as Detroit, became one of the most strategic locations in North America, falling successively under French, British, and U.S. control.

Located on the Detroit and Rouge rivers at the narrowest point of the channel connecting Lake Erie and Lake Huron, and opposite the present-day city of Windsor, Ontario, Detroit evolved from a small fur trade outpost into a regional trade center. Captured by the British in 1760 during the French and Indian War (1754–1763), Detroit again became a center of conflict three years later when tensions between natives and British regarding trade resulted in the unsuccessful five-month siege of the fort by a confederacy of Great Lakes tribes led by the Ottawa chief Pontiac. Detroit remained under British occupation until after the American Revolution. In 1802, it was incorporated as a city and in 1805 named capital of the Michigan Territory. A great fire swept through Detroit shortly after, burning it to the ground. The completion of the Erie Canal in 1825 and the arrival of steam navigation in the area in 1818

Antoine de la Mothe Cadillac landing at Detroit, Lake Michigan, 1701. (Bettmann/Corbis)

opened the region to trade and immigrants from the East Coast and Europe. The Great Lakes became the world's largest inland waterway, with Detroit at its center, and although the state capital was moved to Lansing in 1847, the twentieth century again placed Detroit on the map of the world, thanks to the automobile industry.

Initially intended to block British interests in the region, early Detroit grew rapidly under the French and by 1706 included a church, a barracks for soldiers, a warehouse, a storage area for gunpowder, an icehouse, and a beer brewery. For reasons of safety, convenience, and easy access to water by canoe, land was divided into traditional sections of "ribbon" farms of 400 to 900 feet wide and 1 to 3 miles deep perpendicular to the river. The first streets constructed bore the names of the French farmers (Chene, Beaubien, Dequindre) and ran parallel to the ribbon farm property boundaries. Much of modern-day east side and central Detroit maintains the French pattern, whereas main avenues in northwest Detroit are American style. The only operating entity today that dates to the city's founding in 1701 is Sainte Anne's parish. As the second-oldest parish in the United States, it is preceded only by Saint Augustine's in Florida. Among the most notable priests to serve Sainte Anne's was Gabriel Richard, who came to Detroit in 1796 and acted as a bridge between the remaining French and newly emerging U.S. communities. Richard helped found the University of Michigan in 1817, organized educational instruction for the hearing impaired, encouraged education for Native Americans, brought the first printing press to Detroit, and was elected to Congress in 1823, where he served for two years. Local printers produced religious books in French throughout the nineteenth century to be used by parishioners at Sainte Anne's, and the last French sermon was pronounced there in 1946.

Maureen Waters

See also: American Revolution; Automobiles; Catholic Church; French and Indian War; Fur Trade; Pontiac; Steamboats.
References
Dunnigan, Brian Leigh. *Frontier Metropolis: Picturing Early Detroit, 1701–1838.* Detroit: Wayne State University Press, 2001.
Vander Hill, C. Warren. *Settling the Great Lakes Frontier: Immigration to Michigan, 1837–1924.* Lansing: Michigan Historical Commission, 1970.
Woodford, Arthur M. *This Is Detroit, 1701–2001.* Detroit: Wayne State University Press, 2001.

DEVIL'S ISLAND

The notorious French penal colony in French Guiana on the northeast coast of South America.

The first French effort to colonize Guiana, in 1763, failed utterly when tropical diseases and climate killed all but 2,000 of the initial 12,000 settlers. The survivors found refuge on the three small islands 10 miles off the coast, calling them collectively the Salvation Islands; individually, they were named Royal Island, Saint Joseph Island, and Devil's Island—the last allegedly deriving from the flocks of black birds nesting there. Nearly a hundred years of further effort produced little progress, and in 1854 the French government decided to make Guiana a prison colony to which any male sentenced to a term at *travaux forcés* (hard labor) would be transported. Although most of the prisoners, called *bagnards* from the penal dockyards, *bagnes,* to which they had previously been

Part of Detention House on Devil's Island. Photo shows a part of the main detention house, facing the grand court, where guards are constantly on duty. The cells are veritable fortresses, with heavy steel doors and small openings on top through which air circulates. (Bettmann/Corbis)

condemned, were held on the mainland, the colony and its regime of horrors became known by the expressive and appropriate name "Devil's Island."

To guarantee settlers for Guiana, a sentence of five to eight years required the convict to remain as a free colonist for an equal period, a penalty called *doublage;* for a sentence of any greater length, the convict was prohibited from ever leaving Guiana. Few ever left under any circumstances. Prisoners died so rapidly and in such great numbers that from 1867 to 1887 only convicts from France's other colonies were sent to Guiana; after 1887, based on the arguments that hard labor punishment should be painful and exhausting and that the reputation of Devil's Island would be a deterrent to

crime, all hard labor convicts were transported to the colony. Popular opinion changed by the early 1930s, and in 1938 legislation ordered all hard labor to be served in France. Plans to close the colony were delayed by World War II but were completed in 1946. During its existence, France transported approximately 56,000 prisoners to Devil's Island. Fewer than 10 percent survived their sentence. That France, the most open, liberal government in Europe, produced and sustained this barbaric and repressive penal colony is one of history's great ironies.

Hard labor in Guiana meant cutting timber or constructing roads with only axes and shovels. Attempts to escape were rarely successful. Guards shot to kill. Free colonists were paid a bounty for reporting escapees. Inland tribes were hostile. Dangerous insects, spiders, and reptiles filled the swamps and jungles. Sharks patrolled the seas. Convicts who survived escape attempts were condemned to months of solitary confinement in the so-called tiger-cage cells on Saint Joseph Island, called "the man-eater" because so many did not survive. For long in France, the fate of men transported to Guiana was ignored. The great exception before World War I was Alfred Dreyfus, who was falsely convicted for treason and held on Devil's Island itself from 1895 to 1899. After World War I, the same conditions, sensationalized in leading newspapers and in *The Dry Guillotine,* a chilling account by René Belbenoit, who did manage to escape, seemed less acceptable and led to the decision ending transportation. In 1970, there was one last depiction of Devil's Island, in *Papillon,* the alleged autobiography—many details were challenged—of another escapee, Henri Charrière, which three years later was made into an enormously successful U.S. film starring Steve McQueen and Dustin Hoffman. That readers and moviegoers would cheer for hard labor convicts demonstrated that attitudes toward crime and punishment had changed drastically.

Benjamin F. Martin

See also: Charrière, Henri; Dreyfus Case; Guiana.

References
Charrière, Henri. *Papillon.* New York: Morrow, 1970.
Donet-Vincent, Danielle. *La Fin du bagne.* Rennes: Ouest-France, 1992.
Redfield, Peter. *Space in the Tropics: From Convicts to Rockets in French Guiana.* Berkeley: University of California Press, 2000.
Wright, Gordon. *Between the Guillotine and Liberty: Two Centuries of the Crime Problem in France.* New York: Oxford University Press, 1983.

DEYGLUN, HENRY (1903–1971)

Dramatist and novelist, born in Paris in 1903.

Deyglun spent his childhood in Marseilles and interrupted his studies in 1918 to join the navy. Six months after the end of World War I, he traveled to Paris and was employed at the Théâtre du Vieux-Colombier, where he worked with director Jacques Copeau. At the same time, he sang in a club in Montmartre, Le Lapin à Gilles. He arrived in Montreal in September 1921 and quickly established a friendship with Fred Barry and Albert Duquesne, who were the directors of a theater group at Chanteclerc and then at the Théâtre Saint-Denis. With them, he made his debut as an actor in Canada, and he collaborated with them in the founding of the Théâtre Stella in 1930.

His first play, *Bonne maman* (*Good Momma*), was staged successfully at the Théâtre Chanteclerc in 1926 and was quickly reprised under the title *La Mère abandonnée* (The Abandoned Mother) at the Théâtre Saint-Denis. From 1926 to 1930, he wrote a dozen plays. In 1935, *Gens de chez nous* (*People from Here*), which had first been staged at the Théâtre National, toured France and Belgium in September 1937 under a new title, *Vers la terre canadienne.* At the same time, he embarked on a career in radio and great success at CKAC, then at CRCM (Radio Canada's predecessor). From 1932 to 1940, he wrote several adaptations of dramatic texts for *Le*

Théâtre du docteur J. O. Lambert, Le Théâtre populaire (The Popular Theater), *Le Théâtre Lux, Le Théâtre N. G. Valiquette,* and *Le Théâtre des étoiles* (The Theater of the Stars), while also offering his own comic sketches, such as *Octave et Cyprien* and *Nénette et Rintintin.* He participated in *La Rumba des radioromans* (The Radio Novel Rumba, 1939) and created *Vie de famille* (Family Life, 1938–1947) and *Les Secrets du docteur Morhanges* ("The Secrets of Doctor Morhanges," 1940–1947), radio serializations from which he took several episodes and adapted them for the stage. His greatest successes were, nevertheless, *Le Roman d'une orpheline* (The Novel of an Orphan Girl, 1936), which has been staged more than 2,000 times in Canada, France, Belgium, North Africa, and the United States, and *Cœur de maman* (Mother's Heart, 1936), adapted from his first melodrama, turned into a twenty-episode radio serial, staged at the Théâtre Arcade, readapted for the cinema, and directed by René Delacroix in 1953.

At the start of the 1950s, Deyglun founded the ephemeral Théâtre du Hasard and staged *Jenny Madore* there in 1952. He wrote a second film, *L'Esprit du mal* (The Spirit of Evil, 1954), produced by Richard Jarvis and directed by Jean-Yves Bigras, and he presented further dramatic texts for CKVL radio (1955–1960). Nevertheless, he spent more and more time writing chronicles and memoirs for radio broadcast or for publication in the written press, and he worked on the preparation of a historical account of performance entitled "Les Années folles" (The Crazy Years). The first manuscript was destroyed in a fire and the second, which was unfinished, is held at the National Archives of Canada. Deyglun died of cancer on February 27, 1971.

Deyglun's work includes seventeen theater plays, two novels, and 32,000 pages of radio texts, as well as several newspaper and magazine articles.

Lucie Robert

See also: Montreal; Theater.
Reference
"Dossier Henry Deyglun." *L'Annuaire théâtral* 1, no. 1 (1985).

DION, CÉLINE (1968–)
Québécois and international pop singer.

During the 1990s, Céline Dion became the most glittering, if at times controversial, symbol of the international success of francophone Quebec culture. Her personal itinerary and her worldwide commercial success, particularly in the United States and in France, conferred on her the status of a Quebec icon. In the context of cultural globalization, for the Québécois she symbolizes a small nation and a linguistic minority asserting themselves on the world stage.

Born in Charlemagne, Quebec, on March 30, 1968, Dion began her career at the age of thirteen. In 1982, she achieved her first success abroad when she won the gold medal at an international festival in Tokyo. The following year, her single "D'amour ou d'amitié" (Of Love and Friendship) obtained a gold disc in France. In 1988 in Dublin, she won the Eurovision Song Contest. These successes, however, found little echo in the wider world. A huge star in her native Quebec since 1981, she remained relatively unknown elsewhere at the end of the 1980s.

This began to change in 1990 with her first recording in English, *Unison,* which

Céline Dion sings "My Heart Will Go On" from the film Titanic. *(Los Angeles Daily News/Corbis Sygma)*

sold more than a million copies. Her presence on the soundtrack of the animated Disney film *Beauty and the Beast* (Trousdale and Wise, 1992) gave her in turn her first number one hit single in the United States and sent her second album to the top there and elsewhere round the globe. *The Color of My Love* (1993) outsold her previous albums, with 10 million sales worldwide, surpassing the record set by some sales figures that went back to the Beatles and confirmed her status as superstar. There followed appearances at the opening ceremony of the Olympic Games

in Atlanta in 1996, and again on a film soundtrack, this time on that of James Cameron's *Titanic* (1997), the biggest grossing film of the decade. Spectacular successes continued on the coattails of this unsinkable film, with the albums *Falling into You* (1996) and *Let's Talk about Love* (1997). After an absence of two years, Dion reappeared in March 2002 with *A New Day Has Come,* which achieved similar success.

Dion's international fame in the 1990s was not limited to the English-speaking world. In the middle of the decade, she simultaneously launched herself into the French-speaking European market. In the same way that she had used producers and songwriters to penetrate the U.S. market, she collaborated with a French star, Jean-Jacques Goldman, to establish herself in France. The resulting album, *D'eux* (1995), was a huge critical and commercial success, selling nearly 7 million copies, a first for an album sung in French, and even selling 150,000 copies in English-speaking countries. *S'il suffisait d'aimer* (*If It Were Enough to Love*), another album written and produced by Goldman, was a hit in 1998.

Several factors have helped to hoist Dion to status of heroine for the Québécois. The ideologues of the old French Canada had for long valued large families living a rural life as a mythical rampart against the encroachment of, and assimilation to, the Anglo-Saxon world. Dion explicitly echoes these founding myths, being the youngest of fourteen children from a modest background in a small rural town. The bearer of national "authenticity" for her local audience, she represents a shared memory. At the same time, more concrete factors, such as her worldwide commercial successes, contribute to her popularity in

Quebec, where public opinion tends to celebrate her triumphs as those of a whole people. For while Dion uses the English language in her career, she does not submit to it. Equally at easy in the English- and French-speaking worlds, she happily crosses all barriers, including those of language. Because of her professional success and her continued emphasis in interviews on her "belonging" to Quebec, strong emotional bonds have developed between her and the cultural community of francophone Québécois. On the other hand, intellectuals in Quebec have been reluctant to recognize her value, importance, and significance as a figure around whom cultural identities coalesce.

In the wake of her first successes on the world stage, Dion has been awarded the status of ambassador by Quebec public opinion, and the singer has herself claimed this status. She plays a determining role in the relations between Quebec, France, and the United States.

The numerous expressions of admiration coming out of France for Dion arouse strong, contradictory feelings in Quebec francophones, who for a long time lived their relationship with France in a kind of "distant proximity," characterized by a mixture of envy and affection and a wish for recognition. In semiological terms, the average French person "exists" in two ways in Quebec: as an admirable, superior, and cultured individual, and at the same time as the caricature of the arrogant, pedantic, and conceited *maudit Français* (bloody French). And so the Québécois react with glee at every celebration of Dion's talent that comes out of the French (be the speaker a journalist, public figure, or simple admirer), for approval in this context means that the admirable is returning the admiration and that there is no need to be arrogant. Dion has thus turned to the Québécois's advantage the traditional terms of the relationship with France, and so partially satisfied their long-held quest for recognition.

The relationship with the United States has different premises. There is certainly a love-hate relationship, but the Québécois seek not love from the world's superpower, but rather the proof that they can compete with it. For a long time they had in the economic domain a negative image of themselves. Quebec elites before 1960 hammered in the idea that material prosperity was for English-speaking Protestants. But while Quebec nationalists condemned the album *Unison* as a sellout, others chose to see it as a first stage in conquering the world. Today Céline Dion illustrates the fact that Quebec can win on the world stage. So her successes in the United States are perceived as the jewel in the crown, confirming her symbolic conquest of the world of pop music.

Frédéric Demers

See also: Music (Pop); Quebec; Quiet Revolution.

References

Beaunoyer, Jean. *Céline Dion: une femme au destin exceptionnel.* Montreal: Québec Amérique, 1997.

Demers, Frédéric. *Céline Dion et l'identité québécoise.* Montreal: VLB, 1999.

DISNEYLAND PARIS

Statistics on tourism in France for the late 1990s showed that Notre-Dame de Paris received almost as many visitors per annum as Disneyland Paris. Between 10 and 13 million people annually undertake pilgrimage to the French Disneyland, making it

Mickey Mouse and Minnie Mouse visit the site of the future Disneyland in Marne-la-Vallée (1985). (Alain Nogues/Corbis Sygma)

the most popular tourist attraction not only in France but in the whole of Europe. While the city of Paris often seems close to becoming a gigantic theme park in its own right, the close competition between "Mickey" in the Ile-de-France and the Parisian home of the Virgin Mary exemplifies a number of the issues raised by the Disneyland enclave of U.S. culture in the outskirts of Paris.

In the United States, Disney set up the Disneyland amusement park in Anaheim, California, in 1955 and Walt Disney World in Orlando, Florida, in 1971. In Japan, Tokyo Disneyland was created in 1983. Euro Disneyland was opened in April 1992, and in 2002 a second theme park was added focusing on film, animation, special effects, television, and new audiovisual technologies. Located some 20 miles east of Paris in the Seine-et-Marne department's "new town" of Marne-la-Vallée, these theme/amusement parks have given rise to considerable discussion—much of it impassioned—about culture (French and American) in general, and more specifically, about the appropriateness of such an entertainment center on French soil. In microcosm, Euro Disneyland, or Disneyland Paris—as it was renamed in 1995—is a case study for French debates on cultural values and standards and national identity and globalization. More concretely and prosaically, it is an example of planned local economic development designed to bring employment and infrastructures to a struggling area in the shadow of Paris. The best way to understand Disneyland Paris in real terms is to analyze its creation and development both as economic development *and* cultural symbol, since globalization is as much economic as it is cultural, and the French state's reasoning in supporting the project was grounded in the conviction that leisure, tourism, and culture were integral parts of the new economic landscape.

The Euro Disneyland project was discussed by a number of French governments of both Left and Right during the 1980s and early 1990s. Agreements signed by Prime Ministers Fabius (PS [Parti Socialiste]) in 1985 and Chirac (RPR [Rassemblement pour la république]) in 1997 with the Walt Disney Company contracted the French state to work with Disney's French subsidiary until 2017 in a variety of activities including, but not restricted to, the amusement park. It has been suggested that the Disney theme park should be understood as part of President Mitterrand's policy of *grands travaux,* which throughout his two periods in office endowed France—or Paris—with a number of impressive cultural and architectural monuments of various kinds, such as the Opéra de la Bastille, the Grand Louvre and Pyramids, the Cité de la musique, the Grande Arche at La Défense, and the Très grande bibliothèque (TGB; "Very Large Library") later to become the Bibliothèque de France François Mitterrand. Although there are some similarities between these projects and Euro Disneyland, there are also important differences, and a more appropriate—and enlightening—comparison should perhaps be made with the *"grand stade"* (great stadium) project, which eventually produced the Stade de France in Saint-Denis for the 1998 World Cup Finals in soccer.

Mitterrandian *grands travaux* were in essence intended to be prestigious monuments of and to high cultural values such as

(classical) music, (fine) art and avant-garde architecture and literature, and (elite) knowledge. The main *grands travaux* bequeathed to France by Mitterrand are high-culture, noncommercial iconic institutions intended to reaffirm France's cultural exceptionalism—variously interpreted—in a globalized world. In contrast, the Stade de France, despite strenuous efforts at every stage of its planning, construction, and running to make it a multiuse facility, is firmly linked to sport and popular culture rather than to high culture in any of its forms. Still, the Stade de France is—as the name eventually chosen for it suggests—a symbol of France and an arena for the expression of French sporting prowess and national sentiment, whereas Euro Disneyland/Disneyland Paris—however it is named—is a symbol of American culture.

Much of the furor of discussion raised by EuroDisney focuses solely on the cultural and political symbolism of the French state's encouragement of its location in France. Commentators of both the Left and Right decried the launch of the theme park by suggesting that it was a "cultural Chernobyl" or ironically noting that its timing coincided neatly with the French people's approval of the 1992 Maastricht Treaty on European integration and France's consequent abdication of sovereignty. The left-wing Republican politician Jean-Pierre Chevènement diagnosed France's acceptance of EuroDisney as an act of collective schizophrenia, and the philosopher and sociologist Jean Baudrillard, in an article in *Libération,* interpreted it as being another way in which France was prepared "to dream herself American." These analyses will be discussed below, but first, as background, there are other ways in which "Mickey" engages France in her permanent sociocultural dialogue with the United States.

Under the terms of the agreement of 1987 between the Walt Disney Company and the French state, elements of government and local authority planning policy in the Paris region have to be undertaken jointly with the EuroDisney company. In this way, a new urban center based around an out-of-town shopping mall, new RER station and road links, university campus, and housing is planned for Val-de-Paris in the Seine-et-Marne, amounting to a new *ville nouvelle* (new town). In addition to the disquiet provoked in some Republican quarters at the influence of an American corporation on state *aménagement du territoire* (planning), perhaps more concretely, small shopkeepers and retailers in the area have complained bitterly (as French commerce traditionally has in a Poujadist corporate reflex) that the new commercial center will threaten established livelihoods and employment by the introduction of U.S. retail approaches. This local social and political opposition to the influence and actions of EuroDisney has echoed complaints from the Communist Party and the Communist CGT (Confédération générale du travail) trade union in particular—and other political and union bodies—over the management style prevailing in the theme parks themselves. In the first ten years of its existence, Disneyland Paris was run by five CEOs, alternating between U.S. and French managers, as the human relations difficulties of running an American-inspired business in France have required a certain amount of smoothing out. In particular, Disney rules on the physical appearance of employees conflicted with French expectations of personal freedoms.

The establishment of EuroDisney in 1992 as another bridgehead in France for American popular culture brought a predictable outcry from intellectuals and cultural commentators. The fact that government seemed to be not only permitting but actively encouraging Disney to choose France rather than Spain as the site for their European theme park shocked cultural elites and the general population alike, accustomed as they traditionally were to either state promotion of high culture (in the manner of the novelist André Malraux, when he served as minister of cultural affairs in the sixties) or the Socialist administration's encouragement of popular French cultures "pour tous" (for all, in the manner of Jack Lang, minister of culture, later culture and communication, in the eighties). Wherever Jack Lang had encouraged popular cultural forms such as rap, hip-hop, and ragga, they had at least been French (if originally imported genres) and francophone, and they had essentially been supported by the state rather than by the private sector. EuroDisney did everything wrong: it was U.S. popular culture, at best purveying American interpretations of classics of European children's literature; it was "cultural" distraction provided by an organization driven by the profit motive; it was leisure as an industry. All this meant that for many concerned by globalization and its effects on French culture and society, the theme park at Marne-la-Vallée was another major step toward the Coca-Colonization of France.

What visitors can see at Disneyland Paris is often interesting sui generis. Apart from the unavoidable curiosity of a "Disneyworld" located in the Seine-et-Marne, the park's substitution of pastiche for authenticity and of appearance for reality underscores contemporary questioning of what is to be considered real; the ways in which the stories of Andersen, the brothers Grimm, and even Victor Hugo (in *The Hunchback of Notre-Dame*) are reinterpreted by Disney for European audiences raise issues concerning the conservation of literary heritage. Perhaps more hopefully, the second park's exhibitions on cinema, animation, and new technologies (rather than representations of traditional popular cultural forms of children's literature) and the original exhibitions in which technology and industry are presented as leisure point to a feature of the French demand for theme parks, which some analysts see as an antidote to the much feared U.S.-inspired dumbing down of French civilization. In a market for theme parks that is still growing, there appears to be a demand for attractions that combine amusement with education, just as Disneyland Paris complements its traditional Disney material with other—arguably less trivial—displays, Franco-French theme parks such as Parc Astérix (founded 1990), but more significantly the Futuroscope (Poitiers, 1987), the Cité des sciences (Paris, 1984), and former president Valéry Giscard d'Estaing's Vulcania (Auvergne, 2002) attract visitors to see and learn about nature and technology.

Since the early years of low visitor numbers, financial difficulties, weak stock exchange quotations, and conflicts with the staff and unions, Disneyland Paris has become a highly successful commercial venture. In a context of expanding demand for amusement parks, "Mickey"—and the cultural icons and values it purveys—is more than holding its own both against other parks in France and against the classical monuments of French national heritage such as Notre-Dame and other, lesser *grands travaux* of the past. Disneyland Paris is becoming accepted, politically (the generous state funding, tax breaks, and loans are being forgotten) and culturally, since it has even achieved the consecration (in terms of popular culture) of hosting a stage finish of the Tour de France.

Hugh Dauncey

See also: Anti-Americanism; Architecture; Baudrillard, Jean; Chirac, Jacques; Cinema, 1945 to the Present; Giscard d'Estaing, Valéry; *Hunchback of Notre-Dame/Notre-Dame de Paris;* Lang, Jack; Mitterrand, François; Sport; Tourism.

References

Ariès, Paul. *Disneyland: Le royaume désenchanté.* Villeurbanne: Golias, 2002.

Baudrillard, Jean. "Disneyworld Company." *Libération* (March 4, 1996): 5.

Hauteserre, Anne-Marie d'. "The French Mode of Social Regulation and Sustainable Tourism Development: The Case of Disneyland Paris." *Tourism geographies* 1, no. 1 (February 1999): 86–107.

Philips, Deborah. "Carnival and Control at Disneyland Paris." *Tourism and Tourist Attractions.* Ed. Neil Ravenscroft et al. Eastbourne, UK: LSA, 1998.

Smadja, Gilles. *Mickey l'arnaque: Euro-Disneyland.* Paris: Messidor, 1998.

DJIAN, PHILIPPE (1949–)

French writer, born in Paris on June 3, 1949.

The author of novels and short stories, as well as a song lyricist, Djian has been called "the most read writer of his generation" since his best-selling works of the 1980s, most famously *Betty Blue* (*37,2° le matin*) of 1985. He has lacked critical acclaim, but he is the contemporary French writer most influenced by U.S. literature.

In his novels, a rapid, acerbic style, in which the everyday and the universal mingle, combines with a depiction of landscapes that seem to recall the Americas: forests of firs, which could be in Canada, the northern United States, or the Belgian Ardennes, and arid regions that resemble Texas or Provence. The names he gives to his characters are also elusive: Franck, Patrick, Betty, Eileen, Francis, Ethel. Music is very present in his texts and is more precisely marked: rock, Bob Dylan, and PJ Harvey, among others. Critical hostility and a large readership in the early phase of his career are explained by the important role of sex in his books and the liberties he takes with the French language.

Djian makes no bones about the American influence. In an essay, "Ardoise" (2002), he himself pays tribute to the ten writers to whom he feels in debt, and only two of them are not Americans, Blaise Cendrars and Louis-Ferdinand Céline. The best known are Herman Melville, Henry Miller, William Faulkner, and Ernest Hemingway, but also J. D. Salinger and Jack Kerouac (whose influence is palpable in Djian's style), and less famous figures such as Richard Brautigan and Raymond Carver. Djian's works include a trilogy, *Assassins* (1994), *Criminels* (1995), and *Sainte-Bob* (1997); his most recent work is a volume of short stories, *Frictions* (2003). Djian also writes the lyrics for the songs in French by the Swiss Stéphan Eicher.

As a teenager, Djian traveled around the United States for four months, and even worked at the French bookshop in the Rockefeller Center in New York. He crossed the continent as far as Colombia. After the success of *Betty Blue* and the film adaptation (*37°2 le matin,* directed by Beineix in 1986), he moved in 1989 to Martha's Vineyard where he stayed two years; since then he has lived in Florence, Lausanne, Biarritz, and Paris. He returned to work in the cinema in 2003, as scriptwriter for Luc Bondy's *Ne fais pas ça!*/"Don't Do That!"

Pablo Aiquel

See also: Beineix, Jean-Jacques; Céline, Louis-Ferdinand; Cendrars, Blaise; Dylan, Bob; Hemingway, Ernest; Kerouac, Jack; Miller, Henry Valentine; Remakes.
References
Boudjedra, Mohamed. *Philippe Djian.* Monaco: Du Rocher, 1992.
Djian, Philippe, and Catherine Flohic. *Philippe Djian revisité: Rencontre avec Catherine Flohic.* Paris: Les Flohic, 2000.
Platten, David. *Philippe Djian. 37°2 le matin.* Glasgow: University of Glasgow French and German Publications, 1995.

DORZIAT, GABRIELLE (GABRIELLE SIGRIST) (1880–1979)

Already a well-known theater actress before she went into films, Dorziat was a star of the Parisian night and friend of many authors and theater directors such as Lucien Guitry, Jean Cocteau, and Jean Giraudoux. As early as 1900, Gabrielle Dorziat was ubiquitous on the boulevard stage, appearing in the likes of *La Bourse ou la vie*/Stock Exchange [or Purse] or Life! (1900) by Alfred Camus, which she created at the Théâtre du Gymnase.

Gabrielle Dorziat made her first appearance onscreen in 1921 in a film by Henri Houry, *L'Infante à la rose*/The Infanta with the Rose. It was not, however, until 1935 that she returned to the studios and dedicated herself to the silver screen with regularity. She was seen in *Mayerling* by Anatole Litvak, and then in six other films in 1937 alone. She kept up this rhythm and made no fewer than sixty-six films between that time and 1964. From her point of view, however, her film work was always eclipsed by the theater, and if some successes are remembered, such as Henri-Georges Clouzot's *Manon* (1949), or *Les Parents terribles/The Storm Within* (1948) by Jean Cocteau, in which she played a witty but severe old aunt, many films to which she contributed did not make it into film history.

She devoted herself to theater, and this gave her much public as well as professional esteem, in France and abroad. Thus, after signing a contract in December 1913, she left for New York for the first time on September 5, 1914, shortly after the declaration of war. She was hired to act in *L'Epervier* by Francis de Croisset, scheduled at the Shubert Theater run by William Faversham. After the company went to Baltimore to "try the play on the dogs" (Dorziat, p. 193), as she said, that is, to let the show get into its stride, it played in New York for 136 performances. On the first night, on hearing whistles, she became angry with the public before it was explained to her that whistling was a sign of success, and not the same as booing. From then on, she acquired the habit of having a chat with the public after each show. "I don't know a more hospitable and warm country in the world than America," she used to say. Helped by the jeweler Louis Cartier based in New York, she organized a collection of donations for war-torn France.

Afterward she made numerous tours, playing in English, in the United States, South America, Great Britain, and Canada. She left France after two months of rehearsals for eighteen roles, parts of a reper-toire of twenty or twenty-two plays, in Brazil, Argentina, and Uruguay. The tours were exhausting but sometimes surprising, as in Canada where, after a full month of success, she had problems with local clergy who reproached her for her daring reper-toire. She published her life story in 1968, *Côté cour, côté jardin/*Over the Courtyard or Garden, relating in lively fashion her vast theater and cinema experience.

Roger Bourdeau

See also: Argentina; Brazil; Cinema, 1895–1945; Cocteau, Jean; Theater; World War I.

Reference
Dorziat, Gabrielle. *Côté cour, côté jardin.* Paris/Geneva: La Palatine, 1968.

DOS PASSOS, JOHN (1896–1970)

American writer.

Dos Passos's grandfather was a Portuguese immigrant who settled in Philadelphia as a cobbler. At the age of forty-seven, his father, a respected lawyer and author of several treatises on industrial commerce, married Lucy Addison, a woman from the South. John Roderigo Dos Passos was born of this union on January 14, 1896, in Chicago. His parents took him to Mexico and to Belgium, and then to Britain. Upon his return to the United States, he studied at Harvard and graduated in 1916. On condition that he renounce his intention to enlist in World War I, his father offered him the chance to travel to Spain to study architecture. Dos Passos's essays on his stay there are collected in *Rosinante to the Road Again* (1922). In 1918, he enlisted in the ambulance division in France, a meeting place for authors of the so-called Lost Generation, which included such figures as

John Dos Passos, U.S. essayist, novelist. (National Archives)

Hemingway and Fitzgerald. His wartime experiences gave him the inspiration for his first two novels: *One Man's Initiation* (1920) and *Three Soldiers* (1921), the latter his first success. After the 1918 armistice, Dos Passos traveled farther in Europe, including Paris where he frequented the Montparnasse district. He then abandoned the topic of war and wrote two novels about New York: *Streets of Night* (1923) and *Manhattan Transfer* (1925).

As a reaction against Broadway, he founded the New Playwrights Theater in New York in 1927 with four other young authors; it staged, among other productions, his three plays: *Fortune Heights, The Garbage Man,* and *Airway, Inc.* Pursuing his critique of all forms of oppression, he wrote *The 42nd Parallel* in 1919 and *The Big Money,* which were published together

in 1938 in his *U.S.A.* trilogy, which signaled the end of the Lost Generation.

He published in 1934 *In All Countries,* writings that stemmed from his travels; he then wrote another trilogy, *District of Columbia,* which included *Adventures of a Young Man* (1939), *Number One* (1943), and *The Grand Design* (1949). He also published other works, including *Midcentury* (1961).

Dos Passos adopted in his writing elements of the cinematographic techniques of David Wark Griffith and Sergey Eisenstein, and many other elements—interior monologue, American slang, journalistic information—fed his work, lending it a critical and social foundation whose influence was felt by subsequent generations of European and American authors, including in France the "unanimist" groupe de l'Abbaye founded by Georges Duhamel and Charles Vildrac. Jean-Paul Sartre's novel cycle *Les Chemins de la liberté/The Roads to Freedom* (1945–1947) is indebted to Dos Passos techniques of simultaneity, especially the second volume, *Le Sursis/ The Reprieve.*

Dos Passos died in Baltimore on September 28, 1970, without having completed his final novel, *The Thirteenth Chronicle.* His posthumous publications include *Easter Island* (1971), *The Fourteenth Chronicle* (1973), and *Century's Ebb* (1974).

Aurea Fernandez Rodríguez

See also: Duhamel, Georges; Fitzgerald, F. Scott; Hemingway, Ernest; Mexico; Romains, Jules; Sartre, Jean-Paul; World War I.

References

Hook, Andrew, ed. *Dos Passos: A Collection of Critical Essays.* London: Prentice-Hall, 1974.

Robles Pazos, J. "Prologue" to *Manhattan Transfer*. John Dos Passos. Madrid: Cenit, 1929.

Sartre, Jean-Paul. "A propos de John Dos Passos et de *1919." Situations, I*. Jean-Paul Sartre. Paris: Gallimard, 1947: 14–24.

DOUBROVSKY, SERGE (1928–)

Serge Doubrovsky is best known for his work on life writing. His five volumes of autobiographical writing, including *Fils* ("Son," 1977) and *Un Amour de soi*/A Self Love (1982), have received considerable critical acclaim. Indeed, the most controversial of these works, *Le Livre brisé* ("The Broken Book"), was awarded the Prix Médicis in 1989. Doubrovsky's literary criticism has included work on Corneille, Sartre, and Proust, although he is perhaps best known for his contribution to life-writing theory. In particular, he is reputed to have coined the term *auto-fiction* to refer to an innovative form of life writing. Like classic autobiographies, auto-fictions establish a homology between the author, narrator, and protagonist of a work, and draw their inspiration from real-life experiences. Unlike classic autobiography, however, they recognize the fallibility of memory and the impossibility of telling "the truth" of a life. Doubrovsky's own auto-fictions are highly literary endeavors, reveling in wordplay and textual innovation.

Doubrovsky's relationship with the French Atlantic is both enduring and complex. Since emigrating to the United States in 1955 to take up a temporary post as a French assistant at Harvard, his life has remained in continual flux between France and America. As a professor of French literature, his working life has regularly alternated between the New York and the Parisian branches of New York University. Within his auto-fictional writings, the dual attachment to France and the United States is constructed as not only one of the fundamental organizing features of his life, but also of considerable importance to Doubrovsky's textually constructed identity. The geographical division is cited as the source of considerable angst for Doubrovsky's textual self, who never establishes a coherent home space in either country. On the contrary, he describes himself as living in an *entre-deux* or in-between situation, caught between two cultures and two languages, between his Paris-based mother and his American first wife and daughters.

Within his writing, Doubrovsky seems to attribute the complexity of his relationship with France and the United States to the sense of cultural dispossession that he felt as a French Jew living in Paris during the occupation. At this time, the teenaged Doubrovsky was forced to spend almost a year in hiding in a relative's house in the outskirts of Paris in order to escape Nazi persecution. Although France remains the site of Doubrovsky's literary success and the only place to which the Self he constructs in his texts can contemplate retiring, he is strongly attached to the United States. In his writing, he describes this country in terms of *une terre promise* (a promised land), as a land of opportunity and a melting pot of cultures. Doubrovsky's textual construction of the French Atlantic, then, seems to position France as the Old World, which remains marked by anti-Semitism, and the United States as the New World, in which he is able to transcend his ethnicity through professional success.

Elizabeth H. Jones

See also: World War II.

References

Jones, Elizabeth H. "De la patrie perdue à la patrie recyclée: Home as a Collage of Recycled Cultural Practices in Serge Doubrovsky's *Autofiction.*" *L'Esprit créateur* 42, no. 4 (winter 2002): 17–27.

Robin, Régine. "Trou de mémoire: Le travail de la judéité." *Les Temps modernes,* nos. 611–612 (December 2000–January/February 2001): 192–209.

DREYFUS CASE

The court-martial of Captain Alfred Dreyfus, a French officer wrongly accused of transmitting military secrets to Germany in 1894, attracted little interest throughout Europe and across the Atlantic until the publication in 1898 of the letter beginning "J'accuse," novelist Emile Zola's indictment of the French General Staff. By the following year, the national scandal had erupted into an international affair, triggering demonstrations, largely in support of Dreyfus, from New York to Budapest. The most celebrated case of the epoch, the Dreyfus Affair became inextricably linked with issues of nationalism, anti-Semitism, modern Zionism, the separation of church and state, civil liberties, and more.

In the late summer of 1894, a French undercover agent in the German attaché's office in Paris discovered a memorandum dealing with French military materiel. Comparing the handwriting with that of General Staff officers, the army's intelligence unit rushed to accuse Alfred Dreyfus, a staff probationer, of treason. Scion of a prosperous Alsatian family and a fervent patriot, the captain protested his innocence. But he had no allies in high places. Intensely private and widely disliked, he was also the only Jewish officer assigned to the

General Staff at that time. Court-martialed and then "degraded" in front of crowds shouting "Death to the Jews!" the prisoner was exiled to Devil's Island off the northeastern coast of South America. In 1896, new evidence pointed to another officer as author of the treasonous memorandum, but Ferdinand Walsin-Esterhazy's court-martial, delayed until 1898, ended with an acquittal by unanimous vote. Esterhazy, unlike Dreyfus, enjoyed protection.

Shocked by that injustice, Zola penned his attack on the General Staff. Divisions deepened between Dreyfusards and anti-Dreyfusards, and anti-Semitic riots spread throughout France and French Algeria. Later in 1898, further revelations confirmed that forgeries had been inserted into Dreyfus's court-martial dossier, and after Esterhazy fled to London, the army ordered the Devil's Island prisoner back for a "revision" of his case. Reported to the world by legions of journalists and photographers, that dramatic trial ended with yet another shocking verdict: military judges reconvicted Dreyfus with "extenuating circumstances." Immediate protests from throughout Europe and America (including threats to boycott the Paris World's Fair of 1900) helped prompt the French government to grant the prisoner a presidential pardon in September 1899. Seven years later France's highest court affirmed Esterhazy's guilt and reinstated Dreyfus in the army, complete with the Legion of Honor.

In the United States at the height of the affair, a Dreyfus Propaganda Committee rallied to the prisoner, and Mark Twain joined less notable citizens who sent letters of support. A community of "French-descended Huguenots" based in Massachusetts condemned the intolerance rampant

Captain Alfred Dreyfus, facing left, with three other French military officers, all in uniform. (Library of Congress)

in France, and in the wake of the presidential pardon, Dreyfus received invitations to lecture in the United States. He declined them all, but the symbolic case endured on both sides of the Atlantic. Zionists pointed to the affair as proof of the failure of assimilation and the need for a Jewish state; militant nationalists from Quebec to Languedoc perpetuated the image of Dreyfus as traitorous Jew; and in 1927, in the closing stages of the Sacco-Vanzetti case, civil libertarians looked to the example, as the *New York Times* reported, of "Alfred Dreyfus of Devil's Island fame."

Finally, in both France and America, the affair figured prominently in the history of motion pictures. Pioneer filmmaker Georges Méliès re-created the affair's major events in a fifteen-minute film in 1899 (the longest and most "realistic" of its time), and the American motion picture, *The Life of Emile Zola,* released in 1938, garnered an Academy Award, though that and other films dealing with the affair were banned in France until 1959. And in the plastic arts, as in cinemas, the image of Dreyfus continues to inspire admiration and venom. While a statue of the captain on Paris's Left

Bank commemorates his courage, militant nationalists smear on its base the graffiti of intolerance.

Michael Burns

See also: Cinema, 1895–1945; Devil's Island; Twain, Mark; Zola, Emile.

References

Bredin, Jean-Denis. *The Affair: The Case of Alfred Dreyfus.* Trans. Jeffrey Mehlman. New York: Braziller, 1986.

Burns, Michael. *France and the Dreyfus Affair: A Documentary History.* Boston/New York: Bedford/St. Martin's Press, 1999.

Feldman, Egal. *The Dreyfus Affair and the American Conscience.* Detroit: Wayne State University Press, 1981.

Kleeblatt, Norman L., ed. *The Dreyfus Affair: Art, Truth, and Justice.* Berkeley: University of California Press, 1987.

Dubos, René Jules (1901–1982)

One of the twentieth century's foremost microbiologists and public intellectuals, René Jules Dubos was born in Saint-Brice-sous-Forêt, France, on February 20, 1901, into a family of rural butchers. Dubos showed early academic promise beyond the limits of the one-room school that he attended in his youth in Hénonville, a small farming village. In 1914, on the eve of war, his family moved to Paris, where his educational opportunities were enriched at the Collège Chaptal. After overcoming a series of childhood hardships, Dubos was accepted by the Institut National Agronomique, where he began his formal scientific training. In 1922, unable to accept a scholarship at the Ecole d'Agriculture Coloniale in Paris because his susceptibility to fever made him ineligible to journey to Indochina, René took instead a position in Rome with the League of Nations' International Institute of Agriculture.

In 1924 Dubos met future U.S. Nobel laureate Selman Waksman at a scientific conference in Europe. Having already expressed interest in traveling to the United States to complete his scientific training, Dubos soon accompanied him back to Rutgers University in New Jersey, where he completed a doctoral dissertation on soil microbiology under Waksman's guidance in 1927. Later that year Dubos began his professional association with the Rockefeller Institute in New York City, remaining there for the next fifty years. In his time at the Rockefeller, Dubos carried out pathbreaking research in biomedicine and environmental microbiology dealing with a host of issues involving microbial genetics, enzymology, immunology, and the experimental pathology of pneumonia and tuberculosis. In 1934 Dubos married his first wife, Marie Louis-Bonnet, who died unexpectedly of pulmonary tuberculosis in early 1942. Prior to her death Dubos carried out the most important research of his career involving the discovery of the antibiotic characteristics of tyrocidin and gramicidin. Derived from soil samples of the bacteria *Bacillus brevus,* these were the first of the antibiotics that soon transformed the face of modern medicine. This success resulted in international scientific acclaim and numerous awards, including election to the prestigious U.S. National Academy of Sciences in 1945 and the 1948 Lasker Award.

Dubos spent the war years 1942–1944 at Harvard University working on tuberculosis and simultaneously carrying out top-secret research on biological warfare for the U.S. Army. The recipient of more than forty-one honorary degrees from universities around the world, Dubos is perhaps best remembered today less for his scientific accomplishments than for his authorship of a series of popular yet intellectually rigorous books for nonscientists, most written in the last third of his career. *So Human an Animal,* awarded the 1969 Pulitzer Prize for nonfiction, is representative of his writing style. Making the historical and philosophical evolution of modern scientific practice accessible to lay readers, René Jules Dubos was able to explain the powerful impact such activity had had on both the world's environment and on human society.

Gerard J. Fitzgerald

See also: World War I; World War II.
References
Dubos, René J., and Jean Dubos. *The White Plague: Tuberculosis, Man, and Society.* New Brunswick, NJ: Rutgers University Press, 1986.
Hirsh, James J., and Carole L. Moberg. "René Jules Dubos: February 20, 1901–February 20, 1982." *Biographical Memoirs Volume 58, National Academy of Sciences, 1989.* Washington DC: National Academy of Sciences Press, 1989: 133–161.

DUBUFFET, JEAN (1901–1985)

French painter, writer, sculptor, sometime untrained musician, born in Le Havre, France.

His use of everyday materials and dirt mashed into his pictures marked a key moment in late twentieth-century art. His attacks on academic art were equally influential, whether in the form of his own painted, cartoonlike worlds, free of contemporary perspective, of his writings, or of his championing of *art brut* (raw art), a type of art essentially unacknowledged until his interest in the 1940s. For Dubuffet, like the surrealists, art came from somewhere outside rational experience,

and who better to take us there than the insane, the "untalented," the childlike. Unlike the surrealists, that those who produced the art should be mad was not enough—it would still be the products that counted. This focus on the product can be seen in the vast amount of time he himself spent developing his techniques, ordering his work into series, and collating his own catalogue raisonné. His early work nonetheless set the tone for his career: in these pictures we see flattened landscapes (and often townscapes) with cartoonlike figures, out of scale, sometimes unconnected even with the rest of the specific form of nonperspective set up in the picture's visual field.

Dubuffet was a late starter as an artist, and the French public and critics were equally slow to pick up on his work. He effectively began painting in the 1940s and was very quickly recognized in the United States as an important figure. His pictures sold well from regular shows in Pierre Matisse's New York gallery, and as the leading modernist critic Clement Greenberg was writing about him positively in 1946, Dubuffet represented a major exception at a time when French art was seen as hopelessly behind the times. The Parisian art world persistently rejected Dubuffet's naïve, primitivist pictures and did not know what to make of his use of clay, earth, and dirt within paintings (notably his *Matériologies* series). This use is precisely what caught Greenberg's attention, as he took this interest in the material aspect of a picture (as opposed to a straightforward painting), correctly, as signaling a new departure for "painting." Dubuffet's first major retrospective took place in New York's Museum of Modern Art (MOMA), in 1962. The first staging of his *Coucou*

Bazaar, a moving tableau of his *Hourloupe* series (made up of red, blue, and black lines only, in a continuous pictorial space, or sculpture), took place in New York, in 1973. The American reception of Dubuffet continually contributed to his reputation as a major artist of the twentieth century. Although he stayed in New York (in the Bowery) in 1951–1952, little of the United States features in his work, except the Bowery bums he liked. What singles Dubuffet out as an artist is that amid the portentousness of postwar art, his work is both inventive and humorous (see his portraits and his "Beard" series). Dubuffet died in Paris in 1985.

Paul Hegarty

See also: Painting.
Reference
Dupleix, Sophie, and Daniel Abadie, eds. *Jean Dubuffet.* Paris: Centre Georges Pompidou, 2001.

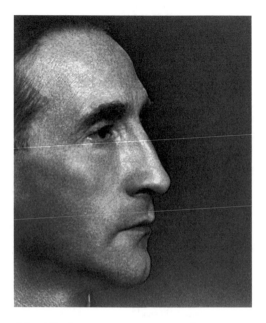

Marcel Duchamp, prominent avant-garde painter and installation artist. (Library of Congress)

DUCHAMP, MARCEL (1887–1968)

Prominent avant-garde painter and installation artist, most often associated with the manifestations of dada, Marcel Duchamp was born near Blanville (Normandy, France) in an upper-middle-class family.

In 1904, he joined his elder artist brothers, Jacques Villon and Raymond Duchamp-Villon, in Paris, where he enrolled at the Académie Julian. His early works were postimpressionist in style. During the following years, Duchamp's paintings displayed the influence of fauvism (*Paradise,* 1910–1911; *Portrait of Dr. R. Dumouchel,* 1910), and cubism (*Chess Players,* 1911). Between 1911 and 1913, he became involved with the group of artists known as the Golden Section, alongside

Fernand Léger, and started using cubist techniques in an attempt to capture movement on canvass (*Sad Young Man in a Train,* 1911; *King and Queen Surrounded by Swift Nudes,* 1912). Duchamp's *Nude Descending a Staircase* (1912), first shown at the Salon des Indépendants, then at the New York Armory Show in 1913, aroused fierce controversies and established Duchamp's reputation in the United States.

The same year, Duchamp created his first installation piece, *Bicycle Wheel* (mounted upside down on a kitchen stool), which announced the famous series of readymades (a concept he launched three years later). The idea of taking banal objects from their everyday environment, and endowing them with an iconoclastic message by signing them and providing a title for what is thereafter displayed as an "art object" (e.g., *Bottle Rack,* 1914), predated the first dada manifestations in Paris, and exerted a powerful influence on avant-garde movements in France and the United States, most notably on postwar pop- and op-art paintings and installations. Duchamp's provocative *Fountain*—1917 (a urinal signed R. Mutt) was refused by the Society of Independent Artists and the Armory Show. As early as 1913, Duchamp started elaborating one of his most complex mixed-media works, *The Bride Stripped Bare by Her Bachelors, Even* (*The Large Glass*), which he officially declared "unfinished" in 1923.

In 1915, he traveled to the United States and met Man Ray, who was to become one of his closest friends and collaborators. From 1920 to 1926, the two artists worked together on a series of experiments with optics and movement: *Rotary Glass Plates* (*Precision Optics*)—1920 and *Rotary Demisphere* (*Precision Optics*)—1925. This project inspired Duchamp's film *Anémic Cinéma* (1926), which he produced with the help of Man Ray and Marc Allégret, and which included a combination of verbal puns and optical effects. During the early 1920s, Duchamp cofounded (with Katharine Dreier) the Société Anonyme, Inc., which was devoted to the propagation of modern art in the United States, and he edited the only issue of the magazine *New York Dada* (1921) with Man Ray. In 1934, Duchamp published the *Green Box*, which contained a series of documents related to *The Large Glass*. During World War II, Duchamp helped Breton organize the 1942 surrealist exhibition in New York City and coedited (with Ernst and Breton) the magazine *VVV*. In 1954, he married Teeny Salter, and in 1955 he became an American citizen. For the last twenty years of his life,

Duchamp worked secretly on a major installation piece, *Etant donnés/ Given,* which has been posthumously exhibited at the Philadelphia Museum of Art.

Ramona Fotiade

See also: Avant-Gardes; Breton, André; Cinema, 1895–1945; Painting; Ray, Man; Sculpture; Surrealism; World War II.

References

Sanouillet, M., and Elmer Peterson, eds. *The Essential Writings of Marcel Duchamp: Salt Seller.* London: Thames and Hudson, 1975.

Schwarz, Arturo. *The Complete Works of Marcel Duchamp.* London/New York: Thames and Hudson/Abrams, 1969.

DUCHARME, RÉJEAN

One of Quebec's most famous and respected writers, Réjean Ducharme was first published in 1966, at the age of twenty-four, by Gallimard.

After having been rejected by Pierre Tisseyre, editor of the Cercle du livre de France in Montreal, Ducharme's novel *L'Avalée des avalés/The Swallower Swallowed,* along with *L'Océantume* and *Le Nez qui voque,* were accepted for publication by Raymond Queneau for the prestigious French publishing house Gallimard. Subsequently to Tisseyre's rejection, Ducharme, following a friend's advice, sent his three manuscripts to France in a single envelope. *L'Avalée des avalés* was listed for the Goncourt literary prize, and although Ducharme did not win the award, he was compared to Rimbaud, Céline, Vian, and Queneau. One of the first Quebec authors to be published in metropolitan France, Ducharme's success participated greatly in the promotion of Quebec literature in Europe as well as in the United States.

Since 1966, Ducharme has published novels (*L'Hiver de force*/Forced Winter [1973], *Les Enfantômes* [1976], *La Fille de Christophe Colomb*/The Daughter of Christopher Colombus [1969], *Dévadé* [1990], *Va savoir*/Go Figure [1994], *Gros mots*/"Swear Words" [1999]), plays (*Le Cid maghané* [1968], *Ines Pérée et Inat Tendu* [1976], *Ha ha!* . . . [1982], *Le Marquis qui perdit*/"The Marquis Who Lost" [1969]), songs (for singer Robert Charlebois), and film scripts (*Les Bons Débarras*/Good Riddance* [1980], which was distributed in France, and *Les Beaux Souvenirs*/Happy Memories [1981]). He is also known as Roch Plante, a pseudonym with which he signs collages made out of recycled materials. Throughout the years, Ducharme has been awarded a number of prizes, among which are: the Governor General's Award for *L'Avalée des avalés* and the Prix de la Province de Québec for *Le Nez qui voque* in 1967, the Governor General's Award for *L'Hiver de force* in 1973, the Prix Belgique-Canada for the entirety of his work in 1974, the Prix France-Québec for *Les Enfantômes* in 1979, the Governor General's Award for his play *Ha ha!* . . . in 1983, the Prix Gilles-Corbeil for *Dévadé* in 1990, and the Prix Athanase-David in 1994.

What most distinctively characterizes Ducharme's work is a fascination for childhood: the author perceives children as imprisoned inside an adult world, against which they must constantly fight to keep their creativity and imagination, a process that he immortalizes through fiction. His hyperbolic writing, which has been described as baroque, is marked by a constant use of neologisms and puns, a style that serves the characters' biting irony. That irony is shared by the author, who, for the last thirty-five years and through-

out his successes, has remained outside of the public realm, refusing to grant interviews or be photographed, and sending a third party to receive awards in his place. This need for privacy, which has been described as the *effet Ducharme* (the Ducharme effect), has always been respected by the public, friends, journalists, and critics. A myth has surrounded the character of Réjean Ducharme since the beginning of his career, a myth that has not only been preserved but entertained within Quebec society.

Martine Delvaux

See also: Céline, Louis-Ferdinand; Charlebois, Robert; Vian, Boris.

References

Laurent, Françoise. *L'Oeuvre romanesque de Réjean Ducharme*. Montreal: Fides, 1988.

Nardout-Lafarge, Elizabeth. *Réjean Ducharme: Une poétique du débris*. Montreal: Fides, 2001.

Schendel, Michel van. *Ducharme l'inquiétant*. Montreal: Presses de l'Université de Montréal, 1967.

DUFRESNE, DIANE (1944–)

Québécois singer and rock music performer.

Dufresne gained popular and critical acclaim with her eccentric stage performances, which combined revealing costumes and erotic lyrics to predictable effect in the buttoned-up Quebec of the 1970s.

Dufresne grew up in Montreal in a modest francophone family. Her mother, who died when Diane was thirteen, would dress her up for family parties, which no doubt contributed to her love of costumes and live performance. As a trainee nurse, Diane was encouraged by her singing teacher to embark on a musical career.

Dufresne's debut was difficult. She first appeared in a Montreal *boîte à chanson* (song club) in 1965, with a repertoire of French *rive-gauche* (Left Bank) artists, but was perceived as being too French. But when she tried her luck in Paris, interpreting the songs of Quebec artists (Gilles Vigneault), she was considered too exotic for mainstream success.

In the meantime, however, she had met the composer and arranger François Cousineau, who became her partner and artistic collaborator. Their first collaboration was for the soundtrack of a soft-porn film (*L'Initiation,* 1970), in which Diane sang with a mock-prudish voice. Her musical career really took off in 1972 with the album *Tiens-toé ben, j'arrive*/Hold on, I'm Coming, written especially for her by Cousineau and Luc Plamondon. Plamondon, a Montreal lyricist, had met Dufresne in the late 1960s. Influenced by American rock music, he sought to leave the rigidity of French and Quebec poetic texts, and considered songs as pretexts for a performance. The single "J'ai rencontré l'homme de ma vie"/"I've Met the Man of My Life" (1972) was intended as a pastiche of pop music, in an album exploring the sexual fantasies and anxieties of contemporary women. Ironically, this song was received as a "classic" romantic pop song and became an immediate success. Today, it remains Diane's most popular (and misunderstood) success.

Nonetheless, Diane had created a powerful artistic persona, winning a Quebec audience through shocking performances. Onstage, she changed costumes constantly, playing a dominatrix and a nun, Barbarella and Joan of Arc, a witch and an aristocrat in a crinoline. She performed stripteases and faked masturbation ("La main de Dieu" [The Hand of God], 1977). Her wide singing range befitted this exuberance, and many commentators saw her as the first "authentic" Quebec show woman, combining erotic lyrics, electric rock music, and outrageous behavior to unsettle the audience.

In 1978, she starred in *Starmania* as Stella Spotlight. An aging sex symbol, Stella was another opportunity for Diane to assert her persona as a crazy, scary, even desperate, seducer. Her success continued throughout the 1980s, as she moved on to writing her own lyrics, while continuing with her distinctive brand of performance. In the 1990s, she added illustration and documentary direction to her list of accomplishments. Two compilations of her music were produced in 2000 and 2003, testifying to her ongoing commercial success.

Barbara Lebrun

See also: Charlebois, Robert; Dion, Céline; Joan of Arc; Music (Pop); Plamondon, Luc; Vigneault, Gilles.

References

Baillargeon, Richard, and Christian Côté. *Une Histoire de la musique populaire au Québec, Destination Ragou.* Montreal: Triptyque, 1991.

Beauvarlet, Geneviève. *Diane Dufresne.* Paris: Seghers, 1984.

Thérien, Robert, and Isabelle d'Amours. *Dictionnaire de la musique populaire au Québec (1955–1992).* Quebec: IQRC, 1992.

DUFY, RAOUL (1877–1953)

French artist born in Le Havre on June 3, 1877; died in Forcalquier on March 23, 1953.

One can classify Raoul Dufy's artistic creations as having affinities to late impressionism, fauvism, and cubism. As an artist, he did not differentiate between the value of high art and the merits of more pedestrian forms of artistic production that his contemporary public enjoyed. This egalitarian approach to culture is evident in Dufy's wide range of artistic work, which includes paintings, watercolors, drawings, wood engravings, lithographs, etchings, ceramic pieces, tapestry cartoons, fabric designs, stage sets, murals, and monumental decorations. Influenced by Henri Matisse and Paul Cézanne, Dufy was a major contributor to the decorative arts. Whatever the medium, in all of Dufy's creations the real coexists with the imaginary without an appeal to tragedy. The resulting ease and lightness of his style have guaranteed his appeal in the many different milieus in which he worked.

Raoul Dufy visited the United States several times, exhibited his work in many major U.S. cities, and completed commissioned work in the States. Dufy exhibited his work in 1913 at the Armory Show in New York as well as at shows in Chicago and Boston. In 1930, Dufy began collaborative work on fabric designs with the Maison Onondaga, in New York. Although he refused to exhibit his *La Fée Electricité* in a New York department store in 1937, Dufy did travel to Pittsburgh, Pennsylvania, as a member of the Carnegie Prize Jury. A year later, he had exhibitions in New York and Chicago.

Dufy was particularly active in the United States during the period between 1949 and 1951. In 1949, he exhibited his work at the Galerie Louis Carré in New York. In 1950, Dufy exhibited in a retrospective of fauvism and also at a show at the Perls Galleries in New York. The same year, Dufy designed scenery for Jean Anouilh's *Invitation au château/Ring Around the Moon,* which was to be produced by Gilbert Miller in New York. In 1951, he exhibited in New York, Pittsburgh, Washington, Chicago, and Richmond, Virginia. Also during the same year, Dufy painted jazz bands in Mexico. In September 1951, Lincoln Kerstein commissioned work from Dufy for the New York City Ballet.

After Dufy's death in 1953, there were several major U.S. retrospectives of his work. In 1953, there was a Dufy retrospective in New York. In 1954, retrospectives were held in San Francisco and Los Angeles.

Matthew Hilton-Watson

See also: Dance; Jazz; Matisse, Henri; Mexico; Painting.

References

Clement, Russell T. *Les Fauves: A Sourcebook.* Westport, CT: Greenwood, 1994.
Perez-Tibi, Dora. *Dufy.* Trans. Shaun Whiteside. New York: Abrams, 1989.

DUHAMEL, GEORGES (1884–1966)

Novelist, essayist, playwright, poet, and physician, whose *Scènes de la vie future* (*America the Menace,* 1930) was a searing indictment of American civilization as commercialization, industrialization, and technocracy run riot with irreparable harm to individualism.

Born in Paris on June 30, 1884, Duhamel overcame poverty and strained family relations to study both literature and medicine. From 1905 to 1908, he was a founding member of the literary commune, the Abbaye de Créteil, and before 1914 had established a minor reputation for poetry and plays. During World War I, he served fifty-one months with a mobile surgical unit close to the trench line. He wrote of these horrors in *Vie des martyrs,*

1914–1916 (*The New Book of Martyrs,* 1917) and *Civilization 1914–1917* (1918), the latter winning the Prix Goncourt. The experience of modern war led him to detest technology, converted him to pacifism, and confirmed his defense of the individual.

Giving up medicine for literature, he won renown for two multivolume novels, *Vie et aventures de Salavin* (The Life and Adventures of Salavin, five volumes, 1920–1932) and *Chronique des Pasquiers* (*Caged Beasts,* ten volumes, 1933–1944), which explored, through the stories of an eccentric individual and a family, what modern society in France had become. This achievement was recognized by his election to the Académie Française in 1935. Duhamel also sought to encourage harmony between French and Germans as an antidote to future war, but by the late 1930s he concluded that Hitler had to be opposed at all costs. Immediately after the 1938 Munich conference, he accused French appeasers of having abandoned the "Descartes line," by which he meant defense of truth and liberty, and in *Positions françaises* (1940), he justified the defense of civilization against tyranny. At the liberation in 1944, he joined the Comité national des écrivains (National Committee of Writers) but resigned in 1946 in disapproval over the excesses committed in purging collaborators. For the next two decades, Duhamel produced a series of novels dealing with the issues of morality and human destiny, but he fell out of fashion. He also continued the social criticism for which *Scènes de la vie future* had made him celebrated, warning in *Problèmes de l'heure* (*Problems of the Hour,* 1957) of the increasing encroachment of the state upon the individual. When Duhamel died on April 13, 1966, at his country home in Val-mondois (Val d'Oise), his writings filled ninety-nine volumes.

Duhamel's condemnation of materialism, commercialism, collectivism, and the worship of technology was the dominant theme in all that he wrote. His most celebrated attack on what he called these enemies of the individual, and for which he was awarded the Grand prix de l'Académie française, was *Scènes de la vie future,* written after a short trip (October–December 1929) to the United States, where he visited principally New York, New Orleans, and Chicago. He fulminated against the ugliness of billboards, automobile graveyards, and pollution. He decried the assembly-line mentality of standardizing everything from manufactured goods to food to opinion. He predicted that the complete embrace of automobiles and cinema foretold the end of originality—of activities such as wandering and the conjuring of personal images—and the imposition of a passivity and enslavement to technology. The result, he warned, would be to create a society in which the collective would completely overwhelm the individual. Above all, Duhamel urged Europeans not to emulate America, but he feared that the lure would be too great to resist.

Benjamin F. Martin

See also: Camus, Albert; Sartre, Jean-Paul; World War I; World War II.

References

Duhamel, Georges. *Light on My Days: An Autobiography.* London: Dent, 1948.

Keating, L. Clark. *Critic of Civilization: Georges Duhamel and His Writings.* Lexington: University of Kentucky Press, 1965.

Knapp, Bettina Liebowitz. *Georges Duhamel.* New York: Twayne, 1972.

Lafay, Arlette. *La Sagesse de Georges Duhamel.* Paris: Minard, 1984.

DUHAMEL, MARCEL (1900–1977)

The French translator, actor, and editor Marcel Duhamel was born in the north of France in 1900, spending most of his life in Paris.

A participant in the surrealist movement during the 1920s, Duhamel began translating modernist U.S. fiction into French in 1930. From 1945 until his death in 1977, he directed the *Série Noire* (black [or dark] series), the highly influential detective fiction series at the prestigious French publishing house Gallimard, which popularized American hard-boiled crime writing in France, and which helped spawn the French critical notion of film noir.

During his post–World War I military service, Duhamel met the future surrealist painter Yves Tanguy and the screenwriter-poets Jacques and Pierre Prévert, who became his lifelong friends. With Duhamel supporting their bohemian lifestyles by working as a manager at the Hôtel Grosvenor, the four shared a house in Paris. It was during this period that Duhamel and the Préverts acquired their appetite for cinema—Pierre's job as a projectionist affording them exposure to the latest U.S. films—and that Duhamel became acquainted with the surrealists; his house soon became the site of numerous surrealist activities, particularly its experimental drawing and word games known as *exquisite corpse*.

Leaving—but never renouncing—the surrealists in 1928, Duhamel sold his house to the surrealist writers Georges Sadoul and André Thirion. Supporting himself through advertising, Duhamel began translating U.S. gangster novels whose modern prose seemed especially sympathetic to his cinematic interests, be-ginning with Raoul Whitfield's *Green Ice* (1931) and W. R. Burnett's *Little Caesar* (unpublished). He continued to translate American modernist fiction throughout his career, including works by Dashiell Hammett, John Steinbeck, Ernest Hemingway, Erskine Caldwell, Richard Wright, and Chester Himes.

During the 1930s, Duhamel participated in the October Group, a worker's theater organization affiliated with the leftist Fédération du Théâtre Ouvrier Français (Federation of French Workers' Theater). Dedicated to proletarian and antifascist politics, the group's membership included Sylvia Bataille and the former surrealists Marcel Jean and Max Morise, with scripts composed by Jacques Prévert or adapted by Duhamel himself. Duhamel traveled to Moscow with the October Group in 1933, winning first prize for France in the International Workers' Theatre Olympiad. In 1935, the group became the ensemble cast for Jean Renoir's film *The Crime of M. Lange,* written in collaboration with Prévert, whose plot centers on a publishing house for American-style popular fiction.

In 1944, the publisher Gaston Gallimard hired Duhamel to direct a new collection of detective fiction in the American hard-boiled style. Launched after the liberation, the *Série Noire* became the popular voice of France's haunted postwar memory, famous for its stark black and yellow covers and for its newly minted French slang. The majority of early titles in the collection were direct translations of American novels by writers like Hammett, James M. Cain, and Raymond Chandler; gradually, the series began publishing works by European authors influenced by this type of genre fiction, such as Albert Simonin. In 1958, at Duhamel's request, the African American writer Chester Himes published his first detective novel in the *Série Noire,* to wide acclaim. The series published its 1,000th title in 1966, garnering extensive critical praise. In 1949, Duhamel launched the *Série Blême* ("pale series"), a parallel collection of suspense thrillers that popularized American authors like David Goodis and Cornell Woolrich. In 1972 Duhamel published a memoir, *Raconte pas ta vie!* (Don't Tell Your Life Story!), which reflects upon his ties with surrealism and the modernist writers he translated.

Jonathan Eburne

See also: Crime Fiction; Film Noir; Goodis, David; Hemingway, Ernest; Himes, Chester; Language; Renoir, Jean; Surrealism; Tanguy, Yves.

References

Blakeway, Claire. *Jacques Prévert: Popular French Theatre and Cinema.* Rutherford, NJ: Fairleigh Dickinson University Press, 1990.

Duhamel, Marcel. *Raconte pas ta vie!* Paris: Mercure de France, 1972.

Fauré, Michel. *Le Groupe Octobre.* Paris: Bourgeois, 1977.

Mesplède, Claude. *Les Années "Série Noire."* 5 vols. Amiens: Enorage, 1992.

DULUTH

Duluth is the westernmost port city on the Great Lakes and the biggest inland port in the United States, with over 1,000 vessels visiting annually. With a population of 86,000, Duluth is the third-largest city in Minnesota and the cultural center of Lake Superior's North Shore. Duluth is nestled in the hills above the outlet of the Saint Louis River and the Minnesota Point peninsula, across the bay from Superior, Wisconsin.

In 1679, Daniel Greysolon, Sieur du Lhut (as he spelled it), came to the local area, then called Fond du Lac. Duluth had set out from Montreal with two goals: to broker a peace between the local Dakotas and Ojibwas, and to explore inland Minnesota. In September 1679, Duluth succeeded in his first goal, thereby ensuring the uninterrupted supply of furs for the French. The following year, Duluth continued his explorations, most notably freeing Jesuit missionary Louis Hennepin from the Dakota. Nearly 200 years later, early citizens of Duluth named their city after Daniel Greysolon.

During the fur trade era, the Duluth area was home to a seasonal Ojibwa village, as well as various fur trade posts. In the 1820s, the fur traders moved out, and the cartographers and politicians moved in. The first treaty between the local Ojibwa and the U.S. government occurred in 1826. Formal surveying and additional treaties cleared the way for settlement in 1854. The subsequent rush of land speculators seemed to bode well for the frontier town, but the dual economic disasters of the 1857 financial panic and the Civil War conspired to delay Duluth's heyday.

In the 1880s, Duluth began to recover once more as the great port for Minnesota's major industries of the era: wheat and lumber. In 1891, the discovery of iron nearby further secured Duluth's fortunes. This time, when a crash occurred in 1893, Duluth survived.

From the early 1900s through World War II, Duluth was a center for the iron ore industry. After the war, however, the local high-grade hematite became scarce and less affordable to mine. For a few decades, the development of taconite processing revived the industry of the North Shore and Duluth, but by 1980 it was clear that Duluth's Iron Age was ending.

Today, Duluth's economy has diversified. Main industries include international shipping, tourism, health care, financial services, and education. An aquarium, zoo, convention center, and revitalized waterfront draw tourists to the city year-round. Echoes of the early French influence can be seen at the annual folk festival and in the use of the fleur-de-lis in decoration.

Nancy O'Brien Wagner

See also: American Civil War; Fur Trade; Hennepin, Father Louis; Minnesota; Montreal; Wisconsin; World War II.
References
Carey, Judge John R. *History of Duluth and Northern Minnesota.* Compiled from *Duluth News Tribune,* 1898.
Cooley, Jerome Eugene. *Recollections of Early Days in Duluth.* Proctor, MN: Published by the author, Journal Printing Company, 1925.
Lydecker, Ryck, and Lawrence J. Sommer, eds. *Duluth: Sketches of the Past; a Bicentennial Collection.* Duluth, MN: American Revolution Bicentennial Commission, 1976.
Sandvik, Glenn N. *Duluth: An Illustrated History of the Zenith City.* Woodland Hills, CA: Windsor, 1983.

DUMAS, ALEXANDRE (1802–1870)

One of the most celebrated nineteenth-century French writers, Dumas is best known for his historical novels *The Three Musketeers* and *The Count of Monte Cristo,* both written between 1844 and 1845. Both works belong to popular culture, and Dumas was among the first French writers who fully used the possibilities of the serial novel. He is credited with revitalizing the historical novel in France, although his abilities as a historical writer were largely disputed because he was not faithful to historical facts, but rather a writer of fast-paced adventure novels.

The grandson of a black slave from Santo Domingo and a military general who served under the First Empire, Alexandre Dumas was born in Villers-Cotterêts, France. His 1843 novel *Georges,* set on Mauritius, deals centrally with questions of race and colonialism. After his father's death in 1806, the family lived in poverty. Dumas worked as a notary's clerk in Villers-Cotterêts and went to Paris in 1823 to find work. Due to his elegant handwriting, he secured a position with the Duc d'Orléans, who later became King Louis-Philippe. An illegitimate son, Alexandre Dumas fils (son), was born in 1824.

As a playwright Dumas made his breakthrough with *Henri III et sa cour/Henri III and His Court* (1829), produced by the Comédie-Française. It met with great success, and Dumas went on to compose a number of additional plays, novels, and short stories. In all, he produced some 250 books with his seventy-three assistants. The story of the king's Musketeers was continued in *Vingt ans après/Twenty Years After* (1845) and *Le Vicomte de Bragelonne, ou dix ans plus tard* (or *Ten Years Later*)/*The Vicomte Bragelonne* (1848–1850).

Dumas lived as adventurously as the heroes of his books. He took part in the revolution of July 1830 and became a captain in the National Guard, caught cholera during the epidemic of 1832, and traveled in Italy to recuperate. He married his mistress Ida Ferrier, an actress, in 1840, but he soon separated from her, after having spent her entire dowry. With the money earned from his writings, he built a fantastic château de Monte-Cristo on the outskirts of Paris.

Alexandre Dumas, one of the most celebrated nineteenth-century French writers, is credited with revitalizing the historical novel in France. (Library of Congress)

Fleeing debt, Dumas spent time in Belgium, Russia, and Italy, where he lived for four years as keeper of museums in Naples and supported Garibaldi's struggle for Italian unity. Dumas died on December 5, 1870, at Puys, near Dieppe.

Other popular works by Dumas include *The Corsican Brothers* (1844) and *The Man in the Iron Mask* (1850). The popular nature of the author's works is all the more attested to as several of his novels were adapted by Hollywood producers and made into major full-length motion pictures. Alexandre Dumas fils (1824–1895) was also a novelist and playwright. His best-known work is *La Dame aux camélias* (*Camille,* 1852), adapted by Giuseppe Verdi as *La Traviata.*

Claudia Wolosin

See also: Louis-Philippe, King of France.
References
Davidson, Arthur Fitzwilliam. *The Memoirs of Alexandre Dumas.* Philadelphia: Lippincott, 1902.
Spurr, Harry A. *The Life and Writings of Alexandre Dumas.* New York: Haskell House, 1973.

DUPLESSIS, MAURICE LE NOBLET (1890–1959)

Québécois politician.

Maurice Duplessis was born in Trois-Rivières, in the parish of l'Immaculée-Conception on April 20, 1890. He was the son of Nérée Le Noblet Duplessis, lawyer and conservative member of parliament in Saint-Maurice from 1886 to 1900, and mayor of Trois-Rivières from 1904 to 1905. He studied at the Collège Notre-Dame in Montreal, at the Trois-Rivières seminary, and in the Faculty of Law at the Université de Montréal (which was, at the time, called Université Laval à Montréal). Maurice Duplessis was admitted to the Quebec bar on September 4, 1913.

He worked as a lawyer for various practices in Trois-Rivières before becoming president of the bar in Trois-Rivières in 1937, and, in 1937 and 1938, president of the bar of the province of Quebec.

He was Conservative Party candidate at the 1923 elections in the Trois-Rivières constituency before eventually being elected under the Conservative banner in 1927, 1931, and 1935. He became leader of the Conservative Party on October 4, 1933. On November 7, 1935, he merged the Conservative Party with Paul Gouin's National Liberal Party in order to found the Union nationale. Maurice Duplessis rapidly eclipsed Paul Gouin both in the party and on the political stage. Maurice Duplessis was elected and reelected member for Trois-Rivières at the Quebec general elections of 1936, 1939, 1944, 1948, 1952, and 1956.

Duplessis was premier of Quebec, president of the executive council, and procurator general of Quebec from August 26, 1936, to November 8, 1939, and from August 30, 1944, to September 7, 1959. At the 1939 general election, Duplessis lost to Adélard Godbout of the Quebec Liberal Party. He was then leader of the official opposition until the general election of 1944.

A nationalist, conservative clerical ideology can to seen to have characterized Duplessis's political work. He left his mark in Quebec history as a charismatic figure, known as *le chef* (the boss), who scorned intellectuals and artists. It must be noted that, under his party, Quebec electoral morals were characterized by generalized partisan corruption. In the history of contemporary Quebec, he is closely associated with the *grande noirceur* (great darkness) period, which went from the end of World War II to Jean Lesage's Quiet Revolution from 1960 onward.

On the international stage, Maurice Duplessis was not very interested in political relations between France and Quebec. He played host to the French president Vincent Auriol when Auriol visited Quebec in April 1951. He adopted an openly pro-American attitude in order to attract U.S. capital and investors to Quebec. Duplessis's detractors accused him of underselling Quebec resources to the Americans. In short, Duplessis had an intracontinental vision without having any real international ambition for Quebec. It was only with the Quiet Revolution that Quebec's

international role became more important, with the opening of a number of delegations, including the Paris one in 1961.

In Quebec historiography, a strong anti-Duplessis sentiment evolved after he died, although, since the mid-1980s, this vision has tended to fade.

Duplessis died in office in Schefferville, on September 7, 1959, at the age of sixty-nine.

Jean-François Béland

See also: Quebec; Quiet Revolution; World War II.

References

Black, Conrad. *Duplessis*. Montreal: De L'Homme, 1977.

Hébert, Jacques. *Duplessis, non merci!* Montreal: Boréal, 2000.

Saint-Aubin, Bernard. *Duplessis et son époque*. Montreal: La Presse, 1979.

DuPont Family

The DuPont dynasty of gunpowder and chemical magnates was founded by Pierre Samuel DuPont (1739–1817), a French Huguenot who became Louis XVI's inspector general of commerce in 1773. Jailed during the French Revolution and suspicious of the directory, DuPont emigrated to the United States, encouraged by his long correspondence with Thomas Jefferson. It was Pierre Samuel's son Eleuthère Irenée (1772–1834), however, who had studied chemistry with Lavoisier, who founded the family's specially constructed gunpowder plant on the Brandywine River in Delaware in 1801 as part of his father's Franco-American land and business holdings. Because of the family's connections to Jefferson, the plant soon had American army contracts and produced powder far superior to any competitor in North America. Despite the accidents and fires that plagued the industry, one of which killed Pierre Samuel, the family flourished, especially after the War of 1812.

Under the leadership of Henry DuPont (1812–1889), the company became entirely American, severing its legal ties to France in 1837 and becoming known for its paternal policies toward workers and increasing political control of Delaware. Henry made all of the DuPont sons work their way up through the company, and he supported their education in chemistry and engineering at the University of Pennsylvania, MIT, and West Point. Henry arranged for the company to sell to both sides of the Crimean War, angering the French tremendously. During the Civil War, the DuPonts, who had sympathies with both the North and South, chose to remain with the Union and provided new, more powerful "Mammoth" gunpowder that armed the *Monitor* against the *Merrimac*. DuPonts also served in both the army and navy, with Colonel Henry A. DuPont's (1838–1926) service and standing in the Republican Party recognized thirty years after the war with the Congressional Medal of Honor and the naming of Washington's DuPont Circle after Admiral Samuel DuPont (1803–1865), who blockaded Charleston.

Forming the "Powder Trust" in 1872, the DuPonts monopolized the gunpowder market in postwar America, driving their rivals out of business and branching out into the new field of nitroglycerine, while a Kentucky branch of cousins invested in textile mills and coal mining. In 1889, Alfred I. DuPont (1864–1935) licensed "smokeless" gunpowder from the Belgian firm Coopals

Pierre Samuel DuPont, founder of the DuPont dynasty of gunpowder and chemical magnates. (Library of Congress)

and Company, which, along with cheaper soda replacing saltpeter in explosives, gave the family an advantage. The Spanish-American War relied on DuPont smokeless powder, while the company made advantageous deals with German and British rivals to keep their domestic market.

By World War I, the DuPonts, under the leadership of P. S. (Pierre Samuel) DuPont (1870–1954), completely dominated Delaware politics, controlling newspapers, a Senate seat, and the turnpike system, and their political clout averted an antitrust suit in 1906. The war made the company enormous profits from gunpowder sales, even though German saboteurs attacked the Brandywine factory in 1915 over their sales to the French and British. Anticipating that World War I was truly a war to end war, the DuPonts branched out into chemicals and automobile manufacturing, acquiring controlling interest in

General Motors in 1922. The family also brought on French censure by offering jobs and refuge to German scientists from I. G. Farben and BASF fleeing the French. These men gave the DuPonts critical trade secrets from the German chemical dye and petroleum industry, and the relationship led to heavy investment in Germany in the 1920s.

The Depression did little to harm the company, which produced a series of tremendous innovations from the mind of chemist Wallace Carothers, including nylon in 1930 and neoprene and Teflon in 1935. Severing their ties to Nazi Germany during World War II, the DuPonts contributed heavily as military contractors, inventing plastic tubing and insecticides, and building Oak Ridge and Hanford as sites for the Manhattan Project.

By 1954, when the DuPonts escaped another antitrust suit, the family had ceased to honor Henry DuPont's spartan and utilitarian policies and had drifted away from active management of the company. Plagued by tuberculosis, hereditary deafness, marital scandals, and political failures, most DuPonts withdrew and lived on their inheritances, as professional managers took over the business and dismantled its huge reach into the auto and coal industries. Many of the family's philanthropic projects remain, including Nemours, a country estate modeled after Versailles and now a children's hospital; many Delaware and Florida public schools, including the first African American high school (1927); and Longwood, another estate, which was donated to the state of Delaware.

As for the Dupont de Nemours company, by the 1980s the chemical industry had matured, and its historic growth rate of twice GNP had moderated: opportunities to create major new products also diminished. Research interests now are focused on technologies such as displays for devices like mobile phones. In 2003, it was a $27 billion company, with 78,000 employees, approximately half of whom work outside the United States, throughout the Americas, Europe, and the Far and Middle East.

Margaret Sankey

See also: American Civil War; Automobiles; French Revolution; Huguenots; Jefferson, Thomas; Kentucky; World War I; World War II.

References

Mosley, Leonard. *Blood Relations: The Rise and Fall of the DuPonts of Delaware.* New York: Atheneum, 1980.

Wall, Joseph Frazier. *Alfred I. DuPont and His Family.* New York: Oxford University Press, 1990.

Winkler, John. *The DuPont Dynasty.* New York: Reynal and Hitchcock, 1935.

DURTAIN, LUC (ANDRÉ NEPVEU) (1881–1959)

French poet and novelist, born in Paris.

Luc Durtain was a constant traveler who visited Asia, Africa, and northern Europe, as well as Brazil, the United States, and Canada in the early twentieth century. Dr. André Nepveu chose the pseudonym of Luc Durtain and began writing poems around 1897. He published ten books of poetry, plus some novels and plays, between 1908 (an early cycle of poems entitled *Pégase*) and 1952. In 1906, Durtain was a member of a literary commune, the Abbaye de Créteil, living for fourteen months with friends such as French writers Georges Duhamel and Pierre-Jean Jouve. Much of his vivid poetry is directly inspired by the places he visited, with enthusiastic descriptions in exalted verse of landscapes, including Niagara Falls, Chicago, and Havana.

Durtain was a joyful poet who wrote with jubilation and whose words were spiced with generous punctuation and stars that could surprise and inspire as well. In fact, Durtain's book of poems entitled *Quatre Continents* ("Four Continents," 1935), with a whole section of poetry named "Suite américaine," synthesizes the poetic essence of Atlantic studies, as well as of Atlanta studies. Here he talks, for example, of the skyscrapers of the "half black city" (Durtain, p. 35), which carries the name of the ocean that has been a willing participant in the slave trade. "Cap Eternité" describes, with various images and clichés, his own fascination for the fjord in the region of the Saguenay River, in Quebec. Here, Durtain talks of steamers breaking through the cold and deep waters, and of the whales that swim alongside them.

While in South America, Durtain wrote another cycle of eight poems entitled "Suite brésilienne" ("Brazilian Suite," including "Atlantique Sud" [South Atlantic] and "Vers Rio de Janeiro" [Toward Rio de Janeiro]) that also appeared in *Quatre Continents,* a book of more than 200 poems, dedicated to his son Pierre. It confirmed Durtain as a landscape poet of the world he visited, with the eyes of a European in America.

Among many recent commentators, French author Serge Faucherau has recognized strong similarities with German expressionist poetry in Durtain's passionate style, a rare phenomenon in French literature from the early twentieth century. In the 1960s, Vincent Gauthier had under-

lined in his thesis many recurrent themes related to "Américanité" in the novels of Durtain (Gauthier, 1966). Sadly, none of Durtain's books are available at the moment, and there seem to be no translations of his works in other languages.

Yves Laberge

See also: Brazil; Duhamel, Georges; Niagara Falls.
References
Durtain, Luc. *Quatre Continents: Poèmes.* Paris: Flammarion, 1935.
Faucherau. Serge, *Expressionnisme, Dada, surréalisme et autres ismes.* Paris: Denoël, 2001.
Gauthier, Vincent. "Luc Durtain et l'Amérique à travers la suite américaine de ses romans." Thèse de maîtrise, Sainte-Foy, Université Laval, 1966.

DUVERGIER DE HAURANNE, ERNEST (1843–1877)

French political theorist and art critic.

Duvergier published an account of his travels throughout the United States and Canada in the last months of the American Civil War. Inspired by Alexis de Tocqueville, he studied the functioning of the social and institutional underpinnings of American democracy during this critical moment in the nation's history.

Born in Paris on March 7, 1843, Ernest was the son of an important member of the Liberal Party, Prosper Duvergier de Hauranne, author of works on political philosophy and representative from the Department of the Cher from 1831 to 1851. The influence of his father was apparent as Ernest developed his talents as a political analyst and theorist as well as a representative of the Cher in the early years of the Third Republic.

The work on his travels in North America was published as a series of twelve articles in the *Revue des deux mondes* (Review of Two Worlds) from August 15, 1865, to April 1, 1866, under the title *Huit mois en Amérique, Lettres et notes de voyage, 1864–1865/Eight Months in America, Letters and Travel Notes 1864–1865.* The articles were written in the form of a daily journal with thematic subheadings. The composite structure allowed him to use his particular experiences in a given site to explore the nature of American democracy in general. For example, during the presidential elections of 1864, he attended electoral meetings in Chicago and from this experience drew conclusions regarding the importance of the party system in U.S. political life. The work also contained occasional critiques of Napoléon III's regime. In a style that resembles that of Tocqueville, he used the American case as an attempt to gain a perspective on the nature of French politics and democracy.

Upon his return to France he continued to write for the *Revue des deux mondes* and became increasingly involved in the opposition to the Second Empire. In 1869 he published two works critiquing the regime, *Le Gouvernement personnel* ("Personal Government") and *La Coalition libérale* ("The Liberal Coalition"). He continued to write articles on politics and art criticism for the *Revue politique et littéraire* and *Revue des deux mondes* and published a final book in 1873 entitled *La République conservatrice* ("The Conservative Republic"), in which he argued that a "conservative republic" was the only form of government that could satisfy the French desire for both equality and order.

In 1870, he was injured in the Franco-Prussian War at Beaune-la-Rolande, for which he was awarded the Légion d'honneur. During the Third Republic he was elected as representative of the Cher on July 2, 1871. He was reelected to this position in 1876, a year before his death on August 25, 1877.

Stephen Sawyer

See also: American Civil War; Tocqueville, Alexis de.

Reference
Bowen, Ralph H. "French Liberalism and American Mass Society, Tocqueville and Ernest Duvergier de Hauranne." *Histoires d'Europe et d'Amérique. Le monde atlantique contemporain: Mélanges offerts au professeur Yves-Henri Nouailhat.* Ed. Michel Catala. Nantes: Ouest, 1999.

DUVIVIER, JULIEN (1896–1967)

One of France's greatest film directors of the classic era, with a career spanning five decades. Duvivier was born in Lille, France, and died in a car crash in Paris in 1967.

Beginning as a stage actor, Duvivier started making silents in 1918, first as an assistant director to Louis Feuillade or Marcel L'Herbier, and then as a director in 1919. However, it was not until the 1930s that Duvivier gained his status as one of the top five French directors, alongside Jean Renoir, Jacques Feyder, René Clair, and Marcel Carné. Duvivier made some twenty-five films in the 1930s alone, giving actors some of their best roles. He directed Jean Gabin in three of his major works of the 1930s, contributing to the actor's myth and stardom: *La Bandera* (*Escape from Yesterday,* 1935) opposite Annabella, *La Belle*

Equipe (*They Were Five,* 1936), and *Pépé le Moko* (1937), also starring Mireille Balin. *La Belle Equipe* and *Pépé le Moko* are highly representative of the period, prime examples of what was happening in society with the election of the Front Populaire in 1936 and in cinema with the distinctive style of "poetic realism."

Duvivier's talent with actors is widely recognized, though often overshadowed by his work with Gabin. The director was, however, also faithful to the great Harry Baur in some seven films, most notably in *La Tête d'un Homme* (A Man's Head, 1933), or other legends, Michel Simon (*La Fin du jour/The End of a Day,* 1939; *Panique/Panic,* 1945) and Louis Jouvet (*Un Carnet de bal/Dance Program,* 1937; *La Fin du jour/The End of the Day,* 1939; *Untel Père et fils/The Heart of a Nation,* 1943), to name but a few. Duvivier indeed directed some of the greatest actors in the history of French cinema, such as Maurice Chevalier, Raimu, Françoise Rosay, Pierre Fresnay, Jean-Pierre Aumont, Fernandel, Danielle Darrieux, Brigitte Bardot, and Alain Delon. Duvivier's skills at directing actors was most apparent when he worked with a large cast in a genre that he favored, the episode or sketch film, such as *Un Carnet de bal, Tales of Manhattan* (1942), or *Flesh and Fantasy* (1943).

The huge international success of *Pépé le Moko,* one of the most remade French films (*Algiers,* 1938; *Casbah,* 1948), ignited the interest of Hollywood studios, which invited the French director shortly after (*The Great Waltz,* 1939). When war broke out, Duvivier returned to Hollywood and became part of the colony of French exiles and refugees who spent the war years in the United States (Renoir, Clair, Aumont,

Marcel Dalio, Gabin, Michèle Morgan, Max Ophuls, and Simone Simon, to take the most famous). The French exile community worked closely together on many projects, and Duvivier's films indeed featured some of them. *Lydia* was produced by Alexander Korda, *Tales of Manhattan* included Marcel Dalio and Victor Francen in its extremely large cast, and Dalio was again in *Flesh and Fantasy,* while *The Impostor* (1943), a war propaganda film, was mainly a vehicle for Gabin.

Duvivier resumed his career in France at the end of the war but never regained his pre-war status, despite some remarkable productions and some huge popular hits like *Le Petit Monde de Don Camillo* (*The Little World of Don Camillo,* 1951), with Fernandel.

Catherine Hellegouarc'h

See also: Boyer, Charles; Chevalier, Maurice; Clair, René; Dalio, Marcel; Darrieux, Danielle; Florey, Robert; Jourdan, Louis; Morgan, Michèle; Pepe Le Pew; Remakes; Renoir, Jean; Rosay, Françoise; Simon, Simone.

Reference

Leprohon, Pierre. *Julien Duvivier.* Paris: Anthologie du Cinéma, 1968.

DYLAN, BOB (1941–)

Born Robert Zimmerman in Duluth, Minnesota, in May 1941, Bob Dylan is frequently hailed as the most significant and influential singer-songwriter of the twentieth century. Dylan's formative influence was the folksinger Woody Guthrie, who had himself been inspired by the prose style of Guy de Maupassant during his brief spell in the armed services in the 1940s. With the influence of Guthrie and the

Singer Bob Dylan. Some critics have compared Dylan's eclecticism with French postmodernism and bricolage, particularly his use of multiple personae, his fondness for open-ended and nonlinear narratives, and his fusion of high and low culture. (Library of Congress)

American folk revival of the late 1950s, Dylan began his career performing and recording ballads, protest songs, and "talkin' blues" in the early 1960s, later in the decade establishing his own fusion of folk-rock when he "went electric" for the albums *Highway 61 Revisited* (1965) and *Blonde on Blonde* (1966). From the late 1960s Dylan's style became more eclectic, shifting from the lyrical *John Wesley Harding* (1968), to the country music of *Nashville Skyline* (1969), to the raw sounds of *The Basement Tapes* (recorded in 1967), to a potent mixture of styles on the mid-1970s albums *Blood on the Tracks* and *Hurricane* (both 1975). In the 1980s and 1990s, when his influence on popular music was less direct, Dylan continued to experiment with styles: fusing folk, rock, gospel, country, old-time, jazz, blues, and Motown, with a lyrical range that draws on a plethora of literary and cultural sources.

Dylan has never favored French culture over other national influences, although he was very pleased to be in France during a European trip in 1964. Critics Aidan Day and Stephen Scobie have compared Dylan's eclecticism with French postmodernism and bricolage, particularly his use of multiple personae, his fondness for open-ended and nonlinear narratives, and his fusion of high and low culture. It can be argued that Dylan's interest in the carnivalesque is deeply rooted in New Orleans culture, while Michael Gray suggests that his blending of musical and lyrical sounds creates a multidimensional aesthetic comparable to Charles Baudelaire's theory of synesthesia, as in lyrics such as "your baby's eyes . . . are tuggin' at your sleeve" from "Ballad of Hollis Brown" (*The Times They Are A-Changin'*, 1964) and "got all those buckets coming out of my ears" from "Buckets of Rain" (*Blood on the Tracks*).

Dylan even gives Walt Whitman's fondness for listing a French spin in "I Shall Be Free" (*Bringing It All Back Home*, 1965) in which American and French pop icons are intermingled, with Brigitte Bardot, Sophia Loren, Cassius Clay, John F. Kennedy, and Elizabeth Taylor standing shoulder to shoulder. At times he draws on distinct French traditions: for example, some of the prose sketches in *Tarantula* (1966) are a direct homage to surrealism and Arthur Rimbaud, and he even manages to find a rhyme for Rimbaud in "You're Gonna Make Me Lonesome When You Go" (*Blood on the Tracks*). But sometimes his allusions to French culture prove subtler than this, as in the tragicomic lyric in "Don't Fall Apart on Me Tonight" (*Infidels,* 1983): "It's like I'm stuck inside a painting / That's hanging in the Louvre." Underlying these examples is Dylan's versatility to creatively fuse a number of cultural impulses, some identifiably French (Baudelaire, Rimbaud, François Villon, Jean Genet), others distinctly American (Whitman, Guthrie, Emily Dickinson, Allen Ginsberg), and others drawn from Hispanic, British, Caribbean, and African sources.

In January 1990, Dylan was made Commandeur dans l'Ordre des Arts et des Lettres (Commander in the Order of Arts and Letters) in France.

Martin Halliwell

See also: Bardot, Brigitte; Baudelaire, Charles-Pierre; Duluth; Genet, Jean; Jazz; Minnesota; Music (Folk); Music (Pop); New Orleans; Surrealism.

References

Corcoran, Neil, ed. *"Do You, Mr. Jones?": Bob Dylan with the Poets and Professors.* London: Chatto and Windus, 2002.

Scobie, Stephen. *Alias Bob Dylan.* Red Deer: Red Deer College Press, 1991.

Shelton, Robert. *No Direction Home: The Life and Work of Bob Dylan.* London: New English Library, 1986.